RECORDS OF EARLY ENGLISH DRAMA

Records of Early English Drama

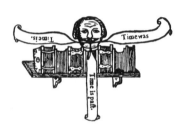

CHESTER

EDITED BY LAWRENCE M. CLOPPER

Introduction
The Records
Appendixes
Translations
End-notes
Glossaries
Index

UNIVERSITY OF TORONTO PRESS

TORONTO BUFFALO

For my mother, my sister, and Pegram

© University of Toronto Press 1979
Toronto Buffalo London
Printed in Canada
Published in Great Britain by Manchester University Press

Library of Congress Cataloging in Publiciation Data

Main entry under title:

Chester.

PN
2596
C48
C4

(Records of Early English Drama)
Bibliography: p.
Includes index.
1. Performing arts – England – Chester – History – Sources.
2.` English drama – England – Chester – History and criticism –
Sources. 3. Chester plays. 4. Chester, Eng. – History –
Sources. I. Clopper, Lawrence M., 1941- II. Series.
PN2596.C48C4   790.2'09427'14   79.16420

ISBN 0-8020-5460-9

The research and typesetting costs of
Records of Early English Drama have been underwritten by the
Social Sciences and Humanities Research Council of Canada.

Contents

Records of Early English Drama

The aim of Records of Early English Drama (REED) is to find, transcribe, and publish external evidence of dramatic, ceremonial, and minstrel activity in Great Britain before 1642.

Acknowledgements

There are many people whose aid and comfort, knowledge and expertise have helped to bring this project to completion. Professor Martin Stevens, my dissertation advisor, has remained a constant source of help and encouragement over the last ten years. Mr Richard Proudfoot and Professor A.C. Cawley supported my efforts at a critical point before the REED project was formed, and Professor Cawley gave a lot of his time to an earlier version of this publication. Professor Robert M. Lumiansky and Dr David Mills have traded information with me, read versions of my commentaries on the documents, and allowed me to read the commentary that they will be publishing in their notes to the *Chester Mystery Cycle* (EETS).

Initially it had been my intention to restrict my work to the records of dramatic performances prior to 1575, the year that the religious cycle was suppressed. When the collection was moved to the REED project, it was necessary to enlarge its scope and to extend the closing date to 1642. Unfortunately, not all of the guidelines for REED were made – nor could they have been made – at the beginning of the project; consequently, there were later changes that I could not undertake to meet entirely by myself.

The Editorial Advisory Board had determined that the series would not publish annual expenditures that remained the same over a period of time; instead, it would publish sample entries and note the remainder. At the suggestion of the outside assessors, and after discussion with the Board, it was decided that all of these entries should be printed even if they were repetitious. The only records at Chester which were affected were the guild expenditures on the Midsummer Watch and Show, records which often ran for fifty years with little change. In order to meet our deadline for copy, Dr Cameron Louis transcribed some of these duplicate entries from xeroxes and then I checked them: records of the Coopers (1618-42), Innkeepers (1584-90, 1592-1603), Mercers (1608-41), and Cordwainers (1578-98, 1599-1615, 1616-41). In England he transcribed the records of the Glovers (1632-41) and Joiners (1579-1642) and the entries in the Tabley House manuscripts and the 'Collectanea Devana'. The latter were checked on the site by Dr Richard Green, who also transcribed several new items turned up through REED bibliographical searching. These entries were then checked against the xeroxes at the REED office or by myself: PRO SP/60/9 and STAC 8/156/22, BL Lansdowne 213, and the Painters' Minute Book.

Dr Bella Schauman checked the majority of the editor's transcriptions against xeroxes and microfilms. Dr Louis checked and resolved in Chester the readings of those entries which could not be photographed, and he and Dr Green completed the manuscript descriptions (foliations, measurements, etc). Dr Schauman and Dr Louis saved the editor from many an error; the accuracy that we hope we have achieved, therefore, is a result of our co-operative efforts.

Some documents claimed the time and expertise of a number of scholars. My colleague, Professor Robert Lewis, helped me with the Coopers' Latin document of 1422. Dr Schauman provided the translations for most of the Latin entries, the remainder being done by Miss Abigail Young. The Anglo-Norman text was established with the help of Professor Alfred David, Dr Louis, Dr Lynette Muir, Mr Peter Meredith, and Professor Brian Merrilees. Miss Young made the translation.

Mr Todd Heather prepared the concordances for the Glossaries and Index. Dr Louis prepared the English Glossary and Miss Young the Latin and Anglo-Norman Glossaries. Mr William Edwards checked the Anglo-Norman Glossary for us. Mr Heather compiled the references to persons and places and the editor extracted the subject headings for the Index. Dr Sally-Beth MacLean put the Index in its final form.

The archivists, guildsmen, and other holders of records were always generous with their time and records. Mrs Elizabeth Berry and Miss Annette Kennett, her successor at the City Archives, bore the heaviest load, but were always helpful in locating records. Miss Kennett, in particular, patiently brought records back into the Archives during the years that our guidelines were changed, and she organized and oversaw the photographing of an enormous number of the documents. Miss Kennett, Mr Simon Harrison, who also helped us with our transcriptions, and the staff of the Archives made every effort to meet our needs even though it was obvious that their normal duties were enough to keep them fully occupied. The staff at the Archives, I should add, has been particularly gracious and friendly through the years.

Some of the guild documents have been deposited with the City Archives, but many of these records remain in guild hands or have been placed in the Guildhall Museum. I would like to thank all of the companies that have made their records available: in particular, Mr Peter Lowe, secretary to the Museum Committee of the Freemen and Guilds and Mr H. Fearnall, formerly president, for their help in making the records housed in the Guildhall available; the Barber-Surgeons' Company; Mr S.K. Tushingham of the Beerbrewers' Company; Mr K.H. Gerrard of the Butchers' Company; Mr R.J. Williams of the Cappers, Pinners, Wiredrawers, and Linendrapers' Company; Mr A. Edwards of the Coopers' Company; Mr F.L. Adams of the Cordwainers and Shoemakers' Company; Mr W.H. Brown of the Wet and Dry Glovers' Company; the Goldsmiths' Company; Mr N.T. Smith of the Innkeepers' Company; Mr K.E. Jones of the Joiners, Carvers, and Turners' Company; the late Mr Fred Parry of the Mercers, Ironmongers, Grocers, and Apothecaries' Company; Mr Hugh Swinnerton of the Painters, Glaziers, Embroiderers, and Stationers' Company; and Mr P.N. Formstone of the Smiths, Cutlers, and Plumbers' Company.

Mr Brian C. Redwood and his staff at the Cheshire Record Office answered many of our queries, gave us assistance in locating records, and made it possible for us to see the manuscripts in the possession of Col. Leicester-Warren, Tabley House. Canon C.E. Jarman and Canon K.M. Maltby, the present librarian of the Cathedral, helped us with the records from the Dean and Chapter. Mr M.R. Perkins, the curator of Special Collections, answered our queries about the Liverpool 'Breviary'.

Records of Early English Drama is particularly fortunate to have Professor Alexandra Johnston as its executive editor and to have many very skilled and knowledgeable persons associated with her. Professor Ian Lancashire can find things that others have missed; he is responsible for adding many items to the rather short initial bibliography, and I am very grateful to him for finding the 'lost' 'Breviary' that is now at Liverpool University. Dr Sally-Beth MacLean has very capably discharged her duties as volume editor; without her eye for detail there would be many points of confusion as well as inconsistencies in the text. She has sent me many a long list of queries, all of which, I hope, have been answered; most important, the text could not have reached its final clean state without her continuous advice. Miss Carolynn Jackson had the unenviable task of typing many of the transcriptions and of setting the final text. She has done this with a considerable degree of accuracy and great patience.

I would also like to thank Miss Prudence Tracy, our liaison with the University of Toronto Press, for her many helpful suggestions over the last four years, and Mr Will Rueter, Miss Jackson, and Dr MacLean for their work on the text design. Dr Helen Wallis and E.J. Huddy, of the British Library, helped with our map. Dr Mary Blackstone did some bibliographical checking for us.

We wish to thank the following institutions for permission to publish extracts from the manuscripts in their possession: the Trustees of the British Library; the Cheshire Record Office; the Chester City Archives; the Dean and Chapter, Chester Cathedral; the Sydney Jones Library, University of Liverpool; Massey College, University of Toronto; and the Public Record Office.

Research of this kind is very expensive; therefore, I am grateful to those agencies that have helped to pay the costs over the years: the National Endowment for the Humanities for a Summer Fellowship, 1972; the American Council of Learned Societies for a Grant-in-Aid, 1974; the American Philosophical Society for a Grant-in-Aid, 1975; the National Endowment for the Humanities for a Research Grant, 1976-7; and the Social Sciences and Humanities Research Council of Canada for its Negotiated Grant. The NEH Research Grant was awarded to help cover costs that could not be met by REED's major underwriter, the SSHRCC. My own institution, Indiana University, provided some typing services.

Finally, Pegram, my wife, has shared most of the ups and downs as this manuscript edged toward its final destiny. I want to thank her for her support and help and patience during my absences of self and mind.

LMC / Indiana University / 1979

The Documents

Original Manuscripts

The city of Chester has retained large quantities of records, most of which do not antedate the mid-sixteenth century. These include the common assembly's ordinances, official papers of the mayor, the city treasurers' reports, records of the various courts, and miscellaneous papers such as petitions and letters to and from the mayor and council.

Chester is also fortunate in having many medieval guilds still active, and some of these have documents relevant to this collection which reach back to the early fifteenth century; however, the majority of the records do not antedate the last quarter of the sixteenth century. The guild account books usually record receipts and disbursements; company books and minute books record guild ordinances and admissions to the fraternity, although the former of these may also include accounts. There are also some early charters and other miscellaneous papers.

Pre-Reformation ecclesiastical records are almost entirely lacking and most are fragmentary, if they exist at all, until fairly late in the sixteenth century. The most important ecclesiastical documents for this collection are the treasurers' reports for the dean and chapter of Chester Cathedral and the churchwardens' accounts for various churches in the city.

CIVIC RECORDS

Assembly Books

Chester, City Archives, AB/1; 1532-1624; Latin and English; paper; ii+382+ii; 400mm x 285mm (340mm x 215mm), 45 long lines; modern rebinding in 8s, each leaf preserved between silk; modern foliation (first 6 leaves lettered A-G, then foliation begins); little ornamentation, initial words of orders written in bold; yellow vellum cover on cardboard, title on spine.

Chester, City Archives, AB/2; 1624-84; Latin and English; paper; i+214+i; 545mm x 280mm (390mm x 210mm), number of lines variable; modern rebinding in 8s, each leaf preserved between silk; modern foliation; little ornamentation; yellow cloth cover on cardboard with white vellum on spine and corners.

The Assembly Books are the official record of the city council and contain the texts of the council's orders. They may also include the resolutions of disputes over customary practices or economic agreements, an occasional rental of city lands, and other related matter.

The first Assembly Book is dated in the manuscript description to 1532-1624, but it is probable that the book was not copied before 1567-8. The first orders begin on f 60 and are dated to Henry Gee's term in 1539-40; Gee's orders continue to f 83, but earlier ones are mixed in with them. There is also a city rental (ff 53-7) from Henry Gee's first term, 1533-4, and this probably accounts for the early date on the manuscript even though there are still earlier orders in it.

More significant for the dating of the MS is the List of Mayors which forms part of the prefatory matter. The List begins with John Arnewaye's term, which is dated 1326 (f 11), and continues in the same hand to 1567-8. Subsequent entries include descriptions of the boundaries of the city, the names and descriptions of the streets (ff 33v-5; copied by Rogers into his Breviaries), and other related matter. The jumbled sequence of orders suggests that the Assembly Book was compiled from the debris of an earlier book or from loose records, and that the prefatory material was added by an antiquarian who either copied the List of Mayors from another source or compiled it himself and who copied or wrote the descriptions of the city's wards, streets, and liberties, which became the staple of all later antiquarian descriptions of the city.

The Assembly Book is similar to but not identical with the one copied into Harley 2150. The most important difference is that AB/1 does not include any Banns for the plays; if it was copied as late as 1567-8, then it is possible that the Early Banns were omitted because they had been superseded by the Late Banns, or, if AB/1 was copied in the late 1570s, because the plays had ceased to be performed.

Assembly Files

Chester, City Archives, A/F/1-24; 1407-1642; Latin and English; paper; loose sheets in varying quantities and sizes; modern pencil foliation; various inks, unbound except for A/F/1 which has a modern red buckram binding, the leaves of which have been preserved between silk. Only A/F/24 has been calendared. The following have been examined; however, it should be noted that not all years are accounted for within the dates given: (♦ indicates extracts in our volume)

♦A/F/1	1407-1535	A/F/4	1576-99	A/F/7	1605-8
♦A/F/2	1536-86	A/F/5	1599-1602	♦A/F/8	1608-10
♦A/F/3	1570-6	A/F/6	1602-3	A/F/9	1610-12

◆A/F/10 1613-18	A/F/15 1629-30	A/F/20 1635-6
A/F/11 1619-23	A/F/16 1630-1	A/F/21 1638-9
A/F/12 1625-6	A/F/17 1632-3	A/F/22 1639-40
A/F/13 1627-8	A/F/18 1633-4	A/F/23 1640-1
A/F/14 1628-9	A/F/19 1634-5	A/F/24 1641-2

The files contain odd notes and papers of attendance at council meetings, rough
minutes by the clerk, drafts of fair minutes which might be used as entries in the
Assembly Books, election notes, and copies and originals of mayors' orders. In the
seventeenth century, petitions to the mayor, aldermen, and assembly are included
in these bundles but are not numbered as A/P (Assembly Petitions) as they were in
the sixteenth century.

Mayors' Books

Chester, City Archives, M/B/1-34; 1392-1652; Latin and English; paper; number of leaves varies;
length varies from 213mm to 350mm, width from 180mm to 225mm (M/B/12 has some leaves
as large as 420mm x 315mm; text area variable throughout); each volume contains from 1 to 12
mayors' books; collation difficult: some fragmentary, many inserts and excisions; early books are
foliated continuously within the volume, but in the later ones each book has a separate foliation;
all volumes repaired and rebound 1935-40; only M/B/1-8 and M/B/28a calendared. The following
have been examined:

◆M/B/1 1392-3; 1393-4; 1397-8; 1398-9◆
M/B/2 1401-2; 1404-5; 1405-6; 1407-8; 1409-10; 1410-11; 1412-13
M/B/3 1414-15; 1415-16; 1417-18; 1418-19; 1419-20; 1420-1
M/B/4 1432-3; 1433-4; 1448-9; 1449-50; 1451-3; 1453-4
◆M/B/5 1454-5; 1458-9; 1459-60; 1461-3; 1466-7; 1467-8; 1468-9; 1469-70; 1470-1; 1471-2;
1472-3; 1473-4; 1474-5◆; 1475-6
◆M/B/6 1475-6; 1476-7; 1477-8; 1483-4◆; 1484-5; 1486-7; 1487-8; 1488-9
M/B/7 1486-7; 1488-9; 1490-1; 1493-4
M/B/8 1494-5; 1495-6; 1496-7; 1498-9; 1499-1500
M/B/9 1500-1; 1501-2; 1502-3; 1503-4; 1504-5; 1506-7; 1507-8
M/B/10 1508-9
M/B/11 1510-11; 1511-12; 1512-13; 1515-16; 1518-19
◆M/B/12 1520-1◆; 1523-4; 1524-5; 1525-6; 1526-7; 1527-8; 1530-1; 1531-2; 1532-3; 1533-4;
1537-8
M/B/13 1536-7; 1538-9; 1539-40; 1540-1; 1541-2
M/B/14 1541-2; 1542-3; 1543-4; 1544-5; 1545-6
M/B/15 1546-7; 1547-8; 1549-51; 1551-2
M/B/16 1551-2; 1552-3
M/B/17 1553-4; 1554-5; 1555-6

M/B/18 1558-9; 1561-2
♦M/B/19 1562-3; 1564-5; 1566-7; 1567-8♦
M/B/20 1568-70; 1570-1; 1571-2
♦M/B/21 1572-3; 1573-4; 1575-6♦
♦M/B/22 1578-9; 1579-80♦; 1580-1; 1581-2
M/B/23 1582-3; 1583-4
M/B/24 1584-5; 1586-7; 1587-8; 1588-9
♦M/B/25 1589-90; 1590-1♦; 1591-2
M/B/26 1592-3; 1593-4; 1594-5; 1595-6
♦M/B/27 1596-7; 1597-8; 1598-9♦
M/B/28 1599-1600; 1603-4; 1604-5; 1605-6
M/B/29 1606-7; 1607-8; 1608-9; 1609-10; 1612-13
♦M/B/30 1613-14♦; 1614-15; 1615-16
M/B/31 1617-18; 1622-3; 1623-4; 1624-5
M/B/32 1626-7; 1628-9; 1630-1
M/B/33 1633-4; 1634-5; 1635-6; 1636-7
M/B/34 1641-2; 1642-3; 1643-4; 1644-5; 1645-6; 1646-7; 1647-8; 1648-9; 1649-50; 1650-1;
        1651-2

Before M/B/5, the books were day to day notebooks of the mayors and sheriffs. Otherwise, the books primarily contain portmote court pleas with some crownmote court pleas. These legal entries, however, do not usually state the nature of the crime, but merely bind the individual over to appear in court. There are also some admissions to the freedom of the city, lists of aldermen, a few assembly orders, and an occasional settlement of a dispute. The formulaic matters – indictments, admissions to freedom – are in Latin; orders, indentures, and other public matters are in English. Many of these books are little more than fragments and debris; others are too faded to be legible.

Mayors' Letters

Chester, City Archives, Great Letter Book, M/L/2; 1599-1650; English; paper (1 parchment leaf, pp 115-16; sheets of varying sizes attached to leaves of a modern bound volume; modern pagination; bound in white leather; contains letters 168-323.

The letters are to and from the mayor and the council on every conceivable matter.

Assembly Petitions

Chester, City Archives, A/P/1-2; 1533-98; English; paper; loose sheets in varying quanities and sizes; modern pencil numeration; various inks.

The collection goes back at least as far as Randle Holme I. Most of the petitions are addressed to the mayor, aldermen, sheriffs, and common council. A/P/2 is two originally separate files of assembly petitions presented to William Aldersey and Richard Rathbone, 1595 and 1598 respectively. The petitions were originally part of the Assembly Files.

Treasurers' Account Rolls

Chester, City Archives, TAR/1/1-3/49; c 1436-1642; Latin, English, and Anglo-Norman; parchment; rolls vary from a single roll made up of serially attached skins to 8 membranes attached at the top; various sizes, the longest being about 8000mm x 180mm (TAR/1/18) and the shortest being 1 gathering of 4 membranes measuring 300mm x 95mm. The following rolls were examined:

TAR/1/1	c 1436	Illegible; rental
TAR/1/2	1460-2	Rental
TAR/1/3	1468-9	Partially illegible; rental
♦TAR/1/4	1472	Rental
TAR/1/5a	c 1493-7	Partially illegible; rental
TAR/1/5b	1507-8	Rental
TAR/1/5c	1507-8	Duplicate of part of TAR/1/5b; rental
♦TAR/1/6	c Henry VII	Partially illegible; rental
TAR/1/7	1547-58	Illegible; rental
♦TAR/1/8	1554	Partially illegible at each end; rental and accounts
♦TAR/1/9	1555-6	Rental and accounts
♦TAR/1/10	1558-9	Rental and accounts
♦TAR/1/11	1563-4	Rental and accounts
♦TAR/1/12	1564-5	Incomplete at beginning; partially illegible; rental and accounts
♦TAR/1/13	1568-9	Rental and accounts
♦TAR/1/14	1571-2	Rental and accounts
♦TAR/1/15	1574-5	Rental and accounts
♦TAR/1/16	1576-7	Rental and accounts
♦TAR/1/17	1587-8	Accounts
♦TAR/1/18	1588-9	Rental and accounts
♦TAR/1/19	1589-90	Rental and accounts
♦TAR/1/20	1590-1	Rental and accounts
♦TAR/1/21	1591-2	Rental and accounts
♦TAR/1/22	1593-4	Partially faded; rental and accounts
♦TAR/2/23	1603-4	Rental and accounts
♦TAR/2/24	1607-8	Mostly faded and illegible; rental and accounts
TAR/2/25	1609-10	Partially illegible; receipts only
♦TAR/2/26	1610-11	Accounts partially illegible; rental and accounts
♦TAR/2/27	1611-12	Fragmentary and damaged; part of a rental down to letter 'K' and payments
♦TAR/2/28	1612-13	Payments partially illegible; rental and payments

TAR/2/29	1613	Rental only
♦TAR/2/30	1613-14	Rental and payments
TAR/2/31	1614-15	Rental and payments
TAR/2/32	1615-16	Rental only
♦TAR/2/33	1616-17	Partially illegible; payments
TAR/2/34	1616-17	Rental only
♦TAR/2/35	1617-18	Payments
TAR/2/36	1618-19	Rental only
♦TAR/2/37	1618-19	Payments
TAR/2/38	1619-20	Rental only
♦TAR/2/39	1619-20	Payments
TAR/2/40	1620-1	Rental only
TAR/2/41	Undated	Three illegible fragments
♦TAR/3/42	1622-3	Rental and payments
♦TAR/3/43	1625-6	Rental and payments
♦TAR/3/44	1626-7	Rental and payments
TAR/3/45	1632-3	Summary of city accounts; accounts of sheriffs
TAR/3/46	1636-7	Rental
♦TAR/3/47	1638-9	Rental and payments
♦TAR/3/48	1640-1	Incomplete
♦TAR/3/49	1641-2	Payments partially illegible; rental and payments

The Treasurers' Account Rolls usually include the receipts from city rentals and other sources of incomes and disbursements. Among the rentals are some for carriage houses. Annual disbursements might include those for morris dancers, the mayor's mount, the dragons and other beasts for Midsummer Show, and the minstrels and waits.

Harley 2158 See ANTIQUARIAN COLLECTIONS (p xlvii)
Harley 2173 See ANTIQUARIAN COLLECTIONS (p xlix)

Portmote Court Rolls; Pentice and Portmote Court Rolls

Chester, City Archives, M/R/4/85; 1428-30 and [1431/2]; Anglo-Norman and Latin; parchment; 1 membrane; 840mm x 295mm (730mm x 265mm); written continuously on both sides; no decoration. The roll is marked on the outside MR 85 and is listed in the Archives' card file as F/R/85; however, in the modern bound indexes, it is listed as M/R/4/85.

These sets of rolls are fragmentary, sporadic in date, frequently illegible, and too numerous to read systematically in the time available. Morris located the entry listed above, but my examination of a few of the rolls leads me to believe that they are unlikely to furnish evidence of dramatic activity. Furthermore, the portmote court entries in the Mayors' Books form a kind of index to the rolls and there seem to be no references to dramatic activity among these entries. The references to plays which do appear in the Mayors' Books are recorded in full in English, and this suggests that play matters would normally be decided by the mayor and council rather than in the courts.

Corporation Lease Book

Chester, City Archives, CHB/3; 1574-1705; English and Latin; paper; ii+261+ii; 420mm x 240mm (405mm x 210mm), average 55 long lines; gathered in 8s, leaves repaired on all sides; modern pencil and ink foliation; initial words of entries often in bold; modern green leather binding; title on spine. Some documents are dated as early as 1507-8; consequently, the date on the spine might refer to the time of compilation.

The book is primarily a lease book which contains copies of grants, leases, bonds, and documents setting up various charities in the city; in addition, it contains Savage's letter to the council and its reply, some articles of incorporation of companies, and other stray items. At the beginning, documents are copied out in full in the language of the original, but towards the end, they are replaced by shortened entries in English.

Miscellaneous

London, PRO, CHES 2/149; 1476-8; Latin and English; paper; 11 membranes attached at top; length varies from 665mm to 850mm (510mm to 665mm), width 285mm (220mm to 230mm), number of lines variable; some membranes written continuously, some written from top on both sides; no decoration.

London, PRO, CHES 2/151; 1479; Latin, English, and Anglo-Norman; paper (parchment covers); 6 membranes attached at top; length varies from 570mm to 820mm (295mm to 760mm), width from 290mm to 295mm (230mm to 250mm), number of lines variable; written continuously; no decoration.

London, PRO, CHES 2/166; 1495-6; Latin and English; paper (parchment cover); 5 membranes attached at top; length varies from 660mm to 790mm (585mm to 635mm), width 280mm (240mm to 250mm), number of lines variable; written continuously; no decoration.

These PRO documents transfer to local officials the Duttons' privilege to hold the Minstrels' Court. During the Dutton heir's minority, the Minstrels' Court resided in the crown prince as earl of Chester.

London, PRO, SP/60/9; 1540; English; paper (2 parchment leaves, ff 170, 242, bound in); i+275+i;

average 310mm x 100mm (text area variable); collation impossible, leaves mounted on binding strips; 6 foliation systems, including modern complete stamped foliation; little decoration; modern binding (front flyleaf and attached f 1 detached from spine).

London, PRO, STAC 8/156/22; 1616; English with Latin dating; parchment; 2 sheets with identifying label stitched through both; smaller sheet: 118mm x 320mm (70mm x 280mm), larger sheet 490mm x 635mm (450mm x 605mm); written on one side only; no decoration.

London, BL, Lansdowne 213, 'A relation of a short survey of 26 counties ...', ff 319-50; early 17th century; English; paper; iii+445+iii; 275mm x 170mm (average text area 225mm x 125mm); collation impossible; modern pencil foliation replacing 2 contemporary foliations (one by individual sections); no decoration; modern binding.

GUILD RECORDS

N B : Records not designated as being in a public repository remain in the possession of the guilds in Chester.

Barber Surgeons' Company, Company Book; 1606-98; English; paper; i+170+i; 335mm x 220mm (315mm x 190mm), average 50 ruled long lines; collation irregular; modern foliation; no decoration vellum binding.

Beerbrewers' Company, Company Book; City Archives, G3/2; 1606-38; English; paper; iii+162+i; 185mm x 290mm (text area variable); collation irregular (1 leaf torn out); 17th century foliation (ff 1-22, 7 omitted) and modern (ff 25-38, 31 repeated), final 126 leaves unfoliated (except ff 105v, 119, 123, 128, 130, 135 in modern pencil); original vellum binding.

Butchers' Company, Company Book; 1656-1812; English; paper; ii+257; 305mm x 190mm (text area variable); mostly gathered in 8s; modern ink foliation; original leather binding.

Cappers, Pinners, Wiredrawers, and Linendrapers' Company, Order Book; 1588-20th century; English; paper; 150 leaves; 285mm x 195mm (235mm x 125mm), average 30 long lines; collation irregular (7 leaves missing); unfoliated; no decoration; original vellum binding.

Coopers' Company, Account Book I; 1568-1617; English; paper, 150 leaves; 305mm x 210mm (280mm x 180mm), average 32 long lines; collation irregular (8 leaves missing, 1 inserted); unfoliated; no decoration; modern paper cover.

Coopers' Company, Company Book II; 1617-50; English; paper 132 leaves; 290mm x 195mm (285mm x 140mm), 38 long lines, collation irregular (4 leaves torn out, several fragmentary); unfoliated; no decoration; original vellum binding.

Coopers' Company, Loose Papers; English and Latin; paper; varying sizes; unnumbered; kept in a folder in the stewards' chest.

Drawers of Dee's Company, Company Book; City Archives, G10/1; 1572-1712; English; paper; 57 leaves; 290mm x 195mm (text area variable); gathered in 6s; 18th century pagination (first 6 leaves unpaginated); no decoration; modern binding. Badly water-damaged, many pages illegible, each leaf repaired with silk. Except for the prefatory remarks, the book seems to date from c 1597. Most of the accounts between 1623-4 (p 52) and 1641-2 (p 56) are missing.

Glovers' Company, Company Book; 1629-1948; English; parchment (first 11 leaves) and paper; ii+565; 340mm x 215mm (text area variable); gathered in 16s; 17th century ink foliation (first 40 leaves), 19th century ink pagination (first 262 leaves), rest of MS unnumbered and mostly blank; no decoration; original leather binding with tooled design.

Goldsmiths' Company, Minute Book; City Archives, G12/1; 1573-1702; English; parchment; viii+48; 265mm x 220mm (200mm x 155mm), 35 ruled long lines; mostly gathered in 6s (10 leaves missing); modern pencil pagination; no decoration; 18th century binding with tooled leather, the back cover bears the date '1723' and the front '1523', but the '5' shows marks of having been either repaired or added over another number.

Innkeepers' Company, Account Book; 1583-1603; English; paper; iii+60+iii; 320mm x 215mm (text area variable); collation irregular; modern pencil foliation; no decoration; entire volume has been rebound and repaired folio by folio with silk, original leather cover over new boards.

Innkeepers' Company, Company Book; 1571-1902; English; paper; 146 leaves; 270mm x 200mm (text area variable); mostly gathered in 12s (2 leaves missing); unfoliated; no decoration; original vellum binding. The book dates from about 1625 when the early orders were copied.

Joiners, Carvers, and Turners' Company, Company Book; City Archives, G14/1; 1576-1756; English; paper; 354 leaves; 415mm x 280mm (text area variable); collation irregular (2 leaves missing); modern foliation; no decoration; modern binding. The first 13 folios contain orders and oaths dated 1576-91.

Joiners, Carvers, and Turners' Company, Minute Book; City Archives, G14/2; 1615-1726; English; paper; i+432; 290mm x 190mm (text area variable); 32 long lines; mostly gathered in 12s (1 leaf missing); paginated; no decoration; original vellum binding.

Mercers, Ironmongers, Grocers, and Apothecaries' Company, Company Book; 1606-67; English; paper; ii+498+ii; 290mm x 185mm (235mm x 155mm), 42 long lines; mostly gathered in 7s and 8s (many leaves torn out); modern pencil pagination; no decoration; original brown leather binding.

Painters, Glaziers, Embroiderers, and Stationers' Company, Account Book I; 1567-1619; English; paper; ii+157+ii; 290mm x 195mm (280mm x 170mm), 32 long lines; gathered in 12s; unfoliated; red ink used in members lists and for initial words; 17th century leather binding.

Painters, Glaziers, Embroiderers, and Stationers' Company, Account Book II; 1620-1706; English; paper except for an initial vellum gathering of 4 and a second of 5 folios which contain copies of orders; 264 leaves; 290mm x 185mm (280mm x 150mm); gathered in 16s; unfoliated; no decoration; original leather binding dated 1621.

Painters, Glaziers, Embroiderers, and Stationers' Company, Minute Book; City Archives, CR63/2/131; 1624-51; English; paper; i+88+i; 190mm x 150mm (text area variable); gathered in 4s; unfoliated; no decoration; rebound in plain brown suede covers, possibly 19th century.

Saddlers and Curriers' Company, Charter; London, PRO, CHES 2/144; 1471-2; Latin and English; paper; 9 membranes attached at top; length varies from 780mm to 860mm (705mm to 720mm), width varies from 285mm to 290mm (235mm), number of lines variable; some membranes written continuously, some from top on both sides; no decoration.

Cordwainers and Shoemakers' Company, Account Book I; City Archives, G/8/2; 1547-98; English; paper, iv+124+iii; 295mm x 210mm (280mm x 155mm), 34 long lines; mostly gathered in 12s (1 leaf missing); modern pencil foliation; no decoration; original vellum binding.

Cordwainers and Shoemakers' Company, Account Book II; City Archives, G/8/3; 1598-1615; English; paper; 100 leaves; 290mm x 185mm (275mm x 170mm); collation irregular (ff 33-4 inserted bifolium); modern pencil foliation; no decoration; original vellum binding.

Cordwainers and Shoemakers' Company, Account Book III; City Archives, G/8/4; 1615-61; English; paper; 260 leaves; 290mm x 190mm (280mm x 155mm); gathered in 6s; modern pencil foliation; no decoration; original vellum binding, front cover and end leaves torn, back cover missing.

Cordwainers and Shoemakers' Company, Waste Book; City Archives, G/8/8; 1639-44; English; paper; 33 leaves; 310mm x 200mm (300mm x 190mm); collation irregular; unfoliated; no decoration; covers and last 2 leaves missing.

The Waste Book contains notes of expenditures, minutes at meetings, and other data which are entered in Account Book III, G/8/4; therefore, no entries were transcribed from this volume.

Smiths, Cutlers, and Plumbers' Company, Account Book I; in BL, Harley 2054, ff 14v-27.

See the description of MS under ANTIQUARIAN COLLECTIONS (pp xlv-xlvi).

Smiths, Cutlers, and Plumbers' Company, Account Book II; 1637-1902; English; paper; ii+428; 505mm x 200mm (text area variable); gathered in 6s; modern ink foliation and pencil pagination; no decoration; original leather binding, now coming apart.

There is no strict division of material in any of these categories: minute books generally contain only orders, admissions to freedom, and apprenticeships; account books only receipts and disbursements; but company books may combine the two.

Unavailable Guild Records

Cappers, Pinners, Wiredrawers, and Linendrapers' Company, Order Book, 1587-1607.
Merchant Drapers' Company, Company Book, 1637-1877.
Saddlers and Curriers' Company, Company Book, 1640-1950.

ECCLESIASTICAL RECORDS

London, PRO, S.C.6/Henry VIII/7384; 1539-41; Latin; paper (parchment covers); 82 membranes attached at top; length varies from 685mm to 830mm , width 285mm, 65 lines average; written on both sides of membrane; elaborated headings mark divisions; mb 1 badly faded.

The document contains a list of Carmelite properties seized at the dissolution.

Chester, Cathedral, Dean and Chapter, Treasurers' Accounts, Vols I-IV; 1541-1644; English and Latin; paper; number of leaves varies from 176 to 225; length varies from 295mm to 310mm, width from 200mm to 210mm (text area variable), 32 long lines; collation irregular (except Vol III, mostly gathered in 16s); modern pencil pagination (Vol II, older incomplete pencil pagination also); no decoration; Vol I rebound in 19th century leaf by leaf in red leather, Vols II-IV bound in green cloth covers on cardboard with titles on brown leather spines and in fair condition, damp-stains, many mutilated pages.

The Cathedral accounts are not continuous and some have been misdated in modern times. The accounts in the first two volumes are fragmentary and rather jumbled, but many of them are dated by regnal year or include a date in the expenditures. The accounts in the last two volumes are more systematic and divide the year into four segments: from the feast of St Katherine to the Nativity; from the Nativity to the Annunciation; from the Annunciation to the feast of St Michael; and from the feast of St Michael to that of St Katherine. The following are the extant accounts:

I Treasurers' Accounts, 1542-59

1 1541-2	3 1545-6	
2 1542-3	♦4 1544-5	

♦5 1544-5   8 1550-1
6 1546-7   ♦9 1555-6
7 1547-8   ♦10 1558-9

II Treasurers' Accounts, 1561-84

1 1561-2   7 1575-6
2 1562-3   8 1576-7 (?) Jumbled
3 1566-7   9 1577-8
♦4 1567-8   10 1578-9
5 1574-5   ♦11 1582-3
♦6 1571-2

III Treasurers' Accounts, 1584-1610

♦1 1584 (St Katherine to Annunciation only)
♦2 1589-90   ♦7 1604-5
♦3 1590-1   8 1605-6
♦4 1591-2   ♦9 1606-7
♦5 1596-7   ♦10 1607-8
♦6 1601-2   ♦11 1609-10

IV Treasurers' Accounts, 1611-44

♦1 1611-12   ♦7 1626-7
♦2 1612-13   ♦8 1627-8
♦3 1614-15   ♦9 1630-1
♦4 1617-18   ♦10 1637-8
♦5 1622-3   ♦11 1638-9 Fragment
6 1625-6   ♦12 1641-2

St Mary's-on-the-Hill Parish, Churchwardens' Accounts
Chester, Cheshire Record Office, Castle, P/20/13/1; 1536-1689; English, paper; 397 leaves; 385mm
x 150mm (375mm x 120mm); mostly gathered in 20s; unfoliated (except first 3 leaves, foliated in
ink); no decoration; original leather binding. Holme made excerpts from these accounts in Harley
1994.

St Michael's Parish, Register
Chester, Cheshire Record Office, Castle, P/65/8/1; 1558-1678; English; paper; 386 leaves; 2
volumes bound together, first volume 300mm x 200mm, second volume 315mm x 195mm (text
areas variable); collation irregular; modern pencil foliation (Vol I only, 1-205); no decoration;
17th century leather binding over wooden boards.

St Oswald's Parish, Churchwardens' Accounts
Chester, Cheshire Record Office, Castle, P/29/7/1; 1575-1629; English; paper; i+47+i; 305mm x
200mm (text area variable); collation irregular; modern foliation; no decoration; modern rebinding.
The MS is a 17th century transcription probably made by Randle Holme while he was churchwarden of St Oswald's.

St Oswald's Parish, Vestry Book
Chester, Cheshire Record Office, Castle, P/29/7/2; 1607-20; English; paper; ii+320+ii; 295mm x
190mm (text area variable); collation irregular (2 leaves missing); original pagination; no decoration;
original leather binding. Contains part of P/29/7/1.

Trinity Parish, Churchwardens' Accounts
In Harley 2177, ff 20v-53.

See the MS description under ANTIQUARIAN COLLECTIONS (pp xlix-l).

The Cathedral records and the churchwardens' accounts include receipts and disbursements; the parish records include accounts, but may also contain lists of
church officers, minutes of meetings, and other matters.

Antiquarian Manuscripts

In addition to the original documents, there are numerous antiquarian copies from
all of the categories named above; however, the general rule seems to be that if an
antiquarian copy exists, then the original has disappeared. Since there are only a
few instances in which both the original and a copy have survived and can be studied
together, the modern scholar may wonder whether he can depend upon the accuracy
of the records. Curiously enough, antiquarians can be trusted because they were
uncritical transmitters of documents rather than synthesizers of materials; nevertheless, we can only assume that the documents they transmitted were copied accurately,
not that the information in the document is accurate. This qualification might seem
to undermine the trustworthiness of antiquarian documents except for the fact
that there has to be a reason for the document to have existed in the first place, and
thus we can trust it to some degree.
    Antiquarian activity in Chester was quite strong as early as the sixteenth century
and to it we owe the preservation of the Whitsun play texts and the history of their
performance, as well as records of other ceremonial and quasi-dramatic activity.
Many of these antiquarian productions had their roots not in amateur dilettantism
but in a concern to preserve the city's history and to maintain its liberties and
customs. Perhaps the earliest documents are the Lists of Mayors and Sheriffs,
which undertook to establish the antiquity of the city's liberties and to fix the
succession of mayors; to these, in later years, were added chronicles or notes of the

significant events in the city's history.

By the end of the century, several antiquarians were at work. Archdeacon Rober Rogers had begun collecting materials for his history of the city but left it uncompleted at his death in 1595; nevertheless, the 'Breviary', which was finished by his son, David, was ascribed to the archdeacon by all the seventeenth-century antiquarians who made use of it. In 1594, Mayor William Aldersey issued a more accurate List of Mayors based on documentary evidence in his and the city's possession; his calendar, furthermore, was the first to place the establishment of the city's liberties in the thirteenth rather than the fourteenth century. George Bellin, the scribe, until 1622, for the Coopers, the Mercers, and the Shoemakers, transcribed and emended Lists of Mayors and copied two of the play manuscripts and the Coopers' pageant, as well as numerous other documents. In the seventeenth century David Rogers and Randle Holme II continued the antiquarian work begun by members of their families.

David Rogers is known solely for his completion of Archdeacon Rogers' 'Breviary' Between 1609 and about 1637, he produced five copies of four different versions of the 'Breviary'. Since the first three and a half chapters of each version are substantially the same, whereas the sections in Chapter IV on the city's plays and customs vary considerably, and whereas the lists of bishops, royal charters, and the like are brought up to David's own day, we may surmise that Archdeacon Rogers produced the early chapters and the early parts of the lists more or less in the form that we have them, and that David produced or augmented the latter sections of the volume. In the title of the last version, David says that he compiled the 'Breviary' from notes left by his father, and since some of the descriptions of the city's customs (eg, the homages to the Drapers), are clearly drawn from extant documents like the Assembly Book, we may surmise that David based his descriptions on notes taken by the archdeacon from records in the possession of the city. David, of course, may have copied some of these records himself, but besides his statement about having used his father's notes, he also implies that he did his work away from Chester and therefore may not have had the access to the records that his father did while resident at Chester Cathedral.

The four Randle Holmes are Chester's greatest transmitters of antiquarian material All were members of the Painters' company and became prominent in the governance of the city, in addition to their involvement in church and guild affairs. They were also heralds, and by far the greatest amount of material that they produced is genealogical records. Although the middle two seem to have been most active, as a group they were responsible for producing or collecting over two hundred volumes of material dealing with Chester, an immense collection of manuscripts which now forms MSS 1920-2277 in the Harley collection. However, the only one of the four who seems to have produced records relevant to the present collection is Randle Holme II, active from the 1630s into the 1660s. Like his father, he seems to have been involved in preparing the city's ancient or standard each year, in helping to revive the city's giants and other creatures for the Midsummer Show, in preparing many of the guilds' standards for the Midsummer Watch, and in performing other tasks associated with his craft. He was also a churchwarden of St Oswald's. He was a very active scribe, who copied, collected, and sometimes annotated every type of record which is relevant to this collection.

Holme seems to be a trustworthy scribe. There are only two antiquarian documents for which the originals still survive and both of these were transcribed by Holme. One is part of the churchwardens' accounts for St Oswald's and the other is a copy of the Painters' Charter. In the first instance, Holme is copying documents in a secretary hand similar to his own and from the same period; in the second, he is copying a court hand from a hundred years before. In both instances, he is totally reliable: in many cases he will copy the same spelling, abbreviations, contractions, and the like, but in others he may make minor spelling variations, expand an ampersand, contract an 'and', or make other similar expansions and contractions. In any event, these minor alterations need not undermine our confidence in the accuracy of the large quantity of records that he was responsible for transmitting.

Although we can be reasonably confident of Holme's accuracy, we cannot be assured of that of other scribes; consequently, it is necessary that we try to make some distinctions about the kinds of records extant and their degree of accuracy. The documents least likely to be transmitted inaccurately are those which simply require the copying of an original text. Among these are guild and churchwardens' accounts of expenditure, ordinances of the city council, and letters and petitions to the mayor and city council. Of course, it is possible for a scribe to make an error in transcription and evidentiary cases ideally should be built either on several bits of the same kind of evidence or on uncontaminated evidence from original sources; in any event, scholars who use these primary antiquarian records should remain sceptical of them and not build their cases on unique references which could be erroneous.

Once a primary antiquarian document of this type has been assimilated into some other kind of production, then we are confronted with a different problem of accuracy. While forgeries of primary documents do take place, it is difficult to imagine that a scribe would sit down and invent lists of expenditure for a guild or an ordinance for the city. The same is not the case for a 'history', for histories, whether consciously or piously, are often fabricated. For example, the antiquarians of Chester piously produced a catalogue of mayors which began with John Arnewaye in 1328. When the Whitsun plays came under attack, the antiquarians claimed that the plays started in Arnewaye's term of office and were produced over a three-day period at Whitsuntide even though we know that, if the plays existed at all in 1328, they were produced on Corpus Christi Day alone. The fraud was partially exposed by Mayor William Aldersey, who claimed that extant documents showed the first mayor to be Sir Walter Lynnett in the time of Henry III and that Arnewaye was mayor from about 1278 to 1288, a fact documented by extant charters; moreover,

Aldersey dropped all references to the invention of the plays from the List he issued
in 1594.

Earlier Mayors Lists seem to have had a wider circulation than the Aldersey List,
but we know that the Aldersey List got to other antiquarians even if it did not
always have the desired results. For example, in the first three versions of the
'Breviary', David Rogers says that the plays were initiated by the first mayor of
Chester about 1328, but in the last two versions he says that they were initiated
in the first year of Arnewaye's term about 1328. From another note in the second
version, it is clear that David came across the information that Arnewaye was not
the first mayor; nevertheless he retained the incorrect date of Arnewaye's term and
passed on the tradition that Arnewaye invented the Whitsun Plays.

This tradition is an easily recognized fabrication – although no one questioned
the story before this century – and F.M. Salter has provided a plausible explanation
for how the story came about.[1] But some antiquarian statements may seem to be
fabrications when they are not, or they may be too hastily dismissed as nonsense on
the grounds that they are self-contradictory. For example, David Rogers does not
always pay enough attention to the documents he is transmitting to eliminate the
contradictions. In his description of the plays, he says that there are twenty-four
pageants and then he appends a list of twenty-five. Salter used this discrepancy as
an illustration of David's untrustworthiness without noting that the Late Banns say
that the cycle contains twenty-four pageants – David's source for the first statement
– whereas the List of Companies and their parts, which circulated as an independent
document, lists twenty-five – David's second source.[2] The differences in computation
depend on whether one counts the Coopers' and Ironmongers' plays as one (as does
MS H) or two (as do the four group MSS HmABR).[3] The point is not that David
is inconsistent or inaccurate but that he copied two traditions, each of which happen
to be accurate within certain limits.

The antiquarians' failure to examine critically the documents that they were
transmitting tends to undermine our confidence in the antiquarians' statements;
nevertheless, when used with caution, antiquarian materials can be relied upon
precisely because the antiquarians were uncritical. One is struck by the fact that the
Chester antiquarians almost always copied what they saw even if it did not make
sense or if it contradicted something else that they had copied. If an antiquarian
merely transmits what he sees, then it is likely that a document has been transmitted
without error from its moment of origin to the time that the antiquarian makes his
copy. This does not mean, unfortunately, that the facts of the document are true
or that they are correctly interpreted, but it does mean that the antiquarian has
probably reported it accurately in the main. Rather than dismiss such evidence,
the scholar should attempt to ascertain whether there is any truth in the statements
despite their possible contradictions. As we have seen, David Rogers' statements
about the number of pageants in the play cycle are not so much inaccuracies as a
confusion of two different phenomena from two different sources. Similarly,

historical reconstructions of the development of the cycle plays are often inaccurate because scholars depend on antiquarians' dates; it is possible for the date to be wrong but for the event associated with it to have happened nonetheless. These antiquarian records, therefore, may seem confused and contradictory, but they may be able to tell us something about Chester's early history.

Although antiquarian evidence can be used to great effect, it would be foolish to rely on it in the same manner that one relies on original documents; consequently, all antiquarian records in this volume are noted in the margin by the letters 'A' (for Antiquarian Compilation) or 'AC' (for Antiquarian Collection). Clearly, original documents should have priority as evidence; antiquarian transcripts of accounts, ordinances, and the like have a high priority also, but they may contain inaccuracies; and antiquarian 'histories' are least trustworthy at face value, but may contain accurate data from a variety of sources which may be accepted as evidence, particularly if it can be substantiated by external or circumstantial evidence.

ANTIQUARIAN COMPILATIONS

Antiquarian Compilations are volumes which have been given some form, such as a history, list of mayors, and the like. The Compilations have been further divided into the Rogers' Breviaries, the Lists of Mayors and Sheriffs, and Miscellaneous.

The Breviaries of Archdeacon and David Rogers

Chester, City Archives, unnumbered MS; 1609; English; vi+123+iv; 290mm x 185mm (260mm x 140mm), 35 long lines; gathered irregularly, most leaves have catchwords; modern pencil foliation; no decoration; modern cardboard binding, green leather on corners and spine, title on spine.

Relevant Contents
Title, 'To the Reader', and, in Chapter IV, the order of entries is: the Shoemakers', Saddlers', and Married Persons' Homages to the Drapers, the Whitsun Plays, the Late Banns, the List of Companies and their Parts, the Midsummer Show, the Sheriffs' Breakfast, and, in Chapter VIII, a note on John Arnewaye and Randulph Higden.

Provenance
The provenance is uncertain before the mid-nineteenth century. The inscription on the flyleaf indicates that the volume was in the possession of George Wilbraham of Delamere House, Cheshire, in 1849, and it was still reported to be there in 1874.[4] It is not clear when it entered the City Archives. Mrs Elizabeth Berry, former archivist at Chester, reported to me that the volume was not in the list of corporation records compiled by Fergusson Irvine in 1906, but that the volume was rebound by Mr Lamacraft in October 1938. Since there is no reference to the volume in the corporation minutes between 1906 and 1938, where other gifts and purchases are recorded, it is possible either that Irvine overlooked it or that it was acquired between

these dates but not entered in the minutes.

London, BL, Harley 1944; c 1619; English; paper, i+117+i; 200mm x 145mm (approximately
200mm x 120mm), 43 long lines; leaves pasted singly on modern binding strips; modern pencil
foliation, correcting older ink foliation which runs 1-129 (f 3 - end flyleaf; missing 61-7, 71, 107,
114, 126); coloured drawings of coats of arms; red leather BL binding on boards, title on spine;
some damp-stained leaves.

Relevant Contents
Identical with the preceding entry.

Provenance
The volume apparently entered the Holme collection in the seventeenth century and
remained there until it was incorporated with the rest into the Harley collection.

Chester, Cheshire Record Office, DCC 19; c 1619; English; paper; iii+125+ii; 180mm x 140mm
(165mm x 110mm), 26 long lines; mostly gathered in 8s and 12s (2 leaves missing); ink foliation;
no decoration; modern white vellum cover, title on spine.

Relevant Contents
The MS revises the title, omits the 'To the Reader' and the Late Banns, and adds
new sections on the St George's Day Race and the Christmas Watches. The order
of entries is as follows: the Shoemakers', Saddlers', and Married Persons' Homages
to the Drapers (minor revisions with additional material at the end), the Sheriffs'
Breakfast (revised), the St George's Day Race (1609 version), the Midsummer Show
(revised), the Christmas Watches, the Whitsun Plays (revised), the List of Companies
and their Parts, and, in Chapter VIII, a note on Arnewaye and Higden (revised).

Provenance
According to the Cheshire Record Office calendar of the Crewe (Cowper) collection
the volume was a part of the Cowper collection accumulated by Dr William Cowper
of Overlegh (1701-67), an antiquarian and mayor of Chester. The collection remained at Overlegh until c 1816 when Charles Cholmondeley inherited it and
removed it to Condover. The MS was reported to be in the Cholmondeley collection
in 1876 and was sold along with the remainder of the collection c 1898.[5] The
volume was purchased by the Cheshire Record Office in August 1950 from the
executors of Lady Annabel Crewe.

London, BL, Harley 1948; c 1624; English; paper; i+151+i; 193mm x 146mm (165mm x 116mm
30 long lines; collation irregular (2 leaves missing); modern pencil foliation correcting older ink
numbers which run 1-15 (ff 3-17), 1-136 (ff 18-150), missing 7, 128, 134; no decoration; brown
cloth BL binding on boards, brown leather spine and corners, title on spine; some damp stains.

Relevant Contents

The MS revises the title, but otherwise follows CRO in omitting the preface and Late Banns. It is almost the same as CRO throughout the initial entries, except for some revision and rearrangement at the end of the section on the Homages to the Drapers. The MS continues with, in order, the Sheriffs' Breakfast (revised), the Christmas Watches (revised), the Midsummer Show (revised), the St George's Day Race (1623 version), the Whitsun Plays (revised), the List of Companies and their Parts, and omits the note at the end of Chapter VIII on Arnewaye and Higden.

Provenance

The provenance is the same as that of Harley 1944.

Liverpool, Liverpool University MS 23.5; c 1637; English; paper; 126 leaves; 285mm x 185mm (260mm x 155mm), 45-50 long lines; mostly gathered in 6s and 8s (1 leaf missing, final gathering almost torn away completely), catchwords on recto and verso of all folios; modern pencil foliation (last 27 leaves unnumbered); 17th century vellum binding, title on cover.

Relevant Contents

The MS revises the title and omits the preface, the Late Banns, the Christmas Watches, and the Midsummer Show. It nearly duplicates the Chester Archives MS and Harley 1944 in the entry on the Homages to the Drapers, except that it contains the poem from the CRO MS at the beginning, even while omitting the continuations which appear in both the CRO MS and Harley 1948. It continues with the Sheriffs' Breakfast (revised), the St George's Day Race (revised 1623 version), the Whitsun Plays (revised), and the List of Companies and their Parts.

Provenance

The Revs Samuel and Daniel Lysons printed their *Magna Britannia* in 1810 and said that the manuscript was in the possession of William Nichols of Chester; however, Mr M.R. Perkin, Curator of Special Collections at Liverpool University, reported to me that the bookplate says that Earwaker sold this and other volumes from George Folliott's collection at Stanley Place, Chester, on 1 August 1810. There can be no question that the volume used by the Lysons is the same as the Folliott volume; consequently, they must have seen the book when it belonged to Nichols and it must have passed shortly afterward to Folliott, who then sold it in 1810, or they must have learned that it had been recently sold to Nichols as they were seeing their book through the press. In 1930, the volume was sold by B. Halliday of Leicester to an unnamed person interested in the history of Cheshire.[6] The volume disappeared until it was reported in the HMC Reports as a new acquisition by the University of Liverpool.[7]

Dates of Composition

The Chester Archives unnumbered MS is undoubtedly the earliest of the five copies
it is dated and signed by 'D. Rogers' in the upper left-hand corner of the title page
and at the end of the preface, '3 Iuly 1609'. On f 87, at the end of Chapter VII
which deals with the earls of Chester, there is a reference in the last entry to 'this
presente yeare 1610' and another signature, 'D Rogers; desember 1610'. These
signatures and several references in the text indicate that David Rogers made the
copy between July 1609 and December 1610. The text has been written in brown
ink; however, there are numerous corrections and deletions in black ink, again in
David's hand, and there are additions, in black ink, to the lists of earls, bishops,
and deans which bring the material up to the year 1619. There are abundant
numbers of blank pages at the end of each chapter and at intervals throughout the
text, which suggest that David left space for later additions.

BL Harley 1944 seems to have been transcribed directly from the corrected
Chester Archives copy. The note on the title plate, now almost obliterated, and
the signature at the end of the preface merely give the date '1609'; however, most
of Harley 1944, including the updated lists, is written in the same brown ink and
would appear to have been written at one time in 1619 or thereafter.

More significantly, the short black lines which appear periodically indicate stopping
places in the process of making the Harley 1944 copy. Four of the six marks in
the Banns section, for example, occur at a place corresponding to the end of one
page and the beginning of another in Harley 1944. The black line in the Chester
MS at:

   a) f 18v 'This matter he ...' begins f 22v in Harley 1944
   b) f 19 'If the same ...' occurs on f 22v
   c) f 19v 'This worthie ...' begins f 23
   d) f 20 'The appearinge ...' begins f 23v
   e) f 21 'The Skynners ...' occurs on f 24
   f) f 21v 'And not god ...' begins f 25

The marks at b) and e) do not correspond to the beginning of a page in Harley 1944
The marks at a), d), and f) appear within the page in Chester but correspond to the
beginning of a page in Harley. The other mark, c), is at the top of the page in both
Chester and Harley. In addition, some words crossed through in black ink in Chester
are omitted in Harley. These facts suggest that, although there are a few additions
in the Harley version, the MS was copied directly from Chester; consequently, the
two are almost identical.

It should be noted that the blank pages have been drastically reduced and now
occur only at the end of chapters in Harley. It is probable, therefore, that David
prepared this copy as a presentation copy sometime in 1619.

The Cheshire Record Office MS DCC 19 also seems to have been made by David in 1619 or shortly thereafter; however, there have been several alterations in the text, which indicate, along with the omission of the preface, that David has begun to produce the 'Breviary' in his own right rather than simply transmitting his father's incomplete version. The last date in the original hand and ink is in the final entry in the list of bishops (ff 69v-70), where David mentions that John Bridgeman was made a bishop on 13 June 1619. The 1609 version of the St George's Day Race indicates that David has not heard about the alterations made in the Race in 1623; that is, it is clear from statements that David makes in the text that he is not living in Chester and that he only receives reports about things that have occurred there. The distance between David and Chester probably accounts for his failure to include anything at all about the St George's Day Race and the Show (1610) in the Chester Archives and Harley 1944 copies, even though the latter of these was made in 1619 or thereabouts. The CRO copy must have been made after 1619 but probably could not have been made much after 1623.

Much of the material has been revised and David has enlarged the earlier versions. The addition of the proclamations and more information about the Sheriffs' Break-fast and the features of the Midsummer Show, and the revision of the note on Arnewaye, all indicate that David came into possession of new documents which would have included, at the least, Mayor Aldersey's List of Mayors (1594) and other antiquarian notes.

The Harley 1948 MS was probably made in 1624. It must have been made after 1623 because David says that he has heard about the 'new alteration' in the St George's Day Race; moreover, he refers twice to King James I 'that now is' (ff 52, 126) and to Lord Cary, deputy of Ireland, 'at this present 1624'. All the entries except that for the Whitsun Plays have been expanded or newly added; the play entry has been reduced.

The Liverpool University MS 23.5 is clearly the latest in date. Not only is David's usually tight and clear secretary hand loose, elongated, and shaky – suggesting that of an older man – but this MS contains a revision of the entry on the 1623 St George's Day Race and is the first version of the 'Breviary' to indicate that David knew how much the Saddlers' bell weighed. Although the last bishop whose term he knew was Bridgeman's in 1619 and the last earl is from the reign of James I, the last mayor listed in the main hand is Thomas Throp, 1637, and the MS may be dated to this year.

David's failure to revise the lists of bishops and earls is further evidence that he was not resident in Chester and that he did not have much more information than he did at the time that he made the CRO copy. David probably dropped the section on the Midsummer Show because he knew that it had been suppressed earlier in the century. He seems to be unaware of its revival in the late 1620s, and since he makes no distinction between the Show and the Watch, the latter of which we know to have been continued throughout the period, he must have deleted the entire Midsummer entry on the assumption that it had been totally suppressed. The expanded List of Mayors, however, indicates that David got a revised list, just as he had suggested in his statements in Chapter VIII in the CRO MS. The weight of the evidence suggests that David made this copy about 1637, but that he had not received much new information since he made the CRO copy.

Authorship

David Rogers' contemporaries and succeeding generations of antiquarians associated the 'Breviary' with the Archdeacon Robert Rogers who died about 1595. This attribution arises quite naturally from the titles of the CRO, Harley 1948 and Liverpool MSS, and from the preface in the Chester Archives MS and Harley 1944. The preface and the Liverpool title indicate that at the time of his death, Archdeacon Rogers left a collection of material on Chester which was largely or wholly unassembled and that David put together the material and subsequently added to, deleted from, and otherwise revised it. The question remains of what David did with his father's material and how much of the composition can be said to be his.

The evidence for authorship is laid out elsewhere; however, further study of the MSS has convinced me that a strong case can be made that David revised each version of the 'Breviary' from his father's notes rather than from preceding versions and that David was largely responsible for transmitting materials derived from sources in the sixteenth century.[8] It is clear that much of the material that David transmitted was collected by his father. Most of the first four chapters of the 'Breviary' are written from a third-person point of view, that is, David tells us what his father wrote down. In addition, the entry on the Homages to the Drapers recalls the language of the extant ordinance of 1540 which altered the customs. Similarly, the statement about Henry Hardware and the suppression of the Midsummer Show is derived from the note in the Mayors Lists, the description of the city streets can be found in the Assembly Book, and the remarks about the authorship of the plays and the riding of the Banns echo the title and prefatory section of the Late Banns, especially those of the Bellin copy in Harley 2013 (dated 1600).[9]

The arrangement of the entries and the collations suggests that except for Harley 1944, subsequent Breviaries were not copied from their immediate predecessors; in other words, each new version or edition was taken from the same sources rather than from each other. For example, the Liverpool MS seems to have greater affinities with the CRO MS than with Harley 1948, its immediate predecessor. Although the Liverpool copy revises the sections on the Sheriffs' Breakfast, the St George's Day Race, and the Whitsun Plays, it follows the order of the CRO MS except that it omits the sections on the Midsummer Show and the Christmas Watches; therefore, it may have been revised from the CRO copy or from Archdeacon Rogers' notes. The collations support a general agreement of the CRO and Liverpool MSS against Harley 1948: see the collation notes to p 234, ll 4-5; p 234, l 16; p 235, l 11; p 235, l 17; p 237, l 4 (1st variant); p 237, ll 11-18. However, since the CRO copy and Harley 1948 agree against the Liverpool MS in one instance (p 237, l 1), and since the CRO copy omits material in three places which is included in the Liverpool MS (notes to p 236, ll 2-3; p 236, ll 4-5 (1st variant); p 237, l 4 (2nd variant)), it seems impossible for the Liverpool copy to have been revised directly from the CRO MS. Furthermore, there are two variants in the 'List of Companies and their Parts' which confirm that David made the CRO and Liverpool copies from his notes rather than the latter from the former. The Chester Archives and CRO MSS call the Shearmen's play the 'prophetes before ye day of Dome' whereas Harley 1948, Liverpool MS, and the Early Banns use 'afore' (note to p 251, l 23). Furthermore, the Early Banns and Liverpool alone use 'be' instead of 'weare' in the statements about the divisions of the plays into segments (notes to p 250, l 1 (3rd variant); p 251, l 6). These variants suggest either that David had two different copies of the List of Companies, or more probably, that he changed the older forms 'afore' and 'be' when he copied some, but not all, of the Breviaries. In any event, the variants suggest that the Liverpool version was copied directly neither from the CRO MS nor from Harley 1948, and the number of revisions in the CRO MS indicates that it was not copied from the Chester Archives MS or Harley 1944; consequently, there seems to be a break between the first two copies and the last three, none of which seem to have been taken from either of the first two.

In the title to the Liverpool copy, David says that the 'Breviary' was collected by his father, but that it was 'in scatered notes' and 'Reduced in to these Chapters followinge' by his son, David. If this were the case for the Liverpool MS, then it may also have been the case for the Chester Archives and CRO MSS and Harley 1948. Furthermore, David's procedure of returning to his notes may account for the similarities in phraseology in many of the descriptions at the same time that it explains the discrepancies between accounts. For example, in the early Breviaries David says that the pageant carts had six wheels, but in the later ones that they had four. The Chester Archives copy uses the roman numeral 'vj', which could be a reversal of 'iv'; when David copied Harley 1944 from the Chester Archives MS, he converted the number into an arabic '6'. However, when he wrote the CRO MS, Harley 1948, the Liverpool MS, he used arabic '4'; therefore, it seems unlikely that he copied the last three Breviaries from the Chester Archives MS or Harley 1944, but rather that he returned to his original which must have had 'iv'. Similarly, if David returned to his notes each time that he made a 'Breviary', then we can account for the vehement attack on the plays in the two earliest and the last copies and the total absence of any antagonism in the two intervening copies: his source must have contained the attacks which he did not always copy.

The revisions tell us something about the extent of David's responsibility for the content of the entries. Some entries remain almost unchanged through the entire series of editions; for example, the main body of the entry on the Homages to the Drapers is almost identical in each version of the 'Breviary', and the description is obviously derived directly or through some intermediary from the 1540 ordinance. Other entries change because the custom changed (eg, the St George's Day Race);

still others are altered in order to reduce them to some coherent shape.

The revisions of the Whitsun Play entry suggest that David attempted to make the entry more orderly and that he had more than one source available to him. A comparison of Chester Archives and Liverpool MSS illustrates the greater degree of order and the regrettable succinctness of the Liverpool over the Chester Archives copy: in the Liverpool MS, one sentence is devoted to the maker of the plays, their matter, the time they were first set out, the actors, the time of year they were played, and the manner of performance, and a few sentences to the places where they were performed. The Chester Archives version contains much of the same material but is more disorganized. David tells us about the author, the first performance, the manner of performance (rather awkwardly), the riding of the Banns, the time of performance, and the places of performance along with some comments on keeping the pageants moving. Then he returns to the description of the pageant (again awkwardly), then repeats some details about keeping the pageants moving, and repeats the places of performance, but with an additional place, and then gives more commentary on keeping the pageants moving. The repetition with variation of the playing places suggests that David had more than one source; in addition, the variation in the descriptions of the pageant cart in the four versions combined with a similarity in phrasing in some of the descriptions of the mode of processional presentation suggest that David had a variety of sources which he used in some versions and not in others, or that he was condensing each time from a larger body of notes.

Since some material remains unchanged and can be traced to extant documents, and since some entries like the Whitsun Play entry contain phraseology which can be traced to extant documents, and since David says that he was working with 'scatered notes', we can assume that David had a body of material originally dating from the sixteenth century which he amended or enlarged when a custom was changed, or when he received more information through a new List of Mayors or the like. The variety of description in the Whitsun Play entries suggests that he may have had more than one description of the route and the pageant carts; most of the other information can be traced to the Late Banns. It is probable, therefore, that most of the material in the Breviaries was written or collected by Archdeacon Rogers and that David arranged it into chapters and revised it four times from the archdeacon's notes and additional information which David received from time to time.

There is the possibility that there was an earlier version of Rogers' 'Breviary' which circulated under the title 'An Abrigemente of many Collections ... gathered by that Reuerend Dyvine Master Robert Rogers ... devided into Seauen Chapters' (Harley 2133; CRO: DCC 11). The Harley MS contains a Mayors List which is written in one hand until 1622 and continued in another until 1635; CRO: DCC 11 is in one hand to 1635 and thus may be a copy of the Harley MS. Both MSS postdate David Rogers' first three copies of the 'Breviary' and could be an abridgement of one of them; however, the Breviaries and these MSS differ at a number of points.

Neither of the two MSS contains the word 'Breuary' in its title, even though the title otherwise recalls those of the later Breviaries. Secondly, the Breviaries always have eleven chapters, but these versions are said to have seven when, in fact, they only have four. Their final chapter includes information on the first building of the churches, the erection of the monastery, and the succession of the abbots, bishops, and deans; in other words, the chapter is unified in its focus on ecclesiastical matters. In the Rogers' Breviaries, the sections on the customs and plays are lumped together into Chapter IV along with the building of the parish churches, but the successions of abbots, bishops, and deans are put in subsequent chapters. Harley 2133 and CRO: DCC 11 do not refer to the plays at all; on the other hand, it is odd that David put the section on the plays and customs in the chapter on the building of the parish churches when the other chapters are unified by subject matter, and when he reserved Chapter XI specifically, he said, for those things which could not aptly be placed in earlier chapters.

Harley 2125, ff 76-87v, contains a similar collection of material bearing the title 'The Antiquity, of the Anciante and famous citty of Chester, with many notes collected by some experienced in authors of great antiquitie' (note the similarity to the title of the Chester Archives MS and Harley 1944). This version also ends with the history of the churches of Chester and Randle Holme added immediately afterwards: 'here followed the whittson playes verbatyn as in lib*er* S 201 begining ⟨...⟩ Theis be the Craftes *etc*.' The *incipit*, in fact, does not come from the beginning of any of the extant play texts, but it is the beginning of the Early Banns entry. Holme's note suggests that the collection entitled 'Antiquity' and attributed to a group of anonymous authors may have provided the model for David's including the play section in with the history of the churches (except that David used the Late rather than the Early Banns). Furthermore, this collection may ultimately have derived from some document like the White Book of the Pentice or the exemplar of the book in Harley 2150 which contains the Early Banns; there are similarities between the material which comes before the Early Banns, that at the beginning of these 'Antiquity' collections and the prefatory material in the Assembly Book.

There are a number of MSS which go under the 'Antiquity' title (Bodleian Top Cheshire e-11 [1646]; Add. 11335 [1725]; Add. 29780 [18th century]; Stowe 811 [18th century]. These collections are attributed to an anonymous group of authors and contain many of the same entries as the Breviaries but in a different order. Significantly, the List of Companies and their Parts in the Whitsun Plays, the only reference to the plays, either follows the section on the churches or is included under the chapter entitled 'Of ye first buyldinge of this Cittie of Chester & of the destroyinge of the same' (Bodleian MS). Stowe 811, in fact, says on f 2 that the material is derived from Rogers.

There are also two other MSS which go under the related title 'Briefe notes of the Antiquitye of the famose Cittye of Chester' (Harley 2125; Add. 29779), both of which can be dated to about 1622 and are in George Bellin's hand. The Bellin collection contains many of the same entries in almost the same order as the Breviaries except that they omit the customs and plays and put the earls earlier in the collection than does David Rogers. They include a 'List of Companies' after those sections devoted to the bishops and deans; in other words, they follow the basic pattern of the 'Antiquity' volumes in placing the play reference after the religious material.

Since all of these volumes were produced after David had written the first three copies of the 'Breviary', it is not possible to rule out their indebtedness to the Breviaries; nevertheless, it should be noted that the arrangement of material is different in most cases, and in all cases, including the Bellin collections, the content in the entries differs in numerous details in arrangement and thus could not have been taken directly from Rogers alone. Furthermore, Harley 2133, CRO: DCC 11, Bodleian Top Cheshire e-11, Add. 11335, Add. 29780, Harley 2125, and Add. 29779 all contain Mayors Lists which begin with Lynnett rather than Arnewaye (though the starting dates in the last two MSS differ from the others), whereas David's Breviaries have Lists that begin with Arnewaye. This suggests the possibility that Mayor Aldersey copied his Mayors List (dated 1594) in with these collections and that they circulated separately from David's augmented Breviaries. Aldersey could have obtained a copy of the uncompleted Rogers collection from the archdeacon, or the collection could have been among the archdeacon's sources and some of them came to be identified as his after the Breviaries came into circulation and the antiquarians noted the similarities between the two.

Further study might reveal the relationships which obtain between these MSS, the Breviaries, the Assembly Book, the White Book of the Pentice, the Harley 2150 book, and other early histories like Smith and Webb's *Vale-Royall*, but such a study will be hampered by the antiquarians' practice of copying from one another, of trading material around, and of copying material which itself might have been copied and altered once before. If there were an earlier version of the 'Breviary' or if Archdeacon Rogers simply pirated his collection and some features of its organization from those going under the titles of 'Antiquity' or 'Briefe notes', we need not change our judgement of the authorship of the 'Breviary', since the existence of these MSS compilations would only confirm that the archdeacon transmitted his material from sixteenth-century sources and that his son augmented it from materials collected by his father but not entered into the archdeacon's original version.

Lists of Mayors and Sheriffs
Not all of the MSS listed below are simply Lists of Mayors; the Lists are often contained within antiquarian histories of Chester, most of which are directly descended from Archdeacon Rogers' 'Breviary' or its predecessor. Some contain the List of Companies and their Parts in the Whitsun Plays, but they have no other descriptions of dramatic activity than those entered in the Mayors Lists.

Mayors List 1
London, BL, Harley 1046, List of Mayors and Sheriffs, ff 159v-65; 17th century; English; paper;

ii+242+iii; 287mm x 185mm (text area variable), some double columns; leaves pasted on new binding strips and gathered in 8s; modern pencil foliation, correcting older ink foliation; modern dark brown cloth binding on boards with black leather corners and spine.

Harley 1046 is a book of genealogies except for the List of Mayors. The catalogue begins with John Arnewaye's term in 1320 and concludes with the 1586 entry.

Mayors List 2
London, BL, Harley 1944, ff 67-100. I.

See the MS description for Rogers' 'Breviary' (p xxviii). The List begins with Arnewaye's term in 1328 and is continued in the same hand until c 1637; however, some of these last entries may have been later additions.

Mayors List 3
London, BL, Harley 2057, 'The maiors of chester. the charters of ye Citty with other thinges about ye same'; 17th century; English and Latin; paper; ii+171+iii; 307mm x 194mm (text area variable); leaves restored and rebound as singles; modern pencil foliation, correcting older ink; no decoration; BL binding, brown leather on corners and spine, title on spine.

The list is attributed to Aldersey; it begins with Lynnett in 1241 and continues in the same hand until 1601.

Mayors List 4
London, BL, Harley 2105, 'seuerall things conceringe the citty of Chester'; early 17th century; English and Latin; paper; ii+296+iii; size of leaves variable (largest 310mm x 200mm, smallest 225mm x 140mm); single leaves attached to modern binding strips; modern pencil foliation; older ink foliation (260-550), ff 3-246; no decoration; BL binding with red leather on spine and corners, title on spine.

The List is a fragment which begins with the twenty-first mayor in 1348 and ends with 1580 (ff 87-97). From 1569 to the end, the entries are in various hands.

Mayors Lists 5-7
London, BL, Harley 2125, 'WW Maiors of Chester': List of Mayors and Sheriffs I (ff 23-58), List of Mayors and Sheriffs II (ff 90-157v), List of Mayors and Sheriffs III (ff 173-95); 17th century; English; paper ii+195+iii; 307mm x 217mm (300mm x 143mm), 45 long lines; single sheets bound together; modern pencil foliation correcting older ink numbers; dark red leather BL binding on boards, title on spine; some damage from dampness.

The first List (ML 5) is dated 1622 and Randle Holme, who made a number of annotations on it, says that it is George Bellin's catalogue; it is probably Bellin's hand. The List begins with Lynnett but assigns his term to 1317; it is in one hand to

1623 (f 58) and is continued to 1650 in a second hand (f 74). The second List (ML 6) is derived from an Aldersey exemplar which begins in 1257. The List is in one hand to 1650 (ff 90-157v; probably Randle Holme's) and continued in another to 1705 (ff 158-72). List III (ML 7) is similar to List II but contains little more than the mayors' names and only a single reference to the plays. It was transcribed by Randle Holme and goes only to 1616 (ff 173-95).

Mayors List 8

London, BL, Harley 2133, 'Mayors of Chester ...'; List of Mayors and Sheriffs, ff 10-68v; 17th century; English; paper; 90 leaves; 297mm x 190mm (text area variable); gathered in 8s; modern pencil foliation; 17th century brown leather binding on boards, now loose, with clasp marks.

ML 8 contains two Lists. List I begins with Lynnett in 1241 (f 10) and continues to 1622 in the same hand; however, the List was apparently started in 1615-16 (see f 47v where the numbering of years is reversed to 'tyme expired'), continued by the same scribe until 1622, and then continued by another scribe to 1635. List II, ff 59-68v, simply enrolls the mayors from Lynnett in 1240 to 1509 and then says that all catalogues agree after that point. List I to 1622 is mostly in Holme's hand and List II is entirely in his hand.

Mayors List 9

London, BL, Additional 11335, William Aldersey, 'Antiquitie of the Most Famous Citty of Chester'; c 1724; English; paper; iii+86+ii; 315mm x 205mm (310mm x 175mm), 40 long lines; mostly gathered in 8s (11 leaves missing); modern pencil foliation (single unnumbered leaf between ff 34-5); modern brown leather binding, title on spine.

The MS contains a List of Memorable Events which begins with 1275 and stops at 1645; the reference in the 1642 entry to King Charles 'that now is' suggests the List was originally compiled in this year.

Mayors List 10

London, BL, Additional 29777, List of Mayors and Sheriffs; late 16th century; English; parchment; 14 membranes attached serially; length varies from 250mm to 840mm, width 205mm, number of ruled lines variable; written on one side only; occasional use of red ink, elaborated initials; end of roll faded.

The List begins with Arnewaye's term in 1326; the roll is torn off in the middle of the 1584 entry.

Mayors List 11

London, BL, Additional 29779, 'Briefe Notes of Antiquitye'; 17th century; English; paper; ii+ 63+ii; 289mm x 221mm (280mm x 170mm), 25 long lines; single leaves attached to modern binding; modern pencil foliation; modern leather binding on boards, title on spine.

The List begins with Lynnett in 1318 and is in the hand of List I in Harley 2125, ie, probably George Bellin's.

Mayors List 12
London, BL, Additional 29780, 'Antiquitie'; 18th century; English; paper; 189 leaves; 335mm x 205mm (298mm x 160mm); mostly gathered in 8s; modern ink foliation; multicoloured patterned binding with leather spine and corners, title on spine.

The List of Mayors begins with Lynnett in 1241 (f 93) and is attributed to Aldersey. On ff 113-71 there is a List of Memorable Events in Chester similar to that in Add. 11335 but continued by the scribe to 1771.

Mayors List 13
London, BL, Additional 39925, 'Antiquitie'; late 16th century hand (latest date 1583), with additions in early 17th century hand (to 1623) and continued to 1634; English; paper; iii+170+iii; 335mm x 215mm (285mm x 140mm), 45 long lines; gathered in 8s; modern pencil foliation (3 unnumbered blanks after f 31); no decoration; brown morocco leather, title on spine.

The MS contains an Aldersey List which begins with Lynnett in 1317 (f 12) and continues to 1634.

Mayors List 14
London, BL, Stowe 811, 'Antiquitie'; 18th century; English and Latin; paper; ii+114+ii; 330mm x 205mm (315mm x 180mm); gathered in 8s; modern pencil foliation (2 unnumbered blanks between ff 72-3, 4 unnumbered blanks between ff 77-8, 3 unnumbered blanks between ff 80-1); no decoration; 18th century brown leather binding on boards, gold frame design on covers and spine, title on spine.

The MS is in the same hand as Add. 11335 and contains some of the same material. The List is an Aldersey List and begins with Lynnett in 1241.

Mayors List 15
Chester, Cheshire Record Office, DLT/B 37 (Tabley Liber N); 1644; English; paper; 123 leaves; 185mm x 150mm (170mm x 120mm), 38-40 long lines; mostly gathered in 16s and 20s; modern pencil foliation; no decoration; 17th century vellum binding, title on spine.

The List begins with Lynnett in 1241 and is in the same hand to 1644.

Mayors List 16
Chester, City Archives, P/Cowper [1956] 'Collectanea Devana', Vol I; c 1763; English with a few

Latin entries; paper; iii+233+vi (with some loose unnumbered leaves inserted); 322mm x 204mm (293mm x 168mm); gathered in 12s; modern numbering; no decoration; very worn brown rough calf binding c 80-100 years old, almost illegible title on spine.

The List begins with Lynnett (1242) and was continued by Cowper up to 1758.

Mayors List 17
Toronto, Massey College MS; 1618, with additions in another hand 1617 to 1639; English with a few Latin entries; paper; 170 leaves (126 blanks); 292mm x 195mm (277mm x 165mm); mostly gathered in 12s (1 leaf missing between ff 35-6, ff 105-6 partially torn out; several blanks excised at end); unfoliated; no decoration; 17th century vellum binding on boards.

The MS was purchased in May, 1967 for Massey College Library by Professor Douglas Lochhead from Thomas Crowe Antiquarian Bookseller in Norwich. The List begins with Lynnett in 1241 and continues in one hand to 1616. The title page says that the List was copied by William Ince in 1618.

Mayors Lists without Relevant Entries

Mayors List 18
Chester, City Archives, AB/1.

See the MS description for Assembly Books (p xi). The List begins with Arnewaye in 1326 and continues in the same hand to 1567-8.

Mayors List 19
Chester, City Archives, unnumbered MS.

See the MS description for Rogers' 'Breviary' above (p xxvii). The List begins with Arnewaye in 1320 which Rogers later corrected to 1328. The List continues in his hand to 1618, although the entries for 1615-18 seem to be later additions.

Mayors List 20
London, BL, Harley 1948.

See the MS description for Rogers' 'Breviary' above (p xxviii). The List begins with Arnewaye in 1328 and is continued by Rogers until 1637.

Mayors List 21
London, BL, Harley 1989, 'The Antiquity's: the Earles, the Bishops, Mariors, etc. of the Citty of Chester': List of Mayors and Sheriffs, ff 93-8; 17th century; English; paper; iii+98+iv; 296mm x 193mm (280mm x 135mm), 40 long lines; collation irregular; modern pencil and ink foliation;

brown cloth BL binding on boards, reddish-brown leather on corners and spine, title on spine.

The List is a fragment which begins with Lynnett in 1241 and stops at 1303.

Mayors List 22
London, BL, Harley 2133, List II (ff 59-68v).

The List was transcribed by Randle Holme and resembles ML 7.

Mayors List 23
Liverpool, Liverpool University MS 23.5.

See the MS description for Rogers' 'Breviary' above (p xxix).

Additional Lists
The following Lists were consulted, but since they had only a few entries and these the most common, they have been omitted from the volume.

Cheshire Record Office MSS:

Mayors List 24
DCC 1. The MS is an 18th century copy and contains a List which begins with Arnewaye in 1328 (f 12) and continues to 1633.

Mayors List 25
DCC 3. The List begins with Lynnett in 1242 (f 22) and continues to 1646.

Mayors List 26
DCC 11. The List begins with Lynnett in 1241 and continues in the same hand to about 1635.

John Rylands Library, Manchester:

Mayors List 27
MS 202. The Hassall Commonplace Book (1591) contains a list which begins with Arnewaye in 1326 and is continued in the same hand to 1602.

The calendars of mayors and sheriffs are among the earliest antiquarian documents of Chester. Though some exist simply as lists, most of the calendars also include notes on important events in the city's history.

There are two principal groups of calendars, those which record Sir John Arnewaye and those which cite Sir Walter Lynnett as the first mayor. These can be further subdivided according to the year assigned to the first mayor's term. The earliest Lists are probably those from the Assembly Book (AB/1), Add. 29777 (ML 10), and John Rylands MS 202 (ML 27), all of which list Arnewaye's first term in 1326. Of these the Assembly Book's List is probably the earliest and can be dated to 1567-8, but it is possible that the Harley 1046 List (ML 1) antedates these three (it begins Arnewaye's term in 1320). In any event, David Rogers had a copy of a List corresponding to Harley 1046, but he altered the date from 1320 to 1328 in the Chester Archives 'Breviary' and retained that date in Harley 1944 (ML 2) and Harley 1948 (ML 20), despite the fact that in the CRO 'Breviary', ff 110v-11v, he says that he is aware that most Lists begin with Arnewaye's term in 1329.

Mayor William Aldersey published a new List in 1594 in order to correct the mistaken chronology and to restore Sir Walter Lynnett to his place as the first mayor. The Aldersey Lists were compiled, he tells us in his preface (Add. 29780, f 93), from documents in his own and the city's possession, and thus the List can be regarded as fairly authoritative. Unfortunately, the Aldersey Lists also have the fewest references to dramatic and ceremonial activity, presumably because their author did not make entries for which there was no documentary evidence.

There seem to be three versions of Aldersey's List:

1) Additional 39925, an early seventeenth-century copy, begins with Lynnett in 1317 and this List is undoubtedly the source for George Bellin's Lists in Harley 2125 (ML 5) and Add. 29779 (ML 11), both of which are dated 1622

2) Harley 2125 (ML 6), and the List at the end of the Liverpool copy of the 'Breviary' (ML 23) begin with Lynnett in 1257.

3) Harley 2057 (ML 3), Harley 2133 (ML 8), Add. 29780 (ML 12), CRO: DLT/B 37 (ML 15), Harley 1989 (ML 21), CRO: DCC 3 (ML 25), and CRO: DCC 11 (ML 26) begin with Lynnett in 1241 or 1242.

It is probable, therefore, that Aldersey's List went through three phases: first he added Lynnett to the old Lists which had started with Arnewaye in the 1320s; then he moved Lynnett back to 1257 and Arnewaye to the 1260-70s; and finally, he settled on 1241 as the first of Lynnett's terms.

There are also some compilations attributed to Aldersey (eg, Stowe 811, Add. 11335, Add. 29780) which contain a List of Memorable Events which usually starts about 1275. Since these Lists say that the last performance of the plays took place in 1572, it seems likely that they represent an antiquarian compilation begun by Aldersey sometime before 1575 and thus they antedate the List of 1594. The information in these Lists is sometimes off by several years and often disagrees with the Aldersey Mayors Lists which follow in the same MSS, eg, in Add. 29780 and Stowe 811.

Within the two groups of Lists, there are two distinct methods of dating mayoral terms: the smaller group, made up of Harley 1046, 2057, 2105, and John Rylands MS 202, places the mayor's name under the year in which the majority of his term was served, while the remainder list the mayor's name under the year of his accession. The mayors were elected on the Friday after Saint Denis' Day in October and their terms ran from the fall of one year to the fall of the next (Harley 2009, f 27). Since some of the antiquarians and some modern scholars have not observed this distinction in the dating of terms, errors have crept into our histories. For example, David Rogers says that the last performance of the plays occurred in 1574 rather than 1575 because that is the date of John Savage's term in his List of Mayors. Similarly, Gardiner postulated twice as many performances of the plays as there actually were because he conflated Add. 29777, which uses one dating method, with Chambers' list of dates from other sources.[11] In this volume, the two methods are conflated in order to reflect the actual term of the mayor's office; consequently, there may be some discrepancies between the date cited in the antiquarian entry and the date assigned the entry by the editor. These differences are explained in the notes.

Dating the Entries
Since the antiquarians used two different methods of dating terms and since they tended to say that an event occurred in the year placed beside the mayor's name, it is possible for there to be errors in the dating of specific incidents. Many of these errors are easily resolved by conflating the two dating methods into a single chronology and then adjusting the chronology according to external evidence. This technique is sufficient to resolve almost all the discrepancies in the entries after the middle of the sixteenth century.

The discrepancies up to that time cannot always be so easily resolved because the chronology of the mayors before the sixteenth century is not absolutely certain and because external evidence is often lacking; consequently, there is the problem of deciding whether a mayor's name has been assigned to the right year, and then whether an event associated with his name belongs to his term, or whether it drifted into his term as a result of the different methods of dating terms, or whether it belongs to that year but not that mayor. For example, most Lists associate the invention of the Midsummer Show and a performance of a play before Prince Arthur with the term of Richard Goodman and date both events to 1498. Some Lists place Goodman's term in 1497-8 and others in 1498-9, the latter of which is correct. Almost universally, however, the visit of Arthur is said to have occurred on 4 August 1498 or on 14 August 14 Henry VII. This is clearly impossible since Goodman did not become mayor until November 1498; therefore, the visit either did not occur during his term or it should be dated to 4 August 1499. The problem is complicated by the fact that the Midsummer Show could have begun in 1498 before Goodman came into office and the visit could have occurred in 1500 and been listed under the succeeding mayor's term which began in 1499; thus, both events could have occurred during terms contiguous to Goodman's but could have ended up associated with his terms if an antiquarian had copied the entries from two Lists using two different methods of dating terms.

Fortunately, events seem to have been associated with a mayor's name rather than a date; therefore, I have followed the general rule of dating an entry according to the mayor's known term rather than according to the MS date where these disagree. This procedure is defensible because in those cases where there is external evidence, there is almost a perfect correlation between events and the mayors' names, whereas there are often errors in dating the mayors' terms. In addition, I have retained the association between a mayor and an event assigned to him even when this means moving the event to a different point in the chronology. The reader, therefore, should be aware that the dates of events for which there is no external evidence could be inaccurate and he should consult the notes in order to determine if the MSS give a different date or mayor than the one assigned by the editor. For ease of reference, the editor has inserted the mayor's name in parentheses at the beginning of each entry.

Selecting the Entries
The first List of Harley 2125 was written by Bellin and annotated by Holme from other Lists; consequently, I have given it priority. Otherwise, entries are selected individually on the basis of their content: those which provide the most details or which contain significant variants have been reproduced fully no matter what List they may appear in. Entries which are similar in language but which contain less information are noted only. No attempt has been made to collate the variants since the relationships between the Lists are too complex to allow the establishment of a copy text and the listing of variants; moreover, since all the variant entries are substantively available in the printed text, it did not seem necessary to record minor and accidental variations.

Miscellaneous

Chester, Cheshire Record Office, DLT/B 3 (Tabley Liber C); 17th century; English and Latin; paper; ii+368+ii; 280mm x 185mm (255mm x 140mm), average 45 long lines; gathered in 10s; 17th century ink foliation (Part I, ff 1-53; Part II, ff 11-326); some coloured drawings of arms; 17th century brown leather binding, one clasp and hinge of another.

The MS contains Sir Peter Leycester's collections on Bucklow Hundred in Cheshire which he published in his *Historical Antiquities.*

ANTIQUARIAN COLLECTIONS
Antiquarian Collections are manuscripts which contain material from a variety of

sources but which, unlike Antiquarian Compilations, have no form. The contents of these volumes are so miscellaneous that, with a few exceptions, they have not been given here. For further information, see descriptions in the BL Harley and Additional MSS catalogues.

London, BL, Harley 1968, 'Deeds and Leases'; 17th century; English and Latin; paper; i+38+ii; 360mm x 230mm (320mm x 170mm), 43 long lines; single sheets pasted to modern strips; modern pencil foliation, old ink foliation (540-76) on ff 2-38; some drawings of seals; BL binding with red leather on corners and spine, title on spine.

London, BL, Harley 1989.

See the MS description of ML 21 (pp xl-xli).

London, BL, Harley 1994, 'Church matters & other things concerninge Abbyes nuneryes & Religious houses'; 17th century; English and Latin; paper, some parchment (ff 33-8, 92-9, 156); vii+324+viii; size of leaves variable (largest 406mm x 300mm, smallest 75mm x 120mm); single sheets bound together; modern pencil foliation, older ink foliation (261-572), f 4 - first flyleaf; some ink drawings of seals; BL board binding with brown leather on corners and spine, title on spine. The MS is in Randle Holme's hand.

The churchwardens' accounts for St Mary's, 1537-1639, which begin on f 40, are extant in CRO: P/20/13/1.

London, BL, Harley 1996, 'Notes of severall companyes in Chester', etc; 17th century; English and Latin; paper; ii+283+iii; size of leaves variable (largest 406mm x 290mm, smallest 90mm x 200mm); mostly single leaves attached to binding strips; modern pencil foliation, ink foliation runs from 732 on f 1; no decoration; BL binding with red leather on corners and spine, title on spine.

Mostly antiquarian notes; however, the Cappers' petition, f 120, is original.

London, BL, Harley 2009, 'Charters and Privileges of the County and City of Chester'; 17th century; English and Latin; paper; i+69+ii; 382mm x 272mm (361mm x 191mm), 68 long lines; single leaves attached to 10mm binding strips bound together (some bifolia); recent pencil foliation correcting older ink; no decoration; BL binding with red leather on corners and spine. The MS is in Randle Holme's hand.

Beginning on f 37 are notes of records remaining at the Exchequer of Chester from Richard II's time.

London, BL, Harley 2054, 'notes & chartres, with seuerall things which concerne the Companyes and occupations within the citty of chester'; 1514-1699; English and Latin; paper; 101 leaves; size of leaves variable (largest 310mm x 200mm, smallest 65mm x 250mm); mostly single leaves attached to modern binding strips; modern pencil foliation, older pencil foliation (65-181) on f 3 to last unnumbered blank (2 unnumbered blanks between ff 57-8, 1 unnumbered blank between ff 62-3 and f 101-first flyleaf); sporadic drawings of seals; BL binding with dark red leather on corners and spine. Mostly in Randle Holme's hand.

London, BL, Harley 2057.

See the MS description under Mayors List 3 (p xxxvii).

London, BL, Harley 2065, 'Inquisitions from Henry III to Edward IV'; 17th century; Latin; paper; iii+184+ii; 380mm x 230mm (360mm x 170mm), 52 long lines; mostly single leaves bound together (ff 27, 59 interleaved); modern pencil foliation, earlier ink foliation (1-143, 195-7) ff 22-171, 174; no decoration; BL board binding with dark red leather on corners and spine, title on spine.

London, BL, Harley 2104, 'Notes, Charters, and other things concerning the Companys within the City of Chester'; 17th century; English and Latin; paper; iii+220+iv; 320mm x 195mm (text area variable); mostly single leaves bound together; modern pencil foliation correcting earlier ink foliation; no decoration; brown leather BL binding, title on spine.

London, BL, Harley 2124; 1607; English; paper with vellum flyleaves; ii+142+ii; 190mm x 300mm maximum (text area variable); leaves usually pasted in pairs on modern binding strips (2 leaves missing); modern arabic foliation and 17th century ink foliation (roman numerals, i-lviii; ff 59-62 mis-numbered lxi-lxiv, f 63 to the end numbered in arabic by scribe); no decoration; bound in tan leather, cover embossed with coat of arms of Earl of Oxford, title in gold letters on spine.

The MS is one of the play texts, but the only item of interest to this volume of records is the antiquarian note on the flyleaf.

London, BL, Harley 2150, 'Deedes & customes with other notes conserning the Citty of Chester'; 16th-17th century; English and Latin; paper; ii+219+ii; size of leaves variable (typically 305mm x 192mm): mostly single sheets bound together; modern pencil foliation, ink foliation (307-87) ff 3-83; no decoration; red leather BL binding, title on spine.

Among the miscellaneous items in this MS, most of which were copied by Randle Holme, is a sixteenth-century copy of a book similar to parts of the Assembly Book (AB/1). This book, which contains the Early Banns, has also had additional material inserted into it by Randle Holme. On the basis of the handwriting, I estimate that the book may have been copied as late as the 1570s; however, it could not have been copied before 1555-6 because the order banning Christmas Breakfasts and mumming is in the same sixteenth-century hand as the majority of the document.

The arrangement of entries in Harley 2150 is roughly the same as that in the Assembly Book: Gable Rents (ff 82-3), the city wards (83v-4), some materials from the terms of mayors Gee and Hope (ff 84v-5v), the Early Banns (85v-8v), the city rental for 1533-4 (ff 88v-93v), and then a series of orders commencing with those for Henry Gee, 1539-40, but mixing in earlier ones. The Assembly Book contains some prefatory matter, including an Arnewaye List of Mayors (f 11) which continues in the same hand to 1567-8. Subsequent entries include a description of the meres and boundaries of the city (ff 32-3), the names of the streets (ff 33v-5; copied by Rogers into his Breviaries), a description of the wards (ff 36-7), the Gable Rents (ff 38-40), the fees for various officials (to f 49), the calling of the Christmas Watch (f 52), the rental for 1533-4 (ff 53-7), the City Charter (ff 58-9), and the orders which commence with Mayor Gee in 1539-40. The differences between the two make it apparent that one could not have been copied from the other; it is likely, therefore, that both were copied from one exemplar, which was in a state of disorder, or that they were copied from different exemplars, both of which were near-duplicate copies and were perhaps kept in different places for safety.

We know that the exemplar of Harley 2150 or a copy of it existed as late as the seventeenth century because Randle Holme made additional entries from a book he called the White Book of the Pentice. This White Book could not be the extant Assembly Book, whose original cover was white, because it does not contain the Early Banns and because the folio references which Holme marks in the margin of Harley 2150 do not correspond to AB/1. Since Holme indicates that some portions of the Early Banns had been erased in the book, then we can surmise that Harley 2150 was made after 1555-6 and that its exemplar was discarded and superseded by the present Assembly Book which seems to have been compiled about 1567-8. We can also surmise that the Early Banns were omitted from AB/1 because they had been superseded by the Late Banns.[12]

London, BL, Harley 2158, 'The accountes of the murrengers & Treasurers of the Citty of chester'; early 17th century; English and Latin; paper; ii+255+ii; 302mm x 211mm (text area variable), 40 long lines; gathered irregularly; modern pencil foliation correcting older ink foliation, ff 101-348 (40 unnumbered blanks between ff 1-2, 1 unnumbered blank between ff 10-11, 80-1, 27 unnumbered blanks between ff 11-12, 76 unnumbered blanks between ff 66-7); no decoration; 17th century brown leather binding on boards, now coming apart, title on spine.

This MS contains Holme's transcriptions of the Muragers' Accounts, 1617-54 (ff 2-10v), City Treasurers' Accounts, c 1431-84 (ff 31-66), City Treasurers' Accounts, 1632-44 (ff 67-110), and, in another hand, the city's rental for 1621 (ff 12-30v). The Muragers made an annual payment of two shillings to the Drapers, but since it is nowhere clear what the fee was for, and since Holme notes by the 1620 entry that it is the first time that he has found the entry '& how it Cometh quere', I have not transcribed the accounts. I have transcribed all the guild references in the city rentals even though some of these may not be for carriage house rentals.

The seventeenth-century City Treasurers' Accounts are routine, but the earlier ones from the fifteenth century call for some comment. Randle Holme, who probably numbered the rolls, says that he transcribed them from a group of old rolls which were much decayed and disordered. The dates, as a consequence, are uncertain to some extent: sometimes he seems to have estimated the date on the basis of the entries; at other times he could apparently read the mayor's name or the regnal year or both. I have given the regnal year and the mayor's name whenever Holme notes them; in addition, I have reported the other comments he made about the rolls from which I have taken extracts. In some cases, several different rolls are ascribed to the same years: these may be duplicates, or rolls of unpaid rents (arrearages), in which case they may be dated either to the term in which the rents were not paid or to the subsequent term in which the arrearage roll was drawn up. In other cases, the date of the regnal year and that of the mayoral term contradict one another; however, in all of these cases, the discrepancy arises because the roll was dated to the regnal year in which it was drawn up but refers to a previous term. Since the rolls are not in strict chronological order, I have listed them by roll number and included Holme's notes on the dates:

Roll 1	ff 31-1v	10-15 Henry VI
Roll 2	ff 31v-2	14 Henry VI, John Walsh, mayor 1435-6
Roll 3	ff 32-2v	12 Henry VI, Thomas Wotton, 1433-4; 13 Henry VI, arrearages, Adam Wotton, 1434-5; 14 Henry VI, arrearages, John Walsh, 1435-6
Roll 4	ff 32v-3	10 Henry VI, Richard Massey, 1431-2
◆Roll 5	ff 33-4v	9-20 Henry VI, 1430-42; extracts from 16 Henry VI, Richard Massey 1437-8; 17 Henry VI, Richard Weston, 1438-9; 18 Henry VI, Nicholas Daniel, 1439-40; 19 Henry VI, John Pilkington, 1440-1; 20 Henry VI 1441-2
◆Roll 6	ff 34v-5	17-20 Henry VI, 1438-42
◆Roll 7	ff 35-5v	20 Henry VI, H. Woodcock, 1441-2; 21 Henry VI, John Flynt, 1442-
◆Roll 8	f 35v	19 Henry VI, arrearages, John Pilkington, 1440-1
◆Roll 9	ff 36-7	'Ed 4 tyme & part of H7', on the basis of the hand and the names in the rental; said to be 'a bundle of Rentalls both broke & obscure'.
◆Roll 10	f 37	'before 9 Roll'.
Roll 11	ff 37v-8	no date; said to be much decayed
Roll 12	f 38v	no date; Pentice charges
◆Roll 13	ff 39-40	7 Edward IV, John Southworth, 1467-8; said to agree with Roll 11
◆Roll 14	ff 40-1	Henry VII's reign on the basis of the names
Roll 15	f 41v	4 Edward III, 1464-5; St Mary's Guild receipts
Roll 16	ff 42-2v	16 Henry VI, Richard Massey, 1437-8

◆Roll 17	ff 43-3v	Henry VI, 'about later end H6 & E4'
Roll 18	ff 44-4v	30-3 Henry VI, 1451-5
◆Roll 19	ff 44v-7v	3 Edward IV, arrearages, 1463-4, from Robert Bruyn, 1462-3
◆Roll 20	ff 48-9v	30 Henry VI and 1 Edward IV, John Southworth's second term, 1459-60; for arrearages which would account for the regnal date, 1460-1
	ff 49-9v	2 Edward IV, Robert Bruyn, 1462-3
Roll 21	ff 49v-50	4 Edward IV, Robert Rogerson, 1463-4; probably arrearages made up in 1464-5
◆Roll 22	ff 50-1	3 Edward IV, Robert Rogerson, 1463-4; 5 Edward IV, Richard Rainford, 1465-6; 6 Edward IV, William Lely, 1466-7. The roll is said to be so torn and damaged by wet that little could be discerned.
Roll 23	f 51	no date; said to be indecipherable
◆Roll 24	ff 51v-2v	7 Edward IV, John Southworth, 1467-8
Roll 25	f 52v	8 Edward IV, John Dedwood, 1468-9
Roll 26	ff 53-3v	9 Edward IV, Thomas Kent, 1469-70
◆Roll 27	ff 54-4v	8-10 Edward IV; also noted 10 Edward IV, Thomas Kent, 1469-70
◆Roll 28	ff 55-5v	12 Edward IV, John Spencer, 1472-3
◆Roll 29	ff 56-6v	9-14 Edward IV, 1469-75; arrearages from: 9 Edward IV, for John Dedwood, 1468-9; 12 Edward IV, for John Spencer, 1472-3; 13 Edward IV, for William Whitemore, 1473-4
◆Roll 30	ff 57-8	16 Edward IV, Hugh Massey, 1476-7
Roll 31	ff 58-9v	various to 18 Edward IV
Roll 32	ff 59v-60	15-17 Edward IV, 1475-8
◆Roll 33	ff 60v-1	17 Edward IV, John Southworth, 1477-8
◆Roll 34	ff 61v-2v	19-21 Edward IV, arrearages, 1479-82
◆Roll 35	ff 63-5	18-20 Edward IV, 1478-81
Roll 36	ff 65v-6	22 Edward IV, arrearages, 1482-3

London, BL, Harley 2172, 'Deeds leases for fee farme leases'; 17th century; English; paper; ii+193 +i; 283mm x 187mm (267mm x 145mm), 48 long lines; gatherings irregular; ink pagination (94 unnumbered blanks, first 3 leaves foliated 1-3, followed by 1 unnumbered blank, 96 paginated leaves); no decoration; 17th century brown leather binding on boards, title on spine.

London, BL, Harley 2173, 'What Writtings & Deeds are in the Maior's, Tresurer's & seuerall other chests & Desks in the pentice of the city of chester'; early 17th century; English and Latin; paper; iii+125+vi; 290mm x 193mm (280mm x 130mm), 48 long lines; mostly gathered in 8s; ff 1*-5* modern pencil, ff 1-119 ink foliation (1 unnumbered blank, f 77* follows f 77); BL binding, brown leather on spine and corners, title on spine. Mostly in Randle Holme's hand.

London, BL, Harley 2177, 'A coppy of the Regester Booke of Trinity Church in Chester coppied by me Randall Holme Alderman and Iustice of peace 1653'; 1653; English; paper; i+108+i; 286mm x 184mm (265mm x 139mm), 48 long lines; single sheets bound together; modern pencil foliation and older ink foliation which runs 1-165 (f 3-end flyleaf, missing 7, 15, 19-22, 71-2, 81-3, 103, 105-12, 117-35, 137-42, 145-60, misplaced leaf 119 now first flyleaf); no decoration; red leather BL binding, title on spine.

London, BL, Additional 9442, 'Lyson's topographical Collections: Cheshire'; 19th century; English; paper (with some paste-ons); i+350+ii; 320mm x 240mm (written area variable); collection of mostly single papers bound together with some bifolia; modern pencil foliation (1 unnumbered blank following f 349); no decoration; modern brown board BL binding, red leather on spine and corners.

BL: Add. MSS 9441-3 contain the Lysons brothers' notes for their *Magna Britannia* the notes are on bits of paper of various sizes pasted onto the leaves of the bound volume. Add. MS 9442 contains the Newhall Proclamation from Harley 2124 (f 264 the Late Banns from Harley 2013 (f 266 and following), and on ff 295-5v extracts from Rogers' 'Breviary'. The texts and the title, which they published in *Magna Britannia*, p 584, note u, are the same as those in Liverpool University MS 23.5. The Lysons brothers said that this MS belonged to William Nichols of Chester.

London, BL, Additional 16179, 'Extracts from the Registers and other documents of the city of Chester ...'; 18th century; English; paper; i+90+i; 316mm x 196mm (299mm x 159mm), 30 long lines; gathered irregularly; modern pencil foliation (first 3 leaves unnumbered); no decoration; dappled brown binding with leather on corners and spine.

Dramatic and
Ceremonial Activity

Ceremonial Activity

Two of Chester's earliest customs came about as a result of attacks by the Welsh on or in the vicinity of the city. The annual Christmas Watch is supposed to have started in the time of William the Conqueror. David Rogers reports that the Welsh, being the barbarians that they were, were so incensed by the peace enjoyed by the Normans during Christmas that they attacked the city. Subsequently, an annual watch, instituted for a three day period, required that the possessors of lands descended from lands held by the Normans provide armoured watchmen at the Christmas season. Although Rogers asserts that the watch was intended to protect the city from thieves, unruly persons, and the like, it seems equally clear that it provided an occasion for the ceremonial procession of the mayor and his attendants through the city and the enjoyment of the odd drink or bite of food.

A later attack on Randle Blundevill, earl of Chester (1181-1232), resulted in the custom of licensing the minstrels of Chester.[13] The earl is supposed to have been besieged by the Welsh in Rhuddlan Castle during the reign of King John. He sent his constable to Chester during the Midsummer Fair to bring aid; the constable, however, was only able to find 'a tumultuous Rout of Fidlers, Players, Coblers, debauched persons, both Men and Women', who not only came to the earl's aid, but succeeded in frightening off the Welsh. As a reward, the earl gave the constable power over the minstrels, shoemakers, and harlots of Chester, a feudal obligation which was subsequently passed on to the Dutton family and which resulted in the annual licensing of the minstrels in Chester at Midsummer. The Duttons' rights over the minstrels were recognized by the crown and Elizabeth's Rogue Law specifically exempted the Chester minstrels from its provisions.[14]

Of more obscure origin are the homages at Shrovetide which the Merchant Drapers received from the Shoemakers, Saddlers, and recently married couples. The earliest references to the homages are contained in Mayor Gee's ordinance of 1540 which altered these ancient customs; this document, however, appears to commingle two separate actions. The document has a long preamble extolling the virtues of archery and it would appear that the intent is to recommend archery as a substitute for the old homages; however, the document completely ignores archery and goes on to substitute a foot race for the Shoemakers' football game and a horse race for the Saddlers' homage, and to add the presentation of glaives or arrows of silver by married persons. It is possible that the disquisition on archery is either a preamble to an earlier amendment of the Drapers' homages, or that it was part of the document which instituted the Sheriffs' Breakfast Shoot in 1511-12, but which was joined to Mayor Gee's ordinance when the Assembly Book was newly copied from the debris of an older book. In any event, the only connection between archery and the Drapers' homages is the presentation of silver arrows by the Shoemakers and married persons. These homages continued until a disagreement between the Shoemakers and Saddlers in the early seventeenth century caused a series of actions to be taken one against the other over who was to have precedence in making the homages. The conflict was ultimately resolved by the mayor and council in 1626, when the council agreed that the Shoemakers were to be called before the Saddlers; in addition, the council stated the obligations of each guild and entered the proclamations in the Assembly Book.

Although the ordinance does not offer any explanation, it is possible to make some suppositions about the origin of these customs. It is probable that the homage of the married persons is a later addition to the custom because they are not mentioned in the preamble to the 1540 ordinance and because they do not enter into the seventeenth century dispute. Furthermore, since the council in 1626 examined the precepts of the Shoemakers' and Saddlers' companies and decided that the Shoemakers ought to have precedence, we can surmise that the Shoemakers had some kind of priority over the Saddlers. It is possible, therefore, that the custom arose as a consequence of the Shoemakers and Saddlers separating themselves from the guild-merchant. Originally, the guild-merchant was composed only of merchants; other companies were formed by a royal grant of a charter, or, in the sixteenth century, by the city's grant of a charter. The homages to the Merchant Drapers, therefore, may be token obligations made as a consequence of the Shoemakers and Saddlers being recognized as guilds separate from the guild-merchant.

Mayor Gee's rationale for altering the customs is a humanist one: for unruly games he would substitute profitable exercises. According to chroniclers and antiquarians, the Shoemakers' football game had become so harmful and injurious to the participants that it was thought better to substitute a footrace.

The Midsummer Show is said to have begun during the mayoralty of Richard Goodman in 1499. Unfortunately, we know virtually nothing about the Show until 1564, when we have an agreement between Thomas Poole and Robert Hallwood and the city to provide dragons and elephants for the city; nevertheless, it is probably not mere coincidence that the city should institute a show to coincide with the licensing of the minstrels and the Midsummer Fair. All of these activities could not help but increase the attractiveness – and the profit – of the Fair. The Midsummer Show seems to have included morris dancers and several large animals, the dragon, the elephant, the mayor's mount, and in later years, camels, antelopes, and the like – all provided by the city – and riders provided by individual guilds. Many guilds rode with characters from the cycle plays; thus, the Painters rode with their angels on stilts, the Smiths with Simeon, the Shoemakers with Mary Magdalene and occasionally Judas, the Innkeepers with their alewife and her devils. This latter group is intriguing, for it is believed that the alewife scene in the Harrowing of Hell remains from an older stratum of the cycle, and it would appear that they may be related to some kind of folk custom.[15] The Innkeepers' records suggest that they are part of an activity called 'cuppes and canes', in which the woman, atop a horse, carries a quantity of crockery which the devil breaks with his cane.

Some of these shows – like the Butchers' devil in his feathers, the naked boys, and the giants – raised the religious zeal of Henry Hardware, who suppressed them all in 1600 or earlier; however, subsequent mayors sometimes revived them. The mayor in 1602 is said to have revived the giants, and the Linendrapers that year ordered Balaam and his ass to go in the show. In 1623, the city paid for the giants and other animals, and in 1627 executed an agreement for their production similar to that made in 1564. The characters from the plays, however, were phased out of the show as the plays came under attack, and most did not appear at all in the seventeenth century; thus, the Coopers, Shoemakers, and Smiths had a child ride for them by 1572 and thereafter. The Painters had a child by 1574, but the angel went on stilts periodically until 1594; the Innholders had the woman and devils in addition to their child in 1583-5, 1589, and 1591-6, but not thereafter.

During the life of the Whitsun Play cycle, according to David Rogers, the guilds of the city used to ride the Banns on St George's Day. There is no evidence that any other kind of activity occurred on that day until 1610, when a former sheriff, Robert Amery, instituted the St George's Day Race; to initiate the custom, he also produced a Triumph in honour of the Prince of Wales. The records indicate that the race was run annually thereafter, but there are no records of subsequent dramatic performances.

Dramatic Activity

THE WHITSUN PLAYS

The antiquarians of Chester promoted the belief that the Whitsun Plays were begun in the early fourteenth century, but the evidence refutes itself.[16] The fifteenth-century documents indicate that a play was performed on Corpus Christi Day, but there are no references to the Whitsun Plays before 1519-20. We can be sure that a play was being performed by 1422 on Corpus Christi Day because there was a dispute in that year between the Coopers and Ironmongers over their responsibilities for the Scourging and Crucifixion. Furthermore, the fifteenth-century records indicate that this play was significantly different from the later Whitsun Plays, for it was performed on one day and in one place – St John's, outside the east wall of the city – at the conclusion of a procession from St Mary's-on-the-Hill, located near the Castle in the southwest corner of the city.

It is probable that the plays were not performed at Whitsuntide before 1519, and that it was sometime between 1519 and 1531 that the plays began to be performed processionally over a three day period. The Old Testament sequence of the cycle seems to have been considerably expanded during this period, and the expansion suggests that the old Corpus Christi Play was a Passion play rather than a complete cycle like those preserved at York and in the Towneley manuscript. The cycle continued to be revised and expanded into the 1540s and the clergy apparently continued to perform a play at Corpus Christi until about 1548. During the reign of Edward, perhaps in 1548, the clergy's Corpus Christi Play was suppressed and there were some alterations in the cycle, the most documented of which is the suppression of the Bakers' Last Supper and the production of a Shoemakers' play which included the meeting of Christ with Mary and Martha, the Last Supper, and the captivity of Christ. With the accession of Mary, some of these suppressed plays may have re-entered the cycle, or the cycle was rewritten, or both. In any event, new Banns were written for the cycle which included references to new play material; these Banns were later revised to include even more new play material; and the texts of the plays, as well as the guild expenditures, indicate that the text continued to be revised and altered up to and including the performance in 1575.

That there was a performance in 1575 is remarkable in itself, for the archbishop of York had forbidden the performance in 1572. It is clear that the plays had come under attack within the city before the performances of 1572 and 1575, the first times that there was any interference from outside the city. The performance schedule in the 1560s and 1570s was erratic – plays were performed only in 1561, 1567, 1568, 1572, and 1575 – and Henry Hardware, for example, did not allow a performance of the plays in his first mayoral term in 1559-60. But the opposition was curiously divided, as the events of 1572 indicate. In that year, Mayor John Hankey decided on a performance of the plays and was successful in getting the council to agree to it. Some parties obviously objected and asked that the archbishop intercede to stop the performance. It is not clear who initiated the request, but we cannot conclude that the religious establishment alone attempted to halt the plays because the dean and chapter of Chester Cathedral paid for the construction of a mansion over Abbey Gates and provided beer to the players as they had done at the previous performance in 1568. It is probable that citizens like Henry Hardware and members of the ecclesiastical establishment, the bishop, possibly, together appealed to the archbishop. In any event, the archbishop attempted to halt the performance, but his 'Inhibition' came too late.

A majority of the council must have believed that the archbishop did not have jurisdiction over the performance of the plays in the city and they voted to produce the cycle in 1575. Nevertheless, the mayor and council were not so naive as to believe that everything could be done as it had been in the past; consequently, they moved the performance to Midsummer, produced it on one day rather than three, and in only one place in the city rather than the accustomed four or five. The play was very likely performed before the mayor at High Cross, his usual viewing place, and certainly was not performed before the Abbey Gates, outside which the Midsummer Fair was held. Despite the city's measures – and this apparently included rewriting some of the plays – the archbishop would not condone the performance and had John Arnewaye called to London to appear before the privy council. Unfortunately, no record remains of Arnewaye's appearance before the privy council, and he may, in fact, never have appeared at all. He wrote to the city council to request a certificate that the council and not he alone had ordered the plays, and Henry Hardware, who was then mayor, was honourable enough to send the certificate stating that both Arnewaye and Hankey had acted with the consent of the council. Apparently, this shared 'guilt' satisfied the government, or the city's charter prevented any further action against the mayor. Nevertheless, the message was clear and the plays were never performed in Chester again, except for one performance of the Shepherds before the Lord Strange and other notables in 1577-8.

CONDITIONS OF PERFORMANCE

The twelve guild accounts of expenditure give us a fairly detailed picture of the sequence of events leading up to the performance of the Whitsun Plays.[17] Though the mayor and council were the final arbiters of whether to produce the plays, the companies apparently could petition for a performance by submitting a 'bill' to the mayor. When the decision was favourable, the companies began to ready their materials and to practise their parts. Their first but least difficult task was to ride the Banns. The guilds participated in a yearly procession at Midsummer whenever the Whitsun Plays were not performed; consequently, they could anticipate the demand for costumes and horses for the character who rode with them and be ready to ride in procession by St George's Day, the time David Rogers claims was set aside for the Banns. If the route for the Banns was the same as that for the Midsummer Show, the companies assembled at the Bars outside Eastgate, where the crier read the Banns and called forth the guilds. The route then took them past the prisons at North Gate and at the Castle, where they contributed money to the prisoners. The liberties of the city extended beyond the walls, but by passing through the major streets and by coming to each of the gates, the guildsmen would thereby reconfirm the city's boundaries and freedoms.

This ceremonial function concluded, the companies would begin to prepare their plays by copying and handing out parts ('parcells'), holding trials for roles, and rehearsing from one to three times before their general rehearsal. The mayor, at least in later years, saw all the plays at some point, but whether he visited each separately or saw them as a group is uncertain.

The actors who can be identified are not professionals, but members of the guilds; for example, of the four actors in the 1572 Coopers' account, Hugh Gillam and

Richard Kalle appear in the freemen's rolls;[18] John Stynson is probably the Coopers' alderman, for it was to his house that they retired each Midsummer Eve; Thomas Marser is unknown, but in 1575 apparently, the Coopers desired his performance enough to spend two pence 'apon Thomas marser to get him to pleay'. Should an actor forget his lines, he could be prompted by the bearer of the 'Regenall'.

Each guild owned or rented a carriage which was used for the principal acting area at each stop. The Vintners, Goldsmiths, and Dyers were able to share a pageant because they performed on Monday, Tuesday, and Wednesday, respectively; their sharing of the wagon was, perhaps, facilitated by the fact that each of their plays centred on a tyrant figure who would require a palace.[19] The Coopers, Skinners, and Painters also shared a pageant, but the similarity between set designs is not immediately apparent. There is evidence of painted backdrops and the decoration of the pageant as a whole; a *locus,* however, may have been denoted largely by a single feature. For example, the Smiths paid for a 'fane', perhaps a simple arched canopy with a top to indicate that the building was a temple rather than a church.

As part of the preparation for the plays, the guilds had to take their carts out of storage and assemble them. They might require the work of a wright to put the wheels on and to put the pageant on the undercarriage. In addition, they might require the services of the Painters and Weavers for decorating the cart. After the performance was concluded, the guild dismantled their cart and stored it in their carriage house.

David Rogers says that the carts were open on the top, and it is likely that this means that the sides were opened – as opposed to the closed undercarriage – so that the audience could see into the cart. Some carriages may have had more elaborate roofs than others if, as in the Tailors' play, there was an ascension. However, not all carriages would have been constructed in the same way; for example, the Noah play calls for a unique pageant, and both the Fall of Lucifer and the Doomsday pageant seem to call for a two-tiered cart.[20]

The stage directions and the accounts demonstrate that the action was not restricted to the pageant wagon. Some plays call for the use of live animals in the playing area and the guild accounts substantiate the practice.[21] In 1568, the Painters 'payd for mete for the asse', 'payd toward*es* the fecchyng of him', and 'payd for horsse brede to harvyes [one of the shepherds'] horse'. In 1550, the Shoemakers 'payd ffor dressyng of the chauernes & ffor ye as' and 'payd ... the lade for leydeng the as' in the Entry into Jerusalem. Some of the animals mentioned in the stage directions may have been constructed (Balaam's ass, for example), and since the Midsummer Show had camels, it is possible that the beasts of the magi were camels rather than horses.

On the day of the performance, the guild may have assembled for breakfast and the dressing of their players before they went to the first station at Abbey Gates. David Rogers indicates that they then proceeded to the Pentice at High Cross – the centre of the city where the four streets intersect – and then into Watergate and

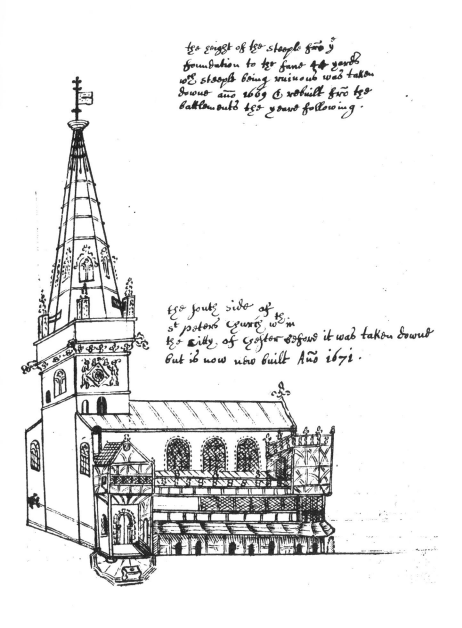

Drawing of the Pentice on the south side of St Peter's Church from BL: Harley 2073 f 88

Bridge Streets where, possibly, they performed at the Watergate and Bridgegate. We can be reasonably sure that this itinerary is correct since the players were in the habit of taking refreshment as they went along; thus, the dean and chapter provided beer for the players at Abbey Gates, and the Smiths had bread in Northgate Street and drink in Watergate Street in 1554, and beer in Bridge Street in 1572. The route follows the natural terrain of the city; at no time are the seven to nine 'poutters' of the carriage required to push it uphill. There is a slight decline from Northgate down to High Cross, but the street remains fairly level from there to Watergate. There is a sharp decline from Watergate to Bridgegate no matter which route is taken, but if the pageants went through the lanes, as Rogers states, then they may have taken a more circuitous but less steep route from Watergate to Bridgegate by way of the Castle. The carriages which were to be used again on the following day could then have been wheeled out Newgate and up to Northgate Street by way of the Eastgate without going up any steep inclines. At the end of the performance, the guild again assembled for refreshment and the undressing of their players.

OTHER DRAMATIC ACTIVITY

The Whitsun Plays were not the only drama in Chester. Although most of the ecclesiastical records prior to the Reformation have disappeared, it is likely that there were liturgical performances in the city. In post-Reformation times, there are records for attending the sepulchre at Easter from the 1530s into the 1540s at St Mary's; Trinity Church kept a sepulchre up to Edward's reign, revived it in the 1550s, and used it until about 1560; St Michael's lists a sepulchre in its inventories from 1550 to 1565; and the dean and chapter of Chester Cathedral paid a Palm Sunday prophet in 1544, 1556, and 1559. Since the entries do not specify that dramatic activity occurred, it must be borne in mind that these references may be to regular liturgical practices rather than to liturgical dramas. The chapter was not averse to seeing secular drama; they entertained the queen's players twice in 1589 and again in 1592, the same year that they heard the earl of Essex's musicians.

The city did not take an adverse stand against plays until late in the sixteenth century. In 1429, there was a performance of a St George's Play; in 1529-30, an 'Enterlude named kinge Roberte of Scissill'; in 1564, an extravagant triumph of the history of Aeneas and Dido; and, in 1588-9, the 'storey of Kinge Ebrauk'. But it was inevitable that antagonism towards the Whitsun Plays should result in the suppression or control of other dramatic activity. In 1596, the city council passed an ordinance which forbade plays and bull-baits within the city, but lest the city become known for being miserly, it allowed the mayor to reward travelling players of the queen with twenty shillings and other noblemen's troupes with six shillings and eight pence. In 1602, it was the ill fortune of Francis Coffin and his troupe to enter Chester when drama was in disfavour and to run into a mayor who knew that Coffin's warrant had been revoked; yet in 1606, the Lord Harforth's men apparently had the foresight to ask the earl of Derby to send a letter to the mayor of Chester on their behalf that they might play in the city.

Apparently the city relented in their decision to ban players altogether, for in 1615 they made another ordinance which only sought to ban performances of players' 'obscene and vnlawfull Plaies or tragedies' from the Common Hall at night. The ordinance is rather curious since it at first implies that the council finds the performance of plays inappropriate in the Common Hall – that is, they seem to object less to the plays than to the performance of them in the Hall. They go on to restrict the playing of tragedies and comedies 'or anie other Plaie by what name soever they shall terme hit' to the daytime, on the grounds that apprentices have been resorting to innhouses to see plays and there waste their masters' substance. Clearly, these ordinances were often ignored; for example, the 1596 ban against bull-baits did not stop the mayor's annual bull-bait for, in 1621, two guilds caused such an affray at the bull-bait that the mayor broke his staff over one guildsman's head in an effort to stop the riot, and later commanded that the two guilds involved undertake the expense of another bull-bait.

Minstrels

In addition to the licensing of the minstrels, which occurred once a year, there were numerous occasions on which minstrels appeared before the citizens of Chester. In 1540, the city ordered that the city waitsmen or musicians were to perform every Sunday, Monday, Tuesday, Thursday, and Saturday in the evening and every Monday, Thursday, and Saturday in the morning. The city gave the waitsmen new gowns each year and in some years paid them to play before the morris dancers at Midsummer.

One of the most prominent waits was George Calley, who was admitted to the freedom of the city without making payment in 1608, and who petitioned to become the city wait in 1613 when the former waits had strangely disappeared. In addition to performing for the city, Calley taught music and dancing and performed at private functions. When Calley was made the city wait, he and his company were entrusted with the city's instruments, a double curtal and a tenor cornet; otherwise, the waits were expected to provide their own instruments, as the dispute in 1591 between Christopher Burton and the other waits against Alice Williams, widow of one of the waits, demonstrates.

Minstrels seem to have been present at every ceremonial and social function in the city. The guilds hired minstrels on their election days, meetings, dinners, and drinkings, on feast days like Corpus Christi when there was a procession, and on other holidays. In addition, many guilds employed minstrels in the Whitsun Plays: of the twelve accounts of expenditure for the plays, ten include payments to minstrels, the Coopers' guild alone not hiring any for their pageant of the Scourging. The dean and chapter of Chester Cathedral hired minstrels for their dinner on audit day and in 1592 entertained the earl of Essex's musicians. Although most music seems to have been presented by local minstrels, the Smiths and Shoemakers paid the baron of Kinderton's minstrels to entertain them in 1557. In any event, the citizens of Chester could hear the waits almost daily and were entertained by music whenever they went to plays and other shows, dinners or meetings, or gathered for social functions.

Conclusion

The city's dramatic and ceremonial activity seems to have peaked in the early decades of the sixteenth century and to have declined thereafter; indeed, by the end of the century, it seems to have lost most of its variety. The Midsummer Show is said to have begun in 1499 and, with the exception of periods in the late sixteenth and early seventeenth centuries, ran until the 1670s; the Sheriffs' Breakfast Shoot began in 1511-12; and the cycle plays, which had been performed on Corpus Christi Day in the fifteenth century, were moved to Whitsuntide about 1519, and the cycle grew considerably between that time and the 1530s. In addition, the city seems to have responded to the new humanist climate and altered many of its customs in 1540 so that they would have more 'profitable uses'. Lastly, the city responded to the shifting religious climate of the day, now supporting the performance of the Whitsun Plays, now repudiating them, until the plays were eventually suppressed in 1575. The new attitudes in religion, however, affected more than just the plays; Mayor Henry Hardware, for example, in 1600, forbade the appearance of the devil in his feathers, the naked boys, 'God in strings', and other parts of the Midsummer Show. Although some of these 'shows' were reinstated by subsequent mayors, they eventually were superseded by more modestly dressed children who rode through the city with guild representatives. By 1642, most of the local play production seems to have ceased and severe restrictions had been placed on travelling companies; in addition, most of the ancient customs had either been suppressed altogether or superseded by customs which might be less offensive to a wider group of people.

Editorial Procedures

Dating the Documents

Some documents in the original are dated Old Style, some by regnal year, some by mayoral term, and some by saints' days or moveable feasts. In order to arrange the documents in chronological order, the editor has converted all dates to modern usage. Events which occur on an annual basis or which are part of a regular accounting year are included within the dates of the accounting year (eg, the Shoemakers' expenditures for Midsummer fall within their accounting year, 11 November - 10 November), and, wherever precise dates within the accounting year are known, these are given in an editorial parenthesis. Documents which record unique events are dated according to the day, month, and year wherever that is possible.

The dating of most of the documents is straightforward; however, some documents are not clearly dated in the MSS and these are discussed in the End-notes. The reader should also see earlier discussions in The Documents section for the dating of the early rentals in Harley 2158 (pp xlviii-xlix), the Rogers' Breviaries (pp xxx-xxxii), and the Lists of Mayors and Sheriffs (pp xliii-xliv).

Chronology

The chronology begins after Midsummer and runs through the following Midsummer. The majority of the Chester records are excerpts from the annual accounts of the guilds, the city, and the churches. Since none of these accounting years corresponds to the beginning of the modern year, it has been necessary to base the chronology on a system of double dates (eg, 1475-6). The second desideratum is that expenditures for the same event appear as close to each other as possible; consequently, the chronology begins after the Midsummer Show rather than at the beginning of the modern year.

There are several impediments to beginning the chronology with 1 January. Many of the guild accounts, for example, contain expenditures for minstrels which cannot be assigned precise dates; all that might be said is that a minstrel was hired sometime between the beginning of the accounting year and some other event which can be dated. In order to preserve some sense of the order of expenditure and in order to maintain a guild's total annual expenditure in one entry, it was thought desirable to enter a guild's account under the day that the guild began its accounting year. When the editor tried to arrange these entries under a single-year chronology beginning in January (eg, January - December 1475 rather than Midsummer 1475 - Midsummer 1476), it was discovered that guilds that began their year before Midsummer showed their expenditure under the year that payment was made (eg, 1475), but those that began their year after Midsummer included expenditures of a year later (eg, 1476) under the preceding year (eg, 1475). This dislocation seemed potentially confusing; therefore, entries taken from documents which observe annual cycles are arranged in the following sequence:

> Drawers of Dee begin on 30 June
> Smiths, Cutlers, and Plumbers begin in July
> Innkeepers begin in August
> Painters, Glaziers, Embroiderers, and Stationers begin on 18 October
> Coopers begin on 20 November until 1589 when they shift their accounting
>   year to 13 January
> City Treasurers' Accounts begin in November
> Lists of Mayors begin in November
> Cordwainers and Shoemakers begin on 11 November
> Beerbrewers begin on 23 November
> Glovers begin on 5 January
> Coopers begin on 13 January after 1589
> Joiners, Carvers, and Turners begin on 25 March
> Churchwardens' Accounts begin at Easter
> Mercers, Ironmongers, Grocers, and Apothecaries begin in May

(Note that some of these begin on the same day each year; others begin on moveable feasts and are dated accordingly in the individual entries.) The effect of this arrangement is to place, for example, all of the expenditures for Midsummer for the same year under one double date; that is, the Drawers of Dee's, Painters', City Treasurers', Cordwainers', Beerbrewers', Coopers', and Mercers' expenditures for Midsummer in 1623 all appear under the heading 1622-3.

This chronology is maintained with the following exceptions and additions:

1) Entries which are not part of any annual accounting cycle are inserted between the appropriate dates in the chronology; for example, the Linendrapers' petition of 13 February 1619 appears under the year 1618-19 and between the entry for the Coopers (13 January) and that for the Mercers (7 May).

2) The Dean and Chapter of Chester Cathedral have four accounting periods

and entries from these records are inserted into the chronology according to each accounting period rather than according to an annual cycle:

St Katherine's to the Nativity (25 November - 25 December)
The Nativity to the Annunciation (25 December - 25 March)
The Annunciation to St Michael's (25 March - 29 September)
St Michael's to St Katherine's (29 September - 25 November)

3) Some of the guilds kept their Whitsun Play accounts separate from their regular accounts; in these few instances, the Whitsun accounts are entered separately from the regular accounts in the chronology.

The other exceptions are early entries from the Lists of Mayors. Since it is impossible to determine if the entries were originally assigned to the year of accession or the year of the majority of the mayor's term, it was decided to list these few entries under the date stated in the MS. Furthermore, in the case of the first several entries, those for 1269 and 1270 and those for 1328 and 1329, there is some question whether these should be regarded as two separate entries or as two versions of the same entry which had been assigned to different years because the manuscripts' predecessors had used different methods of dating mayoral terms; in addition, some MSS contain both entries, and it seemed desirable to maintain all these as separate entries rather than to lump them together under one double date.

Layout

Each document is preceded by a heading with year, MS identification, and folio or page number; antiquarian MSS are noted in the margin as either Antiquarian Compilations (A) or Antiquarian Collections (AC); an editorial sub-heading, within parentheses, gives, when available, the day and month of the event or the day and month on which the accounting year began, and, in the Lists of Mayors, the name of the mayor within whose term the event occurred. Italics indicate information supplied by the editor. When documents from different MSS appear under the same year, they follow the sequence established in the chronology above (pp lxi-lxiii), except for the undated documents in Appendix 1 which follow the order of MSS in The Documents section.

The editor has attempted to preserve the general layout of the MS originals. Headings, marginalia, and account totals are printed in the position in which they appear in the MSS. Right-hand marginalia have had to be set in the left margin of the text, but this transposition is indicated by the symbol ®. The lineation of the original has not been retained in the continuous prose passages.

Where two or more copies of the same document survive, the editor has chosen a base text and collated significant variants at the foot of the page. In all collations, differences in capitalization, form of abbreviation, word-division, and punctuation have been omitted. Collations have not been provided for all the entries in the Lists of Mayors and Sheriffs because all entries which substantively vary in content are printed separately; for further information, see the statement at the end of the MSS descriptions of the Lists (p xliv).

Dittography, emendations, and scribal errors are noted at the foot of the page. Also noted at the foot of the page are readings made by earlier editors of words and phrases which are now obliterated. Peculiarities of MSS (such as decay or damage that affect the reading), scribal idiosyncracies, and problems of dating and provenance are discussed more extensively in the End-notes.

Punctuation

The punctuation of the MSS has been retained. Virgules have been indicated as / and //. MS braces and line fillers have not been reproduced.

Spelling, Capitalization, and Expansion

The spelling of the original has been preserved, as has the capitalization. 'ff' has been retained for 'F'; 'I/J' have been uniformly transcribed as 'I'. It has been difficult at times to distinguish between Randle Holme's capital and lower case 'c' and 's' when he uses the modern forms. The size of some of these clearly indicates that he intended them to be capitals, whereas at other times they are definitely lower case; unfortunately, he also seems to have a median size, and the editor has simply had to guess whether they were closer to capitals or lower case letters. Holme also uses older capital forms and these are always transcribed as capitals regardless of their size. Ornamental or very large capitals in all MSS have been transcribed as regular capitals.

Abbreviated words have been expanded according to scribal practice, with italics to indicate letters supplied. Where there is insufficient evidence in the MS to judge individual scribal spelling habits, abbreviations in Latin have been expanded to standard classical forms, in Anglo-Norman to modern French, and in English to modern British forms. Abbreviations still in common use (eg, 'Mr', 'li', 's', 'd', 'lb', 'etc' or '&c', and 'viz') and ones cumbersome to expand, such as those typical of weights and measures ('ob'), have been retained. 'xp' and 'Xp' have been expanded as 'chr*ist*' and 'Chr*ist*'; 'Ihs' has been expanded as 'Ie*sus*'. The sign ℙ has been consistently expanded as 'es' even when, in the sixteenth- and seventeenth-century records, it follows 'e'. Otiose flourishes such as ♯ and ouↄ have been ignored.

Randle Holme and David Rogers consistently follow the practice of using the ℗ symbol for 'per', 'pre', 'par', and 'pri'. A similar usage appears in the Assembly Books in the document dated 21 November 1575. In these cases, the editor has expanded the abbreviation according to the scribe's practice rather than expanding the symbol as 'per'.

English words in Latin passages have not been declined. Place names, personal names, and surnames have only been expanded to normal spelling when the scribe indicates abbreviation. All superlineated letters have been lowered to the line except when they are used with numerals (eg, x^o, $xxiiij^{ti}$).

Notes

1 Salter, *MDC*, 37.
2 Salter, *MDC*, 57; for further discussion of the point see Clopper, 'The Rogers' Description of the Chester Plays,' 74-5.
3 The MS designations are the standard reference symbols for the five play MSS; see the introduction to Lumiansky and Mills' edition, *The Chester Mystery Cycle*, I, ix.
4 Alfred J. Horwood, 'The Manuscripts of G.F. Wilbraham, Esq., of Delamere House, co. Chester,' *Fourth Report of the Royal Commission on Historical Manuscripts. Part I. Report and Appendix* (London, 1874), 416.
5 Alfred J. Horwood, 'The Manuscripts of Reginald Cholmondeley, Esq., of Condover Hall, Shropshire,' 338.
6 R. Stewart-Brown, 'Annals of Chester,' *Cheshire Sheaf*, 3rd series, 27 (1930), 50.
7 The Royal Commission on Historical Manuscripts, *Accessions to Repositories and Reports added to the National Register of Archives 1974* (London, 1976), 8.
8 For fuller discussion of authorship, see Clopper, 'The Rogers' Description of the Chester Plays.'
9 For the three points, see, respectively, ML 2, ff 90-90v (pp 197-8) and ML 5, f 45v (p 198); AB/1, ff 33v-5; and Salter, 'The Banns of the Chester Plays,' *RES*, 16 (1940), 142-8, or Hermann Deimling (ed), *The Chester Plays*, EETS Extra Series, 62 (1892), 2-9.
10 The entries from this MS were published in a series of notes by W. Fergusson Irvine, 'The Annals of Chester.'
11 *Mysteries' End. An Investigation of the Last Days of the Medieval Religious Stage.* Yale Studies in English, 103 (New Haven, 1946), 79.
12 For further discussion of the document, see the note to the Early Banns entry (pp 517-18); W.W. Greg, *The Trial and Flagellation with Other Studies in the Chester Cycle*, 123-9; Clopper, 'The History and Development of the Chester Cycle'; the Lumiansky and Mills' notes on the plays in their forthcoming second volume of *The Chester Mystery Cycle*.
13 Reported in Sir Peter Leycester's *Historical Antiquities* (see Appendix 2, pp 486-9) and in CRO: DLT/B3, pp 461-6.

14 39 Elizabeth, cap 4: Among others, the law defines as vagabonds common players of interludes and minstrels, but it specifies that it is not intended to disinherit John Dutton of Dutton '... in allowing Minstrels within the Countie Palantine of Chester ... for the gouernment of Minstrels there, and keeping a Court yerely for that purpose ...,' *A Kalender, or Table comprehending the effect of all the Statutes ...,* Fardinando Pulton (ed), (London, 1606; STC 9547), 406, 408.

15 R.M. Lumiansky, 'Comedy and Theme in the Chester *Harrowing of Hell,*' *Tulane Studies in English,* 10 (1960), 5-12.

16 For a fuller discussion of the history and development of the cycle, see Lumiansky and Mills' discussion of the documents in Volume II of their *Chester Mystery Cycle,* and Clopper, 'History and Development.'

17 The details which follow are extracted from the twelve extant guild accounts: Cordwainers and Shoemakers (1550), Smiths, Cutlers, and Plumbers (1554, 1561, 1567, 1568, 1572, 1575), Painters, Glaziers, Embroiderers, and Stationers (1568, 1572, 1575), and Coopers (1572, 1575).

18 J.H.E. Bennett (ed), *The Rolls of the Freemen of the City of Chester. Part I. 1392-1700.* The Record Society for the Publication of Original Documents Relating to Lancashire and Cheshire, 51 (London, 1906), 21, 24.

19 Salter, 'The Banns of the Chester Plays,' 16 (1940), 3-4; MDC, 58-60; Clopper, 'History and Development,' 222-3.

20 Such a cart is feasible, as is demonstrated by the description of the hell cart in the Digby Mary Magdalene, *The Digby Plays,* F.J. Furnivall (ed), p 67, l 357.

21 See the stage directions at IV.1; V.95, 199; VIII.48, 112; XIV.224; and in the H MS at VI.440; and the dialogue at VI.282 and X.274.

Select Bibliography

This short-list includes books and articles with first-hand transcriptions of primary documents. No attempt has been made to list all works cited in the Introduction, textual footnotes, and End-notes.

Anon. 'A Brief Abstract of the Proceedings of the Society,' [1864-72] , *Chester and North Wales Architectural, Archaeological, and Historic Society Journal*, 3, part 12 (1885), 439-554 (see T. Hughes' report, 496-501).

— 'A Company of Players,' *The Cheshire Sheaf*, 3rd series, 59 (1964), 40-1.

B., J.C. 'A Play at Chester in 1529,' *The Cheshire Sheaf*, 3rd series, 10 (1913), 96-7.

Bennett, J.H.E. 'The Grey Friars of Chester,' *Chester and North Wales Architectural Archaeological, and Historic Society Journal*, NS 24 (1921-2), 5-80.

— 'The White Friars of Chester,' *Chester and North Wales Architectural, Archaeological, and Historic Society Journal*, NS 31 (1935), 5-54.

Beresford, Rev J.R. 'The Churchwarden's Accounts of Holy Trinity, Chester, 1532 to 1633,' *Chester and North Wales Architectural, Archaeological, and Historic Society Journal*, NS 38 (1951), 95-172.

Bland, D.S. 'The Chester Mystery Plays,' *The Cheshire Round*, 1 (1967), 232-9.

Boulton, Helen E. (ed and intro). *The Chester Mystery Plays* (Chester, 1962).

Bridge, Joseph C. 'Items of Expenditure from the 16th Century Accounts of the Painters, Glaziers, Embroiderers, and Stationers' Company, with special reference to the "Shepherds' Play",' *Chester and North Wales Architectural, Archaeological, and Historic Society Journal*, NS 20 (1914), 153-91.

— 'The Chester Miracle Plays; some facts concerning them, and the supposed author ship of Ralph Higden,' *Chester and North Wales Architectural, Archaeological, and Historic Society Journal*, NS 9 (1903), 59-98.

— 'The Organists of Chester Cathedral. Part I. 1541 to 1644,' *Chester and North Wales Architectural, Archaeological, and Historic Society Journal*, NS 19 (1913), 63-90.

Broadbent, R.J. 'Annals of the Chester Stage, From the earliest period to the end of the Theatre Royal by Letters Patent (1854).' Transcript in the Liverpool Public Library.

Brown, Arthur. 'A Tradition of the Chester Plays,' *London Mediaeval Studies*, 2, part I (1951), 68-72.

Burne, R.V.H. 'Chester Cathedral in the Reigns of Mary and Elizabeth,' *Chester and North Wales Architectural, Archaeological, and Historic Society Journal*, NS 38 (1951), 49-94.

— 'The Founding of Chester Cathedral,' *Chester and North Wales Architectural, Archaeological, and Historic Society Journal*, NS 37 (1948-9), 37-68.

— *The Monks of Chester. The History of St Werburgh's Abbey* (London, 1962).

C., M. 'Chester Treasurers' Accounts 1612-1619,' *The Cheshire Sheaf*, 4th series, 6 (1974), 28-45.

Chambers, E.K. *The Mediaeval Stage.* 2 vols (London, 1903).

Clopper, Lawrence M. '*The Chester Plays:* Frequency of Performance,' *TS*, 14 (1973), 46-58.

— 'The History and Development of the Chester Cycle,' *MP*, 75 (1978), 219-46.

— 'The Rogers' Description of the Chester Plays,' *LeedsSE*, NS 7 (1974), 63-94.

— 'The Staging of the Medieval Plays of Chester: A Response,' *TN*, 28 (1974), 65-70.

Collier, John Payne. 'The Widkirk, Chester, and Coventry Miracle Plays,' *The History of English Dramatic Poetry to the time of Shakespeare: and annals of the stage to the Restoration* (London, 1831), Vol II, 155-229.

Davis, Ruth Brant. 'The Scheduling of the Chester Cycle Plays,' *TN*, 27 (1972-3), 49-67.

Earwaker, J.P. 'The Ancient Parish Books of the Church of St. Mary-on-the-Hill, Chester,' *Chester and North Wales Architectural, Archaeological, and Historic Society Journal*, NS 2 (1888), 132-48.

— *The History of the Church and Parish of St. Mary-on-the-Hill, Chester, together with an Account of the New Church of S. Mary-without-the-Walls.* Rupert H. Morris (ed) (London, 1898).

Editor. 'Lawsuit about the River Dee Fishery,' *The Cheshire Sheaf*, 1st series, 1 (1879), 319-20.

— 'St. Nicholas' Chapel, Chester,' *Chester and North Wales Architectural, Archaeological, and Historic Society Journal*, 2, part 5 (1858 for 1856-7), 20.

F., H. 'Midsummer Eve and the Watch,' *The Cheshire Sheaf*, 1st series, 1 (1879), 245.

Farrall, Laurence Meakin (ed). *Parish Register of the Holy & Undivided Trinity in the City of Chester, 1532-1837* (Chester, 1914).

Furnivall, F.J. (ed). *The Digby Mysteries.* The New Shakspere Society, Series VII, No. 1 (London, 1882). See 'Appendix to Forewords. Notes on the Chester Plays and Midsummer Watch, from Harleian MSS. 1944, 1948, 2125, &c.,' xviii-xxix.

Greg, W.W. (ed). *The Trial & Flagellation with Other Studies in the Chester Cycle.* The Malone Society Studies (Oxford University Press, 1935).

Groombridge, Margaret J. 'The City Gilds of Chester,' *Chester and North Wales Architectural, Archaeological, and Historic Society Journal*, NS 39 (1953), 93-108.

Halliwell, James Orchard (ed). *Palatine Garland: Being A Selection of Ballads and*

Fragments, Supplementary to The Palatine Anthology (London, 1850).

Horwood, Alfred J. 'The Manuscripts of Reginald Cholmondeley, Esq., of Condover Hall, Shropshire,' *Fifth Report of the Royal Commission on Historical Manuscripts. Part I. Report and Appendix* (London, 1876), 333-60.

Hughes, Thomas. 'Midsummer Show,' *The Cheshire Sheaf,* 1st series, 1 (1879), 243-5.

— 'On the Inns and Taverns of Chester, Past and Present. Part I.,' *Chester and North Wales Architectural, Archaeological, and Historic Society Journal,* 2, part 5 (1858 for 1856-7), 91-110.

— 'St. George's Day at Chester,' *The Cheshire Sheaf,* 1st series, 1 (1879), 204-5.

— 'The Chester Stationers' Company and Midsummer Show,' *The Cheshire Sheaf,* 1st series, 3 (1883), 46-7.

— 'The Joyners', Carvers', and Turners' Company, Chester,' *The Cheshire Sheaf,* 1st series, 4 (1884), 163-4.

— 'The Lord of Misrule,' *The Cheshire Sheaf,* 1st series, 1 (1879), 355-6.

— 'The Whitsun Plays,' *The Cheshire Sheaf,* 1st series, 1 (1879), 230-1.

Irvine, W. Fergusson. 'The Annals of Chester,' *The Cheshire Sheaf,* 3rd series, 29 (1934), 1-2, 7-8, 11, 13, 15, 17, 20-6, 29, 40, 72-7, 79; 30 (1935), 2-4, 7-10, 13-14, 16-17, 19, 23-5, 30, 32, 34, 38, 39-40, 42-5, 47, 49-54, 57, 59-60, 64, 65-6, 68, 72, 73, 75, 77-8, 81, 83, 87-8, 90, 92, 95, 98, 99-100.

Jeaffreson, John Cordy. 'The Manuscripts of the Corporation of the City of Chester, *Eighth Report of the Royal Commission on Historical Manuscripts. Report and Appendix.* Part I (London, 1881), 355-403.

Legg, L.G. Wickham (ed). *A Relation of A Short Survey of 26 Counties Observed in a seven weeks Journey begun on August 11, 1634 By a Captain, a Lieutenant, and an Ancient All three of the Military Company in Norwich* (Oxford and London, 1904).

Leycester, Sir Peter. *Historical Antiquities, in two books. The First Treating in General of Great-Brettain and Ireland. The Second Containing Particular Remarks concerning Cheshire* (London, 1673).

Lumiansky, R.M. and David Mills (eds). *The Chester Mystery Cycle.* Vol I, EETS Supplementary Series, 3 (London, 1974). Vol II (forthcoming) will contain texts of key documents with a commentary.

Lysons, Rev Daniel, and Samuel. *Magna Britannia; being a Concise Topographical Account of the Several Counties of Great Britain* (London, 1810), Vol II, ii.

M., R. 'Christmas Breakfasts and Mummers at Chester, in 1556,' *The Cheshire Sheaf* 1st series, 1 (1879), 354.

Marshall, John. 'The Chester Whitsun Plays: Dating of Post-Reformation Performances from the Smiths' Accounts,' *LeedsSE,* 9 (1977, for 1976 and 1977), 51-61.

Morris, Rupert H. *Chester in the Plantagenet and Tudor Reigns* (Chester, [1894?]).

Nelson, Alan H. *The Medieval English Stage: Corpus Christi Pageants and Plays* (Chicago and London, 1974).

Ormerod, George. *The History of the County Palatine and City of Chester; compiled from original evidences in public offices, the Harleian and Cottonian Mss., Parochial Registers, Private Muniments, unpublished ms. collections of successive Cheshire antiquaries, and a personal survey of every township in the county: incorporated with a republication of King's Vale Royal, and Leycester's Cheshire Antiquities.* 3 vols (London, 1819), 2nd ed, Thomas Helsby (rev), 3 vols (London, [1875]-82).

P., L. and W.F.I. 'The Annals of Chester,' *The Cheshire Sheaf*, 3rd series, 8 (1910), 79, 84, 86-9, 94-6; 9 (1912), 5, 7, 9, 12, 14-15, 17, 20, 22, 24, 26, 29, 32-4, 36, 41, 42-3, 44, 47, 55-6, 58-61, 63, 65, 68, 71, 73.

Salter, F.M. *Mediaeval Drama in Chester* (Toronto, 1955).

— 'The Banns of the Chester Plays,' RES, 15 (1939, 432-57; 16(1940), 1-17, 137-48.

— 'The "Trial and Flagellation": a new manuscript,' *The Trial & Flagellation with Other Studies in the Chester Cycle*, W.W. Greg (ed), The Malone Society Studies (Oxford University Press, 1935), 1-73.

Sharp, Thomas. *A Dissertation on the Pageants or Dramatic Mysteries Anciently performed at Coventry, by the trading companies of that city; chiefly with reference to the vehicle, characters, and dresses of the actors. Compiled in a great degree, from sources hitherto unexplored. To which are added, the Pageant of the Shearmen & Taylors' Company, and other municipal entertainments of a public nature* (Coventry, 1825; rpt Wakefield, 1973).

Simpson, Frank. *Chester City Guilds: the Barber-Surgeons' Company, Chester* (Chester, 1911).

— 'The City Gilds of Chester: The Bricklayers' Company,' *Chester and North Wales Architectural, Archaeological, and Historic Society Journal*, NS 22 (1918), 55-90.

— 'The City Gilds of Chester: The Skinners and Feltmakers' Company,' *Chester and North Wales Architectural, Archaeological, and Historic Society Journal*, NS 21 (1915), 77-149.

— 'The City Gilds of Chester: The Smiths' Cutlers', and Plumbers' Company,' *Chester and North Wales Architectural, Archaeological, and Historic Society Journal*, NS 20 (1914), 5-121.

— 'The City Gilds or Companies of Chester, with special reference to that of the Barber-Surgeons,' *Chester and North Wales Architectural, Archaeological, and Historic Society Journal*, NS 18 (1911), 98-203.

Smith, William, and William Webb. *The Vale-Royall of England. Or, The County Palatine of Chester Illustrated* (London, 1656).

T., G. 'Christmas Watch at Chester,' *The Cheshire Sheaf*, 1st series 1 (1878), 135.

Taylor, Henry. 'The Chester City Companies,' *Chester and North Wales Architectural, Archaeological, and Historic Society Journal*, NS 5 (1893-5), 16-27.

Wickham, Glynne. *Early English Stages, 1300 to 1660.* Volume One 1300 to 1576 (London, 1959).
Z.z 'Ancient Cheshire Games (circ. 1630),' *N&Q,* 2nd series, 2 (1856), 487.

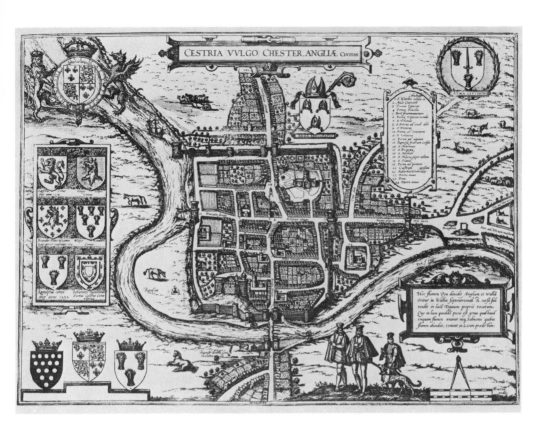

Map of Chester from *Civitatus Orbis Terrarum*, 1572-1618

RECORDS OF EARLY ENGLISH DRAMA

Symbols

A	Antiquarian Compilation
A C	Antiquarian Collection
B L	British Library
C	Chester
C C	Chester Cathedral
C C A	Chester City Archives
C R O	Cheshire Record Office
M D C	*Mediaeval Drama in Chester*
M L	Mayors List
P R O	Public Record Office
R H II	Randle Holme II
*	(after folio, page, or membrane number) see end-note(s)
♦	M S excerpted
®	right-hand marginalia
†	marginalia too long for the left-hand margin
...	ellipsis
⟨...⟩	damaged, lost, or obliterated letters
[ ]	cancellations, deletions, erasures
(blank)	blank spaces in the original where writing might be expected
° °	letters or words added by different or later hand
⌐ ¬	interlineations originally inserted above the line
∟ ⌐	interlineations originally inserted below the line
∧	M S caret
|	change of folio, page, or membrane in passages of continuous prose

N B: The chronology begins after Midsummer (24 June) and runs through the
following Midsummer.

The Records

1268-9

A *Mayors List 9* BL: Add. 11335
f 22v* *(Whitsun) John Arnewaye*

...

The old and Antient Whitson playes played in this city of Chester   5
were first made Englished and published by one Randall Higden
a monke of Chester Abbey, and sett forth and played at, and by
the Citizens of chester charge In the time of S*ir* Iohn Arneway
Knight, and Major of Chester Anno 1268 the last time they were
played was Anno D*omi*ni 1571 mr Iohn Hankey then Major of   10
Chester.

...

1269-70

A *Mayors List 6* BL: Harley 2125   15
f 91v* *(Whitsun) John Arnewaye*

...

In this yeare Whitson playes were invented in Chester by one
Rondoll Higden a monke in the Abby of Chester, and afterwards
set forth in action at the cost and charges of the cittizens which   20
was great charges, and note yat this monke was a pious man, and
a great writer in yat Abby as his bookes yet shew, in great
devotion he and discretion he published ye storie of ye bible, yat
ye simple in their owne language might undestand. /
...   25

•Randle monke
of Chester dyed
31 E 3 1357
wh*ich* is longe
after & this is
not he•

19 / *marginalia in RH II's hand*

1327-8

A   *Mayors List 5* BL: Harley 2125
f 23v* *(Whitsun) John Arnewaye*

The whitson playes . first made by one don Randall °'heggenett' °   5
A moonke, of Chester Abbey °who was thrise at Rome before he
could obtayn leaue of the pope to haue them in the English
Tonge °
...
                                                                        10

1328-9

A   *Mayors List 11* BL: Add. 29779
f 11v* *(Whitsun) John Arnewaye*
...

The whtson playes, invented and made by A worthye man. Called   15
[don] Randall heggnett °'higgden' ° Amonke of Chester Abbey
...

A   *Mayors List 2* BL: Harley 1944
f 67 *(Whitsun) John Arnewaye*   20
...

The whitson playes Inuented, in Chester, by one Rondoll Higden
a monke in Chester abbaye. /
...
                                                                        25

A   *Mayors List 5* BL: Harley 2125
f 23v *(Whitsun) John Arnewaye*
...

The Whitson playes . played openlye . in pageantes by the
Cittizins of Chester . in whitson weeke   30
...

1397-8

A   *Mayors List 6* BL: Harley 2125
f 100* *(Christmas) John de Capenhurst*   35
...

christmas watch & 24 senior or Aldermen named . 25 . 271.
...

5 / °[heggenett] ° *in RH II's hand*   6-8 / °who ... Tonge ° *in RH II's hand*
16 / °[higgden] ° *in RH II's hand*
29 / openlye *BL Add. 29779, f 11v, inserts* three dayes *after* openlye

1398-9
Mayors' Books CCA: M/B/1
ff 55v-6* *(30 May)*

Inquis*icio* capta apud C*est*ri*am* coram Vice*comitibus* Cestr*ie* die   5
Ven*er*is in Crastino corp*or*is chr*ist*i Anno *regni regis* Ricar*d*i
*se*cu*n*di xxij*d*o *per* sacra*mentum* Ricar*d*i de draycote Ioh*ann*is le
Glouer henr*ic*i le coruys*er* Will*elm*i Mody Ioh*ann*is Russell
Porto*ur* Will*elm*i de hulfeld coup*er* Ioh*ann*is Chirche coruys*er*
Ricar*d*i short shippemon Andree le ffremon Rob*er*ti de Thenwall   10
skynner Will*elm*i le Tayllio*ur* & Ricar*d*i del halgh Iur*atores*
dic*unt* sup*er* sacra*mentum* suu*m* qu*o*d Will*elmu*s de Wybunbure
senior henr*icus* de ffelday Webst*er* Thomas Bragot Webster
Will*elmu*s de Stretton Walker Thomas le Challon*er* de
Estegatestrete Thomas de Brymstath heuster Ricar*du*s de   15
Werburton Webster Will*elmu*s Cay Challon*er* Rog*eru*s le Challon*er*
de fforgastrete hug*o* de Thurstanton Weu*er* Ricar*du*s del hope
Weuer henr*icus* huntebach Will*elmu*s Shagh Webst*er* Ricar*du*s
Whyt Walker Will*elmu*s Butt heuster Ricar*du*s Byrne Webster
Ioh*ann*es le Erle Challon*er* Ricar*du*s Gardeyn Walker Will*elmu*s   20
Bryn Walker Will*elmu*s Porter Walker Ricar*du*s de hale Will*elmu*s
Thomassone heuster Ioh*ann*es howell Webst*er* hug*o* Bargeyn
hug*o* de Legh Ioh*ann*es de Ince senior Dauid Broun Webster
Ioh*ann*es mair Walker [Ioh*ann*es de Berkeswell senior] Will*elmu*s
le Sh*er*mon Nich*o*la*u*s le Sh*er*mon Ioh*ann*es le Sh*er*mon Thomas   25
Iakes Sh*er*mon Ioh*ann*es de Shottum Sh*er*mon [hug*o* de Aston
Challon*er*] Ioh*ann*es le challon*er* de SeinctIoneslone Will*elmu*s le
challon*er* [cr⟨...⟩rins le Challon*er* Ioh*ann*es le Smyth Webster]
Ricar*du*s Getegode Webster Will*elmu*s haslore Webster Thomas le
Spencer Walker henr*icus* Denys Webster Ioh*ann*es le Webster   30
de Castellane Symon le Webst*er* de Hawardyn . Ioh*ann*es [de
Bromley] de ffrodesham ˄ ʻWill*elmu*s Capemakerʼ & pl*ure*s
alij *M*agist*r*i textores ven*erunt* vi & armis cu*m* Polaxes baculis
*pre*mitis baslardis & alijs diu*er*sis armitur*is* cogitac*ione pre*meditata
die Iouis in festo corp*or*is chr*ist*i Anno *regni regis* Ricar*d*i *se*cu*n*di   35
xxij*d*o exopposito ecclesiam B*eat*i Petri cestr*ie* p*ariter* congregati
insult*um* fec*erunt* Will*elm*o de Wybunbur*e* Iuniori Thome del
Dame & alijs conpl*ur*imis s*er*uientib*us* suis vocat*is* Iournaymen in
magnam affraiam tocius p*o*pulli Ciuita*t*is contra pacem d*omi*ni
Regis dic*unt* q*uo*d no*n* sunt culp*abiles* et die Iouis p*roximo* post   40

39 / *populli for* populi

festum Apostolorum Petri & Pauli ⟨...⟩o proximo sequenti
compertum fuit per Inquisicionem captam quod Thomas Bragot
Ricardus Whyte Ricardus de Werberton ⟨.⟩illelmus le Chaloner
Iohannes le Chaloner Iohannes Howell Willelmus de Stretton
Hugo Bargayne ⟨..⟩hannes le Smyth Webster & Willelmus   5
Cadewalleshened non sunt culpabiles de insultu predicto set
⟨..⟩cunt quod sunt culpabiles de affraia predicta. Ideo consumatum
est &c. |

Item dicunt quod Willelmus de Wybunbure Iunior henricus   10
Penkyth Walker Iohannes de Merton Iohannes de hull Weuer
Ricardus le Spencer Weuer Iohannes Thomasson Weuer Robertus
de Derbyshyre Walker Thomas del Dame Weuer Ricardus Stubbok
Challoner Iohannes Chestre Iunior Henricus Bragot Iohannes
de Sucton Weuer Willelmus le Smyth Weuer Iohannes de Acton   15
Weuer Reginaldus de Merford Rogerus Pyme Iohannes de holand
Willelmus Wodewarde seruiens Ricardi de hale Thomas Werforde
Iohannes Dernak Weuer Thomas del Mosse Rogerus seruiens
Ricardi de hale Robertus seruiens Willelmi Porter Edwardus
Brounsworde Bellyn seruiens Willelmi Shawe henricus Bragot   20
Hugo Bragot [Willelmus] Nicholaus Ricardus & Dauid seruientes
Ricardi Whyt [Iohannes de londesdale] Thomas de Byrchomley
Iohannes de hale Iunior . Dauid de Moldesdale [Thomas le
Sheuacre Challoner] Iohannes de Chestre senior Willelmus &
Robertus seruientes seruientes Thome de Brymstath Iohannes   25
Gredyn Dauid seruiens henrici Penkyth Willelmus Kydde seruiens
Willelmi Porter Walker Willelmus le Wodewarde seruiens Ricardi
de hale Iohannes Skelo seruiens Dauid Broun

1421-2   30
Coopers' Records C: Loose papers*
(20 April)

Memorandum quod discordia & lis suborte fuerunt inter les
Irenmongers Ciuitatis Cestrie ex vna parte & Carpentarios eiusdem   35
Ciuitatis ex altera parte vtrum vna pars aut alia haberet omnes les
fflecchers . Bowers . Stringers . Coupers & Turnours eiusdem
Ciuitatis ad ipsos auxiliandum in luso Corporis christi eiusdem
Ciuitatis Tandem ex assensu vtriusque partis in pleno Portmoto
tento apud Cestriam die lune proxima post Clausum Pasche Anno   40
regni Regis Henrici quinti post conquestum decimo coram
Iohanne hope maiore Ciuitatis predicte Inquisicio capta fuit ad

sciendum veritatem de materijs predictis vtrum vni parti aut
alteri ⟨.....⟩gi deberent nec ne videlicet per sacramentum Iohannis
de hatton senioris . Willelmi hope . Ricardi Weston . Alexandri
Hennebury . Ade de Wotton . Iohannis de hatton iunioris .
Roberti Wolley Ricardi Lynakre . Willelmi de Pykton Thome de   5
hellesby Iohannis William & Ricardi Thomworth . Iuratorum .
Qui dicunt super sacramentum suum quod predicti ⟨.....⟩chers .
Bowers . Stringers Coupers & Turnours non debent nec tenentur
ludere nec esse participes cum vna parte nec cum alia des
Irenmongers siue Carpentarijs predictis in Paginis suis lusi Corporis   10
christi predicti set dicunt quod tenentur sustentare per semet
ipsos Paginam suam propriam eiusdem lusi videlicet de
fflagellacione Corporis christi cum suis pertinentijs secundum
Originale inde factum vsque ad Crucifixionem eiusdem Iesu
christi prout in dicto Originale continetur . et quod predicti   15
Irenmongers debent Sustentare lusum de Crucifixione vt
predictum ⟨.....⟩stus ⟨..⟩us & predicti Carpentarij Paginam suam
secundum Originale predictum In cuius rei testimonium huic
presenti Inquisicioni predictus Maior sigillum officij sui Maioratus
predicti apponi fecit . datum die & Anno predictis   20

1429-30
Portmote Court Rolls CCA: M/R/4/85
mb 1* *(19 May)*
...
                                                                        25
Placita portmoti Ciuitatis Cestrie tenta apud Cestriam coram
Iohanne Walssh maiore dicte Ciuitatis die lune proximo post
festum sancti dunstani anno regni regis henrici sexti post
conquestum otta ⟨...⟩
    plait a remembrer qe le lvndy proschein apres le fest de saint   30
dunstan lan de regne nostre tressouerein sieur le Roy henry
sisme puis le conquest septyme deuant Iohn le Walssh Mair de la
Citee de Cestre lez viscountz & xxiiij aldermen de dit Citee: de
lassent agrement & bone volunte de Richard de hawardyn &
Richard de Brogheford Seneschalles dez artes de Weuers Walkers   35
Chaloners & shermen de la dit Citee sur vne peticioun en plein
Portemote faitz par lez ditz Maier viscountz ⟨.⟩ xxiiij aldermen
⟨...⟩ ordeigne fust estable & assentira durer perpetaute qe chescun
persone de quele astate ou condicion qil qe ascun dez ditz artes
vse ou occup⟨...⟩ denz le dit Citee soit contributory ⟨...⟩ ou face   40

2 / ⟨.....⟩gi *probably* iniungi

paier tout ⟨...⟩ des quele il est ou serra assese par lez seneschalles
dez ditz artes pur le temps esteauntz de paier A lez costages &
expenses ⟨...⟩ lumeir de nostre dame sancte marie & de corpus
christi & al Iwe de Corpus christi & a lun & lautre de eux a toutz
& achescun fe⟨...⟩ quil auendra le dit lumier estre porte ou le dit
Iwe estre fait & qe celui qi ne voiet la somme a quele il est
assese par lez ditz seneschalles paier deinz moyse ⟨...⟩ le dit
assese fiat qil encourge le forfa⟨...⟩ payne de xiij s iiij d
Cestassauoir vj s viij d a lez viscountz de dit Citee pur le temps
esteauntz & vj s viij d a lez ⟨...⟩ demesne lez artes qe pur le temps   1⟨
serrount & le dit some destre leue par distresse Et qe bene lite si
bene as ditz viscountz pur lez vj s viij d qi a eux apprendra ⟨...⟩
ditz seneschalles pur lez vj s viij d qi a eux apprendra & ⟨...⟩ pur
lez ditz sommes issint assese a distrendre chescun persone qi le
dit somme issait sur luy assese ⟨..⟩ de voier ou paier refuse la dit   1⟨
distresse a chescun fortz qe le dit cas de nonn paument auiendra
danere & tener irreplenisable ⟨...⟩ toutz ioures En temoignage de
quele Mose' ⟨...⟩ ordenance stabissement & agrement endente &
enrolle si bien le dit mair pur lui lez ditz 'viscountz' & xxiiij
aldermen le seal del office de Mairlt ⟨...⟩ lez ditz ⟨...⟩ seneschalles   2⟨
pur eux & toutz lez artifecers dez artes susditz leur seales ount
mys done a Cestre ior & lan susditz
...

1430-1   2⟨

A   *Mayors List 5*   B L : Harley 2 1 2 5
f 27v* *(23 April) Robert Hope*

...

in this yeare was St georges playes playd in chester

                                                                                   3⟨

1437-8

A C   *City Treasurers' Accounts*   B L : Harley 2 1 5 8
f 33v *(November)*

...

Senescallus del Mercers pro redditu de shipyate   viij d   35

...

1438-9

A C   *City Treasurers' Accounts*   B L : Harley 2 1 5 8
f 33v* *(November)*

                                                                                   4⟨

senescallis [pistor] piscatorum cestrie pro quadam

parcell terre   vj d
...

1439-40

AC *City Treasurers' Accounts* B L: Harley 2158   5
f 33v *(November)*
...

senescall*is* sissor Cestr*ie* pro quadam p*ar*cell terre   vj d
senescall*is* piscator pro quadam p*ar*cell terre   vj d
...   10

1440-1

AC *City Treasurers' Accounts* B L: Harley 2158
f 34 *(November)*
...   15

sen*escallis* sissor cestr*ie* pro quad*am* p*ar*cell terre   vj d
...

f 35v *(Arrearages)*
...   20
piscator Cestr*ie* pro quadam p*ar*cell ter*re*   *(blank)*
...

1441-2

AC *City Treasurers' Accounts* B L: Harley 2158   25
f 34v* *(November)*
...

Sissor cestr*ie* pro p*ar*cell terr*e*   vj d
...

piscator Cestrie pro p*ar*cell terr*e*   vj d 30
Senescall*is* mercers pro p*ar*cell terre in shipgate   viij d
...

f 35
... Senescall le mercers viij d   35

1, 8, 9, 16, 21, 28, 30, 31 / parcell *for* parcella
8, 16 / sissor *for* sissorum   9 / piscator *for* piscatorum
21, 30 / piscator *for* piscatoribus   28 / Sissor *for* Sissoribus

1442-3

A C   *City Treasurers' Accounts* B L: Harley 2158
f 35v *(November)*

...

Sen*escallis* le mercers *pro* redd*itu* suo   viij d   5

...

1453-4

A   *Mayors List 5* B L: Harley 2125
f 29* *(November) Nicholas Daniel*   10

In this yeare queene Margrett °ₐ‵wife to H 6'° Came to Chester
vpon p*ro*gresse: with manye greate Lordes and Ladyes with her
They were Graciouslye Received . by the mayor & Cittizins

...   15

1462-3

A C   *Bakers' Charter* B L: Harley 2054
f 36v*

Whitson plays   ... & to be redy to pay for the Costes & expences of the play and   20
light of Corpus Christi as oft tymes as it shall be asseset by the
same stuards for the tyme being ...

A C   *City Treasurers' Accounts* B L: Harley 2158   25
f 49v *(November) (Arrearages)*

...

marchants of chester   iij d

...

                                                                              30

1463-4

A C   *City Treasurers' Accounts* B L: Harley 2158
f 44v *(November) (Arrearages)*

...

the mercers of chester   iij d   35

...

---

12 / °ₐ‵wife to H 6'• *in RH II's hand*

1465-6

A C   *City Treasurers' Accounts* B L: Harley 2158
f 51* *(November)* *(Arrearages)*

...

mercatores Ci*uita*tis Cestr*ie*	*(blank)*	5
drap*ers* Ci*uita*tis Cestr*ie* p*ro* *(blank)*	*(blank)*	
	no more diserned	

...

1466-7   10

A C   *City Treasurers' Accounts* B L: Harley 2158
f 51* *(November)* *(Arrearages)*

...

Mercatores Ci*uita*tis p*ro* mansion Carriagij sui	*(blank)*	

...   15

1467-8

A C   *City Treasurers' Accounts* B L: Harley 2158
f 39* *(November)*

...   20

senescall*is* Tellarie Ci*uita*tis Cestr*ie* p*ro* gardino iuxta		
Truantshole	4d	

...

f 39v   25

Northgate strete 7 E 4

...

senescall*is* de le shermen p*ro* Aysiament Carragij sui	iiij d	

...   30

f 40

Watergate strete

...   35

® ante
mercatoribus

Apronarijs ⌐Meronarijs⌐ p*ro* Aysiamento Caragij ib*ide*m	vj d	
pannarijs p*ro* Consil*io*	viij d	

...

---

14 / mansion *for* mansione   21 / Tellarie *for* Sellarie
29 / Aysiament *for* Aysiamento

f 52

...

Watergatestrete

...

mercatoribus Ciuitatis pro vna vacua placea ibidem   viij d

...

f 52v

...

drapers Ciuitatis Cestrie pro quadam Asyament   viij d

mercatoribus Ciuitatis pro quadam aysiament ad Caragium   viij d

...

Coopers' Records   C : Loose Papers
(12 March)

This script & composicion made by all the maistres & brederin of
the craft of fflecchers & Bowers Within the Cite of Chester ...
Also that euery maistire & iourneman . shalbe contributorie to
pay for the Sustentacion & fortheraunce of the light of Corpus
christi. And othire charges that shall to the playe . of Corpus
christi & othire charges belongyng therto . opon payn of xiij s
iiij d to be leuyed by . way of distresse or enprisonment . of the
person that so offendys or levy of his godys by the styward of
the seid Craftes atte theire eleccion. And that euery person that
shall be made . brothire in any of the seid Craftz . shall paye atte
his entre . to the sustentacion of the seid light & othire charges
xxvj s viij d & that noo person be receyuyd . to the seid
brethirhode in noon othire wyse . nor any Apprentice . to be
take by any maistire of any of the seid Craftes vnto any of the
same Craftz but for terme of vij yeres or above & not vndir
opon payn of brekyng of the othes aforerehersyd. And forfaiture
of xl s to theyre companyes box to be kept & leuyed to the
perfourmyng & vpholdyng of theire light & othire charges in the
fourme aforeseyd ...

10 / Aysament *for* Asyamento   10, 11 / quadam *for* quodam
11 / aysiament *for* aysiamento

1469-70

AC   *City Treasurers' Accounts* BL: Harley 2158
f 56 *(November) (Arrearages)*

... pannar*ijs* Cestr*ie* 4d ...   5

1470-1

AC   *City Treasurers' Accounts* BL: Harley 2158
f 54v* *(November) (Arrearages)*

...   10

pannar*ijs* Ci*uita*tis Cestr*ie*   *(blank)*

...

1471-2

Treasurers' Account Rolls CCA: TAR/1/4   15
mb 1d* *(November)*

...

Wate*r*gatestrete

De Mercatorib*us* Ciuitate Cestr*ie pro* vna vacua placea ib*ide*m vj d   20

...

Saddlers' Charter PRO: CHES 2/144
mb 7 *(8 March)*

                                               25

*Litte*re patentes Edwardus dei gr*acia* Rex Angl*ie* & ffranc*ie* & D*omi*n*us* Hib*er*nie
Sellator*um* Omn*ibus* ad quos *p*resentes *litte*re *p*eruen*er*int sal*ut*em Sciatis
Ciuitat*is* Cestr*ie* q*u*od cum nob*is* sit intimatum *p*er *n*ostros dilectos Subditos
Ric*ardu*m Sadiller & henricum Ellome Senescallos Ric*ardu*m
Ellome Ioh*ann*em yong Ric*ardu*m yong & henricum yong   30
aldermannos & inhabitantes Magistros & occupatores artis &
occupac*ionis* Sellator*um* infra ciuitatem *n*ostram cestr*ie* qualit*er*
*p*er inordinatos intrusiones erecciones & occupac*iones* eiusdem
Artis infra ciuitatem *n*ostram *p*redictam *p*er forincecas *p*ersonas
& *p*op*u*lorum de irrigimine obstinate disposic*ionis* eos non   35
confirmand*o* ad supportand*a* on*er*a & custus ludi & pagine
occupatorib*us* eiusdem Artis & Ciuitatis Assignat*a* pcell*is* ludi
& luminis corpis chr*ist*i in honore eiusdem *p*er occupatores
eiusdem Artis & occupac*ion*is in Ciuitate *p*redicta Annuatim

20 / Ciuitate *for* Ciuitatis   33 / inordinatos *for* inordinatas
37 / pcell*is for* parcellis, *brevigraph omitted MS*
38 / corpis *for* corporis, *brevigraph omitted MS*

sustinend*is* & custodiend*is* nec multimoda alia on*era* annuatim
ordinat*a* in honore dei & ciuitatis n*ost*re *p*redict*e* *per* eosdem
artifices infra ciuitatem n*ost*ram *p*re*dict*am sustentat*a* & sic
n*ost*ri subditi *p*redict*i* grauit*er* sunt deteriorati & ita depaup*er*ati
de bonis suis q*uo*d ipsi eadem on*era* continuare non possunt nec
ea in tempore futur*o* sustinere . absq*ue* fauore . & remedio
n*ost*ris in ea p*ar*te Nos igit*ur* intimam consideraci*on*em ad
*p*remissa . h*ab*entes de gr*aci*a n*ost*ra sp*eci*ali concessimus *p*refatis
Subditis n*ost*ris Senescallis Aldermannis & inh*ab*itantib*us*
magistris & occupatorib*us* eiusdem artis & occupaci*on*is
Sellator*um* & Successorib*us* suis Senescallis Aldermannis &
inh*ab*itantibus magistris & occupatorib*us* eiusdem artis &
occupaci*on*is Sellator*um* infra Ciuitatem n*ost*ram Cestr*ie* tempore
futuro existent*ibus* q*uo*d nulla *p*ersona neq*ue* *p*ersone de *cetero*
durante t*er*mino quadraginta Annor*um* *proxime* sequen*tium*
intrabit aut intrabunt eriget aut erigent nec occupabit aut
occupabunt *p*redict*am* artem & occupaci*on*em Sellator*um* infra
d*ict*am ciuitatem n*ost*ram nec ˄ ʼinʼ aliquo loco ffranchesis
eiusdem absq*ue* voluntate assensu licencia & agreamento
Subditor*um* n*ost*ror*um* *p*redictor*um* & eor*um* Successor*um*
Senescallor*um* Aldermannor*um* magistror*um* & occupactor*um*
eiusdem artis Sellator*um* vel maioris p*ar*tis illor*um* infra *p*re*dict*am
Ciuitatem n*ost*ram inh*ab*itanti*um* sub pena forisfacture Centum
solidor*um* cuiuslibet *p*ersone sic facientis tociens quociens ipse
absq*ue* tali licencia intrabit eriget vel occupabit *p*re*dict*am artem
vel occupaci*on*em absq*ue* voluntate assensu licencia & agremento
sup*radict*or*um* medietate eor*um*dem Centum solidor*um* nob*is*
hered*ibus* & Successoribus n*ost*ris forisfacienda . altera vero
medietate eor*um*dem Centum solidor*um* forisfacienda *p*refatis
Senescallis Aldermannis Magistris & occupatorib*us* eiusdem Artis
& occupaci*on*is Sellator*um* infra Ciuitatem n*ost*ram *p*re*dict*am
*p*ro tempore existen*tibus* ad sustentaci*on*em pagine luminis &
ludi ante dict*i* & *per* n*ost*ros Vicecomites Ciuitatis n*ost*re *p*re*dicte*
*p*ro tempore existent*es* leuand*a* . Et in sup*er* de ampliori gr*aci*a
n*ost*ra concessimus *p*refatis Subditis & eor*um* Successorib*us*
Senescallis Aldermannis Magistris & occupatorib*us* d*ict*e artis
Sellator*um* in ciuitate *p*re*dict*a & ffranchesia eiusdem post*er*im
inh*ab*itantib*us* q*uo*d liceat eis infutur*o* tociens quociens eis de
necessario ordinare fac*ere* & compon*ere* int*er* semet*ipsos decebit
tales ordinaci*on*es & constituci*on*es custodiend*as* infra & int*er*

5

10

15

20

25

30

35

40

15 / durante *for* durantibus (?)

Senescallos Aldermannos Magistros & occupatores eiusdem artis
infra dictam Ciuitatem prout pro oportunitate ordinate
sustentacionis Pagine ludi artis & occupacionis predictorum
Sellatorum infra Ciuitatem predictam & ffranchesiam eiusdem
beneficialius prouidere poterit In cuius rei testimonium has   5
litteras nostras fieri fecimus patentes Teste me ipso apud Cestram
viij die Marcij Anno regni nostri duodecimo

                              per breue de privato sigillo &
                              de data auctoritate parliamenti   10

1472-3

AC *City Treasurers' Accounts* BL: Harley 2158
f 55v *(November)*
...   15

Watergatestrete
...

Mercatoribus Ciuitatis Cestrie pro vacua placa ibidem   vj d
...

panniparijs Ciuitatis Cestrie pro aysament   viij d   20
...

f 56v *(Arrearages)*
... Mercatoribus Ciuitatis pro vacua placea vj d ... pannarijs
Ciuitatis pro Aysiament viij d ...   25

1473-4

AC *City Treasurers' Accounts* BL: Harley 2158
f 56v *(November) (Arrearages)*
...   30
mercatores Cestrie   vj d
...
pannarijs Cestrie   viij d
...
                                                                       35
1474-5

Mayors' Books CCA: M/B/5
f 216* *(3 September)*

Memorandum ⟨...⟩ ther hath ben on Corpus day ⟨...⟩ reign of kyng   40

20 / aysament *for* aysamento   25 / Aysiament *for* Aysiamento

Edward the ffourth ⟨...⟩ and contraversies betwix the bowers &
the ffletchers of the Cety of Chester on that on partie and the
Cowpers of the said cety on that other partie ffor the beryng and
goyng in procession With thaire lightes on the said day which
seidez parties haue agreit thaym & ichon of thaym to abide
perfourme & obeie such ordenaunce dome & awarde as Iohn
Sotheworth Squyer Maire of the Cety aforesaid Shulde make
theryn Wheropon the said maire the iijde day of the monyth of
September of the said Corpus day ye next ensuyng hath herde
the grevaunce & compleyntes of aither of the saides parties by
gode Deliberacion And the said Maire by the Advice of dyvers
of his breder hath ordenet demed & awerdet the saides parties to
be gode ffrendes of & for all the premyssez Also he hath ordenet
& awardet that the saides cowpers & thaire Successors Cowpers
of ye said Cety from hensforth shall bere thaire Lightes yerely
iij lightez on that on side ye pauement and iij on that opposite
from saint maire kirke opon ye hill of ye Cety aforesaid vnto the
Colage of Seint Iohanne next before the lights of the saides
ffletchers & bowers And the ⟨...⟩ & ⟨...⟩chers evenly to bere thaire
lightes ⟨...⟩ides Cowpers by the said Award in ye ⟨...⟩ Yeven the
thridde day of September on the ⟨...⟩ aforesaid /.

1476-7

AC   *City Treasurers' Accounts* BL: Harley 2158
f 58 *(November)*

Watergate street

...

mercatoribus Ciuitatis Cestrie pro vacua placea ter etc.   vj d

...

panniparijs ciuitatis parete pro Aysiament   viij d

...

A   *Mayors List 5* BL: Harley 2125
f 30* *(Christmas) John Southworth*

•by others   ...
about christmas• In this yeare prince Edwarde °ₐ 'sonne to K Ed'° Came to

---

19 / ⟨...⟩: *Morris,* said Bowers   19 / ⟨...⟩chers: *Morris,* Fletchers
20 / ⟨...⟩ides: *Morris,* next to the saide   21 / ⟨...⟩: *Morris,* yere
29 / ter *for* terre   31 / parete *for* pariete (?)
31 / Aysiament *for* Aysiamento   37 / *marginalia in RH II's hand*
37 / °ₐ 'sonne to K Ed'° *in RH II's hand*

Chester at Christmas °in hugh massys tyme°

...

Minstrels' Court PRO: CHES 2/149
mb 11 *(23 June)*   5

Comissio Abbatis Cestrie & Aliorum pro vna Curia histrionum Cestris tenenda

Edwardus &c. Omnibus ad quos presentes littere peruenerint
Salutem Sciatis quod nos de fidelitate circumspeccione & industria
dilectorum & fidelium nostrorum Ricardi abbatis Monasterij
Sancte Werburge Cestrie hugonis Mascy Maioris Ciuitatis nostre   10
Cestrie & Magistri Willelmi Thomas plenarie confidentes
constituimus & ordinauimus ipsos Abbatem Maiorem & Willelmum
Senescallos nostros coniunctim & diuisim ad vnam Curiam
histrionum Cestris in Ciuitate predicta hac vice tantum tenendam
iam in manibus nostris existentem ratione minoris etatis laurencij   15
filij & heredis Rogeri de Dutton nuper domini de Dutton iam
defuncti Et ad facienda & exerccenda omnia que ad officium
Senescalcie predicte hac vice pertinent faciendum Et ideo vobis
mandamus quod eisdem abbati Maiori & Willelmo in omnibus
que ad officium predictum hac vice pertinent faciendum   20
intendentes sitis auxiliantes fortificantes & per omnia
respondentes In cuius rei & Teste me ipso apud Cestriam xxiiij
die Iunij anno regni dicti principis nostri decimo septimo

1477-8   25

AC *City Treasurers' Accounts* BL: Harley 2158
f 61 *(November)*

...

Watergate strete

...   30

mercatoribus ciuitatis cestrie
pannarijs eiusdem ciuitatis

...   held all places & rents
                                                 as Roll 30 ante

                                                                           35

1478-9
Minstrels' Court PRO: CHES 2/151
mb 5d* *(23 June)*

...

Edwardus Primogenitus Edwardi quarti Regis anglie & ffrancie   40

1 / °in ... tyme° *in RH II's hand*

& Domini Hibernie Princeps Wallie Dux Cornubie & Comes
Cestris Omnibus ad quos presentes littere peruenerint Salutem
Sciatis quod nos de fidelitate circumspeccione & industria
dilectorum & fidelium nostrorum Ricardi Soderen Episcopi
abbatis Monasterij Sancte Werburge Cestrie Roberti Natervile
Maioris Ciuitatis nostre Cestrie & Petri Dutton Senioris plenarie
confidentes constituimus & ordinauimus ipsos Episcopum
Maiorem & Petrum Senescallos nostros coniunctim & diuisim ad
vnam Curiam histrionum Cestris in Ciuitate predicta hac vice
tantum tenendam iam in manibus nostris existentem ratione   10
minoris etatis laurencij filij & heredis Rogeri de Dutton nuper
domini de Dutton iam defuncti Et ad facienda & excercenda
omnia que ad officium Senoscalcie predicte hac vice pertinent
faciendum Et ideo vobis mandamus quod eisdem Episcopo
Maiori & petro in omnibus que ad officium predictum hac vice   15
pertinent faciendum intendentes sitis auxiliantes fortificantes &
per omnia respondentes In cuius rei testimonium has litteras
nostras fieri fecimus patentes Teste me ipso apud Cestriam
xxiij die Iunij anno regni dicti principis nostri decimo nono

20

1479-81

AC *City Treasurers' Accounts* BL: Harley 2158
f 62 *(November)*
...   25
the marchants of chester de vnius vacue place terre in grayfrere
lane pro Carriagio suo 2 years vnpayd 19.20 Edward 4   xij d
the drapers of the Citty de redditu alterne shope place terre in
grayfrere lane pro carragio suo 2 years 19.20 Edward 4   xvj d
...   30

f 64v *(Arrearages)*
...
mercatores ciuitatis 2 years 19 20 Edward 4   xij d
pannarijs ciuitatis 2 yeares   xvj d 35
...

---

26 / de ... terre: redditu *probably omitted*

1480-3

AC *City Treasurers' Accounts* BL: Harley 2158
f 63v *(November)*

...

Tho Rokley & Io smyth senescall*is* arte sellario infra C*iuita*tis   5
Cest*rie pro* quod*am* Aysiament Cariagij sui   iiij d

...

f 64

...   10

mercere c*iuita*tis cest*rie pro* placea terre *pro* aysiamento Cariagij
sui 3 yeare   xviij d
pannarie Ciuitatis *pro* redd*itu* alterius placie *pro* Cariagij sui
3 years   ij s
...   15

1481-2

AC *City Treasurers' Accounts* BL: Harley 2158
f 62v* *(November) (Arrearages)*   20

...

marchants of chester for Carrage howse   vj d
drap*ers* of Citty for like   viij d

...

                                                                          25
f 65

...

marchants 21 E*dward* 4 owe   vj d
drapers   viij d

...   30

1482-3

AC *City Treasurers' Accounts* BL: Harley 2158
f 65 *(November) (Arrearages)*   35

... marchants vj d   drap*ers* viij d

...

---

5 / C*iuita*tis *for* Ciuitatem   11 / mercere *for* merceris
11-12 / Cariagij sui *for* Cariagio suo   13 / pannarie *for* pannarijs

1483-4
Mayors' Books CCA: M/B/6
f 72* *(November)*

...

Me*morandum* Ricard*i* Benet mynstrell*i* de pace gerend*a* Rica*rdo*   5
Dalby & Henrico Dalby vsq*ue* pro*ximum* Portmot*um* C*iuitatis*
Cestr*ie* apud Cestri*am* tenend*um* pro*ximum* futur*um* & tunc &c.
vi*delicet* Thomas Dedwode Ioh*annes* Rithebon Edwardus Dolby
sub pena   xl li.

...   1(

Me*morandum* Ricard*i* Dalby de pace gerend*a* Rica*rdo* Benet &
Elisabeth s*eruienti* eius vsq*ue* pro*ximum* Portmot*um* pro*ximum*
futur*um* &c. vi*delicet* Rad*ulph*us Hunt Thomas Trver & Thomas
pena   xl li.

                                                                          1!

1489-90
A *Mayors List 1* BL: Harley 1046
   f 161v* *(November) Rafe Davenport*

   ...

   This yeare St Peters Steeple was pointed, & by ye Parson &   2(
   others a goose was eaten upon ye top thereof and part Cast into
   ye 4 streetes

   ...

A *Mayors List 5* BL: Harley 2125   2!
   f 31* *(November) Rafe Davenport*

   ...

   the Asumption of our lady was playd at the high Crosse befor
   the lo*rd* strange

   ...   3(

A *Mayors List 10* BL: Add. 29777
   item 163* *(November) Rafe Davenport*

   ...

   In this yeare the Assumption of our Ladye was plaid in the   3
   Bridgestrete of Chester before my Lorde Strange

   ...

1495-6
Minstrels' Court PRO: CHES 2/166   4(
mb 3 *(24 June)*

...

Arthurus &c. Om*nibus* ad quos p*re*sentes *littere* p*er*uenerint

Comissio Maioris
Cestrie [&
Aliorum] pro
vna Curia
histrionum
Cestris tenenda

Salutem. Sciatis quod nos de fidelitate circumspeccione &
industria dilectorum & fidelium nostrorum Ricardi Werehall
Maioris Ciuitatis Cestrie Wyllelmi Tatton & hamonis hassall
plenarie confidentes constituimus & ordinauimus ipsos Maiorem.
Wyllelmum & hamonem Senescallos nostros coniunctim &   5
diuisim . ad vnam Curiam histrionum Cestris in Ciuitate predicta
hac vice tantum tenendam tempore mortis Rogeri Dutton
Armigeri . iam defuncti in manibus nostris existentem & de
nobis tenetur per seruicium militare Et ad facienda & excercenda
omnia que ad officium Senescalcie predicte hac vice pertinent   10
ffaciendum Et ideo vobis mandamus quod eisdem Maiori
Wyllelmo & hamoni in omnibus que ad officium predictum hac
vice pertinent ffaciendum intendentes sitis auxiliantes fortificantes
& per omnia respondentes In cuius rei &c. Teste me ipso apud
Cestriam xxiiij die Iunij anno regni dicti principis nostri vndecimo 15
...

1498-9

A   *Mayors List 3* BL: Harley 2057
     f 26v* (November) Richard Goodman   20

midsomer
wach began

In this yeare it apeareth the watch on Midsomer even begonn, ...
prince Arthur came to Chester about the fourth day of August,

whitson playes

the Assumpcion ˚ʹpurificaton`˚ of our Ladie played before the
prince at the Abbay gate, ˚ʌʹ& high Crosse`˚   25

A   *Mayors List 5* BL: Harley 2125
     f 32* (November) Richard Goodman
     ...

In this yeare the Northsyde of the pentise in this cittye was new   30
buylded / prince Aurther came to this cittye ˚ʌʹ3 August 14
H 7`˚ beinge of the age of 14. yeares, and the Storie of the
Assumption of our Ladye was played at the abbey gates and
[nere to] ˚ʹat`˚ the heigh crosse ...

     ˚This yeare the wach on midsomer Eue was first sett out &   35
begonn˚
     ...

24 / ˚ʹpurificaton`˚ *in RH II's hand*          25 / ˚ʌʹ& ... Crosse`˚ *in RH II's hand*
31-2 / ˚ʌʹ3 ... H 7` ˚ *in RH II's hand*
34 / [nere to] ˚ʹat`˚ *cancellation and addition by RH II*
35-6 / ˚This ... begonn˚ *in RH II's hand*

A   *Mayors List 9* BL: Add. 11335
    f 23 *(November) Richard Goodman*
    ...
    The Watch or Midsumer showe began anno Domini 1498 mr
    Richard Goodman then Major. ... prince Arthur elder brother to
    King Henry the 8 came to Chester, the 4 of August, the
    Assumption play was played before him at the Abbey gates the
    25 of august the prince made the Major Esquire, and the 19 of
    September he departed this citty.
    ...   1

AC   *Smiths, Cutlers, and Plumbers' Records* C: Account Book II
    f 1v* *(August-September)*

    Thomas Edyar Smith to Prince Arthur, beinge att the Castle of   1
    Chester, in the xiiij^th yeare of the Raigne of Henrie the Seaventh
    his ffather, then beinge Kinge of England, And att the same tyme
    Prince Arthur gave vnto the sayed Edyar, a Crowned of Silver
    guilt, A Hammer with horshoe and Pincers the Armes of Smiths
    to them and theire Successors fforever. /   2

    1499-1500
AC   *List of Guilds* BL: Harley 2104
    f 4*
                                                                           2
                Drapers
                Drahers of dee
                barburs
                Wry3tus
                Wynteners   3
                Marcers
                goldsm[y]
                goldsmythus and masons
                Smythus
                bucherus   3
                glouers
                Coruisers and barkers
                Baxters
                fflecherus and Cowpers
                hyrunmunggers   40
                Cokus
                Tapsters and hostlers

Skynners
Sadelers
Talyers
ffychemungers
þe Wyfus of þe town assumpcion beate marie   5
Scheremen
Heusters
Weuers & Walkers

1511-12   10

A   *Mayors List 9* BL: Add. 11335
   f 23* *(November) Thomas Smith*

...

The shooteing on Black munday upon the Roodee in Easter
Weeke for a breakfast, by the sherriffes of this citty called calves   15
head & bacon, began first Anno Domini 1511 mr Thomas Smith
major, Hugh clarke and Charles Eaton then sherriffes

...

1514-15   20

Assembly Files CCA: A/F/1
f 5* *(May-November)*

...

      Tempore Iohannis Rathbone Maioris Anno Regni Regis
                Henrici octaui Septimo   25

It is ordred by Iohn Rathbone Maire of the Citie of Chestr &
ales weddinges   his brethern the x[⟨.⟩]iiijti With the holl Counseill of the said
offrynges   Citie for diuerse consideracions & causez profitable theym
movyng that no maner person ner persons inhabityng within the   30
said Citie shall not go ner gedder no compayny out of the said
Citie into the Countrey nother to prest makyng walshe weddynges
ner ales opon ∧'the' payn [of] to h[⟨..⟩]n or theym that doith
so godder x s & of hym or theym that therto so goith vj s viij d
as oft as they so offend & their bodiez to Ward there to remayn   35
dv⟨..⟩ng the mairez pleasure

1515-16

A   *Mayors List 5* BL: Harley 2125
   f 33v* *(November) Thomas Smith*   40

...

the shepards play & the Assumption of our lady was played

in St Iohns churchyard

...

1520-1
Mayors' Books CCA: M/B/12
f 24v* *(4 February)*

5

quarto die ffebruarij Anno xij henrici octaui

This Indenture made the iiijth daye of ffebruary in the xijth
yere of the Reigne . of kyng the eight Betwene Richard laye .
& Edward Taillir Stuardes of Thoccupacion of ffounders &
pewtrers within the Citie of Chester opon the oon partie And
Richard Taillir Smyth & Richard Anderton Stuardes of
thoccupacion of Smyths within the Citie of Chester opon that
other partie. Witnessith that the seides Stuardes & all theire holle
occupacion Apon A-Semble made & Comunycacion had betwene
the seides occupacions for the wele . and goode Zele . of the
same . byn fully condecendet and agreid In manner & forme
foloyng That is to witte from hensfourthe the said Stuardes of
thoccupacions of ffounders & pewtrers for the tyme beyng to
Receyue the Incomes & forfetes of all suche personnes that will
cum in to . the seid occupacion of ffounders & peutrers & be of
theire Brotherhod the Stuardes of thoccupacion of Smythes . in
nowise to intromedill ne haue eny thyng to do therwith And in
like wise the Stuardes of thoccupacion of Smythes . to Receyue
the Incomes . & forfetes of all suche personnes . as will cum in to
the seid occupacion of Smythes . and be . of theire Brotherhod
the . Stuardes of thoccupacion of ffounders and pewtrers . in
nowise intromedelyng ne hauyng eny thyng to do therwith Also
the Stuardes of thoccupacion of ffounders & pewtrers . as the
Stuardes of thoccupacion of Smythes aforseid byn fully
condecendent & agreid to berre & drawe . to whitson playe &
Corpus christi light & to bere to the fyndyng of the preste .
of Seynt loye Chapell and all other Costes as they of olde tyme .
haue donne . & vsed Also the Stuardes of thoccupacion of
ffounders & pewtrers . in the name of all theire holle occupacion
as the [Str] Stuardes of thoccupacion of Smythes . in all the
holle name of theire occupacion byn fully condecendet & agreid
That the Stuardes of aither occupacion for the tyme beyng shall

10
15
20
25
30
35
40

---

11 / kyng the eight *for* kyng Henry the eight

euery yere in the ffeste of Seynt Ioye or within viij dayes . the
seid ffeste of Seynt love Imediatly foloyng yefe afore the
Stuardes of thoccupacion & iiij aldermen of the seid occupacion
A Iuste & a true accompte . of almaner Incomes & forfetes by
theym Receyuet duryng the tyme . they stonde Stuardes So that   5
apon the seid accompte had the prophetes therof shall groo buto
the prophetes of Seynt Ioye Chapell opon the payne of theym
that contrarye to this agrement to forfete to the same vse fyve
poundes of leyfull money of Englond In witnesse wherof to these
Indentures . the Stuardes of aither of the seides Craftes in the   10
name of theire occupacion enterchaungably haue sette theire
Sealles These beyng witnesse Thomas Smyth Maire of the Citie
of Chester Thomas Colburne & Cristofer Werinycham Shirreffes
of the [same] Citie aforeseid & mony other Yeuen at the Citie
of Chester aforsed the daye & yere aboue rehersed   15

1523-4

AC   *Cappers' Petition* BL: Harley 1996
f 120*
                                                                      20

To the right worshipffull & ffull discrete
Dauid Myddelton Maire of the Citie of Chester
And his Cobrethren & Aldermen of the same

Humbly shewen vnto your gode Maystershippes your pouer   25
supplyauntes & besechers the Cappers of this Citie that where
as they of late tyme by the right worshipffull Thomas Smythe in
tyme of hys Mairealtie were onerated & charged to brynge forthe
A playe concernynge the store of kynge balak & Balam the
proffet / And at the same tyme by the sayd Thomas Smythe &   30
hys Cobrethren it was promysed that where as your saydes
pouer supplyauntes ffonde theyme grevyde & gretely hurtyd and
impoueryshed / by reason / that not only the Mercers of the
Sayde Citie but as well dyuerse others occupacions of the same
Citie / do dayly occupye theire sayd occupacion as well in   35
reteyllynge of cowrse wares vnder the price of xvj of the dossen
as aboue / And as yet no reformacion therof can be had / All
thaghe they therfore haue made greate instance & request as well
to your Maystership now in your tyme of mayrealtie as to others
your predecessors as is aforesayd It may please your gode   40
Maystershipps considerynge the greate & importable hurtes &
hyndraunces of your saydes pouer supplyauntes whiche be but

verrey pou*er* men & haue no thynge to lyve by but their sayd
occupac*ion* / other to see for due & lauffull reformac*ion* of the
p*re*mysses or ell*es* to exon*er*ate & discharge theyme of & for the
bryngynge forthe of the sayd playe / Wheof they wolde be right
sorye / yf the meanes myght be fonde that they myght be halle   5
to brynge it forthe / And the remedye therof lyethe myche in
y*our* maystershipp*es* if it wolde please you of y*our* godenes to
putte y*our* ˹gode˺ wyllez & myndes therv̄nto / ffor the ffull &
holle myndes & consent*es* of all & eu*er*y your sayd*es* besechers
is now & at all tymes to come shall be to brynge forthe theire   10
sayd playe And that in theire best man*ner* to the [worship]
pleasure of god worship of Mayst*er* Maire & this Citie Wherfore
they besiche you of y*our* charite other to se for the reformac*ion*
of the p*re*mysses / or ell*es* to take no displeasure w*ith* theyme if
they for lakke of habilitie do not brynge forthe theire sayd play /   15
And this at the reu*er*ence of god and they shall daylye p*ra*ye to
god for you &c.

1529-30

A *Mayors List 8* BL: Harley 2133
   f 39* *(November) Henry Radford*   20

   ...

   The play of Rob*er*t of Cicell was plaied at the high Crosse

   ...
                                                                        25
A *Mayors List 10* BL: Add. 29777
   item 204* *(November) Henry Radford*

   ...

   In this yeare an Enterlude named kinge Roberte of Scissill was
   playde at the highe Crosse in Chester ...   30

1531-2

Assembly Files CCA: A/F/1
f 11* *(14 August)*
                                                                        35
M⟨..⟩orand*um* that the xiiij^th day of August in the xxii ⟨...⟩ kyng
henry the eight It was condescended & agreed befor ⟨...⟩ of the
Citie of Chestr in the Pentice of the same Citie ⟨...⟩ William
Bexwik Stiwardez of the occupac*ion* of vynteners Withi⟨...⟩
kettell & Thomas hasilwall Stiwardez of the occupac*ion* of ⟨...⟩   40

---

4 / Wheof *for* Wherof

of thone p*a*rtie & Iohn Treuo*ur* goldsmyth Stiward of
thoccupac⟨...⟩ Wosewall Stiward of the occupac*i*on of mason
within the Citi⟨...⟩ thother p*a*rtie in forme folowyng That is to
witt The saide*s* S⟨...⟩ & diers for theym & their Successo*ur*s be
agreid & grau*n*ten by these p*re*sentes ⟨...⟩ Stiwardez of   5
Goldsmythez & masons & their Successo*ur*s from hensforth shall
occupie & pecible enioy frome tyme to tyme the Cariage nowe
of the ⟨...⟩ Vynten*er*s & Diers to & for the plaie*z* of the saide*s*
Goldsmythes & masons & ⟨...⟩ Successo*ur*s to be plaied at
Whitsontide to s*er*ue theym for their saide*s* ⟨...⟩ when & as oft   10
as nede shall require without eny lett of the saide*s* ⟨...⟩ of
Vynten*er*s & Diers or their Successo*ur*s ffor whiche Cariage so in
man*ner* ⟨...⟩ Abouesaid to the saide*s* Stiwardez of Goldsmythes
& masons & their Su⟨...⟩ grau*n*ted to & for their saide*z* plaie*z*
frome tyme to tyme as is afor⟨...⟩ saide*s* Stiwardez of goldsmythez   15
& masons [from] for theymself & th⟨...⟩ ben agreid couena*un*ten
& grau*n*ten by these p*re*sente*s* to content ⟨...⟩ cause to be paid
vnto the saide*s* Stiwardez of Vynten*er*s & Diers ⟨...⟩ st*er*ling at
the makyng herof / And from hensforth yerely ⟨...⟩ fynd kepe &
susteyn the Thrid p*a*rte of all & eu*ery* rep*a*rac*i*on ⟨...⟩ necessarie*z*   20
belongyng or in eny wise app*er*teynyng to the same ⟨...⟩ shall
require & also to content & pay or cause to be paid yerely from
the thrid p*a*rt of all the rente*s* due or to be due for the house
wher⟨...⟩ said Cariage now standeth or herafter shall stand

                                                              25

Assembly Files CCA: A/F/1
f 12*

The p*ro*clamac*i*on for the plaie*s* newly made by Will*i*am Newhall
          ⟨...⟩ pentice the first yere of his entre   30

fforasm⟨...⟩ as of old tyme not only for the Augmentac*i*on &
incres ⟨...⟩ faith of o ⟨...⟩ auyo*ur* iesu Crist & to exort the mynd*es*
of the co*m*mon people ⟨...⟩ doctryne th⟨...⟩f but also for the
co*m*menwelth & p*ro*speritie of this Citie a play ⟨...⟩ & diu*erse*   35
stor⟨...⟩ of the bible begynnyng with the creac*i*on & fall of

A/F/1, f 12 *missing readings supplied from BL: Harley 2013, f 1:*
30 / ⟨...⟩: clarke of the   32 / fforasm⟨...⟩: for as much
33 / ⟨...⟩: of the holy & Catholick   33 / o ⟨...⟩ auyo*ur*: our Sauiour
34 / ⟨...⟩: to good deuotion & holsome   34 / th⟨...⟩f: therof
35 / ⟨...⟩: & declaration   36 / stor⟨...⟩: storyes

Lucifer & endy ⟨...⟩ iugement of th⟨.⟩ world to be declared &
plaied in the Witsonweke was devised & m ⟨...⟩ henry ffraunses
°⸌somtyme⸍° monk of this °⸌ ´dissolued⸍° monesty who obteyned
& gate of Clement then beyng ⟨...⟩ daiez of par⟨...⟩ & of the
Busshop of Chester at that tyme beyng xlᵗⁱ daiez of pardon   5
g ⟨...⟩ thensforth ⟨.⟩ euery person resortyng in pecible manner
with gode devocion to here & se the s ⟨...⟩ frome tyme to tyme
asoft as they shalbe plaied within this Citie °[And that euery
person ⟨...⟩ disturbyng the same plaiez in eny manner wise to be
accursed by thauctoritie of the s⟨...⟩ pope cleme⟨...⟩ bulles vnto   10
suche tyme as he or they be absolued therof]° / Whiche plaiez
were d⟨...⟩ to the honour of god by Iohn arneway then mair of
this Citie of chester & his brethern & holl cominal⟨..⟩ therof to
be bro⟨...⟩ forthe declared & plaid at the Costes & chargez of
the craftes men & occupacons of ⟨...⟩ said Citi⟨.⟩ whiche hitherunto   15
haue from tyme to tyme vsed & performed the same accordin⟨...⟩

   Wherefore Maister mair in the kyngez name straitly chargeth
& commaundeth that euery person & ⟨...⟩ of what esta⟨..⟩ degre
or condicion so euer he ⟨..⟩ they be resortyng to the said plaiez
do vse th⟨...⟩ pecible witho ⟨...⟩ akyng eny assault affrey or   20
other disturbans wherby the same ⟨...⟩ shalbe disturbed & that no
manner person or persons who so euer he or they be do vse or
we ⟨...⟩ Vnlaufull wepons within the precynct of the said Citie
duryng the tyme of the said p⟨...⟩ °[not only opon payn of
cursyng by thauctoritie of the said Pope Clement bulles but also]°   25
opon payn of enprisonment of their bodiez & makyng fyne to
the kyng at maister mairis pleasure ⟨...⟩ god saue the kyng &
maister mair &c.

                              per me W Newhall factum tempore
                              Willelmo Sneyde draper secundo tempore   30
                              sui maioralitatis

A/F/1, f 12 to l 25, *missing readings supplied from BL: Harley 2013, f 1:*

1 / endy ⟨...⟩: ending with the generall   1 / th⟨.⟩: the
2 / m ⟨...⟩: made by one Sir   4 / ⟨...⟩: bushop of rome a iooo
4 / par⟨...⟩: pardon   6 / g ⟨...⟩: graunted from
6 / ⟨..⟩: to   7 / s ⟨...⟩: sayd playes
9 / ⟨...⟩: or persons   10 / s⟨...⟩: sayd
10 / cleme⟨...⟩: clemants   12 / d⟨...⟩: deuised
13 / cominal⟨..⟩: cominalty   14 / bro⟨...⟩: brought
15 / ⟨...⟩: the   16 / accordin⟨...⟩: acordingly
18 / ⟨...⟩: persons   18 / esta⟨..⟩: estate
19 / ⟨..⟩: or   20 / th⟨...⟩ themselues
20 / witho ⟨...⟩ akyng: without making   21 / ⟨...⟩: playes
23 / we ⟨...⟩: weare any   24 / p⟨...⟩: play

AC **Trinity Churchwardens' Accounts** BL: Harley 2177
f 19v* *(Lands given to the church)*

...

Impr*imis* a howse in the Greyfrerys lane lyinge next to the grey
frers gate except 2 howses to put Charyches in.   5

...

1533-4
Assembly Books CCA: AB/1
f 53v *(November) (Northgate Street)*   10

...

The occupac*i*on of smeythys for A place to sett ther Carage
adioynyng to the Shermen vnder the Wall*es* nygh vnto A toure
Cauled the Dyllys towre   iiij d
The occupac*i*on of the Shermem for A place to set ther   15
Carage   iiij d

...

f 55 *(Love Lane)*

...   20

The occupac*i*on of tailltor*es* for a Cariage house   iiij d

...

The occupac*i*on of the Sadlers for a place called truant*es* hole
by yere   iiij d
...   25

f 56v *(Grey Friars Lane)*

...

The occupac*i*on of the drap*ers* for a c*er*ten place to bild a house
on which they put ther Cariage in nyghe to ye yate of the ffreres   30
minor*es* by yere   viij d
The occupac*i*on of the mercers for a certen place to bild A house
on in the which the put ther caryage   vj d

...

                                                                               35

1534-5
AC **Painters, Glaziers, Embroiderers, and Stationers' Charter**
BL: Harley 2054
f 87v*
... & for as much as þe seu*er*all crafts arts & facultis of Painters   40
Glassiers Imbrauderers & Stationeres haue by thesse humbel

---

15 / Shermem *for* Shermenn; *minim omitted, MS*

petecion desired þat þe might bee incorpureted into one body by
grant vnder þe citty seale / It also appereinge to vs þat þe haue
bine tyme out of minde one Brotherhood for the costs & Expences
of þe plae of þe shepperds Wach with þe Angells hyme &
likewayes for otherr layinge out conserninge þe wellferr &   5
prosperetie of þe saide citty // It is therfore orderred & declarred
bie Iointe consent of vs þe Maior Aldermen & common consell
þat þe saide Painters Glassiers Imbrauderreres & Stationers &
therre succesors from hence forth & foreuer shalbee taken &
reputed as one speciall company of þe said citty ...   10

A C   *Trinity Churchwardens' Accounts*   B L : Harley 2177
      f 20v *(28 March)*

      ...   15

rec of mr bomvell of the gift of his wife a fyne napkyn of Calico
cloth trelyd with silk to Couer the Crosse in ye sepulcre

...

1535-6   20
St Mary's Churchwardens' Accounts   C R O : P/20/13/1
f 2v *(16 April)*

...

Item payd for ij cordys to the pascall   ij d
Item payd for naylys pynes and [the thred] Thred to Heng   25
the sepulcur   ij d

1536-7
St Mary's Churchwardens' Accounts   C R O : P/20/13/1
f 4 *(1 April)*
                                                                            30
...

Item for naylis thred And pynnys Agaynist Ester   j d ob

...

1537-8   35
St Mary's Churchwardens' Accounts   C R O : P/20/13/1
f 5* *(21 April)*

...

Item for sowyng the [chur] churche clothis Agaynist the
Ester   ij d   40
Item for a Corde to the vayle cloth   j d
Item for Naylis & pynnys to the sepulcer   j d

Item for a torche agaynist palme sonday   ij s

...

Item for paynting of adam & Eve *with* a paxe   ij d

...

                                                        5

1538-9
Carriage House, Property of the Carmelite Friars
PRO: S.C.6 / Henry VIII / 7384
mb 82*

...   10

Reddi*tus* domus Carpentarij ib*ide*m *pro* Pagentibus suis
imponend*is (blank)* ...

St Mary's Churchwardens' Accounts CRO: P/20/13/1
f 6v   15

...

Item for naylis & pynnis to the sepulc*er*   j d
Item for a corde Vnto the vayle   ij d

...

                                                        20

AC   **1539-40**
      Early Banns BL: Harley 2150
      ff 85v-8v*

...

These be the craftys of the Citie the whiche craftys bere the   25
charge of the pagyns in pley of corpus chr*isti* [pena] °pena°
x li. & °were the Auntient whitson playes in chester sett out at
the charges of theis occupations yearly playd on munday Tewsday
& wensday in whitson weeke beinge first Inuented & putt into
English by Rand Higden a monck of chester Abby°   30

Barkers or tanners	the falling of lucyfer
Drap*ers* and hosiers	the creac*i*on of the world
Drawers of dee & wat*er*leders	Noy and his Ship
Barbers °ˏ´wax`° chandlers	Abram & Isack 35
and leches °or Surgions°	
Capp*ers* wyerdrawers & pynners	kyng balac & balame *with*
	moysez
wright slaters tylers dowbers	Natiuitie of o*ur* Lord
& thacchors	40

26 / [pena] *deleted by RH II*   35 / Barbers: b *altered from* k

Paynters brotheres & glasiours	the Shepards offeryng
Vynters & marchauntes	king herod & the mount victoriall
Mercers & spycers	iij kinges of Colyn °Colon°

These ix playes °ᴧ 'and pagents'° Aboue written
be plaid on the fyrst day

Goldsmythis & masons	the sleying of the children of Isarell °by ᴧ 'Herod'°
Smythes ffurbours °ᴧfurbisher, [or cutlers]° & pewters	purificacion of our Lady
Bochers	the pynacle with the woman of canany
glauers & parchement makers	the rising of Lasare from deth to lyff
Corvesers °or showmakers°	the comyng of crist to Ierusalem
Bakers & mylners	cristes monday where he sat with his Appostles
Bowers fflecchers stryngers cowpers & turners /	Scorgyng of cryst
Ironmongers and ropers	crusyfing of [god] °Christ°
Cokes tapsters & hostelers °& Inkeepers°	the harowyng of hell

Theze ix playes °ᴧ 'or pagents'° Aboue writen
be plaid apon the secund day /

Skynners cardmakers hatters poynters & gyrdlers /	the resurreccon
Sadlers ffusters	castell of Amyas °'Emaus'° & the Appostles
Tailers	Assencion of crist /
fflesshe mongers	whitsonday the making of the crede
Shermen	profettys Afore the day of dome

---

4 / Colyn *underlined by RH II*
23 / [god] *deleted by RH II*
35 / *first* s *altered from* x *in* fflesshe

hewst*ers* & belfounders   Antecrist
Weyuers & walkers   domez day

       plaid Appon the thrid |

On corpus chr*ist*i day the collegis and prestys bryng forth A play
at the Assentement of the Maire /
   Prouided Alwais that it is at the lib*er*tie and pleasure of the
mair w*ith* the counsell of his bretheryn to Alter or Assigne any
of the occupac*on*s Aboue writen [Aboue] to any play or pagent
as they shall think necessary or conuenyent /
   ffor asmyche as of old tyme not only for the Augmentac*i*on &
incresse of the holy and catholyk ffaith of our sauy*our* cryst Iesu
and to exhort the myndes of the comen peple to gud deuoc*i*on
and holsom doctryne ther of but Also for the comen welth and
pr*o*speritie of this Citie A play and declarac*i*on of many and
dyuers stories of the bible begynnyng w*ith* the creac*i*on & fall of
lucifer & endyng w*ith* the gen*er*all Iugement of the world to be
declared & playde now in this whison weke / whiche playes were
deuised to the hono*ur* of god by Iohn Arneway sometyme Maire
of this Citie of Chestr & his bretheryn & holl comynaltie therof
to be brought forth declared and plaid at the costys of the
craftys men and occupac*on*s of the said Citie whiche herunto
haue from tyme to tyme vsyd and p*er*formed the same
Accordingly / wherfore mr Mair in the king*es* name straitly
chargith and comaundyth that eu*er*y p*er*son and p*er*sons of what
astate degree or condic*i*on so eu*er* he or they be resorting to the
said playes do vse theym selff peceably without making any
Assault Afrey or other disturbans wherby the same playes
shalbe disturbed & that no man*ner* p*er*son or p*er*sons who euer
he or they be do vse or weyre eny vnlaufull vepans w*ith*in the
pr*e*cinct of the said Citie duryng the tyme of the said playes
Apon peyne of imprisonyment of theire bodies and making
fyne to the king at Maisters Maires pleasure / ˄ ˈandˈ god saue
the kyng ∘mr mair Mayre etc / ∘

                             5

                             10

                             15

                             20

                             25

                             30

                             35

35 / *RH II altered* mair *to* maisr *and added* Mayre etc

The comen bannes to be *pro*claymed & Ryddon *with*
the stewardys of eu*er*y occupac*i*on

Lording*es* Royall and Reuerentt
Louely ladies that here be lentt
Sou*er*eigne Citizins hether am I sent   5
A message for to say /

I pray you all that be p*re*sent
That you will here *with* good intent
And lett your eares to be lent   10
Hertffull I you pray

Our wurshipffull mair of this Citie
with all this Royall com*in*altie   15
Solem pagens ordent hath he
At the fest of whitsonday tyde

how eu*er*y craft in his decree
bryng forth their playes Solemplye   20
I shall declare you brefely
yf ye will Abyde A while |

•Tanners• The ∧ wor*shipffu*ll⌐ tanners of theis towne   25
Bryng forth the heuenly manc*i*on
Thorders of Angellz and theire creac*i*on
According done to the best
And when thangellz be made so clere
Then folowyth the falling of lucifere   30
To bryng forth this play *with* good chere
The tanners be full prest

•Drapers &   You wurshipffull men of the draperye
hosiers•   loke that paradyce be all redye   35
Prepare also the mappa mundi
Adam and eke eve

•waterleaders and   The water leders and drawers of dee
drawers of dee•   loke that noyes shipp be sett on hie   40

25 / theis *altered to* thys *by RH II*   26 / mancion *altered to* manshion *by RH II*

that you lett not the storye
And then shall you well cheue

°Barbursurgions and Tallow chandlers°

The barbers and wax chaundlers also that day
of the patriarche you shall play   5
Abram that putt was to Assay
To sley Isack his sonne

°Cappers and linnen drapers°

The cappers & pynners forth shall bryng
balack that fears and mightie kyng   10
And balam on An Asse sytting
Loke that this be done

°wryghts and slaters°

youe wrightys and slaters wilbe fayne
bryng forth your cariage of marie myld quene   15
And of octavyan so cruell and kene
And also of Sybell the sage
for fynding of that Royall thing
I graunt you all the blessing
of the high imperiall king   20
Both the maister and his page

°Paynters Imbrautherers & glasiers°

Paynters glasiars & broderers in fere
Haue taken on theym with full good chere
That the Sheppardes play then shall appere   25
And that with right good wyll

°marchants and vinteners [and]°

°The vynteners then as doth befall
bringe forth the 3 kings Royall
of Colyn or pagent memoryall
and worthy to appere   30
there shall you see how thos kyngs all
Came bouldly into the hall
before Herald proude in paulle
of Crysts byrth to heare | 35

°marcers°

The mercers worshipffull of degre
the presentation that haue yee
hit fallyth best for your see

28-p 37, l 36 / all material within • • in RH II's hand
29 / marginalia i altered from e in vinteners

by right reason & skyle
of caryage I haue no doubt
both within and also without
it shall be deckyd yat all the Rowte
full gladly on it shall be to loke   5
with sondry Cullors it shall shine
of veluit satten & damaske fyne
Taffyta Sersnett of poppyngee grene

•Goldsmyths   The gouldsmyths then full soone will hye   10
and masons•   & massons theyre Craft to magnyfye
theis 2 Crafts will them applye
theyre worshipp for to wyne
how herode king of Galalye
for that Intent Cryst to distrye   1
Slew the Inosents most Cruely
of tow yers & within

•Smyths furbors   Semely Smythis also in Syght
and Pewterers•   a louely Caryage the will dyght   2
Candilmas dey for soth it hyght
the find it with good will

•Butchers•   The butchers pagend shall not be myst
how Satan temped our Sauyour Cryst   2
it is an history of the best
as wittneseth the gospell

•glouers•   Nedys must I rehers the glouer
the giue me gloues and gay gere   3
the find the Toumbe of Lazarey
that pagend cometh next

•Coruisers or   also the Coruesers with all their myght
Showmakers•   the fynde a full fayre syght   3
Ierusalem their Caryage hyght
for so sayth the text

•Bakers and   and the bakers also be dene
milners•   the find the Maunday as I wene   4

21 / dey *altered to* day   34 / *marginalia* i *altered from* e *in* Coruisers

it is a Carriage full well besene
as then it shall appeare ǀ

Coupers Stringers flechers bowyers with great honors
flechers Bowyers the Cowp*ers* find the Tormentors   5
and Turners
Ironmongers that bobbyde god with gret horrors
and Ropers‧ as he sat in his chere
The yronmongers find a Caryage good
how Iesu dyed on ye Rode
and shed for vs his precyus blud   10
the find it in fere

‧Kookes‧ Cryst after his passion
brake hell for our redempcion
that find the Cockes & hostelers of this towne   15
& that with full good chere

‧Skynners also the Skynners they be bowne
Cardmakers with great worsap & renowne
Poynters and
girdlers‧ they find the resurection   20
fayre may them befall

‧Sadlers Sadlers & foysters haue the good grace
Foysters‧ the find the Castell of Emawse
where Crist appered to Cleophas   25
a faire pagend you shall see

‧Taylyers‧ also the Tayler's with trew Intent
haue taken on them verament
the assencyon by one assent   30
to bringe it forth full right

‧fysshe mongers‧ fysshemongers men of faith
as that day will doe their slayth
to bringe there caryage furth in grayth,   35
wytsonday it hight ǀ∘

‧wyues‧ The wurshipffull wyffys of this towne
ffynd of our Lady thassumpc*i*on

24 / *marginalia* F *altered from* s *in* Foysters

It to bryng forth they be bowne
And meytene with all theyre might

•shermen•   The Shermen will not behynd
Butt bryng theire cariage with good mynde   5
The pagent of prophettys they do fynd
That prophecied ffull truly
Off the comyng of Anticrist
That goodys ffaith wold resist
That cariage I warrand shall not myst   10
But sett forth full dewly

•Hewsters or
Diers•</i>   The hewsters that be men full sage
They bryng forth A wurthy cariage
That is A thing of grett costage   15
Antycryst hit hight /

•Weuers &
walkers•</i>   They weyuers in Euery dede
ffynd the day of dome well [they] may they spede
I graunt theym holly to theire neede   20
The blysse of heuen bright

Souereigne syrs to you I say
And to all this ffeyre cuntre
That played shalbe this godely play   25
In the whitson weeke
That is brefely forto sey
vppon monday tuysday and wennysday
Whoo lust to see theym he may
And non of theym to seke.   30

•erazed in the
booke•</i>   Also maister Maire of this Citie
withall his bretheryn accordingly
A Solempne procession ordent hath he
to be done to the best
Appon the day of corpus christi   35
The blessed sacrament caried shalbe
And A play sett forth by the clergye
In honour of the fest |

18 / Euery *altered to* Vuery *by RH II*
31-p 39, 19 / *marginalia and lines drawn by RH II*
37 / g *altered from beginning of long* s *in* clergye

Many torches there may you see
Marchaunty and craftys of this Citie
By order passing in theire degree
A goodly sight that day 5

They come from saynt maries on the hill
the churche of saynt Iohns vntill
And there the sacrament leve they will
The south as I you say

whoo so comyth these playes to see 10
with good deuocion merelye
hertely welcome shall he be
And haue right good chere

Sur Iohn Aneway was maire of this Citie 15
when these playes were begon truly
god grunt vs merely
And see theym many A yere
Now haue I done that lyeth in me
To procure this solempnitie 20
That these playes contynued may be
And well sett fourth Alway

Iesu crist that syttys on hee
And his blessyd mother marie / 25
Saue all this goodely company
And kepe you nyght and day

Assembly Books CCA: AB/1
ff 64-5* *(10 January)* 30

In the tyme of *(blank)* beyng mayre of the Kinges Citie of
Chester in the xxxjj yere of Kinge Henry Theght
    For as moche As by the ffeate and exercise of the Kinges
subiectes of this his Realme of Englond in shouting in longe 35
bouz ther hath contynually rison & growen & ben within the said
gret multytude of good Archers / which hath not onelye defendid
this Relme & the subiecktes therof Ageynest the cruell malyse &
danger of ther outward enymyes in tyme hertofore passed / But
allso wyth lytell nomber and pussance in Regarde haue done 40

25 / *marginalia and line drawn by RH II*

for shooting in
long Bowes
‸'this citty'
beinge of ould
famous for it

manye noble octes And discomfitures of warre Ageynest the
Infidels & others / And furthermore subdued & Redused dyuers
and manye Regions & countries to ther due obeysaunce to the
greate honor fame & Suertie of this relme And subictes of the
same And to the teryble drede and fere of all strange Nacyons   5
Anythyng to attempt or do to the hurte or damage of them or
eny of them / And albyit thad dyuerse good statutes and
ordenaunces be prouided as Well in the tyme of our Right dere
Souering Lorde Kinge Henry the eyght now being as in tyme of
his noble progenitors kinges of this Realme conserning th   10
mantenaunce of archary and shouting in Long Boues / yet
neuertheles archari and shouting in Longe boues is Lyttyll vsed
but Dalye menyssheth decayeth and abaytyth mor and more to
the grete subuersion of the common Welthe of this the kinges
Realme and His Louing subictes of the same & to the greate   15
bouldenes of all outward enymyes Geuing all childryn yonge
men and all other to excersise the same fete smaule corage to
vse the same / But other vnlaufull gaymes prohibeted by the
kinges highnez and His Laues In tender consederacion of Which
most godlye feate & exercise in shouting in longe bouez and for 20
Reformacion of the saide inconuenientes and dyuerse other
happening Sodenly opon many gode & laudable vsagez Afore
tyme vsid Wherof hath Rison & dary dothe & is lyke to do greate
enui malys and other inconuenientes / And to thentent to set
fourth and preferre The Same godlye feate and exercyse of   25
shoouting in Longe boues and to Reveve the saide auncent fayme

An order for ye
sports on
shroftusday &
agreed on by
ye drapers,
sadlers &
showmakers

of this the kinges citie of Chester It is ordenyd Assentyd &
Agreid by henry Gee mayre of the Citie of chester the aldermen
sheriffes and comon Counsell of the Same Citie And at an
Assimble houlden Within the Said citie In the pentyce ther the   30
tent daye of Ianuarij In the xxxj yere of the Reing of our most
Dere Souereng Lorde now being Kynge henry theyght Wyth Ther
full assent and Consent and allso of the hole occupacyons of
Drapers Sadlers and shoumaykers of (blank) ı wythin the Saide
Citie That the said occupacions of shoumacres which Alwayez   35
tyme out of mannz Remembranc haue geuen and delyuerid
yerlye vpon teuesday Commonly caulyd shroftteuesday otherwyse
Gottedesday at After nonne of the same vnto the drapars Afore
the mayre of the citie at the cros vpon the Rode hee one bale
of Lether Caulyd a fout baule of the value of iij s iiij d or Aboue 40
to pley at from thens to the Comon haule of the Said Citie And
further At pleasure of euill Disposid persons // Wherfore hath

Ryssyn grete Inconuenynce ffromhensforth shall yerlye vpon
the said Teuesday geue and delyuer vnto the said Drapars Afore
the mayre of the Said Citie for the tyme being at the Said playce
and tyme Syx °॰ ꞌgleauesꞌ॰ of Siluer to the value of euery of them
vj d, or Aboue to the order at the discresion of the Drapars and   5
the mayre of the said citie for the tyme being To whom shall
Run best and fvrthest vpon foute befor them Vpon the said Rode
hee that Day or anye other Daye after at the Draperes pleasure
with the ouersight of the mayre for the tyme being / And allso
that the Said occupacion of sadlers within the Said Citie Which   10
be all the same tyme of no mans Remembrance haue geuin &
delyuerid yerlye the said place & tyme euery master of them
vnto the said Drapers ofor the mayre for the tyme being Apayntyd
Baule of Wood with floures and armes vpon the poynte of a
spere Being goodly Arayd vpon hors bake Accordingly   15
fromhensforth shall the said teusday houre & place gyue &
delyuer vnto the said drapars Afor the mayre for the tyme being
vpon horsbak a bell of Syluer to the valu of -- iij s iiij d or Aboue
to be ordred as is aforsaid by the Drapres & the mayre of the
said citie for the tyme Being to Whome shall Rune best & furthest   20
vpon horsbak before them the said Daye tyme & place / And
that allso euery man that hayth bene maryed within the Said
Citie Sithus Shraffteusday last past shall vpon the said Shrafft
teusday next to com At the said tyme & place geue and Delyuer
vnto the said Draprs Afor the mayre now being An Arrow of   25
Siluer To the value of fyue pence or Aboue in value & Recompence
of Such baule of Silke or veluit / which he being maryed As is
Aforsaid should or ought then to gyue or delyuer according |
And by the auncient & laudable vse and costome of the sayde
Citie by all the same tyme of no mans Remembranc to the   30
Contrarye vsed & Approuid / And that also ffromthensforth
euery man Which herafter shalbe maryed within the said Citie
Shall in Lyke manar vpon the said Shraff teusday next after
his maryage at the said tyme and place Geue & delyuer vnto the
sades drapers Afor the mayre of the said Citie for the tyme   35
being A Lyke arrow of Syluer to the value of v d or aboue in
Recompenc of the said baule of Silke or veluit vsed and
accostomyd to be geuen & delyueryd as is aforesaid / Which
arroues of Siluer so to be geuen & delyuerid in Recompence of
the said baules of sylke or veluit In manar & forme Aforsaid   40

4 / °॰ ꞌgleauesꞌ॰ *added in RH II's hand*

shall from hensforth yerly that daye or other dayes After be
ordred by the said Draprs & the mayre for the tyme being to &
for ye preferment and setting forth of the Said fete / And
exercyse of shouting in Longe boues And in Avoyding of the
saides Inconuenyentes eny vse prestripcion or other thinges   5
Afore tyme hadde & vsed to the contrary herof not withstanding
And further it is orderid and fully assentyd that the said
occupacion of draprs & ther Sucssesors shall from hensforth
kepe & performe this ordenances and euery Artycle therin
conteynid in manar and form [folouing] Aforsaid ordred &   10
mayde / And allso the said drapers And ther Sucssessors shall
kepe yerly ther recreacyon and Drinking in Lyke manar and
forme as the same occupacons and ther predecessors tyme out
of mynd haue vsed to do without eny contradiccon or lett /
And that allso the said occupacion of Shoumacres & thaocupacyon   15
of Sadlers & ther Successors and allso euery man now being
maryed and herafter to be maryed within the said Cytie as is
Aforsaid and euery of them shall in Lyke manar obserue and
kepe this ordinaunce and euery orticle therof yerlye from
hensforth from tyme to tyme with out anye gruge Let or   20
contradiccion vpon payne of uery of Them So offending to
forfyt to the aldermen and stewardes of tha occupacion of
Drapars for the tyme being x li. tocins quocins without any
pardon therof or any parcill therof according to The auncyent
& Laudable Costome & vsage of the said Citie Allwayes vsed   25
And Approuid

A   *Mayors List 5* BL: Harley 2125
     f 35* *(10 January) Henry Gee*

...   30

•silver bell &
gleeves offered• The Balls and foote ball: accustomed to be offered to the mayor .
were layde awaye and gleeves of silver offered by the shomakers
in the rombe of them . and for the sadlers ball a siluer bell
which were offered one Shrove Tusedaye to mr mayor . besydes
silver gleaves geven to the drapers by all such persons as are   35
yearely maried in this Cittye

...

31-2 / *marginalia in RH II's hand*

St Mary's Churchwardens' Accounts CRO: P/20/13/1
f 7v *(28 March)*

...

Item paide for pynnys & naylis to the sepulcur   j d ob

5

AC   *City Waits* BL: Harley 2150
f 108 *(April-November) Henry Gee*

...

•An order for
Citty Waytes
when to play &
not when the
list •

Also where as the waytes of this Citie ought to serue and sapplie
their facultie with diligent attendaunce in goode order for the   10
worship and pleasure of the Citie and for bycause that no certen
of ordre Owres nor tymes hath heretofore beyn especially
lemytted vnto theym they haue for the moost part vsed toke
their owne libertiez and to goo / & not goo when it pleased best
theym selffes wherby good ordre hath not beyn obserued ner the   15
•on Sunday
munday Tusday
thursday and
Saterday in
the eueninge •
Citie by theym serued as they ought to be / wherby it is ordeyned
that from hensforth euery sonday monday tuysday thursday and
saturday the said waites shall goo Aboute and play in the evenyng
in suche circuite placys and Owres as hath beyn accustomed in
•on munday
Thursday and
Saturday in
the morninge•
tymes past / And euery monday thursday & saturday in the   20
mornyng they shall goo and play in lyke maner / And this rule
and ordre to be kept contynually heraftur except that speciall
sickenes or extreme weddur lett theym or ellz that Appon some
other their resonable sute to be moved vnto the Mair and his
bretheryn they obteyne lycence for A ceason as case shall require   25

A   *Mayors List 16 Collectanea Devana* CCA: P/Cowper [1956] I.188*
(24 June) Henry Gee

In this Mayorelty . Mathew Ellis of Overleigh, and Thomas   30
Browne of Netherleigh, within the precincts of the city of
Chester, having each married a daughter of Sir Piers Dutton of
Dutton in Cheshire, the two weddings were kept at the same
time, and with much festivity at Dutton=Hall, from whence the
Gentlemen brought their Brides, on tuesday, the 24th of Iune,   35
which being the Feast of St Iohn Baptist, and the day, upon
which the Minstrelsy of the City . and County, are annually
licensed at Chester, by the Lord of Dutton: The Company
before: mentioned were met, on their return from Dutton=
Hall, at Flookers=brook=bridge, by the Steward of Dutton,   40

9, 16, 20 / *marginalia in RH II's hand*

attended by the Pursevant and Standard:bearer of that Family, each properly habited, and having the several Insignia used at that Midsummer solemnity, preceded by all the licensed Musicians, with white scarves across their shoulders, rank'd in pairs, and playing ˄ ʿonʾ their several instruments, this procession marched before the Gentlemen and their Guests, quite thorough the city, to their respective Mansions where plentifull Entertainment was provided on that occasion. --- Sir P: Leycester, and Mr Holmes MS.

1540-1
State Papers of Henry VIII PRO: SP 60/9
f 15
...
Exbursment*es* made [by] for the Char*ges* in conveying the kyng*es* Treasure by Mr Walter Cowley from london in to Ireland
...

f 15v
To the Wayt*es* or Mynstrell*es* At Chester ij s

St Mary's Churchwardens' Accounts CRO: P/20/13/1
ff 8v-9 *(17 April)*
...
Item for pyns & nayl*es* to the sepulcre j d |
Item for a Corde to the vale j d
...

1541-2
St Mary's Churchwardens' Accounts CRO: P/20/13/1
f 10 *(9 April)*
...
Item for a Corde to the vale j d
...
Item to Ric*hard* leche for make the sepulcre light*es* x d
...

1542-3
St Mary's Churchwardens' Accounts CRO: P/20/13/1
f 11v *(25 March)*
...
Item a corde to the [Vay] Va˄ʿyʾle j d
...

1543-4
Dean and Chapter CC: Treasurers' Accounts I
p 132 *(6 April)*

...

Item on palme Sonday to the passynares in wynne	viij d	5
Item ffor iij days ffoloyg	xij d	
Item to iiij men which carid the canaby	iiij d	
Item a payr off glovys ffor the prophet with his brikffast	iij d	
Item ffor makyng off the carege	iiij d	
Item ffor skowryng the candylstykes with other gere	ix d	10
Item ffor iiij stavys to the canaby	v d	

...

p 73 *(Christmas)*

		15
Item to William Cally for the watche	xij d	

St Mary's Churchwardens' Accounts CRO: P/20/13/1
f 14 *(13 April)*   20

...

Item for a corde for the vayle	j d	

...

	25

1544-5
Dean and Chapter CC: Treasurers' Accounts I
p 76 *(29 March)*

...

Item opon palme Sonday to the passyners in wyne	viij d	30
Item for iij days folowynge	xij d	
Item to iiij men which caried the Canaby	iiij d	
Item for a payre of gloves to the prophet on palmes Sonday		
& for his breakefast	iij d	
Item for skowrynge the Kandilstickes with other thynges	ix d	35
Item for iiij staves to the Canaby	v d	

...

St Mary's Churchwardens' Accounts CRO: P/20/13/1
f 15 *(5 April)*   40

...

Item for A corde to ye veyle	j d	

...

1545-6

A C   *Trinity Churchwardens' Accounts* BL: Harley 2177
f 21v* *(25 April)*

...

payd 23 May for bearinge the Crosse & baners of the Crosse xvj d   5

...

for pyns & thred to make the sepulcre ij d ...

A   *Mayors List 4* BL: Harley 2105
f 95 *(Whitsun) William Holcroft*   10

...

In this yere mr holcroft died & mr Iohn Walley was chosyn
mayor & the plaies went that same yere

A C   **Smiths, Cutlers, and Plumbers' Records**   15
BL: Account Book I Harley 2054
f 15* *(Corpus Christi Day)*

... to Ran Crane on Corpus Christi day   4d   for makinge our
lights xiij d ...   20

1546-7

A C   **Smiths, Cutlers, and Plumbers' Records**
BL: Account Book I Harley 2054
f 15* *(July)*   25

...

[1574]   for potinge the Carag out of the hasthel   vj d
1547   for lights on Corpus christi day 1547 2 Copes for the lights   x d
           Spent at ⸢mr⸣ Tho Aldersey Tauarne on midsomer eue   xiij d
           ...   30

Cordwainers and Shoemakers' Records
CCA: Account Book I G/8/2
f 1v *(11 November)*

...   35

Item ffor vj geyffes of selver   iij s
Item spend ouer the shotte on gotedes monday   ij s viij d
Item geyuen to ij menstrells in Thomas pellyn hous   vj d

...

Item geyven to ye menstrels on corpos creste day & on   40

36 / geyffes *for* gleyffes

medsomer daye   ij s

...

Item spend wyene wye payd mester dotton ffor caryng awye
the carch   viij d

...   5

St Mary's Churchwardens' Accounts CRO: P/20/13/1
f 18 *(10 April)*

...

Item payde for ij burdes to mend the sepulcher   j d   10

...

AC *Trinity Churchwardens' Accounts* BL: Harley 2177
f 22* *(10 April)*

...   15

for caring the baners in the Crosse weeke   xij d
for carring the Cope on Corpus christy day   1d

...

for Carringe the baners on the general procession day   v d

...   20

1547-8

AC *Smiths, Cutlers, and Plumbers' Records*
BL: Account Book I Harley 2054
f 15 *(July)*   25

...

to mynstrells at Rondolfs pasewalls wedinge Robyn borys
wedinge & hugh Stokens weding   xx d
to mynstrells on Corpus christy day & drinking   vj s
Spent in the northgate when wee were there   4s 8d 30
for a quart wyne at mr Rafe Aldersey tauarn   iiij d

...

Cordwainers and Shoemakers' Records
CCA: Account Book I G/8/2   35
f 7 *(11 November)*

...

Item geyven at the drenkeng of wyllyam semcoke to a
menstrell   iiij d

...   40

Item payd ffor vj gleyves   iij s
Item payd ouer the shotte on gotedes monday   xxj d

Item payd to a menstrels the same daye .... iiij d
Item payd to ij menstrels in the stuardes house .... viij d
...

f 7v   5
...
Item on corpos creste daye to a menstrell .... iiij d
Item spend ye same daye on oure brethern .... iiij d
Item spend on the shereffes .... vj d
...   10
Item spende at necolas smyth wydeng to a menstrell .... ij d
...

1548-9
Cordwainers and Shoemakers' Records   15
CCA: Account Book I G/8/2
f 10* *(11 November)*
...
Item geyuen to a menstrell on mertens even .... vj d
Item geyuen to a menstrell on oure month dey .... viij d   20
...

f 10v
...
Item geyuen to a menstrel on corpos creste dey .... viij d   25
Item spend in peter tounges hause .... vj d
Item spend on gotedes mondey ou*er* oure shoute .... iij s iiij d
...
Item payd to a menstrell ye thorsdaye affter .... iiij d
...   30

1549-50
Cordwainers and Shoemakers' Records
CCA: Account Book I G/8/2
f 13v *(11 November)*   35
...
Item peyde to the the menstreles on martenes dey .... xij d
...
Item spente on menstreles at wyllyam acokes drenkeng .... xij d
Item peyd ffor a pottel of wyene .... vj d   40

37 / the the MS *dittography*

Item peyde to the wyettes of shorresbere   xij d
Item peyd to the menstreles that dey that wye toke in wyllyam
leneker   xij d

f 14   5
...

Item peyd ffor gleyves   iij s iiij d
Item peyd ffor beff & chesse   v s
Item spende at the [ele] eyldermans housse on ex wyenesdey
ouer the shotte   v s 10
Item sspende the thovrdey after   viij s
...

f 14v
Item spende at the good man hardborens on oure bretheren xij d 15
Item spende at wyllyam Rychardssons apon menstreles   viij d
Item spend the same tyme to the wyettes of shuresbere   xij d
Item peyde at wyllyam aucokes deyner   v s
Item to the wyettes   viij d
...   20
Item spend at wysson ttyde on the sumakers of shovressbere
                           iij s iiij d
...

Item spend ouer the shotte ʽonʼ [s] ssent martens even   iij s
Item geyven to the wyettes   vj d 25
...

ff 16-16v* *(Whitsun)*
Ihesu
The expense to oure pley   30

Item peyd ffor Reydeng the banes   xix d
Item peyd ffor a dosyn bordes to the carych   ij s viij d
Item peyde ffor ij plankes for lasses   viij d
Item payd ffor iij gyse & haffe a sper   xij d 35
Item peyd ffor neyles   viij d
Item peyd ffor ffreytyng of the weyles   xvj d
Item peyd ffor wryght notte & the beyrech   iij s iij d
Item peyd ffor iij stryke of wyete   x s iij d
Item peyd ffor ij eyrdes & a hauffe of flaxson clauth to make   40
meyre madelentes coute   xxij d
Item payd ffor bakyng of godes brede   iiij s viij d

Item payd ffor beffe to oure generall Reyherse   iij s iij d
ˈspend over the shouteˈ   xvij d
Item payd ffor glaues to the pleyers   iiij s
Item payd ffor ssetteng op of oure stepoll & ffor tember   xvij d
Item payde ffor the pleyers breykeffaste   viij s iiij d   5
Item payd ffor dreynke to the pleyers [& poters of ye carych]
    ij s viij d
Item paid ffor geyldeng of godes ffase & ffor peyntyng of the
geylers ffasses   xij d
Item payd ffor dressyng of the chauernes & ffor ye as   viij d   10
Item peyd ffor the menstrells wages   ij s iiij d
some lviij s   Item peyd ffor payntyng & gyldyng of the pleyeng geyre   v s |

Item payd ffor gryndyng the wyette   ij d   15
Item payd ffor ij cordes   ij d
Item payd ffor soupe   j d
Item spend at the bryngeng vp of oure charych   vj d
Item payd ffor wyne to the barkers   xx d
Item payd to the potters of the carych   xviij d   20
Item payd ffor drenke to the potters of the carych   ij s
Item payd ffor the marchantes ware   iiij d
Item payd for wypcord & pake thryd & chonchyse   vij d
Item payd ffloures   j d
Item payd to the lade for leydeng the as   j d   25
Item payd ffor [beyche] beyryches   iiij d
Item to god   ij s
to mare madeline   x d
to martha   viij d
to Iodas   xvj d   30
to vj chelder of esaraell   iij s
to keyffase   x d
to anas   viij d
the to kneythtes   viij d
to the geyler   xvj d   35
to the geylers man   xiiij d
to the Reygenall beyrer   xij d
Item payd ffor wyne that Roger glouer & perse toung
dranke   iiij d
    40
some xxj s iiij d

1550-1
Cordwainers and Shoemakers' Records
CCA: Account Book I G/8/2
f 17 *(11 November)*

...

Item payd to the clerke of sent mertens   ij d
Item payd to a menstrel in Thomas pellyn   vj d
Item payd on oure month dey to a menstrel   viij d

...

f 17v
Item payd for vj gleyvese   iij s vj d
Item payd ffor beffe at goutted   iij s iiij d
Item payd ij menstrels at goutted   vj d

...

Item payd to a menstrel on corpos creste dey   viij d

...

f 18
Item geyuen to a menstrel in Rychard telston   vj d
Item geyuen to a menstrel in Rayffe wya nam   vj d

...

1551-2
Cordwainers and Shoemakers' Records
CCA: Account Book I G/8/2
f 19v *(11 November)*

...

Itam paid to the mynstrell on martens daie   viij d

...

Itam paid to the mynstrell at *our* monyth   viij d

...

Itam on guttides mondaye to the mynstrel*les*   vj d
Itam for *our* gleaves   iij s iiij d
Itam Over the shotte on guttydes mondaie   iiij s iiij d

...

Itam to the mynstrell at Roger Glouers weading   viij d

...

Itam to the mynstrel*les* at Rob*ertes* smythes weding   xij d

...

1552-3
Cordwainers and Shoemakers' Records
CCA: Account Book I G/8/2
f 21 *(11 November)*

... 5

Item geyven to the wyete men on martens dey   vj d

...

Item peyd to myles nokan ffor makyng the gleyues   iij s iiij d
Item peyd ffor chesse & ffeche at goted   iiij s iiij d
Item spend on gottedes mondey & the tholydey after at ovre   10
alldermanes bradbornes havsse ouuer the shovtes in brede &
ale   v s ob.
Item spend at ovre alldermans bradborns hovsse on ex Wensdey
ouer the shoute   xxj d
...   15

f 21v
Item geyven to the menstreles on ex wensdey   xij d
Item geyven to wyllyam luter on gottedes mondey   iiij d
Item geyven to the Wyettemen the thovrdey affter   viij d   20
Item geyven the same dey ffor waffarnes   iiij d

...

Item geyven to a menstrel at Rayffe Warnames hovsse   vj d

...

Item geyvene to a menstrel on medsomer eve at nethe   vj d   25
...

f 22

...

Item peyde to the menstreles on martenes en at nethe   xiiij d   30
Item spend ouer the shovtte on martenes en   viij d

A C *Trinity Churchwardens' Accounts* BL: Harley 2177
f 23 *(2 April)*

                                                                      35

... payd for the Starr ij s ... for pentinge ˄ 'the star' & and
autercloth ij s ...
payd for paper and writtinge of Senses & solens to the Starr   4d

...

to the clarke for wachinge the sepulcre   ix d 40

...

1553-4

AC *Smiths, Cutlers, and Plumbers' Records*
BL: Account Book I Harley 2054
ff 14v-15* *(July)*

1554

...

payd Rand a Crane in yonge Rafe goodmans howse   xij d
                             was ther minstrell

...

to Rand Crane at mr bradfords dinner xij d & on St loys day xij d   10

...

Spent at Io plemers howse when mr maior came to loke what
harnise euery man had   viij d

whitson plays   for ridinge the banes xiij d the Citty Crier ridd
spent at potyng aute off Carriges at Rich barkers   4d   15
we gaue at geting aute of the Carriag   4d
we gaue for an axeyll tre to Rich belfounder   vj d
for an other axelltre to Ric hankey   iiij d
payd for dressing of the Carriage   x d
for Ropes nelles pyns sope & thrid   x d | 20
for wheate ij s ij d for malt iij s 4d for flesh ij s x d
for flesh at the breckfast & bacon   ij s 8d
for 6 chekens x d. for 2 cheeses xvj d
Item we gaue for gelldinge of Gods fase   xij d
Item we gaue botord to the players 4d for bred in northgatestreat   25
ij d
we drank in the watergate street vj d at Io a leys x d. at Ric
Anderton founderer xij d at mr dauison tauarne xiij d
to the mynstrells in mane   ij s
we gaue to the porters of the Caryegs ij s, for gloues xiij d   30
we gaue to the docters   iij s 4d
we gaue to Ioseph   viij d
we gaue to letall God xij d we gaue to mary x d to damane x d
we gaue to the Angells vj d, to ould sermond iij s 4d
we gaue to barnes & the syngers   iij s 4d   35
for more wheate 18d malte ij s ij d flesh 3s 4d a chese ix d
to Randle Crane in mane   ij s
spent at mrs dauison tauarne ij s jd, for the charges of the
Regenall xij d
to the skayneares   iij s 40

...

Cordwainers and Shoemakers' Records
CCA: Account Book I G/8/2
f 24 *(11 November)*

...

Item peyde ffor vj gleyffes	iij s iiij d	5
Item peyde ffor beffe & chesses at govtted	ij s viij d	
Item peyd ovuer the shoutte at gotted	xiij d	
Item peyde to the menstreles at gotted	viij d	
Item spende at Iohn bradbornes at gotted	xx d	
Item geyven the same tymy to the menstreles	vj d	10

...

Item peyd to the menstreles on medsomer evne	viij d	

...

Item spende at gotted at Thomas pyllyn	iiij s vj d	
Item spende over the shotte on martens even	v s xj d	15
Item geyven on martens even to the menstreles	xij d	

...

A *Mayors List 10* BL: Add. 29777
item 228* *(Whitsun) John Offley*   20

...

Also this yeare the Playes were playde

...

1554-5   25
AC *Smiths, Cutlers, and Plumbers' Records*
BL: Account Book I Harley 2054
f 15v* *(July)*

...

a Smyth Kept payd to mynstrells at marriage of Io harrson daughter   4d   30
a Tauerne   payd same day in our Aldermans tauarne   iiij d

...

f 16

                          payments 1554   35

payd at the drinkinge of hugh Masse to mynstrells   4d

...

to mynstrells on Corpus Christi Day   xx d
                                                                        40
layd downe that day more then we receued 3s 4d for our lights

vj s Carring vj d for horsbred to Semeons horse 4d for gloues
for him ij d, to prisoners same day ij d

...

Treasurers' Account Rolls CCA: TAR/1/8   5
mb 3 *(November)*

...

The Watergate Strete

...

The stewardes of the drapers for their Caredge house buylde   10
vpon the Citiez grounde nere to ye greye frere lande ende   viij d
The stewardes of the marsers for ye Caredge house vpon ye
Citiez landes   vj d

...
                                                                           15

mb 4

...

Item payde for Saynte georges daye   xx s vij d

...

Item payde for mydsomer wache for the Caredge of the pagions   20
and paynters   xxviij s vj d

...

mb 5
                                                                           25
...

Item payde to mr Thomas Smythe for vij yardes of Clothe to
the wettemens gownys   xxxix s viij d

AC *Trinity Churchwardens' Accounts* BL: Harley 2177
    f 23v *(14 April)*   30

...

to the clarke for washinge the Sepulcre

...

1555-6   35
AC *Smiths, Cutlers, and Plumbers' Records*
    BL: Account Book I Harley 2054
    f 15v* *(July)*

...

to Sir Io smyth for the Reggenall   ij d 40

...

Assembly Books CCA: AB/1
f 85* *(November)*

breckfast*es* vpon
chri*st*emas day
to be Left &
mu*m*ing in time
of chri*st*enmas

Whereas heretofore of late tyme yt hathe been vsed that diu*er*se
of the worshipfull of this Citie haue caused breckfast*es* to be
made in ther houses vpon Christenmasdaie in the mornyng before
dyvyne s*er*uice endyd by reasone wherof madye dysorderid
p*er*sons haue vsed them selue*es* Rayther all the daye after idellie
in vyse & wantonne*es* then yeuen them Selue*es* holy to
contemplacion & prayre the same Sacryt holye & prynsepaule
feate according to ther most bounden dutye vnto god the sone
redemer of the worlde who as that daye came into this worlde
and was borne of *our* blessed virgyn marye for the redemption
of all mankynd and to the intent the same feste maye be the
better & more hollier kept according to thorder of god & his holy
churche mr mayre by theadvyse of his worshipfull brethern
thaldermen of this cytie haue thought good that those
breckefast*es* banckytt*es* the same christenmee*es* daye in the
morning shall not be vser and kept herafter, and you shall
vnderstand that this ys not meyuyd but that euery man y*at*
will vpon other daye*es* conuenyent may bestoue the same coste
vpon ther frind*es* and pore nyghbore*es* as lyberally as thaye
haue byne accoustomyd other yere*es* before [th] tyme to the
prayse of god and contentac*ion* of ther neighbore*es*, and allso
that no mann*er* p*er*son or p*er*sones go abrode in this citie
mu*m*myng in any place w*i*thin the same citie ther fayse*es* being
coue*ry*d or disgysed and that no man*er* of p*er*son or p*er*sone*es*
w*i*thin this citie suffer any p*er*son or p*er*sone*es* to playe at any
vnlaufull gayme*es* w*i*thin his or ther house or house*es* w*h*ich
be p*ro*hibityd by any laue or statute w*i*thin this realme vpon
payne of imp*ri*senment of ther bodye*es* & makinge fyne according
to the statut*es* in that case prouidyd

Treasurers' Account Rolls CCA: TAR/1/9
mb 4 *(November)*

The Watergate Strete

...

The steward*es* of the drap*er*s for their Caredge howse buylde
vpon the Cittiez grounde ner to the grey frere lane end   viij d
The steward*es* of the marsers for theyr Caredge howse vpon ye
Citiez land*es*   vj d

...

5

10

15

20

25

30

35

40

mb 5

...

Item paide to mr mayre to paye for the wayttmens gouns

xlvj s viij d

...   5

Cordwainers and Shoemakers' Records
CCA: Account Book I G/8/2
f 26 *(11 November)*
...   10

Item geuen to westeid the minstrill the same day   iiij d
Item spend the same daye ouer the shotte at dener   xx d

...

Item payd for gleaufe*es* one gotete*es* daye   iij s iiij d
...   15

Item geuen to the wettmen and other to mynstrylle*es* one the
thoursday in the skluesynge daye*es*   xij d
Item ˄ ⸢more⸣ lede doune that was ouer the shote the same
daye   ij s ij d
...   20

Item geuen to the presoners one sent gorgeday   ij d

...

f 26v
Item apon cobescristye day geuen to shacrofte*es*   xij d   25
Item that we gaufe the wettmen the same day   viij d
Item geuen to amynstryll y*at* plaide afore vs one medsomer
[day] euen   xij d
Item that we spende ouer the shotte the same nyght that we
layd doune   xxj d   30
Item geuen to the presoners one mydsomer euen   ij d

...

It*em* spend ou*er* the shovtte on mertens evn   ix d
It*em* geyven to a menstrell   ij d

...   35

Dean and Chapter CC: Treasurers' Accounts I
p 274 *(Christmas)*

Item to a syngynge man þat was here all Christenmas by the   40
com̄mandemente of mr dayne & þe canons   iij s vj d

28 / x *of* xij d *written over* v

p 279 *(29 March)*

...

First to Thomas barines for a pottell of malvesey and a pere of
gloves for the prophet vpon palme sondaye   xiiij d

...

AC   *Trinity Churchwardens' Accounts* BL: Harley 2177
       f 25 *(5 April)*

       ...

1556 1557   other payments for the first yeare   1(

       ...

       for wachinge the sepulcre one night to the clarke iij d for charcole
       & franconsens agaynst ester: for dressinge the sepurcure & after
       in berrage ij d. for takinge downe the clothes about the sepulcar
       ij d   1$

       ...

       ## 1556-7

AC   *Smiths, Cutlers and Plumbers' Records*
       BL: Account Book I Harley 2054   2(
       f 15v* *(July)*

       ...

       rec at the hands of the occupation   48s 4d
       payd to Io Plumber ij s viij d to R Crane same tyme viij d
       to mr maior to the hande   xx s 25
       same day to Sir Law smythes bally   v s
       Spent on our bretheren *present* at payment of mr maior &
       Sir L Smyth baly   xij d
       to the Ringers on St loys [day] euen ij d to belman ij d to the
       preests on St loys day vj d   30
       Spent same day at mr dauisons tauarne   xviij d

       ...

       for makinge of a bill to putt to mr Maior on St Georges day ij d
       to prisoners same day ij d
       for 6 new topps & payntinge all the spayres new to *willia*m   35
       framo   iiij s x d
       for dressinge the banners & for fringes   xx d
       to Rich gest for 13 new speres vj d for neles to nele the banners
       on j d
       for carryinge of the lights on Corpus christi day vj d to Ran   40
       Crane the minstrell ij s

on midsomer eue to the prisoners ij d Spent same day in Simon
mounforts howse xv d
the same night to Ran Crane   4d
for makinge a bill to put to mr maior for the makinge of our
harnes   ij d   5
...

Cordwainers and Shoemakers' Records
CCA: Account Book I G/8/2   10
f 28 *(11 November)*
...

Item paide vnto Shalcroste the mynstrill   vj d
Item paide vnto Barine of kyndertones mynstrilles   viij d
...   15
Item paid to the prisonares on Midsomer Even at   ij d
...

AC   *Trinity Churchwardens' Accounts* BL: Harley 2177   20
f 25 *(18 April)*
...

for Carringe the Crosse banner on st George day. 1d. for
Carryinge 3 banners in Cross weeke iij d ...
                                                                                                     25
for hollyns to make the hollyn agaynst Christmas & Sences vnto
the Starre with a chales of paper   8d
for Cressets to sett in Candles & makinge balls to the sences   j d
for wyred Candles to the hollyn   xv d
for weshinge 2 sirplus & thrid to sow on the faunounce   ix d ob. 30
for nayles & pynns at seurall tymes for the sepulcar & Alter
clothes etc.
for Settinge vp & takinge downe the sepulcar   4d
...
for 4 Staues to Carry the Canopye vij d & payntinge the same vj d   35

f 25v
...
for francomsence & charcole agaynst easter   4d
wachinge the Sepulcar 2 nights   4d   40
payd a wright for a frame for lightes vnto the Sepulcre   4d
...

1557-8

A C   *Smiths, Cutlers, and Plumbers' Records*
BL: Account Book I Harley 2054
f 15v* *(July)*

...

to barne a kyndertons mynstrells in Symon founders howse on St Loy day	xij d

...

to the waytmen	viij d

...

on midsomer Eue at night at simon founders	3s 4d
on Corpus christi day for Caringe lights vj d to seuerall mynstrell	*(blank)*
to William luter minstrell & Rand Crane	x d

Memorandum the Company neuer mett at Tauarne or any howse without musick

...

Cordwainers and Shoemakers' Records
CCA: Account Book I G/8/2
ff 29v-30 *(11 November)*

...

peyd ffor gleyues on gouttedes dey	iij s iiij d
peyd ffor beffe & chesse ouer & beside the shutte	iiij s iiij d
Item spend the same dey at a later shoutte	xx d
Item geyuen the ssame dey to the menstreles	viij d
Item geyvene to the menstrelles on exwendey	vj d
Item geyven to the menstreles on the thoursdey	viij d
Item geyven at sir Rychard ankokes	iij s iiij d
Item geyven to the menstreles at sir Rychardes	vj d
peyd ffor a gaulen of wyne at Sir Rychardes	xvj d

...

peyd to the preyssoners on sene gorge dey	iiij d
peyd to the preyssoners on corposscryste dey	iiij d
peyd to the menstrell on corposscryste dey	viij d
spend ouer the shutte the ssamedey	iij s iiij d

...

peyd ffor mendeng the tormentors heydes	x d

...

peyd ouer the shutte on mertens euen	ij s x d
peyd to the menstreles the ssame even	xviij d

...

AC   *Trinity Churchwardens' Accounts* BL: Harley 2177
f 26v *(10 April)*

....

for wyer candles wax candles etc. Scouring candlesticks wachinge
the Sepulcre at Ester etc.   *(blank)*   5
for a pully to the Starr & setting it vp   4d

...

1558-9

AC   *Smiths, Cutlers, and Plumbers' Records*   10
BL: Account Book I Harley 2054
f 16 *(July)*

...

giuen the mynsrells at Io huntingtons dimer   xij d

...   15

to the minstrells on St Loyes day when Rich barker Smyth
made his dinner   ij s
for wyne we gaue to the wiues same day   x d

...

to prisoners on St geo day   ij d   20
to lutter the mynstrell when *willia*m Ionson made his dinner
                                         viij d

...

Treasurers' Account Rolls CCA: TAR/1/10   25
mb 5 *(November)*

...

The Watergate Strete

...

The steward*es* of the drapers for their Caredge howse buyld vpon   30
the citiez grounde nere to the grey frere lane ende   viij d
The steward*es* of the marcers for their Caredge howse buyld on
citiez land*es*   vj d

...

                                                      35

mb 9

...

Item payde to the surde berere and to the masse berere at
mydsom*er*   xx s

...   40

14 / dimer *for* dinner, *minim omitted MS*

Item payde to the levelokers for sente George daye   xxv s
...

Cordwainers and Shoemakers' Records
CCA: Account Book I G/8/2
f 33 *(11 November)*
...

Item oure gleuys   iij s iiij d
Item spede oure the showte on gowtyt mondaye   ˊv sˋ [vij d]
Item spnde on the mynstrellys the same day   xiij d   :
Item to the gogyllyr   ij s
Item at my alldermanys to the gogyllyr   viij d
Item at Raufe Vernanes to the gogyllyr & to my myssterellyes xx d
...
Item to the pare [of] on sente gegese daye   iiij d   ▮
...

f 33v
...

Item spende on sentmartn eue ower the shote   vj s iiij d   2
Item on the same nyght to the mynystrelys   xvj d
...

Dean and Chapter CC: Treasurers' Accounts I
p 316 *(Christmas)*   2
...

Item to Randle Bennet for watchyng with þe mayr & shyryffes
christenmasse Even & day & saynt steuens day at nyght   xij d
...
                                                                           3
p 318 *(19 March)*
...

Item for a payr off gloues for the prophet Apon palme Sunday ij d
...
                                                                           3
AC   ### Trinity Churchwardens' Accounts BL: Harley 2177
f 27 *(26 March)*
...

payd to Rafesonne Greff makinge the Roode & mendinge the
Mary & Iohn   xij s 4▮
payd to Rich leche for payntinge the Rode & the Mary & Iohn
                                                            14s

for Carriinge the Crosse & banners in the Crosse weeke   4d
for Senses for the Starr   j d
for wax to make tapers 18d wachinge the Sepulcre at ester viij d
...

  5

1559-60

AC   *Smiths, Cutlers, and Plumbers' Records*
BL: Account Book I Harley 2054
f 16 *(July)*

...   10

layd downe on St loys day to the shott & mynstrells in the
Aldermans howse   6s 3d
that day Rich whitley made his dimer to mynstrells   vj d
...

Spent on Corpus christi day more then the shott came to ix s   15
viij d to mynstrells xij d
on midsomer eue at night to prisoners iiij d Spent at Aldermans
ij s ij d minstrells xij d
...

more to the presoners   ij d   20
...

f 36v
...
more payde to the menstreles at Wyllyam skerse denner   xvj d li.   25
...

Cordwainers and Shoemakers' Records
CCA: Account Book I G/8/2
f 36 *(11 November)*   30
...

payde to the mestreles at Rychard howyt drynkynge   iiij d
...
spende ouer the shot on gottyes monde   v s ij d
more to the mestrels on the same daye   xij d   35
more payde at the aldermones hose ouer the shote   xviij d
more to the mestreles on the same daye   xij d
more payde at wyllyam Rychardsoun hose ouer the shote iiij s ij d
more to the mestreles on the same daye   xvj d
more payde [of] for oure glefes   iij s iiij d   40

---

13 / dimer *for* dinner, *minim omitted MS*   16 / *tittle through the* ll *in* mynstrells

geuen to mester planton in wyne	xij d
more payde to the mestreles at Ry*chard* cokes weddyng	xij d
more payde to the mestrel on medsomar heuen	viij d

St Michael's Parish Register CRO: P/65/8/1
f 1v *(14 April)* *(1560 Inventory)*

...

Item a fframe [of] y*at* was the sepultere

...

f 2

...

Item a stare in the kepynge of wyllyam ssymcocke

...

AC *Trinity Churchwardens' Accounts* BL: Harley 2177
f 27 *(14 April)*

... for Karringe the banners in Crosseweeke ij d

...

1560-1
Cordwainers and Shoemakers' Records
CCA: Account Book I G/8/2
f 39 *(11 November)*

The expenssys

It*em* on sent martyns daye at Ry*chard* snytes denner to the menstreles	ix d
more the same daye spende	iij d
...	
more spende ower the shote on gottets mondaye	vij s ij d
more to the menstreles the same daye	xv d
more spende ower the shote on ex wensdaye at the aldermones	
	xx d
more spende ower the shote at Robart branes	v s [d]
more payde to the menstreles on the same daye	iij s
...	
more spende at Ry*chard* knghyts weddynge to the mynstrel	vj d
more at Ihon hoghtes weddynge to the mynstrel	vj d
...	

f 39v

...

payde to the menstreles on mycommer heuen	xij d
more for ij potteles of sake ower the shote	ij d
more for bere to the stuwarts of the gornemen and the	5
hobbehorssys	iiij d
more to the presoneres	j d ob.
more ouer the shote at the makynge op of the playe	ij d ob.

...

more spend ouer the shote on martens heuen	xij s iij d ob. 10
more to the menstreles	xvj d

...

St Michael's Parish Register CRO: P/65/8/1
f 8v *(6 April)* *(Inventory)*   15

...

Item a fframe 'yat' was the sepulkar

...

f 9   20

...

Item a stare whyche ys in the kepynge of wyllyam symcoke

...

AC ***Smiths, Cutlers, and Plumbers' Records***   25
BL: Account Book I Harley 2054
ff 16v-17* *(Whitsun)*

The names of the Company 1561 & receued of them
of hugh Massy 13s 4d   30
rec of Mr Moumfort Alderman ij s 4 ob.

Rich skryuener	Irrian Ryder	Tho Towers
Io parsyuall	Robert vrmeston	William Ionnson
Io plunner	Io dooe	hugh massy	35
Io Robynson	Io ball	Io harrison wife ij s ij d
Rich barker	Meowe Trafford	Rich barker wife
Roger ledsham ij s 4d	Rich smyth	Robert hancock
gilbert Knowes	Rich newall	
Robert Crockett	Rich brasse ij s	all the rest ij s iiij d	40

35 / plunner *for* plumer, *extra minim MS*

Rafe smyth   Rand latton   ob. apeece
William loker   william clyffe
law gesley   Io huntington
hugh Stokton ij s

rec of the Iurneymen v s
of the Iurneymen at the generall rehearse xvj d
payd on election day in our Aldermans howse vj s vj d to
mynstrells 4d
to mr Tho Massy for Tymber 8s 9d to carter & men to gett
it out 7d ob.
for wod to make welles 3s 4d
Cost vs the rydinge the banes our horses & ourselues of the
which symyon was one ˄ ⸢ij s⸣
payd for the first rehearse at Io huntingtons howse vj d

whitson play

busnesse

for paper to Coppy out the parcells of the booke v d
berrage of our wheles 9d ob.
spent hyring the Cartwrights in Geff Cokes sellor ij d quarta
spent at deliueringe forth of the parcells & gettinge pillers 4d ob.
payd for making the welles to the Cartwright 7s 4d to mr boydle
for bords and other tymber v s
payd the wright for makinge the Carriage & for berrag 8s 5d
for nayls vj d
for drink in barkers after the rehearse xviij d
payd Io byrth for beaffe agaynst the generall rehearse 6s 8d
for 3 ould cheeses 4s
for frettinge the wheles & nayles xviij d,
for going to warne the occupations spent 4d
Spent in Sr Rand barnes chamber to gett singers iij d
Spent at Robert Iones at rehearse xix d, to William lutter at
genrall rerearse 4d ob.
for 6 Crokes for Alle at genrall rehearse x s a crocke of Small ale
& 2 gallons xx d
a hoppe of wheate to the genrall rehearse ij s iij d
to Iames Tayler for bread & cakes for genrall rehearse ij s vij d
for wyne to the sayd rehearse ij s vjj d
for an other hoppe of wheat agayne the whyttson tidde ij s iij d
when we brought oure Carragge to the wayevers howse vj d
payd the wrights for settinge the wheles viij d, & Carriage forth
of the water [viij d] ⸢j d ob.⸣
for a pound of gray sope for the wheles iij d
for 2 chekens vj d. for naylles to dresse the Carriage iij d ob.
for makinge a faxe payntinge & dressynge the pillers gere & a

Crowne for Mary *(blank)*
for 3 Curten Cowerds iij d for pynnes iij d
for flesh for a breckfast at whitsontyde 3s 8d
for glowes ij s viij d |
for guildinge of litle Gods face xij d   5
for makinge the players to drinke in the watergate street v d
for drinke to the players in the bridgstret iij d
to Io layes wife for drinke xij d to Io dooes for drink xij d
to the minstrells 3s 6d payd for drinke for ther breckfast before
they play & after they had done when the were vnbowninge   10
them iij s
payd the porters of the Carriage xviij d
payd to Symyon 3s 4d
payd to S*ir* Io Genson for songes xij d. to the 5 boyes for singing
ij s vj d   15
to the Angell vj d
to dame Anne x d to Tho ellam xij d
to the first docter xvj d to the 2d xij d to the 3d docter xij d
to the lyttell God xvj d
for redyng the auRygynall ij s   20
to the skynners iij s, to the weuers 4s to hugh Stoken xviij d
to W*illia*m loker for plleyinge xvj d. to Robe*r*t Crockett for a
lord iij d
to Io dowes for drink xvj d
spent in the Tauarne on Midsomer euen in mr Moumforts tauarn   25
ij s 4d
payd in stuards howse same night xij d
to the p*ri*soners in Castell iij d
spent at makinge vp our buke xvj d

                                                                        30

in all vij li. viij d ob.

A *Mayors List 12* BL: Add. 29780
   f 130* *(Whitsun) William Aldersey*
   ...   35

   This yeare the playes called Whison playes were played ...

   1561-2
AC *Smiths, Cutlers, and Plumbers' Records*
   BL: Account Book I Harley 2054   40
   f 17 *(July)*
   ...

   Spent on electionday in mr mounforts vij s & to 3 mariners &

minstrell ij s vj d

...

giuen 3 mynstrells in Io persyualls   xij d

...

for rent to the weuers 4s   <u>this was for Carriage place</u>

...

Cordwainers and Shoemakers' Records
CCA: Account Book I G/8/2   1
f 41 *(11 November)*

The exsspences of thythes

It*em* payde to the mensteres on martenes dyee   xvj d   1

...

more payde at radhes drynkynge to the menstreles   vj d
more payde at hethes drynkynge to the menstreles   xvj d
more payde for the glayfes   iij s iiij d
more payde ouer the shote on gottes mondaye   vij s ij d   2•
more for howre bretheren shotes the same daye   ij s vj d
more on ex wenssdaye for the shotes & besyde the shot viij s iiij d
more at wyllyam Lynykeres howse for the shot and besyde
the shot   vij s vj d
and for the menstreles for the iij dayes   iiij d   2.

...

more for the gyldynge of godes fase on medsomare heue   x d
more to the prysoneres the same daye   iiij d
more spende on the playeres on mydsomar heue   iij s
more to the menstreles the sam daye   xvj d   3•
more spende on the shomakeres of shorsbere   ij s

...

f 41v
more on sante martenes heu at nheghet ˄'for' [ower] the shot   3.
                                                               xvj s
more to the menstreles the same nheghte   viij d

...

1562-3

Cordwainers and Shoemakers' Records
CCA: Account Book I G/8/2
ff 43-3v *(11 November)*

...   5
Item payde for beffe agaynste guttedes monde   v s
Item geven to the menstrelles the same daye   xij d
Item spende over the shotte the same daye   xj s x d
Item spende the same daye in sacke   xx d
Item payde for oure glevys   iij s iiij d   10
Item spende over the shotte in oure alldermans at gutted   x s
Item geven the menstrell the same day   viij d |
Item spende at gutted in wyllyam lays howsse over the shotte x s
Item spende the same day in sacke   xx d
Item geven the menstrels the same day   xij d   15

...
Item geven to wyllyam levter on corpus crysty daye   iiij d
Item given to the presonars on mydsomar even   iiij d
Item spente on the brethren when whe vente abovte on
mydsomar even   vj d   20
Item geven the menstrell the same nyghte   ij s
Item geven the [the] cheldren that dansed the hobbe horses
                                                                  iiij d
Item spende over the shotte ∧ ʿon corpus crysty dayʾ [the same
nyghte]   xij d   25
Item spende on mydsomar even over the shotte   v s
Item spend in settyng out of mare modelan on mydsomar
even   xx d
...

                                                                         30
f 44

...
Item geven the menstrell on martens even   viij d
Item payde over the shotte the same nyghte   v [d] s
...   35

St Michael's Parish Register CRO: P/65/8/1
f 17v *(11 April) (Inventory)*

...   40
Item a frame that was the sepulcre
...

1563-4

AC *Smiths, Cutlers, and Plumbers' Records*
BL: Account Book I Harley 2054
ff 17-17v *(July)*

...

payd in mr Mountforts xi s to minstrells 4d

...

spent at our aldermans howse on midsomer eue viij d more v s j d
payd for our Carriage howse 4s rent |
to prisoners on midsomer eue 4d to mynstrells viij d
to the 2 docters xij d to litle God 4d for suinge litle gods horse
iij d
for guyldinge the litle gods face xij d

...

Treasurers' Account Rolls CCA: TAR/1/11
mb 3 *(November)*

...

The Watergate Streat

...

The stuard*es* of the drap*eres* for ther careage house bouild vpon
the Citize ground nere to the greffrer lane end   viij d
The stuardes of the m*er*cers for ther careage house vpon the
Citize landes by yere   vj d

...

mb 4

...

Item paid mr mayre at midsom*er* for the trivmthe   xxvj s. viij d

...

Item paid to houghe gillome for daunsinge at midsom*er*   vij s.
Item paid Thomas yeaton for gonne poulder at the trivmthe
by master mayres apoyntment   xiiij s.

...

Cordwainers and Shoemakers' Records
CCA: Account Book I G/8/2
f 45 *(11 November)*

...

Item payd vnto a menestrell by the consente of our alldermane
and the rest of the bretherne at thomas dycheres daughteres
wedynge   xij d

Item payd for our gleeves at shrostyde   iij s iiij d
Item spend vpon goottedes moundaye in beffe and over and
bescyde the shotte   xij s
Item more for ij potells of secke   xxij d
Item spend at my alldermanes vpone exwenesdaye over and   5
besyde the shotte   viij s
Item spend over the shotte at Rondull a Crones house one
thouresdaye   ix s
Item payd more the same tyme in wyne   xxij d
Item payd vnto the mestrelles for all the iij dayes   ij s vj d   10
Item payd vpon corpus crystye daye overe the shotte the some
of   vj s
...

f 46   15
...

Item payd vpon mydsomer yeven ffor the setynge ffowrthe of
marye modeand and Iudas the some of   xvj d
Item geven vnto the presoneres of the castell   iiij d
Item spend over the showte vpon mydsomer yeven in moneye   20
the some of   iiij s iiij d
Item ffor the copynge ˄ ʾoutʾ of the oregenall now in money the
some of   iij s iiij d
Item payd vnto menstrelles vpon mydsomer yeven the some
of   xvj d   25
...
Item geven to the menstreles on martens even   ij s
Item spende the same nyghte at oure alldermans   xiij s viij d
...

        30

AC   *Midsummer Giants* BL: Harley 2150
f 208* *(21 April)*

    Memorandum of an order & agrement made at the last
    assembly holden the xxjth daie of Aprell in Anno Domini   35
    1564 Betwene Sir Laurence Smith knight Maier of the citie
    of chester the aldermen and comen counsaill of the seid
    cittie of thon partie And Thomas Poole and Robrt halwod
    of the citie aforeseid Painteres of thother partie concerning
    the wache vpon the eve of St Iohn baptiest   40

Imprimis the seid Thomas Poole & Robrt hallwod doth covenant

& graunt to & with the seid Maier Aldermen & commen Counsaill
of the seid Cittie & theire successores that they the seid Thomas
p⟨...⟩ and Robrt halwod shall & will yerely during theire Naturall
Lives vpon their proper costes and charges at & vpon the Even of
Saint Iohn baptiest bring ffurth repare & have in redines for the
wache afforeseid all suche ornamentes as hereafter ensueth
according as the seid wache here to fore hathe ben set furth,
withall furnytures thervnto belongeng videlicet ffoure Ieans, won
vnicorne won drombandarye, won Luce, won Camell, won Asse,
won dragon, sixe hobby horses & sixtene naked boyes, And the
same so being in A Redines shall bere & carie or cause to be
borne & caried during the seid wache from place to place
according as the same have ben vsed vpon their proper costes
& charges. In consideracon whereof the seid Maier Aldermen
and comen coumsaill doth covenant & graunt for them & their
successores to & with the seid Thomas Poole and Robert halwod
that they the seid Maier Aldermen & comen Counsall & their
successores shall well & trewly content and paie or cause to be
contented & paied vnto the seid Thomas Poole and Robert
halwod yerely during their Naturall Lieffes the Somme of ffourtie
Shillinges of good and Lefull money of england in & vpon the
feast of Saint Iohn baptest in one hole & entire payment, In
wittnes whereof either parties to otheres have Sett herevnto
their handes & Seales the Daie and Yere ffurst Above Written.

(signed) Thomas pole   *(seal)*   *(seal: WK)*   *(signed)* Robart hallwod

A   *Mayors List 5* BL: Harley 2125
f 39* *(Midsummer) Lawrence Smith*

this year the sunday next after midsomer there was a triumph
deuysed by william Crofton gentleman & mr mane master of
Art of the history of Aeneas & dido of carthage which was
played on the Rode eye & 2 forts Raysed & a ship on the water
with sundrey horsmen well apoynted.
...

A   *Mayors List 8* BL: Harley 2133
f 42v *Lawrence Smith*
...
Vpon the sonday after Midsomer day The historie of Aeneas and

15 / coumsaill *for* counsaill

queene Dido was plaid vpon the Roods Eye And were set out by
William Chroften gentleman and one mr Manne In which Tryumph
there made 2 fortes and shippinge on the water, besides many
horsemen well armed & appointed.

...   5

A   *Mayors List 10* BL: Add. 29777
item 238* *Lawrence Smith*

...

In this yeare the Sondaye next after Mydsomer daye there was   10
A Tryvmpth devysed by wyllyam Croften gent and one Mr man
Scholemaister of the ffree Schole of the historye of Aeneas and
Qeuene Dido of Carthage, in which Trivmpthe vppon the Roode
Eye was Two ffortes and A Shippe vpon the water with sundrye
horssemen well Armed & appoincted   15

...

St Michael's Parish Register CRO: P/65/8/1
f 22v *(2 April)* *(Inventory)*

...   20

Ittem a frame that was the Sepulchere

...

1564-5

AC   *Smiths, Cutlers, and Plumbers' Records*   25
BL: Account Book I Harley 2054
f 17v *(July)*

...

midsomer euen

30

® it semed
Companys vsed
then no banners
but part of the
plays

for Guildinge of Gods face   xij d
payd God & the 2 docters   xij d
for horsbread v d to mynstrells xij d
Spent in our Alderman screueners that night   vj d
... rent of Carriage howse iiij s   35

...

Treasurers' Account Rolls CCA: TAR/1/12
mb 1 *(November)*

...   40

The Watergate streate

...

The stuardes of the drapers for ther careage house vpon the

Citize landes by yeare   viij d
The stuardes of the mercers for ther careage house vpon the
Citize landes at the grefrerlane end by yere   vj d
...

mb 2*
...

Item paid houghe gillome for dansinge at midsomer by mr
mayres apoyntment   vj s viij d
...

Item paid to hallowed the paynter & his ffellowes for ther
worke donne at midsomer in mr bamvelles dayes   xxxj s.
...

Cordwainers and Shoemakers' Records
CCA: Account Book I G/8/2
f 48 *(11 November)*
...

Item payde for the gleives at gutted   iij s iiij d
...

Item payde on guttedes monday at the stwartes for beffe and
ovar and besyde the shotte   x s
Item for a pottell of secke   xij d
Item payde at oure alldermans on wennes day ovar and be syde
the shotte   x s
Item for a pottell of secke   xij d
...

Item payede the menstrelles for the threye days iij s iiij d
Item payede the menstrell on mydsomar even   xvj d
Item spente on mary modelande and Iudas   xvj d
Item geven the presonares on mydsomar even   iiij d
Item geven to Iudas the same nyghte   iiij d
Item geven the menstrell at master bunbarres medens weddynge
                             viij d
...

f 48v
...

Item spende at the alldermans on martens even   ix s
Item to the menstrelles the same nyghte   ij s
...

1565-6

AC   *Smiths, Cutlers, and Plumbers' Records*
BL: Account Book I Harley 2054
f 17v *(July)*

...   5

for guildinge of litle Gods face xij d for 3 payre of gloues &
horses for the docters & litle God xvj d more to the Docters &
litle God for theyr payns xij d
more when we went about the towne to the prisoners at Castle
                                                                              4d   10
spent on midsomer eue at wach at Towers howse 4d at mr
Mountfords after wach 4s
to mynstrells   xvj d
... rent of Carriage howse iiij s
                                                                                    15

A   *Mayors List 12* BL: Add. 29780
f 130* *(Whitsun) Thomas Grene*

... this yeare Whitson playes were played ...
                                                                                    20

1566-7

AC   *Smiths, Cutlers, and Plumbers' Records*
BL: Account Book I Harley 2054
f 18 *(July)*

...   25
for gloues for the docters & litle god on midsomer eue   vj d
gilding Gods face   xij d
other ordnary expences for midsomer euen as before
...
                                                                                    30

Cordwainers and Shoemakers' Records
CCA: Account Book I G/8/2
f 50v *(11 November)*

...
Item payde the menstrell the same day   xij d   35
...
Item payde for the gleves at gutted   iij s vj d
...

f 51   40
...
Item payde for belles on mydsomer even   vj d

Item payde for gloves that nyghte xij d
Item payde the menstrell*es* that nyghte xij d
Item spente that nyghte at oure alderman*es* viij d
Item payde the presoner*es* that nyghte in the castell iiij d
Item payde thomas newton that nyghte j d
...
Item payde the menstrell on martens even xij d
Item payde that nyghte att oure alldermans vj s iiij d
...

1

Assembly Files CCA: A/F/2
f 10* *(14 December)*

       temp*ore* willi*a*m snede milit*is* maior*is* Ci*uita*tis
       Cestr*ie* xiij^cio die decembris Anno Regni Eliz ⟨.⟩

1

fforasmuch as in the time of Iohn Rathburne Late mayer of the
Citie of Chester at an assembly ther holden the xxviij^th of aprell
An*no* R*egni* R*egis* henrici viij^ti octaui it was ordered and decred
by the said mayer alderme*n* and como*n* counsaill of the seid
Citie that no man*er* of p*er*son or p*er*sons inhabiting or resident
w*i*thin the seid Citie shuld gether or cause to be gethered or
assembleh any compeny to any prest, offering wedding or ale
to be had or said w*i*thin this Cytie vpon paine of x s of him or
the*m* that so gathereth or assembleth or causeth such assemble
or gathering to be had or made and to him that so is gathered and
assemblid vj s viij d for eu*er*y time that eny p*er*son therin
offendeth and to be further punished at mr mayer*es* plesure /
And forasmuch as the said order synce the making thereof haue
not ben obs*er*uid in all point*es* as it ought to haue ben but p*art*ly
neglected wherto great inconveniences have ryson and growen
for remedie wherof it is now ordered by the seid S*ir* willi*a*m
snede knight mayer of the Citie of Chester thalderme*n* Sheriff*es*
and comi*n* Counsaile of the seid Citie at an Assembly holden
in the Comi*n* hall w*i*thin the seid Citie the daie and yere first
aboue wrytten that the same order shall stande be firme stableshed
'and' [n] put in execuc*i*on and eu*er*y article sentence point and
clause therein conteyned to remaine and continue in force and
vertue fromhensfor⟨.⟩ for ever vpon paine and forferture of the
seu*er*all Somes before in the seid ord*er* expressed.
...

2
2
3
3
4

A C *Smiths, Cutlers, and Plumbers' Records*
BL: Account Book I Harley 2054
ff 18-18v* *(Whitsun)*

                the recets of the bretheren for the plays   5

of mr fomder for the plays ij s viij d	willm Iohnson ij s viij d
of mr Alder*man* Screuener	Io andro
of mr knowles	hughe masse
Robert Croket	Tho hollme 10
Roger ledsham	Io Kempe
Io bradshae	Rich brasse ij s vj d
Io Robenson	Gye Cormell
william Rychardson	Tho Symcocke
Robert hancoke	Rog Callcote 15
Io ball	Io hatton iij s
yerreon Ryder	daue founder iij s
hughe Stoken ij s vj d	william Cradocke
meehoo Trafforte	widow hareson o
Robert hormeson	widow perceuall iij s 20
Io doo	harry Seston xx d
Ric smythe	Io smyth xx d
Ric Richardson	
Rondull Lawton	of 6 Iurneymen xvi d apeece
Tho Towres	all the rest aboue ij s viij d 25
all rest ij s viij d apeece	apeece

1567   the moneys layd downe for our play by william Richardson &
             Tho Towers Stewards

                                          30

             inter alij

             for our bill we put vp to mr mere for the pleys ij d
             to Newton for the banes j d for bred for our horses that day we
             Rod the banes xij d   35
             for gloues & drinke iiij d
             spent on mr chanter in mr pooles Tauarne iij d for prisoners in
             Castell iij d
             Spent at the heringe of the payers x d. at rehersinge vnder St
             Iohns xiiij d   40

7 / fomder *for* founder, *one minim omitted MS*

at rehearsinge before mr major ij s vj d
spent after the chosinge of the litle god x d to 2 of clarkes of
the menster viij d
spent on the sonday morninge at the hearinge of the Docters
& litle God 4d   5
for the steple & the Trestle or forme iij s viij d
for gettinge the Carriage out of the Axeltree viij d & settinge
in of the Carrige into the weuers howse viij d
for a whole chese ij s vj d a bushell of malt 4s 4d for a barrell
& quart of beare v s viij d 3 hoopes of wheate 4s 8d for gorse   10
Salt buter Safforn & a spyte x d
for gildinge Gods face xij d to x porters of the Carrage ij s viij d
to the stewards of the Iorneymen for wachinge the Carrage all
night viij d |
payd one for Carringe of the Regalls ij d. for mending the   15
Crowne & diadem x d
for 2 parcells ij d for mending 2 faxes viij d to mynstrells ij s
to the players Robert Rabon xvj d to the litle god xvj d to the 2
docter xij d to the 3 docter xij d to Ioseph xij d to dame Anne
xij d to the Angell viij d   20
to mr white 4s to mr chanter xij d to william Couper xij d for
gloues for the players iij s
for alle & Spent a Aldermans tauarne ij s for Skynnes for play
iij s to Hugh stocken ij s Rich brasse ij s

                                                                                                         25

A *Mayors List 11* BL: Add. 29779
   f 25* *(Whitsun) William Snead*

   ...

   In this yeare the whitson playes were played in this Cittye by   30
   the Cittizins of Chester ...

1567-8
Painters, Glaziers, Embroiderers, and Stationers' Records
C: Account Book I   35
f 38* *(18 October)*

                                                    °midsomer show whitson plays°

   ...

   Item payde oft the menstrell at my brodar wette Denner   viij d
   ...   40

---

37 / *heading in RH II's hand*

Item pade oute for the menstrells at welliam sheuenton wed͞ing
                                                         iiij d

...

Item a pone messomar nighte at ouare aldarmane	v s vj d
Item the same feste amesomar nighte in wyne	viij d
Item pede to the pressonars	ij d

...

Item pade to Rychard daeby and [the mynstrells] for mydsomer
nyght   viij d

Cordwainers and Shoemakers' Records
CCA: Account Book I G/8/2
f 52 *(11 November)*

...

Item payde the menstrell at thomas byrchenhedd*es* drynkynge
                                                       xij d

Item payde the same day to the menstrell at Robarte askers   vj d

...

Item payde at gutted for the gleves	iij s viij d
Item for oure drynkynge on gutted*es* monday	xviij s
Item payde the menstrell*es* that day	ij s
Item payde newton & the presonar*es* y*at* day y*at* whe rode ye banes	v d

...

Item payde the menstrell*es* on mydsomar even	ij s
Item payde the presonar*es* that nyghte	iiij d
Item spente on the brethren at the barr*es* that nyghte	vj d
Item payde for gonne powder	xvj d
Item payde for mare modeland*es* horsse & hyr Rydynge	xvj d
Item spente at oure alldermans that nyghte	iiij d
Item spente at the borroenge of mare modeland*es* Saddell	iiij d
Item spente at the stwarte symcock*es* that nyghte at the wacche	vj d

...

f 52v

...

Item payde the menstrell*es* on martens even   xij d

...

---

1 / t *written over* r *in* menstrells

A *Mayors List 5* BL: Harley 2125
f 39* *(November) Richard Dutton*

... mr mayor kepte a verye worthy howse, for all Comers dureinge
all the tyme of Christmas, with a lorde of misrule and other   5
pastymes in his cittye °as the witson plays°
...

Mayors' Books CCA: M/B/19
f 45v* *(30 April)*   10
...

Memorandum that the xxx^th daie of Aprell in Anno decimo
Elizabeth &c. mr Randall Trever gent*leman* was called before
the maior of the Citie of Chester and was demaunded for the
originall booke of the whydson plaies of the said Citie who   15
then and ther confessed that he have had the same booke w*h*ich
book he deposeth vpon the holy evangelist of god that by
comaundeme*n*t he deliu*er*ed the same booke againe but where
the same is now / or to whom he then deliu*er*ed the same book /
deposeth likwise he knoweth not. /   20

Mayors' Books CCA: M/B/19
ff 52-2v* *(5 June)*

                     v^to die Iunij 1568 /   25

Memorandum that whereas varyaunce *prese*ntly dependeth
betwene Iohn whitmore esquier vpon thon p*ar*tie And Anne
webst*er* wedow tenaunt to Georg Ireland esquier vpon thother
p*ar*tie for and concerning the claime right and title of A mansion   30
Rowme or place for the whydson plaies in the Brudg gatestrete
wit*h*in the Cyty of Chester w*h*ich varyaunce hath ben here wayed
and considered by Ric dutton esquier maior of the cyty of
chester & w*illia*m gerrard esquier Record*er* of the same cyty
by whom it is now ordered that forasmuche as the said m*is*tres   35
webster & other the tenu*n*tes of the said mr [m*is*tres] Ireland
have had their plac*es* and mansyons in the said place now in
varyaunce in quiet sort for ij [yeres] ^'tymes' past whan the said
plaies were plaied / That the said Anne webster in quiet sort for
this *prese*nte tyme of whydsontide during all the tyme of the   40

6 / °as ... plays° *in RH II's hand*

said plaies shall enioy and haue her mansyon place and the said
place & Rome now in varyaunce: Provided alwaies that the
having of the [said] possessyon of the said Rowme place or
mansyon shall not be hurtfull nor preiudice to nether of the said
parties in whom the right of the said premisses is or hereafter   5
shalbe found or proved to be: And also yt was | then further
ordered by the said maior that after the feast of pentecost next
coming at some convenient tyme an Indifferent enquest shalbe
charged and Sworne for the triall of the right of the said Rowme
or place now in varyaunce And that in case yt be found by such   10
enquest that the said mr whytmore hath better right to the
said premisses thann the said mr [tenuntes] Ioreland & his
tenuntes: yt is ordered that then the said mistres webster shall
content and pay vnto the said mr. whytmore so much money for
the said Rowme[s] and place as hath ben accostomed for this   15
one yere to be payed ₍ˆ₎ ˹heretofore˺ within the said cyty of
chester

(signed) Richard Dutton
william gerrard

20

Painters, Glaziers, Embroiderers, and Stationers' Records
C: Account Book I
ff 35-7v* *(Whitsun)*

for whytsone playes the yeare of oure   ˹whitson plays˺   25
lord God A thousant fyue hundreth
thrye score & eyght then mayre of the
Sytte of chester mr Rychard dutton   ˹[1568]/1567˺

furst payd for the Reste of A counte at oure firste metyng   ij d   30
Item payd to the sharemon for the dressyng of oure skynes   viij d
Item payd to Gryffe talyer for makyng of oure huddes   xij d
Item for oure horssees at the Rydynges of the banes xvj d [viij d]
Item to the prysoners   j d
Item to newton for Rydyng of the banees   j d   35
Item [for ij ⟨...⟩ of ⟨...⟩]   [⟨...⟩] d
Item spentt at Thomas Ionsons to speke with mr Chaunter for
shepertes boyes   ij d
Item payd for paper to coppye the orrygenall   ij d
Item payd at oure first Rehersse at oure Aldermans   xvj d   40

25 / ˹whitson plays˺ *in RH II's hand*   28 / ˹[1568]/1567˺ *in RH II's hand*

Item payd for the Rest of A counte at a meting A nenest
Ry*ch*ard garralt for the Rest of A shote   v d
Item spente at Ry*ch*ard halowod*es* A boute the hyryng of the
caryge   iiij d
Item spente at mr hankyes A bowte mr bryd   vj d   5
Item spente at master hankyes at A Rehersse the same daye v d |
Item spente at oure Aldermans the same daye   xij d
Item sppente at oure aldermans when we Re hersed bofore
mr mayre   ij s vj d
Item spent at oure Aldermans the furst tyme we mett in the   10
Come*n*hall   xx d
Item spent for boreyng of Coueryng & A naked chyld   ij d
Item payd for mogges   ij s vj d
Item payd to the beryg for payntyng of oure ox & asse & our
pye in the co*mm*on hall   iiij d   15
Item payd for A best*es* baly to dener   x d
Item payd for wosshyng puddyng*es*   j d ob.
Item payd for Coppyng of oure orygenall   xij d
Item spente at Iohan Cockes to borrow bottell*es*   ij d
Item payd for botter to the playe   viij d   20
Item for Chesse   v d
Item payd for nayles   iiij d
Item payd for A corde   ij d
Item for whystel*es*   j d
Item for pynnes   j d   25
Item for poynt*es*   j d
Item spente at Ry*ch*ard halewod*es* vpon wytson Sondaye in
drynke   iiij d
Item spente to sane daye vpon the shepert*es* Boyes   ij d
Item payd for brydd*es*   ij d | 30
Item payd for crabefysshes   ij d
Item for mendyng Trowes Cote   ij d
Item for Coppyng A p*ar*sell   iiij d
Item for potes of ale ˄ ˊat Ry*ch*ard halewod*es*ˋ when we dressed
oure playes & when we made oure capes & cot*es*   vj d   35
Item payd for bred to the playe   iiij d
Item payd for bere to them y*at* puted the Caryge   [iiij d] vj d
Item payd to viij putters of the caryge   ij s
Item payd to the mynstrell*es*   ij s iiij d
Item payd to Ioseff   x d   40
Item payd for mete for the asse   viij d
Item payd toward*es* the fecchyng of him   iiij d

Item payd for horsse brede to harvyes horse   iiij d
Item payd to Iohan howtton for A qarter of vele   xvi d
Item for a qarter of corsse vele   viij d
Item for a bestes bely & calues fette   viij d
Item for a Mydcalffe And Anox tonge   viij d   5
Item for a calues hed   iiij d
Item for a grone   iij d
[Item for A ⟨...⟩ of ⟨...⟩   vj d]
[Item to the mayde ⟨...⟩ for A ⟨...⟩ hed   iiij d]
Item for a Tuppes hed   ij d   10
Item for Ale at Iohan Cokes   iiij d
Item to oure ladyees wayges   viij d
Item to iiij sheperdes boyes   ij s viij d
Item for the hyre of oure Caryge   iiij s
Item for a payre of pumpes And Trowes shewes   xvj d | 15
Item to Rychard chalewoddes wyffe for xv[j] hagays   vij d
Item to her for bacon   vj d
Item to her for a calues hed   iiij d
Item to her for brede & ale ‸ ʹin the mornyngʼ to the puteres
& the mynstrelles And at oure supper   iiij s   20
Item for parbolyng of the garbyge   xvj d
Item [to iiij sheppertes boyes   ij s viij d]
Item for a quarter of A lambe to Iohn howton   x d
Item for v haggassys to Rammesdalees wyffe   ij s ij d
Item for a garnyshe for the lyttell chyld   ij d   25
Item for one pottell of bere at oure alldermans   ij d
Item payd to the mynstrelles vppon mydsomer euen   vj d
Item to the prysoners the same tyme   j d
Item to Rychard halewoddes wyffe for brede vppon mydsomer
euen   viiij d   30
Item to her for [⟨...⟩ the] drynke the same tyme   ij s viij d
Item for A pottell of whytt wyne   vj d
Item for samontt   ij s iiij d
Item to the eldest sheppertt   ij s
Item to the socond sheppertt   xx d   35
to the thryd sheppertt   xx d
Item to trow   ij s [ij d]
Item to trowes boye   vj d
Item to tow shepperttes for goyng vppon mydsomer euen   x d
Item to the tow sheppertes when the [sheppertes whytsone]   40
banes were Rydden   x d
Item to him that Rydeth the orrygynall   xij d

I*tem* to the angell   vj d

the sum ys iiij li ij s vj d ⌐

The hole some of the whytsone playes And all the Char*ges* of   5
oure occupacyon ‸ ⌐excepte quarteryg*es*⌐ from Saynt ludedaye
vntyll the vth of Iuly ys iiij li. ij s vj d wyche ys for euery
brother — v s vj d
whereof Thomas powle ys bated in his p*ar*te   iij d
I*tem* Mem*o*randum that Rych*ard* Calye ys indetted to the   10
occupacyon for whytsone playes   v s v d
I*tem* due to him for income brydren   ij s ix d
I*tem* he ys behind for Char*ges* vppon Sayst luke daye   iij d
...
                                                                    15
f 37v
         for oure expensys sencys the vth of Iuly when we
         Recond for wytsones playes *(blank)*
furst payd for the Rest of a shott at Thomas gylones the vth
of Iuly   ij d   20
...

Dean and Chapter CC; Treasurers' Accounts II
p 52* *(Whitsun)*
...   25
Item paid for a brode clothe againste the witson pleaes vj s viij d
Item for a barell of bere to yeue to the pleares to make them to
drincke   vj s
Item for packe threed at witson daye to hange vp the clothe   ij d
...   30

AC *Smiths, Cutlers, and Plumbers' Records*
    BL: Account Book I Harley 2054
    ff 18v-19* *(Whitsun)*
                                                                    35
another reseveste of the bretheren for the plays
Reseved of mr mounfort ij s ij d Called before mr founder
of oure allderman scrifnor 2s ij d
of mr knowlles   *willia*m Ionson
of Robe*r*t Coket <u>ante Crocket</u>   Io Andro   40

10 / M *of* Mem*o*randum *written over* Rec.   13 / Sayst *for* Saynt

Ro ledsame
Io brosho bradshaw ante
Ric newas
wm Richardson
Robert hankock
Io ball
herryen Ryder
hu Stoken
meo Traffort
x Robert ormson mort
Io doo
Rich smythe
Rich Robynson 0
Io honteton
Ron Laton
Tho Towers

hu masse
tomas holmes
Io kemp
Gye Cromell
tomas simkoke 5
Rog kalket
Io haton
dauid mounfort ante founder
wm Cradok
wido Robinson 10
wido persuow xij d
Io smythe
Tho haswall
Ed borlay
Rich ledsham 15
Rich Ionson

all ij s ij d apeece

1568   these byn the somes of monaye that ware lade doune by Ric 20
newhous & william Ionson about our playes thys yere which
is the ix yere of our Reyne

Anno domini 1568

 25

for our byll we put vp to mr meare ij d
for gloues & horsbred when we rid the banes xviij d,
Spent on the chanter & clarke of the mynster v d at our first
reherse at Alderman skruenors ij s 4d to prisoners in Castell 4d
giuen to mr mere to wards the makinge of a new booke xij d 30
at the hyerynge of the Menstrells & Consell of Simion iij d
Spent at Gilb flowers vpon mr wite & Sr Rondle barnes vij d
for 2 bosshell malt vij s 4d ob. for wheate ij s ij d ob., 2 ould
cheses ij s 8d
for beefe at our generall reherse viij s x d 35
for a pound of grey sope iij d
for boled mete for them that broght the new cheses xij d
for kakes at our generall reherse ij s spice vij d salt iij d viniger
3d for bourne 4d for bacon on tewsday moring for players
brekfast x d 40
for vele same tyme 14d chekens xvj d bred viij d
to griff Yeuans wife to pay for wessing the Curtens 4d

for neles pinns nedles cords ix d. to io men for portage of
Carrag ij s 6d
to the prentis when we gat in our Cariage to drink viij d
to the Right for gettinge the Carriag off & on viij d
to mr Rond barnes 3s 4d to mr wyte for singinge 4s   5
to mary 2s to Ioseph xij d to litle god xvj d |
for gylding Gods face on midsomer euen xij d
to newton & prisoners vj d
to the docters & litle god xij d to menstrells ij s
for gloues to litle god & docters ix d   10
spent at mr mounfforts iij s ij d
...

A   *Mayors List 8* BL: Harley 2133
    f 42v* *(Whitsun) Richard Dutton*   15
    ...

    This yeare the Whitson playes were plaid and Diuers other
    pastimes

A   *Mayors List 10* BL: Add. 29777   20
    item 242* *Richard Dutton*
    ...

    In this yeare the same Playes were playde & well set forthe, ...

1568-9   25
AC *Smiths, Cutlers, and Plumbers' Records*
    BL: Account Book I Harley 2054
    f 19 *(July)*
    ...

    on st Loys day to 2 mynstrells   viij d   30
    ...

    Treasurers' Account Rolls CCA: TAR/1/13
    mb 3 *(November)*
    ...   35
                        The Watergate Strett
    ...

    The Steuartes of ye Drapers for a carage howse bylt on the
    cittiz ground of yerely rent   viij d
    ...   40
    Item for the mercers carage howse of yerly rent   vj d
    ...

mb 4

...

Itam paid the mores dansares at mydsomer	vj s viij d
Itam paid the mynstrells which plaid before them	xvj d

...

Cordwainers and Shoemakers' Records
CCA: Account Book I G/8/2
f 54 *(11 November)*

...

Item payde for the gleves at gutted	iij s viij d

...

Item payde for settynge forthe of mare modelante	xvj d
Item geven vnto the presenores at the castell	iiij d
Item geven vnto the menstrelles on mydsomer even	[xi] ij s
Item spente at oure alldermans that nyghte	vj d

...

f 54v

Item a pottell of secke at Rychard wyllsons denne	x d
Item geven the menstrelles the same day	ij s

...

Item payde the menstrell at alexander wylldyges denner	viij d

...

Item geven the menstrelles yat nyghte	xvj d

...

Coopers' Records C: Account Book I
f 1* *(20 November)*

...

Item for the hyre of too copes & men to were them & pennes and for the wrytyngs & for drenke whan ye were in dreseng & vndreseng on medsomer euen	ii s iiij d
more spend on ye company in thomas lenekers the same nyght	xvi d
Item spend in the wedo thropes on the company ix d	
Item payde to master mare for on halfe yere for the hauen	viii s
more spend in Iohn stynsons on ye company	xiii d
Item to the presoners on medsomer euen	ii d

...

1569-70

AC *Smiths, Cutlers, and Plumbers' Records*
BL: Account Book I Harley 2054
f 19 *(July)*

...   5

for horsmete to the horses at midsomer   iij s
to the docters and some of the Company iiij d minstrells ij s
to the 2 dougters & litle god & j d *Sir* Rob*ert* Spent   xiij d
to prisoners at Castell   ij d
for gildinge of gods face   xij d   10

...

to weuers for rent of Carrage howse   iiij s

Painters, Glaziers, Embroiderers, and Stationers' Records
C: Account Book I   15
f 41 *(18 October)*

                        ᵒmidsomer show no whitson play ᵒ

...

It*em* to Thomas newton   i d
It*em* to our mynstrell   ij d   20
It*em* to A nother mynstrell   vj d
It*em* to the prysoners   ij d
It*em* to oure Aldermans wyffe for oure Charges vppon mydsomer
euen   vj s
It*em* for the ᴧ ⌜iij⌝ shepp*eretes* way*ges*   xviij d 25
It*em* for a payre of gloues to the angell   ij d

...

Cordwainers and Shoemakers' Records
CCA: Account Book I G/8/2   30
ff 56v-7 *(11 November)*

...

It*em* payde for the gleves at gutted   iij s iiij d
It*em* spente at the Resevynge of the gleves   ij d

...   35

It*em* payde for settynge forthe of mary modeland   xviij d
It*em* spente on mydsomar even at oure alldermans   xv d
It*em* geven the presonar*es* that nyghte   iiij d
It*em* payde for bere that nyghte at symcock*es*   ij d |
It*em* payde newton the same nyghte   j d   40

17 / ᵒmidsomer ... play ᵒ *in RH II's hand*

Item payd the menstrel*les* the same nyghte   ij s   vj d
Item payd mayster whytte for oure song*es*   iiij d

...

Item payde for vyne & the menstrel*les* at wyllyam burgaynes
dennar   iij s   vj d   5
Item payde for vyne & the menstrel*es* at Iohn poop*es* dennar   ij s

...

Item payde the menstrel*les* on martens even   ij s   viij d

...

   10

Coopers' Records   C: Account Book I
f 1v* *(20 November)*

...

Item payde to wyllyan rogerson for the lone of to copes   iiii d
more payde to them that caryed them and for drenke whan the   15
were in dressenge and oon dressenge   xx d
more spend on the companye at nyght whan the from the wache
in Iohn stynsones   ii s   vi d
more to the preseneres   ii d
Item spend on the companye in Iohn stynsones ye xii of Iuly   xii d   20

...

A C   *Trinity Churchwardens' Accounts*   BL: Harley 2177
f 28v* *(26 March)*

...   25

sould to Thomas sheuyntons sonne the belman & Tho Dychers
sonne 3 Course vestments & a course Stremer to make players
garments   viij s

...

   30

1570-1
A C   *Smiths, Cutlers, and Plumbers' Records*
BL: Account Book I Harley 2054
f 19v *(July)*

...   35

           Myddesomer Euiene

for our syne xvj d. for things that went to dresse our child vij d
to cryor j d prisoners iiij d mymstrells ij s   ij d   charges of our
harneys xviij d   40

14 / wyllyan *for* wyllyam, *minim omitted MS*
39 / mymstrells *for* mynstrells, *extra minim MS*

other expences at Ald*erman* Scryuenors mr Mountforts & Tho
Towers   *(blank)*

...

Painters, Glaziers, Embroiderers, and Stationers' Records
C: Account Book I
f 45 *(18 October)*

...

                                        ᵒmidsomer show no whitson plays ᵒ

                                                                                                    10

furst payd to the mynstrell*es* vppon Saynte luk*es* daye at oure
aldermans   xij d

...

It*em* for towe men goyng on the stylt*es*   xij d
It*em* [⟨...⟩] ´spent`ₐ at Robert halewood*es* vppon mydsomer   15
euen   j d
It*em* spente goyng to the barrs vppon the same tyme   iij d
It*em* geuen to the prysoners the same tyme   ij d
It*em* spente vppon mydsomer euen in gudchere   iiij s
Item payd to the mynstrells the same tyme   xvj d   20

...

Coopers' Records C: Account Book I
f 2v* *(20 November)*

...   25

more payd to the menstreles and to the presoners at medsomer
                                                                                          vj d
It*em* spend on the companye on medsomer ewen in thomas
lenekers   xv d
more spend on the companye in the wedo thropes   vj d   30

...

1571-2
AC *Smiths, Cutlers, and Plumbers' Records*
BL: Account Book I Harley 2054   35
f 19v *(July)*

...

® about 1571   ffor the Banes
for dressinge our huddes xiiij d for gloues same day x d
to the Cryor j d for horsbred same day xij d   40

9 / ᵒmidsomer ... plays ᵒ *in RH II's hand*

Spent at our Ald*ermans* same day xiiij d at May kynnes ij d
when I went to borrowe a [toule] touyle iij d
for the playes
layd downe about seekinge our players xvj d
for p*arch*ment to make a new orriginall booke 3s 6d   5
for beefe for our gen*rall* rehearse 7s 8d. 2 cheeses 3s. 6 Cart
clouts & nayles vij d
for nayles to nayle the bords of the Carrage 4d for 2 stays for
Carrage ij d
for Tallow for wheles ij d pinns for the Axtrees ij d   10
hoope wheat ij s. bred same day 10d
at first reherse 22d. at second rehearse ij s ij d
when we went to mr Maiors about the plays vij d
for Ale to our genrall rehearse x s. beare ix d for spices for the
meates 4d   15
to the waytes & our musysyens xij d to mynstrells vj d
for dressinge the fane & diadem xviij d
for ynckill pynns & nayles to our Carriage
for a rybben for our scotchen iij d. for gloues iij s ij d
for dressinge our Carriage & after our play spent at our   20
Ald*ermans* ij s 4d
to the minstrells for our pagent 3s 4d. for sope to wash
clothes x d
for small beare in bridgstreet iiij d

The names of
the Players. Symion. Dame Anne. 2 Angells xij d Ioseph. Mary xviij d   25
Deus xvj d primus docter xvj d 2 docter 3 docter
for the clergy for the songes 4s 2d for breckfast on Twesday
morning 8s gildinge of litle gods face viij d, porters for Carriage
xviij d to the clarke for lone of a Cope an Altercloth & Tunecle
x d. for redinge the orrignall book ij d to the skynners iij s for   30
bringinge of the Carriag home & Spent on mynstrells & porters 4d

Painters, Glaziers, Embroiderers, and Stationers' Records
C: Account Book I
ff 47-8* *(18 October)*   35

® •Whitson plays
went this yeare
1572 and
mesomer show
also p*er* accounts• for Whissone playes the yeare of our Lorde god
a thowssande fywe hunderthe seuente and ii
The mayre of the sytte of Chestar
Mastar Ihon hankye   40

37 / *marginalia in RH II's hand*

Item for our horssces at the Rydyng of the banes   xvi d
Item for papare   i d
Item for ryddyng the banes   i d
Item for the reste of a shoute at the fyrste rehersce   vi d
Item spende on the iiij syngarse at rondylle ynces   ij d   5
Item for xiiij yerthen moges   iij s
Item spende at Tomas Lyncarsse for the baryage of the cariage
      vi d
Item pede to doosse wyfe to yarneste the hagoosscys   xij d
Item spentte in Wyllam dones   iiij d   10
Item spette in Tomas Lynecars   i d
Item spentte in Rychart twyssces spekynge for the asse   i d
Item before the generall reherce in Robart halewodes   vi d
Item lede done goinge to loke for skynnes   ij d
Item lede done at the generaulle rehersce denar   vj s   15
Item payde to Rogare Colarke for ij yarne stabylles   iij d
Item payde for iiij wyestlles   ij d
Item payde at the hyrynge of the caryages   i d
Item payde for ij chessces   v d
Item for a gambone a bacone & iiij fytte   vi d   20
Item for ij gannokes from Waryntone   ij d
Item spente goynge to borow bogyttes   ij d
Item for a besstes tonge & iiij colfes fytte   viij d
Item for bouttare   viij d |
Item for a houlle   iiij d   25
Item payde to doosses wyffe for lethes & leuarse   xij d
Item payde 'for' gettyng wedes   ij d
Item spend at gettynge cattes an bottylse   iiij d
Item payde for a topes yede   iij d
Item for nelles corde pynes pynttes & paketryde   ix d   30
Item for the as lede doune   xij d
Item for pentynge the houke & ass the styltes and the stare   xij d
Item for crabes   i d
Item for a lawne a velle   vi d
Item for a tryne platar   iij d   35
Item to viij pottarres of the caryages   ij s x d
Item to petar a moston for troues shone makyng & for hys
penes an labore   xvi d
Item for bayre that Rochart doby hade   i d
Item for payntes to bone the pleares   ij d   40
Item payde to the mynstryles   ij s
Item for ij wystyles for trowe   ij d

Item for the brekefast to the plears & pottares of the caryags

            v s viij d

Item for brede & bear to the plle   x d

Item to master brearwood for hortyng of skyngnes   vi d

Item payde to Robart radeborne   xij d | 5

Item payde to dosse wyfe for hagocyes   vi s viij d

Item payd to the sheppertes Boyees   iiij s

Item to Roger Calcotte for a Ierne to the caryge   ij d

Item a skynne to trowes shewes   vj d

Item to trowes boye   vj d   10

Item to our lady   vj d

Item to Iohan casker for a lord   iij d

Item a pott of beare   j d

Item payd for the caryge   v s iiij d

Item for harvyes wages   xx d   15

Item for tuddes wages   xx d

Item for Trowes wages   ij s

Item for the wages of the [⟨...⟩] ˹angell˺   [⟨...⟩ d] vj d

Item for Rydyng the orygenall   xij d

Item for drynke to the players   iiij d   20

Item for a payer of lether garteres   vj d

Item for a shype hoke   vj d

Item for goyng vppon the styltes at Rydyng the banes   vj d

Item for a nother payer of Sewes for trowe   xvj d

[9 li iij s ⟨.⟩ d]   25

              3 li - 3s - 2d

...

f 48v*

      More layd out by the stewertes for the   30

      charges of the whole yeare 1572 ...

...

Item for Ale in wyllyams fronwayes on mydsamer euyn before

the wache wentte   iiij d

Item to the prysoners   ij d   35

Item for our mynstrelles   xij d

Item for the Rest of A shott at Robert waytes   iij d

...

Item to the waytemen   iiij d

...   40

6 / y of wyfe *written over* e

Treasurers' Account Rolls CCA: TAR/1/14
mb 3 *(November)*

...

The Stuardes of the drapers for acarage housse byld opn the
cittes Landes of rent for the same   vi ⟨.⟩   5

...

Item the mercers carege howse yearly rent   vj d

...

mb 5   10
Item payd the moris dancers at mydsomar   vi ⟨.⟩

...

mb 6

...   15

Payd for vj yardes quarter of cloth for the wetmen [iii] at vij s
v d a yard   xlvj s iiij d ob

...

Cordwainers and Shoemakers' Records   20
CCA: Account Book I G/8/2
f 60 *(11 November)*

...

Item payde vnto the menstreles at Rawffe hylltons drynkynge
                                                                    xij d   25
Item payd the menstrelles at wyllyam fletcheres drynkynge xvj d

...

Item geven vnto the menstrelles at Rychard Pammertons
drynkinge   xx d
...   30
Item geven the menstrelles in Iohn Dalaheys   ij d
Item payde for the geves   iij s iiij d
Item spente on the golldsmythe   ij d
Item spente on oure brethren at Rondoll hynces   xvj d
Item geven the weattemen the same day   iiij d   35

...

ff 60v-1
Item spente on the [myd] mynstrelles on mydsomer even   v d
Item geven to the presoneres & thomas loker   vj d   40
Item payde the menstrell the same nyghte   ij s vj d

...

Item geven the menstreles at Rawffe hylltons [drynkynge]
denner   v s viij d
Item geven the menstreles at wyllyam fletcheres denner   xx d
...
Item geven vnto the menstrelles at Rychard pemmertons denner   5
                                                     xvij d |
Item geven the menstrelles on martens even   iij s iiij d
...

Coopers' Records C: Account Book I   10
ff 3-3v* *(20 November)*
...
Reseuyd of the paynters and of the skyners for the caryge
                                                    x s iiii d
...   15
                    lede done of expenses

In primis the herryng of the playeres and leuerynge of persells
to the holle ys   ix d
Item spend of the Ryddyng of the banes & other thynges   xii d   20
Item spend at the forst Reherse & ye delyueryng of oure gerre
to ye payntter   x d
Item coste the brekynge of the caryge the bernggyn yt up to ye
stuerdes doure   xviii d
Item too selles to the caryge the pryse   ii s viii d   25
more payde to Iohn croulay for the makyng of ye caryge and
nayles   iiii s
Item for ye carynge ye welles to the water and frome & ye
berygh of ye caryge   vii d
more spende whan ye payntars came to garne ye bereghe and at   30
the seconde Reherse in the stuardes lenekers   ix d
Item for ieren & byndyng of a welle & one stable one neue
welle and the dresyng of one howlde welle the wyche commes
to   v s i d
more spende in gresenge of the caryghe ʿwellesʾ & grese to yt the   35
ladar & the settyng vp of yt one the welles   xiiii d
more for frettes & for axeltre penes   viii d
Item spende at the brengeng vp ʿof ytʾ to ye menster gatte for
cordes & penes to sette vp the howsynge of the caryghe   ii s
more spend at dener one the company & one players and at   40
nyght whan the vndressed them and all the daye   vii s iiii d |
payde for the carynge of pylates clothes   vi d

payde to wyllyam Rogerson for ʿaʿ cope & a tenekell   vi d
payde to wyllyam trolloke by ye consant of ye company   vii d
payde to vii men putters of the caryghe   ii s iiii d
payde to hugh gyllam   vi s vii d
payde to Thomas marser   ii s iii d
payde to Iohn stynson   ii s iii d
payde to Rychard kalle   xvi d
payde to hugh sparke for ryedyng of the Ryegenalle   ii s
Item payde to Iohn proulay for the brekyng of ye caryghe   vii d

the some ys in all yat the playes lyes in xlix s x d

more payde to Iohn Ioanson for laynge the caryghe in hys seller   1●

    xviii d

more spend at ye takyng done of yt & ye laynge in of yt   vii d
Item payde for the payntyng of oure gere   iii s viii d
Item spend one sante edmondes daye on the companye   iii s x d

...   1●

more payde ʿforʿ the armes one medsomer euen   xii d
Item a perre of gloues to the chylde yat caryede the armes &
a quarte of wyne to hys mother and for the makynge of hys
cloke   xi d
more to wyllyam Rychyrson and to the presoners   iii d   2●
more to Rondul thrope for the bryngyge upe of the horse   i d
spende in Iohn stynson one medsomereuen   xxii d
more spende at ye Reseuynge of the paynters & skyners mone

    vi d

...   2●

Dean and Chapter CC: Treasurers' Accounts II
p 120 *(Whitsun)*
...
Item for ₍ʿye hyreʿ of a clothe for ye mansyon ouer ye gates   vj s   3●
Item for cordes   xvj d
Item for a barrell of byre to ye players   viij s
...

A   *Mayors List 1* BL: Harley 1046   3●
f 163v *(Whitsun) John Hankey*
...
This yeare the Maior would needs haue the playes (commonly
called Chester playes) to goe forward, againste ye willes of ye

---

2 / *first* l *of* trolloke *written over* u   2 / v *written over* ii *in* vii d
4 / v *written over* ii *in* vii d

Bishops of Canterbury Yorke & Chester

...

A *Mayors List 5* BL: Harley 2125
f 39v *John Hankey*   5

The Whitson playes were played this yeare / °to the dislike of many°

...
                                                                        10

A *Mayors List 8* BL: Harley 2133
f 43* *John Hankey*

...

This yeare whitson playes were plaied, And an Inhibition was
sent from the Archbishop to stay them but it Came too late.   15

...

A *Mayors List 10* BL: Add. 29777
item 246* *John Hankey*

...   20

In this yeare the whole Playes were playde thoughe manye of
the Cittie were sore against the settinge forthe therof

...

                                                                        25

1572-3
A C *Smiths, Cutlers, and Plumbers' Records*
BL: Account Book I Harley 2054
f 20 (*July*)

...   30

to the waytemen at our Aldermans howse   vj d

...

giuen on that brought vs gere for the child that ridd on midsomer
euen   vj d
for our signe   ij s 4d   35
other ordnary expences as at other tymes   (*blank*)

...

7-8 / °to ... many° *in RH II's hand*

Painters, Glaziers, Embroiderers, and Stationers' Records
C: Account Book I
f 51 *(18 October)*

°midsomer show only no whison plays°

...   5

•1573• payd for ij pot*tes* of Ale att Thomas barkers vppon mydssomer
euen   ij d
It*em* to wyllyam Ryc*hard*son at the barres   j d
It*em* to the prysoners at the castell   ij d
It*em* to the prysoners at the northgate   j d   10
It*em* to the mynstrell*es*   xij d
It*em* sspente at our Aldermans   xviij d
It*em* ffor horssebread to the horsse that the boye Rode vppon ij d
It*em* payd to Ryc*hard* dobe for going vppon the stylte*es*   vj d

...   15

It*em* to Edward dobe for goyng vppon the styltes at mydsomer
[ij d]

...

Cordwainers and Shoemakers' Records   20
CCA: Account Book I G/8/2
f 63 *(11 November)*

...

Item spente on thursse day after gutted*es* day in Rondull hynces
over the shotte   iiij s j d   25
Item payde for a quarte of meathe to m*aster* Recorder the same
day   iij d
Item geven the weete men the same day   xij d
Item payde for the gleves   iij s iiij d
Item spente on the goldesmythe yt made the gleves   iiij d 30
Item geven the stewart*es* of the Iornemen for there attendance
vj d

...

Item spente at Iohn dalaheys howsse that day that wee pwynted
oure bannar shullde bee   iij d 35
Item payde for makynge of oure banner   ij s viij d
Item payde the menstrel*es* on mydsomer even   iij s iiij d
Item payde the same nyghte for a quarte of whyte wyne   iiij d
Item geven hym that Rode & carreed the bannar a payre of

---

4 / °midsomer ... plays° *in RH II's hand*   6 / *marginalia in RH II's hand*
34 / pwynted: *sic MS*

gloves & a payre of pompes   xij d

Item to wyllyam Rycharson at the barres   j d

...

f 63v   5

...

Item geven the presoner*es* on mydsomer even   iiij d

...

Item geven the mynstrell*es* on martens even   xx d

...   10

Coopers' Records C: Account Book I

f 4v* *(20 November)*

...

It*em* payde ffor the armes and arsedo*n* the bereghe to the   15

makynge off yt   iiij s vj d

...

more gaue ij peneworthe off horsebred to mr ffransus one

medsomer euen   ij d

It*em* spende one medso*m*mer ewen one the companye in Iohn   20

stynson   iiij s

more in sake   xij d

It*em* a payre off gloues to the chylde that caryed the armes and

a bowe   vj d

more ffor the staffe off the armes   iiij d 25

...

It*em* spende on the menstrelles at Iohn Ioanson maryge   iiij d

...

It*em* spende one the company in Rychard layes dener ffor

seke   vj d 30

more to the wettmen   vj d

It*em* payde to the presoneres in the castyll and in the norgatt

                                                        iiij d

...   35

1573-4

AC *Smiths, Cutlers, and Plumbers' Records*

    BL: Account Book I Harley 2054

    f 20 *(July)*

    ...   40

for mynstrells at Ann Stokens wedinge   iiij d

... to mynstrells on St Loyes day xij d

...

Midsomer euen

for a payre of hosse for him that ridd viij d makinge his apparell
viij d
for gloues 3d horsebred for the horse iiij d to Cryor at barrs j d
to prisoners at castell & norgate viij d
spent at mr mounforts ij s viij d at Alderman Stokens ij d
for Arsedyne & dressinge of our signe vj d to mynstrells xvj d
for goinge to hooton & poole to fach gere for the child 4d
...

Painters, Glaziers, Embroiderers, and Stationers' Records
C: Account Book I
f 53 *(18 October)*
...

Item spent at the dressyng [A] of the chyld vppon mydsomer
euen   ij d
Item to wyllyam Rychardson at the barres   j d
Item to the prysoners at the castell   ij d
Item to the prysoners at the northgate   ij d
Item to the mynstrelles   xij d
Item for our banket at our Aldermans housse   iiij s iiij d
...

f 55*
...

for the pley euerye man hathe payde that is croste   iij s iij d
...

f 56*
...

ytem for thomas poolles child bycose he plednot our god   iiij d
...

Cordwainers and Shoemakers' Records
CCA: Account Book I G/8/2
f 64 *(11 November)*
...

Item payde for the gleves at gutted   iij s iiij d
Item payde the mynstrelles in oure stewarte Inces on thursday
aftr gutted   viij d

Item payde the ˹stewart*es* of˺ Iornemen for there paynes the
iij days   iiij d
Item payde the same day in oure stewarte Inc*es*   xvj d
...
Item payde the mynstrell*es* on mydsomer even   ij s vj d   5
Item spente on the menstrell*es* in dave dymcock*es*   ij d
Item payde the crier at the barres   j d
Item geven the presoner*es* on mydsomer even   iiij d
Item spente in oure alldderman cook*es* howsse before the wacche
                                                                  vj d   10
Item payde the chylde that Rode for hys paynes   xij d
Item payde for a payre of gloves for hym   j d
Item geven hys fote man for ledynge hys horsse   iiij d
Item geven the presoner*es* in the northegate on mydsomer
even   ij d   15
Item payde for horsse bredd   iiij d
...

f 64v
...   20
Item payde the menstrell*es* on martens even   xvj d
...

1574-5
Assembly Books CCA: AB/1   25
f 151 *(20 July)* *(Watergate Street)*
...
The Caryadg howse for the Mercers now conu*er*ted to A Stable
w*hich* was graunted to mr moris williamz and now the steward*es*
hath it the yerely Rent   vj d   30
The steward*es* of the drap*er*s for their caryadg howse in rerag*es*
for viij yeres Rent / of the yerely Rent of   viij d
...

                                                                           35
AC *Tailors' Carriage House* BL: Harley 2172
    p 17* *(10 August)*

16 QE   Rich Dutton maior etc grant in fee farme to Rob*er*t hill Tayler
⊛ wolfegate   the whole buldinge or howse called the Taylers Carriage howse   40
⊛ ffleshmonger lyinge on the south p*art* to alane called ffleshmonger lane nere
lane the Taylors to the land called wolfes gate or new gate now in tenure of the
Carriage howse

fee farme

ij s vj d

Aldermen & stewards cetus sutar*um* vestiar*um* infra d*i*ct*am*
Ciuitat*um*, contayinge in length v yards in bredth 3 yards &
halph paying ij s vj d at 2 feasts St mih & ladyday prouiso as
before dated 10 Aug 16 Q Elz
    The Thropp sergant a*n*d claues attorney to deliuer possesion

in latyn   Red lib*er* 8

A C   *Drapers' Carriage House* B L : Harley 2172
           p 17* *(15 October)*

in latyn

® Watergatstret
fee farme
®Croftes

® grafrer wall

xij d rent

Rich Dutton maior etc grant in fee farme to Edward Martyn
drap*er* that whole wast place of land lyinge [by] ˄ ⸢in⸣ the watergate
⸢strete⸣ betwene that place on the south & a lane leding from
that place to the Croftes vpon the Est & a certayn stone wall
called Grayfreere wall w*hi*ch place adioyneth to that wall &
vnder the wall comonly called the drap*ers* Carriage howse
contaying in length xj yards in bredth 5 yards paying yearly
xij d at lady day & mich p*ro*uiso as aboue in barrow dated
15 october 16 Q Elz
…
                              lib*er* Ruber 24

Treasurers' Account Rolls C C A : T A R / 1 / 15
mb 6 *(November) (Watergate Street)*
…
nich*o*lus white pro dom*o* p*ro*xim*o* adiacen*te* cuid*am* dom*ui*
voc*ate* drap*ers* carighouse   iij s iiij d
…
Senescal*lis* del m*er*cers pro dom*o* Cariag   vj d
…

mb 7
Iohanni Allen vni ex*tra* vicinet*um* ad soluend*am* tunic*am* Thome
bennet paver et pro lez waitmes gownes   vij li. x s vij d
Senescallis del sadlers pro feod*o* suo   vj s viij d
…

2 / Ciuitatum: *sic MS*   3 / 2 *altered from* 4
32 / Cariag *for* Cariagii

Cordwainers and Shoemakers' Records
CCA: Account Book I G/8/2
f 66 *(11 November)*

...

Item payde the mynstrell*es* on martens day   xx d   5

...

Item geven the menstrell*es* at willyam Kerk*es* drynkynge   vj d
Item payde for the gleves   iij s vj d
Item payde for Ryngynge curfer   ij s
Item for berreiche of the gleves   ij d   10

...

Item geven the menstrell*es* on throfte thurseday   viij d
Item spente the same day over the shotte   viij d
Item geven the [menstrell*es*] stewart*es* of the Iornemen for there
paynes thosse days   viij d   15

...

f 66v

Item geven the menstrell*es* on mydsomer even   ij s vj d   20
Item payde the presoner*es* in the northegate & the castell   viij d
Ite*m* payde the crier   j d
Item spente on the menstrell*es*   j d
Item for the horsse & aReeyenge hym that Rode on mydsomer
even   xviij d   25
Item payde for payntynge the banner   xvj d
Item payde hys fote man   iiij d

...

(St Martin's Eve)
Ite*m* payde the mynstrel*es* the same nyghte   ij s iiij d   30

...

Assembly Files CCA: A/F/3
f 25* *(30 May)*   35

assembly in the common hall   • xxx^v die maij 1575

...

whether the accostomed
plaes called the whitson   40
plaes shalbe sett furth &
plaied at mide*summer* next or not

meet to be plaid °and to begyn°   not meet
monday °´sonday`° after mid*summer* day next °1575°

0 0 0 0	0 0 0
0 0 0 0 0	0 0 0
0 0 0 0	0 0 0
0 0 0 0	0 0 0
0 0 0 0	12
0 0 0 0	
0 0 0 0	
0 0 0 0	
0	
33	

agreid they shall be sett furth
in the best fayssion with such   1!
reformac*ion* as mr maior with
his advice shall think meet &
convenient

20

Assembly Books CCA: AB/1
f 159v* *(30 May)*

...

Ad congregac*ion*em tent*am* in [interior pentice] ´*Commun*i Aula
p*l*ac*itorum*` *Ciui*t*atis Cestrie* [ib*idem* tent*am*] xxx*m*o die May   25
Anno *Regni Regi*ne Elizab*eth* &c. xvij*m*o

⟨.⟩greed vpon that   At whiche assembly yt was ordered Concluded and Agreed vpon
the plaies Called   by the said Maior aldermen Sheriff*es* and Comon Counsaile of
whitson ⟨.⟩laies   the said Citie That the plaies Comonly Called the whitson plaies   30
at mid*summer*   At Midsom*er* next Comynge shalbe sett furth and plaied in such
next ⟨.⟩halbe set   orderly man*er* and sorte as the same haue ben Accostomed with
furth and plaied   such correction and amendem*ent* as shalbe thaught Convenient
by the said Maior And all Charg*es* of the said plaies to be
supported and borne by thinhabitant*es* of the said Citie as haue   35
ben heretofore vsed.

...

1 / °and ... begyn° *probably correction by the same scribe*
2 / °´sonday`° *probably correction by the same scribe*
24 / interior *for* interiore

AC   *Order for the Whitsun Plays* BL: Harley 1989
f 26* *(30 May)*

30 may in Com*mon* hall xvij QE

                                             5

whitsun playes   that wheras the whitsone plays had byn forborne that at
midsomer next the should be playd & set forth in such order &
sort as they haue byn acustomd with such corection & amendment
as shall be thought Conueniet by the maior & the Charges of the
sayd plays to be suported [to be suported] by the Inhabitants   10
of the Citty as hertofore hath byn vsed
...

AC   *Smiths, Cutlers, and Plumbers' Records*
BL: Account Book I Harley 2054   15
ff 20v-1 *(Midsummer)*

    ...
spent on the players & other things necessisary xij s
Spent at Tyes to heare 2 plays before the Aldermen to take the
best xviij d   20
for drink at our generall reherse v s
led out att medsamar yeuan to the presnars ij d in northgate
for thryd to sowe the bowes ger that went afore hus att
mydsamar ij d
for horsse bred for the nag he red apon 4d   25
our bangket when we Cam ffrome the wache vj s
for tallow for the Carrage iij d
to the menstreleles at our generall rehers and midsamar and
with our pagan v s
to litle god 20d to oure marye xviij d to our 2 docter xvj d   30
for Sop to wache our gere we borrowed viij d. for penes &
nayles xij d
for bere at mr burgeses viij d
for 9 men to Carry our Carryche & one tressell & 2 that did help
me in the mornnge 3s 9d ob.   35
for making the bewes gowne 4d for knetting of our bewes house
tat Rid before vs at Midsamar viij d
for the banes & dring at the barrs xij d at medsamar yuen to
presnars 4d
for the syne & ffaxe xij d   40
for the copes & clotthe xij d |
to 3 of the synngares xiiij d spent at Io dowes xvj d

at the banes for glowffes & to the plears & Aldermen at bringinge
of our pagen forth 3s 2d
on of the syngares had for his panes & gloffes xvj d
to Io a shawe for lone of a docters gowne & a hode for our
eldest docter xij d   5
payd for our ffirst angell vj d
for dryngke at dressinge our Carrge vj d
to Seameon iij s. to our frest doctor xvj d to our tret doctor
xij d to our dame An x d
to gossep xvj d to secon angell vj d   10
to the skenars iij s

...

Painters, Glaziers, Embroiderers, and Stationers' Records
C: Account Book I   15
ff 59-60* *(Midsummer)*

ffor whytson playes in the yere of oure lorde god . 1575 . and in
the same yere soure Iohn sauyche mayre of this syte of chester /

    °22   20
    1575
    1597/°

Item for bred to oure horses when wye rede the banes   viij d
Item to rycharson at the banes rydeng   j d   25
Item to the presnars at the castell   j d
Item to the berynge of the caryge   v d
Item I layde downne at the Reherse by sovre mr mayre   xij d
Item for bere to the pleares at the same reherse   j d
Item ffor ij got skynes ffor trow shous   [iiij d] iij d   30
Item for xij erthen moges   xxj d
Item for the hayare of the ij bardes and trowes cape   vj d
Item for wystelles   ij d
Item layde down [at my] at my alderman halwods for the reste
of the shot one medsomers ˹eue˺   xvj d   35
Item to the menstrelles   xij d
Item to the presnares in the castell   ij d
[castell] to the presnares in the northe gate   j d
Item for snyges   j d
Item for the brebynge of the botell   ij d   40
Item in neles pynes *and* pakethryde   vj d

34 / one ... ˹eue˺ *interlined in MS*

Item payd to anderasone	iiij d	
Item for [⟨.⟩] pouder for the sengers	vj d ∣	
Item for the leg[e] loyne and tonnge of velle	xv d	
Item for the topas hed and the groyne	ij d	
Item for the caules fyte	j d	5
Item for the boylange and dressynge the garbyche	xij d	
Item for vj hagosses	iiij s vj d	
Item for ij chysses	iiij d	
Item for the copynge of a parsell	iiij d	
Item for vij poutters of the caryche	ij s iiij d	10
Item for peter of mosten for makynge of troules shoues and		
hys paynes	xij d	
Item iij shepardes boyes	iij s	
Item for troulles boye	vj d	
Item to Iosefe	xij d	15
Item to marye	vj d	
Item to ouer angell	vj d	
Item for a Ianokes	ij d	
Item for cakes	iiij d	
Item for bouter	vj d	20
Item for drynke to the ples	x d	
Item to rychard dobye for goynge one the styltes at the banes		
rydenge	vj d	
Item ffor goynge one the styltes one medsomare eue	vj d	
Item for the mynstrell to the plase	ij s	25
Item in borowenge tangkeres bages	ij d	
Item for wedes	ij d	
Item for the souper to the pleares	v s	
Item [f] bystoued one drynke to the pouters when the playe		
was donne	vj d ∣	30
Item for troulles wages and hys shoues	iij s	
Item payde for the caryge	vj s iiij d	
Item spend at the same tyme	iij d	
Item for hankyns wages	ij s	
Item for harvyes wages	xx d	35
Item for toudes wages	xx d	
Item for the rydenge [of the] of the regenall	xij d	
Item that the pleares at my aldermanes house	ij d	
Item to my alder man halwod for the makynge the bohye and		
pentenge the styltes	[viij d] x d	40

39 / bohye for boy (?), or a mistranscription of balye as in next item? The o is closer
to an r than an o in this scribe's hand

Item for a paste balye   viij d

      the some is lj s xj d

Roger framwall is vn paid this yere 1575
Item for the pleayse   iij s iij d
...

Coopers' Records C: Account Book I
f 7* *(Midsummer)*

Item Receaved of the stuardes of the paynters for our cariadge
                                                          v s iiij d
Item Receaved of the stuardes of the hatmakers & skyners vj s 8d
...

ff 7v-8*

...

Item spent in our aldermans at the rydinge of the banes	xij d
Item spend in horsbred	vj d
Item paied for wryttinge the parceles	vj d
Item paied for ij peare of gloves	vj d
Item spend apon Thomas marser to get him to pleay	ij d
Item geven William Rycharson	j d
Item spent at the receavinge custome	iij d
Item spent at the fyrste rehearse	vj d
Item spend at the secunde rehearse	xij d
Item spend at the thred rehearse	xij d
Item paied for a peare of whelles	iiij s
Item geven the presonars when we rode the banes	ij d
Item paied for nealis to the cariadge	xij d
Item spend at the dressinge the cariadge	x d
Item paied for the payntinge the playars clothes	ij s viij d
Item spend on margery gybban to get our regynale	ij d
Item paied vnto Robart slye for helpinge at the cariadge	v d
Item spend at our generall rehearse	ij s x d
Item for a borde to the cariadge	iiij d
Item for nealis to neale the hingis	ij d
Item spent at the Bringinge vp the cariadge	viiij d
Item spent on [med] Rychard Doby	ij d |
Item spent on Edwarde porter & for ij copes	viij d

Item nealis pynnis and cordes & drynke at the bowinge our

cariadge   vj d
Item at the fyrste dresnge dresinge the cariadge for cordes   ij d
Item for newe housinge to our cariadge   vj d
Item for thre clapes of Iren to the cariadge   xvj d
Item for the mendinge of arrates vysar   iiij d   5
Item spent at the Bowninge of the players   ij d
Item paied for drynke to the players   ij s
Item spent at the vnbowninge of the players in drynke & bred
                                                               xij d

Item paied vnto pylat and to him that caried arrates clothes &   10
for there gloves   vj s vj d
Item paied vnto the turmenters   iiij s vj d
Item paied vnto annas   xxij d
Item paied the putters of our cariadge   ij s viij d
Item paied the wright for settinge vp our cariadge & takinge yt   15
done and asonder   ij s x d
Item spend at the takinge downe of our cariadge on som of our
compeny   xij d
Item spend at the receavinge of our mony for the cariadge of
the paynters   iiij d   20
Item entringe a accion agaynste Ihon ashewode and for the
arestment of him   viij d
Item more spent when we went to paye the players   vj d
Item paied houghe sparke for redinge the regynall   ij s
Item spent on medsomer even apon the compeny   v s iiij d   25
Item spent at the Bowninge of our boye to ryde Before us   viij d
Item geven the presonars on medsomer even   vj d
...

A   *Mayors List 1* BL: Harley 1046   30
    f 164v* *(Midsummer) John Savage*
    ...

    this year the said Sir Iohn Sauage caused ye popish plaies of
    Chester to bee playd ye Sunday Munday Tuesday and Wensday
    after Midsummer day in contempt of and Inhibition and ye   35
    primates letters from yorke and from ye Earle of Huntington,
    for which cause hee was serued by a purseuant from yorke, ye
    same day yat ye new Maior was elected, as they came out of ye
    common hall, notwithstanding the said Sir Iohn Sauage tooke
    his way towards London, but how his matter sped is not knowne   40

2 / dresnge dresinge *MS dittography*

Also Mr Hanky was serued by the same Purseuant for ye like
contempt when hee was Maior, diuers others of ye Citizens and
players were troubled for ye same matter

A   *Mayors List 5* BL: Harley 2125
f 40v *John Savage*

The whitson playes played in pageantes in this cittye ᵒat midsomer
to the great dislike of many because the playe was in on part of
the Cittyᵒ   1ᵒ

A   *Mayors List 8* BL: Harley 2133
f 43v* *John Savage*
...

The whitson playes were plaid at Midsom*er*, and then but some   1ᵍ
of them leaueinge others vnplaid w*hi*ch were thought might not
be Iustified for the sup*er*stition that was in them. Allthough the
Maior was enjoyned not to p*ro*ceed therein
...
                                                                                20

A   *Mayors List 10* BL: Add. 29777
item 249* *John Savage*

... The playes calld whitson playes were at mydsomer sett forthe
to the misliking of manye   25
...

1575-6
AC   *Smiths, Cutlers, and Plumbers' Records*
BL: Account Book I Harley 2054   30
f 21* *(July)*
...
rec of the accounts of the pleayes   xj s iij d
...
for 5 pynttes Seke on St Lowes daye at mr monforttes   xv d   35
to mynstrells   viij d
...
at coming in of Tho Kemp v s vj d to menstrelles xij d
...

8-10 / ᵒat ... Cittyᵒ *in RH II's hand*

The Armes ffor the showe

® first banner
they had at
midsomer

for selke to the same ij s viij d. for fring xij d for sowinge it vj d
for paper & wyer for the same   ij d ob.
for the workmanshepe of the same   x s 4d
for dressinge the child xiij d. for hose & shewes for chyld xiiij d
for yelow thred & pines   3d
on medsomer effe peayd at mr mownfords 4s 5d. to menstrelles
ij s
...

Painters, Glaziers, Embroiderers, and Stationers' Records
C: Account Book I
f 61v *(18 October)*
...

Item paid for the Compayne on sent lukes daye att Richert
Dobies dynner as here after folowethe
Item for a potell of secke   xij d
Item [for] to the waytes men   vj d
...

Item paid one mydsomar even to Richardson att the barse   j d
Item paide to the pryssoners in the castell and in the norgate iij d
Item pade to edwarde dobye for going on the styltes   xij d
Item paid for dressing the boye   vj d
Item paid to the mynstrell   vj d
Item spend att our aldermans house on mydsomar even vpon
the mynstrell and the Companye   vj d
...

Mayors' Books CCA: M/B/21
f 187v* *(30 October)*

    Apud Ciuitatem Cestrie xxvto die octobris
    Anno Regni Regine Elizabete &c. xvijmo

Whereas Andrew Tailer of the said Citie Tailer vsinge the
occupacion of Diers within the same Citie was taxed and sossed
to beare with the Compeny of Dyers by the same compeny for
the charges in the setting furth of their parte and pagent of the
plaies sett furth and plaied in this Citie at midsomer laste past
comonly Called whytson plaies and by the said Compeny rated
and appointed to paie for that entent iij s viij d which he refused

to paie And whereas vpon the complainte of the said Compeny
of diers againste the said Andrew to the right worshipfull S*ir*
Iohn Savage knight late maior of the same Citie in the tyme of
his mairalty whervpon the same Andrew beinge Called before
the same then maior in that behalf denied to paie the same And
therfore the said Andrew Tailler was then and ther by the said
then Maior Comytted to warde where he hethervnto hath
remayned And whereas Iohn Banester and Edmunde Gamull
gent*lemen* Cam before henry hardware maior of the said Citie /
willi*a*m Gerrard and *willia*m Glaseor esquiers Aldermen*n* of the
same Citie and others the Iustices of peace w*i*thin the same
Citie the daie yere and place firste aboue remembred and willed
that the said Andrew Tailer vpon paym*ent* of the said iij s viij d
might be of his said imp*ri*sonment enlarged [w*hi*ch so] whervpon
now the said Iohn Banest*er* & Edmund Gamull haue paied and
discharged the said iij s viij d for the said Andrew and vpon such
paym*ent* the said Andrew Tailer the said daie yere and place
was of his said imp*ri*som*ent* enlarged and sett at libertie by the
said now maior the said aldermen and others of the Iustic*es* of
peace aforesaid

Corporation Lease Book CCA: CHB/3
f 28* *(10 November)*

After my right hartie Comendacons where it hathe bene enformed
to the prevey Counsell that I caused the plays laste at Chester
to be sett forwarde onely of my sellf w*hi*ch your sellues do
knowe the contrary And that they were by comon assemblie
apointed as remayneth in Recorde ffor the easinge and qualefyinge
all controuersees growen abowte the same I am moste hartely
to desyre you to sende me a Certificate vnder your haund*es* and
Seale of your Citie to testefy that the same plays were sett
forwarde as well by the counsell of the Citie as for the comen
welth of the same whereby their hono*urs* may be the better
satisfied thereof and hopinge thereby to reduce all suche matters
quiett as are risen nowe againste me and mr hankye whom you
muste make mencyon of in the Certificate as well as my sellf
whiche I pray you may be sente me with as muche convenient
speede as is possible So for this tyme I bidd yow farewell at
London the xth of november 1575

Your lovinge ffrende
Iohn Savage ./.

Assembly Books CCA: AB/1
ff 162v-3* *(21 November)*

Tempore p*refati* henrici hardware maio*ris* C*iuitatis* C*iuitatis*
p*redicte* ad congracio*n*em ib*idem* tent*am* in Interior*e* Pent*ice*   5
eiusdem C*iuitatis* die lune videl*icet* xxj die novemb*ris* Anno
R*egni* Regi*n*e Elizabeth &c. xviij.

A request by S*ir*
Iohn Savag
knight to have
c*er*tificat
tow*c*hing his
setting furth of
whitson plaies

Whereas informacon was geven to the saide maior and certein
others his bretherne on the behallf of Sir Iohn Savage knighte   10
that he shuld be Charged to haue sett furthe and caused to be
plaide the accostomed pageons and plays Called the whitson
plays in the tyme of his maioraltie at midsomer laste of himsellf
to satisfy his owne will and pleasure and contrary to his othe and
dutie without the assente or consente of the reste of his bretherne   15
and of the Common counsell of the same / And whereallsoe the
saide Sir Iohn Savage hath addressed his letters to the saide
maior and his bretherne thaldermen requestinge them vnder
the Cities seale to certefy the trueth therein together with the
transcripte of an order therof taken / whervpon this assemblie   20
was called and the p*re*misss hearde wayed and considered And
wherallsoe at this assemblie Iohn hanky ald*erman* enformeth
the same that he was burthened with the like offence viz for the
settinge furthe him sellf of the whitson plays without any assent
or consente of the aldermen and comen counsell in the tyme of   25
his late maioralty of this City that is to say the xiiijth yere of
the raigne of the quenes ma*ies*tie that nowe is / who allsoe made
requeste that this assembly wolde allsoe Certefy with him the
man*er* howe the saide plais were sett furth in his late maioralty
whether of him sellf or by assente and consente of the aldermen   30
and com*m*en counsell of this Citie w*hich* allso beinge likewise
wayed and considered And for that the appereth of Recorde
entred in the booke of the orders of this Citie a certen conclucion
order and constitucion made in the tyme of the maioraltie of
the saide Sir Iohn Savage aucthorisinge him with assent of   35
thaldermen Sheriff*es* and comon counsell of the saide Citie to
sett furthe the saide plays in the saide tyme of his maioralty
And for that allsoe it is confessed by this whole assemblie that
the saide Iohn hanky in the tyme of his maioralty of the saide
Citie did sett furthe the said plays by thassent and consente of   40

4 / C*iui*tatis Ciuitatis MS *dittography*

the aldermen sheriff*es* and com*m*en counsell of this Citie and so
waranted and auctorised so to doe by assemblie / It is nowe the
day and yere firste above remembred ordered concluded vpon
and agried by the saide maior the aldermen Sheriff*es* sheriff*es*
peeres and com*m*on counsell of the said City That certificate
shalbe made from and in the name of the corp*oraci*on of this
Citie and vnder the com*m*en seale of the same City p*ro*portinge
the saide informaci*on And that at suche request*es* as before
suche certificate is made that the saide surmys*es* alledged againste
the saide Sir Iohn Savage and Iohn hankie are vntrue And that   1
the saide play*s* set furthe in their seu*er*all maioralties was seu*er*ally
don by thassent consente good will and agreamente of the
aldermen sheriff*es* sheriff*es* peeres and Comen counsell of the
saide Citie and so determyned by seu*er*all orders agried vpon in
open assemblie acordinge to the auncyent and lawdable custom   1
of the saide Citie whereunto and for the performance wherof the
whole Citizens of the Citie are bounde and tyed by othe as they
are to other their orders And that they the saide Sir Iohn Savage
and Iohn hanky nor either of them did nothinge | in their seu*er*all
tymes of maioralties towchinge the saide plays but by thassent   2
consent and full agreamente of the aldermen sheriff*es* and comen
counsell of the saide Citie in the sellf safe same manner and
forme as the same nowe is penned and redd to this assembly /
And it is further ordered that aswell the saide seu*er*all let*t*ers
of the saide Sir Iohn Savage towchinge his saide requeste As   2
allsoe the saide such certificate shalbe entred verbatim in the
saide booke called the table booke of the saide City for the
inrolment*es* of all the indentures leases and ded*es* concerninge
the land*es* of the saide Citie All w*hi*ch was and is so don*n*e
acordynglie. /   3●

Corporation Lease Book CCA: CHB/3
f 28v* *(21 November)*

To all true chr*ist*en people to whom this p*rese*nte writinge shall   3●
come to be ⟨...⟩ hearde or redd henrie hardware nowe maior of
the Citie of Chester and the Citizen ⟨...⟩ the same Citie sende
gretinge in our lord god everlastinge. forasmuche as it is enfo⟨...⟩

4, 13 / sheriff*es* sheriff*es* MS *dittography*   17 / tyed *altered from* byed
CHB/3, f 28v *missing readings supplied from* Harley 2173, ff 107v-8:
36 / ⟨...⟩: seen   37 / Citizen ⟨...⟩: Citizens of
38 / enfo⟨...⟩: enformed

vnto vs the saide maior and Citizens on the behallf of Sir Iohn
Savage knight ⟨...⟩ it is reported that he the saide Sir Iohn Savage
knighte beinge the yere laste paste maior of the saide Citie did
then of his owne power and aucthoritie in the s⟨...⟩ tyme he was
maior to the great abuse of the same office vnleafullie and by   5
ind⟨...⟩ and synistre ways and meanes cause and procure to be
plaide within the same C⟨...⟩ Certen pagions or plays comonlie
there called witteson playes for the satisfying of his owne singuler
will luste and pleasure to the great coste and Charges los⟨..⟩ and
harme of the Citizens and inhabitauntes of the saide Citie And to   10
their no li⟨...⟩ impouerishemente And not by the orderly assente
of his then bretherne the aldermen ⟨...⟩ the comen counsell of the
saide Citie as he shoulde and oughte to haue donne nor to ⟨...⟩ for
the wealth benefite and comoditie of the same Citie acordinge to
his dutie ·/. All which surmyses we well knowinge to be vntrue   15
and that the saide Sir Iohn Sav⟨...⟩ knighte did nothinge the saide
laste yere duringe the tyme he was maior as is aforsa⟨...⟩ in or
abowte the settinge furth of the saide pagions or plays but only
acordinge to an order concluded and agried vpon for dyuers good
and great consideracons redoundinge to the Comen wealthe   20
benefite and profitte of the saide Citie in assemblie there holden
acording to the auncyente and lawdable vsages and customes
there hadd and vsed fur above ⟨...⟩ remembraunce by and with
the assente consente and agreamente of his saide then bretherne
the aldermen of the saide Citie and of the comen counsell of the   25
same ⟨...⟩ in execucion and accomplishemente of the saide order
To the performance wherof both the saide Sir Iohn Savage and
we all that were then Citizens and freemen of the saide Citie were
bounden and tyed by our othes so as we be to all our orders
taken and made in and by our asse⟨...⟩ And therefore at and   30
vpon the mocion and re⟨.⟩ueste made vnto vs in our assembly
holden ⟨...⟩ day of the date of these presentes on the behallf of
the saide Sir Iohn Savage we the saide m⟨...⟩ and Citizens haue
caused the tenor and transcripte of the saide order to be here

CHB/3, f 28v missing readings supplied from Harley 2173, ff 107v-8:

2 / ⟨...⟩: that   4 / s⟨...⟩: saide
6 / ind⟨...⟩: indirect   7 / C⟨...⟩: Citie
9 / los⟨..⟩: losse   11 / li⟨...⟩: litle
12 / ⟨...⟩: and   13 / ⟨...⟩: and
16 / Sav⟨...⟩: Savage   17 / aforsa⟨...⟩: aforsaide
23 / ⟨...⟩: mans   26 / ⟨...⟩: did
30 / asse⟨...⟩: assembly   32 / ⟨...⟩: they
33 / m⟨...⟩: maior

wri⟨...⟩ as folowethe / Ad congregacionem tentam in communi
aula placitorum Ciuitatis Cestrie xxxº die mai Anno Regni
Regine Elizabeth &c. xvijº / At which assemblie it was ordered
concluded and agried vpon by the saide maior aldermen sheriffes
and common counsell of the saide City that the plays comonlie   5
called the whitson plays at mydsomer nexte cominge shalbe
sett furth and plaide in suche orderly manner and sorte as
the same haue bene accustomed with suche correcion and
amendemente as shalbe thought conveniente by the saide maior
And all charges of the saide plays to be supported and borne by   10
thinhabitauntes of the saide Citie as haue bene heretofore vsed /.
And in wytnes that this is a true copy and transcripte of the
saide order and warrante whereby and in accomplishment wherof
the saide Sir Iohn Savage did cause the saide pagions and plays
to be sett furth and playde as is aforesaide which did begyn the   15
xxvjth of Iune laste paste in the afternone of the same day and
there contynued vntill the wednesday at eveninge then nexte
folowinge / And that allsoe this presente day in our saide assembly
holden and kepte within the pentice of our saide Citie acordinge
to the good and lawdable vsages & accustomes aforesaide Iohn   20
hanky one of the aldermen and late maior of the saide City to
wytt in the xiiijth yeare of the quenes maiestes raigne that
nowe is made his humble peticion to the saide assemblie that it
might please the same to publishe by theis presentes by what
warrante he the saide Iohn hanky caused the saide plays to be   25
sett furthe & plaide in the aforesaide yere that he was maior
as is aforesaide of the same Cittie Which saide peticion consideringe
the same is verey reasonable thaught mete to grante the same
And therefore the saide maior and citizens doe publishe and
declare that it was this day confessed by the saide assembly   30
that the saide Iohn hanky alderman did in the tyme of his
saide maioralty cause the saide plais to be sett furth and plaide
onlie by vertue and in execucion of an order taken by assemblie
of the saide Citie holden there the xxixth of aprill in the saide
xiiijth yere of the quenes maiestes raigne that nowe is And by   35
and with the consente and assente of his saide bretherne the then
aldermen of the saide City and comen counsell of the same And
allsoe in wytnes hereof we the saide maior and Citizens haue to
thes presentes sett the comon seale of the saide Cit⟨.⟩ dated at

CHB/3, f 28v *missing readings supplied from Harley 2173, ff 107v-8:*
1 / wri⟨...⟩: written   39 / Cit⟨..⟩: Citty

the saide Citie the xxjth day of november in the Eightenth yere
of the raigne of our soueraigne ladie Elizabeth by the grace of
god of england fraunce and Irelaund quene defendor of the
ffaith &c. /.

5

Cordwainers and Shoemakers' Records
CCA: Account Book I G/8/2
ff 68-8v *(11 November)*
...

In primis payde the Whetemen on martens day	vij d	10
Item payde peter cally the same day	vij d	
Item payde shurlocke the menstrell	iiij d	
Item payd thomas fidler the same day	iiij d	
...		
Item payde for gleves	iij s vj d	15
Item payde for the bariage of the gleves	ij d	
Item payde for Wheetemen at gutted	vj d	
Item geven the stewart*es* of the Iorneme for sarvynge vs	vj d	
Item payde the wheete men at wyllyam symcock*es*	vj d	
Item payde the shyrreff*es*	ij s	20
Item payde the iiij sargans	xvj d	
Item payde for arfflaye donne for the syne	ij d	
Item payde the menstrell*es* on mydsomer even	ij s vj d	
Item payde the chyllde that Rode	xviij d	
Item payde hys fote man	iiij d	25
...		
Item payde the presoner*es* in the castell	viij d	
Item spente at the stewarte Inc*es*	viij d ⏐	
Item payde the crier at mydsomer a penny	j d	
...		30
Item payde the menstrell*es* at peter bemott*es* drinkynge ij s	iiij d	
...		
Item payde the menstrell*es* on martens even	xij d	
...		

35

Coopers' Records C: Account Book I
f 9 *(20 November)*
...

Item more R*eceaved* for a peare of the cariage whelles iiij s	viij d	
...		40
Ite*m* that yt coste us for lokinge for a boye to ryde on medsom*er*		
even	vj d	

Item that we gave the childe a peare of gloves iij d
Item that we spent the same daye we warned the occupation ij d
Item payed for horsbred that we gave the horse the childe
rode on iiij d
Item geven the prisonars at castell iiij d   5
Item geven the prisonars at norgate ij d
Item geven william rycharson ij d
Item for the drynkynge one medsomer even iiij s vj d
...

  10

Joiners, Carvers, and Turners' Records
CCA: Company Book G 14/1
f 15 *(25 March)*
...   15

Item payed for ij hudes for vs the ij stuardes vj s
Item payed to the mynstreles at mydsomer xij d
Item payed to the presoneres in the castell iiij d
Item payed to pole to the berege for makinge our armes v d
Item geven to the presoneres in the northegate ij d   20
Item payed for a wyer to the baner iiij d
Item payed for a peare of to the boye apone mydsomer even that
Rid afore the compenye vj d
Item payed for a pere of gloves to the boye ij d
Item payed for a staffe to the banere iiij d   25
Item payed for grene silcke j d
...
Item that wee stuardes haue payed for makinge of the banner
iij s iiij d
...   30

1576-7
AC *Smiths, Cutlers, and Plumbers' Records*
BL: Account Book I Harley 2054   35
ff 21-1v *(July)*
...
of our sister hancocke for the please xv d of Robert Crockett
xv d of Ric locker xv d
of 2 smythes in hanbridge for the please ij s viij d   40
...
of Io Andro for please xv d

payments

to the wayte men on the election day xij d to them when Tho
Kemp made his dimer xij d
the same day a pott*ell* of sack to vs a pott*ell* to our wiues & a   5
pottell to mr maior   iij s
spent same day at mr leauelokers tauarne v s iij d to the mynstrell
vj d |
to 3 mynstrell vpon St Loye Ieuen at our Ald*erman* stokens   ix d
...   10

for pott sack & pott clar at Tho locker dinner xx d to weytes
xij d to other minstrells 4d

...

for horsebred when I went to borow gere for the child to ride
before vs   4d   15
for lace pynns & threed to stych the Iuells   4d
for dressinge our signe   ij s vj d
for hose & showes for child   xiiij d
for gloues for child & footman   v d
on midsomer eue for 3 pott bere 3 pott Ale   vij d   20
to Cryer j d Spent in gatharing our play mony xviij d prisoners
at Castell iiij d
at norgate   ij d
to the mynstrells   ij s
payd an ouerplus at Ald*erman* mounforts on midsomer eue xvj d   25
...

Painters, Glaziers, Embroiderers, and Stationers' Records
C: Account Book I
f 66 *(18 October)*   30

...

Item payd to W*illia*m Rychardson at the barres   j d
Item to the prysoners at the castell   ij d
Item to the prysoners at the northgate   ij d
Item payd for iiij pott*es* of alle at wyllyam framwayes vppon   35
midsoner euen before the wache was vppon the sheper*es* and
other*es*   iiij d
Item to a mynstrell to goe before vs   vj d
Item payd in our Aldermans howsse to make vppe the shott
vppon mydsomer Euen   xij d   40

4 / dimer *for* dinner, *minim omitted MS*

Item for payntyng the stylltes   [vj d]

...

Item to the ij shepert*es* for going vppon the Syltes   xx d

...

Treasurers' Account Rolls CCA: TAR/1/16
mb 4 *(November)*

...

Nicho*lus* white pro domo pr*o*xim*a* adiacen*te* cuidam dom*ui*
voc*ate* drapers cariadge howse   iij s iiij d   10

...

Senescal*lis* del mercers pro domo Cariag sua   vj d

... Et solut*um* Ioh*anni* hankie ald*ermanno* p*ro* toga Ric*ardi* veale
officiar*is* Ciui*tatis* p*redicti* p*er* mand*atum* p*redicti* maior*is* xxiiij s   15
iiij d. Et solut*um* Senescall*o* del sadlers pro campanilla sua p*er*
mand*atum* maior*is* vj s viij d ...
    Et solut*um* Thome Gillam pro saltaci*one* sua voc*ata* daunseinge
lud⟨.⟩ voc*ato* morris dawns ad vigi*l*i*tatem* s*an*cti Ioh*ann*is Baptiste
vl*timam* preterit*am* vj s viij d. ...   20

Cordwainers and Shoemakers' Records
CCA: Account Book I G/8/2
f 70 *(11 November)*

...   25

Ite*m* payde for the gleves the thrid day of marche   iiij s
Ite*m* payde the waytemen in oure alld*er*man Inc*es* the viij^th day
of marche   viij d

...

                                                                 30
f 70v
Item payde Robarte leche for payntinge the banner   ij s vj d
Ite*m* spente on Robarte leche to the berrage   ij d
Ite*m* payde the crier at the barres   j d
Ite*m* payd the presoner*es* in the caster & in the northegate   viij d   35
Ite*m* payde the chyllde that Rode before the occupacion   xviij d
Ite*m* payde for a pottell of secke at oure alldermans   xij d
Ite*m* payd the mynstre*es* at mydsomer   ij s vj d
Ite*m* payde for bere in oure alldermans the same nyghte   ij d

...   40

12 / Cariag *for* Cariagii

Item payd the mynstrelles at peter bennettes dynner xx d

...

Item geven the mynstrelles on martens even xij d

...

Item geven the mynstrell at edward yonges denner viij d 5

...

Coopers' Records C: Account Book I
f 10v *(20 November)* 10

...

Item payd for dressing the singne on medsomer Eve to william
fromond xij d
Item payd for a peare of gloves to the child viij d
Item spent when the child was drest ij d 15
Item spent in the aldermans house ij d
Item for Inkle ij d
Item for dressing the bridell and for the lone of the sadle clothe
vj d
Item payd to the cryer at the bars j d 20
Item to the prisoners at the Castell ij d
Item to the prisoners at the northgate ij d

...

Item for a quart of sacke at the bringung home of the boye vj d
Item spent on thomas Radford desyring his good will for the 25
childe in Robert Annions house iiij d
Item spent on the company on midsomer Eve iiij s

...

30

Joiners, Carvers, and Turners' Records
CCA: Company Book G14/1
f 16 *(25 March)* 35

...

Item geven to the presoneres vpon mydsomer even iiij d
Item geven to the presoneres in the northe gatte vpon mydsomer
even iiij d
Item geven to the cryer at the bares iij d 40

...

Item payed to the mynstreles vpon mydsomer even viij d

...

Painters, Glaziers, Embroiderers, and Stationers' Records
C: Account Book I
f 67v* *(3 May)*

...

Robert Waytt is fyned for that he did promysse the Company
that his man shuld goe vppon the Styltes vppon mydsomer eueen
ˏ ˋ1577ˋ and keptt bothe his man and the Styltes from vs And
went in to the Ile of man *with* them And [⟨...⟩] he [⟨...⟩] caused vs
to be at xviij d more charg*es* vntyll we had neded   xij d

...   1(

1577-8

AC   *Smiths, Cutlers, and Plumbers' Records*   1(
       BL: Account Book I Harley 2054
       f 22 *(July)*

...

Spent on mr bauand requestinge his sonne to ryd at midsomer
wach   vj d
for tryminge the banner   vj d   2(

...

the rest ordnary dutyes for midsomer

...

                                                               2(

Painters, Glaziers, Embroiderers, and Stationers' Records
C: Account Book I
f 68 *(18 October)*

...

I*tem* furste for mydsomer euen for buckeram to set the Armes   3(
vppon   iiij d [xij d]
It*em* a payer of gloues   ij d
It*em* for dressynge the boye   iij d
It*em* at the barres   [ii]j d
It*em* for the castell   ij d   3!
It*em* at the northgate   ij d
It*em* to the mynstrell   vj d
It*em* spentt vppon the mynstrell   ij d
It*em* for horse bread for the boyes horsse   ij d
[It*em* payd for Ryc*hard* dobes charges]   4(

...

Cordwainers and Shoemakers' Records
CCA: Account Book I G/8/2
f 72v *(11 November)*
...

Item payde the mynstrell at harre youmg*es* drinkinge	xx d	5

...

Item payde Willyam Richarson on mydsomer even	j d	
Item payde Robarte leche for paynntinge the banner	ij s iiij d	
Item payde the presoner*es* in the castell	vj d	
Item payde the presoner*es* in the north gate	vj d	10
Ite*m* payde the menstrell*es* the same nyghte	ij s vj d	
Item payde the chyllde that Rode before the company	xviij d	
Item payde for horsse bredd to the horsse	ij d	
Item payde for bereage of the gleves	ij d	
Item payde for the gleves	iiij s	15
Item geven the menstrell*es* in oure allderman Inc*es* howsse	xvj d	

...

f 73
...

		20
Item payde the mynstrll*es* on martens even	xx d	

...

Coopers' Records C: Account Book I
f 12 *(20 November)* 25
...

It*em* paid for a payre of gloves to the child	iij d	
It*em* paid for a payre of shues	vij d	
It*em* for a payre of hose	xij d	
It*em* for the hyre of a sadell cloth	iiij d	30
It*em* to him that lead the horse	iiij d	
It*em* to the cryer	j d	
It*em* to the pri*s*oners at the castell	iiij d	
It*em* to the pre*s*oners at the northgate	ij d	
It*em* spent at the dressing of the boy	iij d	35
It*em* for Inkle to dresse the horse	j d	

...

5 / youmg*es* for young*es, extra minim MS*

A *Mayors List 3* BL: Harley 2057
f 29v *(July)* *Thomas Bellin*

...

Restored the auntient Custom of midsomer wach

...   5

Joiners, Carvers, and Turners' Records
CCA: Company Book G14/1
f 19 *(25 March)*

                                                                                         10
Item payd for a peare of gloves for the boye that did Ryd vpone
mydsomer even   iij d
Item geven to a boye to ffeche a chene for the boye that did
Ryd vpone mydsomer even   iiij d
Item geven to the cryer at the bares   iij d   15
Item geven to the presoneres in the castell   iiij d
Item geven to the presoneres in the northe gatte   ij d
Item geven to the mynstrell to goo a ffore vs vpvne mydsomer
even   xij d
...   20
Item payd for a pere of Red lether soes to the boye that dyd
Ryd   x d
Item geven to a boye that dyd Lead the horse one mydsomer
even and for bred to the horse   iiij d
...   25
Item geven to the mynstrelles at the same dener   xvj d
...

A *Mayors List 5* BL: Harley 2125
f 41 *Thomas Bellin*   30
...

"the scollers of
the freescole
also playd a
comody before
them at mr
maiors howse"

Alsoe he entertayned . the Earle of Darbie and his sonne
ffardinando . Lord Strange, two nightes at his howse he caused
the Sheappeardes playe to be played at the hie Crosse / with
other Trivmphes one the Roode Deey.   35
...

A *Mayors List 8* BL: Harley 2133
f 44* *(Midsummer)* *Thomas Bellin*

...   40
In Iulie the Erle of Darbie ye Lord strange with many others

32 / *marginalia in RH II's hand*

Came to this Citie and were honorablie receaued by the Maior
and Citizens. The sheppards play was plaied at the high Crosse
and other Tryumphs on the Roods eye ...

5

1578-9
Painters, Glaziers, Embroiderers, and Stationers' Records
C: Account Book I
f 70 *(18 October)*   10

...

payd to *willia*m Ry*card*son att the barres vppon mydsomer
Euen   j d
payd to the prysoners at the castell   ij d
payd to the prysoners at the northgate   ij d   15
payd to a mynstrell the same tyme   vj d

...

20

Cordwainers and Shoemakers' Records
CCA: Account Book I G/8/2
f 74v *(11 November)*

...

In prims geven vnto the wayte men at harre young*es* denner xvj d   25

...

Item geven to the beriage of the gleves   ij d
Item payde for the gleves   iiij s
Item geven the wheete men on shrofte thursday   xvj d
                                                                    30
Item payd the cryer on mydsomer even   j d
Item geven the presoner*es* in the castell   vj d
Item geven to the presoner*es* in the northgate   viij d

...

Item payde the mynstrell*es* on mydsomer even   ij s vj d   35
Item payde the chyllde that Rode before the occupacc*i*on xviij d
Item payde for horsse bredd to the horsse   ij d

...

f 75   40

...

Item payde the wheetemen & shurlocke   xx d

...

Coopers' Records C: Account Book I
f 13 *(20 November)*

...

It*em* payed at Rycchart sawndars dyn*n*er ffor a pottell of wyn
        xv d   5
It*em* payed at the same dyn*n*er to the mynstrel*es*   xij d

...

f 13v

...   10

It*em* payed at the alderman*es* on midsomer Ewyne one the
compa*n*ye   iiij s
It*em* payed ffor the borrowynge of the horsse & dressynge of
hyme   x d
It*em* payed to the pryssoner*es* on mydsomar Ewene   vj s   15
It*em* payed ffor the bowes hosse & sewesse & apayere of glowes
       xij d
It*em* payed to the you*n*ge mane y*at* stayed the baye apone the
horsse   iiij d
It*em* payed at wyllyam penye*es* dyn*n*er to the myn*n*strel*es*   xij d   20
It*em* payed at thomas gardenars dyn*n*er to the mynstrel*es*   xij d.
It*em* payed at Raffe conpares at a wedynge to the mynstrel*es*
       iiij d

...

   25

A   ***Mayors List 10*** BL: Add. 29777
item 253 *(November) William Jowett*

...

In this yeare the said Sheriffe David Mountforde dyd wynne the
Standerd on the Roode Eye on Shrofte Tuesdaye ... Also the   30
Earle of Derby, the Lorde mountegle & the Lorde Strange came
to Chest*er* who were by ye said maior well enterteynd

...

1579-80   35
Painters, Glaziers, Embroiderers, and Stationers' Records
C: Account Book I
f 73 *(18 October)*

...

It*em* spent aboute the companyes 'bysenes in' muney our   40
aldermans a geneste mydsomer   iiij d
It*em* on mydsomer euen in the stewardes house for alle   ij d

Item at the bares at the castell and the northe gate   v d
Item for the ouer [p] plous of a shotte at our aldermans on
mydsomer euen   viij d
Item to the mynstrel   vj d
Item for goynge one the stiltes   vj d   5
...

Cordwainers and Shoemakers' Records
CCA: Account Book I G/8/2
f 77 *(11 November)*   10

...

In primis payde the mynstrell*es* on martens day   xviij d

...

Item payde the mynstrell*es* at Roger chantres drincking   iij s
...   15

Item payde the mynstrell*es* at thomas newbett*es* drincking   viij d
Item payde for the gleves   iiij s
Item for the berrage of them   ij d
Item payde the menstrell*es* at gutted   xij d
...   20

f 77v

...

Item for dressynge the banner & the berrecche   xviij d
Item payde the presoner*es* in the castell   vj d   25
Item payde to the presoner*es* in the northegate   iiij d
Item pade the mynstrell*es* on mydsomer ever   ij s vj d
Item payde the chyllde that Rode   xviij d
Item payde the horsse bredd   iiij d
...   30

Item payde the crier at the barres   j d

...

Item payd the mynstrell*es* at the shirreffes   vj d
Item payde the menstrell*es* at Roger chantrell*es* dynner   xvj d
Item payd the mynstrell*es* at petr bockosos dynner   xvj d   35
Item payde the tomler that day   ij s

...

f 78v

...   40

In primis payde at necolas bockeses dynner to the mynstrell*es*
      ij s ij d

...

Item to the mynstrell*es* at Richard tyftons & edward bennet*es*
drinckinge   v d

...

Item for the gleves & the berricche of them   v s iiij d   5
Item to the wheatemen at guttes in oure allderman Inc*es*   xvj d

...

Item to the menstrell*es* on mydsomer even   ij s vj d
Item for a pottell secke the same nyghte   xij d
Item payde the presoner*es* of the castell   vj d   10
Item to the presoner*es* at the northegate   vj d

...

Item payde the chyllde that Rode on mydsomer even   xviij d
Item for a horsse the same nyghte   iiij d
Item to the crier at the barres   j d   15

...

f 79
...

Item spente on martens eve   xiiij s   20
Item payde the menstrell that nyghte   xxij d

...

Coopers' Records C: Account Book I
f 14v *(20 November)*   25

...

It*em* payed to Roger fframo ffor payentynge of the banere   xij d

...

It*em* payed to the man y*at* helde the chylde on ye horsse   iiij d
It*em* payed to the onower of the horsses in horsse brede   iiij d   30
It*em* payed ffor a pottell of wyne to brynge mr gam*m*well   xij d
It*em* gywene to the presoner*es* on mydsomar Ewene   vj d

...

It*em* spent on mydsomer Ewen on the compeny   ij s

                                                                     35

Mayors' Books CCA: M/B/22
f a-v *(7 February)*

                    7mo feb Shroftestewsday

                                                                     40

        mr Maior
        mr Poole   mr Sheriff Brid

mr Grene

mr Balle

mr hanky

mr Lea

mr harvy

mr Bellin

mr Ryerson

mr Hammer

mr Brerewod

mr Bavand

mr Stiles

5

The persons aforesaid addressed their Letters to mr Peter
Warburton esquier declaring the greate abuse of his Man drink   10
water in Cominge to the maior and clayming of him the brode
Arrow and fflight after those games were (amonges others)
differed vntill Sonday next by proclamacion saing they were his
due albeit vnshot for and that this was the daie and yat the maior
cold not differ the tyme and that the maior did him wrong yet   15
wold he haue the same with diuers others presumpteous and
disobedient words and being demaunded by mr grene whether
he knew to whom he spake said he spake to the maior who did
him wrongs if he wold not deliuer vnto him the said ij gaines
and yet not herewith contented thrust him self amonges the   20
Iustices of peace in his going with covered hed & them sonderd
and encownterd with them and being comaunded by An officer
to geve place refused the same other by comaundement or
dutie / And shewed his master that for his sake his man was
pardoned of his imprisonment at that tyme and praied his   25
opinion towching his said man

Joiners, Carvers, and Turners' Records
CCA: Company Book G14/1
ff 22-2v *(25 March)*   30

...

Item geven to the minstrerells at the same gouse svttinge   vj d

...

Item payed for a peare of gloues for the boye that dyd Ryde
at mydsomer   iij d | 35
Item payed for a peare of sheues to the chylld that dyd Ryde
one mydsomer even   vij d
Item payed for a peare of howse to hime that dyd Ryde   vj d
Item payed for hyer of velvete that made the chyllds clocke
                                                               xviij d   40
Item geven to the minstrells one mydsomer euen   ij s vj d
Item payed for mendinge the staffe   ij d

Item geuen to the cryere at the bares iij d
Item geven to the presoneres in the castell and the northgate vij d
...

1580-1 5

Cordwainers and Shoemakers' Records
CCA: Account Book I G/8/2
f 80v *(11 November)*

...

Item payde for the gleves iiij s viij d 10
Item spend at the berynge of them ij d
Item payde the waytemen at gutted xvj d

...

Item geven maystris powell a quarte of wyne for borroenge a
horse on mydsomer even v d 15

...

Item payde the crier at the barres on mydsomer even j d
Item geven the presoner*es* in the castell & in the northe gate
the same nyght xij d
Item geven maystris powell*es* man for waytinge on the horse that 20
nyghte vj d
Item payde the myllstrel*es* the same nyghte to playe before
vs ij s vj d
Item payde for a pottell of secke the same nyghte xij d

... 25

Item payde for a payre of bot*es* for the chillde that Rode on
mydson ⌈even⌉ xij d
Item payde for leadinge the horsse on mydsomer even iiij d
Item geven maystr powell a quarte of wyne to hys wellcome
whom v d 30
Item payde Robarte halewud for Reparinge & dressinge the
banner ij s iiij d

...

f 81 35

...

°Item paied the weatemenne one marten evene xvj d°

...

Coopers' Records C: Account Book I 40
f 15v *(20 November)*

...

In prymys for dressynge *our* sygne o medsomer even ij s iiij d

more lede downe for dressynge the boye	vj d
more for Apeare of gloves to the boye	jjj d
more for horstebred and aboye to dresse the horse	vj d
more to the cryer	j d
more geven the prysoners	iiij d
more geven the prysoners at the norethgate	iij d
more pead the charges of *our* companye at wyllyam nyclas howse	xix d
more for a man to Attend vpon the boye	vj d

...

Joiners, Carvers, and Turners' Records
CCA: Company Book G 14/1
f 23 *(25 March)*

...

Item payed at mydsomer even for a peare of hose shewes and gloves for the boye that dyd Ryde	xvj d
Item geven the cryer at the bares	iij d
geven to the pressoneres in the castell and northegate	vij d
geven to the mynstrelles to goe a fore our compenye	ij s vj d
payed for a potell of secke to the compenye one mydsomer even	xij d

...

payed for the hyer of velvete to make thè chylld a clocke	xviij d
payed for ij potelles of alle at the aldermane taskeres one mydsomer even vnto the compenye	iiij d
geven to the boye that dyd lead the horse	ij d

...

1581-2
Painters, Glaziers, Embroiderers, and Stationers' Records
C: Account Book I
f 76v *(18 October)*

...

Item payd edward dobye for goinge on the styltes	xij d
Item payd vnto the menstrell	vj d
Item payd to the presoneres	iiij d
Item payd to the Cryer	j d

...

Cordwainers and Shoemakers' Records
CCA: Account Book I G/8/2
f 82v *(11 November)*

...

Item geven the wheate men at the stewarte lynglays howsse
on martens day   vj d

...

Item payde for the gleves at gutted   iiij s viij d
Item payde for the beriage of the gleves   iiij d
Item geven the wheate men at oure alldeman Inces on thurs day   1
aftr guttedday   ij s

...

Item payde thomas Richerson on mydsomer even at the
barr*es*   j d
Item geven the presoner*es* in the castell   vj d   1
Item geven the presoner*es* in the northegate   vj d
Item geven the mynstrell*es* on mydsomer even   ij s vj d
Item geven maystr powell man for hys paynes   vj d
Item geven maystr powell a quarte of sacke to hys wellcome
whom   vj d   2
Item spente at Rauffe edggys howsse on mydsomer even   xiij d
Item payde for a pottell secke at oure allderman layes howsse
on mydsomer even   xij d
Item payde Robarte halewudd for mendinge the banner   xij d
Item geven thomas harper a payre of shoys & a payre of pompes   2
                                                                                        x d
Item geven wyllyam lov for leadynge the horsse   iiij d

...

f 83   3

...

Item geven the wheate men on martens even   xvj d

...

Coopers' Records C: Account Book I   3
f 16 *(20 November)*

...

that we lead downe at midsomer Euen as followethe

for a pere of hose to the boye   viij d   4
It*em* for aper of showes   viij d
It*em* to dresse the boye in silk & semet   iiij d

Item for the horse hire	vj d	
Item to hym that lad hym	vj d	
Item for a pere of gloues to the boye	iij d	
Item for a pottle of sake in the stewartes	xij d	
Item for the dressinge of the signe	xviii d	5
Item to the crier	j d	
Item for bere on midsomer in my aldermans	x d	
Item for quart of wyne	iij d	
...		
		10

Joiners, Carvers, and Turners' Records
CCA: Company Book G14/1
f 24 *(25 March)*

...		
for a payre of shooes	vj d	15
...		
for a paire of gloves	iiij d	
...		
To the presoners	iiij d	
To the mynstrells	xx d	20
...		
spent at Iames Kempes dyner in wyne to the mynstrells	vj d	
...		
to the presoners on midsomer eve	iiij d	
...		25

1582-3
Painters, Glaziers, Embroiderers, and Stationers' Records
C: Account Book I
f 78v *(18 October)*

...		30
payd at the barres vppon mydsomer Euen	j d	
att the castell	ij d	
at the northegate	ij d	35
to a mynstrell	vj d	
...		
payd for the charges vnppo mydsomer euen at our Aldermans howsse	iiij s	
...		40
payd to Edward dobe for goinge vppon the Styltes	xij d	
...		

Cordwainers and Shoemakers' Records
CCA: Account Book I G/8/2
f 84v *(11 November)*

...

Item payde for the gleves	iiij s viij d
Item payde the bereche of the gleves	iiij d
Item geven the wheate men for plaeng in the *com*men hall & in the alldermans	ij s vj d

...

Item geven the waytemen at Rauffe alyns drinckynge	xvj d	1

...

Item payede for a payre of gloves for the childe	iij d

...

Item geven the presoner*es* in the castell	vj d	
Item geven the presoner*es* in the northegate	vj d	1

...

f 85

...

Item geven the menstrell for playeng before vs on mydsomer even	ij s vj d	2
Item payde for horsse bred	iiij d	
Item geven maystris hope a quarte of wyne when she broght her sonne	iiij d	
Item payde for makyng the mandelion breches & bownyng the childe	v d	2
Item payde Rauffe alyn for a payre of buskens for the childe	ij s	
Item payde the foteman	iiij d	

...

Item payde for martens even	xiiij s	3
Item geven the wheatemen	xviij d	

Coopers' Records C: Account Book I
f 17 *(20 November)*

...

		3
It*em* at willi*am* Congles diner to the mintrels	xij d	

...

It*em* for dressing the singe	ij s	
It*em* for the boyes house & showes that Ride	xviij d	
It*em* paid for dressing the boye	xvj d	4
It*em* paid to the Criere	j d	
It*em* for a peare of glowes to the boye	iij d	

Item paid to the towe Iayles   vij d
Item to towe men that did atende vpon the horse & the child
                                                viij d
Item [p] paid for the horse horse breid   vj d
Item spent on the compeny on midsomer evene   ij s   5
Item at Raff copers diner in wyne   xviij d
Item to the minstrel at the same diner   ij *(blank)*

...

Dean and Chapter CC: Treasurers' Accounts II   10
p 304* *(14 May)*

Item payd the xiiijth of maye vnto Mr Rogers whiche he gaue
to the Earle of Essex players when they woulde haue played
in Mr Deanes howse   ij s   15

...

1583-4
Innkeepers' Records C: Account Book
f 6* *(August)*   20

...

Item payed for the charges of our corporacion as well for the
sealle as for the drawinge and empossinge withe the fote for the
same and our charges vppone mydsomer even   xlvj s ij d

...   25

ff 9-9v

...

Item payed vnto vj boyes for Caryinge dysaneates a fore our
compenye   xiij d   30
Item payed for iiij peare of gloves to iiij boyes that dyd Ryd a
fore our compenye at ij d a pese   viij d
Item payed to iiij foutmen at iiij d a pese   xvj d
Item payed for a peare of gloves to the womane that dyd Ryde
afor our compenye   iij d   35
geven to heare for heare paynes   iiij d
geven to a mane to a tend vppone heare horse   iiij d |
Item payed for dresinge the pye and the horse head   vj d
spen at the borowinge of the deye manes a parell for hime that
dyd lead the womanes horse   [iiij d] ij d 40

4 / horse horse *MS dittography*   7 / l *in* minstrel *written over* s

payed for borowinge a cussocke for the womane   iiij d
payed for potes for the womane   xvj d
payed for iij Canes   vj d
payed for oure drinkinge a fore the watche and after vppone
our compenye   vij s   5
payed for wyne to our compenye   vij d
...

Painters, Glaziers, Embroiderers, and Stationers' Records
C: Account Book I   10
f 79v *(18 October)*
...

payed for a payer of gloues to the child that Rode on mydsomer
euen   iij d
also for a payer of showes to the same child   x d   15
geuen to the prissnors at the casstel and northegate   iiij ⟨.⟩
payed for horse bred on midsomer euen   ij d
payed to rycherson at the bars   j d
payed to the mynstrel on mydsomer ⟨.⟩ euen   vj d
...   20
payed to the mynstrels at thomas Chalners dyner   xij d
...

AC   *City Treasurers' Accounts*   BL: Harley 2173
f 90* *(November)*   25
...

mr Robert brerewood late maior oweth by his accounts 129 li.
19s. ⌈4d⌉ more he oweth mony which he receued by lone of the
Aldermen sheriffs & Comon Counsell when the Earle of leicester
came to chester 46 li. 13s. 4d   30
     for a hogshed of wyne for my lord of Leicester 3 li. 5s for
beare 24s for bankitinge stuff provided for the lord of leister &
mr brerewood had for his owne vse. v li. which is to be deduct
only 30s for Ipocrise:
     in his payments we find to be allowed for the Cupp & gould   35
giuen to the Earl of Leicester 49 li. 11s. 6d.
...

f 91

Disbursements 1583 inter alij   40
...
for the wayte men or citty waytes gownes   v li. xvj s
...

f 91v

...

maiors mount   to Tho pole for payinting or triminge mr maiors mount xxiij s 4d
to citty drumer   xij d
morris dancers   to the morris dauncers   vj s viij d   5

...

Cordwainers and Shoemakers' Records
CCA: Account Book I G/8/2
f 86 *(11 November)*   10

...

Item payde for the gleves   v s

...

Item geven the wheatemen at gutted   ij s
...   15
Item payde the mynstrelles on midsomer even   ij s vj d
Item payde to the presoneres in the castell & the presoneres
in the northegate   xij d

...

Item for a payre of buskens for the childe that Roode   ij s   20
Item for a payre of gloves to hym & makynge his breches   vj d
Item for a quarte of secke on mydsomer even   vj d
Item payde the men that whente before vs when the lorde of
lesciter came to chestr & tendnide the childe   xij d
Item payd willyam mason for leadinge the horsse   iiij d   25
Item payde for horsse bredd to *Mais*tr hurlstons horse   iiij d
Item payd the crier & for ale at the barres   iij d

...

f 86v   30

...

Item for a pottell secke on martens even   xij d
Item geven the wheatemen   xviij d

...   35

Coopers' Records C: Account Book I
f 18 *(20 November)*

...

It*em* payed ffor wyne at thomas hitthi*es* dyner   xij d
It*em* payed to the mynstrell*es* at the same dyner   vj d   40

...

It*em* payed at the bowrounyng of the boye   iiij d
It*em* payed at the bownnynge of the boye   xvj d

Item payed ffor a payer of hosse to the boye   x d
Item payed ffor a payer of shewes   x d
Item payed at the bryngyng of the chylde hom   iiij d
Item payed ffor ledyng of the hores & houldynge the chylde
                                                               viij d   5
Item payed ffor hores brid to the hores   iiij d
Item payed the pryssonares   vj d
...
Item payed ffor the dryssyng of the syne   xviij d
...   10
Item payed ffor the compenye on mydsomare Ewen   ij s vj d
...

Joiners, Carvers, and Turners' Records
CCA: Company Book G 14/1   15
f 27v *(25 March)*

...

payed more for a peare of gloves for the boye that dyd Ryd a
fore our compenye   iiij d
payed for thryd and pynes one mydsomer even . to sowe the   20
chylldes clothes vpone hime   j d

...

payed for the boyes shewes at mydsomer   viij d
payed to the cryer at the bares   j d ob.
geven to the presoneres at the castell iiij d and to the presoneres   25
at the northe gate iij d some is   vij d

...

AC   *Order to Entertain the Earl of Leicester*   BL: Harley 1989
       f 27 *(13 May)*   30

       ...

       13 may order was taken how the E of leicester should be
       entertayned what gifts giuen him & banquet made him & for
       present suply of mony euery Alderman to lend xx s euery
       sheriff & sheriffpeere xiij s iiij d euery of the forty vj s viij d.   35
       but after at asente the j Iune the banquet was turned into a
       Cup to be giuen him & 40 Angells in it. the Cupp was latly
       bought by mr Io Tylson and valued at xviij li and for more
       security of the Citty because great resort was to see the Earl
watche wach was ordred to be for tewsday & wensday night of honest   40
       citizens in harnesse videlicet xxiiij for bridgseete xxiiij for forest
       street xij for norgate street & xij for Watergate street and that

all Companyes in their best aparell vpon wensday should atend
mr maior at high Crosse furder to be ordred by him

A   *Mayors List 5* BL: Harley 2125
    f 42* *(3 June) Robert Brerewood*   5

    ...

The Earle of Leaicester, ◦⸢Chamberlein of Chester,⸣◦ the Earle
of Essex, the Earle of Darbye: ◦⸢& Lord North⸣◦ Came to this
Cittye out of walles . and were honorablye received ◦⸒& had a
speech at high crosse⸒◦ by mr mayor and Cittizins in theire   10
scarlett*es* & velvett Coates . mr mayor did dyne them all . at
his howse and after banquited in the pentise / The Earle of
Leicester pr*esent*ed by the mayor . as the Cittyes geifte . with
A fayer ◦‸⸢standing⸣◦ silver Cupp ◦⸢duble gilt⸣◦ & 40 li. Elizabeth
Angells w*i*th it.   15

    ...

A   *Mayors List 9* BL: Add. 11335
    f 23* *Robert Brerewood*

    ...   20

Robert Earle of Lester a great favorite of Queen Elizabeth came
to Chester the 3 of Iune accompanyed with the Earle of Derby,
the young Earle of Essex, the Lord North, and alsoe mett and
attended upon, by most of the Gentlemen in this shire in their
whole trayne, as was thought fifteen hundred horse he was   25
received by the major and his brethren sherriffes peers and forty
at the Crosse, he lay in the Bishops palace and dined with the
major the 4 of Iune, and presented by the citty with a guilt
cup and 40 Angells of gold in the same he departed the 6 of Iune
anno D*omi*ni 1583 mr Robert Brerewood Major   30

    ...

1584-5
Innkeepers' Records C: Account Book
f 12 *(August)*   35

    ...

It*em* payed for arisedene and for reperinge of our baner   viij d
It*em* payed for potes and for the Cane aganest mydsomer even
and for Iron to bynde the cane   ij s viij d

7 / *marginalia,* ◦⸢Chamberlein ... Chester⸣◦ *in RH II's hand*
8 / ◦⸢& ... North⸣◦ *in RH II's hand*   9-10 / ◦⸒& ... crosse⸒◦ *in RH II's hand*
14 / ◦‸⸢standing⸣◦, ◦⸢duble gilt⸣◦ *in RH II's hand*
39 / i *altered from* v *in* ij s

Item payed to the womane for Rydinge iij d and for a peare of
gloves for heare vij d
Item geven to a mane to Leade heare horse   iiij d
Item spente in borowinge of a dye manes Cote   ij d
Item payed for a peire of hose and sues and a peare of gloves
for the Chyld that dyd Ryde afore our Companye   xix d
Item payed to ij men, to a tend vpone the chyld and the horsse
and one to Carye the Cvpes   ix d
Item spent at Insses withe owte the bares one mydsomer even
vppone parte of our bretherne   vj d   )
Item spent at our aldermane Iohn shawes afore the watche   vj d
Item geven to the Cryer at the bares   j d
Item geven to the pressvneres at the Castell iiij d and at the
northe gate iiij d some is   viij d
Item spent at our stvard sysses howse after the wache vppone   )
our bretherne   v s
Item payed for ij peare of gloves to the to the stuardes at iij d
a peare   vj d
Item payed for horsbred the womane Ryde vppone at mydsomer
                                                      iij d   2)

Painters, Glaziers, Embroiderers, and Stationers' Records
C: Account Book I
f 83 *(18 October)*   2
…
Payd for Cloathe to the stuardes hoodes and the makinge of them
                                                      vij s vj d
Payd for apayre of Buskyns to the childe   xij d
Payd for apayre of Glooves to the childe   iij d   3
…
Payd for the Lace to the buskkyns   ij d
Payd at the Barres   j d
Payd at the Castle & northgate   iiij d
Payd to the mynstrelles   xij d   3
Payd vppon mydsomer eve for the Drinckinge for the Companyes
the childe & ye mynstrells   ij s vj d

17 / to the to the *MS dittography*

Cordwainers and Shoemakers Records
CCA: Account Book I G/8/2
f 87 *(11 November)*

...

Item geven the two companes of musicions at thomas ball*es* drinckynge	xx d

...

Item geven the musicions at thomas lenard*es* drinckynge	xviij d

...

Item payde for the gleves at gutted	v s
Item payde for the bericche of the gleves	· iiij d
Item geven the wheatemen at gutted at oure allderman Inc*es*	ij s

...

f 87v

...

Item for a payre of buskens for the childe at mydsomer	ij s
Item for a payre of gloves for hym	iiij d
Item payde for a dosen of horsse bredd to the horsse	iiij d
Item geven the crier at the barres	j d
Item geven the presoner*es* in the castell	vj d
Item geven the presoner*es* in the northegate	vj d
Item payde the mucicions at mydsomer	ij s vj d
Item payde the fote man for ledinge the horsse	vj d
Item geven the taylor for dressinge the childe	iij d

...

Item payde the musicions on martens even	ij s iiij d

...

Coopers' Records C: Account Book I
f 19 *(20 November)*

...

It*em* payed at the borowynge of the boye	iiij d
It*em* payed at the bown*y*nge of the baye	x d
It*em* payed ffor a payere of hosse	viij d
It*em* payed ffor a payere of shew*ees*	x d
It*em* payed at the bryngynge home of the chylde	iiij d
It*em* payed ffor houldynge of the chyld on horssbake	iiij d
It*em* payed ffor horssebrede to the horsse	iiij d
It*em* payed to the pryssonar*es*	vj d
It*em* spynt on the company one mydsomar Ewen	iij s
It*em* for dressynge of the syne	xvj d

Item ffor a payer of glowes to the baye   iij d
...

Dean and Chapter C: Treasurers' Accounts III
p 1 *(November-December)*
...

Item for charges at our Audyt & dynner   vj li. xiij s. iiij d
Item to the mvsicions the same daye we had our Dynner   iiij s.
...

p 2
...
Inprimis paid the xxviijth of December vnto hugh skynner for
a watchman atendinge on the maior in Christmas tyme   xij d /
...

A C ***Mayor Brerewood's Address to the Watch*** BL: Harley 2150
f 5v* *(24 December)*

the speech of mr Robert brerewood Maior 1584 vpon
Christmas Eue at the maiors wach but was made by
mr William Knight then clarke of the pentice and by
the sayd maior learned by hart & by him pronounced:
for although he could nether write nor read yet was of
exelent memory & very braue & gentile partes otherways:

out of the
office in mr
Knights booke

The homagers or wach beinge Called he Sayd

Stand neere good fellows and heare your charge

Most of you as I vnderstand are such as are well accquinted with
this kind of seruice therfore I will vse but few words at this tyme
   you represent by this your apparances the stulls & places of
such honourable and worshipfull personages as haue byn called,
whos Auncestors & themselues tyme out of mynd rightly haue
done this manor of seruice & homage to the maior of this citty
for this night and to the sheriffs for the tow next nights, for the
better preseruation of this citty and as this manor of seruice
first arosse, as I learne in tyme of warrs with the welch: this
citty beinge most endangered by the Enimy at christmas tyme,
so it is Contynued of duty for such termes, for that euery
Artificer and other persons in this citty agaynst this holy feast

of christmas accustomed to be paynfull and wakfull in their
trades & occupations and now theis holly days expect rest and
quietnesse, therfore you are to vse yourselues as wachmen
hauinge the Care & charge of this citty reffered to you, vnder
your lords & masters, and diligently and paynfully to shew your   5
selues herin and ouerssee that no hurt or hindrance happen or
come to this citty or Inhabitants therof duringe your tyme of
wachinge nether by fier nor by any lewd Roges or vacobonds or
other disordred persons in robbinge of shopps stealinge or
Conveighinge out of backsides or otherways nor wandringe   10
abrode gamninge drinkinge or disordringe them selues at any
vndue tyme, yf you find or know of any such suppresse them,
and if you see Iust cause Comitt them to ward, so as they may
be forth Cominge in the morninge to answare their misdemenares.
also I charge you all to behaue your selues trustyly in this seruice   15
as to your dutyes appertayneth & to deuide your selues into
seuerall Companeys throughout the Streets & lanes within this
Citty wherby you may the better acomplish this seruice & with
all if you shall perceaue any mans children or seruants in any
place to vse themselues wantonly or otherways not as they   20
ought or is conuenient or any other persons disordringe
themselues; reforme them ⌃'in' orderly sort if the shall resist
you, vse them as the rest & in this doinge you shall discharge
your duties or otherways you endanger thos for whom you now
serue, of their Tenures the hould of this citty for this seruice,   25
as also be assured your selues to receaue seuere punishment to
be Compelled by body or goods to make recompence for your
neglences: (thus leauinge) trustinge you will ⌃'be' haue your
selues like honest men hauinge due regard to this your charge
& so farwell.   30

...

Joiners, Carvers, and Turners' Records
CCA: Company Book G14/1
f 28 *(25 March)*   35

...

Item payed for a peare of shewes to the boye that dyd Ryd
afore our compenye one mydsomer even   viij d
payed for a peare of gloves for the same boye   iij d
spent at william Stevensones in ffachinge vp the horse   ij d   40
geven to the Cryer at the Bares   j d
geven to the Wedowe Bovlton   iiij d

geven to the presoneres at the Castell   iiij d
geven to the presoneres at the northegate   iij d
geven to the mynstreles one mydsomer even   ij s vj d
payed for Wyne one mydsomer for our compenye   xvj d
...
payed for sowinge the boyes Covte   j d
payed for a peare of hose for the boye   viij d
...
payed for grese for the horse the boye Ryd vppone   ij d
...   10

1585-6
Innkeepers' Records   C: Account Book
f 13v *(August)*
...   15

Item paid for a yeard and a quarter fyne Calico Clothe for the
banner   iij s viij d
Item paid for ∧⌈grene mockadone⌉ [fringe] to the same [xvj d]
                                         viij d
Item paid for a staffe and wier to the same the some of   iiij d   20
Item paid to Thomas Poole for the workemanship som of
                                   vj s vij d
Item paid to the Widowe ellis for iij yerdes of ffryng the some of
                                        xvj d
Item a beuarage to Thomas poole ⌈by promyse⌉   xvj d   25
Item to the wyffe of Thomas poole for sowynge the frynge to
the baner & the sockett   xij d
Item spent at our Alderman howse at our metynge vpon
mydsoner euon   xviij d
Item payd to the mynstrelles   xviij d   30
Item spent vpon the chyld & hys foote man after the Wattche
                                         viij d
Item gyuon to the prysoners at the castell and at the northgate
                                         xij d
Item for apayre of hoses & shewes for the child   xiiij d   35
Item payd for spanlyes to sowe vpon the bande of the chylde
                                         iiij d
bestowed vpon them which dressed the chylde in wyne & sugar
                                     xj d ij d
Item to the Cryer at the barres   j d   40
Item for apayre of gloues for the chylde   iiij d
Item to hys foote man   xij d

Item for apottell of wyne to mr Chamberlayne for hys consell

              xij d

Painters, Glaziers, Embroiderers, and Stationers' Records

C: Account Book I   5

ff 84-4v *(18 October)*

...

Item for apeyre of Buskyns to the childe	xvj d	I d	
Item spent at the borowing of twoe chaynes of goulde	ij d		
Item paid for flues to dresse the boyes capp	iiij d		
Item for pynnes to dresse the boy	j d	I d	
Item for drinke at the dressing of the boy	ij d		
Item paid for apeyre of gloves	iiij d		
(entry cut off)	ij d |		
Item to the minstrell	vj d		
Item to the presoners	iiij d		
Item to Richardson	j d	I d	
Item for apottle of secke	xvj d		
Item for apottle of Claret wyne	x d		

mydsomer chardges (left margin, lines 8–9)

mydsomer charges hetherto ./ (left margin, lines 17–19)

line 10 (margin right)

line 15 (margin right)

...

line 20

Cordwainers and Shoemakers' Records

CCA: Account Book I G/8/2

f 89 *(11 November)*

       25

...

Item payde for the gleves at shrofte tyde	v s
Item payd to the berecche of the gleves	iiij d
Item geven to the wheate men at shrofte tyde	ij s vj d

...

Item payde for a payre of gloves for the childe at mydsomer	iiij d
Item payde for arsladyne to put on the saddell clothe	vj d
Item for a payre of buskens for the childe	xx d
Item payde for flewes for his bande	ij d
Item payde for halffe an ellne of grene taffata for the childes breches	iij s
Item payde for a girke for the childe lase & buttons	iij s iiij d
Item geven the taylor for dressinge the childe	iiij d
Item payde for a dosen of horsse bredd	iiij d
Item geven the crier at the barres	ij d
Item geven the presoneres at the castell	xij d
Item geven to the presoneres at the northe gate	xij d
Item geven the musicioneres at mydsomer	ij s vj d

line 30, 35, 40 (margin)

Item geven the two fote men for leadinge the horsse   xij d
...

f 89v
...

Item payde to the musicions on martens even   ij s
...

Coopers' Records C: Account Book I
f 20 *(20 November)*   1
...

Item payede at the borrowynge of the boweye   v d
Item payede at the bownnynge of the boye   vj d
Item payede ffor a payere of hosse   viij d
Item payed ffor a payere of shewees   x d   1
Item payed at the bryngeynge home of the boye   ij d
Item payed ffor leadyng of the horsse & howledynge ye boye
              viij d
Item payed ffor horsse brede to ye horsse   iiij d
Item payed to the pryssonares   viij d   20
Item spente on mydsomares ewen on ye companye   iiij s
Item payde ffor dryssynge of ye syne   xvj d
Item ffor a payere of glowes to ye boye   iij d
...

Item payed ffor wyne at thomas crystyanes dynere   xviij d   25
Item payed to the mynstreles   xviij d
...

Joiners, Carvers and Turners' Records
CCA: Company Book G14/1   30
f 29 *(25 March)*
...

Item payed for a pynt of wyne at mr llodes at the dresinge of
the boye   iij d
Item payed for a peare of hose to the Boye that dyd Ryd   viij d   35
...

Item geven to the presoneres at the Castell iiij d and to wedowe
bovlton iiij d and to the presoneres at the northe gate iij d
some is   xj d
geven to the mynstreles one mydsomer even   xiiij d   40
payed for a peare of gloves to the Boye that dyd Ryd   vj d
payed for a peare of shewes to the same boye   ix d

spent vppone mydsomer even . at the stuard harye skasbryckes
howse at in the presen*tes* of the Compenye   xx d
payed to Iohn denesberye for spungyes to sowe one the boyes
clocke   ij d
payed for cape papper to lape our banner in   iij d   5

...

geven to the mynstreles at *our* govse svttinges   xij d

...

payed for horsbrede to the horse the boye Ryd vppone   ij d
geven to Raphe barlowes wyffe to drepe the boye   iiij d   10

...

Item leaid dovne for wyne at Iohn Rabarnes dener   xvj d
Item geven to the mynstrelles at the same dener   xij d

...
                                                                                15

1586-7

Innkeepers' Records C: Account Book
f 16v *(August)*

...

Item for one Iryon to *our* banner   ij s   20
Item [for] payd for*e* the child hose   viij d
Item payd for a peyre of showes   viij d
Item for a peyre of gloves for the child   vj d
Item payd at the glou*er*stone to ye *prisners*   iiij d
Item payd at the norgate to the *prisoners*   iiij d   25
Item payd to the Cryer at the bares   j d
Item payd to the mynstrell   xvj d
Item payd for makinge the Child*es* rep*arile* & dressinge ˹hym˺
Redy appon mydsom*er* eive⟨.⟩   xij d
Item payd for ij footmen   xij d   30
Item for vj⁰ potes of drynke to the byryche   vj d
Item spent [afore] at *our* company cominge downe before the
Child went vp to the barres & after wards brought ˰˹him˺
whome againe at the stuward howse   viij s viij d
...   35

Painters, Glaziers, Embroiderers, and Stationers' Records
C: Account Book I
f 87 *(18 October)*

...   40

Item for aneln of fyne holland Cloathe for our Banner   v s
Item for threyde to hem yte and for the ylott holes   j d

Item to the Taylor for the settinge on of the fringe to the Banner
iij d
Item to the presoners at the Castle and the northgate as
accostomed   vj d
Item to the Smyth for the Iron rodde that beareth vpp the   5
Banner   vj d
Item to the Crier at the Barrs   j d
Item to the Bereache at the workinge of oure Banner spent
at our aldermans   ij s viij d
Item spent at abereach to the taylor at ye setting on of the fringe   10
to ye banner   ij d
Item to the mynstrelles   xij d

...

Item for the staffe to Carrye the banner   x d
Item spent at our Aldermans vpon mydsomer eve   ij s viij d   15

...

Cordwainers and Shoemakers' Records
CCA: Account Book I G/8/2
f 91 *(11 November)*   20

...

Item pead for the gleves at shrofte tid   v s
Item spent at the berege of the gleves   iiij d
Item geven to the weatmen at shroftyd   ij s

...   25

Item pead for a peare of gloves for the chyld at mydsormer   iiij d
Item spent at *Maistris* pyllins a bowt the chyld   iiij d
Item pead for a peare of buskins for the chyld   xx d
Item geven the prysenars at castell on mydsomer Eve   xij d
Item geven the prisenares at the northgate   xij d   30
Item geven to thomas Rycharsun at the bares   j d
Item geven the musisiones for pleinge before vs   ij s vj d
Item pead for a pottell of sacke at my alderman leas on
mydsomer Ive at night   xx d
Item pead to the futman for weating on the chyld   vj d   35
Item pead [fo] Ihon ley for leding the horse   vj d

...

f 91v

...   40
Item geven to the weatmen at martines Ive   ij s

...

Coopers' Records C: Account Book I
f 21 *(20 November)*

...

Item pead for wyne At Iohn scownses dyner	ij s vj d
Item pead for suger	vj d.
Item pead to the mynstrylles	ij s
Item At the northgate	vj d

...

f 21v

Item pead to my Alderman nyckis	xij s
Item for lassee And choryed	xiiij d
Item for Buttones And sylke	ix d
Item for halfe A yarde bluee cottone	iiij d
Item spende *(blank)*	ij d
Item for makyng the cyldes clothes	iij s
Item spend At rafe cowpers	iij s iiij d
Item spend on mydsomer ewen	vj s
Item for dressynge the syne	xix d
Item for Apeare of hosse to the boye	xiiij d
Item for hoosse bred	iiij d
Item for Apeare of showes to the boye	x d
Item to the mynstryll	iiij d
Item to the cryere	j d
Item to the prysoners	vj d
Item Apeare of glowes to the boye	iij d
Item At the Boynynge of the boye And At sevrall tymes in warnynge the companye	xij d

...

Item oure fowtman on medsomer evene	vj d

...

Joiners, Carvers, and Turners' Records
CCA: Company Book G14/1
f 30 *(25 March)*

...

payed for a peare of gloves for the Chylld that Ryd afore our Compenye at mydsomer	iiij d
payed for a peare of hose and shewes to the boye	xviij d
Item geven to the Cryer at the bares ij d and at the Castell to the presoneres iiij d and at the northe gate iiij d some is	ix d
Item geven to the mynstrelles one mydsomer even . to goo a	

fore our Compenye   xviij d

...

payed at willim garffylldes to the mynstreles   [x d] xij d

...

5

1587-8

Innkeepers' Records   C: Account Book
f 20 *(August)*

...

spent in provydinge for a Chylld ∧ 'to Ryd afore oure companye'   10
the some of   xiij s iiij d
payed for makinge of a newe Rode to our syne   iij d
payed for a peare of hose for the Chylld that Ryd fore ouer
Compenye one mydsomer even   x d
payed for a peare of shewes for hyme   viij d   15
payed for a peare of gloves for hyme   iiij d
payed for a lether sockete to pute the end of the staffe into
carye the syne withe   ij d
payed to ij ffute men to a tend vppon the Chylld at iiij d a pese
                                                           viij d   20
payed for a quart of wyne to the Ientill women that drest the
Chylld   vj d
payed over the shoost at the vndressinge of the Chylld at Iohn
myllneres howse   iiij d
payed to the mynstrell to playe afore our Comepanye one   25
mydsomer even   xij d
geven to the Cryer at the bares   j d
geven to the pressoneres at the Castell iiij d and at the northe
gate iiij d some   viij d
payd at the stuardes howse one mydsomer even at the presentes   30
of our bretherine   iij s viij d

Painters, Glaziers, Embroiderers, and Stationers' Records
C: Account Book I
f 90 *(18 October)*   35

...

Item to the wayet*es*   xij d

...

Item geven to the mynstrell*es* att stuert*es* Raufe hallwodes
dener att his wedding   viij d   40

...

It*em* paid for a paire of buskins to the boye   xvj d

Item paid for pymes and thride to bowne the boye   ij d
Item paid for a paire of gloves to the boye   ij d
Item paid for drincke att the bowninge of the Childe   ij d
Item paid to the prissoners in the Castell and norgate   iiij d
Item paid at our aldermans Allens for our bankett and wyne   5
on mydsomar even   iij s iiij d
Item paid to the mynstrelles   xviij d
Item paid for horse brede to the horse   iiij d

...

Item spent att alderman framwall on mydsomar even   xij d   10

...

Treasurers' Account Rolls CCA: TAR/1/17
mb 4 *(November)*

     15
...
Item to mr Thomas fletcher draper for xix yardes [⟨..⟩] tinge a
halffe clothe this xviijth of december to make iiijor gownes to
the wetemen and one to Iesper gyllome and acote to Richerd
crofote at vij s iiij d the yarde is   vj li. xv s viij d
     20
...

mb 4d

...
Item payed for v elles of Redd yallowe and blewe sassenet for
the Aunciante and for the staffe and other furniture to the same   25
the some of   iiij li.
Item to the stuardes of the sadlers towardes their bell   vj s viij d

...

Item the 25 of Iune to Thomas poole for tryminge of mr maior
his mounte   xxiij s iiij d   30

...

Item to Thomas gyllome and Robert smythe for their morreys
daunsinge at mydsomer   vj s viij d

...

     35

Cordwainers and Shoemakers' Records
CCA: Account Book I G/8/2
ff 93-3v *(11 November)*

...
Item pead for the gleaves at Shorofte tyd   v s   40

---

1 / pymes *for* pynnes, *minim omitted MS*

Item spent at the berege of the gleves   iiij d
Item geven to the weatmen at shorfte tyd   ij s

...

Item for cotten and lynan linige and lase to sett vpon the chyldes
hose at mydsomer [and]   ij s   5
Item for the makinge of of them howse   vj d
Item for arsedine for to trime the sadle clothe   viij d
Item for a peare of gloves for the chyld   iiij d
Item for a peare of buskines for the chyld   xx d
Item for a Dosen of horse bred   iiij d   10
Item geven to Rycharsin at the bares   ij d
Item geven at the northgatt   xij d
Item geven at the castell   xij d |
Item geven to the mususiones one mydsomer Ive   ij s vj d
Item geven to the futtman for ledinge the horse   vj d   15
Item spent at the Dressinge of the chyld   iiij d
Item pead for a gallon of sacke at alderman leas vpon mydsomer
Ive   iij s iiij d

...

Item spent at alderman Insis one martins Ive   xx s   20
Item geven to the weatmen   ij s

...

Coopers' Records C: Account Book I   25
ff 23-3v* *(20 November)*

...

Item Layde Downe on mydsomer even in ale bred & Chese   v s
Item at attyring the boy spent   iiij d
Item for a paire of hose   vj d | 30
Item to the footman   iiij d
Item for a paire of gloues   ij d
Item borrowing the horse spent   ij d

...

Item for buckeram to the banner   xv d   35
Item for fringe   x d
Item fore the Iren & stafe   v d
Item for the making & paynting the same   iiij s

...

Item more among the Company at the Earle of Darby his   40

Comyng in   xviij d

...

Joiners, Carvers, and Turners' Records
CCA: Company Book G 14/1   5
f 31 *(25 March)*

...

payed for a peare of shewes to the boye that Ryd afore our
compeyne one mydsoner even   viij d
payed for a peare of hose for hyme   iiij d 10
payed to the Cryer at the bares   ij d
payed to the presnores at the northe gate iij d and at the castell
iij d   vj d

...

payed for a peare of gloves for the boye that Ryd afore our   15
compenye   ij d
payed to the mynstrell one mydsoner even   ij s vj d
payed to willim modsleye for his horse for the boye one
mydsomer even   iiij d
payed to gryffithe ap shone to a tend vppone the Chylld   iiij d 20

...

1588-9

Innkeepers' Records C: Account Book
f 22v *(August)*   25

...

Itt*em* for a pair of showes to the boy that Ride at midsomer
                                                            viij d.
Itt*em* for apair of hoose and gloves to the boy   xij d.
Itt*em* Speent at our aldermans howse one midsomer Even when   30
we went to the watche to fetche him down   vij d.
Itt*em* given to the Crier at the barres   j d
Itt*em* given to the prisoners at the ´Castle` [barres] and at the
northegatte   viij d
Itt*em* for a sokett to hold the bannr*e* staffe   ij d   35
Itt*em* for horse bread to the horse that the boy Rid vpon   iiij d
Itt*em* to two footmen to load the horse   vj d
Itt*em* to the minstrels to play befor oure company   xvj d
Itt*em* for the drinckinge to our bretheren befoer the watche and
after the watche was Doon when the brought whom the Childe /   40
And Lickewise to the minstrels and foot men At oure steward*es*
howse   vij s ij d /

...

Painters, Glaziers, Embroiderers, and Stationers' Records
C: Account Book I
f 91 *(18 October)*

...

In pr*im*is paid at our brothers thomas prickett dynner for wyne
and to the mynstrelles   vij s iiij d

...

It*em* spent att the Coninge in of the erle of darbye   xij d

...

It*em* spent on mydsomar even in wyne   ij s ij d
It*em* geven att the Castell & northgate   viij d
It*em* geven to the mynstrell   vj d
It*em* paid for a paire of buskins for the Chylde   xvj d
It*em* paid for a paire of gloves   iij d
It*em* paid for drincke flues and pynnes att the boning of the
Chylde   viij d
It*em* paid for horse bred and the leder of the horse   iij d
It*em* paid for a Cloke to the Chylde so hitt Remaying to the
Company   v s

...

It*em* spent att Ihon walkers dyner and the mynstrelles   iij s x d
It*em* to the mynstrells att thomas gyllns wedyng   xij d

...

Treasurers' Account Rolls CCA: TAR/1/18
mb 3 *(November)*

...

vnpaide Nycholas white Marchant for a house Next Adioyninge to the
drapars Cariadge howse p*er* Ann*um*   iij s iiij d
[The steward*es* of the drap*er*s for their Cariadge house   viij d]

...

[The steward*es* of the m*er*cers for their Cariadge house   vj d]

...

mb 5

...

It*em* to mr. ffletcher drap*er* the xjth of december for xviij
yeard*es* of sadd nerve Collored broade Cloth att vij s iiij d the
yearde Viz for three of the eldest waytte men x yeard*es* for iij
gownes iij yerd*es* for towe Coate Clothes for towe of the Yonger

---

8 / Coninge *for* Cominge, *minim omitted MS*

Wayttmen . iij yerdes and halfe for agowne for gesper gyllam and
one yearde and halfe for a Coate cloth for Crofoote keper of
the Conduitte and ys Some   vj li. xij s

...

Item ffor playinge vppon the drvme before mr mayor vppon   5
goodtid*es* tewsedaye last past is Some   vj d
Item the xijth of februarie to the steward*es* of the Sadlers
toward*es* their Bell is Some   vj s viij d

...
                                                                10

mb 6

...

Item the xxiiij° of Ivne to thomas poole for settinge forth of
the Mount before mr mayr on mydsom*er* even is some   xxiij s iiij d
Item the xxvth of Ivne to the morres dauncers ffor daunsynge   15
at the Watche before the Shereffes is some   vj s viij d

...

Cordwainers and Shoemakers' Records

CCA: Account Book I G/8/2   20
f 95 *(11 November)*

...

Item. payd for Gleaves at Shroftyde   v. s.
Item. Spent at the berridge of the same gleaves   iiij d
Item. geven to the weatmen, at the Alderman Inces howse   25
                                                      ij. s vj d

...

f 95v

...   30

Item. payd for a payre of gloves, for the Childe, on midsomer
even   iij d
Item. payd for horse breade   iiij d
Item. payd for threede to sett one Arsedine, one the Childes
foote Clothe   j d   35
Item. payd for a fydder for the boye   viij d
Item. payd to Thomas Richarsonne for Callinge vs, at the Barres
                                                         iiij d
Item. geven to the Priesoners at the Castle   xij d
Item. geven to the Priesoners at the Northgate   xij d 40
Item. payd for a potle of Claret wyne on midsomer Even, at
Alderman leys   xij d

Item. payd for a potle of Sacke the same tyme xx d
Item. payd to the minstrels for playing before vs iij s
Item. payd for a payre of Buskins for the Childe xx d
Item. spent at the dreshinge of the Childe iiij d
Item. payd for dresshinge the Staffe to Robert leeche the same 5
tyme viij d
Item. payd to a foote man vj d

...

Item. Spent at alderman Inces, one martins Eve xx. s
Item. geven to the weatmen ij. s 10

...

A *Mayors List 5* BL: Harley 2125
f 43* *(November) Robert Brock*

...   15

also a play was playd at high crosse called the storey of Kinge
Ebrauk with all his sonne but such rayne fell it was hindred
much

...

...   20

Coopers' Records C: Account Book I
f 24* *(20 November or 13 January)*

...

Item Receiued more of the Cowpers vppon mydsomer evine vj d

...   25

Item payd for a payre of hosse for the boye that dyd Ryde
vppon mydsomer evine xiiij d
Item payd for a payre of shewes for hime viij d
Item for a payre of gloves for hime iij d
Item payd for horsse bredd for the horsse iiij d 30
Item to the prysoners at Castyll & northgate vij d
Item to the mynstrell iiij d
Item spent vppon our Company at mydsomer evine iij s iiij d

...

...   35

Joiners, Carvers, and Turners' Records
CCA: Company Book G 14/1
f 32 *(25 March)*

...

mydsoner even.   40

Item spent at dicler Ioynores in spekinge for aboye to Ryd afore

our compenye at mydsomer	ij d	
Item payed for a peare of gloves for the Chylld	ij d	
Item payed for a peare of hose for hyme	xj d	
Item payed for a peare of shewes for hyme	viij d	
Item payed for a pottell of wyne and svgare	xiiij d	5
Item geven to the Cryer at the bares	ij d	

Item geven to the pressoneres at the Castell and at the northe
gate   vj d

Item geven to the mynstrelles to gooe afore our compenye   ij s

...   10

Item geven to the mynstrells at the govse shewtinge   xij d

...

f 32v

...   15

mydsomer even.

payed for a peare of hose to the boye that Ryd a fore our Compenye	viij d	
payed for a peare of shewes for hyme	viij d	20
geven to the Cryer at the bares	ij d	
geven to the pressoneres at the Castell and at the northe gate	vij d	
payed for a peare of gloves to the boye	ij d	
payed to the minstrells to playe afore our compenye	xxij d	
payed to povell for pentinge of the staffe	j d	25
payed to a tellyer for sowinge the boyes clothes	iij d	
spent one mistris kaye at the bounying of the boye	ij d	

...

Assembly Books CCA: AB/1   30
f 192 *(1 June)*

...

•A cup and xl Angels presented to the Erle of Leicester•

At which daie mocion was made, whether more Convenyent in stid of the former Banquet appoynted, at the laste former Assembly to be prepared for the Erle of leycester to haue that   35 faire standinge Cupp, which Mr Iohn Tillson, nowe hath bought and that Cupp, with xlie Angells of goolde to be presented to his honor, not not, which Cupp is valued after xviij li. or that aboute, yet wilbe had for lesse as is supposed, And vpon consideracion and good advisemente therof had, And vpon   40 vnder standinge, that his honor delyteth not in banquettes, neyther shalbe occasyoned to stay the tyme therof in this Cittie.

It is at this Assembly fully concluded and agried vppon by the
saide Maior, The aldermen, Sherifes and Comon Counsaile of
the said Cittie, That the saide Banquett shalbe spared, and that
the saide Cupp . and nomber of Angelles shalbe presented to his
honor in the humbleste manner in the name of this Cittie, in   5
remembrance of his honorable goodnes to this Cittie and for
Contynuaunce thereof./

f 192v

...   10

And for the better shewe tattende vppon Mr Maior, It is allso
ordered that all Aldermen and Stewardes of euery occupacion
shall made ready all their seuerall Companies in the beste order,
with one personne of euerye Companie to kepe them in order,
well attyred, to attend vpon Mr Maior, vppon wednesdaie nexte,   15
at five a Clock in the aforenoone, at the highe Crosse to be
ymployed, as Mr Maior shall appoynt /

...

1589-90   20
Innkeepers' Records C: Account Book
f 24 *(August)*

...

Item for dressinge our boye that Ryde   iiij d
Item hose showes for our boye   xvj d   25
Item for glowes for our cheld   iiij d
Item the man that tendyd the childe   vj d
Item to the cryer at the barres   j d
Item to the prysoners at the castell and at the northgate   viij d
Item in bowrowinge the dyvelles ^'clothes' spent   ij d   30
Item for the two men that weare them   xij d

...

Item the woman that Ryd with them to breake the goddertes
                                                               viij d
Item the man that carryed the baskett   iiij d   35
Item our banor staffe & Rode   vj d
Item our canne trymmynge   ij d
Item for two dosen of goddertes   xvj d

...

Item the horse for our chield in bread & gresse   iij d   40
Item spent on mydsomer eaven on oure companye   vj s ij d

...

Dean and Chapter CC: Treasurers' Accounts III
p 45* *(29 September-25 November)*

...

Item to the Queen's players at the appoyntment of Mr Deane &
the Chapter   xx s   5

...

Painters, Glaziers, Embroiderers, and Stationers' Records
C: Account Book I
f 93 *(18 October)*   10

...

Item in primis at Nicholas halewoodes house for A quarte of
Seck one our accompte daye viz St luke   x d
Item to the Musicians at the same tyme   vj d
...   15
Item Spent at Thomas Chaloners at the amendinge of our
Banner   vij d
Item Spent at the fetchinge awaie of ye banner   vj d

...

Item to the Crier on mydsomer eve at ye barres   ij d   20
Item to an Impotent old man on midsomer eve   ij d
Item at the Castle and the Northgate   viij d
Item for hose and Shooes to the Child   xviij d
Item for pynnes and Glooues   iiij d
Item spent at the dressinge of the child   iij d   25
Item for horse Bread on midsomer eve   ij d
Item to the musicians on mydsomer eve   xx d
Item Spent on mydsomer eve at our supper   iiij s iiij d
Item for Wyne at the verey Same tyme   xij d
...   30

Treasurers' Account Rolls CCA: TAR/1/19
mb 2 *(November)*

                                                                          35

... Et solutum pro novemdecem virgatis et quarter panni lanei
pro tribuenis Ciuitatis predicte vocatis le waytmen et Jasper
Gillam et Crowfot vij li. ... Et solutum Ricardo Bromley et
Laurencio warmincham Senescallis occupacionis del Sadlers date
per Ciuitatem ad partem faciendam le horse bell vj s viij d Et   40
solutum Raimundo Stockton pro le gun powder xl li. Et solutum
pro Cariagio inde ij s ...

Cordwainers and Shoemakers' Records
CCA: Account Book I G/8/2
f 96v *(11 November)*

...

(St Martin's Day)   5
Item giuen to the waitmen the same daye   xvj d

...

Item giuen for Gleves at Shroftide   v s
Item giuen to the barrage   iiij d
Item giuen to the waitmen at *our* Alderman Inc*es* house at   10
Shroftide   ij s

...

f 97

                                                                15
Item giuen for a payre of gloves for ye childe vpon Midsom*er*
evine   iiij d
Item ˄ ˈspentˈ for apparelinge the Childe   v d
Item for a payre of buskinges for the childe   xx d
Item for two footmen for to attend vpon the Childe   xij d   20
Item for the horsbread   iiij d
Item spent at widdowe Eages house vpon Midsom*er* evine   vj d
Item giuen to Thomas Richardson for callinge vs at the barres
                                                               iiij d
Item giuen to the pr*i*soners of the castell   xij d   25
Item giuen to the pr*i*soners of the Northgate   xij d
Item giuen to the Musitiones   ij s vj d
Item giuen to [thre] 4 Musitioners the same daye   vj d
Item giuen for a potell of Sacke sent for to our Ald*er*men Leas
house the same daye   xvj d   30
...
Item giuen to the waitmen vpon Martins evine   xvj d
Item giuen to Calie the same night   xij d
...

                                                                35

Dean and Chapter CC: Treasurers' Accounts III
p 78 *(25 December)*
...

Inpr*i*mis to Io*h*n Welch for iij night*es* attendinge vpon the
maior in Christmas   xij d   40
Item for the loane of harnes   viij d
...

Coopers' Records C: Account Book I
f 25 *(13 January)*

...

Charges Lead out on midsomer even as folloeth

5

Item payd for a payre of hosse for ye boye yat did Ryde for ye Compeny	ix d
Item for a payre of showse for ye Boye	x d
Item payed for a payre of gloves for ye boye	ij d
Item for horsebred for ye horss	iiij d	10
Item to ye foote man	iiij d
Item geuen to ye Cryer at ye Bares	j d
Item geuen to ye presseners of ye Castell and ye norgate	viij d
Item geuen to ye minsterell	vj d

15

1590-1
Painters, Glaziers, Embroiderers, and Stationers' Records
C: Account Book I
f 97 *(18 October)*

...

20

Item in pr*im*is To the Waytes and for Wyne the daie af*ter*
St Luk*es* at *our* bro*ther* Edmundes dynner at *our*
Aldermannes   iij s ij d tch

...

Item for apayre of hose to the child for mydsoom*er* eve	xij d	Im	25
Item for apayre of Shoos to the child	viij d	Im
Item for apayre of Glooves to the child	iij d	Im
Item to the mynstrell*es* for mydsomer eve	xxij d	Im
Item to the presone*rs* at the northgate & ye Castle	vj d	Im
Item spente at the bowninge of the childe at mr *william* holland*es*	iij d	Im	30
Item spent at *our* aldermans vpon the minstrell*es* & the child	xij d	Im
& such as cam thether af*ter our* pro*cessione*		
Item geaven the youngman that ledd the horse for ye child	ij d	tc	35
Item geven the Crier at the Barrs	ij d	Im
Item for horse bredd to the horse wee borrowed	ij d	tc

...

34 / & such ... pro*cessione interlined*

Dean and Chapter CC: Treasurers' Accounts III
p 80* *(29 September-25 November)*

...

Item to the Quene Ma*jestes* players   xx s x d

...   5

Treasurers' Account Rolls CCA: TAR/1/20
mb 7 *(November)*

...   10

It*em* payd for xix yard*es* & a quarter of cloth for the wayte
men Iesper Gyllam and Crofoote   vij li.

...

mb 8   15

...

It*em* to Rychard Bromley & Lawrence Warminsham steward*es*
of the sadlers gyven by the Cittie toward*es* there bell   vj s viij d

...

It*em* to Iohn waring for playing vpon the droimme before   20
mr maior at shroftyde   viij d

...

It*em* payd to Tho*mas* Poole paynt*er* for dressing mr maiors
mount and the Geyant*es* and beast*es* at midsom*er*   xliij s iiij d

...   25

It*em* for playing on the drum*me* at midsomer   viij d
It*em* to the morris danc*ers*   vj s viij d

...

                                                                                                          30

Cordwainers and Shoemakers' Records
CCA: Account Book I G/8/2
f 99 *(11 November)*

...

(St Martin's Day)   35
Item payed to the Musitioners the same daye   xij d

...

Item payed for the glaves   v s
Item giuen for the barage of the glaves   iiij d
Item giuen to the watmen at *our* Alderman Inc*es* house at   40
Shroftide   ij s

...

f 99v

...

Item payed for linen clothe	xj d
Item payed for mendinge the staffe	iij d
Item payed for makinge the dublet bumboist and buttons	iiij s
Item payed for a payre of gloves for ye childe	ij d
Item giuen to Ricerson the Crier	iiij d
Item giuen to the prisoners at the castell	xij d
Item giuen to the prisoners at the Northgate	xij d
Item for horsbreade	iiij d
Item payed for iij Quartes of Sacke vpon Midsomer Evene	ij s vj d
Item payed for the Musitioners for playnge before vs	ij s vj d
Item payed for a payre of buskins for the childe	xx d
Item payed for leadinge the horse	vj d

...

f 100

...

Item giuen to the waitemen vpon St Martins Evene   xx d

...

Dean and Chapter CC: Treasurers' Accounts III
p 106 *(Christmas)*

...

Inprimis to Walshe for 3. nights attendance vpon mr Maior in
Christmas   xij d
Item for the loane of Harnesse   xij d

...

Coopers' Records C: Account Book I
f 26v *(13 January)*

...

mydsomer even Item payed for a peare of hose to the boye   x d
Item payed for a peare of shewes to the boye   x d
Item payed to the Cryer at the bares j d and and to the presoneres
at the Castell iiij d and at the northe gate iiij d some is ix d
Item geven to the horse in brede   iiij d

...

Item geven to a minstrell to playe afore our Compenye   vj d

35 / and and MS *dittography*

Item geven bestowed vppone our Compenye after the watche

iij s iiij d

f 27

...

Item Receved of ye Cowpers on midsomer even   xiij d

...

Item Receved of Thomas Braband for owre Carredge   iij s

...

Joiners, Carvers, and Turners' Records
CCA: Company Book G 14/1
f 33 *(25 March)*
...

mydsomer . even .

Item payed for the Chyllds hose xj d and for his shewes ix d
some is   xx d
Item geven to the minstrells to playe a fore our compeny one
mydsomer even   ij s
payed for wyne to the Ientillwomen that drest the chylld   iiij d
spent at Iohn sysses howse at the byinge of the dvblete   iiij d
payed for a peare of gloves for the Chylld   ij d
geven to the pressoneres at the Castell iij d and at the northe
gate iij d and to the Cryer at the barres ij d   viij d
payed for dvblitte for the Chylld   ix s vj d
...

Mayors' Books CCA: M/B/25
f 45 *(28 May)*
...

Apud Ciuitat*em* Cestr*ie* xxviij° die Maij Anno R*egi*ne Elizabeth
&c tricesimo tercio Coram Will*el*mo Massy maior*is* Ciu*itatis*
Cestr*ie*

At w*h*ich day matter was in question betwene Ales Willi*a*mz
late wief of Thom*a*s Willi*a*mz Late one of the waytsmen of the
said Citie vpon thone party and chr*isto*fer Burton and Willi*a*m
Madock the other waitesmen of the said Citie for and Conserninge
their instrument*es* of musick viz the how boies the Recorders
the Cornet*es* and violens whereof the said Ales Claymeth a p*ar*te
as to her said late husband in his lief tyme belonginge w*h*ich

they deny to yeld vnto: But are Contented and soe are now
Agreed and it is now fully ordered by Assent that the said
instrum*entes* shall from hensfurth forever remayne Continue
and bee the owne proper good*es* of the said Waitesmen and of
the s*ur*vivour of them and of Will*ia*m Will*ia*mz late sonne of the   5
said Thom*as* Will*ia*mz And of henry Burton sonne of the said
chr*ist*ofer When they shall haue s*er*ved out their yeres as
Apprentices to the said exercise and to the s*ur*vivour of them
and the survivour of eu*er*y of them and of the survivinge sonne
of eu*er*y of them experienced or to be experienced in the said   10
excercise and Apt and fitt for the same s*er*vinge w*i*thin the said
Citie or ells to remayne foreuer to the said Citie At the
Appoyntm*ent* and Admittance of the maior of the said Citie
for the tyme beinge
                                                                          15

1591-2
Innkeepers' Records C: Account Book
f 29v *(August)*

...

Inp*r*imis payed for the boyes hose & shewes	ij s iiij d	20
Item payed to Thomas poole for ouer banner	iij s	
Item payed to Iasp*er* Gillam	xij d	
Item for gloves for the boye	viij d	
Item payed to the woman that Ridd	viij d	
Item payed to the two devilles	viij d	25
Item payed to the foote men	viij d	
Item payed for coierse cuppes	xvj d	
Item payed for the boyes garters	xij d	
Item to mr Gamulles man for bringinge the Ciertall	iij d	
Item payed for apound of gonnpother	xvj d	30
Item for the womans gloves	iij d	
Item spent when the Child was in Dressinge in wyne and kakes		
	[xij d] viij d	
Item payed for ouer [dring] Drinckinge before & after ouer		
goinge to the barres	v s iiij d	35

...

Painters, Glaziers, Embroiderers, and Stationers' Records
C: Account Book I
f 99 *(18 October)*   40

...

Item geaven to the musicians vppon St Lukes daie	xij d	

...

Item for askynne to make the boye a Ierkine for mydsom*er*   vj d
Item for the makinge of the Ierkyne for the boie   xiiij d
Item spent for all the Companie at the widdowe Ieffreys ij s vj d
Item more for apaire of hose to the boie at midsomer   xij d
Item more for apaire of shooes to the boie at midsom*er*   viij d
Item paid to the musicians at mydsomer   ij s vj d
Item paid at the Barrs on midsomer Eve to the Crier   ij d
Item geven to the presoners at the Northgate   iiij d
Item to the presoners at the Castle   iiij d
Item deliuered to Robert waytes wief to helpe her child   v s.
Item geaven to the man that ledd the horse at midsomer   iiij d
Item for dressinge the Staff . for mydsomer .   vj d
Item spent on mydsomer eve for beeyre to ye companie   x d.
Item for breade at the tyme to the Companie   iiij d.
Item more at the same tyme for a Wort to ye Companie   vij d
Item geven to the hench man for his pains & borrowing of
apparell   xvj d

...

Dean and Chapter CC: Treasurers' Accounts III
p 109* *(29 September-25 November)*
...

Item bestowed vpon the earle of essex his musitions   ij s.
Item for wyne & sugar   ij s.
Item to the Quenes players   xl s.

...

Treasurers' Account Rolls CCA: TAR/1/21
mb 7 *(November)*
...

Item to the stuard*es* of the sadlers toward*es* their bell   vj s viij d
Item for playinge one the drome at shroftide   vj d
...

Item to henry hamnet for gesper gyllome his gowne & for 13
yard*es* di. to the weatement & their Boyes   vj li. vij s
...

Item to morreys dauncers at mydsomer   vj s viij d
...

Item to Thom*as* poole paynter for his Dewe for mydsom*er*
watche   xliij s iiij d
...

Item to walche for carryinge the Auntient at mydsom*er*   ij s

Item to tyttle for playinge one the dromme then   xij d

...

Cordwainers and Shoemakers' Records
CCA: Account Book I G/8/2   5
f 103 *(11 November)*

...

Inprimis / payed for a potell of Sacke at Thomas Tilstons diner
      xx d
Item giuen to the waite men At the fore fore said diner   ij s   10

...

Item payed for the glaves   v s
Item payed for berrige of the glaves   iiij d
Item giuen to the waitemen vpon shroft thursdaye at our
Alderman Inces house   ij s   15

...

f 103v

...

Item payed to Thomas Ricerson for callinge vs at the barres   iiij d   20
Item giuen to the prisoners at the Castle   xij d
Item giuen to the prisoners at the Northgate   xij d
Item to the Musitioners for plainge before vs   ij s vj d

...

Item payed for apayre of gloves for the childe   iij d   25
Item payed for a payre ˄ ʻofʼ buskins   xx d
Item payed to the footeman for leadinge the horse   xij d

...

Item payed for horsbread   iiij d
...   30

Dean and Chapter CC: Treasurers' Accounts III
p 137 *(25 November)*

...

Item to the Waytes   xij d /   35

...

p 138 *(Christmas)*

...

Inprimis to Iohn Wealch for 3. nightes attendinge vpon the   40
maior & Sheriffes in Christmas   xij d /

10 / fore fore MS *dittography*   22 / e of giuen *altered from* g

Item for the loane of harnes xij d /

...

Coopers' Records C: Account Book I
f 27v *(13 January)*

...

midsomer
euen

Item payde for a payre hosse for the Boye that did Ryde Before
owre Company x d
Item payde for a payre of showss for ye Boye x d
Item payde for a payre of glooves for the boye iij d
Item payde for horssbred for ye horsse iiij d
Item spende at the dressinge of the Boye vj d
Item payde to ye foottman iiij d
Item payde to the Cryer at the Barres j d
Item geven to ye prisseners at ye Castle and norgat viij d
Item payde to ye minstrell iiij d
Item payde for dressinge owre Bannar iij s
Item spende on owre Company after ye watch iij s iiij d

...

Joiners, Carvers, and Turners' Records
CCA: Company Book G14/1
f 36 *(25 March)*

...

Item Spente at the attyringe & setting . fowrth of the childe ij d
Item geaven to the presoners of the Castle and the northegate vj d
Item paide to the Mynstrelles vppon mydsomer Eve xij d
Item paide for apaire of hose to the child that rydd before ye
companye xj d

...

Item geaven to aboye that led the horse for the child at
midsomer ij d
Item geaven to the Cryer at the Barrs . for the Companie ij d
Item for apeyre of Shoes and apeire of glooves to the child xj d
Item more to the Mynstrelles on mydsomer Eve xij d

...

Joiners, Carvers, and Turners' Records CCA: Minute Book G14/2
f 9 *(3 June)*

At ameetinge 1592 the 3 of Iune
It was ordered that euerie Brother shall fynde a man in harnesse

vppon midsomer even nexte to come /
    Also that the drinckinge or Banquet shalbe haill after the going
about vppon Mydsomer eve, at the house of William Stevensone,
...

5

1592-3
Smiths, Cutlers, and Plumbers' Records C: Account Book II
f 2v* *(3 July)*

                          Midsomer Eve   10

17 Item it is fullie agreed vpon the same daye, that everie Brother
of our Companie shall Come With an Armed Manne to the
Common Hall lane End before the Watch to attend vpon the
Aldermen and stewardes and the rest of the Brethren in payne   15
of fforfeytinge   ij s. vj d.
...

Assembly Petitions CCA: A/P/1/38
(13 July)   20

    To the right worshipfull Mr Thomas Lynyall Maior of
    the Citie of Chester & to the Aldermen sheriffes &
    comen councell thereof

25

In moste humble wise, besecheth your worships Your Orator
Thomas Beedle Bowier. and maker of Instrumentes of Musick:
That whereas your said Orator is A verey poore man brought
vp in the occupacion of a Bowier and in the trade of makinge of
Instrumentes of Musick and Longe staves, for her Maiestes   30
seruice, which said trade he is moste desyerus to set vp, vse and
occupie within the said Citie, if he Might obtaine the freedom
thereof, beinge moste desyerus to end the rest of his time heere:
with your worshi⟨...⟩ good favours: where fore your [worships]
ˊOratorˋ moste humb⟨...⟩ besecheth your worships that it wold   35
please the same to graunte to your poore orator the freedome
of this ˄ˊCityeˋ and to admitt him into the liberties of the said
Citie as A freed[ome] man And in consideracion therof your
Orator will constraine him self to geve to this incorporacion
xxvj s viij d and become A dutifull Citizen tradinge and   40
occupiinge as is Aforesaid and will daily pray to god for your
worships

(*Endorsement*) Thom*as* Bedle Bowier and maker of
Instrum*entes* of Musick humblie craveth the freedome
of this Citie proferringe to geve for the same xxvj s   viij d

°graunted 13 Iuly 1592°   5

Innkeepers' Records C: Account Book
f 33 (*August*)

...

Item for mendinge o*ur* Can to the Cowp*er* and smyth	xj d	10
ffor a peire of garteres for the boy	ij s vj d	
ffor showes and hoose	ij s x d	
ffor Arsedine to dresse the boy and the horse sadle cloth	xiiij d	
ffor gloves to the boy	viij d	
ffor ˄ ʹvᵗʰ dozenʼ Cupes to breake	ij s vj d	15
ffor sylke and [thed] threde to dresse the child	vj d	
ffor wyne shouger and L cakes		
ffor dressinge the boy	xij d	
ffor dressinge the Banner	ij s viij d	
ffor a Peare of gloves to the woman that ˄ ʹ[⟨...⟩]ʹ Ridd (*blank*) &		20
his waggs	viij d	
Item to the tow foot men	viij d	
Item to the tow Deviles	viij d	
Item to the minstrells	ij s iiij d	
Item A pounde of gonnpowder	xvj d	25
Item to Iesp*er* gillam for Cuttinge the Tinsild	viij d	
Item for Drynke at y*at* tyme	iiij d	
Item for the Drynkinge appon mydsom*er* even of o*ur* company		
	viij s	
Item geven to mr gammll man for bringinge the Curtall	iij d	30
Item for tow penworth horsbread	ij d	
Item at glover stone to ye pr*isners*	iiij d	
Item to the norgate	iiij d	
Item to The Cryer at bares	ij d	
...		35

Painters, Glaziers, Embroiderers, and Stationers' Records
C: Account Book I
f 101 (*18 October*)

...   40

Item in pr*im*is for apaire of hose   xvj d

---

30 / gammll *for* gamull, *extra minim MS*

Item apayre of shooes	x d
Item for a Ierkyne	iij s viij d.
Item to the Crier.	ij d

...

Item for fringe to the Banner & sowing	xvj d	5
Item for Drincking on mydsom*er* eve	v s./	

...

for the painting the staff	vj d

...

On mydsomer eve to the musicions	ij s	10

...

To the preesson*ers* at Castle & Northgate	viij d

...

Cordwainers and Shoemakers' Records   15
CCA: Account Book I G/8/2
ff 105-5v *(11 November)*

...

Inpr*i*mis / payed for a potell of wyne at *ou*r Alderman Incis		
house the xiijth daye of November	xvj d	20
Item payed to the Musitioners the same daye	ij s	

...

Item giuen to the Musitioners at the time that Iohn Burchenhead	
made his drinkinge	ij s

...   25

Item payed for Glaves	v s iiij d
Item giuen to the Musitioners at shroftide	ij s

...

Item payed for a quarte of sacke w*hi*ch was bestowed vpon		
Mr Brocke for lendinge a Cappe & other Iewels for the		30
childe	viij d |	
Item payed for a payre of glooves	iij d	
Item payed for a payre of buskins	ij s	
Item payed at dressinge the Childe	iiij d	

...   35

Item payed to Ric*er*son the Crier	iiij d
Item giuen to the pr*i*soners at the Castell and Northgate	ij s
Item spent vpon Midsom*er* Even at *ou*r Aldermans house	ij s vj d
Item giuen to the footmen	xij d

...   40

Item payed for horsebread & shooinge ye horse	viij d
Item payed to the Musitioners	ij s vj d

...

Coopers' Records C: Account Book I
f 28 *(13 January)*

...

midsomer even | It*em* spend on owre Company on midsomar euen afteer the watche | iij s iiij d
Item for 'on' payre hosse for ye chylde | xx d
Item for on payre showsse for ye chylde | xij d
Item for on payre Gloves for the chylde | iiij d
Item for horss Bread | iiij d
Item fo to ye prisseneres at ye Castle and norgate | viij d
Item for on quart sacke when wee Brought whom ye chyld | viij d
Item to ye cryer at the Barres | j d
Item spend when the chylde was on dressinge | iiij d

...

Joiners, Carvers, and Turners' Records
CCA: Company Book G 14/1
f 38 *(25 March)*

...

Item in pr*im*is one payre of hose for the Child | xvj d
Item for apayre of glooves to the Child on midsom*er* eve | vj d
Item for apayre of shooes to the same Child | xiiij d
Item to the mynstrel*les* on Mydsomer Eve | ij s
Item geaven to the p*res*oners at Castle & Northgate | vij d
Item geaven to the Cryer at the Barrs | ij d
Item geaven to apoorewoman at glou*er*stone | iij d
Item for aquarte of wyne at *our* banquet | vj d
Item to the mynstrel*les* at Thom*as* Edmund*es* dynn*er* | xviij d

...

Item more to the mynstrell afterward*es* the same tyme | ij d

...

1593-4

Innkeepers' Records C: Account Book
f 35 *(August)*

...

Item payed for vj doussen of Cvppes to searve afore Compenye one mydsomer even at iij d a doussen some is | xviij d
Item payed for horsbred for the horse the womane dyd Ryde vppone one mydsomer even | iiij d
payed for a littell Cane to hange abowt the womanes necke one mydsomer even | ij d

payed for a brode bande of Lace for the Cane iij d
payed for payntinge the cane ij d
spent at the Bares vppone our companye afore ye wache iiij d
payd to the Cryer at the Bares iiij d to the presoneres at the
castell iiij d to the presoneres at the northe gat iiij d xij d. 5
payed to the mynstrell to goe afore our companye xij d
payed to the womane that dyd Ryde x d
payed to iij men wheare of ij weare dye men and the other dyd
carye the potes in a [⟨.⟩] baskete xv d
payed for a peare of gloves to the womane that dyd Ryd iiij d 10
payed for our drynkinge one mydsomer even at nyght afore
the wache vj s

Painters, Glaziers, Embroiderers, and Stationers' Records
C: Account Book I 15
f 104 *(18 October)*

...

Item in pri*m*is on St luk*es* daie to the musitians xij d
Item for mydsomer eve Chardges in meate drinck &c. iij s vj d
Item for horse breade on mydsomer Eve iiij d 20
Item paide to the mynstrell on mydsomer eve vj d
Item to the presoners at Castle & Northgate viij d
Item to the Crier at the Barrs iiij d

...

Item to Edward dawbie for going on stiltes ij s vj d 25
Item spent at the Dressing of the Childe iiij d

...

Item for apeire & hose and shooes to the child xx d
Item for apeire of glooves to the Childe iij d
30

Treasurers' Account Rolls CCA: TAR/1/22
mb 3d *(November)*

...

Item to the stuard*es* of the sadlers this ixth of february toward*es*
their bell vj s viij d 35

...

Item to tyttle for playinge one the drome at shroftyde vj d

...

Item to Thomas poole paynter for his yearelye fee for setting
fourthe the watche at mydsom*er* xliij s iiij d 40

...

Item to the morrys dauncers at midsom*er* vj s viij d

...

Item to tyttle for the playinge one the drome at mydsom*er*   xij d
Item to welche for carryinge the Auntient at mydsom*er*   ij s
Item for mendinge the staffe of the antient beinge broken   iij d

...

Item to mr maior for clothe had of hime for the iiijor *seriantes*
gownes and for the wheate mens gownes   xiij li. xiij s vj d

...

Cordwainers and Shoemakers' Records
CCA: Account Book I G/8/2
f 107 *(11 November)*

...

Inp*r*imis, payed at Mr Edward Benetes house the daye Iohn
Birchenhed had his Din*er* to the Musition*er*s   xvj d   1

...

Item giuen to the Musitioners at Thomas Iohnsons drinkynge xij d
Item payed for the glaves   v s
Item giuen for the berige of the glaves   iiij d
Item giuen to the watemen at Shroftide   ij s   2

...

f 107v

...

Item payed for a payre of gloves vpon Midsom*er* even for the   2
childe   iij d

...

Item for dressinge the childe   ij d
Item payed to the Crier at the barres   iiij d
Item giuen to the p*r*isoners at the Castell and Northgate   ij s   3
Item payed to two footemen   xij d
Item giuen to the Musitioners the same night   ij s vj d
Item payed for a potell of sacke the same night   xvj d
Item payed for a payre of buskins for the child   xx d

...   3

Item giuen to the Musitioners at William Vrinstons Din*er*   ij s

...

A   *Mayors List 5* BL: Harley 2125
     f 43v *(November) David Lloyd*   4

...

This yeare mr mayor Rode the libertyes of the cittye / and he
gate all the Scollers leave to playe that they / might goe with

hem. to thende they might remember the same ...

Coopers' Records C: Account Book I
f 29 *(13 January)*

...   5

[Inprymes bovght a shvtte of a parille a genste messemer even ⟨...⟩]
Item peed for a perre of shovsses for the chilld   x d
Item peed for a perre of hosses for the child   xij d
Item for a pere of Glovffes   ij d
Item for triminge the staffe for the bannare   iiij d   10
Item Ledovne for ovre compenye a pone messemer evene   iiij s
Item peed for horsse bridd   ij d
Item Gave vnto the fouteman that held the child   iiij d
Item gave vnto the criare at the barsses   ij d
Item gave vnto the prisinars at the castille and nore gatte viij d 15
Item gave vnto the menstrillis   viij d

...

Item peed for hirre of a horsse at the Ridinge of the lebertis   x d

...
                                                                      20

Joiners, Carvers, and Turners' Records
CCA: Company Book G14/1
f 40 *(25 March)*

...

Item for apaire of Shooes to the child for mydsomer eve   25
                                        [jx iiij d] ix d
Item for apayre of hose for the Child at the same tyme   xiiij d
Item for apaire of Glooues to the childe for mydsomer eve iij d
Item paid to the mynstrelles on mydsomer eve   ij s
Item paid to Lewis Bennett for leading the child   iiij d   30
Item paid for horse breade on mydsomer eve   ij d
Item paide for the Company at the Northgate & the Castle vj d

...

Item for the fetching of the horse out of the Countrey   iiij d
Item geaven to the Crier . at the Barrs   ij d   35

...

1594-5

Innkeepers' Records C: Account Book
f 37 *(August)*   40

...

Item payed for the hyer of a horse to Ryde wythe mr main
abowt the lybertyes of Chester ˊtheˊ20ˋ[23] of septemberˋ   x d

...

Item spent the aldermane Bryde in Borowinge the dye manes
svte a gaynest mydsomer even   iiij d

...

mydsomer even Item payed for vij doussen of Cvppes to bee Brocken one
mydsomer even withe the womane that Ryd afore our compenye
                                                    [xij d] [xiiij d] xx d
Item payed for the hyer of the horse the womane Ryd vppon
a fore our Compenye and for horsbred   x d
payed for the hyer of ij dyemenes cotes and for there houdes   1
the some of   xij d
payed to the mynstrell to go a ffore our compenye one mydsomer
even   xij d
Item payd to the womane that Ryd afore our compenye   x d
payed for a neve peare of gloves for the womane   iiij d   1.
payed for ij dyemen to a tend vppone the womane and for a
mane to Carye the Cvppes   xvj d
payed for our banckete one mydsomer even afore the wache to
the bretherne and after the wache whene the came whome   x s

                                                                    20

Painters, Glaziers, Embroiderers, and Stationers' Records
C: Account Book I
f 106 *(18 October)*

...

Item for the boyes Hose at midsomer   j s. x d   25
Item ffor a paire of Gloves   o iiij d
Item A payre of Shewes   o x d
Item ffor paintinge of the Staff   o iiij d
Item to the Crier at the Barres   o ij d
Item to the prisoners at northg and Castle   o viij d   30
Item to the musitions   j s ij d
Item to the 3 men that Guyded the boy   j s iiij d
Item to him that brought the horse   o ij d

...

                                                                    35

Cordwainers and Shoemakers' Records
CCA: Account Book I G/8/2
f 108v *(11 November)*

...

Inprimis, payed for wine the same daye, Thomas Iohnson makinge   40
his diner   ij s viij d
Item giuen to the Musitioners the same daye   xvj d

...

Item giuen to the Musitioners at shroftide   ij s

...

f 109

Expences vpon Midsomer evene

Item a payre of gloves	iij d
Item for silke & lace	iij d
Item payed to the Crier	iiij d
Item giuen to the prisoners at the Castell & Northgate	ij s
Item giuen to the footemen	xij d
Item giuen to the Musitioners	ij s vj d
Item In Saike	ij s viij d
Item the childes buskins	xx d
Item for dressinge of the staffe	viij d

...

Coopers' Records   C: Account Book I
f 30 *(13 January)*

...

Item ledovn for a perer of hosses for the child at messemare	xvj d
Item for a pere of svsse at the sam tym	x d
Item ped for bred birer and a chesses at that tym	v s iiij d
Item ledovn for the compenye in ovre allderman lynikars	viij d
Item gave vnto the Criare at the barsses	ij d
Item gave vnto prissenars at the Castille a norgate	viij d
Item ped vnto the menstrille	vj d
Item ped for a pere of glovsses for the child	iij d
Item ped for tryminge the staffe for ovre banare	vj d

...

AC   *Players' Warrant*   BL: Harley 2173
f 81 *(16 February)*

a warrant for a Company of players to passe & play by from
Edward Lord dudley 41 QE. 1595

To all maiors sheriffs baliffs Constables & all other her maiesties
officers & louinge subiects greetinge wheras by virtue of the last
act of parlament houlden at westminster it was enacted that no
players should be permited to play or trauell in the Cuntrey in

the quality of playinge without the warrant & seale at Armes of a
lord baron or some greater personage, know ye therfor that I
Edward sutton baron of dudley haue thought it good to licence
& Authorize and by theis presens doe licence & authorise my
seruants francis Coffyn and Rich bradshaw to trauell in the
quality of playinge & to vse musicke in all Cittys Townes &
Corporations within her maiestyes dominons giuinge them free
liberty to discharge any that shall trauell in my name but
theirselues & their Company which I also authorise / further I
request you the rather for my sake to ayde them with your   1
Countenances & presens & to lett them haue your Towne halls
or other places fitt for their exersize as to other noble mens
men of the like quality hath byn granted hertofore & to lett
them passe without lett molestation or Contradiction so longe as
the behaue themselues well & honestly & to be debard from none   1
exept it be in the tyme of diuine seruice which I thinke nether
fitt nor convenient in wittnesse wherof I haue herunto put to my
hand & seale the 16 of february in the 41th yeare of her maiesties
1595
                    E Dudley   the seale broke   2

endorsed on the back
Memorandum that francis Coffen & others within named who
were licenced to play as the lord dudleys seruants did repayre to
this citty for that purpose 10 no 1602 & for as much as I am   2
Credbly enformd the lord dudly had long since discharged the
sayd Coffen & licensed certayn others with words of reuocation
of this warrant which was shewed vnto me I haue therfore taken
the same from them giuinge them admonitions nether to play in
this citty nor els where opon payne of punishment according to   3
the lawes & statutes in that Case provided
                    xi nou 1602   Hugh Glaseour maior
...

Joiners, Carvers, and Turners' Records   3
CCA: Company Book G 14/1
f 42v *(25 March)*
...

            ffyrst paid for the Busquyns to the Child   ij s   4
            moore paid for Glooves to the Child   iij d
            moore to the mynstrells on mydsomer eve   ij s vj d

	for aquart of Sack . at the Banckquet	viij d
Item	to the preesoners . at the Northgate	iij d
	to the Presoners . at the Castle	iiij d
	to the Cryeour at the Barrs	ij d
	spent at the attyringe of the child for aquart of ˌwyneˌ	vj d
	spent on ij men . for the leading & conducting the child	vj d

...

1595-6
Innkeepers' Records C: Account Book
f 40 *(August)*

...

Item payed for goddartes to bee Broken at mydsomer   xviij d

payed for a peare of gloves for the womane that Ryde afore our
compenye one mydsomer even   iiij d

geven to the horse the womane Ryd vppone in brede iiij d and to
the myllner for fechinge hyme owt of the ffelldes iiij d some
is   viij d

geven to the stuartes of the weaveres for the dye manes covte
and heade pese   vj d

spent vppone our compenye one mydsomer even withe owt the
bares and vppone the womane and the die mane & harnest
men   x d

payed to the womane that Ryd afore our compenye   x d

payed to the mane that caryed the dye manes covte   vj d

payed to the boye that caryed the cvppes   iiij d

spent in Charges affore the wache and afte the wache vppone
the harnest mene and the Rest   iiij s

[sp] payed to our mynstrell to playe a fore our compenye   xij d

Assembly Petitions CCA: A/P/2/4
(17 October)

> To the right worshipfull Mr William Aldersay maior of
> the Citie of Chester and the Aldermen sheriffes & common
> Concell of the same Citie

In moste humble wise besecheth your worships Your poore
suppliant christofer Burton late one of the waitmen of the same
Citie That whereas your said suppliant hath longe time ben

admitted for one of the company of waitemen attending your
worships by your worships good likinge & appointement and
therin continued maried with an honeste mans daughter [s]
within this Citie and by her hath a great nomber of smale children
and being brought vp in the same exercise & having none other   5
trade to get his living with all was vpon Abuses him self dysplased
and deprived thereof worthely deservinge the same for which
abuse he is abaished and reformed and is by the want of the said
office fallen into great want & pouertie as also into debt not
hable to recover nor any waies to maintane his wif & children   10
but to suffer them to goe abegging except your worships reliff
in this behalf / wherfore your said suppliant moste humbly
besecheth your worships for godes sake & in the name of charitie
to restore your said suppliant to the said charg as one of the
waites of this Citie as formerly he hath bene for the better reliff   15
of him his wief & children & your supplant wilbecom most
dutiful & behaue him self according to his dutie and will daily
pray to god for your worships & his wief & children shall doe
the like
                              °differred°   20

Painters, Glaziers, Embroiderers, and Stationers' Records
C: Account Book I
f 108 *(18 October)*

...   25

Item to the Cryer on mydsomer eve   ij d
Item to the presoners at bothe places   viij d
Item to The mynstrells on midsomer eve   x d
Item for ij paire of glooves to the ffoteman and to the childe
that roade for vs   vj d   30
Item for hose and shooes to the childe   ij s
Item for rybband to tie about the childes hede   ij d
...

Cordwainers and Shoemakers' Records   35
CCA: Account Book I G/8/2
f 110v *(11 November)*

...

(St Martin's Day)
Inprimis the said day for wine at Dauy Allens dinner   xx d   40
Item giuen to the Musitioners the said daye   ij s
...

Item giuen vnto Christopher the waite man   xij d

...

Item payde to the Musitioners the same daye Richard Wildinge
had his drinkinge   xviij d

...   5

Item payed for a pottell of Sacke at Bradford Thropes drinkinge
         xx d

Item giuen to the Musitioners the same daye   ij s

Item giuen to the Musitioners at Shroftide   ij s vj d

...   10

Item payed for the glaves   v s

Item giuen to the barage of the glaves   iiij d

...

f 111   15

...

Expences vpon Midsomer Even.

Item for bowning the childe   iiij d

Item for gildinge the staffe   vj d   20

Item for a payre of gloves   viij d

Item for a payre of buskins   ij s vj d

Item spent at Woodcoches   iij d

Item for leadinge the horse & houldinge the childe   xij d

Item for horse bread   iiij d   25

Item giuen to the Crier   xij d

Item giuen to the prisoners at the Castell   xij d

Item giuen to the prisoners at the northgate   xij d

Item giuen to the Musitioners   ij s vj d

...   30

Glovers' Records C: Company Book
p 9 *(10 January)*

...

An Order concerninge Midsomer Eve   35

Memorandum It is ordered and by Consent of the whole
Companie agreed vppon That whosoeuer Cometh not personallie
vppon Midsomer eve to attend vppon the Maior of the Cyttie
att the Watche, and goeth not the Circuite with the rest of his   40
Bretheren according to auncient Costome (except he haue
areasonable and Iust Cause to the Contrarie) shall forfeite and

pay for afine ffive shilling*es* And what brother soeu*er* bringe they
not forth his harnest man vppon the foresaid even accordinge
to old Custome, Shall pay for his fyne xij d And that the
Steward*es* Shall att the next meetinge after bringe in the names
of all such as offend and breake the order /

...

Coopers' Records C: Account Book I
f 31 *(13 January)*

...

It*em* ped for bred beare & ches at messemar	vj s viij d
It*em* ped for a pere of svches at messemare for the chyld	x d
It*em* ped vnto the menstrille at that daye	viij d

...

It*em* ped for a pere of hoves for the chyld at messemar	xij d

...

It*em* gave vnto the criare at the bares	ij d
It*em* gave vnto the pressnares at the castill and norgatt	viij d
It*em* for lonne of the horsse at messemare	viiij d

...

Joiners, Carvers, and Turners' Records
CCA: Company Book G14/1
f 44v *(25 March)*

...

Item ffirst payd ffor a payre of busquins to the child	ij s
Item payd ffor a payre of gloves	x d
Item payd ffor aquarte of wine & sugar att the dressinge of the child	viij d
Item payd to the cryer att the barres	ij d
Item given to the prisoners att the castle & the northgate	vij d
Item payd ffor aquart of wine att our*e* banquett	vj d
Item payd to aman to lead the horse & to cary the banner	iiij d
Item payd to the musicke ffor ther play	ij s vj d

...

Item geaven to the Cryer at the barrs	ij d
Item geeven . to the presoners at the Castle	iiij d
Item geeven to the presoners at the Northgate	iij d
Item geaven to the mynstrells	ij s

...

Painters, Glaziers, Embroiderers, and Stationers' Records

C: Account Book I
f 13v* (7 June)

...

at a metinge
the x of aprill
1610 by consent
of the wholl
companey that
this order shall
stand firmly
without altering
and the companey
to mett (.)t aney
howere the
steuards shall
apoynt the same
daye•

It was ordered and Agreed: by a generall consent that every   5
brother should betweme the Howres of ffoure and five a Clock
on the Eive of St Ihon Baptist personally A peire in theire best
Attire with a man ffurnished redy to geve theire Attendantes
on theire Alderman and by theme to be directed ffurder and for
Default therof it is by consent Aforesaid Agreid that Every   10
person so offendinge shall pay ffor Every his offence ij s v d

...

1596-7

Innkeepers' Records C: Company Book   15
ff 41-1v (August)

...

payed to the minstrelles after our meitinge at our brother scuelles
howse by the a povyntmente of our alderman and bretherne the
23 of Ianuarye   vj d   20

...

payed to Robert lyche for makinge ij denens heades   x s |
payed for viij yeardes of canvas to make ij dye menes Covtes
of at vj d a yeard   iiij s
payed for makinge of theme   ij s   25
geven to the beredge of the Covtes and heade pesses   xj d
payed for the pentinge of the ij covtes beinge Layed in oryell
                                                                 vj s viij d
payed for viij dousen of Cvppes to brecke at iiij d a Dousen
some is   ij s   30
payed for pentinge of the Clvbe   viij d
geven to the Cryer at the Bares iiij d at the northgat iiij d at the
castell iiij d   xij d
geven to the womane to Ryd afore our compenye   x d
payed for a pere of gloves for the womane   iiij d   35
payed to ij dye mene   xij d
payed to amane to carrie our cvppes   iiij d
payed for the horse brede for the horse and to the myllner   viij d
payed for pines to drese the womas clothes abowte heare and to

---

5 / marginalia: p of companey corrected from y
22 / denens for demens; minim omitted MS

piyne the dye [mes] menes covtes   j d
payed for bred dryncke and chese for the womane ij dye mene
and he that caryed cvpes withe the harnest mene   [x] s vj s
...

Assembly Books CCA: AB/1
f 243v* *(8 October)*
...

•Playes and
bearebea*tes*
restrayned•

Alsoe where by daylie experience it hath fallen out what great
inconvenences there haue Arrysen by playes and bearebea*tes*   10
within this Citie besides how the Magistrates in open pulpitt*es*,
Haue bene exclaymed vpon for sufferinge the same within this
Citie prouinge the same playes and bearebea*tes* contrary to
god*es* Lawes and the Comen Wealth ffor reformac*ion* whereof
it is nowe fully ordered by this whole Assembly, that hensforth   15
within this Citie there shalbe neither play nor bearebeat vpon
the Cities charges, and that noe Citizen hensforth vpon payne
of punishm*ent* and fyne shall repayre out of this Citie nor out
of the Lib*er*ties or franches thereof to any play or bearebeate
And yet notwithstandinge because yt shall not be alledged that   20
this restraynte is for sparinge of the treasury of this Citie, It is
ordered that it shalbe Lawfull for the Maior of this Citie for the
tyme beinge to appoynt to be geuen in rewarde to her Ma*iestes*
players repayringe to this Citie twentie shillinges and to any
noble mens players sixe shilling*es* eighte pence and not aboue /   25
...

Assembly Petitions CCA: A/P/2/30
(8 October)

                                                  30

     To the right wor*ship*full mr Willm Aldersey Maior of
     the Citie of Chester and the Aldermen Sheriff*es* &
     Comon Councell of the same Citie

In moste humble wise, besecheth your wor*ships* your [your]   35
poor seru*a*nt and daily beadman chri*sto*fer Burton late one of
the waite*s* within the said Citie attendinge your wor*ships* That
where y*our* orater heretofore hath ben of the same compeny
And for some Cause was of the said compeny restrained & from
them put out And having none oth*er* meanes to maintaine him   40
self & A nomb*er* of smale motherles childre*n* then by the said
trade Therfore your orater moste humblie besecheth y*our* wor*ships*

for god*es* sak and in the Name of Charitie to restore y*our* orator
to the Compeny of y*our* wor*ships* waytmen *with*in the same Citie
and as one of that nom*ber* as form*erly* he was for the better
Maintenans of him self & his poore smale Childre*n* and y*our*
orat*er* will both daily pray to god for y*our* wor*ships* as also will   5
so conforme him self in the maner of his livinge As y*our* wor*ships*
shall therby the better like of him / Also y*our* orat*er* putteth
y*our* wor*ships* to vnderstand that where y*our* orat*er* sonne is by
y*our* wor*ships* put over to the said waitmen to vse that trade and
to saue for his paines & travell certaine Somes of money w*hich*   10
y*our* wor*ships* intended to be bestowed towards the relef of his
poore brethre*n* & susters / he the same boy so wantonly and
extraordenaryly daily wasteth his such gaine and money as
neith therw*ith* doeth him self good nor any of his / Wherfore
y*our* orat*er* moste humbly besecheth y*our* wor*ships* all to take   15
order that the waytmen maie paie over such money due to the
boy to this y*our* orat*er* that the same may be expended as is
most nedfull for his the boys benefit & good & to the relif of
the rest of his brethre*n* & susters And this for god*es* love

                                                                          20

   °8 october 1596 Mr Maior will take order for the better
   gouernment of the Boy°

Painters, Glaziers, Embroiderers, and Stationers' Records
C: Account Book I   25
f 109 *(18 October)*

...

It*em* in pr*im*is vpon St Lukes daie at *our* brother Basnett*es*
dynner for apotle of Secke at wydow Alcok*es*   xx d.
It*em* to the waytes of the Cittie The same daie   xviij d   30
It*em* spent on Wyne at *our* brothers hanckok*es* din*er*   xx d.
It*em* geven to the mynstrells at y*at* tyme   xij d
It*em* for apayre of hose to the childe at midsom*er*   xij d
It*em* for apaire of Shoes to the same childe   x d
It*em* for Gloves   v d   35
It*em* bestowede on him that ledd the horse   ij d
It*em* for makinge apayre of breeches   ij d
It*em* to the presoners at bothe places   viij d
It*em* for horse breade   iiij d
It*em* for breade and Cheese at the steward*es* house   xx d   40

14 / neith *for* neither

Item at *our* ald*erman* Leches for ale   vj d
Item at the Barrs   iij d
Item to the musicians on the eve   xviij d
Item more for ale on midsom*er* eve at *our* ald*erman* Leches

                                                        ij s ij d

...

Cordwainers and Shoemakers' Records

CCA: Account Book G/8/2

f 112v *(11 November)*

...

(St Martin's Day)

Item giuen to the musitioners the same day   iij s
Item spent in wine vpon the cremacon daye Bradford Throppe
makeinge his din*er*   iiij s iiij d
Item giuen to the Musition*er*s   xij d

...

Item payed for glaves   v s
Item giuen to the barige of the glaves   iiij d
Item giuen to the Musitioners at shroftide   ij s vj d

...

f 113

...

Item payed for a payre of hoses for the childe vpone Midsom*er*
Even   xviij d
Item payed for a payre of gloves   vj d
Item payed for a payre of shoes   vj d
Item payed for arsideine   vj d
Item payd for gildinge the staffe   vj d
Item payed for horsbread   iiij d
Item spent in drinke at the bares [vpon ye child]   v d
Item giuen to the Crier at ye barres   iiij d
Item giuen to the pr*iso*ners at the Castell   xij d
Item giuen to the pr*iso*ners at the Northgate   xij d
Item giuen to two men for leadinge the horse   xx d
Item payed for sacke vpon Midsom*er* even at the banket at
our Aldman Mr Allens house   xx d
Item giuen to the Musitioners the same daye   ij s vj d

...

f 113v

...

Item giuen to the Musition*ers*   ij. s

...
                                                                              5

Dean and Chapter CC: Treasurers' Accounts III
p 171 *(Christmas)*

...

Inprimis the xxviij^th day of December to Richerd Woodes for
3 nightes attendinge vpon ye maior & Sheriffes in Christmas xij d. 10
Item to Richerd Richerdson for loane of harnes   xx d.

...

Coopers' Records C: Account Book I
f 32 *(13 January)*   15

...

Inprimis for making our baner and for all things belonging to
it   ij li. iij s x d
Item paied for the boyes cloues   x s
...   20
Item our charges on midsomer Eve and for hosse and sues for the
boye and other charges   xvij s iiij d

...

Joiners, Carvers, and Turners' Records   25
CCA: Company Book G14/1
f 49 *(25 March)*

...

Item in primis for Cloathe to make our Banner vpon   iiij s
Item for the ffringe to the same Banner   xx d   30
Item for Buckram to the socket and soyinge the banner   x d
Item geaven to the Berrage at the making the banner   iiij d
Item paid for apaire of Stockinges to the child that Roade
                                                            ij s viij d
Item for apayre of Shooes to the same childe   xij d   35
Item payd for Gloves   iiij d
Item payd ffor aquart of white wyne bestowed in borrowing the
boy   viij d
Item bestowed on mr Oldfeldes man that attended the childe in
gloves   iiij d   40
Item paid to Lewis for Carrynge the banner   iiij d
Item paid for leading of the horse   ij d

Item geaven to the Cryer at the barrs   ij d
Item geeven to the presoners at the Castle   iiij d
Item geeven to the presoners at the Northgate   iij d
Item geaven to the mynstrells   ij s

...

Innkeepers' Records C: Company Book
f D-3v *(8 June)*

The viij^t of Iune
1597

None to be
absent from the
watch on
Midsomer eve

Item It is ordered and agreed vpon That euerie Brother of the
said Companie that shall be absent at the watch vpon Midsomer
Eve at the howre appoynted shall forfeitt for euerie offence
ij s, And the Aldermen — iij s iiij d a peece

penaltie
for a brother
— ij s
for an Alderman
— iij s iiij d

...

1597-8

Innkeepers' Records C: Account Book
f 47 *(August)*

...

Item paide to Iohn owen ffor taffyta one yearde   xij s vj d
Item pade for silke ij ownsses for our frynge and sylke to sett
it one with all   iij s [vij d]
Item payde for takeinge downe of our staffe   iij d
Item payde for makinge of our frynge   iiij d
Item payde ffor hosse and shooes for the chylde   ij s
Item paide ffor apayre of gloues ffor the chylde   iiij d
Item ffor ^'them at'[the] castle ^'to' the cryer and the north
gate   xij d
Item spente at the Lossinge of our wach vpon them that weatede
vpon the chylde and gevn the mvsykke   xx d
payde to the [vusicke] musycke   v s
ffor makinge of our banner
Item to paye vnto the Smyth   xxvj s viij d
for makinge Iron Rodds

...

Painters, Glaziers, Embroiderers, and Stationers' Records
C: Account Book I
f 112 *(18 October)*

...

Item for hose shooes and gloues to the childe	iiij s	5
Item spent at the dressinge of the childe	iiij d	
Item to two men to guyde the horse	x d	
Item to the prisoners and Crier	x d	
Item spent in ale one midsomer Eue at mr Williams	iiij d	
Item to the minstrells one midesomer eve	ij s	10
Item for ˄'our' bankett one midsomer eve at our Alderman		
leeches	v s	
Item for mendeinge the banner	xij d	

...

		15

Cordwainers and Shoemakers' Records
CCA: Account Book I G/8/2
f 115v *(11 November)*

...

(St Martin's Day)		20
Item payed to the Musitioners	xviij d	

...

f 116

		25
payed for ye Glaves	v s	
Item for the barage of ye same	iiij d	
Item giuen to ye Musitioners at shroftide	ij s	

...

Expences vpon midsomer even		30

Item halfe a barell of beare	viij s	
Item for bread	v s iiij d	
Item for Chise	vj s x d	
Item payed for ye horse	xij d	35
Item for the footemen	xij d	
Item for the shoos	xij d	
Item for the hoses	xx d	
Item for the gloves	iiij d	
Item giuen to ye Musitioners	ij s vj d	40

...

Coopers' Records C: Account Book I
f 32v *(13 January)*

...

Item spende and Lede oute on medsseumeer Eyne for house
and shause and oudor chares   xiij s x d   5

...

Joiners, Carvers, and Turners' Records
CCA: Company Book G14/1
f 52 *(25 March)*   10

...

Item for apaire of hose to the childe that Roade at midsomer
                                                        xxij d
Item for apaire of Shooes to the same childe   xiij d
Item for apaire of Glooves for the same childe   v d   15
Item spente at the bounninge of the childe in white wyne &
suger   x d
Item at the barrs to the Criere   ij d
Item . at bothe presons bestowede Castle & Northgate   vij d
Item to the ij men . for holding the child & leading the horse   20
                                                        viij d
Item to the Mynstrelles on Mydsomere eve   iij s

...

1598-9   25
Innkeepers' Records C: Account Book
f 47v *(August)*

...

(Election Day)
Item geven vnto the mvsyssyons the same daye   iiij s   30
Item paide vnto the smyth for makinge of an Iron Rode for our
Banner   xij d
Item paide for a staffe to Rowle our Banners vpon   iiij d
Item payde to symon Smyth for a staffe   x d

...   35

Item payd for staffe for our banner   x d
Item Cloth to make our typpetes   xv s
Item ffor makinge, silke and Lasse   iij s viij d
Item ffor apayer of gloves   vj d
Item ffor Lone of a cape to the boye   xij d   40
Item Leade out for ale without the barres bestowed vpon the
compaynye   xx d

Item geven to wodcocke and the prisoners   xvj d
Item ffor Lone of a feather   vj d
Item payde to the mvsicke   v s
Item payd for apayer of spures   vj d
Item bestowed vpon the companye and them that weated vpon   5
the chyld after our wach in beere   x d
Item ffor ij that weated vpon the Chyld   ⟨...⟩
[Item payde for anewe staffe for our banner]

Painters, Glaziers, Embroiderers, and Stationers' Records   10
C: Account Book I
f 114 *(18 October)*

...

Item for the Childes apparll the oute sydes lyneinges bumbast
lase buttons and for the makeinge   xxiiij s   15
Item for the hose shues and gloues to the Childe   ij s x d
Item to a man to guide the horse   iij d
Item for horse bread to the horse   ij d
Item to ⌃ʻtheʼ prisoners of the northgate and Castell and to
the Crier   x d   20
Item to the musisions on midsomer Eve   ij s
Item our Banquett on midsomer Eve at our alderman ʻda*n*byeʼ
     iiij s

...

   25

AC   *City Treasurers' Accounts* BL: Harley 2173
f 92v *(November)*

...

for the wetemens gownes   v li. xix s
...   30

Cordwainers and Shoemakers' Records
CCA: Account Book II G/8/3
f 3v *(11 November)*

   35

Item giue for wine at Rauffe Tonges drinkinge   ij s
Item giuen to the musitions ye same daye   ij s

...

f 4   40

...

Item payed for glaves   v s

Item giuen for barage of the glaves   iiij d
Item giuen to the musitions at shroftide   ij s vj d
Item giuen to Henry Shurlocke   vj d
Item giuen to the stewardes of ye Iovrnemen of ye shomakers
for servinge at shroftide in the gate   xij d   5
...

f 4v

...   10
Item for a payre of breeches for the boye at midsom*er* viij s vj d
Item for Cuttinge makinge & lacinge the briches   [xvj d] ij s
Item for Cop*er* lace for Ierkinge & breeches   ij s iiij d
Item for a Ierkine & a payre of shoes to mr Allen   vj s
Item for a payre of hoses   ij s iiij d   15
Item for a payre of gloves   x d
Item payed for a boord to ye Curier   v s viij d
Item payed to mr Benet for a Cloke to the Curier   viij s
Item lent to the Curier   vj s
Item payed to the Carpender   ij s ij d   20
Item spent at mr Winnes vpon the Curier   iiij d
Item giuen to the Crier   iiij d
Item giuen to the p*riso*n*er*s of the Castell & northgate   ij s
Item giuen to the musitions   iiij s
Item giuen for wine at midsom*er* Even   iiij s   25
Item for dressinge the staffe   viij d
Item for tinsill for the staffe   ij d
...

                                                                                          30

Mayors' Books CCA: M/B/27
f 17v *(17 December)*
...

Memorandu*m* that the xvijth day of December 1598 Mr maior
w*i*th the assent of the Aldermen his bretheren did deliu*er* vnto   35
Richard Woodcock Cryer a tymber mast typt at both endes and
embellished [⟨.⟩] in the middest w*i*th silver where of Thomas
Richardson late Cryer had the vse and Custody to be kepte and
vsed by the said Richard Woodcock as the Cities good*es* and to
be redeliu*er*ed backe to the same Citie vpon demaunde.   40
...

Coopers' Records C: Account Book I
f 33 *(13 January)*

...

Item fore [a] halfe a barrell of beare   iiij s
Item for brede   ij s   5
Item for chese   xxj d
Item for a peare of hose and a peare suse and a peare of gloues
      ij s vj d
Item at barese and the Caltele and the norgate   xvj d

...   10

Assembly Books CCA: AB/1
f 253* *(1 March)*

...

Order taken towchinge the intertaynment of the earle of Essex earle marshall of England

At which assembly mr Maior Declareth that he is credible   15
enformed that the Right Ho*norable* the Erle Marshall of England
will speedely repaire to this citie to take shippinge for Ireland
And moueth that some such order may be taken for the receipt
and entertaynem*ent* of the saied Erle as may be both befittinge
soe honorable a personage and tend to the credite of the citie   20
vppon whose motion it is by the same Assembly agreed and
ordered that there shallbe prepared at the ou*er* sight and
appointmt of Mr Dauid lloyd and Mr William Aldersay Ald*ermen*
for the said Erle a good banquett vppon the cities Chardges and
that a siluer cupp of x li. or xx ty marks price shalbe bought   25
and fortie Angells of gould alsoe prouided vppon the cities
chardges and putt into the saied cupp and soe be p*re*sented vnto
his Ho*nor*

Joiners, Carvers, and Turners' Records   30
CCA: Company Book G14/1
f 55 *(25 March)*

...

Imprimus payd . ffor a payre off stockings for the childe w*hich*
Roade ffor the company   ij s viij d   35
Item payd for apayre of shooes   xij d
Item payed for apayre off gloves   iiij d
Item for ij men for holdinge the child & leadinge the horse   viij d
Item spent in dressinge of the childe in wine & sugar   x d
Item payed to the cryer att the barrs   ij d   40
Item given to the prysoners of the castle & northegate   vij d

Item payd to the minstrells on midsom*m*er eve   ij s vj d
...

A   *Mayors List 2* BL: Harley 1944
      f 90 *(1 April) Richard Rathbone*   5

This yere the Earle of Essex, as Genarall for Ireland, againste
the greate rebell Tirone, came to Chester, accompanyed, with
the Earle of Southampton the Earle of Rutland, the Earle of
Killdare, the lord Graye, and the lord Mounteagle, with many   10
other knight*es.* and great p*er*sons, at whose Comeinge into the
Cittie the Mayor & Aldermen mett, them in the streete, in theire
scarelett gowns, the Earle of Essex lay in the Bishopps pallace
and, soe after aseason, they dep*ar*ted for Ireland
...   15

A   *Mayors List 12* BL: Add. 29780
      ff 63-4* *Richard Rathbone*
      ...

Robert Devereux, Earle of Essex, a great favorite of *Queen*   20
Eliza*beth* came to this Cittie, the first of April as her Majesties
Leiuetenant Generale of Ireland. Accompanyed with the Earles
of Rutland and Southampton, the Lord Audeley, Lord Grey
Lord Cromwell, Lord Monteagle, he laye in the bishops palace
he was banqueted in the pentice. with all his | Attendence and   25
he was presented by the Citty with a Guilt bowl. and 60 Angells
of Gould in a fine purse. by Mr. Thomas Greene being the
Anchantste Alderman the Mayor being Sicke and Absent. Anno
Do*m*ini 1598 Mr. Richard Rabone then Major.
...   30

      St Michael's Parish Register CRO: P/65/8/1
      f 139* *(8 April) (Inventory)*

Item a table & a frame   35
...

1599-1600
AC   *City Waits* BL: Harley 2054
      f 101 *(25 July)*
                                                                    40
                          At the Citie of Chester the xxv^th day of
                                                         Iuly 1599

Whereas Variance and Controuersie heretofore hath growen and
bene dependinge betwene George Cally of the said Citie musitian
vpon thone partie and Robert Cally of the same Citie Musitian
brother of the said [Rob] George vpon thother partie The said
parties doe agree and doe promyse either to other. to Contynue   5
be and remayne of one Consorte. and to play vpon their
instrumentes together still in one Company and be lovinge and
frendlie thone to thother during ˄ ʼ& toʼ thend of their naturall
lyves without separation or departure one from another / And
where the said Georg hath two boyes and the said Robert but   10
one boy they haue Concluded and Agreed to devyde their gaynes
arrising by their play in force folowing That is to say that the
said Georg shall haue three partes of the gaine and the said
Robert two And that whensoeuer the said Robert shall haue an
other boy or that the said Georg shall departe with thone of his   15
boyes soe as they shall either of them ˄ ʼhaueʼ a lyke number
of boyes that then the gaynes shall equally be devyded amongest
them without fraud or deceipt Dated at the day and yeare
aforesaid
                                                                    20
Witnesses of this agreement

   Thomas Drewe   George calley
   William Bird   Robert Callye
   Richard Bavand   25
   William Walter
   Davye Lloyd
   Thomas Fletcher

Innkeepers' Records C: Account Book   30
ff 50-50v *(August)*
...
paid by the aldermens appointment for dyvers gentlemen that
weare eatinge the venyson mr ffrancis bestoed on the Company
at Steward Alcockes   xx s   35
...
paid to the musicke the same tyme   iij s. iiij d.
...
paid to mr. Cise vpon thelexcion daie for settinge out the woman
at midsomer vj s. vj d and for Chardges against the bakers by   40
order from the Company iiij s vj d   xj s.
...

(Midsummer)

p*ai*d the same tyme by order of the Company to Rob*er*t Innce in almes	ij s. vj d.
p*ai*d for a paire of Buskins for the Boye	iij s iiij d.
p*ai*d for a paire of Spurrs and gloves for the boye	xij d	
p*ai*d for ale for the Company at humphry Ellis	[xviij d]
p*ai*d to woodkocke and at the gates	xvj d
p*ai*d to the leader of the house	ij s vj d
p*ai*d to ffloode for Carryinge the banner	x d
p*ai*d to Randle holmes for keapinge the banner and for newe payntinge the staffe	ij s
Spent in gatheringe the alehowse money	xvij d
p*ai*d to the musicke	v s

...

Painters, Glaziers, Embroiderers, and Stationers' Records
C : Account Book I
f 115 *(18 October)*
...

It*e*m for hose shooes gloues and spent athe dressing of the Childe and for Ribens to the shooes	iij s iij d
It*e*m spent at our Alderman Leeches at our goeinge vp vppon midsomer eve	iij d
It*e*m to the Crier and to the prisoners of the Castle and northgate	x d
It*e*m payd for the Caryinge of the banner	iiij d
It*e*m to the musysions vpon mydsomer Eve	iij s
It*e*m layd out for wyne at our Supper vpon mydsomer Eue	iij d
It*e*m for our supper vpon myddsomer Evee	vj s viij d
It*e*m for the amendyinge and Repayreinge of our banner and layeinge of the staff in oyle Cullers	ij s

...

Cordwainers and Shoemakers' Records
CCA : Account Book II G /8/3
f 6v *(11 November)*
...

It*e*m payed to the Musition*er*s vpon St Martins daye	ij s

...

f 7
...

It*e*m giuen for *our* glaves	v s

...

Item giuen to the Musitioners at shroftide ij s vj d

...

f 8 5

...

Item payed for a payre of hoses for the child at Midsomer
and gloves ij s
Item for a payre shoes xvj d
Item giuen to the Crier iiij d 10
Item giuen At the Castell & Northgate ij s
Item giuen for a gallen of Sacke iij s iiij d
Item giuen for a pottell of Sacke xx d
Item in bread v s iiij d
Item In Chise v s viij d 15
In prunes xviij d
Item halfe a barell of beare iiij s
Item for suger xvj d
Item for bringinge the childes apparell to Iohn grines houses ij d
Item gildinge the staffe iiij d 20
Item spent at Mr Williams house ij d
Item spent at Iohn grynes house ij d
Item at bownynge the childe xv d
Item giuen to the Musitioners iiij s
Item giuen for leadinge the horse xij d 25
Item giuen in horse bread vj d
Item for dressinge the childe ij d
Item for a quarte of sacke x d

...

30

A   *Mayors List 2* BL: Harley 1944
ff 90-90v *(November) Henry Hardware*

...

This mayor was a godly zealous man, yet he gott ill will amonge
the Commons, for puttinge downe some anchant orders, in the 35
Cittie and amonge some Compaiyes, especially the shooemakers,
whoe he much opposed, he caused the giantes which vse to goe at
midsomer to be broken, The bull ringe at the high crosse to be
taken vp, The dragon and naked |boyes he suffered not to goe
in midsomer showe nor the diuell for the Butchers, but aboye to 40
ride as other Companyes,, he restrayned their leauelookers,

36 / Compaiyes *for* Companyes, *minim omitted MS*

for sendinge wine, on the [eu] feastifull dayes, accordinge to theire anchant vse and Custome.

...

A *Mayors List 5* B L: Harley 2125
f 45v* *Henry Hardware*

The Mayor was a godlye ₒ ˹ouer˺ₒ zealous man, and kepte a verye worshippfull and A plentefull howse, he ruled well, yeat he gate greate yll will Amonge the commons. for Appooseinge hym selfe   ⟩
Againste some companyes ₒ ˹espetialy the Showmakers˺ₒ orders and agaynste oulde customes of this cittye.

he caused the Gyanntes, in the Mydsomer show to be put downe ₒ ˹& broken˺ₒ and not to goe, The devill in his fethers ₒ ˄ ˹to ride   ⟩
for the buchers but a boy as ˄ ˹others had˺˺ₒ he put Awaye. and the Cuppes and Cannes. And dragon and Naked boyes. ₒ˹but caused a man in complet Armor to goe before the show in their steed˺ₒ he caused the bull Ringe to be taken vpp And the Leave Lookers were restrayned, for sendinge wine Accordinge to the   2
Aunciente vse and Custome of this Cittye

...

A *Mayors List 8* B L: Harley 2133
f 46 *Henry Hardware*   2

...

This Maior for his tyme Altered many ancient Customs as ye shootinge for the sherifs Breakefast the goinge of the gyants at Midsomer etc. and would not suffer any playes beare Baits or Bullbaites ...   3

A *Mayors List 15* C R O: DLT/B/37
f 67 *Henry Hardware*

...

Also the saide Mayor caused the giantes not to goe at midsomer   3
watche, but in stede a man in armore on horse backe, in white armor. Also in the same showe he put downe the diuill ridinge for ye butchers and caused a boy, to ride for them as the reste of the companyes. he also put downe the cuppes and cannes, with diulls in the same showe, Also the dragon with naked boyes,   4

8-19 / ₒ... ₒ *insertions in RH II's band*

he put downe alsoe in yat showe, he also tooke vp the bullringe
at the highe crosse & he also opposed ye shoemakers, and woulde
haue them to receaue britheren yat serued theire times to come
in amonge them for iij s iiij d, he also restrayned the leauelookers
from sendinge wine accordinge to theire anchante custome, he   5
firste tooke ye toole from the sergents

Coopers' Records C: Account Book I
f 34 *(13 January)*
...   10
Item for halfe a barril of beare   iiij s
Item for brede   ij s
Item for Chese   ij s
Item for a peare of hose   xvj d
Item for a peare of shvse   xij d   15
Item for a peare of glovse   iij d
Item gave to ovr fote mane   iiij d
Item for dresing of the syne agenste medsore   v s
Item for papre to lape the syne in   j d
...   20
Item for Charges on medsem*er* eyn at the bare*es* and the norgate
and the Castele   xi d
the pyperse and the horse   ij s viij d
...
                                                                      25

Joiners, Carvers, and Turners' Records
CCA: Company Book G 14/1
f 58 *(25 March)*
...
Item payd for the boy to ryde att midsomer for hose & shues   30
& gloves   ij s ix d
Item payd att the barrs, & the prisoners of the Castle & northgate
                                                        ix d
Item payd to the minstrells vpon midsomer eve   ij s vj d
Item payd for grasse & bread & for on to lead the horse   vij d   35
...

1600-1
Innkeepers' Records C: Account Book
f 52 *(August)*   40
...
payd to wodcocke and the gattes   xvj d

payd for a paier of buskines for the boye   iij s iiij d
payd for a paier of glowes   iiij d
payd to the leder of the horsse   ij s vj d
payd to randell holmes for kepinge the baner   xij d
payd to the musicke   v s
spent in gatheringe the allemonye   xvj d

...

Painters, Glaziers, Embroiderers, and Stationers' Records
C: Account Book I
f 118 *(18 October)*

...

Item for Sacke and Clarrett wyne at william pooles dynner   xvj d
Item for the musysions at that tyme   ij s

...

Item for hose shooes and gloues to the Child   ij s viij d
Item spent at the dressing of the Child   ij d
Item geven to a man for leadyng the horse   iiij d
Item spent at our alderman holmes the same tyme   ij d
Item geven to the Cryer at the bares   ij d
Item to the prisoners of Castell and northgate   viij d
Item vpon mydsomer eve for musicke   xviij d
Item that nyght for our drinkinge   vj s

...

Cordwainers and Shoemakers' Records
CCA: Account Book II G/8/3
f 9 *(11 November)*

...

Item to the wetemen   ij s

...

f 9v

...

Item payd for the gleues   v s
Item spent vpon the barrich   ij s

...

f 10

...

Item for gildinge the stafe   iiij d
Item for trimmige the childe   ij d

Item spent in bouninge the childe   xij d
Item for hose and gloues for the child   ij s ij d
Item for the childes shoues   xvj d
Item for chise for our cumpaney   v s.
Item for brede for our cumpaney   v s   5
Item for pruines   ij s
Item for sugere   xx d
Item for beare   v s.
Item spent vpon Iohn Grine   xiiij d
Item giuen to the crier at the barse   iiij d   10
Item giuen to the prisoners of the castill   xij d
Item giuen to the prisoners of the norgate   xij d
Item giuen to the fotemen   xij d
Item giuen for horse brede   vj d
Item giuen for wine for our cumpaney   iij s iiij d   15
Item giuen to the musiners   iiij s

...

f 11

...   20

Item for musicke   iij s

...

Coopers' Records C: Account Book I
ff 36-6v *(13 January)*   25

...

Imprims paide for owr dinner at widdow Cowpers oon the
twenthe daye laste   ix s viij d
Item paide for wyne the same tyme   ij s
Item paide to the musisiners   xij d   30

...

Item paide to the musisuners at Robert markes dinner   ij s vj d
Item payd to the waitemen   vj d

...

Item payd at Richard bennets dinner for wyne and to the   35
musisiners   iiij s vj d

...

Item payde for our Charges on midsomer even   viij s |
Item payde for the Chyldes [gloves] hose   xv d
Item payde for the Chyldes shous   xij d   40
Item payd for on payre gloves   iij d
Item payd for gloves for the foote men   viij d

Item spent at barsse on our Company   viij d
Item to the Cryer   j d
Item to the priseners at the Castel and norgate   x d
Item for horse bred   iiij d
Item to the pyper   vj d   5
...

Joiners, Carvers, and Turners' Records
CCA: Company Book G14/1
f 60 *(25 March)*   10
...

Item payd for apayre off stockings for the boy w*hich* did ryde
for the companye   iij s vj d
Item payd for apayre off . shues for him   xviij d
Item payd for apayre off gloves for him   v d   15
Item payd for a quart of wine & sugar att his dressing   viij d
Item given to the tuo footmen, w*hich* led the horse   viij d
Item given to the Cryer att the barrs   ij d
Item given to the prysoners of the Castle   iiij d
Item given to the prysoners of the northegate   iij d   20
Item payd to the minstrells for our*e* musick   iij s
...

1601-2
Innkeepers' Records C: Account Book   25
ff 54-4v *(August)*
...

(14 June at a meeting)
paid for musicke the same daye to geo Cally   ij s vj d
...   30
paid for apayre spurres for *our* boy   vij d
...

midsom*er* even   spent at Iames Brvsters in beare and ale vpon *our* company and
watchmen   iij s
[pai] given to Iohn deane in wyne 'for hemself' and oates for his   35
horse . that the boy ryd vpon at the watche   xiij d
paid to davy Allen for apayre of buskyns for the boy to ryde
with   iij s iiij d
for laces for the same   ij d
[for four payre of spurres   vij d]   40
for half ayard riben to fasten the chaynes   j d.
paid to *our* musicke at the watche   vj s
paid for a drinkinge at *our* comyng home from the Watche vpon

part of the compay   iij s iiij d
given to Richard Woodcock at the northgat and Castell   xvj d
to Randle holmes for dressing *our* bann*er*   xij d
[⟨...⟩]
spent in gathering the ale house money   ij s ij d   5
to aman that led *our* horse that *our* boy rid on and to Cary the
banner   ij s
[for riben for the ⟨...⟩   ⟨...⟩ d] |
paid for Ryben for to Dresse the horse mane   vj d
paid for apayre of gloues for the boy   vj d   10

...

paid to holmes for a new Iron rodde for *our* banner   xij d

...

Painters, Glaziers, Embroiderers, and Stationers' Records   15
C: Account Book I
f 118v *(18 October)*

...

Item for hose shooes and gloues to the Childe that Rode ij s viij d
Item for horse breade to the horse at Mydsomer   iiij d   20
Item for one to guyde the horse   iiij d
Item to the Cryer and to the prisoners of the northgate and
Castell   x d
Item to the musysyons   ij s vj d
Item to Aron dawbye for goeing vpon stiltes   xij d   25
Item for our Banquett vpon mydsomer Eue   vij s

...

Cordwainers and Shoemakers' Records
CCA: Account Book II G/8/3   30
f 11v *(11 November)*

...

(St Martin's Day)
Item given to the waitemen   ij s
...   35
Item paid for gleaves   v s iiij d
Item given to the waitemen   ij s vj d

...

f 12   40

...

Item for cheese   v s.
Item for prunes   xviij d

Item for bread	iiij s
Item for Sugar	vj d
Item given at the Castle	xij d
Item given at the Northgate	xij d
Item for secke	ij s vj d
Item given to the Musitions	iiij s
Item to mr Glasiers man	xij d
Item to Richard Halliwell	vj d
Item for shoes	xiiij d
Item for Riban	ij d
Item paid for Ale at mr dimmockes	iij d
Item for gloves	iij d
Item for hose	xvj d
Item given to Richard Woodcocke	iiij d
Item for beere	v s
Item given to mr maior for peter Burkesey his children	x s
Item given to mr Iustice a pottle of secke and a quarter of sugar and a pottle of wite wine	iij s ij d
...	
Item given to the Callis	ij s
...	

f 12v
Item given to the waitmen	xij d
...	

Dean and Chapter CC: Treasurers' Accounts III
p 207 *(Christmas)*

...

Inprimis payd ye 29th of December vnto the watchman attending iij nightes vpon ye maior & Sheriffes in Christmas	xij d
Item for Armor hyred for ye watchman	xiiij d /
...	

Coopers' Records C: Account Book I
f 39 *(13 January)*

...

Imprimis payde for wyne at Thomas harrison his dinner	iij s
more to the minstrells the same tyme	ij s vj d
...	
more spende on oure Company in Widdow Cowpers	ij s
more geven to the minstrells the same tyme	vj d
...	

f 39v

...

more payde for oure Charges on midsomer even	viij s	
more payde for on payre hose for the Chylde	xiiij d	
more payde for on payre shouse	xiiij d	5
more payde for on payre gloues	iiij d	
more payde to ij footeme	x d	
more payde for horsbredd	iiij d	
more payde to the pyper	vj d	
more payde to the Cryer	j d	10
more geven to the norgate and the Castle	xiiij d	
more for gildinge oure staffe and an Iron pin	vij d	

...

15

Joiners, Carvers, and Turners' Records
CCA: Company Book G 14/1
f 63 *(25 March)*

...

Imprimis laide out for three quarters of Clothe to make our		20
tippit*es* to mr Littler	xij s	
Item to Bedle for a newe staffe	vj d	
Item for the makinge of ye tippit*es* & lace to them	iij s vj d	
Item for a paire of stockens for ye childe w*hi*ch did ride		
	iij s iiij d	25
Item for a paire of Spanishe leather shoes	ij s	
Item for colouringe & silueringe ye staffe & mendinge the banner		
	xiiij d	
Item for gloues for the boie	vj d	
Item to the prisoners of the Castle & Northgate	vij d	30
Item to the Crier at the Barres	ij d	
Item giuen to the minstrels	iij s	
Item for Wine and sugar at the dressinge of ye Childe	viij d	
Item to two me*n* to laide the horse	x d	

...

35

Item paide to three sort*es* of Mynstrels at our dynner at		
Alderma*n* Kenderickes house	iij s vj d	

...

f 63v

40

...

Item paide for Edward Iones vppo*n* midsomer Eve	iiij d	

...

A C *Linendrapers' Order for Midsummer*
Rupert H. Morris, *Chester in the Plantagenet and Tudor Reigns*
pp 324-5* *(21 May)*
...

Whereas the Companye of Bricklayers within this citty are to be   5
at charges in settinge forth of the Showe or Watch at Mydsomer
of Balaam and Balaam's Asse, whereunto as well the freemen of
the Lynnen-drapers, brickemakers, and bricklaiers of this cittye,
as also the forreners [non-freemen] inhabitinge within this
cittye, and using the trades aforesaide, have bene accustomed to   10
bee contributarye. These are to authorise Roberte Ridley | and
George Antrobus, Aldermen of the Companye of Bricklayers,
and Roberte Goodaker and Thomas Markes, stewards, to collecte
of everye of the said persons aforesaide all such somes of money
as they have bene heretofore accustomed to paye and as hath   15
bene accustomed to bee collected towards the charges aforesaide.
...

A *Mayors List 5* B L : Harley 2125
f 46* *(Midsummer) John Radcliffe*   20
...

he sett out the Giants & midsomer show as of ould it was wont
to be kept
...

                                                                        25

1602-3

Innkeepers' Records C : Account Book
f 56 *(August)*
...

paid the xxiij^th of Iune 1603 for apare of hose [the] for the boy   30
that rid for our compay   xx d hc
paid for a pare of spanish lether shooes for h⟨.⟩   xv d hc
paid for tyes for the same   vj d hc
paid for ryben to dresse the horse   vj d hc
paid for apint of wyne for use of the hat for the boye   iij d hc   35
paid for apaire of gloues for the boy   vj d hc
paid to Randle holmes for keping our banner   xij d hc
[more he demandeth for paynting the staff]
paid for beare at Iames Brosters alderman wache   ij s hc
paid to the Lender of the horse & dressing him   xij d hc   40
paid to woodcock   iiij d hc
paid to the prisoners at the castle   vj d hc

paid to the prisoners at northgate   vj d hc

given to Bryan at the northgate   ij d hc

paid to Georg kally for our musicke   vj s hc

paid for a banquet to our compay aftr the wache   iij s hc

...   5

for loane of the saddle for the boy   j d hc

spent in travelling to procure necessaries for the boy   iij d

spent in gathering the alehouse money   xiiij d

...   10

Painters, Glaziers, Embroiderers, and Stationers' Records
C: Account Book I
f 121 *(18 October)*

...

Item for horsbread to the horse that Caryed the Childe vpon   15
mydsomer Eve   iiij d

Item for paynteing the banner staffe   vj d

Item for salueringe of the lase of the Childs apparrell   ij s

Item for the musike vpon Mydsomer Eve   xxij d

Item for stockings for the Childe   xviij d   20

Item for the shooes   xij d

Item to moyses dalby for goeinge vpon the stilts   xij d

Item for a sokett to [y] Carry the howr glase   ij d

Item to the prisoners and to the Cryer   x d

Item our supper vpon Mydsomer Eve   vij s   25

...

Cordwainers and Shoemakers' Records
CCA: Account Book II G/8/3
f 13 *(11 November)*   30

...

(St Martin's Day)
Ittem payde to the musycenors the same day   ij s vj d

...

(at a dinner)   35
Ittem given for musicke   ij s

(at a dinner)
Ittem given for musicke   ij s

...   40

Ittem payed for our gleaves   v s

Ittem given to the Barrage   viij d

...

Itt*em* given for musicke at shroftyde   ij s ij d

...

f 13v   5

...

Itt*em* payde for our boyes shoes at midsom*er*   xij d
Itt*em* payde for his hose   xx d
Itt*em* for his gloves   vj d
Itt*em* payd for dressinge of him   vj d   10
Itt*em* spent at mr dymocke   iiij d
Itt*em* given to the Cryer   iiij d
Itt*em* given to the prysoners at Castle   xij d
Itt*em* to the prisoners at the northgate   xij d
Itt*em* payde for dressinge of the staffe   vj d   15
Itt*em* payde for musicke at midsom*er*   iiij s
given to the man that leid the horse   xij d

...

Coopers' Records C: Account Book I   20
f 41 *(13 January)*

...

It*em* Inprimes payd at mydsomer for the bankytt   viij s
It*em* payd for a paire of hosse for the Child that dyd ryd   xvj d
It*em* paid for a payre of shewes for the Chillde   xij d   25
It*em* payd for a payre of glowes for hime   iiij d
It*em* payd to the fotte men   vj d
It*em* paid to the boye that dyd lede the horse   iiij d
It*em* paid for horsse breade to the horse   iiij d
It*em* payd for good dalle at the bares   xij d   30
It*em* payd to the mynstrell one mydsomer evine   vj d
It*em* payd to the Cryer at the bares   ij d
It*em* payd at the Castell and at the norgatte   xiiij d
It*em* paid to the sheryffes   ix s

...   35

It*em* payd for wine at Iohn anterbous his diner   ij s
It*em* payd to the mynstrells the same tyme   xviij d
It*em* payd at Kathren Cowp*er*s one the v of august for bread
and drinke   v s
It*em* payd to the mynstrell the same tyme   ij s   40

...

Joiners, Carvers, and Turners' Records
CCA: Company Book G14/1
f 66 *(25 March)*

...

Item for a peare of hoose for the childe that did Ride at midsomer	iij s iiij d	5
Item for a peare of shoes & Ribbins to them	ij s vj d	
Item for a peare of gloues	vj d	
Item for wine and sugar at the dressinge of the boie	viij d	
Item to the Cryar at the barres	ij d	10
Item to the prisoners of the Castle and Northgate	vij d	
Item for silueringe of the stafe	xij d	
Item gaue to the minstrels	iij s	
Item to the fotemen yat lade the horse	xij d	

... 15

1603-4
Painters, Glaziers, Embroiderers, and Stationers' Records
C: Account Book I
f 123 *(18 October)* 20

...

Item payd at Richard Bakers dyner for Wyne and to the
mynstrells iij s iij d

... 25

Treasurers' Account Rolls CCA: TAR/2/23
mb 6d *(November)*

...

Payd more to Iasper Gyllaume by the apoyntment of mr Maior
beeing dew to him att midsomer last as Captaine of the watch 30
in monney vj s viij d

...

mb 7
Payd more the xv^t day of ffebruary 1603 to Richard Innce and 35
Edward dauies stewardes of the company of Sadlers. and was.
towardes the payment of the silver bell for the horse Rase att
Shrovetyde laste 1603 in money vj s viij d

...

Paid to the drummer on shrouetuesday xij d 40

...

Cordwainers and Shoemakers' Records
CCA: Account Book II G/8/3
f 16 *(11 November)*

...

Itt*em* given for the gleaves and barrych   vj s   5

...

Itt*em* geuen to the wetmen at Srovetyd   ij s vj d

...

Itt*em* geven to the mynstrylles on mydsomar Eyve   iiij s
Itt*em* spent vpon the mynstrylles the same tyme   [⟨...⟩] ij s   10

...

f 16v

...

Itt*em* spent and geven the xiij daye of septembar beying ovre   15
meyting daye to the wetmen and for macking the hall Clayne
                                                             ij s vj d

...

Itt*em* spent and geven to the wetmen at ovre meytyng tha xviij
daye of septembar   xij s iiij d   20

...

Itt*em* spent and geven to the wetmen and henrye Shorlock the
viij daye of novembar being our meyting daye   ix s iiij d

                                                                         25

Coopers' Records C: Account Book I
f 43v *(13 January)*

...

It*em* payde for wyne at Iohn Kenmons dinner   ij s viij d
It*em* payde to the minsterlls the same tyme   ij s vjj d   30
It*em* payde for alle the same tyme   iij d

...

Joiners, Carvers, and Turners' Records
CCA: Company Book G14/1   35
f 67v

...

Imp*ri*mis for a paire of hoose for the Childe y*at* Ride at
midsomer   iij s ij d
It*em* more for a paire of shoes   xvj d   40
It*em* for a paire of gloues   xij d
It*em* for Ribbins to tie the shoes   iij d

It*em* to two men to laied the horse	viij d
It*em* for wyne and sugar	viij d
It*em* to the mynstrells	iij s
It*em* to the Cryar at the Barres	ij d
It*em* to the prisoners of the Castle & Northgate	vij d 5

...

A   *Mayors List 5* BL: Harley 2125
f 47* *(Midsummer) John Aldersey*

...   10

no midsomer wach by reason of Sicknesse was sett forth /

...

1604-5
Cordwainers and Shoemakers' Records   15
CCA: Account Book II G/8/3
f 21 *(11 November)*

...

(at a dinner)

giuen to ye weetmen	ij s 20

...

(at a dinner)

more geven to the waytmen the same tyme	ij s
more paide for our gleeves v s, and xij d to the barage some is	vj s

...   25

f 21v *(4 November at a dinner)*

...

Item geven to the waytmen the same tyme	ij s

...   30

A   *Mayors List 5* BL: Harley 2125
f 47 *(November) Edward Dutton*

...

no fayer   Noe fayer kepte at mydsomer, neither the watch sett out w*hich*   35
was Lamentable /: all this by reason of the sickenes of the
plague / God remove it farr from vs / ·nether any waches at
Christmas Eue·

...

11 / *entry is in left margin*
37-8 / ·nether ... Eue· *in RH II's hand*

Dean and Chapter CC: Treasurers' Accounts III
p 242 *(Christmas)*

...

Inprimis payd to the watchman Atending iij nightes vpon the
maior and Sheriffes in Christmas & for Armour   ij s iiij d./   5

...

Coopers' Records C: Account Book I
f 44v *(13 January)*

...   10

spent at Roger
lea his diner

Inprims paid for William Sanders his Dinner   vij d
more paid for iije pottells of dubble beare   vj d
more for a gallone of wine   ij s
Item more to the minstrells   ij s vj d
more for a pottell of Alle   ij d   15

...

1605-6

Painters, Glaziers, Embroiderers, and Stationers' Records   20
C: Account Book I
f 126v *(18 October)*

...

Item mending the Childs apparell   viij d
Item for ˰ ʿa new hower glasse and᾿ mending the Case   v ⟨.⟩   25
Item for hose and shooes to the Child   ij s iiij d
Item for a sokett to hould the banner   ij d
Item for garters and gloves to the Child   ix d
Item for mending the banner and Collering the staffe   xviij d
Item to the prisoners of the Castle and northgate   viij d   30
Item to the Cryer   iij d
Item for our bankett on mydsomer Eve   vij s
Item for the musike   ij s vj d
Item for the lone of a hatt at mydsomer eve   xij d
...   35

Cordwainers and Shoemakers' Records
CCA: Account Book II G/8/3
f 2v

...   40

Items in Stewards possession in 1606

...

more one dublett and one payer of breech of Taffyta

[more one collored hatt lyned with greene Taffyta.]
more our collors in sylke with our companyes armes

...

f 22v *(11 November)*   5

...

Item giuen to george kellye and his companye   ij s vj d
Item giuen to the waytmen   xviij d

...

Item giuen to the kellyes at the cominge in of danyell thropp   10
beinge the xxiij^th day of Ianuary 1605 the some of   ij s

...

Item paid for gleeves at shrofetyd   v s
more giuen to Iohn lingley to the barrage   xij d
Item giuen to the waytemen at the same tyme   ij s 15
Item giuen to the Iorneymen for theire attendance at that
tyme   xij d

...

f 23   20

...

Item paide for our boy ^'for his stockinges' that did Ryde at
the watch at mydsomer   ij s
Item paid for Ahatt for our boy at midsomer   iiij s
more paid for one paier gloves   vj d 25
more for one paier shooes   xviij d
more giuen to the Crier at the barres   vj d
more giuen to the prisoners at the Castell and the Northgate   ij s
more giuen to the two foote men   xx d
more paid for musicke one mydsomer even   iiij s 30
Item paide for dressinge the staffe   viij d
[‹..›jth Iuly 1606] Item paide for one pottell of Sacke vpon mydsomer even at our
drinkinge after the watch   xx d

...

Item giuen to the waytmen & to the kellyes at our Alderman   35
pembertons sonnes comy in to the companye   iiij s

...

f 23v

...   40
(St Martin's Eve)
Item paid to the waytmen the same night   ij s vj d

...

Coopers' Records C: Account Book I
ff 47-7v *(13 January)*

...

Midsomer Accomptes	paid for a cheese	iij s iiij d
	paid for vj li. of prunes	xviij d	5
	paid for a quartr of a li. of suger	v d.
	paid for a payer of stockinges for the child	xviij d
	paid for dressing the staffe	xij d
	paid to the cryer	ij d	
	geuen to the prisoners at the Castell	iiij d	10
	geuen to the northgate	vj d
	spent at henrye Phillipes	vj d
	paid for Riboning for the childes shues	iij d
	geuen for lone of the childes hatt	viij d
	paid for a payer of gloues to hime that held the child	viij d	15
	geuen to him that lede the horse	vj d
	paid for horse meate	vij d
	geuen to the drommer	xij d
	paid for a C ˄ ʿdʾ wayffers	xij d
Midsomer Accuntes endes	paid for the childes shoes	xij d	20
	paid for bread	xviij d
	paid for drinke	iiij s viij d

...

Mercers, Ironmongers, Grocers, and Apothecaries' Records 25
C: Company Book
p 19* *(2 May)*

...

Item payde Roberte Smyth Tayler for makeinge a Taffita gowne
for the ladye   vij s 30
Item paide for ij payer of stockinges   ij s viij d
Item payde for two payer of spanishe lether shues   iij s iiij d
Item payde for aquarte of wine at mr Conwayes at the dressinge
of the boye   vj d
Item paide for two payer of gloves   ij s j d 35
Item paide to three men to leade the horses   xviij d
Item payde vnto the prisoners in the Castell   xij d
Item paide vnto the prisoners of the Northgate /   xij d
Item payde the Crier   iij d
Item paide for one payer of frenshe garters for the boye ij s vj d 40
Item one dossine sylke poyntes   xvj d
Item payde for makeinge the Taffyta shute for the boye to

Roger handcoke Taylor   iij s

...

f 20

                                                                        5

...

Item more for the ladyes gowne three yardes of Russett Iene
fustian at   iij s
Item paide for two yardes of buceram at   ij s
Item more xij yardes of whall bone   xij d
Item for .9. skynes of collered sylke at   xiij d ob. 10
Item ij yardes Dur gould parchement Lace weayinge A quarter
and Dur of an ounce at   ij s vj d
Item ij dossin gould buttons   ij s
Item ij yardes more of goulde parchement Lace weayinge
Aquarter and dram at   ij s j d 15
Item Dur quarter yarde grine serge at   iij d
Item for the boyes sute .3. quarters yarde Course Canvas at   vj d
Item iij dossine watched sylke buttons at   ix d
Item iiij skaynes of sylke at   vj d
Item quarter pound Right bumbast at   v d 20
Item paide Rondall Houlme for keepinge our banner and
Colloring the staffe in oyle collor   iiij s

...

Item paide mr Owen mercer for Taffyta for the boyes sute
and the ladyes gowne the some of   lix s. 4d 25

...

p 21

...

Item p̂ [de]`ayde to Roberte Smyth for the ladyes gowne j   30
yarde [d] quarter saccloth at 10d per yarde is   xv d
Item [⟨...⟩] more j skayne soeinge sylke at   j d ob.
Item more for the winges of the gowne 19 yardes of Rybine
at 20d per dossine is   ij s viij d
Item in greene thrid   j d 35
Item more iiij skaines of seawater sowinge sylke greene at   vj d
Item j payer of bentes   ij d
Item j payer of fustian Trunke sleeves at   ij s x d
Item iij yardes of welshe Cotton bought of Iohn Anyon at   iij s
Item iiij yardes of white Ienes at   iiij s 40

...

Item paide for a staffe for stremer for our companye xvj d. and

for payntinge the same 18d some is   ij s x d
Item paide for cakes one mydsom*er* even   ij s
Item for vj li. prunes   xviij d
Item more j potter of Clarrett wine j pottell of white wine and
one pottell of sacke at   iij s viij d   5

...

1606-7

Drawers of Dee's Records CCA: Company Book G10/1
pp 19-20* *(30 June)*   10

...

p*a*id for making a new staffe for the bann*er*   xij d
p*a*id for painting the staffe   vj d
p*a*id for prunes   ix d
p*a*id for a payer of shoes for the child   xx d   15
p*a*id for 1 payer of stocking*es* for the child   xxij d
p*a*id for ⟨.⟩ a payer of gloues for the child   vj d
p*a*id in streking the chains of old iewells & other necessaries
for the child   xij d
p*a*id for bread beare & cheese after the banquett   v s viij d   20
p*a*id for a quarte of wine & suger at dresseng the child   viij d
for a pottell of wine at the banquett   xij d
geuen to the Crier   ij d
geuen to the prisoners at the castell   vj d
geuen to the ⟨..⟩ison*er*s at the Northgate   iiij d   25
p*a*id for a fall ⟨...⟩ for ⟨...⟩ pa⟨...⟩ at ⟨...⟩ banquett   ij s ij d |
geuen to ⟨..⟩ footemen w*h*ich went w*i*th the Child   xvj d
p*a*id for ⟨...⟩ at the watch   iij s

Painters, Glaziers, Embroiderers, and Stationers' Records   30
C: Account Book I
f 129 *(18 October)*

...

It*em* spent at vid Basnetts vpon St lukes day   vj s
Item to the musicke at the same tyme   iij s   35
Item payd for wyne at the same tyme   xviij d
Item spent at Rob*er*t Thornleys dyn*n*er in wyne   ij s vj d
It*em* at the same tyme for musicke   ij s vj d

...

It*em* for hose shewes and gloues . for the Child vpon mydsomer   40
eve   iij s

34 / vid *for* widow

Item to the Cryer vpon mydsomer eve   iiij d
Item to prisoners of the Castle and northgat   viij d
Item for sylvering the Lase of the Chylds [lase] Clothes at
mydsomer   xx d
Item for musike vpon mydsomer eve   ij s vj d   5
Item for our bankett vpon mydsomer eve   vij s

...

Cordwainers and Shoemakers' Records
CCA: Account Book II G/8/3   10
f 27v *(11 November)*

...

Item paid for sixe gleeves to Iohn lingley the gouldsmyth and the
beriage withall some is   vj s
more [for] giuen to the stewards of the Iorney men for theire   15
attendance at 'Shroftyde'   xij d

...

Item paid for one paier of showes for the boye at midsomer xvj d
Item paid for j paier of stockeinges   xvj d
Item paid for his gloves   vj d   20
Item paid for mendinge the Collors   vj d
Item giuen to mr brynes man vpon mydsomer even   ij s vj d
Item giuen to the Crier at the barres   vj d
Item giuen to patricke & william Coldocke   xij d
Item giuen to the musioners   iiij s   25
Item given to the prisoners at Castell & northgate   ij s
Item given to william siddall   iiij d
Item paid for poyntes   iiij d

...
                                                                      30

f 28
Item paid for sacke vpon mydsomer even   ij s

...

AC *City Order for Gowns* BL: Harley 2150   35
    f 162v* *(November)*

        an order for wearinge of Gownes
        caused to be sett downe in this forme
        by mr Phillip Phillips Maior 1606   40

All Iustices of Peace within this Citty of chester theis seuerall
days and feasts followinge are to weare their Scarlett Gownes &

thos feastes and dayes all other Aldermen theie not ʌ ˈbeingˈ
Iustices of peace to weare their Murrey Gownes & also sheriffs
& sheriffs peeres for euery thos days to were their best Gownes
& like order to be obserued at other tymes so often as mr Maior
shall appoynt vpon payne of xij d for euery defalt

All Saintes	Purification day	Trinity Sonday
5th of nouember	Coronation day	midsomer eue
mr maiors wach	Easter day	5th August
Christmas day	Loue sunday	& at mr maiors
mr maiors feast	Ascension day	appoyntment
new years day	Whitsonday	
Epiphanye or 12th day		

...

A   *Mayors List 11* BL: Add. 29779
f 34* *(November) Philip Philips*

...

'Dauncing one
a Rope°

A strange man Came to this Cittye and his wife & the did daunce
vpon A Rope . Tyed overCrosse the streete: with other pleasante
trickes: which was rare to the behoulders. /

...

Beerbrewers' Records CCA: Company Book G 3/2
ff 8-8v *(23 November)*

...

Item for Taffeta for the banner for the Companies vse at
mydsommer   xiij s vj d
Item to Randle Holmes for paynting the banner   xl s
Item a staffe for the banner   xx d
the yron for the banner   xiiij d
Item fringe for the banner   ij s viij d
Item for buckram to make a Sockett for the banner   iiij d
Item a payre of stockinges for the boy that ryed at Mydsommer
     xxij d
Item a payre of shues for him   xx d
Item gloves for him   ix d
Item layd out in travelinge to procure a Chayne against mydsomer
for the Childe   xij d
Item for a pottle of wyne and Suger at the dressinge of the

19 / *marginalia in RH II's hand*

Childe   xx d
Item for Cheese and bread at the banquett at mydsommer
                                                            iiij s vj d
Item for stronge beere at mydsommer   ij s viij d |
Item for prunes and Sugar   xiiij d   5
Item payd to mr. back for a Samon for the banquett   iiij s
Item for a gallon of wyne for the company at our banquett
one mydsommer even   ij s viij d
Item given to the Cryer at the barres   iiij d
Item to the prisoners at the Castle   vj d   10
Item to the prisoners at the northgate   vj d
Item given to two footemen one mydsomer even to attend
the Childe   xvj d
Item to the musick one mydsommer even   v s
...   15
for a Saddle lost one mydsommer even at mr Rattclyffes   v s
...

Dean and Chapter CC: Treasurers' Accounts III
p 284 *(25 November)*   20
...
Item to the waites at our audit   xij d
...

Mayors' Letters CCA: Great Letter Book M/L/2   25
no 184 *(2 December)*

To his Loveinge ffrende the maior of the Cittie of Chester
theese deliuer
                                                                             30
This Companey beinge my Lord of Harforth his men and haveinge
beine With mee, Whose retorne and abode for this Christmas
tyme I expecte, I ame to desire that if theire occutione bee to
Come to the Cittie that youe Will permit them to vse theire
quallatie Lathome my howse this ij^th of december 1606   35

                                    °your Loving frend
                                    william Derby°

post Creipt I would Request you   40
to lett them haue the towne
hall to playe in Ile vale

Coopers' Records C: Account Book I
ff 51-1v *(13 January)*

...

geuen to the Minstrells at Will*i*am fishers . the third of August   iij s

...

Midsom*er* Accompt*es*	paid for the child*es* hoes	xviij d
	paid for shoes for the child	xviij d
	paid for Riboning for the child*es* shoes	iiij d
	paid for iiij li. prunes	xij d
	paid for dressing the staffe	viij d
	paid for a payer of gloues for the child	iiij d
	paid for walnut*es*	iiij d
	paid for ij° footemen	xij d
	spent at henry Phillipes	ij s
	paid for d. a barr of beeare	v s
	paid for a cheese	ij s. viij d
	geuen to the northgate	vj d
	geuen to the Castle	iiij d
	geuen to Sidall	ij d
	geuen to the Musitioners	xxj d
	geuen to the Crier	iiij d
	paid for bread	xxij d
	paid for wine	ij s ij d

...

spent at Tho*mas* Tomlinsons Dinner	ffirst spent at Thomas Iohnes in beare	xxij d
	in Wine	xx d
	geuen to the minstrells	ij s vj d

...

Joiners, Carvers, and Turners' Records
CCA: Company Book G14/1
f 74 *(25 March)*

It*em* for dressinge of the stafe	viij d
It*em* for shoes and Ribbins for ye Childe	ij s
It*em* for hoose for the Childe that did Ride at midsomer	ij s
It*em* for gloues and pointes	xj d
It*em* for minstrels	xvj d
It*em* for two fotemen	x d
It*em* spent in wyne and sugar at the dressinge of the Chield	viij d
It*em* to the Cryer at the bares	ij d
It*em* to the Prisoners of the Castle and Northgate	vij d

...

Item bestowed vppon wyne at Edwarde Heidockes dynner xvj d
Item more for musicke at the same dynner xij d

...

Mercers, Ironmongers, Grocers, and Apothecaries' Records 5
C: Company Book
p 33 *(8 May)*

payde and disbursed, against mydsomer watch viz /

10

Item paide for ij payer of shues . for the two children ij s vj d
Item paide more for two payer of stockinges ij s iiij d
Item payde for two payer of sweete gloves xviij d
Item more for two payer of sylke garters iij s
Item iiij yardes .2d. Rybin at 6d. for sue ties ij d for two skynes 15
sylke .2d. x d
Item xij li. prvnes .2s. for cakes .2s.6d. for comfettes 10d.
some is v s iiij d
Item to the prisoners at castell and Northgate ij s
Item to the Crier 4d. more to two poore men. 6d some is x d 20
Item payde to the piper. ij s more for beere at the barres 4d
some is ij s iiij d
Item for iiij *ounces* synamond xiiij d
Item payde for one quarte of wyne at mr Cases . and one quarte
at mr lyttlers beinge at the dressinge of the two children xvj d 25
Item paide for two pottells of wine clarrett one pottell of white
wine and one pottell of sacke for the company at v s. viij d
Item payde Rondall hoolmes the hearalde at armes the thirde
day of Iuly 1607 for payntinge the two banners new. 43s 4d
and for layinge the staves in oyle, & to his man given 8d some 30
is xliiij s

...

A C *Smiths' Order for Midsummer* BL: Harley 2054
f 24 *(6 June)* 35

...

the 6 day of Iune 1607 Item it was then ordred by the full &
whole consent of the company that euery brother which shall at
® •to goe in   any tyme herafter at any Midsomer wach or at their departure
their places   from any meetinge goe out of descent order but duly keepe 40
orderly •   there places accordinge to their Callings & seigniorityes shall
forfeitt for euery such offence vj d

...

1607-8
Painters, Glaziers, Embroiderers, and Stationers' Records
C: Account Book I
f 130 *(18 October)*

...

Item for hose shooes and gloves to the Child that Rydd	ij s x d
Item for our bankett on mydsomer Eve	vij s
Item to the prisoners and Cryer at the same tyme	xij d
Item for a blacke fither	xvj d
Item for musike at mydsomer	xij d
Item for mendinge the banner	xij d
Item to Thomas Gyllam	vj s viij d

...

Treasurers' Account Rolls CCA: TAR/2/24
mb 2 *(November)*

...

paid vnto William hancock and nicolus hallowoodd paynteres
the xxvij° of maij and was to repayre the gyuntes againste
the show at mydsomer   xliij s iiij d

...

paid for the Carrege of the drum on myesomer eue   xij d
paid Thomas Welsh for carryinge the antient   ij s vj d

...

Drawers of Dee's Records CCA: Company Book G10/1
p 30 *(10 November)*

...

10 [october]
nouember

geuen to Iohn Garnett towardes the Making of the banner   xx s
geuen to the bearebruers vpon Agrement for our Companie
towardes the [sh]ow at midsomer   vj s viij d

...

Cordwainers and Shoemakers' Records
CCA: Account Book II G/8/3
f 31 *(11 November)*

...

Inprimis paide vnto the waytemen by the Aldermens appoyntment
at william Gregoryes   xij d
Dynner in money
Item paide the same tyme to pemburton þe waiteman   xij d
Item paide the same tyme to George kellye and his companye

by the Aldermens appoyntment   ij s vj d

...

Item paid for vj gleaves   vj s

...

Item given to the wayte men at shrove thursday   ij s vj d   5
Item given to the stewards of the Iorneymen at shrove Tyde xij d

...

f 32   10
Item paide for our boye . that did Ryde vpon midsomer even
for one paier gloves & sylke pointes at   xx d
Item paide for one paier stockinges & a paier shues at   iij s iiij d
Item paide for a hatt for our boye & for one fether   iiij s vj d
...   15
Item giuen to the cryer   vj d
Item giuen to william sidall   iiij d
Item at the Castell & northgate to the prisoners   ij s
Item paid for sue ties of sylke Ryben   iiij d
Item paid to the man that lead the horse vpon midsomer even   20
                                                         iij s [vj d]
Item more paid for the removing of the horse sues   vj d
Item giuen to the two Iorney men for houlding & attendinge
the childe   xij d
Item spente the same daie at our drinkeinge one pottell seacke ij s   25
Item giuen to the musioners   iij s
Item spente at the dressinge of the Childe vpon midsomer even
                                                         ij s vj d

...   30

f 32v
Item giuen vnto the kellyes the vth august 1608 beinge the kinges
daie at A dynner   ij s
...   35

f 33
...
(St Martin's Day)   40
Item paid vnto Roberte kelly for musicke   ij s
...

Beerbrewers' Records CCA: Company Book G3/2
ff 11-11v *(23 November)*

...

Item for a payre of stockinges for the childe that rydd at
Mydsomer   ij s vj d
Item for a payre of shues for the childe   xv d
Item for gloves for the Childe   viij d
Item for wyne and suger at dressinge of the Childe   ij s
Item charges in procuring a Chayne and other Iewells for the
Childe   xij d   1
Disbursements

Item payd to Randle Holmes for the keepinge of the banner xij d
Item given to the Cryer at the barres   iiij d
Item given to the prisoners at the Castle   vj d
Item given to the prisoners at the Northgate   vj d
Item for bread and Cheese for the banquett one Mydsomer   1
even   iiij s
Item for stronge beere at the banquett   ij s
Item for prunes and suger the same tyme   xiiij d
Item for three quartes of wyne at the bankett   ij s
Item given to two footemen to leade the horse and guide the   2
Childe one Mydsomer even   xvj d |
Item for Musicke one Mydsomer even   ij s vj d
...

Dean and Chapter CC: Treasurers' Accounts III   2
p 314 *(25 November)*
...

Item to the waites   xij d
...

                                                                    30

p 315
...

(at Christmas)
Imprimis to the wachman [⟨...⟩] to attend the mayor &
sheriffes   ij s 35
...

Coopers' Records C: Account Book I
f 53v *(13 January)*
...   40
Midsomer
accomptes

ffirst for half a barr of dubble beare   vij s
paid for a cheese   iij s ij d

p*ai*d for a payer of shoes for the child	xviij d	
p*ai*d for a payer of hoes for the child	xviij d	
p*ai*d for iij li. of prunes	[ij d] vij d	
p*ai*d for a payer of gloues for the child	iiij d	
p*ai*d for bread	ij s vj d	5
spent at the Barres	v d	
geuen to cryer at the barres	iij d	
geuen to Suddall	ij d	
geuen to the prison*ers* at the castell	iiij d	
geuen to the Northgate	vj d	10

paid for a pottell of seck bestowed vpon the Companie at
Midsom*er*   ij s.

geuen to the Minstrels	xij d	
paid for suger & sinomon	iiij d	
paid for horse bread	iiij d	15

...

°spent at William Catterall his dinner one gallone of wyne price
                                                          ij s viij d

more a pottell of secke	ij s	
more a pottell of Alle	iiij d	20
more gaue the muisickiconeres	iij s°	

...

Joiners, Carvers, and Turners' Records   25
CCA: Company Book G 14/1
f 77 *(25 March)*

...

Item paied for one paire of Stockens for the Childe y*at* Rode at
Midsomer   iij s iiij d   30

It*em* more for one paire of shoes	xviij d	
It*em* for gloues	ix d	
It*em* for Ribbins for the Shoes	ij d	
It*em* for payntinge the staffe	viij d	
It*em* to the mynstrels	iij s	35
It*em* to the Cryer at the barres	iiij d	
It*em* to the Prysoners of the Castle and Northgate	vj d	

...

Item spent & bestoed at Ric*ard* Calcot*es* Dynner in wyne and
Ale and to the Mynstrels   v s   40

...

Item for two fotemen to leade the horse   viij d

St Oswald's Vestry Book CRO: P/29/7/2
p 31 *(27 March)*

...

Item spente vppon the Synginge men of the Queare goinge with
the Vicar & parishioners vppon procession in Cyttie & Countrey

iij s iiij d

...

Mercers, Ironmongers, Grocers, and Apothecaries' Records
C: Company Book   1(
p 41 *(6 May)*

...

Inprimis paide at midsomer at the watch at our drinkinge for
suger sinamond cloves & comfettes   iij s viij d
Item paide for cakes   iij s iiij d   15
Item paide for 9 li. prvines   ij s vj d
Item paide for one potter seake   ij s
Item paide for two gallans & one pinte of white wine and clarett
& venaker   v s x d
Item paide for doble beere   iiij s   20
Item paide for two paier of hoose at   iij s
Item paide for two paier shues for the children at   ij s vj d
Item paide for two paier silke garters for the two children   iij s
Item paid for two paier gloves for them   j s iiij d
Item paide for silke Riben Laces poyntes and pynnes for them   25
xxj d
Item paide for one velvet girdle for the boye   xij d
Item paide at the barres castell & Northgate   ij s vj d
Item more paide vnto Lame siddall   iiij d
Item paide vnto the men that did attend the children & theire   30
horses   iij s
Item paide to kellsall the officer & other watchmen that did
attend the londoners ⌐at midsomer⌐   iij s

...

35

Assembly Files CCA: A/F/8
f 18*

To the right worshipfulle the maior Aldermen
sheriffe and Common Counsell of the Citie of Chester   40

The humble petition of Thomas ffisher Musitioner

shewinge

That he was borne and broughte vpp in the Citie aforesaid, That
his graundfather and all his Auncestor⟨.⟩ before him were Freemen
of the said Citie and therefore the petitioner meaninge to lead   5
the reste of his life in the same Citie is desirous to become a
freema⟨.⟩ thereof

That the qualitie he professeth is Musicke and that he is
ignoraunte and not experienced in any trade neither will vse
or exercise any whereby anie Companie of tradesmen in the   10
said Citie mighte receive preiudice

The petitioner doeth therefore earnesly beseeche
your worships to graunte at this assembly That
he maie be made a freeman of the said Citie And   15
he will not only paie such imposicion as his poore
abillity will extend to but will ever praie for your
prosperities

°not fitte with a generall vote / °   20

1608-9
Drawers of Dee's Records CCA: Company Book
p 31 *(23 June)*   25
...

23 Iunij paid for a fishe bestowed vpon the bearebruers and our selves
after midsomer   v s
geuen to the stewardes of the bearbruers vpon agrement for
our Companie at midsomer showe vj s [vij d] viij d 30
...

Assembly Books CCA: AB/1
f 302v *(20 September)*
...   35

•George Cally And at the same assembly It is graunted vnto George Callye
graunted to be Musitioner vpon his humble petition exhibited in regarde he
free gratis• was borne broughte vpp and hath all his life tyme hitherto
dwelled in this Citie That he shalbe admitted into the Liberties
thereof and made a freeman of the same Citie gratis and   40
withoute payinge anie thinge therefore
...

Painters, Glaziers, Embroiderers, and Stationers' Records
C: Account Book I
f 132v *(18 October)*

...

Inprimis on St Lukes daye at Iohn framwalls dyner for wyne
    iiij s vij d
Item to the wayets the same tyme   ij s vij d

...

Item for hose showes and gloves for the Child at mydsomer
    iiij s vij d   1
Item for Rybans to the horse heade   iij d
Item to the Cryer   iiij d
Item to the prisoners of the Casle and northgate   viij d
Item for our bankett on mydsomer Eve   vij s
Item for Ale at the same tyme   xx d   1

...

Cordwainers and Shoemakers' Records
CCA: Account Book II G/8/3   2
f 38 *(11 November)*

...

(St Martin's Day)
Item givin to Richard barlow man pickeringe for singinge   vj d
...   2

f 38v *(26 January)*

...

Item geven to Roberte kellye   ij s [iij d]
...   3
Item geven for the v. gleeves   v s
Item geuen to the berage   xij d
Item geven to the waytemen in the Comen hall   ij s

...

Item [s] geven to the Iorneymen for theire paines at Shrovetyde   3
    xij d

...

f 39

...   4
Item spente . at Alderman younges house vpon midsomer even
at our drinkeinge after the watch In an overplushe   x s iij d

Item spente *without* the out the barres   xij d
Item to the Crier   vj d
Item giuen to Sidall   iiij d
Item spente at geo Kellies house on the even   ij d

                                                                                        5

f 39v

...

Item geven to the prisoners at the Castell & the Northgate   ij s
Item geven to mr massyes foure men . *which* did Attende the
boy *which* Ryde for vs   iiij s   10
Item geven [ge] danyell wright *which* held the staffe   vj d
Item geven Roberte kellye & his companye for our musicke   iiij s
Item spente the same tyme in seacke   xx d
Item paide for dressinge our staffe   xviij d
Item paid for one paier shooes for our boye one paier stockeing*es*   15
shue ties and gloves   vij s

...

Item giuen to Roberte Kelly and his fellowes in Tho Inces   ij s
...

                                                                                        20

Beerbrewers' Records CCA: Company Book G 3/2
ff 14-14v *(23 November)*

...

Item payd for a payre of stockinges for the Childe that rydd at
mydsom*er* for the companie   ij s vj d   25
Item for a payre of shues the same tyme   xv. d
Item for gloves for the Childe   viij d
Item for wyne and suger at dressing the Childe   ij s
Item Charges in procuring Chaynes and other necessaries for
the Childe   xij d   30
Item payd to Randle holmes for the keeping of the banner   xij d
Item given to the Cryer at the barres   iiij d
Item given to the prison*er*s at the Castle   vj d
Item given to the prison*er*s at the northgate   vj d
Item for bread and Cheese at the banquett one mydsom*er* even   35
as hath beene allowed in form*er* yeares   iiij s |
Item for strong*e* beere at the banquett one mydsom*er* even   ij s
Item for prunes and suger the same tyme   xiiij d
Item for foure q*uar*tes of wyne the same tyme   ij s viij d
Item given to two footemen to attend the Childe   xvj d   40

1 / without the out the MS *dittography*

Item to a man to leade the horse   vj d
Item for musicke to goe with the companie one mydsom*er*
and at the bankett   v s
Item for a Samon more then the drawers in dee sent   xx d
...

AC   *Trinity Churchwardens' Accounts* BL: Harley 2177
f 39 *(Christmas)*

...

28 nou*ember* 1608 for 5 sheets of plate 20d. 2 li. ˆ'3 onz' of
wyer xij d on p*oun*d yellow wyer xij d Small neyles vj d: to a
Tinker for makinge the Candlestickes for the Starr and nayling
them on xij d for a Cord for the Starr ˆ'8d' to the Smyth
for his work xviij d. for a pully with Iron stables & hooke ix d.
for a glass lanthorne for the Starr vij s. for carriage of longe
lathers from Estgate to & frow 4d to Rafe davis Ioyner for
makinge the Starr vij s

...

to nicho hallowood for payntinge the Starr   4s
...

Coopers' Records C: Account Book I
f 54v *(13 January)*

...

Midsommer accompt*es*	gaue for a cheese	iij s iiij d
	gaue for halfe a barrell of beare	vij s
	gaue for a payre of hose for the childe	xvj d
	gaue for a payre of gloues for the childe and for the footeman	ix d
	gaue for three pound pruines	viij d
	gaue for a payre of shoes for the boye	xxj d
	gaue for bred	ij s ij d
	more spent at the barres	xiij d
	gaue to the cryer at the barres	iiij d
	gaue to Syddall	ij d
	gaue to the prisoneres at the castell	iiij d
	gaue to the prisoneres at the northgate	vj d
	paid for a quarte of alle at the banquitte	iij d
	gaue for a pottell of secke	xxij d
	gaue to the musickesoneres	viij d
	gaue for sugar	iij d
	gaue for sinomon	iij d
	gaue for horse bred	iij d

gaue to the mane for leadinge the horse iiij d

Joiners, Carvers, and Turners' Records
CCA: Company Book G14/1
f 79v *(25 March)* 5
...

Item for a payre of shoes and ribbens for the Childe which did
ryde at midsomer ij s
Item more for hose xviij d
Item for gloues vj d 10
Item spent in Wyne and suger at the dressinge of the childe x d
Item . to the Muscicans xvj d
Item to three men to leade the horsse xij d
...

15

f 80
Item spent at Richard Coes dynner in Wyne iij s iiij d
...
Item to the Musitians at the same dynner iij s
... 20

Mercers, Ironmongers, Grocers, and Apothecaries' Records
C: Company Book
p 43 *(5 May)*
... 25
Item paide the 13 maye 1609 for blacke Taffita . sylke . and
Reben . for the repayringe of the Tippittes 00-04-08d
Item paide Lewes williams for doinge the Tippettes 00-02-06
Item paide for a neale and halfe of white taffyta & foure skeanes
of sylke . for the repayringe of the boyes clothes 00-01-09 30
Item paide for two payer of shooes for the Children 00-02-04
Item paide for two payer of gloues for the Children 00-02-00
Item paide for two payer of hoose for them 00-04-08
Item paide for one yarde greene Reben for the boyes clothes
00-00-02 35
Item paide hugh Iones for his worke 00-01-02
Item paide for iij yardes ½. tincill Reben 00-01-02
Item paide for vj li. prewnes 12. ounces Comfettes 00-02-11
Item paide for Cakes and spice for the same 00-04-10
Item paide for wine and beere 00-08-00 40
Item paide for muzicke 00-08-00
Item paide mr Holmes for keepinge the banners 00-02-00
...

p 44

...

Item giuen to the prisoners at the Castell & Northgate	00-	1-	0
Item paide for beere at the barres	00-	1-	0

...

A   *Rogers' Breviary*   CCA: unnumbered MS
unnumbered folio* *(3 June)*

1609 Iuly: 3
I began to write
D Rogers

> A Breuary or some fewe Collectiones of
> the Cittie of Chester . gathered out of some
> fewe writers, and heare set down. And re
> duced into these Chapters followinge.

...

Chapter 4)

4   Of the buldinge & changeinge of some parishe Churches in
    Chester, Certayne lawdable exercises and playes of Chester.

...

f 1*

To the Reader

Gentle Reader I am boulde to presente vnto your sighte a breuary
of Chester that Anchient Cittie, the which howsoeuar it be not
profitable, for anye yat seeke deuine consolation. yet it maye be
delightefull ‸ 'to' [m] any, that desire to heare of antiquitie,
[the] which worke heare followinge was the collectiones of a
lerned and Reuerende father within this Cittie: [the] which
worke I muste craue the readers hereof not to [⟨...⟩] contemne,
because of the defectes herein, assuringe you, that whatsoeuar is
wantinge, either for lerninge or Readinge it is not for the wantes,
yat weare in the author hereof, for both this Cittie and these
partes did [fullye] knowe his full abillitye and sufficiencie in
those respectes And therefore I alledge . the Resones yat moued
the Author to this worke, And the reson whye it is not perfected

Collation   CCA: unnumbered MS, ff (one) unnumbered, 1, 17-23, with BL:
Harley 1944, ff 3, 4, 21-6v *(1944)*; CRO: DCC 19, ff 34v-6 *(CRO)*; BL:
Harley 1948, ff 18-18v, 58-67 *(1948)*; Liverpool: Liverpool University MS
23.5, ff (one) unnumbered, 24-7v *(L)*:   27 that desire] that [seeke] desire
1944   36 is] was *1944*

in that perfection yat he Intended [⟨...⟩] craueinge pardon for
any thinge herein: Either nakedly or Improperly set downe.
The resons that moued hime heareunto, as I conseaue was,
because he was heare borne. and his predicessors also, and some
of them beinge of the beste rancke within this Cittie. and also   5
because he himselfe was a continuall resident within this place.
And did desire the continuall honor wealthe and good estimation
of this. anchiente Cittie. But the Reson whye it was not perfected.
was the ereuokeable will of God. whoe before he coulde finishe
this, or many much more excellente and deuine treatises, called   10
hime and gathered hime to his fathers in a tymely death and full
of dayes, And soe he lefte this and manye more of excellente
vallue, vnfinished, euen as abodye without a head: Therefore
againe I craue the Readers hereof to Impute the defectes herein
to the vnskillfull writer, whoe indeede is altogether vnfitt to   15
take anye such matter in hande, whoe wanteth both learninge
and readinge in this kynde to finnishe up this treatise, and also
I maye bouldlye saye wanteth tyme, to combine it in that fashon
which it requireth [⟨...⟩] craueinge only but acceptacion for my
desyre. willinge to displease none. but desiringe yat ₍ᴧ₎ ʼallʼ defectes   20
herein may be Imputed to the vnskyllfull writer. and if any good
effecte, that it be imputed to the Author. And thus wisheinge the
honor and perpetuall good estate of this moste anchiente and
Righte worshipfulle Cittie, I euer reste a continuall well wisher,
obliged in all loue as God nature, & reason byndethe mee: 25

per David Rogers:
1609
Iuly 3ᵗʰ 1609

Collation continued: 7 good] *omitted 1944*   10 this] *omitted 1944*
11 hime and] him [awaye] and *1944*   14 defectes] defectes [to the] *1944*
18 it] *omitted 1944*   29 Iuly 3ᵗʰ 1609] 1609 Iuly *1944*

ff 17-23*

Chapter .4.

Now for the lawdable exersises yearelye
vsed within the Cittie of Chester.

Memorandum that whereas the companye and occupation of
the shooemake-ers within the Cittie of Chester. tyme oute of

the homage of
a footeball was
offered to the
company of
Drapers, before
the maior, and
not to the maior,

the memorye of man vpon tuesedaye commonly called
shrouetuesedaye, or otherwise, Goteddesdaye on the afternoone
of the same daye. At the crosse vpon the Roode Dee. before the
Maior of the same Cittie, did offer vnto the companye of the
Drapers. of the Cittie of Chester. an homage. A ball of lether
called a foote ball: of the value of iij s iiij d or there aboute.

There is no reson
by any truly to

And by reson of greate hurte. and strife which did arise amonge
the yonge persones of the same Cittie. while diuars partes weare

Collation continued: 4 for] of *L*   4-5 Now ... Chester.] Now of the
lawdable exercises and playes of Chester, yerelye there vsed: *1948; between
the heading and the entry, CRO and L insert the following poem:* Certamina
elympyca: Istamina nehemia Ellis:† (1) | Sacrap*er* Arginas certamina quatuor
vrbes (2) | Su*n*t, dies facta viris, et duo coelitibus: (3) | vt Iouis et Phœbi,
melicertæq*ue*, Archemoriq*ue* (4) |proemia; oliuaster, poma, apiu*m*, picea (5)|
(CRO base text: 2 Sacrap*er* for Sacra per 4 vt] et *L* 4 melicertaeque] er *altered from*
ir, *CRO* 5 poma, apiu*m*] pono opiu*m L)* 7 M*emorandum* that] *omitted 1948*
8 the] *omitted L* 8 Chester.] *CRO and L add* did yearelye; *1948* did
yerelye 8-9 tyme ... man] (time out of the memorie of man no man
remembringe the origenall thereof) *1948* 9 the memorye] the *omitted*
CRO, L; 1944 adds and deletes mynde 9 *marginalia]* The oulde homage
by ye shomakes to ye drap*er*s in Chester *CRO;* The ould homage of ye
Shomakers: *1948; omitted L* 9 called] *omitted L* 10 otherwise] *omitted*
1948 10-11 on ... daye.] at afternoone *CRO L* 12 same] *omitted 1948*
12 did] *omitted CRO L* 12 companye of the] the *omitted CRO L* 13 of
the Cittie] of the same Cittie *CRO 1948 L* 14 there aboute] aboue: *CRO;*
1948 adds the w*hi*ch when it was receaued, the drapers did giue the same ball
pr*e*sentlye there to be played for, by the shooemakers & sadlers, to bringe
the said foote ball to any of the 3 howses either of the mayor or either of
the Sheriffes, then that side to wine the same ball: 16 hurte. and] *omitted*
CRO L 17 *marginalia]* omitted L; 1944 omits *reson and alters* firste *to*
origenall; *CRO reduces the note to* The vse of ye ould homage; *1948*
reduces to ye new homag now: to ye drapers:

be giuen of the
firste of these
homages donne
to the drapers by
the shooemakers
sadlers and all
maried *persones*
but the custome
of antiquitie and
the charge of the
same homages of
anchant tymes.
but these
customes are of
as greate force
beinge truly
anchant as any
Record or deede
of specialtie
which and proued
by the custom
belongeinge to
the crowne.
which may not
be denied

taken with force and stronge hande to bringe the saide Ball. to
one of these three howses. that is to saye to the Maiors howse.
or to any one of the Sheriffes howses for the tyme beinge.
muche harme was donne some in the greate throunge fallinge
into a transe. some haueinge theire bodies brused & crushed, 5
some theire, armes, heades. and legges broken and some otherwise
mayemed or in perrill of theire liffe; Now for to auoyde the
sayde Inconuenienses, And also to tourne and conuerte the saide
homage to a better vse: It was therefore thoughte good by the
Maior of the saide Cittie. and the Reste of the com*m*on counsell. 10
to make exchange of the saide Ball as followeth: That in place
thereof theire shoulde be offered by the Shooemakers. vpon the
same shroue tuesedaye vj gleaues of siluer. the which gleaues the
appoynted to be rewardes to such men as woulde come and the
same daye and place passe and ouerrunne on foote all others. 15
And the saide gleaues weare presentlye deliuered acordinge to
the Runinge of euerye one. And this exchange was made when
Henrye Gee. was Mayor of Chester, an*n*o domini .1539. an*n*o
.32. Henry the 8. ...

Collation continued: 2 one] any *1948* 2 these] the *1948* 2-3 that ...
beinge.] *omitted 1948* 3 to] *omitted CRO L* 3 Sheriffes howses] *CRO
omits* howses; *1948 adds* aforesaid *after* howses; *L adds* twoe *before*
Sheriffes 4 the] *omitted 1944* 4 fallinge] fallinge, fallinge *L* 6 and] or
CRO L 7 or] and *1948* 7 theire] *omitted L* 7 Now] *omitted 1948 L*;
Now *begins a new paragraph in CRO and against it in the left margin is*
change of ould homage 8 to tourne and] *after* and *1948 has added and
deleted* conc 9 therefore] *omitted CRO 1948 L* 9 by] to *CRO L*
10 Cittie.] *CRO adds* Aldermen 10 counsell.] *1948 adds* with the
concente of the said drapers, 11 Ball] footeball *CRO L* 12 shoulde]
omitted L 12 by the] *CRO adds* said 12-13 vpon ... tuesedaye] vnto the
Drapers, before the maior the same day & place, *CRO;* [the same ˄'day'],
vnto the drapers, the same [and] Shrouetuesday *1948; omitted,* to ye
drapers *added L* 13 vj] vj [gl⟨...⟩] *1944* 14 rewardes to] rewardes vnto
CRO 1948 L 17 when] in the time when *L* 18 Henrye] mr Henrie *CRO;*
mr Henry *1948* 18-19 an*n*o domini ... 8.] ano domini: 1539: ano: 32:
henry: 8: *1944;* anno domini: *(blank)* the: 31 yeare of king Henry the 8:
CRO; beinge the 21th yeare of the raigne of kinge Henry the 8th: And
the yeare of our lord God: 1539: *1948;* Anno domini 1539. And in ye 31:
yeare of kinge Henry the .8. *L*

Also whereas the companye and occupation of Sadlers within the same Cittie of Chester did yearely bu custome. tyme out of the memorye of man. the same daye hower and place. before the sayde Mayor. did offer vpon a trunchon or staffe or speare. vnto the companye of Drapers a certayne homage called the sadlers ball. profitable for fewe vses or purposes as it was.

This homage as is saide before was torned into a siluer bell wayeinge in siluer *(blank)* at the leaste. The which bell was ordayned to be the rewarde for that horse which with speede runninge there shoulde runne before or ouerrunne all others And there presently shoulde. be | geuen the same daye and place. This alteration was made the same tyme, and by the same Mayor like as the shooemakers footeball was before exchanged into vj siluer gleaues.

Collation continued: 1 of] of the *CRO 1948 L*   2 *marginalia*] The sadlers ould homage to the Drapers: *CRO 1948; omitted L*   2 same] *omitted 1944 CRO L*   2 bu *for* by   2-3 tyme ... man.] *omitted CRO*   2-3 the memorye] the *omitted L;* [mynde] the memorie *1944*   4 sayde ... staffe or] said Maior, Offer vnto the said Company of Drapers within the said Cittie of Chester *CRO;* said Mayor vnto the Companye of Drapers in Chester did offer vpon the trunchon of a staffe or *1948;* Mayor, offer vpon a Trinchon: staffe, of *L*   4-5 vnto ... Drapers] *omitted CRO 1948*   4-5 vnto ... homage] acertayne homage to the drapers of the Cittie of Chester *L*   6 ball] *1948 adds* beinge a ball of silke of the bignes of abowle, which was profitable for few vses or purposes as it was: The which ball the said Drapers did Caste vp amonge the throunge, to gett it who coulde, in which thronge also much hurte was done, the same mayor & Aldermen with consent of the drapers aforesaid did alter and Change: 8 This ... before] As before is said *CRO;* beinge a ball of silke of the biggnes of a bowle, *L; begins a new paragraph only in MS*   8 This ... bell] That in place thereof the said Company of Sadlers shoulde offer before the mayor vnto the Drapers, abell of siluer. *1948*   9 *marginalia*] The change of this ould homage: *CRO;* The new homage to the drapers: *1948; omitted L*   9 in ... leaste] *(blank)* at the leaste *1948;* about 2. oz. as is supposed of siluer. *L*   9 which bell] which saide silver bell *L*   10 ordayned] *1948 adds* also   10 speede] spedy *L*   11 runninge] *L misreads* ruinge   11 or ouerrunne] *omitted CRO 1948 L*   12 same] *omitted L*   13 made] made at *CRO;* made 'at' *1948*

Also whereas of custome whereof mans memorye now liueinge
can-not remember the origenall and begininge. The same daye
hower and place. and before the mayor of Chester for the tyme
beinge euerie person that was maried within the liberties of
Chester and dwellinge els where: And euery person dwellinge   5
within the liberties of the saide Cittie and married els where.
did offer vnto the companye of Drapers likewise a balle of silke
of the bignes of a boulle. The same Mayor torned the same
boulles of silke into siluer arrowes, The which arrowes they
tooke order shoulde be giuen to those which did shoote the   10
longest shoote with diuars kyndes of arrowes. for which homages
the Drapers ˄ ʼby custome likewiseʼ doe feaste the mayor. the
companyes of Sadlers and shoemakers. vpon shroue tuesedaye
after the homages be performed and those games played. with
bread and beere and the nexte ˄ ʼdayʼ after in the afternoone.   15
beinge Ashewensedaye. with leeckes and salte. and the 3 daye
after yat with a [banquete] bankett ˄ ʼall which areʼ in the
common hall of the same Cittie.

The forfett of
not offeringe
this siluer arrow
or gleaue to the
Drapers on shroue
tuesedaye. next
after any mariage
is 10 li. by the
maried person
so offendinge.

All persones
maried within the
liberties of Chester
ad dwellinge ells
where and all
persones dwellinge
within the
liberties of Chest
and maried els
wheare are to
deliuer vp a
gleaue to the
wardens of the
Drapers. or to
forfet to the
drapers x li. now
it is sertayne if
the forfett be to
the drapers then
the homage of
all is donne vnto
the Drapers,

Collation continued: 1 of] of auncient [time] *CRO 1948*; of ˄ ʼanʼ Anchant
L 2 marginalia] The oulde homage of all maried persons to ye drapers
CRO 1948; omitted *L* 3 of Chester] *omitted 1944 CRO 1948 L* 4 that
was] which is *CRO L*; yat is *1948* 4 liberties] Cittie *CRO* 5 Chester]
the said Cittie *1948 L* 5-6 and ... Cittie] and liberties thereof, or dwelled
within the Cittie the yeare before, *CRO*; and dwelled els where, or that
dwelled within ye Cittie the yeare before *1948*; dwellinge wheresoeuer
without, And all those that [for the] dwell within the saide Cittie *L* 6 and
... where] & was maried els where *1948*; for one yeare befor and marye
else wheare *L* 7 offer] offer likewise *1944 CRO L* 7 vnto the] the said
CRO 7 vnto ... likewise] likewise an homage to the said Companye of
drapers, before the mayor *L* 7 likewise] *omitted 1944*; within ye Cittie
of Chester *CRO*; in Chester an homage *1948* 8 marginalia] *omitted L;*
1944 has & for MS misreading ad, *adds* els *after* or (17) *and omits* to (21);
CRO reduces the note to The new homage to ye drapers of maried persons:
and 1948 to The new homag to the drapers: 8 marginalia Chest *for* Chester
8 the bignes] the quantitie *1948*; the like bignes *L* 8 boulle.] boulle fitt
for few vses: *CRO*; boulle profitable for few vses or purposes: *1948* 8 same
Mayor] said maior *CRO* 8 Mayor torned] mayor with concente of the
drapers afforesaid, did torne *1948* 8-9 same boulles of silke] same balles at
the same time *CRO*; said balls *1948*; same balls *L* 10 be giuen] be the
rewardes giuen *1948* 11-18 for ... Cittie] *omitted CRO L;* as ye flighte,
ye brod arrow & the buttshafte,: *1948* 14 the] these *1944* 15 beere and]
and *omitted 1944* 16 salte] salte & bread & beere: *1944* 16 3] thirde
1944 17 yat] *omitted 1944* 17 are] are ˄ ʼkeapteʼ *1944* 18 the] this *1944*

.

These exchanges
of these homages.
donne to the
company of
Drapers was as
it semeth
moderated on
both sides by the
wisdome of the
Cittie. that both
should haue theire
due namly the
homage done to
the Drapers. and
the benifitt
thereof. should
be for the publike
recreation of the
whole Citti there
assembled. for
which there
wisdome is
commended:

This exchange was made as before is mentioned of shooemakers footeballe. and sadlers ball. And the silke balls of all the maried persons. In the which exchange there appeared greate wisedome in those Anchant and sage senators. In whome was seene greate studye and regarde to torne the aforesayde thinges vnto so profitable excersises: So that thereof the moste commendable practises of walike feates. As of Runninge of horses and shooetinge of the broade arrowe. the flighte and the butchafte in the longe bowe with Runninge of men on foote. are there yearely vsed which is doone in uerye fewe, if anye Citties of Englande so farre as I doe vnderstande; |

Now of the playes of Chester called the whitson playes. when the weare played and what occupationes bringe forthe at theire charges the playes. or pagiantes.

Heare note that these playes of Chester called the whitson playes weare the worke of one Rondoll. a moncke of the Abbaye of Sainte Warburge in Chester. whoe redused the whole historye of the bible into englishe storyes in metter. in the englishe tounge. and this monke in a good desire to doe good published the same. then the firste Maior of Chester. namely Sir Iohn Arnewaye knighte he caused the same to be played. the manner of which playes was thus they weare deuided into 24 pagiantes acordinge to the companyes of the Cittie. and euerye companye broughte forthe theire pagiant which was the cariage. or place which the played in. And before these playes there was a man

Collation continued: 1 *marginalia*] *omitted L; 1944 has* Draper *for* Drapers (9); *CRO reduces the note to* The commendation of this exchang: *and 1948 to* Comendation giuen by mr Robert Rogers, in this exchange: 1 exchange] Change *1948* 1 of] of the *CRO 1944 1948 L* 2 sadlers] the sadlers *CRO L* 2 all the] all *1944* 2-3 And ... persons] *omitted CRO 1948 L* 3 In the] For *L* 3 wisedome] *1948 adds* of 4 In ... seene] who had *CRO 1948 L* 6 excersises] vses and exercises *L* 6 thereof] there is three of *L* 7 practises] exercises, and practises *L* 7 walike *for* warlike 7 As of] As runninge of men on foote, *CRO 1948 L* 7 of horses] of [men on] horses *CRO* 7 and] And ye *1948* 9 with ... foote.] *omitted CRO 1948 L* 9 there yearely] *transposed CRO 1948 L* 10 doone] vsed *CRO* 10 if anye] (if in any) *CRO 1948 L* 11 doe] *omitted CRO 1948 L* 16 or] & *1944* 19 *marginalia* are] are now *1944* 25 pagiantes] pagiantes or partes *1944* 26 the companyes] the number of the Companyes *1944* 28 And] And yerelye *1944* 28 playes] *omitted 1944* 28 man] man fitted for the purpose *1944*

w*hi*ch did Ride as I take it vpon St Georges daye throughe the
Cittie and there published the tyme and the matter of the playes
in breeife the weare played vpon mondaye tuesedaye and
wensedaye in whitson weeke And thei firste beganne at the
Abbaye gates. and when the firste pagiante was played at the   5
Abbaye gates then it was wheled from thense to pentice at the
highe crosse before the maior and before that was donne the
seconde came. and the firste wente into the watergate streete. &
from thense vnto the Bridgestreete and so one after an other tell
all the pagiantes weare played appoynted for the firste daye. and   10
so likewise for the seconde and the thirde daye. these pagiantes
or carige was a highe place made like a howse with 2 rowmes
beinge open on the tope, the lower rowme theie. apparrelled and
dressed them selues. and the higher rowme[s] theie played. and
thei stoode vpon vj wheeles. and when the had donne with one   15
cariage in one place theie wheled the same from one streete to
another. firste from the Abbaye gate. to the pentise. then to the
watergate streete. then to the bridge streete. through the lanes
& so to the estegatestreete. And thus the came from one streete
to another. kepinge a directe order in euerye streete | for before   20
thei firste Carige was gone from one place the seconde came.
and so before the seconde was gone the thirde came. and so tell
the laste was donne all in order withoute anye stayeinge in anye
place. for worde beinge broughte howe euerye place was neere
doone the came and made noe place to tarye tell the laste was   25
played :

Heareafter followeth the Readinge of the Banes which was reade
before the begininge of the whitson playes beinge the breeife
of the whole playes   30

Collation continued: 3 breeife] breife which was called the readinge of
the banes. *1944* 6 to] to the *1944* 9 so] soe all *1944* 14 and] and in
1944 19 the] the [lanes] *1944* 21 from one place] *omitted 1944*
22 and ... tell] and so the thirde, and so orderly till *1944* 28ff Heareafter
...] *only the 'Breviary' in the base MS and Harley 1944 contain the Late
Banns; in addition, there are copies in BL: Harley 2013 (Chester Plays), ff
1*, 1-3v (R) and Bodl: Bodley 175 (Chester Plays), ff 1-2v (B)* 28-30
Heareafter ... whole playes] The Reading of The Banes 1600 The Banes
which are Reade Bee Fore The Begininge of the Playes of Chester 1600.
4 June 1600 *R; omitted B*

The Banes. /

Sir Iohn Arnewaye the first maior of Chester first sett oute the whitson playes *anno* domini; 1329. beinge made by a moncke na*m*ed Rondoll. of the Abbey of St warburge

Reuerend Lordes and Ladyes all
That at this tyme here assembled be
By this message vnderstande you shall.   5
That sometymes there was Mayor of this Cittie
S*i*r Iohn Arnewaye knighte whoe moste worthelye
Contented him selfe to sett out in playe
The deuise of one Rondoll Moncke of Chester Abbaye   10

This moncke was of the most esteimed a godly man and religeose in those dayes

This Moncke not Monckelyke, in scriptures well seene
In stories traueled with the beste sorte
In pageanttes sett forthe apparante to all eyne
Interminglinge therewithe onely to make sporte
Some thinges not warranted by anye wrytte   15
Which glad the hartes he woulde men to take hit

the matter of the play he made in xxiiij *partes* or playes. here he is co*m*mended for his worke

This matter he abreuiated into playes xxiiij^tie
And euerye playe of the matter gaue but a taste
Leaueinge for better learned, ye cercumstance to acomplishe   20
ffor all his proceadinges maye appeare to be in haste
yet alltogether. vnprofitable his labor he did not waste
ffor at this daye an euer. he desearued the fame
Which fewe Monckes deserue[d] proffessinge the same |
    25

This moncke without fere of marterdome sett out in enlishe the storye of the testament, the bible that men mighte vnderstand and beleue:

These storyes of the testamente at this tyme you knowe
In a co*m*mon englishe tonge neuer reade nor harde
yet thereof in these Pagiantes to make open showe
This Moncke and noe moncke was nothinge affrayde
W*it*h feare of burninge. hangeinge. or cuttinge of heade,   30
To sett out that all may Deserne and see
And parte of good belefe. beleue ye mee, /

Collation continued: 3-p 242, l 15] *omitted B*   7 knighte] *omitted 1944*
9 one] one Done *R*   11 not] *omitted R*   13 apparante] apparently *R*
13] *after this line, R has* the olde and newe testament with liuelye comforth
16 glad the hartes] to gladd the hearers *R*   19 a taste] taste *1944*
20 learned] learninge *R*   23 an] and *R*   23 desearued] deserveth *R*
24 fewe] all *R*   24 deserue[d]] deserves *R*   24 the same] that name *R*
26 *marginalia,* testament, the bible] testame*n*te with ye bible *1944*   27 a
common] comon *1944*   29 noe] *omitted R*   30 burninge. hangeinge.]
hanginge breninge *R*   32 parte of good belefe] parte good be lefte *R*

As in this Cittie Dyuars yeares the haue bine set out
So at this tyme of Pentecoste called Whitsontide
Allthoughe to all the Cittie followe labore and coste,
Yet god giueinge leaue, y*at* tyme shall y*o*u in playe
ffor three dayes togeather begine on mondaye   5
See these Pageantes played to the beste of theire skill.
Wherein to supplye all wante. shalbe noe wante of good will.

As all y*at* shall see them shall moste welcome bee
So all y*at* doe heare them. we moste hu*m*blye praye   10
Not to compare this matter or storye
With the age or tyme wherein we presentlye staye
But to the tyme of Ignorance whearein we doe straye
And then dare I compare y*at* this lande throughout
None had the like. nor the like durste set out   15

If the same be lykeinge to the co*m*mons all
Then oure desyre is satisfied, for y*at* is all oure gayne
If noe matter or shewe. thereof enye thinge speciall
Doe not please but mislycke ye moste of the trayne   20
Goe backe againe to the firste tyme I saye
Then shall y*o*w finde the fine witte at this daye aboundinge
At y*at* daye & y*at* age, had uerye smale beinge

Condemne not oure matter where groosse wordes y*o*u heare   25
which Importe at this daye smale sence or vnderstandinge
As sometymes postie, bewtye, in good manner or ·in feare
with suchlike wilbe vttered in theare speaches speakeinge
At this tyme those speches caried good lykinge
Thoe if at this tyme y*o*u take them spoken at that tyme   30
As well matter as wordes, then all is well. fyne |

These playes weare uerye chargeable to the Cittie and had greate labor to make them readye.

here he confesseth that the liued in the tyme of Ignorance wantinge knolege to vse the holy thinges of god arighte. yet this mo*n*ke had a good Entente to doe good thoe blyndly he did shew it

he sayeth y*at* if neither matter or shewe, doe (.)ffecte the Companye then his labor was loste for to please the companye was all his gaine. In antiant tyme there was noe such excellent & curiose wittes.

he desires y*at* the grosse wordes herein vsed ˄'not' to be conde*m*ned, for now in oure age and tyme the seeme strange & grosse yet the weare the same wordes, which we now vse ˄'thoe' with more fine wordes a*n*d exellent speech.

Collation continued: 5 begine] begyninge *R*   7 Wherein] wher *R*
7 wante. ... wante] wantes ... wantes *R*   9 *marginalia*, here he] *heare 1944*
9 *marginalia*, doe] *omitted R*   13 to] in *R*   13 doe] did *R*   14 And then
dare] then doe *R*   15 durste] dost *R*   17 *marginalia*, (.)ffecte] *affect 1944*
17 *marginalia*, excellent & curiose] *transposed 1944*   18 satisfied] to
satisfie *R*   19 enye thinge] *omitted R*   21 againe ... I saye] I saye ... againe
R   25 *marginalia*, age and] *omitted 1944*   26 Importe at] Impart as *1944*
27 sometymes] some tyme *R*   27 bewtye] lewtie *R*   30 if] *omitted R*
31 As well] *as wee 1944*   31 all is well] is al well and *R*

Sir Iohn
Arnewaye the
first maior set
out these plays
and, caused the
companyes to
make the cariges
for them to
play in. euery
companye at
theire owne
charges.

The worthie
companye of
the Tanners
playe.

The welthie
Drapers playe.

The simple
waterleaders &
drawers in Dee.

The antient
Barbers and
Waxe Chandlers
playe.

This worthie knighte Arnewaye, then mayor of this Cittie
This order tooke, As declare to yow I shall
That by xxiiijᵗⁱᵉ occupationes, Artes, Craftes, or misterye
These Pagiantes shoulde be played after brefe rehearesall.
ffor euerye Pagiante a Cariage prouided withall.   5
In which sorte we purpose this Whitsontyde /
Oure Pagianntes into three partes to deuide

1   Now yow worshipfull Tanner yat of Custome olde
The fall of Lucifer did trulye sett out
Some writers awarrante your matter therefore be bolde   10
Lustelye to playe the same to all the route
And if anye therefore stande in anye dowbte
your Author his Author hath youre shewe lett bee
Good speeche fine playes with Apparell comlye   15

2   Of the Drapers you the welthie companye
The creation of the worlde. Adam & Eue.
Acordinge to your welthe sett oute wealthelye
And howe Cayne his brother Abell his life did bereaue   20

3   The good simple Waterleaders & drawers of Dee
See that in all poyntes your Arke be prepared
of Noe and his Chilldren the whole storie
And of the Vneuersall floode by you shall be playde   25

4   The sacrefise yat faithfull Abraham of his sonne should make
you barbers & waxe Chandlers of antiente tyme
In the 4ᵗʰ Pageante with paynes ye did take
In decent sorte sett out, the storye is fyne   30
The offeringe of Melchesadecke of bread & wine
And the preseruation thereof sett in youre playe
Suffer yow not in enye poynte the storye to decaye

Collation continued: 3 by] *omitted 1944*   5 prouided] *to be provyded R*
10 *marginalia*] worshipfull Tanners *R*   10 trulye] *omitted R*   13 therefore]
therof *R*   15 playes] players *R*   18 *marginalia*] drapers *R; playe omitted*
1944   23 *marginalia*] water leaders drawers in dee *R*   23 in ... Arke] your
Arke in all poyntes *R B*   27 of] *to R*   28 *marginalia*] Barbers Wax
chaundler's *R; playe omitted 1944*   29 with] with the *B*   29 did] doe *R*
32 preseruation] presentacion *B*   33 decaye] take Awaye *R*

Cappers and
Linan Drapers.
playe.

5 Cappers and Lynen Drapers, see that ye forthe bringe
In well decked order that worthie storye
Of Balaam & his Asse & of Balaacke the kinge
Make the Asse to speake and sett hit out lyuelye |

5

The Lusti
wrightes and
Sclaters playe

6 Of Octauyan the emperower. yat coulde not well allowe
The prophesye of antiante Sybell the sage
you Wrightes & slaters with good players in shewe
Lustely bringe forth. your well decked Caryage
The birth of Christe shall all see in that stage
In the scriptures a warraunte. not of the midwiues reporte
The author tellethe his author. then take hit in sporte

10

The Deckeinge
Paynters and
Glaseers playe

7 The appearinge Angell. & starr vpon Cristes birthe
The Shepperde poore of base and lowe degree
you Paynters and Glaseers. decke out with all myrthe
And see that Gloria. in excelsus. be songe merelye
ffewe wordes in the Pagiante. make merthe trulye
ffor all that the author had to stand vppon
Was glorye to god on highe & peace [t] on earthe to man

15

20

The worthie
Marchantes and
Vinteners playe.

8 And yow worthie marchantes vinteners yat now haue plentye
    of wine
Amplye the storye of those wise kinges three
That through Herodes lande & realme by yat starr did shine
Soughte the sighte of ye sauioure. that then borne shoulde bee

25

The worthie
Costely and
fine mercers
playe

9 And you worthie mercers. thoughe costelye and fyne
ye tryme up your Cariage as custome euer was
yet in a stable was he borne that mightie kinge deuine
Poorelye in a stable betwixte an Oxe and ane Asse

30

Collation continued: 1 forthe] *omitted 1944*   2 marginalia] cappers Linen
drapers *R*   7 *marginalia*] wrights slaters *R; 1944 has* slaters *for* Sclaters
9 well decked] *omitted 1944*   11 In the] In *1944;* yf the *R B*   12 in]
omitted 1944   15 *marginalia*] Painters Glassiers *R*   15 The Shepperde] to
Sheapeardes *R*   18 the Pagiante. make] that pageante makes *R*   19 author]
Alter *R*   20 on highe] Aboue *R*   20 on ... man] ˄'in earth' [to god &] man
B   23 of wine] *omitted B*   24 *marginalia*] merchants vintners *R*
24 Amplye] Amplifye *R B*   24 wise] *omitted 1944*   25 yat starr] ye starr
1944; the starr that *R B*   28 worthie] worshippfull *R*   29 *marginalia*]
worshipfull Mercers *R*   31 stable] stall *B*

10

The
Goldesmythes
and Massons.
playe.

Yow Goldesmythes and Massons make comlye shewe
How Herode did rage at the retorne of those kinges
And howe he slewe the tender male babes
Beinge vnder twoe yeares of Age /

5

11

The honest
Smythes playe /

Yow Smythes honeste men. yea & of honeste arte
How Criste amonge the Doctors, in ye temple did dispute
To sett out your playe comlye. hit shalbe youre parte
Gett mynstrelles to that Shewe pype Tabrett and fflute |

10

12

The Butchers.
playe

And nexte to this yow the Butchers of this Cittie
The storye of Sathan yat woulde Criste needes tempte
Set out as accustomablie vsed haue ye
The Deuell in his ffeathers. all Rugged and rente

15

13

The wett and
drye glouers.
play.

The death of Lazarus and his riseinge againe
yow of Glouers the whole occupation
In Pageon with players orderlye let hit not be payne
ffinelye to aduance after the beste fashon.

20

14

The Coruysers
or shooemakers
playe.

The storye howe to Ierusalem our sauioure tooke the waye
yow Coruysers that in number full menye be
With your Ierusalem carryage shall sett oute in playe
A commendable true storye. and worthye of memorye

Collation continued: 2 *marginalia*, Goldesmythes] Goldsmiths *R*; gliteringe
goldesmythes *1944* 3 tender] small tender *R B* 3 babes] babes beinge *B*
4 Beinge] *omitted B* 4 Age] Age a most blasfemus thynge *B* 6 yea]
omitted R 7 *marginalia*] smiths *R* 8 your playe] in playe *R B* 9 fflute]
[flute] harpe *B* 11 the] *omitted R B* 12 *marginalia*] Buchers *R*; The
stoute Butchers playe *1944* 12 woulde Criste needes] woulde needes
Christe *1944*; christe woulde needes *R B* 13 vsed] *omitted R* 14 Rugged]
ragged *1944 B*; Ragger *R* 17 *marginalia*] Glouers *R* 18 Pageon] pageantes
1944 21 howe] howe that *R* 22 *marginalia*] Corvisors *R* 22 full]
omitted R 24 true storye] storye true *B* 24 of] *omitted R*

The Bakers.
playe

15 And howe Criste *our* sauioure at his laste supper
Gaue his bodye and bloode for redemtion of us all
y*ow* Bakers see y*at* with the same wordes you vtter
As Criste himselfe spake them to be a memorall /
Of y*at* deathe & passion within playe after ensue shall 5
The worste of these storyes doth not fall to y*our* parte
Therefore caste god*es* loues abroade with accustomed
    cherefull harte

The ffletchars,
boyers Cowp*ers*,
stringers, and
Irnemongers,
playe.

16 Y*ow* ffletchares, Boyeres, Cowp*ers*, stringers, & Irnemongers 10
See soberlye ye make oute Cristes dolefull deathe
his scourginge his whippinge, his bludshede & passion
And all the paynes he suffred till the laste of his breathe
Lording*es* in this storye consisethe oure chefe faithe,
The Ignorance wherein hathe us manye yeares soe blinded 15
As though now all see the pathe playne
yet the moste parte cannot finde it.

The Cookes,
playe.

17 As oure belefe is: y*at* Christe after his passion
Decended into hell. but what he did in that place 20
Though oure author sett forthe after his opynion
yet creditt y*ow* the beste lerned. those he dothe not disgrase
we wishe y*at* of all sortes the beste you imbrace
y*ow* koockes with y*our* Cariage see y*at* you doe well
In Pagiante sett oute the harrowinge of hell / | 25

The Skynners.
play.

18 The Skynners before y*ow* after shall playe
The storye of the Resurrection
How Criste from deathe arose the thirde daye
Not altered in menye poyntes from the olde fashion 30

Collation continued: 2 *marginalia*] Bakers *R*; The proffitable Bakeres playe
1944 2 bloode] his blood *1944* 3 with the] with *omitted B*; the *omitted
1944* 5 after ensue] ensue after *R* 6 these storyes] this storye *B* 6 doth]
doe *1944 R* 7 accustomed] *omitted 1944 R* 11 *marginalia*] fflechers
bowyers coopers stringers Iron mongers *R*; *for* Irnemongers *B has* Iremong*ers*
altogether 11 oute] of *R B* 14 consistethe] conscisted *B* 15 manye
yeares soe] soe many yeres *1944*; so manye yeres *B*; *omitted R* 16-17]
omitted R B 16 now] *omitted 1944* 19 yat] *omitted 1944* 20 *marginalia*]
cookes *R* 22 he dothe] doth he *R* 23 you] you may *1944* 28 *marginalia*]
skinners *R* 29 arose] rose *R*

19 The Sadlers and ffrysers playe.	The Sadlers and ffrysers shoulde in theire Pagiante declare The appearance of Christe his traueyle to Emaus His often speeche to the woman & his desiples Deere To make his risinge [to] agayne to all the worlde notoriouse

5

20 The Taylors. play	Then se yat you Taylors with Cariage decente The storye of the assention formallye doe frame Wherebye yat gloriose bodye in Clowdes moste ardente Is taken vppto the heauens. with perpetuall fame /

10

21 The ffishmongers playe	This of the oulde & newe testamente to ende all the storye which oure author meaneth at this tyme to haue in playe, yow ffishemongers to the Pageante. of the holye goaste well see That in good order it be donne as hathe bine allwaye /

15

22 The shermens playe.	And after those ended yet dothe not the Author staye But by prophettes shewethe forthe howe Antechriste shoulde rise Which yow Shermen see sett out in moste comlye wise.

23 The Diers and hewsters playe.	And then yow Diers & hewsters. Antechriste bringe out ffirste with his Doctor that godlye maye expownde Whoe be Antechristes the worlde rownde aboute And Enocke. and. Helye persones walkinge on grownde In partes well sett yow out the wicked to confownde which beinge vnderstanded Christes worde for to be Confowndethe all Antechristes and. sectes of yat degree /

20

25

24 The weauers. playe the laste of all,	The commynge of Christe to geue eternall Iudgmente yow weauers laste of all your parte is to playe Domesedaye we call it. when the omnipotente Shall make ende of this worlde by sentance I saye On his righte hande to stande god grante us yat daye And to haue yat sweete worde in melodye Come hither, come hither, venite benediciti	

30

Collation continued: 1 ffrysers] ffusterers *R*   2 *marginalia*] sadlers
ffusterers *R*   2 appearance] Appearances *R*   3 woman] women *R B*   3 &]
and to *R*   4 agayne] *omitted 1944*   7 *marginalia*] Taylours *R*   7 formallye
doe frame] formerly to fame *B*   8 ardente] orient *R*   12 *marginalia*]
ffishmongers *R*   13 the Pageante] that Pageant *B*   13 goaste well] crose
will *B*   16 yet] yt *R*   16 Author] storie *R*   17 *marginalia*] shermen *R*
18 see] *omitted R*   21 *marginalia*] diers Hewsters *R*   24 well sett yow] set
R B   29 *marginalia*] wauers *R;* playe ... all *omitted 1944*   29 is to] is for to *R*

The conclusion
of banes. he
wisheth heauen
to the beholders
of these playes,

To which reste of Ioyes and Celestiall habitation
Grante us free passage that alltogether wee
Acompanyed with Angells & endles delectation
Maye continuallye lawde god & prayse yat kinge of glorye

5

Conclusion of the Banes

he wisheth men
not to take the
sighte of the
playe only but
to conceaue of
the matter so as
it mighte be
profitable. and
not offenciue.

The sume of this storye Lordes & ladies all
I haue breifelye reapeated & how the muste be played
Of one thinge warne you now I shall
That not possible it is these matters to be contryued
In such sorte and cunninge & by suche players of price
As at this daye good players & fine wittes. coulde deuise
ffor then shoulde all those persones that as godes doe playe
In Clowdes come downe with voyce and not be seene
ffor noe man can proportion that godhead I saye
To the shape of man face. nose and eyne
But sethence the face gilte doth disfigure the man yat deme
A Clowdye coueringe of the man. a Voyce onlye to heare
And not god in shape or person to appeare
By Craftes men and meane men these Pageanntes are playde
And to Commons & Contrymen accustomablye before
If better men and finer heades now come what canne be sayde
But of common and contrye players take yow the storye
And if anye disdayne then open is the doore
That lett hime in to heare, packe awaye at his pleasure
Oure playeinge is not to gett fame or treasure,

10

15

20

25

All that with quiett mynde
Can be contented to tarye
Be heere on Whitson mondaye
Then begineth the storye.

30

finis   DR

Collation continued: 1 Ioyes] wayes *R B*   2 *marginalia,* banes] the banes
1944 2 free] all free *B* 6-34 Conclusion ... DR] *omitted R; R has the
colophon:* Amen finis deo gracias per me georgium Bellin 1600
6 Conclusion ... Banes] *omitted B* 9 *marginalia,* not ... playe only] not
only ... play *1944* 12 cunninge] commyng *B* 13 this daye] these dayes
B 13 players] preserve *B* 14-34 ffor ... DR] *omitted B*

And thus muche of the Banes or breife of the whitson playes in Chester for if I shoulde heare resite the whole storye of the whitson playes. it woulde be tooe tediose for to resite in this breauarye. As also the beinge nothinge profitable to anye vse excepte it be to showe the Ignorance of oure forefathers: And to make us theire offpringe vnexcusable before god that haue the true and sincere worde of the gospell of oure lord ʹandʹ [and only] sauioure Iesus Christe. if we apprehende not the same in oure liffe and practise to the eternall glorie of oure god the saluation and comforte of | oure owne soles. Heare followeth all the   1(
companyes as the were played vpon there seuerall dayes. which was. Mondaye. Tuesedaye, and Wensedaye in the Whitson weeke. And how many Pagiantes weare played vpon euerye daye at the Charge of euerye companye.

                                                                          1⁹

The companye. or trades that playe.	The storye yat euerye companye did Acte.

Collation continued: 9 god] god and *1944*   14 *The list of companies and their parts appears in all MSS of the 'Breviaries' and in the following: BL: Harley 2150, ff 85v-6, Early Banns (EB); BL: Harley 2125, ff 14-15, Breiffes of Chester (2125); BL: Add. 11335, ff 16-17, Antiquitie (11335); BL: Add. 29779, ff 8-8v, Breife Notes (29779); and CRO: DLT/B37, ff 23-4v (B37)* 16-17 or ... playe.] that Ioyned together *CRO;* that broughte out their pagiantes *1948; omitted L EB*   16-17 The storye ... Acte] The partes that each company played *CRO 1948; to* storye *1944 adds* or matter; *omitted L EB; instead of* The storye ... Acte, *the other MSS have the following headings:* Now follow, what occupationes, bringe forth at theire charges. the playes of Chester, and on what dayes, theye are played. yearely. these playes weare sett forthe. when the are played, Vpon, monday. tuesdaye and, wensedaye in the whitson weke *L;* The Ioyninge of all the trades of oulde tyme. as the played the whitson playes. and the partes the playd, one Monday Tusedaye and wensdaye in whitson weeke, as followeth *2125 29779;* The Anchant Whitson playes in Chester were set forth att the charges of these Occupations sett forth and played yearly. on Munday Tuesday and Wednesday in the Whitson weeke being first Invented, and put into English by Randle Higden a monke in Chester Abbey. *11335; B37 differs from 11335 as follows: B37 adds* coste and *before* charges, *deletes* sett forth, *deletes the before* Whitson, *adds* made and *before* Invented, *adds* tounge *after* English, *adds* one *after* by, *alters* monke in *to* monke of, *and adds* in anno domini 1269 *at the end. The entry continues:* The Companyes, as they then Ioyned & and the partes that they played, at theire owne Costes, here followe

1	Barkers & Tanners	bringe forthe	The fallinge of Lucifer	
2	Drapers & Hosiers		The Creation of the worlde	5
3	Drawers in Dee & Waterleaders		Noah and his Shipp	
4	Barbers Waxechandlers Leeches		Abraham and Isacke.	10
5	Cappers Wyerdrawers Pynners		kinge Balack & Balaam with Moyses.	15
6	Wrightes Sclaters Tylers Daubers Thatchares		Natiuytie of oure Lord	20
7	Paynters Imbrotherers Glasiores		The Sheperdes Offeringe		25
8	Vinteners Marchantes		kinge. Herod and the mounte victoriall,	30
9	Mercers Spicers		bringe forthe the three kinges of Colin.	

Collation continued: 1 Barkers] k *altered from* b *in L*   1 bringe forthe]
omitted EB 11335; B37 adds the   7 in] *of 1948 L EB 2125 11335 29779
B37*   7 Noah] Noy *1948 EB 2125 29779 B37;* Noe *L*   11 Abraham]
Abram *1948 EB*   12 Leeches] *omitted 2125 29779*   25 Imbrotherers]
Brotherers *1948 L 11335 B37;* bruderers *2125 29779*   28 Herod] Harrald
1944; herolde *2125 29779*   31 bringe forthe] *omitted L EB 2125 11335
29779 B37*

These .9. Pageantes aboue written weare played
vppon the firste daye. beinge. Mondaye.

1	Gouldsmythes Massons	The Destroyeinge of the chilldren by Herod. /
2	Smithes forbers Pewterers	Purification of oure Ladye
3	Butchares	The Pinackle with the woman of Canan. /
4	Glouers and Parchmente makers	The risinge of Lazarus from death to liffe. /
5	Coruesters or Shooemakers	The comeinge of Christe to Ierusalem. /
6	Bakers Mylners	Christes maundy with his Desiples. /
7	Boyers ffletchares Stringers Cowpers Turners	The scourginge of Christe
8	Irnemongers Ropers	The Crusifieinge of Christe

Collation continued: 1 Pageantes] playes *EB*   1 aboue written] *omitted 2125*   1 weare] be *L EB B37*   2 vppon] on *B37*   2 beinge. Mondaye.] *omitted L 2125 11335 B37;* beinge monday in whitson weeke *CRO 1948*   4 Destroyeinge] slayeinge *CRO 1948 L EB 2125 11335 29779 B37*   4-5 by Herod] by herolde *2125 29779;* of Isarell *EB*   12 Canan.] canany *EB B37;* Canay *11335;* Canahan *29779*   14 and] *omitted L*   14 risinge] arisinge *L*   14 Lazarus] Lasare *EB;* Lawzerous *B37*   14 from death] *omitted 2125*   15 liffe] *MS* fife *corrected by later hand to* liffe   17-18 or Shooemakers] *omitted EB*   20 Bakers] Bakers and *L B37*   20 with his Desiples] where he sat with his Appostles *EB*   25 The] *omitted L*   25 Christe] god *EB*   29 Irnemongers] Ironmongers & *L B37*

9	Cookes Tapsters Hostlers Inkeapers	The harrowinge of hell. |

5

These .9. Pageantes aboue written weare played
vppon the second daye. beinge tuesedaye.

1	Skinners Cardemakers Hatters. Poynters Gyrdlers	The Resurrection
2	Sadlers fusters	The Castell of Emaus and the Apostles.
3	Taylors	The Ascention of Christe
4	ffishemongers	Whitsondaye the makeinge of the Creede. /
5	Shermen	prophetes before ye day of Dome
6	Hewsters Bellfownders	Antechriste
7	Weauers Walkers	Domes daye

10

15

20

25

Collation continued: 4 Inkeapers] *omitted EB*   6 weare] be *L EB B37*
6-7 played ... tuesedaye.] playd one Tusedaye the .2. daye *2125 29779*;
played on the seconde day *B37*   7 vppon] on *1948*   7 beinge tuesedaye]
omitted 11335; beinge tuesedaye in whitson weeke *CRO 1948 L*
11 Resurrection] Resurecion of christe *2125*   18 The] *omitted L*
23 before] afore *1948 L EB B37*   25 Hewsters] Hewsters and *B37*
28 Weauers] Weauers and *L B37*

These .vij. Pageant*es* weare played vpon the third daye beinge
wensedaye and these whitson playes weare played in Chester
a*nn*o d*o*mini .1574. S*ir* Iohn Sauage knighte beinge mayor of
Chester. w*h*ich was the laste tyme that the weare played. And we
haue all cause to power out oure prayers before god that neither
wee. nor oure posterities after us. maye neuar see the like
Abomination of Desolation, with suche a Clowde of Ignorance
to defile with so highe a hand. the moste sacred scriptures of god.
but oh the merscie of oure god. for the tyme of oure Ignorance
he regardes it not [As well in euerye mans *p*articular corse as
also in general corses] And thus muche in breife of these whitson
playes.

Of the midsomer showe
or watch in Chester.

Heare we maye note that the showe or watche. on midsomer
eaue called midso*mm*er showe. yearelye now vsed within the
Cittie of Chester. was vsed in the tyme of those whitson playes.
and before so farre as I canne | Vnderstande for when the whitson
playes weare played. then the showe at midsomer wente not.
And when the whitson playes weare not played. then the
midsomer showe wente onlye: As manye now liueinge canne
make theire owne knowledge proofe sufficiente: But since these
playes at whitsontyde weare put downe And the midsomer
showe wente onlye. there hath binne taken awaye some thinges
and reformed that weare not decente: wherein the wisedome and
godlye care of those Magistrates that did remoue awaye thinges
either sinfull or offensiue. is to be com*m*ended. and by all
Religeose magistrates there steepes to be troden in In as muche as

The midsomer ^'show' as antiant as the whitson playes. if not more aitiant :

when the midsomer showe wente then the whitson playes wente not.

when the whitson playe wente then the showe at midsomer wente not /

Collation continued: 1-2 These ... wensedaye] These .7. pagiantes aboue
written weare played vpon the third day beinge wenseday in whitson weeke
CRO L; plaid Appon the third *EB;* These vpon wensdaye the 3. daye *2125
29779;* The Seaven pagiantes were played on the third day *11335; B37
omits* beinge wensedaye. *For the variants on the remainder of this passage
in CRO, 1948 and L, see the conclusion of the play entry in each.* 4 that]
omitted 1944 8 moste] *omitted 1944* 10-11 [As ... corses]] *omitted
1944* 11 these] ye *1944* 20 Vnderstande] vndersta‚nde, *is the last word
on f 23, MS with* nde *in normal catchword position; omitted 1944* 22 the]
the [midsomer sho] *1944* 28 that] *omitted 1944*

manye things reformed in the midsomer showe. by mr H Hardware sometymes maior of Chester. As the Diuell Ridinge in fethers before the butchars. A man in womans apparell with a diuel waytinge on his horse called cappes & canes. with other thinges which weare Reformed & amended /

the Intende all theire actions to god*es* glorie and the rule or liue of p*er*fection. the which howsoeuar it cannot be atayned vnto in this liffe. yet it is the marke that we are all to aime at. In the which I com*m*end the gouernemente of mr Hen [Hardware] Hardware esq*uire* sometymes mayor of Chester whose gouernemente was godlye, wherein he soughte the redresse of manye abuses as namelye in the midsomer showe he caused somethinges to be reformed and taken awaye. that the watchmen of oure soules ˄ ⸢or Deuines⸣ spake againste as thinges not fitt to be vsed. for the which he deserued Iuste com*m*endation. howsoeuar the vulgar [or baser sorte] of people did oppose themselues againste the reformation of si*n*nes not knoweinge that Antiante sinnes oughte to haue new Reformation. And antiquitye in thinges vnlawfull or ofensiue is not reson to mantayne the same: But for the Decensie of the midsomer showe as it is now yearely vsed. I referre it to the Iudgmente of those whoe are more Iuditiouse

5

10

15

Now of the Sheriffes breakefaste
wh*i*ch the shoote for yearely. vpon Mondaye in ester weeke

20

The Shereffes breakefaste is an aitiante custome. the Reson thereof none knoweth

Now conser*n*inge the Custome tyme oute of the memorye of man noe men now liueinge canne remembar the origenall of the same. The Shereffes of the Cittie of Chester doe yearelye vpon mondaye in ester weeke. commonlye called [Blatke] Blake mondaye vpon the Roode Dee before the mayor and the Aldermen of the same Cittie. doe shoote for a breakefaste of Calues heades and Bacon. commonlye called the Shereffes breakefaste. The Maior and the aldermen with all other Gent*lemen*. yeomen. or goodfellowes takeinge parte withe the one shereffe or with the other. And when the haue ended the game. the Shereffe. that is a winner. He goethe vp firste

25

30

Collation continued: 1 *marginalia,* by mr ... Chester] before mr H: Hardware & in his tyme, *1944* 1 *marginalia,* Ridinge in] in his *1944* 1 *marginalia,* cappes & canes] *1944 adds* god in stringes, 3 that] *omitted 1944* 4 the] *omitted 1944* 4 Hen [Hardware]] [Hardware] *partially erased in MS and* Hen *overwritten at beginning;* Henry *1944* 10 the] *omitted 1944* 11 [or baser sorte]] sorte *1944* 20 yearely] *omitted 1944* 22 of] of [mynde] *1944* 26 *marginalia,* custome.] *1944 adds* and laudable 27 breakefaste] *1944 adds* or dinner 30 yeomen.] *omitted 1944* 32 firste] *omitted 1944*

ˆ'through ye streete to ye common hall' and all on his side that
be winners withe arrowes in theire handes. The loosers side
followinge after with bowes in theire handes. to the hall of the
same Cittie where | the take parte alltogether of the same
breakefaste or Dynner the loasers payeinge. 4d apeice. and the   5
winners side ij d apeice towardes the Charges of the saide
breakefaste: The which Custome beinge there yearelye vsed the
tyme beinge, very seasonable the practise and game lawefull.
The ende thereof beinge the comforte societye and refresheinge
of the Cittisens. So farre as I conseaue it deseruethe not onlye   10
continuance but also commendation /

...

f 105

... In the time of the firste maior of Chester whoe is thoughte to   15
be Sir Iohn Arnewaye the Whitson playes weare made by a
Monke of Chester, and was by the saide maior published and sett
out at the charges of euery company with theire pagiantes as
is afore expressed, And the said monke Rondulph whoe did make
the saide playes lyeth buried in the marchantes Ile [of] within   20
the Cathedrall Church of Chester.

1609-10
Drawers of Dee's Records   CCA: Company Book G 10/1
p 39   *(30 June)*   25

...

paid for afish bestowed vpon the bearebruers   iiij s

...

Painters, Glaziers, Embroiderers, and Stationers' Records   30
C: Account Book I
f 134v   *(18 October)*

...

Item payd for shewties for the bayes shewes   ij d
Item payd for showes for the Child at medsomar   xvj d   35
Item payd for hosse for him   xiiij d
Item payd for gloues for him   vj d

Collation continued: 1-2 that be winners] *omitted 1944*   3-4 to ... Cittie]
to ye saide hall *1944*   9 societye and refresheinge] *transposed 1944*
19-21 And ... Chester] *a variant of this note on Arnewaye can be found
at the end of the CRO entry under 1619*   19 Rondulph] Rondoll *1944*

Item payd for our banket vpon medsomer Eue   v s

...

Item payd at the bares Castell and northgate   xij d
Item payd for musicke vpon medsomer Eue   xij d
Item payd for a quart of sacke on medsomer Eue   x d   5
Item to mr Amery for St george   xx s

...

Cordwainers and Shoemakers' Records
CCA: Account Book II G/8/3   10
f 46 *(11 November)*

...

(St Martin's Day)
Item geven to Roberte kelly the same tyme   ij s
...   15
Item paid for sixe gleeves and berrage to the gouldsmyth v s viij d

...

ff 46v-7
...   20
Item giuen to the waytemen At my Alderman Sales at shroftyde
                                                                       ij s
Item paide to the kellyes the same tyme   ij s vj d

...

Item paid to the stewards of the Iorneymen for theire attendance   25
at shroftyde vpon the company   xij d

...

Item [spente] paide for Taffyta for the boyes clothes against
mydsomer   xiiij s
Item paid for lyninges to the same sute   iij s viij d   30
Item spent at Richard partingtons for the teyler   ij d |
Item paide for the makinge of the same sute & for sowinge
sylke and berrage   iiij s iiij d
Item paide for one paiere of stockeinges   xx d
Item paide for one paier gloves & sylke poyntes   xviij d   35

...

Item paide for one paier shooes for the boye and silke Rybyn ij s

...

Item giuen to the Crier at the barres   vj d
Item giuen at the Castell and Northgate   ij s   40
Item giuen to three men which did attend the boye   xviij d
Item giuen to Roberte kellye   iiij s

Item paide for [one pottell] five pint*es* seacke at alderman
young*es* vpon midsomer even   ij s j d
Item giuen to will*i*am sidall   iiij d
Item giuen to Iohn Tylston for the lone of ahate for the boye
                                                                        vj d
...

Item spente at an overplushe at Alderman young*es* vpon
mydsom*er* even at our drinkinge   xj s v d
...

                                                                         1

Beerbrewers' Records CCA: Company Book G 3/2
ff 17-17v *(23 November)*
...

and to the Wait*es*   xij d   1
...

and to the Wait*es*

for pruns & suger   xiiij d.
for stokings & gloves for the Child   ij s iij d
for garters & shoes & strings   [ij s viiij d] xx d
at the dressinge of the Child a q*u*art of Clarite wyne   viij d   2(
at the bankett a ˊgalon ofˋ [pottle] of Clarit & a quart of sack
                                                                  iij s jvj d
geven to the m*aste*r musitions   v s
for beere   [ij s] [vj s iiij d]
payd for keepinge the Banner   xiij d | 2:
payd to ˄ˊthemˋ that led the hors   viij d
payd to him that Caryed the banner   vj d
payd to one that tended the Child   vj d
[payd for the Lone of a hat   xij d]
geven at forgate to the Cryer   iiij d   3(
geven at norgat   vj d
geven at the Castle   vj d
[for Cakes & Cherys   ix d]
for bred   xviij d
for samont more then the drawers in deee sent   viij d   35
bestowed vpon mr Robert Amery by the Companie   l s
...

midsom*er*
accompt*es*

this l s g*i*ven to
Mr Am*e*rie
toward*es* the
race to be
p*er*petuallie
Contynued vppon
St Georges day
and toward*es* the
Charge of the
bells & Cupp &c.

22 / jvj d *for* vj d

Dean and Chapter CC: Treasurers' Accounts III
p 343 *(Christmas)*

...

Inprimis payd to ye Watcheman attendinge the maior & Sheriffes
3 nightes at Christmas & for Armor hyred for yat purpose   5
                                        ij s. iiij d.

...

Coopers' Records C: Company Book II
f 56v *(13 January)*   10

...

⟨...⟩arg	
To dossen poyntes	ij d
for dressinge the stafe	xij d
spent at henry Phillipes	iij d
gaue to the Cryer at the bares	iij d 15
gaue to Siddall	iij d
gaue at the Castell	iiij d
gaue at the northgate	vj d
gaue to the minstrelles	xij d
for j quarte sacke	x ˹[ij]˺ d 20
for bread	iij s iiij d
for j half barrell beare	vij s
for Ribininge for the boyes shoes	vj d
for the Chese	ij s viij d
for a payre of stockins for the Childe	xvj d 25
for mendinge the iron	iij d
for iij li. prunns	viij d
for j payre shoues	xviij d
for iij payre gloues	xvj d
for sinomon	iij d 30

...

Joiners, Carvers, and Turners' Records
CCA: Company Book G14/1
f 82v *(25 March)*   35

...

Item for the Childes stockinges	ij s iiij d
Item for his shoes	xviij d
Item for his gloues	viij d
Item for tyes for his shoes	iiij d 40
Item for a quarte of Wyne and suger at his dressinge	x d
Item payd to three men to attend the Childe	xij d

Item to the Musitian   xviij d.
Item for a quarte of Renish Wyne   xij d.
Item to the Cryer iiij d to the prisoners of the Castle iiij d and
to the prisoners of the Northgate iiij d in all   xij d
...   5

AC   *Assessment for the St George's Day Race*   BL: Harley 2150
f 185* *(23 April)*

what the Companys gaue toward St Georges Rase for the   10
Contynuance of a bell or Cupp

The beerebruers iij li. 9s   the mercers & Ironmongers
The Inhoulders 9 li. xj s.   iij li. x s
the drapers ij li. x s   the smythes xx s   15
the bakers ij li.   the glouers. ij li.
the showmakers ij li.   the shermen xx s
the lynen drapers xx s   the Ioyners x s
the Taylers xx s   the Tanners xx s
the barbours xx s   the coupers xiij s iiij d   20
the paynters xx s & mr holme
their Alderman of his owne gift v s
the feltmakers & skynners ij li. x s   36 li. 8s 4d

euery horse that run putt in xx s but at last it wore all out as   25
appereth by the seuerall maiors for the same & what the bell
cost now all gone & the citty when any race is out of the
Thresury maketh it vp saue the horses money.

                                                                liber Ruber 214.215.   30

AC   *St George's Day Show*   BL: Harley 2150
ff 186-6v*

The maner of the showe that is if god spare life & health shalbe   35
seene by all the behoulders vpon St Georges day next being the
23th of Aprill 1610. and the same with more Addytion to
Continew being for the kynges crowne & dignitye and the
homage to the kyng & prynce with that noble victor St george
to bee Continued for euer: God saue the Kynge.   40

Item ij men in greene Evies set with worke vpon their other habet

with blacke heare & black beard*es*, very owgly to behould and
garlan´d´ vpon their head*es*. with great Clubs in their hand*es*
with fier work*es* to scatter abroad to mantaine way for the rest
of the shewe. /

Item j on horseback with the buckler & headpeece of St George
and iij men to guide him with a drum. before him for the honor
of Engle Land.

Item j on horsebacke called fame with a trumpet in his hand &
iij me⟨.⟩ to guide him. & he to make an Oration with his habit
in pompe

Item j called mercury. to descend from aboue in a cloude his
wing*es* and all other matters in pompe. & heauenly Musick with
him and after his oration spoken to ryde on horseback with the
musicke before him

Item j Called Chester with an Oration & drums before him his
habit ⌃ ˊin pompeˋ

Item j on horseback with the kynges Armes vpon a shield in
pompe

Item j on horseback conserninge the king*es* crowne & dignity
with an oratio⟨.⟩ in pompe.

Item j on horseback with a bell dedicated to the kynge being
double gilt with the kyng*es* Armes vpon / caried vpon a septer
in pompe. and before him a noise of trumpet*es* in pompe

Item j on horseback with the princes Armes vpon a shield in
pompe

Item j on horsback with an Oration for the prynce in pompe

Item j on horseback with the bell dedicated to the princes
Ar⟨...⟩ vpon it in pompe & to be caried on a septar. & before the
b⟨...⟩ a noyse of trumpett*es*

Item j on horseback with the Cup for saint George caried vpon
a septar in pompe

Item j on horseback with an Oracyon for St George in pompe. |

Item St George himselfe on horseback in Complete Armor with his flagg and buckle in pompe & before him a noyse of drums.

Item j on horseback called Peace with an Oration in Pompe

Item j on horseback Labelled P[ompe] ∧ ˈlentyeˈ with an Oracion in pomp

Item j on horseback called Envy with an Oration whom loue will Confect. in Pompe.

Item j on horsebact called Loue with an Oration to mantaine all in pompe. /

Item the maior & his brethren at the pentes of this Cittye with their best apparell & in skarlet & all the Orations to be made before him & seene at the high crosse as they passe to the Roodye wherby grentlemen shall be Runne for by their horses for the ij bells on a double staff & the Cup to be Runne for at the Rynge in the same place by genntlemen & with a greater mater of showe by Armes & shott with more than I can recyte. with a banket after in the Pentis to make welcome the genntlemen. and when all is done then Iudge what you haue seene & soe speake on your mynd, as you fynde; The Actor for the presente.

Robart Amory.

Amor is loue and Amory is his name
that did begin this pompe and princlye game
the Charge is great to him that all begun.
[let him be satisfyed now all is done.]
°who now is Sattiffited to see all so well done°

---

8 / La of Labelled *written over in*   21 at *written over by*
33-4 / [let ... done.] *crossed through and line 34 added by Randle Holmes. The second word of line 33 appears to be* hide *but must be a slip for* him.

Assembly Files CCA: A/F/8
f 38*

    To the right Wor*ship*fu*l*l William Leicester Maior of the   5
    Cittie of Chester, the Aldermen Sheriff*es* and comen
    Councell of the same Cittie

The humble petition of Robert Amerie Iremonger [Shewinge]   10
Late Sheriffe Shewinge /

That the Peticion *with* the lykeinge and approbation of diuers
iudicious persons *with*in this Cittie, for the good of the same, at   15
home, and grace thereof abrode, and for a perpetuall establishm*en*t
of a yearelie horsse race & runing at the ringe at the roode eye
vpon St George his day by gentlemen of Worshipp and qualitie.
The exercize & practize Whereof chieflie tendinge to the seruice
of his Ma*ie*stie as occasion shall requyre; and to the ‸ ˊpresent˺   20
delight & Comforte of his people, did lately to this Peticion*er*s
greate trouble & Charges procure three Bell Cupps of silver to
be made, *with* other shewes and devyses, for the better settinge
forth of the said games to this Peticioners Charge the some of
C li. at the leaste   25

    The Peticioner moste humblie besecheth y*our*
    wor*ship*s in regarde the greateste parte of the
    said Charge is bestowed vpon thinges extant,   30
    w*hi*ch are to remayne to future ages for the
    good of the said Cittie That y*our* wor*ship*s
    would be pleased to giue order and directions
    for an assessm*en*t and Collection of such money
    as this Peticioner therein hath disbursed, as to   35
    y*our* wor*ship*s shall seeme moste expedient,
    And he will euer pray to God for y*our*
    wor*ship*s prosp*er*itie

        40

    °this peticion beinge read throughte not fitt to
    passe to elec*ci*on & voic*es* at an assemblie /°

A   *Mayors List 11* BL: Add. 29779
f 35* *William Leicester*

...

•St george Race /•   St Georges Bells of Silver, and Race of Runinge horses with
Runinge at the Ringe. and other pleasante showes. Invented
by mr Roberte Amerye Iremonger. and some tymes sheriffe
of this Cittye and A Cittizin borne / all these at his Coste: with
the dyall and the two smiters at the Clocke of St peters Church
in Chester /

...

Mercers, Ironmongers, Grocers, and Apothecaries' Records
C: Company Book
p 51 *(4 May)*

...

Inprimis paide for the two Children Againste the watch at Midsomer for ij payer of shooes .2.s 6d & two payer of vsted hose .4s. some is	vj s vj d
more for two payer of gloves & Ryben for them	ij s iiij d
more for viij yardes of Tincill Reben	iij s iiij d
more for j yarde ½ Reben & Inckle i d	iij d
more j yarde halfe of Cobweb Lawne at	j s viij d
more for pynnes and ½ yarde Reben	o v d
more one payer of garters for the Ladie	o iiij d
more geven five men y*at* attended the Children	ij s iiij d
more at the barres for beere	xij d
more to the Crier	o iiij d
more to the prisoners	xij d
paide to two messengers w*hich* were sente to borrow thing*es* for the Ladye	ij s vj d
more paide for Muzicke	iiij s
more for beare and wyne	xij s
paide for one quarter of fustian for the. La. wire	o iij d.
paide for prewnes Comfett*es*. suger synemon and Spice for the Cakes	ix s vj d
paide for a cage wyre	o - ix d
paide for Cakes	iiij s

...

4 / *marginalia in RH II's hand*

1610-11
Drawers of Dee's Records CCA: Company Book G10/1
p 40 *(30 June)*

...

geuen to mr Amery ⟨...⟩ mr maiors request by the Companie of   5
drawers in dee the some of   x s

...

p 41 *(1 August)*

...   10

paid for a fish geuen to the bearebruers vpon midsomer even
iiij s geuen back viij d
geuen more to the bearebruers   vj s viij d

...   15

AC   *Leavelookers' Accounts* BL: Harley 2158
f 80 *(October)*

...

giuen Shermadyne for baytinge the beares at high Crosse   x s
...   20
payd the Stewarts of the Drapers accustomed at Shroftyde   ij s

...

payd for wine for the Calues head feast   iij li. viij s
payd for wime on witsonday   iij li. xvj s

...   25

for paynting the Giantes & hobby horses at mydsomer   xliij s 4d

...

Painters, Glaziers, Embroiderers, and Stationers' Records
C: Account Book I   30
f 136 *(18 October)*

...

Item payd at Thomas shevingtons dynner for wyne   iij s
Item for musike and given to the Cooke   iiij s iiij d
...   35
Item for silvering the Childs Clothes   ij s
Item for those shooes and gloves to the Child   ij s vij d
Item given at the barrs Castle and northgat   xij d
Item for musike on mydsomer eve   ij s vj d
Item for our drinkinge one mydsomer eve   vij s 40

24 / wime *for* wine, *extra minim MS*

Item this yeare to Thomas gillam   vj s viij d

...

Treasurers' Account Rolls CCA: TAR/2/26
mb 3 *(November)*

...

paid to him more for being captaine at midsom*er*   vj s viij d

...

paid to the steward*es* of the paintors for the gyaunt*es* at
midsomer   xliij s iiij d   1
paid for Carrying the Citties Cullers at midsom*er*   ij s vj d
paid for Carrying the Drume   xij d
paid to the steward*es* of the sadlers for the bell at shroftid
     vj s viij d

...   1

Cordwainers and Shoemakers' Records
CCA: Account Book II G/8/3
f 52 *(11 November)*

...   2●

(St Martin's Day)
Item Geven to Roberte kelly and his Companye for musicke at
the same dynner   ij s vj d

...

   2.

f 52v

...

Item paide for our gleaves & berrage   vj s iiij d

...

Item paide to the waytemen   ij s   3●
Item paide to the kellyes   ij s
Item paide to the Iorneymen for theire paines   xij d

...

f 53   3!

...

Item paide for gloves and poyntes   xij d
Item spente aboute the boye   vj d
Item for goeinge into the Cuntrie to borow acheane   vj d
Item for one paier shooes & stockings for the boye   ij s viij d   4●

7 / him *refers to the yeomen of the Pentice*

Item for sylke Rybyn	xvj d	
Item spente At harrye phillippes at the barres	xv d	
Item giuen to Woodcoke the Crier	vj d	
Item giuen to William siddall	iiij d	
Item giuen to the Castell & Northgate	ij s	5
Item giuen to the three men for Attendinge our boye & horse		
	xviij d	
Item paide Roberte Kellye for his musicke	iiij s	
Item paide for starchinge the boyes bande	iij d	
Item paide for wine	ij s ij d	10
Item paide at an overplushe vpon midsomer even vpon our		
bankett at Alderman Inces	ix s	

...

(at Robert Jenson's entering the company)
Item more paid vnto Robert kellye at the same tyme	ij s	15

...

f 53v

...

Item giuen to the prisoners in the Castell	ij d	20

...

Beerbrewers' Records CCA: Company Book G 3/2
ff 20v-1 *(23 November)*

...		25

(at a dinner)
paid for musicke to George Callie	iij s iiij d	
paid to Robert Callie	ij s vj d	
paid to the Waites	xviij d	
...		30

<table>
<tr><td rowspan="12" style="vertical-align:top">midsomer
accomptes</td><td>paid for a payer of stockinges for the Child</td><td>ij s vj d.</td><td></td></tr>
<tr><td>paid for a paier of shoes for him</td><td>xv d</td><td></td></tr>
<tr><td>paid for gloues</td><td>viij d</td><td></td></tr>
<tr><td>paid for wine and suger at dressing the Child</td><td>ij s.</td><td></td></tr>
<tr><td>spent in procuring a cheine and other Iowells for the Child xij d. |</td><td></td><td>35</td></tr>
<tr><td>paid to mr holmes for keping our banner</td><td>xij d</td><td></td></tr>
<tr><td>paid to the cryer at the barres</td><td>iiij d</td><td></td></tr>
<tr><td>geuen to the prisoners at the northgate</td><td>vj d</td><td></td></tr>
<tr><td>geuen to the prisoners at the Castell</td><td>vj d</td><td></td></tr>
<tr><td>...</td><td></td><td>40</td></tr>
<tr><td>paid for bread & chese at the banckett</td><td>iiij s vj d</td><td></td></tr>
<tr><td>paid for strong beare</td><td>iij s vj d</td><td></td></tr>
</table>

paid for prunes & suger   xiiij d.
paid for a gallone of wine   ij s viij d
geuen to ijᵒ footemen to tend the Child   xvj d
geuen to one that lead the horse   vj d
paid for musick vpon midsomer even   v s.
paid for Salmon more then the Companie of drawers in dee did
allowe   ij s. viij d

...

Coopers' Records   C: Account Book I
f 59v *(13 January)*

the 5th of August ...
being the kinges
day

ffirst for wine   ij s x d
geuen to the musicioners   ij s.

2ᵒ die Septembr 1611

spent at Raph Cowpers dinner in Wine   ij s x d
on musick   ij s vj d

...

f 60

...

Midsomer
Accomptes

ffirst paid for a payer of shoes for the child   xvj d
paid for prunes   viij d.
paid for a payer of gloues   viij d.
paid for Riboning   vj d
paid for a payer of stockinges   xvj d.
paid for horsebread   viij d.
paid for Cheese   ij s viij d.
paid for alle at the barres   viij d
paid to the Cryer   ij d.
paid at the Castell   iiij d
paid at the northgatte   vj d
paid to the Minstrells   viij d
paid for half a barrel of beare   v s.
paid for bread   iiij s iiij d.
paid for Sinomon   iij d.
paid for mending the Iron staffe   iij d.

...

Joiners, Carvers, and Turners' Records
CCA: Company Book G14/1
f 84v *(25 March)*

Midsomer euen   Item payd for the boyes hose and shoes   ij s x d

Item for a quarte of sack and suger	xij d
Item to the musitians	xvj d
Item to the Cryer at the Barres	iiij d
Item to the prisoners at the Castle and Northgate	viij d
Item for a pottle of wyne at the Banquett	xvj d
Item for Ribbandes	iiij d
Item to three men for leadinge the horsse	xij d

...

Item for wyne at Hughe Inkellit*es* dynner	iij s

...

Item to the Musitians	ij s

...

Item for wyne at Edward Calcott*es* dynner	iij s
Item to the Musitians	ij s

...

Mercers, Ironmongers, Grocers, and Apothecaries' Records
C: Company Book
p 55 *(4 May)*

...

paide the 19 Iune for two payer of hoose for ye Children	ij s viij d
paide for two payer of gloves for them	j s iiij d

...

paide for one yarde & 6d Reben for the childe	o ix d
paide for Comfett*es* j li. ½ sugar j li. ½ Sinemond 2 oz. codling*es* 6d	xj viij d
paide for ½ li. suckett and princebiskie	j s viij d
paide for vij li. prewnes at	j s ix d
paide for 2 C d walnvtt*es* at	j s iiij d
paide for wyne and beere	xij s oo
paide at the barres for beare	j s
paide the Cryer	iiij d
Given the prisoners	j s
paide to Thomas werall that followed the boye	o. vj d

...

paide for Cakes and spice	iiij s o
paide for Musicke	v s iij d
paide for ij yardes of Reben	iiij d

...

Assembly Books CCA: AB/1
f 312 *(20 June)*

...

•An order touchinge the alteration of the showe or watch at Mydsommer•

Att which Assemblie the faire at midsommer neere approchinge vppon the eue Whereof it hath beene vsuallie accustomed *within* this Cittie That ashewe or Watche should bee by the maior & Citizens *per*formed & kepte whereupon it was then & there proposed by mr Maior whether the said shewe were fitt to goe vppon the Saterdaie althoughe the faire then fell out to bee vppon the Sundaie w*hi*ch beinge then propounded it was Conceaued by manie in the same assemblie y*a*t it Would greatlie extend to the prophanitie of the sabboth W*hi*ch Cause beinge referred to voich it was by the most then p*re*sente thought fitt that the said Watche or shewe should not bee *per*formed vppon the Saterdaie in respecte it had beene for manie yeares last past still *per*formed vppon midsommer Eve, by reason whereof it seemed distastfull vnto manie to alter that time or daie, /.

...

A   *Mayors List 8* BL: Harley 2133
f 47 *(Midsummer) Thomas Harvey*

Midsomer Eue being on the Sonday Mr Maior Caused the watch to be sett forth the day before Allthough that some were vnwillinge thereof.

...

A   *Mayors List 12* BL: Add. 29780
f 156* *Thomas Harvey*

...

This y*ea*r middsummer Even being upon a Sunday the Watch was ridden upon ye saterday for the Eve and ye fair upon the munday ...

1611-12
Drawers of Dee's Records CCA: Company Book G10/1
p 42 *(30 June)*

...

geuen to the Companie of bearebruers   vj s viij d

...

Painters, Glaziers, Embroiderers, and Stationers' Records
C: Account Book I
ff 138-8v *(18 October)*

...

Item spent on St Lukes day at *Mistris* Rathburnes in Musick   ij s   5
Item spent at *our* Alderman Holmes the vth of November beinge
the kinges day   iiij d

...

Item spent at Thomas Humfreys dynner in Wyne   iiij s
Item spent in Musick at the same tyme   ij s vj d   10

...

Item for stuffe for the Childes Coate   xvj d
Item for Buttons   iiij d
Item for silke for the button holes   ij d
Item for Inckle for the Childes Clothes   vj d   15
Item for makeinge of the Childes Clothes   ij s vj d
Item for the Childes shoes   xiiij d
Item for lyninge to the Childes Clothes   iiij d
Item for gloues for the Childe   vj d
Item for rybandinge to the Childe   vj d   20
Item for stockinges for the Childe   xv d
Item for a quarte of Wyne at dressinge of the Childe   vj d
Item given him that ledd the horse   vj d
Item given to the Crier at the barres and to the Prisoners at the
Castle and Northgate   xij d   25
Item giuen to the Musick   ij s vj d |
Item for poyntes   vij d
[Item for pynnes   j d]
[Item for Arsedyne for the garland]   j d
Item for gildinge of the Childes Clothes   iij s   30
Item payd for a pyke of Iron for the staffe   [xj d] ij d

...

Item for wyne at Midsomer   iij s
Item for *our* feaste at Midsomer   vij s
Item for stronge drinck at the same tyme   ij s   35
Item for wyne at Thomas Allertons the vth of Auguste   x d

...

Treasurers' Account Rolls CCA: TAR/2/27
mb 1 *(November)*   40

...

Paid for 13 gall*ons* of Clarett & one potle of white wine at the

venison feaste xxvij s and for 3 gall*ons* of sacke xij s   xxxix s
Paid to Kelly for musique at the venisin feaste   v s

...

Paid for makinge the Bulringe   ij s

...

Cordwainers and Shoemakers' Records
CCA: Account Book II G/8/3
f 57 *(11 November)*

...   1(

(at a dinner)

h   Item paide the same tyme vnto Roberte Kellye and his companye
for musicke   ij s vj d

...

w   Item paide to Roberte Kelly and his Companye for theire   15
musicke at Ald*erman* Inces house the xiij^th daye Ianuarye 1611.
when danyell wright came into the said Companye to be
Abrother   ij s

...   20

f 57v

...

o   Item paid for five gleaves to Iohn lynglay   v s
o   Item giuen hym to the berage   xij d
w   Item giuen to the Iorneymen for theire Attendance at   25
Shrovetyde   xij d
o   Item giuen vnto the waytemen . vpon shrove tuseday after the
Race at our Ald*erman* Inces   ij s
Item more giuen to Roberte kelly & his Companye at the same
tyme at our Alderman Inces   ij s   30

...

f 58

...

midsomer.   paide for one payer of shooes for our boye at midsomer   xvj d   35
paide for his stockin*ges*   xiiij d
paide for his gloues   viij d
paide for poyntes and sue tyes   iiij d
paide to Roberte Kellye & his companye   iiij s
Spente *with*out the barres   ij s ij d   40
geuen to the Crier at the barres   vj d
geuen to will*iam* Siddall   iiij d

geven to the prisoners at the Castell & Northgate   ij s
geven to mr whytheads man for leadinge the boyes horse   vj d
geven to two men for tendinge the boye   xij d
Spente at An overplushe at our Alderman Inces vpon midsom*er*
even at our drinkinge   xij s x d   5
...

f 59

...

(St Martin's Eve)   10
paide vnto Roberte Kelly at his companye the same tyme   ij s
...

Dean and Chapter CC: Treasurers' Accounts
p 19 *(25 November)*   15

...

It*e*m to ye waytes of ye Cittye at ye Audite tyme /   ij s.

...

p 20 *(Christmas)*   20

...

Inp*r*imis payd to ye watchman attendinge the maior & Sheriffs
iij nights & for Armore   ij s vj d.

...

          25

Coopers' Records C: Account Book I
ff 62-2v *(13 January)*

...

Midsom*er*
accompt*es*

pa*i*d for the child*es* shoes   xvj d
pa*i*d for his hose   xiiij d.   30
pa*i*d for Riboning for the child*es* shoes   iij d.
pa*i*d for a payer of gloues for the child   iiij d
geuen to the ij⁰ footemen that ‸ ʳwentʼ [led] the Child*es* horse
          viij d
pa*i*d for point*es* for the child*es* hose   ij d   35
pa*i*d for mending the banner to mr holmes   iij s iiij d.|
pa*i*d for bread.   iiij s.
pa*i*d for drinke   v s.
pa*i*d for cheese   ij s xj d
pa*i*d for prunes   vj d   40
pa*i*d for horse bread   iiij d
pa*i*d for Riboning for the horse   ij d

spent in bread & drinke at the barres vpon the Companie	xvj d
geuen to the cryer	iiij d
geuen to the Castell	iiij d
geuen to the northgate	vj d
geuen to Siddalle	ij d
geuen to the piper	vj d
paid for alle at the banckett	iiij d

...

Goldsmiths' Records CCA: Minute Book G12/1
p 13* *(8 February)*

Item that the viij^t of ffebruarie 1612 it is agreyed by the whole
Consent of the Compeney of the Gouldsmythes that ffor the
brood Arrowes shall waygh everie Arrowe viij d and ffor the
makinge of everie Arrowe iiij d soe that yf any shall sell vnder
xij d and ffor everie defalt that shalbe ffounde by ether Alderman
or Stewardes ore any of the Compeney shall pay [vnto] vnto
the Aldermane and Stewards of the Compeney ffor the time
beinge ffor fforfeture xij d and ffor deniall of the premises yat
shalbe lawffull for the Compeney of the gouldsmyths with the
Alderman and Stewardes to odistresse of any thinges in his shope
to the valewe of xij d whom shalbe found in deffault And that all
the gleues yat the drapers shall Receive everie yeare by mariags
shalbe broken

Iohn lynglay	Alderman
Robert Smith	Thomas price
Richard wormynshamme	stward
Griffith Edwardes	
Richard Gregorie	
Iosephe Lingley	

...

Joiners, Carvers, and Turners' Records
CCA: Company Book G14/1
f 86 *(25 March)*

...

Item paied for the boies hoose yat did Ride vppon midsomer

22 / MS reading o in odistresse uncertain. It may be for the indefinite article a and
should read a distresse of, ie, a confiscation of

Eve	xviij d	
It*em* for his shoes	xvj d	
It*em* for Ribbins for his shoes	iiij d	
It*em* for Ribbins for the horse heade	vj d	
It*em* to the prisoners of the Castle and Northgate	viij d	5
It*em* to the Crier at ye bares	iiij d	
It*em* for the hier of a hatt	vj d	
It*em* paied to the Musitions	ij s	
It*em* for a quarte of wyne and sugar at our banquet	viij d	
It*em* for a quarte of wyne & suger at the dressinge of the boie		10
	viij d	
It*em* to three men for leadinge the horse	xij d	
...		
It*em* paied to the musitions	ij s	
...		15

Assembly Books CCA: AB/1
f 316 *(17 April)*

...

•The games and
recreations on
Stt George his
day to haue
contynuance by
the onelie
direction of the
maior and
cittizens•

Allso at the same Assemblie it is thought fitt and soe ordered 20
that those sportes and recreac*i*ons vsed of late within this Citie
vpon Saint George his daie, shalbe from hencefourth vsed and
Continued in such decent and Comendable manner as by the
Maior for the time beinge and his bretheren shalbe appoincted
and allowed of as a pleasure or recreation performed and daie 25
by Direction of the Maior and Citizens, and not by anie priuate
or particuler person whatsoever

...

Mercers, Ironmongers, Grocers, and Apothecaries' Records 30
C: Company Book
pp 61-2 *(8 May)*

midsomer.

...

i	more delivered to katheryn blease the .23. Iune 1612 vj yardes		
	of Crimson silke Riben for the ladies sute	ij s	35
i	It*em* more ij ounc*es* of sinamonde of 4. ounc*es* of suger	xviij d.	
i	It*em* more the same daye. 4. yardes ½ silke Rebin at	xviij d	
i	more one yarde of Silke Reben at	vj d	
i	more one skine of Cremson silke	ij d	
i	more paide for Codling*es* for our bankett	iiij d	40

34-40 / i *marginalia refer to Johnson, one of the two stewards for the year*

i	more paide for one Cheese wayinge 9 li. and halfe at ij d ob. p*er* li. is	ij s	
	...		
b	paide vnto peter pennant for three quarters of the yarde of taffyta . for the ladies gowne	ix s	5
b	paide for halfe a yarde of Buckrom	v d	
	paide for 3. quarters of the yarde of sackcloth	vj d	
	paide for .2. yardes of whall. bone	iiij d	
	paide for .2. yardes of goulde lace	ij s vj d	
	paide for one quarter of greene serge	vj d	10
	paide for .6. skines of greene and yellow silke	viij d	
	paide for .3. quarters of fustian	ix d	
	paide the Taylor for alteringe the gowne	ij s vj d	
	paide for one paier of gloves for the ladie	xvj d	
	paide for one paier for the boye	viij d	15
	paide for .2. paier of Shooes for the Children	ij s vj d |	
	paide for .2. payer of stockin*ges* for them	ij s iiij d	
	paide vnto 6. men that did attende the Children	iij s	
	paide the Crier at the barres	vj d	
	Geven to poore siddall beinge alame man	ij d	20
	Geven to the prisoners of the Castell	xij d	
	Geven to the prisoners of the Northgate	xij d	
	paide vnto the musicke	v s	
	paide for Cakes and suger	iiij s vj d	
	paide for xij li. prvines	ij s	25
	paide for Comffyt*tes*	iiij s	
	paide for Conceates	vj d	
	paide for Biskett breade	vj d	
	paide for Suckett*es*	vj d	
	paide for one gallon of sacke	iiij s	30
	paide for one gallon of Clarett wine	ij s	
	paide for beere	vj s	
	paide for suger and Rose water	vj d	
	paide for two payer of gloves	viij d	
	...		35

1-6 / i *and* b *marginalia refer to Johnson and Blease, the two stewards for the year.*

1612-13
Drawers of Dee's Records CCA: Company Book
p 43 *(30 June)*

...

geuen to the bearebruers vpon midsom*er* even   vj s viij d   5

...

Painters, Glaziers, Embroiderers, and Stationers' Records
C: Account Book I
f 140 *(18 October)*   10

Item paid for the Companies two new banners   l s

...

Item [spent at a] ∧ ⌈for the⌉ feast on midsomer Eue   vij s
Item for strong beare   ij s vj d   15
Item for musick   ij s vj d
Item to him that ledd the horsse   xij d
Item for gloues for the Childe   v d
Item Hose for the Childe   xv d
Item shoes for the Childe   xv d   20
Item at the Castle Barres and Northgate   xij d

...

Treasurers' Account Rolls CCA: TAR/2/28
mb 2 *(November)*   25

...

paide to the Stewardes of Sadlers towardes the Bell at
Shrovetyde   vj s viij d.

...

paied to Gueste for druminge on Shrovetewsday   xij d   30
paied for plaisteringe and Rushinge the gallery on shrovtusday
                                                    iij s iiij d
paied for takinge vp and settinge downe the pales at rood dee
                                                      xvj d
...   35
paide to Routhe for settinge vp the pales after mr Sherriffes
whitbyes horsse race   viij d

...

mb 3   40

...

paied to the Paynters for midsomer Shew   xliij s iiij d

...

paied to Thomas wealch for Carrieng the Auntient at midsomer

ij s vj d

paied the Drum*m*er the same tyme   xij d

...   5

Cordwainers and Shoemakers' Records
CCA: Account Book II G/8/3
ff 67-7v *(11 November)*

...   1(

paide for gleaves   v s

spente at berrage of the gleaves   xxj d

...

Geven to the waytemen. at the stewarde Gregoryes howse at
shroftyde   ij s | 15

Geven to Roberte kelly the same tyme   ij s vj d

paide vnto the stewards of the Iorney men. for theire attendance
at shrofetyde   xij d

...   2C

f 68

...

midsomer charg   paide for one paier of stocking for our boye   xxij d

paide for the boyes gloves   x d

paid for his shooes   xviij d   25

paide vnto the men for tendinge the boye   ij s

paide for one yarde of silke Reben   xij d

Spent at the barres   ij s vj d

given to the Crier   vj d

Given to willi*a*m Sidall   iiij d   3C

Given to the prisoners of the Castell & the Northgate   ij s

Spente in wine at the bankett   xxj d

Geven to the musioners Rob*er*t kelly and his Company   iiij s

[s] paide for mending our banner and staffe   ix d

Spent at An overplushe at our bankett   xj s vj d   35

...

Beerbrewers' Records CCA: Company Book G 3/2
f 27 *(23 November)*

...   4(

midsomer accompt*es*.

pa*i*d for a payer of stocking*es* for the Child   ij s vj d

p*ai*d for a payer of shoes for him	xvj d.
p*ai*d for a payer of gloues for him	viij d.
spent at dressing of the Child	ij s.
spent at pro*c*uring a horse and for Iwells for the Child	xij d
p*ai*d for keping o*ur* banner	xij d
geuen to the cryer at the barres	iiij d.
geuen to the Northgate	vj d
geuen to Castell	vj d
p*ai*d for bread and cheese at o*ur* banquett	iiij s vj d
p*ai*d for ryboning / & for the horse and ryboning for the Child*es*	
shoes	xiij d.
p*ai*d for strong beere	v s.
p*ai*d for prunes & suger	xiiij d.
p*ai*d for wine	ij s vj d
p*ai*d to ij⁰ footemen that lede the child*es* hose	viij d
p*ai*d for Mvsicke	v s.

...

Dean and Chapter CC: Treasurers' Accounts IV
p 54 *(25 December)*

...

Inprimis payd to ye Watchman attending iij nightis upon ye
maior · · · · · ij s vj d

...

Coopers' Records C: Account Book I
f 65v *(13 January)*

...

midsomer accompt*es*

p*ai*d for accheese	ij s x d
p*ai*d for bread	iiij s
p*ai*d for drinke	iiij s.
p*ai*d for shoes for the child	xv d [j d]
p*ai*d for a payer of hoes for the child	xvj d
p*ai*d for gloues	iiij d
p*ai*d for point*es*	ij d.
p*ai*d for ryboning for the child*es* shoes	ij d.
p*ai*d to mr holmes for keping the banner	xij d.
p*ai*d for horsebread	iiij d
spent at the barres	ix d
geuen to the cryer	iiij d
geuen to old siddall	ij d

geuen to the Castell	iiij d
geuen to the Northgate	vj d.
geuen to the pip*er*	viij d.
p*ai*d for walnutt*es*	ix d
p*ai*d for prunes	vj d. 5

...

Joiners, Carvers, and Turners' Records
CCA: Company Book G 14/1
f 88 *(25 March)* 10

It*em* paied for a case for the banner	xiij d
Item for shoes for the Childe	xviij d
It*em* for stockens	iij s
Item for gloues	viij d 15
It*em* spent at our Aldermans house one Midsomer Eve	xij d
It*em* paied for a pottle of wyne at our banquet	xij d
It*em* for two quart*es* of Ale	iiij d
It*em* for a quarte of wyne and Sugar at ye Dressinge of the Childe	viij d 20
It*em* gaue to mr Boothes ma*n*	xij d
Item to two foteman	viij d
Item paide for Musicke	iij s
It*em* to the Cryer and to the prisoners of ye Castle & Northgate	
	xij d 25

...

Mercers, Ironmongers, Grocers, and Apothecaries' Records
C: Company Book
pp 66-8 *(7 May)* 30
...

paide at mr Leycester shoppe the 19. Iune 1613 for v yardes halfe of Braunched stuff for the boyes sute .at. 5s. 6d p*er* yarde is	xxvij s vj d
paide for one yarde of Canvas the 21. Iune 1613	viij d 35
paide for 3. dossen silke bottons and .4. skynes sylke	xiiij d
paide the 22. Iune for one yarde of Rebin	iiij d
paide the same daye for one standinge Collor	xx d
paide for apples	vj d
paide for xij li. prvines	ij s vj d 40
paide for j li. powder suger	xvj d

...

paide for .6. yardes of iij d Rebin   xviij d
paide for one payer of hoose and shooes for the boye   iij s iiij d
paide for .2. yardes one q*uarte*r of 6d. Rebin   xiiij d
paide for. apayer of gloves for hym y*at* tended the boy   vj d
paide for beere at the barres   xij d   5
paide vnto the Crier . to the prisoners of the Castell northgate
and to lame Siddall   iij s
paide for the Musicke   v s |
paide for one dossen sylke poyntes for the boyes sute   xviij d
paide for makinge the Ierken doblet and hoose for the boye   iij s   10
paide for .3. oun*ces* synamond and .6. oun*ces* suger   xx d.
paide more for apples   vj d
paide for wafers   vj d
paide for Marmalat   xviij d
paide for Cakes   iiij s   15
paide for A Cheese   ij s
paide for orrenges and Leemons   vj d
paide for beere   v s
paide for Claret wine and sacke   vij s
...   20

Blease paide the 17. Iune 1613. in wine suger and bread   ij s viij d
paide for beiskie bread the 23. Iune 1613   x d
paide for suckett   xj d. |
b   paide for ij li. Comfett*es*   iiij s
b   paide for Conceates   vj d   25
b   paide for one payer of gloves for the geirls   xv d
b   paide for .2. payer of gloves for the two men   viij d
b   paide for the geirle for her hoose and shooes   iij s vj d
b   paide vnto the men. that did attende the geirle   xviij d
...   30

1613-14
Drawers of Dee's Records CCA: Company Book G 10/1
p 45* *(30 June)*
...   35
geuen to the beare bruers   x s
...
geuen to the bearebruers in fishe monye against midsomer   x s
...

21-9 / Blease *and* b *marginalia refer to one of the stewards for the year*

Assembly Books CCA: AB/1
f 322v *(30 July)*

...

And fynallie at this Assemblie George Callie Musitian exhibiteth
his Peticon Deseringe that he and his felowe Musitians may be
admitted waytes of this Cittie in steede of the Waytes now
absent fyndinge Instrum*ent*s of his owne Charg to p*er*forme
the service w*hich* is deferred to be graunted vntill it may be
vnderstoode what are become of the ould waytes

Painters, Glaziers, Embroiderers, and Stationers' Records
C: Account Book I
f 142 *(18 October)*

...

payd for apayer of hose for the Child medsomer eue	xvi d
payd for the Childes shoes	xvi d
payd for Ribeing for the Childes shoes	iij d
payd for gloues for the Child	vi d
payd at the bars Castel and northgat	xij d
payd for the banket on medsomer eue	vij s
payd for musicke on medsomer eue	ij s vi d
payd for a quart of seke and a quart of ^'Clarret' wine	xx d
payd for strong alle	xij d

...

Mayors' Letters CCA: M/L/6/102
(November)

To the Right worshippfull William Aldersaye maior of
the Cittye of Chester

Certeyne Greiffes shewed vnto your good wor*ship* by
the Companye of Tallowchaundlers of this Cittye

your good worshipp shall truely vnderstand: that wee the
Tallowchaundlers and Barbers of this Cittye. beinge made one
companye and meetinge to gether. divers tymes at our meetinge
howse. as conc*er*inge the good of our companye. and the
Common wealth of this Cittye / The saide Companye of barbers
by theire more voyces contrarye to our myndes and alsoe
contrarye to our orders of Auncient tyme, hath admitted into
our companye or brotherhood of our trade divers *per*sons:

which hath not served. accordinge to our Auncient orders as
others hath done here to fore. which hath bene and is to our
greate hynderance and losse. /

...

ffourthly: that whereas yt is an order Auncient in ˄ ˹the˺ said   5
companye that vpon the kinges holy dayes. and At the watch
vpon midsomer even. that we the said Tallowchaundlers and
barbers: shoulde attende to gether. vpon your worship and
vpon other maiors for the tyme beinge the said barbers at such
tymes: doth vtterly refuse vs. and doth Companye themselves.   10
with the pa⟨..⟩ters grasiors ymbroderers and Stacioners and leaves
vs. beinge few in nomber. to our greate greiffe

...

Treasurers' Account Rolls CCA: TAR/2/30   15
mb 3 *(November)*

...

payed to Squire for playinge on the Cornett vpon the kinges
day   xviij d
                                                                      20
...

Payde to Squire the Cornett player by mr Mayors appoyntment
to gett him out of the Cittye   vj s viij d

...

payed to Gueste for Braceng the drum and druminge at mr
mayors watche   xij d   25

...

mb 4

...

Payed to the Company of Sadlers for the bell on Shrofftuesday   30
                                                          vj s viij d

...

Payed for takinge vpp the Pales and settinge them downe on
Shrovetewsday last   xvj d
                                                                      35
mb 5

...

payed to Gest for druminge on Shrovetewsday   xij d

...

payed to Nicholas hallwood and William handcock by warrant   40
vnder mr Mayores hand for tryminge the Cittyes Mounte
                                                          xxvj s viij d

...

mb 6

...

paied to the paynters for dressinge & repayringe midsomer
shew   xliij s iiij d

...

payed to Guest for druminge at midsomer   xij d

...

paid to Walshe for bearinge the Auntient at midsomer   ij s vj d

...

                                                                                                10

Cordwainers and Shoemakers' Records
CCA: Account Book II G/8/3
f 74

...

Inprimis paide vnto Roberte Kellye and his companye vpon   15
Saint martens daye at night & the night after at the other
stewards howse for musick   iiij s

...

more geven to Roberte Kellye & his companye   ij s

...   20

f 74v

...

Shrovetyde   paide for sixe gleaves and the beirage   v s x d
              paide to george kellye and his companye at shrovetyde ij s vj d   25

...

Geven vnto Roberte kelly   ij s

...

Geven vnto the Stewards of the Iorneyme for their Attendanse
at Shrovetyde   xij d   30

...

ff 75-5v

...

Spent. at. Mr Willam Gamull. for one quarte of. seacke: in   35
speakinge for his sonne to Ryde at midsomer   xij d

...

Midsomer   [paide for ⟨...⟩   iij s iij d
Charges   paide for v ⟨...⟩   ⟨...⟩ s ⟨..⟩j d
⟨...⟩   paide for halfe abarill of stronge b⟨.⟩re   ⟨...⟩   40
              paide for orenges and ⟨...⟩   ⟨...⟩
              paide for ⟨...⟩ ij of walnuttes   xx d

paid for brede and stronge beere   v s ij d

paide for *white* suger   ix d

paide for Currentes   vj d

pade for the loone of Iugg*es*   ⟨...⟩ d

paid for ⟨...⟩   ⟨...⟩ d   5

paid ⟨...⟩   ij d

p⟨..⟩d for veneger   vj d

paide for wafers   viij d] |

midsomer /.   paide for the buskyns for the boye   iiij s

paide for Carnation sylke Rebyn to tye them   xvj d   10

pade for the boyes Gloves   viij d

paide to the three men for theire Attendance   xviij d

paide to woodcocke at the barres   vj d

paide to the prisoners of the Castell   xij d

Geven to will*ia*m Sydall   iiij d   15

paide for one pottell of sacke   ij s

paide more for one pottell and one pint sacke   ij s vj d

paide for musicke   iiij s

Spente *with*out the barres at the watch   ij s vj d

...   20

paide at an overplushe at the bankett vpon mydsomer even   xvj s

...

Beerbrewers' Records CCA: Company Book G 3/2

f 30 *(23 November)*   25

...

midsom*er*   ffirst paid for a payer of stocking*es* for the Child   ij s vj d

accompt*es*   p*ai*d for a payer of shoes for the child   xvj d

p*ai*d for a payer of gloues for the child   ix d

spent at dressing the Child   ij s   30

spent at p*ro*curing a horse for the child and for other necessaries

    xviij d

p*ai*d for keping o*ur* banner   xij d

geven to the Cryer at the barres   iiij d

geuen to the priso*ner*s at the Castell   vj d   35

geuen to the priso*ner*s at the northgate   vj d

p*ai*d for bread and cheese at the banquet   v s.

p*ai*d for point*es* and Ryboning for the Child   xij d

p*ai*d for strong beare   v s.

p*ai*d for prunes and suger   xviij d   40

p*ai*d for wine at the banquett   ij s vj d

geuen to ij⁰ footemen that led the Child*es* horse   xvj d

paid for musicke   v s.
paid for walnut*es* wafers nut*es* & gingbread   xvj d
p*ai*d [for] more then was allowed for a samond from the drawers
in dee   xvj d

...

AC   *Trinity Churchwardens' Accounts* BL: Harley 2177
     f 42 *(Christmas)*

...

to Rich hynde Tallowchandler for 2 li. candles to furnish the   1
Starr anew   *(blank)*

...

Coopers' Records C: Account Book I
f 67v *(13 January)*   1

...

Midsomer   ffirst paid for [horsehier for] the Child ^ ⌐shoes⌐   xvj d.
accompt*es*   paid for the Child*es* gloues   iiij d.
paid for ij° payer of gloues for the footemen   x d.
paid for prunes   vij d   2
paid for Cheese   ij s viij d.
paid for bread   iiij s.
paid for beare   v s.
paid for Riboninge   iij d
paid for horse bread   iiij d   2
paid for point*es*   ij d
paid to Rondell holmes for keping the banner   xij d
spent at the barres   x d
geuen to the cryer   iiij d
geuen to Sciddall   ij d   3⬤
geuen to the Castell   iiij d
geuen to the Northgate   vj d
paid for Musicke   xvj d

...

   3⬤

Joiners, Carvers, and Turners' Records
CCA: Company Book G14/1
f 90 *(25 March)*

...

It*em* for a paire of shoes for ye Childe y*at* Ride at midsomer   4⬤
     xiiij d
It*em* for a paire of stockens   xiiij d
It*em* for a paire of gloues   xv d

Item for musicke   xviij d
Item for a pottle of Wyne at the banket   xij d
Item to the Cryer & to the prisoners at ye Castle and Northgate
                                                                   xij d
Item for a quarte of wyne at the dressinge of the Childe   vj d   5
Item for a Ribbine to tie at the horse heade   vj d
Item for paintinge the staffe   vj d

...

Mercers, Ironmongers, Grocers, and Apothecaries' Records   10
C : Company Book
p 73 *(6 May)*

...

Imprimis payde the 22th daye of Iune Anno 1614 for. vij li. of
prunnes   xvij d   15
payde for iij oz of Sinamound   xv d
payde for halfe pounde of sugar   viij d
payde for ij li. of Comfettes   iiij s
payde for prince and. biskett breade   xj d
payde for quarter pounde of Conseates   ix d   20
payde for ij C of Wallnuttes   xij d
payde for Beare   vij s
payde for Wyne   v s
payde for Cakes   iiij s
payde for Cheese   *(blank)*   25
payde for ij paere of stockinngs for the towe Childrenn   iij s x d
payde for j Yarde of vj d broade Ribbenn and j Yarde of iij d
breade ribbenn   ix d
payde for a paere of gloves for the ladye   x d
payde for ij paere of glooves for her men   xij d.   30

...

Mayors' Books CCA : M/B/30
f 22* *(30 May)*

...   35

Memorandum that the day and yeare abovesaid vpon the [ad]
former admittance of George Cally Musitian and the reste of his
nowe Company to be Waytes of the said Cittie Mr Maior did
deliuer vnto the keepeinge and Custodie of the said George
Callie for the vse of the same Cittie one double Curtayle wantinge   40
a staple of brasse for a reede, and one tenor Cornett beinge
the Citties instrumentes

...

1614-15
Drawers of Dee's Records CCA: Company Book G10/1
p 45 *(30 June)*

...

geuen to the bearebruers in fishe & monye Against midsomer   x s

...

AC *Trinity Parish Register* BL: Harley 2177
f 84* *(10 July)*

...   1•

® brake his neck
goinge downe a
payre of stayres
by the church

Iohn brookes Mason who poynted the steple 1610 & made many
showes & pastymes on the steple of Trinity & also on the topp of
St peters steple as many thousands did wittnesse dyed 10 Iuly &
bur. 11 Iuly in the church yard

...   1!

Painters, Glaziers, Embroiderers, and Stationers' Records
C: Account Book I
f 144v *(18 October)*

2•

Inprimis payd [for] to the Musitians at *our* feaste vpon St Lukes
day   iij s iiij d

...

Item payd for the Childes hose who ridd at Midsomer   xij d
Item for his shoes   xiiij d   25
Item for his gloves   vj d
Item to the Musitians   ij s vj d
Item payd At the Barres Castle and the Northgate   xij d
Item for the Banquett   vij s
Item for a pottle of Clarett Wyne and a quarte of Sack   ij s iiij d   3C

...

Treasurers' Account Rolls CCA: TAR/2/31
mb 3 *(November)*

...   35

Item paied the Company of the Sadlers for the bell offered at
Shrovetide   vj s. viij d.

...

Item paied Guest for druminge on Shrove Tewsday   iiij d
Item paied for removinge the pales at the roodee for the   40
horsserace on shrouetuesday and for placeinge of them agayne
                                                             xvj d.

...

mb 4

...

Item paied by mr maiors appoyntment, for a pottle of Sack and
suger spent in the pentice at the Cominge vpp from the Roodee,
from Sct Georges Race   ij s vj d.   5

...

Item paied Guest the drummer for drumminge on St Georges
day   xij d.
Item paied for takeing downe the pales at the roodee, and for
settinge vp of them   xvj d.   10

...

Item paid to Nicholas halwood paynter, by the appoyntment
of Mr maior, for tryminge of the Iyantes at midsomer last
                                                       xliij s. iiij d.

...   15

Item paied Gest for his Drumminge at midsomer showe   xij d

...

mb 5
                                                                        20
...

Item paied Thomas walsh for carryinge the Citties Ensigne on
midsomer eve   ij s. vj d.

...

AC   *City Treasurers' Accounts* BL: Harley 2158   25
     f 20 *(November)*

...

              Watergate Street vpon both sidees

Item for a stable sometymees the Mercers carridge howse per   30
annum   iij s iiij d
more for voyd grownd sometymees the drapers carriadge howse
per annum   xij d

...
                                                                        35

Cordwainers and Shoemakers' Records
CCA: Account Book II G/8/3
f 81 *(11 November)*

...

more paied vnto Roberte kelly at the same dynner for musicke   40
and at night   iiij s

5 / Georges Race *italicized MS*

...

paide for the sixe gleaves the xvth feabruarye 1614 beinge of a
greater & Larger Sise and biggnes then the haue bene heretofore
& of a new stampe   vj s
more spente at the bringinge of them home   xij d

f 81v *(Shrove Tuesday)*

...

paid to george kelly the same daye   ij s
paid to Roberte Kellye the same daye   iij s

...

f 82

...

Midsomer Charge 23. Iune 1615

Inprimis paide for one payer of stockinge for the boye that did
Ryde   xij d
paid for his shooes   xx d
paide for Rybyne for his shoe tyes   vj d
paide for poyntes   ij d
paide & spent at Iohnsons *without* the barres   iij s
paide to woodcocke the Cryer   vj d
paide for the boyes gloves   x d
paide to lame sydall   iiij d
Given to the prisoners at the Castell   xij d
Geven to the prisoners at the northgate   xij d
Geven to three men that did leade the boye   xviij d
paid for seacke   ij s vj d
paid for musicke   iiij s
paid for mendinge of our banner   xiiij d

...

paide at an over plushe at our bankett at the watch   xiiij s

Beerbrewers' Records CCA: Company Book G 3/2
ff 31-1v *(23 November)*

<table>
<tr><td>Midsomer
accomptes</td><td>paid for a payer of stockinges for the Child</td><td>ij s vj d.</td></tr>
<tr><td></td><td>paid for a payer of shoes for the Child</td><td>xviij d</td></tr>
<tr><td></td><td>paid for gloues for the Child</td><td>ix d</td></tr>
<tr><td></td><td>spent at dressing the Child</td><td>ij s.</td></tr>
<tr><td></td><td>spent in getting a horse for the Child & for other necessaries</td><td>xviij d</td></tr>
</table>

p*ai*d for keping the banner	xij d.	
p*ai*d for musicke	v s
[p*ai*d for Cakes	ij s]
p*ai*d for beare	v s.
p*ai*d for ˄ ʿbread and ʾ Cheese	vj s [viiij d.] 5
p*ai*d for prunes suger & sinomon	xviij d
p*ai*d for Wine	ij s
p*ai*d for pepp*er* and vineger	ij d.
geu*en* to a man that led the horse	vj d
geu*en* to ij° footemen	xvj d 10
geu*en* to the cryer at the barres	iiij d
geu*en* to the Castell	vj d
geu*en* to the Northgate	vj d
p*ai*d for Riboning for the Child*es* shoes	vj d
...	15
p*ai*d to the drawers of dee more then they allowed for a samond	
	ij s viij d
[spent at getting a Cheyne & other Iuells for the child	xij d]
...	
	20

Dean and Chapter CC: Treasurers' Accounts IV
p 88 *(25 November)*

...

It*e*m payd to George Callye musicion at ye Audyte	ij s

... 25

p 89

...

Inp*r*imis payd Dece*mber* 29th to ye watchman attendinge iij	
nightes ye maior & Sheriffes & for Armore hyred for y*a*t purpose	30
	ij s vj d

...

Assembly Files CCA: A/F/10
f 53* *(November)* 35

Ciuitas	To the Right Wors*h*ipp*fu*ll Thomas
Cestr*ie* 1615	Throppe maior of the Cittie of chester
	the Aldermen sheriff*es* sheriffspeeres and
	Common Counsell assembled 40

5 / vj *written over* iij (?)

The humble Peticion of George Callie shewinge /

That the Peticion*er* was borne and received his education w*i*thin
the said Cittie, and by your Wors*h*ipps especiall favors was
ad⟨..⟩tted into the lib*er*ties of the same Cittie and made a free
member thereof, and sithence received and approoved of to bee
the Citties Waite and as the servant of the said Cittie to haue
the rule and especiall gou*er*ment of the same Companie, beinge
five in nomber

That the Peticion*er* hath heretofore and at his presente   1⟨⟩
professed musicke and the arte and facultie of teachinge to
daunce and by the practice thereof and his owne diligence hath
not onelie manteigned himself his wife Children and familie
w*h*ich are Tenn in number at the least but hath allso obtained
& pro*c*ured a good respecte and estimacion from men of the best   1⟨⟩
sort & gen*er*all fashion truelie sensible and respectiue of the like
faculties /

That one Iohn ffarrar ⟨Thomas Squier Richard Bell and
Nicolas Webster⟩ a meere strangers vnto the Cittie [doth] ⟨haue⟩
of late intruded theimself into the Companies & societies of   2⟨⟩
seu*er*all p*er*sons in the said Cittie, and doth arrogate vnto himself
the said arte of dauncinge & the teachinge thereof ⟨and the
science of musicke⟩ to ther distaste & greatt dislike of dinogte⟩
to the wronge & pr*ei*udice of the peticion*er* (as hee conceaueth),
& to the incoragement & evill example of others /   2⟨⟩

The Peticion*er* doth therefore most humblie desire &
beseech your Wors*h*ipps that as hee is your Wors*h*ipps
servant and a free Citizen of the Cittie hee maie receiue
your fauorable respecte and Countenance & that the   3⟨⟩
said ffarrar & all others maie in such case bee discouraged
& all altogether suppressed from ye pro*f*esion & practice
of the arte & facultie afforesa*i*d

⟨...⟩ blie of the said Cittie and the peticion   3⟨⟩
⟨...⟩

---

36 / ⟨...⟩ *entire last line faded*

Coopers' Records C: Account Book I
ff 70-70v *(13 January)*

...

Midsomer accomptes

5

paid for acheese	iij s iiij d
paid for hose. shoes & shoe ties & gloues for the Child	ij s viij d
paid for pointes	iij d
paid for beare	v s.
paid for bread	iiij s. 10
paid for Walnutes prunes & apples	xiij d.

...

geuen to the musicioners	x d.
paid for ijᵒ quartes of Wine	xvj d.
geuen for keping the banner	xij d. 15
spent at the barres vpon the Companie [xij d ⟨...⟩ d xv d] xv d	
geuen to the northgate	vj d |
geuen to the Castell	iiij d
geuen to the Cryer	iiij d
geuen to Siddalle	ij d 20
geuen to Sir Henry Boothes man for dressing the horse	iiij d
paid for ijᵒ payer of gloues for the footemen	xvj d

...

Joiners, Carvers, and Turners' Records   25
CCA: Company Book G 14/1
f 92 *(25 March)*

...

Item for Hoose and shoues for ye Childe yat did Ride vppon midsomer Eve	iiij s 30
Item for gloues	ix d
Item for Dressinge the stafe and the trunche	xij d
Item spent on the boies mother when we Receiued ye staffe	iiij d
Item paied to the Cryer & to the Castle and Northgate	xij d
Item spent at Alderman Salisburies	xij d 35
Item for Musicke	ij s
Item spent in Ale at the banquet	xij d
Item spent at ye Dressinge of the boie	vj d
Item for a Ribbine for the horse heade	iij d
Item to Thomas Bedles man to lead the horse	iiij d 40
Item to olde Sidle	ij d
Item spent vppon mr Pilkinton when we went to entreat him	

that his sonne might Ride   iiij d

...

1615-16
Drawers of Dee's Records CCA: Company Book G 10/1
p 46 *(30 June)*

...

29 of aprill   geuen to the beare bruers   x s

...

1

Painters, Glaziers, Embroiderers, and Stationers' Records
C: Account Book I
f 146 *(18 October)*

...

payd vpon St Lukes ‸ ʼforʼ ij pottls Sake & one potle Clarret   1
                                                        v s iiij d
payd for musike the same daye   iij s iiij d

...

payd on mydsomer Eve for all things Concerning the boye
horse and musik   viij s ij d   2
payd for the bankett   vij s
To the Cryer ‸ ʼon mydsomer Eveʼ   vj d
given at the Castle and northgat   viij d
for Ale and wyne on mydsomer Eve   iij s

...

2

Assembly Books CCA: AB/1
f 331v* *(20 October)*

          20 Oct 1615   Thomas Throp Mayor   3

...

•Alsoe Plaiers to
be allowed to
plaie in the
comon Hall nor
in the night after
vjᵉ of the Clock
in the eveninge• Moreover at the same Assemblie Consideracion was had of the
Comon Brute and Scandall which this Citie hath of late incurred
and sustained by admittinge of Stage Plaiers to Acte their obscene   3
and vnlawfull Plaies or tragedies in the Comon Hall of this
Citie thereby Convertinge the same, beinge appointed and
ordained for the Iudiciall hearinge and determininge of Criminall
offences, and for the solempne meeting and Concourse of this
howse, into a Stage for Plaiers and a Receptacle for idle persons.
And Consideringe likewise the many disorders which by reason   4
of Plaies acted in the night time doe often times happen and fall
out to the discredit of the government of this Citie and to the

greate disturbance of quiet and well disposed People, and beinge
further informed that mens *servant*es and apprentices neglectinge
their *Master*s busines doe Resorte to Innehowses to behold such
Plaies and there manie times wastfullie spende thar *Master*s
goodes ffor avoidinge of all w*h*ich inconveniences It is ordered   5
that from hensforth noe Stage Plaiers vpon anie pretence or color
Whatsoever shalbe admitted or licenced to set vp anye Stage in
the said Comon Hall or to acte anie tragedie or Commedie or anie
other Plaie by what name soever they shall terme hit, in the said
Hall or ‸ ⌈in⌉ anie other Place w*i*thin this Citie or the Lib*er*ties   10
therof in the night time or after vj⁽ᵉ⁾ of the Clocke in the eveninge.

Cordwainers and Shoemakers' Records
CCA: Account Book III G/8/4   15
ff 6-7 *(11 November)*

more geven vnto Roberte kelly for musicke   ij s vj d
...
paid for our gleeves   ⟨.⟩ | 20
payde to the waytemen at shroftyde   ij s
payde vnto Thomas hough   iiij d
paid to Roberte Kelly   ij s
...

mydsomer   Inprimis paide for one payer stockeng*es* gloves and poyntes for   25
           the boye   ij s v d
           paid for his shooes   xiiij d
           paid for shooe tyes and silk Reben for ther horse heade   ix d
           paide for the loone of Ahat for the boye   vj d
           Spente at the barres   xviij d 30
           Geven to the Cryer   vj d
           Geven to will*ia*m Siddall and apoore man   vj d
           Geven to the prisoners at the Castell and Northgate   ij s
           Geven vnto hugh Richardson by the appoyntm*en*t of the two
           Aldermen and the Companye the some of   v s | 35
           Geven to a man for bringe the horse that the boye Ryde one and
           for goeing w*i*th vs about the towne   xij d
           Geven to two men for tendinge the boye   xij d
           Geven to Roberte kelly for musick   iiij s
           paide for one firken of doble beere   iij s vj d 40
           paide for white bread and Cakes   xij d
           payde for mendinge of our banner and silke   vj d

paide for mendinge the staffe   ij d
...

Beerbrewers' Records CCA' Company Book G3/2
ff 36v-7 *(23 November)*

paid to mr holmes for dressinge the banner which he alledged
was in the default of william hutchins & Rondell higgenson   vj s.
more paid to mr holmes for kepinge the banner according to
Custom and is to performe the keping of it during his lief for   1
xij d a yeare, the same being brought to him within A day after
Midsomer watch   xij d
...

Midsomer   paid for a payer of stockinges for the Child   ij s vj d
accomptes   paid for a payer of shoes for the Child & for Riboning   vj d.| 1
              paid for a payer of gloves for the Child   xv d.
              spent at dressinge the Child as formerly hath bene allowed   ij s.
              spent on prouiding a horse for the Child and for other necessaries
              as formerly hath bene allowed to other stewardes   xviij d
              geuen for Mvsick vpon Midsomer even   v s.   2
              paid for beare to the Companie & the Men   v s.
              paid for bread and Cheese   vj s.
              paid for Wyne   ij s.
              paid for apples prunes Comfettes & other necessarie prouicion
              for the Companie as formerlie allowed   xx d.   2
              geuen to the Men that lede the Childes horse   xxij d
              geuen to the cryer at the barres   iiij d
              geuen to the prisoners at the Castell   vj d
              geuen to the prisoners at the northgate   vj d
              paid to the drawers of dee more then they allowed for a salmon   3
                                                                      ij s x d
...

Coopers' Records C: Account Book I
f 71 *(13 January)*
...

Midsomer   first for beare   iiij s.
accomptes.   for bread   ij s
              for musick   xx d.
              spent at henry phillipes   ix d   4
              geuen to Siddall   ij d
              to Rondle Iuett   ij d

to the Castell	iiij d
to the Northgate	vj d
at dressing the child	iiij d
for poin*tes*	iij d
for Riboning	vj d 5

...

f 71v

...

geuen to [Rob] the Musicionrs at Robert Nicholas dinner	ij s. 10
spent at the same tyme	viij d
for dressing the Child*es* horse	vj d
for horse bread	iiij d
paid to mr holmes for dressing the flag and the staffe & for	
keping of the same	ij s. 15
to twoo foote men that led the child*es* horse	xvj d
for a payer of gloues for the Child	ix d
spent for berrag of the child*es* clothes	iiij d

...

for a payer of shoes	xviij d 20
for nvtes & prunes	x d

...

for stocking*es* for the child	xxij d
for Cheese	ij s viij d

...   25

Joiners, Carvers, and Turners' Records
CCA: Company Book G14/1
f 94v *(25 March)*

...   30

Item paide for stocking*es* and shooes for the Childe vppon	
Midsomer Eve	iiij s
Item paide for gloues and shooe tyes for the Childe	xvj d
Item paide for a quart of Clarrett wyne at the dressinge of the	
Childe	viij d 35
Item giuen to Mr duttons man for dressinge the horse	iiij d
Item giuen to two footemen to Attend the Boy	viij d
Item spente at the Barrs	iiij d
Item giuen to the Cryer	iiij d
Item spent and giuen to Sibdall a poore man at Trinite Church	40
	iiij d
Item giuen to the prisoners in the Castle and the Northgate	viij d

Item paide to the Musicke   xviij d
Item paide for wyne at the Banquett on Midsomer Eve   viij d
...

Mercers, Ironmongers, Grocers, and Apothecaries' Records
C: Company Book
pp 83-4 *(3 May)*
...

midsomer | paide for beere at wilson howse at the barrs before the watch
at midsomer   xij d   ￫
payde vnto the Crier for Callinge the Companye   vj d
Geven to olde Siddall. a poore Lame man   vj d
Geven to the prisoners at the Castell   ij s
Geven to the prisoners at the Northgate   ij s
Geven by the Companyes Appoyntment to apoore man   ij d   1
Geven vnto two men that attended the boye   xij d
payde for musicke   vj s viij d
payde for a quarte of wine and suger sente to mr Mayor by
mr drinkwaters appoyntment   viij d
payde for two payer of gloves for the Children   xx d   2
payde for a Collor for the boye   xij d
payde for one dossen of poyntes for the boye   vj d
payde for two payer of Shooes for the Children   ij s viij d
payde for two payer of hoose for them   ij s viij d
payde for two yardes of sylke Rebyn for shoe tyes   xij d   2
payde for apayer of garters for the boye   xviij d
payde for ayarde of Rebyn for the horse head   vj d
payde to the two men that attended the Ladye   xij d
payde for two payer of gloves for them   xij d
                                                                              3

.For the Banquett /

vij li. of pruines   xviij d
more one quarter of Sinomonde   iiij d
more j li. of Suger   xviij d | 3
more j li. 2 quarter of Marmalatt at   ij s
more j li. ½ of Conseates at   iiij s
more for Wafers   ij s
more for Cakes   ij s
more for Cheries   xiiij d   4
more for. Wall Nuttes   vj d
more for two quartes of seacke   ij s

more for beere   ij s iiij d

...

Joiners, Carvers, and Turners' Records CCA: Minute Book G 14/2
p 10 *(11 June)*   5

...

It is ordered that the Company shall meete at Alderman
Salisburies house vppon Midsomer Eue before the Watch
accordinge to Antient Custome And after the same watch to
repayre to Steward Beedulphs house to the Banquett   10

Innkeepers' Records C: Company Book
f D-5 *(14 June)*

The xiiijth of Iune   15
Anno Domini 1616

An enlargement   Item fforasmuch as at divers tymes heretofore Many of the
of an order for   Bretheren of our Companie have not given theire Attendance
Attendance on   with theire Watchmen vpon Midsomer Eve Although divers   20
Midsomer Eve   orders to that end have hereto fore bene made Therefore it
is now at this present Meetinge ordered and agreed vpon by the
greater parte of the Companie now present, That all the Bretheren
who doe not excercise or follow any other Trade within this
Citie, aswell those that are free of other Companies, as those that   25
are free [asw] onelie of this Companie shall with theire Watchmen
everie Midsomer Eve, Attend the Aldermen and Stewardes for
the tyme beinge duringe the whole tyme of the Watch And if
any Brother shall himself be absent from the said watch he shall
forfeite to the Companie the somme of ij s, and euerie Alderman   30
that shall be Absent to forfeit the somme of — iij s iiij d
      (They and euerie of them haveinge noe lawfull Cause to the
Contrarie) And euerie brother That shall want his watchman to
forfeite the somme of — xij d

                                                                        35

Midsummer Show PRO: STAC 8 156/22*

... vpon the xxiiijth daie of Iune a greate ffaire is kepte in the
Cittie of Chester, and that vpon the xxiijth daie of Iune beinge
the daie next before the ffaire and in the eveninge of the same

---

7-10 / It ... Banquett *written in right-hand column in MS*

daie diuers pagentes and shewes are yearelie made in the ‸ ˋsaied˺ Citty of Chester, which are Comenlie Called the Midsomer Watch, and that by reason thereof great Multitudes of people doe allwaies Come and resorte vnto the saied Citty of Chester yearelie vpon the saied xxiijᵗʰ daie of Iune. ...

1616-17

Drawers of Dee's Records CCA: Company Book G10/1
p 47 *(30 June)*

...   1

geuen to bearebruers at midsomer   vij s

...

Painters, Glaziers, Embroiderers, and Stationers' Records
C: Account Book I   1
f 148 *(18 October)*

...

Item shooes for the Child that rid	xiiij d
Item gloues	viij d
Item riband to hang iewels in	iiij d
Item riband for the hors	vj d
Item at dressing the Clid ˚quart Claret suger˚	viij d
Item to the musicke	ij s
Item to iij men that tended the boy	iij s
Item the bars Castle and Northgate	xiiij d
Item for our banquet on midsomer eue	vij s
Item strong beere	ij s
Item quarte sacke and ij quartes Claret	ij s

...

Item for our part of the rent of the phenix   xij d

...

Treasurers' Account Rolls CCA: TAR/2/33
mb 2 *(November)*

...   3

Item paied the xxvjᵗʰ daie of ffebruary 1616. by the appoyntment of Mr Maior to Mighell Iones and Richard Ince being Stewardes of the Sadlers towards their bell   iiij s

...

Item pade to Roger Guest for drumminge on Shrove tewsday xij d
Item paied to the keeper of the Rood dee, the sixt daie of marche for [takinge] downe the pales & for setting of them vp

agayne   xvj d

...

Item paide the xxj of Aprill 1617 for a banquett vpon Blake
munday by mr Green   vx s
Item paide to Roger Guest the xxiij of Aprill 1617. for druminge
on St George day   xij d

...

mb 2d

...

Item paied the xxvij. of maie 1617. to Nicholas hallwood toward
the settinge forthe of the Gyantes & showe against midsomer
                                                        ij li. iij s j d

...

Item paied to Thomas wealch the younger for Carrieng the
Citties auntient ˄ 'at the watch'   ij s vj d
Item paied to Nicholas hallwood and Robert Thornley by the
appoyntment of mr maior the 17. of Iulie 1617.   xxij s 8d

...

mb 3

...

Item paide Mr Alderman Litler and Mr Rutten for xiiij yardes
and ahalf of Clothe to make the waytemen gownes and the
boyes Cloakes at viij s per yarde   j li. xvj s

...

Cordwainers and Shoemakers' Records
CCA: Account Book III G/8/4
f 11v *(11 November)*

...

paide for our gleaves at shrofetyde   vj s
paid to the berag of the gleaves   ij s
paid to george kelly for musicke at shrovetyd   iij s
Given to the stewardes of the Iorneymen for theire attendance
at shrofetyd   xij d

...

f 12

...

paide for Aquarte of seacke at mr Maiors Taverne when wee
seased vpon two paier of childrens shooes at Thomas fletcher

the Cobler   xij d

...

f 12v

...   5

midsomer. / paid for apayer of stockinges for our boye   xvj d
paid for silke Rebyn   vj d
paid for poyntes   vj d.
paid for the loone of Ahatt for the boye   vj d
Spent at Iohnsons without the barres   ij s   10
Geven to the Cryer at the barrs   vj d.
Geven lame sydall   iiij d.
Geven at the northgate   xij d
Geven at the Castell   xij d
Geven mr Glasiers man for leadinge the horse   vj d   15
paid for wine at our bankett   ij s vj d
Geven to Roberte kelly for musicke   iiij s
Geven to two men for tendinge the horse   xij d
paid for Rebyn for the horse   vj d

...   20

f 13
paid for the boyes shooes   xvj d
Spent at Alderman younges   xx d
Spent vpon an over plushe at our banquett   xvj s v d   25
Spent more at Alderman younges vpon gorges daye   ij s vj d

...

Beerbrewers' Records CCA: Company Book G 3/2
ff 40v-1 *(23 November)*   30

payd for a Samon more then iij s iiij d which the drawers in
dee allowe   ij s viij d
payd to mr holmes for keeping the banner for on yeare   xij d
mydsomer
accomptes. for a payre of shoes for the Child and rybbening   xx d.   35
for a payre of hoose for the Child   ij s viij d
for a payre of gloves for the Child   xv d.
spent at dressinge of the Child as formerlie hath beene allowed ij s
payd and layd out in provyding of a horse and other necessaries
for the Child, as hath beene allowed to other stewardes   xviij d   40
geven for musick vppon mydsomer even   v s.
for beere vppon mydsomer even for the Companie & theire

men	v s.
for bread & Cheese	vj s
for wyne	ij s
for apples prunes comfettes and other necessarie provicion	
for the companie as formerlie hath beene allowed	xx d 5
given to [fo] three men to leade the Childes horse	xxij d
given to the Cryer at the barres	iiij d
given to the prisoners at the Castle	vj d |
given to the prisoners at the northgate	vj d
...	10

Coopers' Records C: Company Book II
ff 4-4v* *(13 January)*

...

midsomer	Item paide vnto mr hoolmes. for our flagg	xij d 15
	Item paide for apayer of stockinges and shooes for the boy	
		ij s vj d
	Item paide for Rebyn	ix d
	Item paid for horse bread	iiij d
	Item paid for apayer of gloves for the boye	x d 20
	Item paid for poyntes	iij d
	Item paid for two payer of gloves for the two men that did	
	attende the horse.	xij d
	Item paid to aboye for dressinge the horse	ij d
	Item paid for two pounes of pruines	v d 25
	Item paid for Suger	ij d
	Item paid for wall Nuttes	v d
	Item paid for Cheese	iij s
	Item paide for bread	iij s vj d
	Item paid for beere	iiij s 30
	Item paid for the loone of Ahatt for the boye	xij d
	Item paid for Musicke	ij s vj d
	Item paide for apayer of gloves. which were geven to mr	
	haddocke	xij d |
	paid for drinke at the barres	vj d 35
	paid to the Cryer	iiij d
	Geven to william Siddall alame man	ij s
	Geven to Rondall Iewett	iij d
	Geven to the prisoners of the Castell.	iiij d
	Geven at the Northgate	vj d 40
	paide to Thomas Greiffyth gloves which was vnpaid the yeare	
	paste	iiij d

payde for one pottell of Clarett wyne. at our banquett   xij d

...

paide to Roberte kelly for muscke the same tyme   ij s vj d

Spente at Roberte boydells howse the xxiij^th day of August

1617. at the king*es* Cominge to Chester   iij s   5

...

Joiners, Carvers, and Turners' Records

CCA: Company Book G14/1

f 96 *(25 March)*   10

...

Item paid for stockinges for ye Childe vppon midsomer eue   ij s

Item paid for stockinges for ye same Childe   iij s iiij d

Item paid for gloues for ye Childe   xij d

Item spent in wyne and sugar at ye dressinge of ye Childe   viij d   15

Item paid for mendinge of ye Banner   vj d

Item paide for Musicke   ij s vj d

Item spente at Henry Phillps *without* ye Barrs   vj d

Item spente at The Aldermans house   vj d

Item giuen to ye Cryer at ye Barrs   iiij d   20

Item giuen to ye prisoners at the Castle   iiij d

Item giuen to Siddall a poore man   ij d

Item giuen to ye prisoners at ye Northgate   iiij d

Item giuen to two men for leadinge ye horse   viij d

...   25

Mercers, Ironmongers, Grocers, and Apothecaries' Records

C: Company Book

p 91 *(2 May)*

...   30

Inp*rimis* ij p*ar*re of childers hose   iiij s vj d

It*em* ij p*ar*re of childers gloues   xvj d

It*em* a yard 6d ribyne. ij skaynes yellow silke   viij d

It*em* vpon too men. ij p*ar*re gloues   xij d

It*em* a p*ar*re of silke garters   ij s   35

It*em* to the officers. at midsomer   ij s

It*em* to mr warberton the macebearer   ij s

more. ij li. Cumfet*tes* at 2s p*er* li. is   iiij s

more j li. Suger at   xx d

more one ounce Synamon at   iiij d   40

more payde for wafers   ij s

more for Stronge beere   iij s iiij d

more for 8 li. pruines	ij s
more marmelate	ij s
more for two yardes of Riban for shooe ties at	xij d
more ½ li *preserue* *(blank)* at	xx d
more one dossen broade poyntes	xvj d
more for pynnes to dresse the girle	ij d
more paide to wilson wife at the barrs	xij d
more paide to the Crier at the barrs	xij d
more geven to olde Siddall	vj d
more geven vnto mr Rondall. Iewett	xij d
more geven to the prisoners at the Castell	ij s vj d
more geven to the prisoners of the Northgate	ij s vj d
more paide for our Musicke	vj s viij d
more paide to three men to attende the Children	xviij d
more paide for kakes	ij s
more paide for fyttinge of the boyes dublett	vj d
more paide for 4. quartes of Seacke and one quarte of Clarrett wine	iiij s vj d
more for two payer of Shooes	iij s

p 92

...

paide to aboye at Rondall Inces that played some Trickes   vj d

...

Joiners, Carvers, and Turners' Records CCA: Minute Book G14/2
p 14 *(14 June)*

...

It is Agreed that the Company shall meete at the Alderman
Salisburies house accordinge to An*n*tient Custome euery Brother
with his watchman And the Banquett to bee at Steward Calcotts
house euery brother to pay iiij d a peece as hath bene vsuall

...

A   *Mayors List 17* Toronto: Massey College MS
f 33v *(Midsummer) Edward Button*

...

This yeare the maior Caused vppon Midsomer euen the divell to
ride before the companye of the butchers, with other divels
leadinge of him, as alsoe the woman with Cuppes and Cannes

29 / capital I *in left margin next to entry*

before the inhouldiers, with other divells leadinge of them with
other toyes in the like nature which hath bin layd downe to my
remembrance 16 or 17 yeares by grave and wise magistrates,
that went before, and now sett vp this yeare by this maior to the
greate dislike of them which are well disposed both Meinesters   5
and People. /

...

1617-18

Drawers of Dee's Records CCA: Company Book G10/1   10
p 48 *(30 June)*

...

geuen to the bearebruers   x s

...

15

Joiners, Carvers, and Turners' Records CCA: Minute Book G14/2
f 15 *(2 July)*

...

C   Mr Heidocke hath laid downe vj d for his man Cominge shorte
of the watch vppon Midsomer Eue But by a generall Consente   20
of the whole Company the same is giuen him agayne.

...

Assembly Books CCA: AB/1
f 336* *(23 July) Edward Button*

25

•C l to be leuied   Allsoe at the same Assemblie th[at]ᴧ're' was Conference had
for the   concerning the repaire of the kinges Maiestie in his progresse
Intertainment   vnto this Citie, what Course should be fittest for his entertainment
of his Maiestie
and how the   and where money should be paid and in readines for the   30
same shalbe   disbursement of the necessarie charge for that busines, It is
assessed•   therefore ordered and agreed vpon that the somme of C li shalbe
                       raised taxed assessed and Collected in manner followinge viz.
                       euery Iustice of the peace shall lend v li. euery Alderman v.
                       markes euery Sheriffes peere xl s and euery one of the fortie and   35
                       Comon Counsall xx s and all the seuerall sommes aforesaid
                       shalbe brought in and to the hands of the Threasurers paid in
                       the Inner Pentice with in this Cittie at or before the end of one
                       weake next Comminge, and that Mr William Gamull and Mr Iohn
                       Ratcliffe Aldermen and Iustices of peace Mr Charles ffitton and   40

19 / *marginal letter* C *indicates that this item is third in the list of entries for 2 July*

Mr Edward Kitchin Aldermen Threasurers of the same Citie,
Mr Nicholas Ince Alderman Mr Randle Holmes Mr William
Sparke and Mr Iohn Annion shall appoint Comand and oversee
the streetes to be Cleansed, houses to be outwardly beautified
the Conduit and Pentice adorned a Carpet prouided, the Comon   5
Hall Colored and florished and other such necessaries to be
prepared if his Maiestie should happilie by his presence soe honor
this Citie, as they in their Iudgementes and discretions should
thincke most meete fitt and Convenient and as might yeeld
vnto his Maiestie the best Contentment   10
...

AC *Trinity Churchwardens' Accounts* BL: Harley 2177
f 44v *(23 August)*
...   15
for rushes & Sand 23 August to Straw the street before the
church against our gratious soueriane Lord Kinge Iames Cominge
to the City with many of his noble the same day in the
afternoone   *(blank)*
...   20

A *Mayors List 8* BL: Harley 2133
f 47v* *(23 August) Edward Button*
...
Our Citie was graced with the Royall presence of our soueraigne   25
kinge Iames who beinge Attended with many honorable Erles
Reuerend Bishops and worthy knights and Courtiers besides
all ye gentry of the shire Rode in state through the Citie ye
23 of August, beinge mett with the sherifs peeres and Common
Councell of ye Citie euery one with his foote Cloth well mounted   30
on horsebacke. All the trayned souldiers of the Citie standinge in
order without ye Eastgate. And euerie Company with theire
ensignes in most seemelie sorte did keepe theire seuerall stations
on both sides of the Eastgate streete The Maior and all the
Aldermen took theire places vpon a scaffold, rayled and hunge   35
about with greene And there, in most graue and seemelie Manner
they Attended the Comeinge of his Maiestie At which tyme
(after a learned speech deliuered by the Recorder) The Mayor
presented vnto the kinge a faire standinge Cuppe with a Couer
dubble guilt, and therein 100 Iacobins of goulde And likewise   40
the Maior deliuered the Cities sword vnto the kinge, who gaue
it vnto the Maior againe, And the same was borne before the

kinge, by the Maior (beinge on horsebacke) And the sword of
Estate was borne by the right ho*nora*ble Will*ia*m Erle of Darbie
Chiefe Chamberleine of the Countie Pallatine of Chester The
kinge Rode first to the minster where he alighted from his
horse And in the west Ile of the minster he heard an oration   5
deliuered in lattin by a scholler of the free [schoole] schoole
After the said oration he went into the Queere And there (in a
seate made ˌᶜfor ye kingeˀ in the higher end of the Queer) [on]
he heard an Anthem songe And after Certayne prayers [for]
the kinge went from thence to the Pentice, where a sumptuous   10
banquet was p*re*pared on the Cities Cost w*hi*ch beinge ended
the kinge departed, to the Vale Royall And at his dep*ar*ture
[⟨...⟩] the order of knighthood was offered to mr Maior But he
refused the same

                                                                   15

A   *Mayors List 9* BL: Add. 11335
     ff 23v-4* *Edward Button*

The 23 August 1616 Edward Button Esq*uire* Innkeeper being
then Major of Chester, King Iames came purposely to see this   20
cittie the Major and Aldermen standing on a scaffold in their
scarlett gownes in the Eastgate street near the honey stairs, the
companyes of this Cittie attending with their Banners, where
after a speech made to his Majesty by the Recorder on the
scaffold, then being mr Edward Whitby, his majesty was there by   25
him presented with a guilt bowl and cover worth about £10
with a hundred peices of gold in it being one hundred pound |
his majesty went to the Quoire and heard service and from
thence on foot he went through the shoemakers Row in the
Northgate street to the pentice, where he was banqueted and   30
after he rode on horsebacke through the cittie. the major carrying
the Citty sword affore his Majesty and William Earle of Derby
did bear the Cheker sword before him alsoe his majesty Went
that night to vale Royall to bed.

                                                                   35

A   *Mayors List 12* BL: Add. 29780
     ff 161-2* *Edward Button*
     ...

The Kings Majesty came the 22 Day of Aug*u*stt to the Sea Hall to
S*i*r George Calveley and there had a banquett, and from thence   40

13 / [⟨...⟩] *full line deleted MS*

the same day |to the Citty of chester, where he was banquetted
in the pentice and presented with a Cupp of Gold by the Citty,
and from thence went to Vale Royal the same night being
saturday were he rested till munday and then came to Nantwich
that night and so away   5

...

Painters, Glaziers, Embroiderers, and Stationers' Records
C: Account Book I
ff 150-50v *(18 October)*   10

...

Item for stuffe for the Childs breeches	iiij s viij d
Item for Cotton and the making	ij s ij d
Item for silvering	ij s
Item for hose shooes and gloues for the Child	iij s v d 15
Item for gloues for the Aldermen & stuard*es*	iij s iiij d
Item for the banquet on midsomer eue	vij s
Item for pottle sack and pottle Claret	iij s iiij d
Item ij pottles beere	viiij d
Item to the musicke	j s vj d 20
Item to S*ir* George Beuerlet man that led the horse	ij s vj d	
Item riband for the horse head	ij d
Item for arsedine	ij d
Item spent at dressing the Child	iiij d
Item at the bars Castle and northgate and to a poore man j s iiij d 25	

...

Treasurers' Account Rolls CCA: TAR/2/35
mb 3 *(November)*
...   30

Item paied for takinge downe the pales at the roodee on Saynt
Georges daie   xij d.
Item paid the drum*m*er for carryinge the drum*m*e y*a*t day   xij d.
Item paied vnto Nicholas hallowed and william handcock for the
Citties worke against midsomer Eve by mr maiors appoyntment   35
the viij^t of maie 1618   xliij s. 4d.

...

mb 4

...   40

Item paied vnto Gest for druminge at midsomer watch   xij d
Item paide the xxvjth of Iune 1618 to the Steward*es* of the

paynters for tryminge and settinge forth the Citties mount on
midsomer Eve   xxxvj s. 8d
...

Item paied to Thomas welch Cooper for Carringe the Citties
fflagge or Ensigne on midsomer Eve   ij s vj d   5
...

mb 5-6
...

Item paid to mr Alderman Litler the xxij. of december 1617 for   10
xiiij yardes quarter & half a quarter of Broadecloth to make the
waitemen gownes and the boyes Clokes at viij s the yard   v li. xv s.
...

Item paide vnto hamnett Bennett one of the Stewardes of the
Company of Sadlers on the xijth of ffebruary 1617 for the   15
Augmentinge of the Bell for shrovetewsday by master maiors
appoyntment   vj s viij d
Item paid to Roger Guest the drommer that day   xij d
Item paide vnto two Laborers for takinge downe the pales at
the roodee on Shrove tweseday & for settinge them vp the same   20
day   xij d
...

Cordwainers and Shoemakers' Records   25
CCA: Account Book III G/8/4
f 18 *(11 November)*
...

Inprimis payde the xjth daye of November Anno domini 1617.
beinge S martens daye. vnto Roberte kelly and his companye   30
for musicke   iiij s iiij d
...

f 18v

...   35
paide for our sixe gleaves   vj s
paide to the berrage of them   viij d
Spente at Iohn Androwes vpon gutteds daye in the Companye
of the Sadlers   iiij d
Spente at mr Buttons. vpon Ashewednesday when wee were   40
disappoyntd of our drinking at the Comon hall by the drapers
then the Sadlers being all in Companye   ij s iiij d
paide to george kellye for musicke at shroftyde   ij s vj d

paide to Roberte kelly for musicke the same tyme & daye   iij s
Spente at an over plushe the same daye at our drinkinge at
mr Inces   ij s
paide to Thomas hough   iiij d
paid for one pottell of seacke the same tyme   ij s   5
...

f 19
...

paide / At that tyme the Companye did dyne at daniell Throppes   10
for Musicke   xviij d
...

Spente when we wente to agree with mr hoolmes as conceringe
the makeinge of our New banner to be fynished against
midsomer 1618   xij d   15
paide for an Ellne of greene Taffyta for the banner   xiiij s iiij d
paide for buckrom   viij d
...

paide vnto Roberte Kelly for musicke the 2th Iuly 1618 when
foure brethren Came into our Companye   ij s   20
paide. vnto mr Rondall hoolmes painter: for makinge of Anew
banner for the Companye against midsomer 1618   iij li. v s o d
paide to the beriage of our new banner   xiiij d

mydsom paid for Apayer of stockinges for the boye: ij s
paid for his shooes   xvj d   25
paid for shoe tyes   vj d
paid for Reben for the horse head   vj d
paid for the boyes gloves and poyntes   xiiij d
paid to the men that did at tende. the Child   xviij d
...   30

f 19v
Spente At Iohnsons without the barres   ij s viij d
paid to the: Cryer. at the barrs   vj d
Geven to olde sydall   iiij d   35
Geven to the prisoners of the Castell and Northgate   ij s
paid to Roberte Kelly for our musicke   v s
Geven to the man that brought Ahorse for our boye   xviij d
paide at Anoverplushe. at our bankett vpon midsomer even
ˊand for wineˋ   xj s ij d   40
...

paid for one pinte of wine at the dressinge of the Childe   iiij d
...

Beerbrewers' Records CCA: Company Book G 3/2
f 44 *(23 November)*

...

Midsomer
accomptes.

paid for a payer of shoes for the Child	xx d
paid for a payer of hooes for the Child	ij s vj d
paid for a payer of gloves for the Child	ix d
spent at dressing of the Child as formerly hath been allowed	ij s.
paid and laid out in prouidinge of a horse & other necessaries for the Child as hath beene allowed to other stewardes.	xviij d
geuen to the Mvsicioners. vpon midsomer even	vj s.
paid for beare vpon midsomer even for the Companie and ther men	v s.
paid for bread and Cheese	vj s.
paid for wyne	ij s iiij d
paid for apples prunes Comfetes & other necessarie prouicion for the Companie as formerly hath beene [p] allowed	xx d

(marginal line numbers: 5, 10, 15)

...

f 44v

geuen to three men that lead the Childes horse	xxij d
geven to the Cryer at the barres	iiij d
geu to the prisoners at the Castell	vj d
geuen to the prisoners at the Northgate	vj d

...

paid to mr holmes for keping the banner for on Yeare	xij d

(marginal line numbers: 20, 25)

...

Dean and Chapter CC: Treasurers' Accounts IV
p 120 *(25 November)*

...

Item to the waites & other musike	iiij s

(marginal line number: 30)

...

p 121 *(Christmas)*

...

Item paid to the wachman attending 3 nightes vpon the mayor & sherives & for Armor for yat purpose	ij s vj d.

(marginal line number: 35)

...

4 / shoes *written over* hooes

Coopers' Records C: Company Book II
f 9 *(13 January)*

...

(John Tottye's dinner)
paide To Thomas williams and his companye for Musicke at the   5
same dynner   ij s vj d

...

midsomer charge

paide for the Loone of the Childs hatt   xij d   10
paide for one dozin of poyn*tes* for the boye   iiij d
paid for apayer of gloves for the boye   x d
paide for two payers of gloves for the two men that lead the
boyes horse   xvj d
paid for apayer of shooes for the boye   xvj d   15
paide for his stocking*es* and shoe tyes   xvij d
paid for Rebin for the horse   vj d
paid the Cryer   iiij d
paid at the Castell and Northgate and to old sydall   x d
Geven to Rondall Iewett   iiij d   20
paid for musicke   ij s
paid for beere and bread at our banquett   vj s vj d
paid for Cheese   ij s iiij d

...
                                                                 25

f 9v
paid for prvines   viij d
paid for Apples   vj d
paid for suger   ij d
paid for one quarte seacke and one quarte Clarrett at *(blank)* xx d   30
...

[paide vnto mr hoolmes painter for keepinge and new tryminge
of our staffe w*hich* beares our flagg   iij s]

...

paide vnto mr hoolmes for repayreinge of our banner   vj s. x d   35

...

Joiners, Carvers, and Turners' Records
CCA: Company Book G14/1
f 98 *(25 March)*   40

...

Item paid for paintinge the staffe of the Banner against midsomer

Eue for the watch   xij d
Item paid for a paire of Bootes for the Child   iij s iiij d
Item paid for Ribboninge for the Child   xiij d
Item for wyne bestowed at the dressinge of the Boy   vj d
Item for a paire of gloues for the Child   xij d   5
Item giuen to the Cryer at the Barres   iiij d
Item giuen to the prisoners of the Castle and the Northgate viij d
Item giuen to Sibdall a poore man   ij d
Item giuen to Three men to Attend the Child   xiiij d
Item paid to the Musicke   ij s   10
Item paid for three quartes of wyne for the Company at the
Banquett vpon Midsomer Eue   xviij d
Item for Beere bestowed vpon the Watchmen on Midsom*er* Eue
at Alderman Salisburies house   xij d
...   15

Mercers, Ironmongers, Grocers, and Apothecaries' Records
C: Company Book
pp 97-8 *(8 May)*
...   20
At midsomer for watch

Comphett*es* ij li. at   0-4-0
Suger j li. a   0-1-6
Synamonde two ounces at   0-0-8   25
Prunes xij li. at   0-2-6
Marmalott j li. j oz. at   0-2-0
Wett Suckett   0-1-0
Conseit*es* halfe apound at   0-1-8
Waffers   0-2-0   30
Stronge beere   0-6-0
j pottell of Sacke. 3. quartes of Clarett   0-4-0
payde for apayer of stocking*es* for the Ladye   0-3-0
payde for apayer of shooes for her   0-1-6
payde for Rybon for her shooes   0-0-4   35
payde for Rybon to tye her Iewells   0-1-0
payde for apayer of gloues for her   0-2-0
payde for Rybon for her horse head   0-1-0
payde the man that leade her horse and Caryed the Coolers 0-1-0
payde two men that held the Ladye   0-3-0   40
payde for 4. payer of gloves for the men   0-3-0
payde for apayer of gloves for the boye   0-0-6

payde for apayer of bootes for the boye   0-5-0
payde two men for atendinge the boye   0-2-0
Spente in beere at the barres at wilsons howse   0-1-0
Geven to the Crier at the barres   0-1-0 |
Geven to Siddall the Cobler   0-0-6   5
Geven to Randall Iewell   0-1-0
Geven to the prisoners of the Castell   0-2-0
Geven to the prisoners of the Northgate   0-2-0
Geven to the musicke   0-6-8
Geven them more for playinge to some of the Company that   10
came in after the were were payde   0-0-6
payde 3. men for watchinge the londoners at midsom*er* fayer

                                                                 0-5-0

...
                                                                          15

Joiners, Carvers, and Turners' Records CCA: Minute Book G14/2
p 20 *(8 June)*
...

It is Agreed that the Company shall meete at Alderman Salisburies
house vpon Midsomer Eue Accordinge to Antient Custome   20
euerie brother with his Watchman And the Banquett to bee at
William Pues house and euery brother to pay iiij d a peece
towards the same.
...
                                                                          25

1618-19
Drawers of Dee's Records CCA: Company Book G10/1
p 48 *(30 June)*
...

geuen to the bearebruers   x s   30
...

Painters, Glaziers, Embroiderers, and Stationers' Records
C: Account Book I
f 152 *(18 October)*   35
...

It*em* for gloues for the Ald*er*men and stuard*es* at midsomer
                                                           iij s iiij d
It*em* for hose shooes and gloues for the Child   iij s x d
It*em* for riben and shooeties   x d   40

11 / were were MS *dittography*

Item spent at dressing the Child   v d
Item at the bars Castle and northgate   j s o
Item for the banquet on midsomer eue   vij s o
Item for a pottle of sacke and ij pottles Clarett   iiij s o
Item to the musick   ij s vj d
Item to the men that led the horse   j s vj d
Item for three pottles of beere   j s o
Item for loane of the hat and fether   vj d
...
Item to william handcocke for gilding the little phenix   xvj d   1
Item paied for our part of the rent of the phenix   j s
...

Treasurers' Account Rolls CCA: TAR/2/37   1
mb 3 *(November)*
...
Item paied more for Tenne yardes and ahalf of brode clothe
for the Three Waytemens gownes at eight Shillinges the yarde
                                                  iiij li. iiij s.   2
Item paied for fiue yardes of Brode Clothe to make the Two
boyes of the waitemen Cloakes and for seaven yardes of Brode
cloth to make Adam and the night bell man gownes in all is
xij. yardes at vij s the yarde is   iiij li. iiij s
...   2
Item paid vnto hamnett Bennet and Thomas Williams ye stewardes
of the Sadlers to augment the Bell at Shrovetide Anno 1618
                                                          vj s viij d
...
                                                                      3

mb 4

Item paied vnto Roger Guest for his drominge on Shrove Tewsday
                                                             xij d
Item paid for takinge downe the pales against that daie and   3
setting them vp   xvj d
...
Item paid to the paynters the xth of maie 1619 for the payntinge
of the giantes &c at midsomer   xliij s iiij d.
Item paid for the taking vp & setting downe of the pales at the   4
roodye on St Georges day   xvj d
...

mb 5

...

Item paid the 23 of Iune to Guest for druminge at the Watch

xij d

5

...

Item paied the painters for settinge forthe the maiors mounte

xxvj s. 8d.

...

Cordwainers and Shoemakers' Records   10
CCA: Account Book III G/8/4
f 26 *(11 November)*

...

more Geven vnto Roberte kellye for Musicke   iiij s
more Geven vnto Bruse the piper   xij d   15
more Geven vnto Thomas hough   iiij d

...

ff 27-7v

...   20

Spente. as concerninge the busynesse. aboute the drapers   xx d

Shrovetide   paid for sixe Cleaves   vj s
paid to the berrage   viij d
Geven to Thomas hough   iiij d
paid vnto George kellye for musicke   ij s vj d   25
paid to Roberte kellye for Musicke the same tyme   ij s viij d
paid for one pottell seacke. and one pottell Clarett wyne the
same daye   iij s

...

Mydsomer Charge   30

paide for the Loone of Ahatt for our boye   vj d
paide for his gloves   xij d
paide for his stockinges   ij s
paide for one dozin silke poyntes   xvj d   35
paid for silk Ryben for his shooes   vj d
paid for his shooes   xviij d
paid for Ryben for the horse head   vj d
paide vnto three men that Attended the boye   xviij d
paid to mr. hoolmes for keepinge of our banner   xij d   40
paid vnto the man that brought the horse   xviij d
paide at the dressinge of the boye for one pint wine   iij d

paid at widdow Iohnsons. for breade & beere. for the Company
ij s vj d |

paid to the Crier at barrs	vj d
paid to olde Sidall	iiij d
Geven to the prisoners at Castell & Northgate	ij s
paid for our Musicke	v s
paide at Anoverplushe at our bankett	xij s ix d
pade for thre quartes of seacke	iij s

...

1

Beerbrewers' Records CCA' Company Book G 3/2
ff 47-7v *(23 November)*

Midsomer
accompt*es*.

paid for a payer of shooes for the Child	xx d
paid for a payer of hooes for the Child	ij s vj d 1
paid for a payer of gloves for the Child	ix d
Item spent at dressing the child	ij s.
Item spent in prouiding a horse for the Child & for other necessaries	xviij d
Item geuen to the Musicions vpon midsomer Even	vj s.	2
Item paid for beare vpon midsomer even	v s.
Item paid for bread & Cheese	vj s.
Item paid for wynne	ij s iiij d
Item paid for apples & other thinges	xx d.
Item geuen to three men that led the Childes horse	xxij d 2
Item geuen to the cryer at the barres	iiij d
Item geuen to the prisoners at the castell	vj d.
Item geuen to the prisoners at the northgate	vj d

...

Item geuen to mr holmes. for kepinge the banner   xij d 3

...

Coopers' Records C: Company Book II
ff 13-13v *(13 January)*

...

3

Mydsomer Charges /

payde for the Loone of the Childes hatt	xiiij d
payd for one dozin poyntes	iiij d
payde for his gloves	x d 4
payde for two payer of gloves for the two men that leade the boyes horse	xij d

payde for the boyes shooes	xviij d
payde for his stockinges and shoe tyes	xx d |
payde for Sylke Rebyn for the horse heade	iiij d
payde the Cryer at the barres	iiij d
payd at the Castell Northgate and to olde sydall	x d
payde for our Musicke	xx d
payd for beere and bread at our banqueitt	vj s viij d
payde for Cheese	ij s vj d
payde for prvines	viij d
payde for Aples	vj d
payde for suger	ij d
payd for one pinte seacke and a quarte of Clarett	xij d
Geven vnto greiffeith Iones apayer of gloves	vj d

...

AC *Linendrapers' Petition* BL: Add. 16179
ff 25-6 *(13 February)*

...

The Linnendrapers by petition set forth that they have been an
ancient Company by the name of the Aldermen Stewards and
Brethren of the Company of Lennendrapers by prescripcion and
also confirmed by charter from the Citty 6. °Ed. 6.° and they so
continued till the Year 1603. That by the Order of ˄ ⸢the⸣ then
Mayor and Justices the Bricklayers were admitted to joyn with
them in setting forth the pageants for Midsummer Shew but by
many Years experience have been found troublesome and
unserviceable to their Company many of them being very poor
and unable to contribute to the defences of the priveledges
of the Said Company and therefore desired that the Bricklayers
might be seperated from them and that the petitioners might be
restored to their ancient priveledges of being a distinct Company
the House being satisfied of the truth thereof and that the
Bricklayers made many | Irregular Eleccions and disorders in
their Company. Ordered that they be Secluded and debarred
from being any longer Members of the Said Company of
Linnendrapers or meeting with them as such and that the
Linnendrapers be a Company of themselves as they have antiently
been.

...

Joiners, Carvers, and Turners' Records
CCA: Company Book G14/1
f 100 *(25 March)*
...

The disbursments

Imprimis paid for a paire of shooes for the Child that did Ryde
for the Company on Midsomer Eue   xvj d
Item for a paire of stockinges   xiiij d
Item paid for a paire of gloues   ix d   1⟨
Item paid for a paire of shooetyes and garters   vj d
Item paid for a hatt   iij s iiij d
Item paid for a Ribbon for the horse head   iiij d
Item spent in wyne at the dressinge of the Child   viij d
Item spent vpon the Companye in Beere   iiij d   1⟨
Item giuen to the Cryer at the Barrs   iiij d
Item giuen to Sibdall a poore man   ij d
Item giuen to the prisoners of of the Castle and the Northgate
                                                           viij d
Item giuen to the Musitians that did Attend the Company on   2⟨
Midsomer Eue   iij s
Item paid to three men to Attend the Child   xij d
...

Mercers, Ironmongers, Grocers, and Apothecaries' Records   2⟨
C: Company Book
p 105 *(7 May)*
...

Item payd for apayre of gloues for the boy   ix d
Item to 3 men for ffollowinge the horse with the boy   iij s   3⟨
Item payd for musicke   vj s viij d
Item to the prisoners in the northgatte & in the Castell iiij s [d]
Item to siddall the Cobler   vj d
Item j yard Ribin to the horse head   viij d
Item j pere shoes for the boy   xvj d   3⟨
Item for Ribin for his shoes   vj d
Item j pre hos for the boy   xvj d
Item to the Crier at the barrs   xij d
Item spent at Raph Wilsons house   xij d
Item 3 pre gloues to the men that ffollowed the horse at xviij d   4⟨
Item to a man for waching at the londoners shopps   vj d

18 / of of MS *dittography*

Item to the Cunstable for bringing Garrett to the northgatte xij d

...

Item dj barrill bier	vij s
Item waffers	ij s
Item Cakes	ij s
Item ij li. comffettes	iiij s
Item j li. Marmelad	ij s
Item dj li. Conseates	xx d
Item dj li. Wett suckett	xij d
Item xij li. prunes for	ij s vj d

Item j pottell of sacke & j pottle Clared Wine by the appointment
of the aldermen   iij s
Item j li. suger   xviij d
Item 2 oz Cinamon   viij d

...

p 106

...

Item payd mr Holmes per mr Drinkwaters direcon for 2 banners
                                                                   v li. vj d

...

Item paid at Midsomer Aginse for the Lady shoes	xiiij d
Item for apayre of hos for her	xviij d
Item for Ribin for her shoes	vj d
Item for a paire of gloues for her	xij d

Item for 3 payre of gloues to 3. men that did attend the lady
                                                                     xviij d
Item Ribin for her horse head   xij d
Item for Ribin to tye her Iewells and Triming her head   xxij d
Item to the man that leade [the] her horse & Carried the banner
                                                                       xij d
Item payd 2 other men that did attend the lady   ij s vj d
Item given a mayd that did attend the lady while she was in
Towne and Came with her   xij d

...

Joiners, Carvers, and Turners' Records CCA: Minute Book G 14/2
f 27 *(21 May)*

...

B Alderman Salisburie   all these haue denyed to Come to
   steward Calcot   the Banquett that of Custome [h]

---

40 / *marginal letter* B *indicates that this item is second in the list of entries for 21 May*

Edward Heidocke   hath Bene on midsomer Eue, And
[Robt]'Willam' ap Hugh   doe desire that the Cost in that
Richard Walker   kinde may hereafter be spared

...

Assembly Books CCA: AB/1
f 347v *(1 June)*

...

Allsoe att the Same Assemblye the Petycion proferred by some
of the ffortie or Common Councell of the Cittie for and in the
name of the reste Prayinge they mighte ryde vppon there
fotclothes vppon Midsomer eve in the tyme of the Watche
yearely. and ever after was by the whole Assemblye, for some
Consideracons reiected and thought vnfitt to be graunted to the
said petyconers. /

·fforties: their peticion to ride on their foote Clothes at Midsomer ·

A   ***Rogers' Breviary*** CRO: DCC 19
unnumbered folio*

A breauary or Collectiones of the moste anchant Cittie of Chester
reduced into these chapters followeinge: by the reuerend:
mr Robert Rogers Bachlor in diuinitie, Archdeacon of chester,
and one of the prebundes of the Cathedrall Church in Chester:
written a new by his sonne DR: a well willer to that anchant
Cittie

...

*(The account of the homages to the Drapers is nearly identical to
those in the* CCA: *unnumbered* MS *'Breviary' and has been
collated with it (see pp 234-8). The* CRO MS *continues:)*

ff 36v-42v

...

Now the Custom of the said Company of Drapers was Aunchantly,
after the balls offered by ye Shoemakers & sadlers & the

Collation CRO: DCC 19, ff 36v-7v, with BL: Harley 1948, ff 60-60v
(1948): 34-p 321, l 14 Now ... shew:] *Rogers rewrote and rearranged these
three paragraphs and transferred them to the end of the section on the
homages in 1948, ff 60v-1v (see pp 351-3)*

1 / d *of* Heidocke *written over another letter*

~ 'foteball' playe ended, to meete togeather all the 3. Companyes
of drapers Shoemakers and sadlers, at the charge of the drapers
in token of societie,

ye drapers
charges now:

But as this alteration. is more commendable soe the Charges to
the worthie Company of drapers is more Chargeible, for now the   5
said drapers doe the same Shrouetueseday after the games be
ended. they doe feast the maior & Aldermen in the Common hall
of the said Cittie, & the 2. Companies of Shoemakers & sadlers,
with bread beare ij dayes & the iij day with abanquet:

The Drapers of the Cittie of Chester haueinge these homages   10
done to them, they haue alsoe the forfeture if any neclect the
same, beinge: x li.: of which they haue many anchant recoueries,
and also yerely by those that neclecte the same homage as theire
presidentes doe shew:

                                                                    15

    The proclamation commanded by ye maior of
    Chester, yerely at the Rood dee, when the
    people are assembled to see these exceseses
    performed on Shrouetusday yerely:

                                                                    20

A proclamacion
on Shroue:
tuseday:

Oes: Oes: Oes: The right worshipfull: The Maior of the Cittie
of Chester willeth and requireth and in his maiesties name
straitely chargeth & Commandeth | all. manner of persons of
what degree or callinge soeuer he or they be, here this daye
assembled for the comfort and recreation of his maiesties   25
Subieckes. That they and euery of them obserue and keape his
maiestis: hignes peace duringe the time the games be in playeinge
vpon paine and perill that shall fall thereon xc:

Collation continued: 16-19 The ... yerely:] The proclamations and the
manner vsed to this daye, here followe: The mayors Proclamation on ye
Rood de on Shrouetuedaye, before these homages be deliuered ad the
games played *1948* (be *written over* de; *the* u *of* deliuered *lacks a minim;*
ad *for* and *1948*) 21 marginalia *and* Oes: Oes: Oes:] *reduced in 1948 to
the marginalia* Oyes: *under which RH II added* thrise 22 his] ye kings
1948; RH II added Queens *above* 23 manner of persons] *RH II underlined*
manner of persons *and added above* & euery person & persons *in 1948*
24 this daye] *between* this *and* daye *in 1948, RH II interlined* or shall
assemble themselues to see the Auntient Games hertofore accustomed to
be played as on this day 26 Subieckes] *RH II added* then present *in 1948*
26 them] *RH II added* ~ 'doe' *in 1948* 27 peace] *Rogers adds* & be of
good behauiour *in 1948*

An other proclamation for the homages
of maried persons. to the drapers:

All manner of persones that haue bene maried within the Cittie
of Chester and dwell els where or maried els where and dwell
within the same Cittie this last yere past, Come forth and doe
your homages in deliueringe vp. your gleaues vpon payne of ten
powndes:

for the Shoemakers,

1

The Alderman and stuardes of the Shooemakers within ye Citti
of Chester Come forth and doe your homage. in deliueringe vp.
your gleaues. and presentmentes vpon paine of ten powndes:

1

for the Sadlers:

The Aldermen and stuardes of the Sadlers within the Cittie of
Chester Come forth and doe your |homage with your horse and
bell, vpon payne of ten powndes:

2

Of the Shereffes breackfast:

Whereas time out of the memori of man no man liueinge
rememboringe the origenall: The ij sherefes of the Cittie of
Chester doe yerely on monday in ester weke commonly called

2

Collation continued: 1-2 An ... drapers:] for all maried persons: *1948;*
O yes *marginalia 1948; in 1948 the proclamation for married persons
follows that of the Sadlers.* 7 your] *Rogers adds* seuerall *in 1948* 12] O
yes: *marginalia 1948* 12 stuardes] *Rogers adds* of ye societie & Companye
in 1948 12 Shooemakers] *RH II added* Cordwinders *above in 1948*
14 ten powndes:] *below this entry at the bottom of f 60, RH II added to
1948:* mr knight onst clarke of the pentice sayth that this Custome was
obserued before his tyme tyme out of Mynd: & that in Considration of this
homage the Company of Cordwenores in the sayd City be free from the
trialls in matters between party & party before mr maior & the Sheriffs
16] O yes: *marginalia 1948; against the entry itself RH II added* this Called
first in mr Knights notes 18] stuardes of the Sadlers] stuardes of ye
societie and Companye of Sadlers *1948* 20 ten powndes:] *Rogers shifts
the proclamation for the married persons to this point and concludes the
entry with the rewritten paragraphs which appear at the beginning of this
section. See the entry for the Harley 1948 'Breviary', pp 351-2.*

blake monday, [doe] doe prouide abreakefast of Calues heades
and bacon, and there on the Roode dee partes are taken by
gentlemen, yeomen, & good fellowes with one shereffe or the
other, an equall number of archers on both sides, and there doe
shoote for the same breakefast, which ended the winners side   5
paye ij d apeice, the losers: 4d the all take parte thereof, at the
Common hall of the said Cittie, which Custome soe vsed, the
time beinge veri seasonable, the ende being the amitie and
societie of the Cittizens there deserues not only Continuance
but also greate Commendation: | 10

Of St Georges day:

In the yere of our lord :1609: mr William Lester mercer beinge
maior of Chester, one mr Robert Ambrye Irnemonger, somtime   15
a Shereffe of the Citti of Chester, with the consent of the mayor
and Citti caused: 3. bells of siluer [⟨...⟩] or Cuppes of siluer of
agood value to be made, the which weare appoynted to be yerely
on that day runne for by horses vpon the Roode dee, that horse
that was firste, to haue the best bell, and ˄ʳyat horseʼ[hor] that   20
came second to haue the second bell, And for the third bell it
is the same day runne for by gentlemen at the ringe, who ruinge
there and takeinge the ringe haue it for that yeare, And so the [t]
other 2. bells also, and they are broughte in the same day twelue
monthe, And soe remayne foreuer: 25

Of the showe at midsomer:

Of the midsomer show, beinge of like antiquitie no man liueinge
rememboringe the origenall it hath continued euer to be   30
performed on midsomer | eaue. except the eaue. fell on the
sonday then the maior hath [g] performed it the day before In
which show many thinges, which weare offensiue hath bene
taken awaye. and reformed by the Instance of worthy Preachers,
whoe spake against som thinges formerly vsed. bot for the   35
decensie of it now, it is moste Comendable, rich, and beautifull,
The like in few Cities of this lande:

Of Christmas watches:

                                                                    40
The cause of which is very anchant, for the ould brittons the

22 / ruinge for runinge

Walshmen, beinge at warres with this Citti, beinge soe often
molested with brvyles it beinge the only place in these partes for
defence, the said walshe men, came in the nighte at Christmas
time and burned and destroyed A greate parte of this Cittie,
wherevpon, A stricte watch was at that time euer kepte, And
with the Conqueror Came in 4. britheren videlicet Neele lord
of Halton. Constable of Cheshire Hadard lord of Dutton. marshall
of Cheshire Edward lord of Haw˄ˊaˋrden. stuard of Cheshire
Hebard lord of Donham Chamberlayne of Cheshire To ˄ˊallˋ
these it should seime the Conqueror gaue | greate landes, To   1•
haue theire aydes to defende this Cittie. as neede shoulde require,
yet the same landes are at this daye come to the possession of the
Earles of Oxenford & Derbye, mr Port. and diuers otheres, whoe
yerely by theire deputies doe theire seruices and homages at the
Mayores watch Courte, and there be called to serue in respecte   1:
of the tenure of the same landes, which landes are Called ye
Gable rent, and oughte to be at the seruice of the Cittie vpon any
occasion,: The which oulde custome now vsed is torned to the
seruice of watcheinge the Cittie from danger of fire robbers, or
other violent misdemenors, wharby peace might be broken, or   2•
God dishonored, at soe sacred afeast, where vpon the watchcourt
beinge ended, the state of that Cittie doe vsuallye, banquett
togeather, as the time requires, and ˄ˊasˋ Ciuill societies vnited
togeather by those anchant and lawdable customes, whoe metinge
in such a state of solemnitie, doe Ioyne in frendly concorde,   2:
by banquetinge togeather to theire Iuste deserued praise and
commendation |

Now of the Whitson
playes in Chester: 3(

ye origenall of   Concerninge the whitson playes of Chester The origenall of them
ye whitson   was. In the time of Sir Iohn Arneway. who by most copies was
playes: the first maior of Chester, about anno domini :1332: then the
                     weare firste played and sett forthe: The Author or maker of   3:
ye author.   them was one Randoll A monke of the Abbay in Chester. whoe
                     made the same in partes as it was:
ye matter   The matter of these playes weare the historie of the bible,

---

8 / a of Haw˄ˊaˋrden *written above a letter which has been blotted out*
12 / yet *written over* iet (?)

composed by the said author in a holy deuotion, that the simple
mighte vnderstand the scripture, which in those times was hid
from them:

ye Actors

    The actores or players, weare the Companies or trades men of
the Citti of Chester, who at theire owne Costes and Charges, sett   5
forth and alsoe played the same playes yerelye: the last time they
weare played in Chester was: anno domini :1574: | Sir Iohn
Sauage beinge maior of Chester mr Iohn Allen & mr William

the time of ye
yere when they
were played

Goodman beinge shereffes: The time when they weare played
was, 3 dayes togeather, on monday: Tueseday: & Wenseday in   10
Whitson weeke,

The [time of]
ₐ'places'ₐ'where'
ye played

    The places where they weare played were in euery streete of
the Cittie, that all people that would mighte behoulde the same:

The manner [of
ye playes] how
ye plaied.

The manner of these playes was, euery Company made a Pageant
on which they played theire partes, which Pagiant was a scaffolde,   15
or a high foure square buildinge, with .2. rowmes a higher and
alower, the lower hanged aboute richly and closse, into which,
none, but the actors came, on the higher they played theire
partes beinge all open to the behoulders, this was sett on .4.
wheeles, and soe drawne from streete to street, they first beganne   20
at the Abbay gates, where when the first pagiante was played, it
was wheled into an other streete, and the second pagiant came in
the place thereof and so till all the pagiantes for the day weare
ended, soe into euery streete and, it was soe orderly attended,
that before the | one Pagiant was played an other came in place   25
to satisfye the beholders in euerye streete at one time: Also
euery yere that these playes were played, on St. Georges day
before, was the banes read, which was a man did ride warlike
apparaled like st. George throughe euery streete, with drume
musicke and trumpetes, And there was published that the playes   30
were played that yeare, And that the breife or banes of the playe
was reade what euery Company should playe, which was called
the Readinge of the bannes, the wordes of which conclusion
was this:

                                          35

         All those that be minded to tary
         On monday, tweseday. & wensday in whitson
         weeke begines the storye:

for the better explaninge I haue here sett downe the, Companies   40
seuerall Pagiantes and partes the played, in those whitson playes:
...

(The entry is concluded with a list of companies and the parts they play; see the collation in the 1609 'Breviary' entry, pp 248-52.)

ff 112v-13*

...

In the [time] ˄ˊyereˋ when this S*ir* Iohn Arneway was mayor of Chester, the whtson playes made by a monke of Chester Abbay named Rondoll, was by the said maior published and caused to be sett forth and played at the Charges of euery Company within the said Cittie with theire Pagiantes as in the former Chapters is fully expressed, And the said Rondoll the author in the p*ro*louge before his booke of the whitson playes doth shew more fully. And the said monke Rondoll who did make the said playes lyeth buried within the marchantes Ile within the Cathedrall Church of Chester

...

1619-20
Drawers of Dee's Records CCA: Company Book G 10/1
p 49 *(30 June)*

...

geuen to the bearebruers   x s

...

Painters, Glaziers, Embroiderers, and Stationers' Records
C: Account Book I
f 154 *(18 October)*

...

It*em* geven in berage at dressing the phenix Caried at Midsom*er*   ij s o

It*em* for arsedine   o iij d

...

It*em* paied at severall times for Charges disbursed about the phenix   xvij s x d

...

Midsom*er* eues Charges	It*em* for gloues for the Ald*er*men and stuard*es*	iij s iiij d
	It*em* shooes and gloues for the Child	iij s x d
	It*em* riband and shooeties	o x d
	It*em* at dressing the Child spens	o v d
	It*em* at the bars Castle and Northgate	j s o
	It*em* for *our* banquet on Midsom*er* Eue	vij s o

Item pottle sacke and pottle Claret   iij s o
Item to the musicke   iij s iiij d
Item to one that led the horse   j s vj d
Item three pottles of beere   j s o
Item for loane of a hat and fether   o vj d   5
Item to William handcoke for gildinge the little phenix   j s iiij d

...

Treasurers' Account Rolls CCA: TAR/2/39
mb 3 *(November)*   10

...

Item paid the xxviijth of ffebruary vnto Thomas williams steward
of the Sadlers Towardes the Bell at Shrovetyde   vj s viij d.
Item paid to Guest for drumminge vpon Shrove tewsday   xij d
Item paid to the keeper for taking downe the pales at the roodee   15
and setting them vp againe   xvj d
Item paid to mr Leauelooker Goose for a xj yardes & half of
broadcloth for the waytmens gownes at viij s the yarde iiij li. iiij s
Item paid to him for the 2 boyes Cloakes being iiij. yardes xxxij s
...   20

mb 4
...
Item paid to Guest for beatinge the drum at Midsomer watche
                                                              xij d.   25

...

Item paid to Nicholas hallwood and william hancock for
payntinge the maiors mounte   xxvj s.

...

Item paid to Thomas wealch for Carryinge the Auntient at   30
midsomer watch   ij s. vj d

...

Cordwainers and Shoemakers' Records
CCA: Account Book III G/8/4   35
f 32 *(11 November)*

...

payde vnto Roberte kellye & his Company at Stewarde Enyalls
howse   ij s
...   40
more geven vnto Roberte kelly for musicke   ij s

...

f 32v

payde for powther and match at mr Sheriffe Incces watch. he
beinge our Alderman   v s iij d

...

paide to Roberte kellye for musicke at the Cominge in of Iacob
Carter   ij s.

...

payde for our gleeves and berrage at Shroftyde   vj s viij d
payde to george kelly for musicke   ij s vj d
more geven to Roberte kelly the same tyme for musicke   ij s   1(
payde at An over plushe after our drinkinge at shrovetyde at
mr Sheriff Inces howse   v s

...

f 33   1:

Midsomer Charges.

Inprimis Geven vnto mr hoolmes for keepinge our banner   xij d.
paid for apayer of Stockinges for the boye   xxij d
paid for his shooes   xvj d   2(
paid for apayer of gloves   viij d
paid for sylke Reben for the boyes shoe tyes and for the horse
head.   xij d
paide for one dozin poyntes   vj d
paid for hyering ahatt for the boye   vj d   2:
Spent at dressinge of the boye   iij d
Spent without the barrs for drinke   ij s viij d
more giuen the Cryer   vj d
more giuen willm Sidall   iiij d
more geven at Castell and Northgate   ij s   3(
more giuen to the men that attended the boye & horse   xviij d
paid for our musicke to Roberte kelly   iiij s
paid for wine at our banquit midsomer even   ij s vj d
paide at an over plushe at our banquiett one midsomer even
                   14s - 4d   xiiij s iiij d   35

...

Beerbrewers' Records CCA: Company Book G 3/2
f 49v *(23 November)*

                                                    40

Midsomer
accomptes.
     paid for a payer of shooes for the Child   xviij d.
     paid for a payer of hoes for the child   ij s iiij d.

p*ai*d for a payer of gloues for the child	x d
spent at dressing of the Child	ij s.
spent in pr*o*uiding a horse for the Child & for other necessaries	
	xviij d
geuen to the Musicion*ers*	vj s
p*ai*d for beare vpon midsom*er* Even	v s.
p*ai*d for bread and Cheese	vj s.
p*ai*d for wyne.	ij s.
p*ai*d for prunes & apples and other thing*es*	xx d
geuen to three men that led the horse	ij s.
geuen to the Crier at the barres	iiij d
geuen to the prison*ers* at the Castell	vj d
geuen to the prison*ers* at the Northgate	vj d

...

geuen to mr holmes for keping the banner.	xij d

...

Coopers' Records C: Account Book I
ff 16v-17 *(13 January)*
...

Midsomer Charges

payde for the loone of Ahatt for our boye y*at* did Ryde	xij d
paid for one dossen of poyntes	iiij d
paid for his gloves	x d
paid for 2. payer of gloves for the two men	xij d
paid for the boyes shooes	xxij d
paid for his stockinges and shoe tyes and Reben for his horse	
head	ij s
paid for drinke at the barres	x d
paid the Cryer at barrs	iiij d |
paid at the Castell Northgate and to olde Sydall	xij d
paid for our Musicke	xviij d
paide for beere and bread at our banquiett	vj s
paid for Cheese	ij s
paid for pruines	viij d
paid for apples.	vj d
paid for Suger & Synamond	iiij d
paid for one quarte Clarett & w*hi*t wine	xij d

...

payde at the dynner of Thomas lynaker The first August 1620	
one quarte seacke and one pottell w*hi*t wine	ij s

13 l

paide the same tyme for our musicke   iij s
...

Joiners, Carvers, and Turners' Records
CCA' Company Book G 14/1
f 101v *(25 March)*

Disbursements 1619

1(

Imprimis paid for a paire of stockin*ges* and garters for the Child
vpon Midsomer Eve   xx d
Item for gloues and Ribbonninge   xxj d
Item for a dozen of poy*ntes*   iiij d
Item paid to the Musitians   xx d   1⁵
Item paid for a paire of shooes for the Child   xiiij d
Item given to the Cryer at the Barres   iiij d
Item given to the Prisoners at the Castle and Northgate   viij d
Item given to Sibdall a poore man   ij d
Item paid for a hatt for the Child   iij s vj d   2(
Item paid to three men to Attend the Child   xij d
Item spent in Wyne at the dressinge of the Child   viij d
...

25

Mercers, Ironmongers, Grocers, and Apothecaries' Records
C : Company Book
p 111 *(5 May)*
...

payde for one payer of gloves and hoose and shooes for the   3(
Ladye   iij s x d
payde to three men for Attendinge the Ladye   iij s
payde for three payer of gloves for the three men   xviij d
payde for Musicke   vj s viij d
payde vnto the prisoners at the Castell and Northgate   iiij s   3⁵
paide to willi*a*m Sidall the Lame Cobler   vj d
Spente at Raffe wilsons howse *with*out the barres vpon the
Companye   ij s vj d
Geven vnto the Cryer at the barrs   xij d
payde for sylke Rebine for the horse heade   ix d   4(
payde for shooe tyes and silke Rybine for the ladyes head   iij s
...

p 112

...

3. Iuly 1620.

payde for halfe abarill of beere at   vj s vj d   5

...

paide to mr drinkwater for prunes and Comfett*es*   xj s
payde for wafers   ij s
payde for Cakes   ij s
payde for one potter seacke one pottell Clarett   iiij s   10
paide for j li. Suger at   xviij d
payde for two ounces Synamond   viij d
payde for fetchinge furniture for the Ladye and for thuse of
them   xv d
payde to mr hoolmes for keepinge the two banners. for the yeare   15
       ij s

...

payd for halfe [Ell blue] and Crimsyn taffyta for two Tippett*es*
       vij s iiij d
paide for makinge them and sil: ij s vj d   20

...

p 113

...

payde by Iames battrich one of the stewardes for gloves   25
stockinges and shooes the some of   x s

...

1620-1
Drawers of Dee's Records CCA: Company Book G10/1   30
p 49 *(10 July)*

...

geuen to the beare bruers   x s

...

   35

A   *Mayors List 5* BL: Harley 2125
ff 52v-3* *(2 October) Hugh Williamson*

...

Bullbayte   A bull baytinge at the heigh Crosse the 2th daye of october
Accordinge to Auncient Custome. for Mr mayors fare well out   40
of his office. it Chaunced a Contention fell out betwixt the
Bowchers and bakers of this Cittye aboute there dogges then

feightinge. The fell to blowes. and in the tumulte of manye
people. woulde not be paciffyed Soe that mr mayor. seeinge
theire greate abuse being Cittizins. Coulde not for beare but he in
person hym selfe. wente out of the pentise. Amongst them to
have the peace kepte. They in theire Rage. [but] . lytill did
Regarde hym. lyke rude and vnbroken fellowes, were in thende
parted. and the begynners of the sayde brawle being exsamyned
and founde out were Commytted to the North gate / mr mayor
smott freely Amongst them & broke his whyte staffe, and the
Cryer Tho knowstley brake his mase & soe the brawle ended / |

After the Tumulte and fallinge out of the aforesayde Butchers
and bakers, knowing the had offended and done Amisse /
Broughte out vnto the bull Ringe one other bull vpon the vth
october 1619: and there made verye fayer playe / in the
presentes of mr mayor and his brethen Sir Thomas Savage and
other gentlemen then presente who had before dyned with mr
mayor at his howse /

Soe after the bull baytinge. Sir Thomas Savage knight &
barronett and alderman of this Cittye, sente vnto the bowchers
and bakers .xx s. to drinke to geather & to be frendes his worshipp
heareinge before of the Contenticion: which the toke thankefully
and spente merrilye / prayinge god to blesse hym & all his
Chearefullye

...

Painters, Glaziers, Embroiderers, and Stationers' Records
C: Account Book II
p 1 *(18 October)*
...

Given to a berrage for seuerall workes aboute the Phenix for midsomer shew	xviij d.
[paid for powder at the same tyme	xij d.]
To three men for carrieng the Phenix & for Leadeinge the horsse	xviij d.
paid to sir Henry Bunburies man for his paynes aboute the horsse	xviij d.
paid to Siddall a poore man	iiij d.
paid to the barrs Castle & northgate	xij d.

...

paid for gloves to ye Aldermen & stewardes	iij s iiij d.
Shoes ˄'hose' and gloues for the Child	iij s. x d.
paid for Riban & Shooeties	x d.

spent at dressinge the Childe   v d.
for our banquett at midsomer eve   vij s.
a pottle of sack & a pottle of Clarrett   iij s.
To the musick   iij s. 4d
ffor stronge beare   xij d.   5
ffor loane of ahatt   vj d.

...

Cordwainers and Shoemakers' Records
CCA: Account Book III G/8/4   10
f 39 *(11 November)*

...

more geven vnto Roberte kellye for musicke at Iacob Carters
dynner   ij s
more paide to hym for musicke at Stewarde Tottyes the same 15
nighte   ij s

...

paide for musicke at Stewarde morgans howse   ij s

...
    20

f 39v

...

payde for musicke. at mr Inces. when willm Locker came into
the companye   ij s

...
    25

Shrouetyde. /   paide for our sixe gleaves at shrovetyde and the berrage to the
gouldsmith   vj s viij d
paid for our musicke at shrove tyde to the waytemen   ij s
paide to george kelly & his Companye for our musicke at mr
Inces. the same tyme   iij s 30
paid at mr Inces after. our Drinkinge one the Thursdaye at an
over plushe   vj s
paid the same tyme for one pottell of seacke   ij s

...
    35

f 40

...

Mydsomer Charge 1621

+paid: for orrenges and cheese   vj s 40
+paide for apples   *(blank)*
paid for apynte of wine at the dressinge of the boye   iij d

paide for the Loone of Ahatt for our boye   vj d.

paid for his gloves   viij d.

paid for his stockinges   ij s.

paid for one dozin silke poyntes   xvj d.

paid for silk Reben for shooe tyes   vj d

paid for his shooes   xviij d

paid for Reben for his horse   vj d

paid to thrie men that Attended the boye   xviij d

paid ∧ ˙to˙ [for] the man that brought the horse & did dresse hym

      xviij d

paid the Crier at the barrs   vj d

Geven to olde sidall   iiij d

Geven to Ablynd boye   ij d

Geven to the prisoners at the Castell and Northgate   ij s

paid for our musicke   v s

paid for .3. quartes seacke   iij s

paid at an over plushe at our banquiett·one midsomer even xviij s

...

Geven vnto the 3. men [yat men] that tended the horse. beinge
verye vnruly at the barrs to drinke   vj d

f 41

...

Spent one. the Companye. at the barres one midsomer even at
Iohnsons   xij d

...

Beerbrewers' Records CCA: Company Book G 3/2
ff 55-5v *(23 November)*

...

<table>
<tr><td>midsomer
accomptes</td><td>ffirst paid for a payer of shoes for the Child</td><td>xxij d</td></tr>
<tr><td></td><td>Item paid for a payer of stockinges for the Child</td><td>xxij d</td></tr>
<tr><td></td><td>Item paid for a payer of gloues for the Child</td><td>xiiij d</td></tr>
<tr><td></td><td>Item spent at the dressing of the Child</td><td>ij s</td></tr>
<tr><td></td><td>Item [geuen] spent in prouiding of a horse for the Child. to
rid vpon</td><td>xviij d</td></tr>
<tr><td></td><td>Item geuen to three men that led the horse</td><td>ij s.</td></tr>
<tr><td></td><td>Item paid for prunes Comfettes apples & other thinges</td><td>xx d</td></tr>
<tr><td></td><td>Item paid for bread and Cheese</td><td>vj s</td></tr>
<tr><td></td><td>Item paid for beare</td><td>v s.</td></tr>
<tr><td></td><td>Item paid for wine</td><td>ij s vj d</td></tr>
<tr><td></td><td>Item geven to the mvsitioners</td><td>vj s</td></tr>
</table>

Item paid for a Salmon more then iij s iiij d which the drawers
in dee allowe   ij s viij d |
Item geuen to the Cryer at the barres   iiij d
Item geven to Siddall   ij d
Item geven to the prisoners at the Castell   vj d   5
Item to the prisoners at the northgate   vj d
Item geuen to mr holmes for keping the banner   xij d
Item geuen to mr holmes for dressing the staffe   xij d.

...
                                                                     10

Coopers' Records C: Company Book II
f 21 *(13 January)*

...

Inprimis .payde: at: the greene dragon at Robert martens dynner
the 13th Ianuarye 1620 for one pottell whit wine and one   15
pottell Clarett   ij s viij d
paide the same tyme to george kellye and his Companye for
Musicke   iij s iiij d

...
                                                                     20

f 21v
                    Midsomer Charges 1621

payde for the boyes stockinges shoe tyes and poyntes   ij s iiij d
paide for his gloves   xij d   25
payde for his shooes   xx d
paide for two payer of gloves for the two men   xij d
paide for Cheese   ij s
paide for bread   xviij d
paide for halfe abarill beere   iiij s   30
paide for prvnes & nottes & suger & Sinamon   x d
paide for apples   vj d
paide for two quartes wine   xij d
paid for ale at the barres for the Companye   iiij d
paide to the Crier at barrs   iiij d   35
paide at Castell & northgate to the prisoners   x d
paid to olde sidall & the blinde boye   iiij d
paide for our musicke   xviij d

...

paide for Gune powder and match for our men at Midsomer   40
                                                       iiij s iij d
paid to the syxe men that did Carrie our Armour   ij s

paid to the Cuttler for Cleaninge our Armor   iiij d

...

paide vnto Nicholas hullwood for dressinge of our flagg staffe

     xij d

Joiners, Carvers, and Turners' Records
CCA: Company Book G14/1
f 104 *(25 March)*

...

Disbursements   1

...

Item for a hatt for the Child that did Ride for the Company on
Midsomer Eve   iij s viij d
Item paid for a paire of stockinges for the Child ˈand gartersˈ

     xviij d   1

Item paid for gloues and for Ribbonninge   xviij d
Item paid for a paire of shooes for the Childe   xviij d
Item giuen to the Cryer at the Barrs   iiij d
Item given to the prisoners at the Castle and Northgate   viij d
Item given to Sibdall a poore man   ij d   2(
Item paid for starchinge a Cloth to Couer the Saddle   ij d
Item spent in wyne at the dressinge of the Childe   vj d
Item paid to three men to Attend the Child   xij d
Item paid vnto the Musicke   xviij d
Item paid for a Pyke for the staffe   ij d   2!

...

Item paid for the dinners of xxix[en] persons the xxvij[th] of
Nouember at ix d a peece   xxj s ix d

...

Item giuen to the Musicke the same tyme   iij s iiij d   3(

...

A   *Mayors List 5* BL: Harley 2125
f 53v* *(1 May) William Gamull*

   3!

[merrye maye
day.]
A pleasante shoe sett out vpon [maye daye morninge] ˑˈmunday
in witson weekˈˑ of younge men Cittizins. Sett out by mr
ffraunc*es* Gamull & [on Thomas Gamull: brethiers children]
ˑˈRandle holmeˈˑ[beinge two ⟨...⟩ God blesse them bauth] ˑˌ&
others of bridstreet.ˑ   4(

36-p 337, l 3 / *cancellations and interlineations by RH II*

merrye St Iames   An other shew sett out vpon St Iames daye by the Cittizins
day.   ·´of forgat street`·verye pleasant to the behoulders & proffytt
                    to the Cittye be reason manye Cuntree people Came in to see it

                    ...
                                                                                    5

Mercers, Ironmongers, Grocers, and Apothecaries' Records
C: Company Book
p 119 *(4 May)*

...

payde. for our boye at midsomer watch for one payer hoose one   10
payer shooes. and one payer of gloves and one payer of garters
                                                                vj s
payde for 3. men attendinge the boye   iij s
payde for 3. payer of gloves for the 3. men   xxij d
payde for musicke   vj s viij d   15
payde to the prisoners of the Castell and northgate   iiij s
payde to lame Siddall. and the blynde boye that played one
Adrome   xij d
Spente at Rauffe wilsons howse at the barres vpon the Companye
                                                               xij d   20
payde to the Cryer at the barres   xij d
payde. for Carnation Rybyne silke for the horse   xij d

...

pp 120-1   25
payde for halfe a barill of beere at our banquiett at mydsomer
                                                               iiij s
payde for iij li. Comffettes   v s
payde for Suger plates and marmilate   ij s viij d
payde for j C allnottes   iij d   30
payde for orrenges and Lemons   x d
payde for one dozin prvines   ij s
payde for Cakes   ij s
paide for j li. suger 16d and for Cloves & mace iij d   xix d [.]
payde for 2. ounces Synamon   viij d   35
paide for one pottell Seacke and one pottell Clarrett wine   iij s
paide for iiij C wafers   ij s

...

payde for one ell quarter and a nayle mixte taffita at 15.s per
ell   xix s vij d   40
Item ij dossen and two yardes of sylke & silver Lace at iij s vj d
per dozin   viij s viij d

more one quarter halfe q*uarte*r of soinge sylke at   xj d
more one q*uarte*r ell Canvas at   v d
more one yarde Ieane fustian at   xj d
more iij neyles powldauie at   ij d
...
payde for makinge the gowne   iiij s
payde for the berrage   iij d |
more in hookes and eyes   ij d
more halfe A dozin of bone   ix d
more one payer of wollen hoose   xx d   1
more two yarde 6d Ribine at   x d
more halfe Ayarde silke Ribine   v d
more two yardes and halfe of fine 6d Ribine at   xiij d
more one yarde and halfe 2d ferrett Riben   iij d
payde for gloves   ij s   1
more .4. yardes 2d Ribine   viij d
more 3. yardes 2d Ribine   vj d
...
payde for one payer shooes   xx d
payde for 3. payer of Gloves for 3. men   xviij d   2●
...

1621-2

Drawers of Dee's Records CCA: Company Book G10/1
p 50 *(30 June)*   2●

...

geuen to the bearebruers   x s

...

AC   *Plans for a Show* BL: Harley 2057   3●
f 36* *(1 August)*

The order of our Showe

ferst 2 woodmen with &c. /   35●
St. George fighting with ye dragon &c. /
[E⟨...⟩y] °'tyme'° et [vices] °'fame'° the leaders of ye 9 wortheys
[men then speake] °.then Eternity. °°faling at variance°
The 9 wortheys in Compleat Armor with Crownes of gould on
there heads, euery on hauing his esq*uire* to beare before him his   40●
sheild and penon of Armes, dressed according as there lords
where accostomed to be; 3 Issaralit*es*, 3 Infidels, 3 Christians &c. /

After theme fame to declare the rare vertues and noble deedes
of the 9 worthye women. /
The 9 worthy women euery one adorned after there Cuntrey
fashion, each one hauing her page before her bearing there
Armes. &c. /   5
next the 4 vertues sitting on a mount in the 4 Corners therof.
a height aboue them the 3 graces in treangle wise
on the top of the mount shall stand Eternity ther speaker, this
mount being a pagient for Visus, because it delites [your yrs]
the eyes. &c. /   10
After them Lingua, because shee could not be permitted to make
the 5 scences 6 is fittest to be ther speaker, /
1 seeinge, hauing her pagiant bfor her. &c. /
2 smelling, adorned with flowers, before whome shall be led tow
   bloodhounds &c. /   15
3 hearing, before whom shall goe musick Incident thervnto. &c. /
4 Tastinge with a Cornucopia of frute in her hand, before whom
   shall ride an Ape on horse backe eating of Apples &c.
5 Touching. before whom shall be borne a torteaux. &c. /
After them 4 seasons of ye yeare   20
Tyme there speaker. /
1 ver in a greene gowne. after whom shall follow fawckners with
   hawckes on there fistes leadinge there spaniels, &c. and huntsmen
   with hares on there staues there hownds following them. &c. /
2 oestas in a yellow gowne adowened with Flowers after whom   25
   shalbe drawne a cart with hay corne frute and flowers with other
   thinges apertayning to the season. &c. /
3 Autum in a tawny gowne with faded leaues after whom shall
   be drawne, ferst a plowe then a man soing otes after him the
   harrow   30
4 Hyrms in a furd gowne a furd cap houlding his handes ouer a
   Chafindish of fier, with men after him dressed according to the
   season &c. /

all the showe aboue saide to ryde on white and red horses. /   35

The soulders each man with a white Iacket, ₍˄˒St Georges [chros]
crose on ther' red breeches, white stockens red garters with each
thing compleat. & ⟨...⟩
                                                                         40
[wee would intreat your worshippes to keepe this note in your
   owne handes lest it bee too Common in the mouthes of our

aduisaryes, which wee would not haue them to know our plot
&c. /]

°this show was Intended to be made vpon the pettion to mr
Recorder but shortley it fell off and nothinge was done therin
aug 1 1621 °

Painters, Glaziers, Embroiderers, and Stationers' Records
C: Account Book II
p 3 *(18 October)*

...

payd for the Childs hose	xv d
payd for showes	xviij d
payd for Ribands for showtyes	vj d
giuen for berradge to the Childes Clothes	iiij d
spent at the dressinge of the Child	iij d
payd for Ribands for the horse head	vj d
payd for tape for the eschochions	j d
giuen at the barres, Castell and northgate	xij d
giuen 3 men for Carringe of the banners	xviij d
giuen to him that led the horse	vj d
giuen to the man that tended the Child	xij d
giuen to the minstrell	xij d
payd for drinke for the Company and there men	ij s vj d
giuen in berradge for the garland and Phenix	xij d
payd for gloues for the Aldermen and Stuards	iij s iiij d
payd for gloues for the Child	xij d
payde for socket*es* for the [pa]pikes	xviij d
payd for layinge of 12 pikes in coler	xij d

...

Cordwainers and Shoemakers' Records
CCA' Account Book III G/8/4
f 47 *(11 November)*

...

more giuen to Roberte kellye in handbridg at Stewarde Iensons howse	ij s

...

more paid to Roberte kelly at Stewarde Lynialls howse	ij s

...

3-5 / *additions in RH II's hand*

f 47v

...

Shrovetyde /

payde for our sixe silver gleeves	vj s	5
payde for the berrage of them	xvij d	
payde to the waytemen	ij s	
payde to Roberte kellye	ij s vj d	
Spente at An overplush at mr Inces after our drinkinge one the.		
Thursdaye	xj s	10

...

f 48

x Midsomer Charge x

15

payde for sylke poyntes for the boye	xij d	
payde for wine at the dressinge of our boye	xij d	
payde for the boyes stockinges	xviij d	
payde for his shooes	ij s vj d	
payde for sylke Rebyne. for the boye & horse head	xv d	20
payde for his gloves	vj d	
payde vnto the thre men thatt attended	xviij d	
Spente vpon the Companye without the barres	ij s ij d	
more geven to the. Cryer at barrs	vj d	
more geven to apoore blynde boy	ij d	25
more geven at the Castell & northgate	ij s	
payde for one pottell seacke	ij s	
payde for our musicke	iiij s	
payde to mr hoolmes for keepinge the banner	xij d	
more for mendinge the iron of it	ij d	30
more bestowed vpon mr. Inces. maydes	xij d	
payde at an overplushe [at mr. Inces] at our banquitt ˈone		
midˈ	xx s	

...

35

Beerbrewers' Records CCA' Company Book G 3/2
f 59 *(23 November)*

...

paid for the Childes shoes	xvj d	
paid for a payer of hose for him	xx d.	40
paid for a payer of gloues for him	xvj d.	
spent at dressing the Child	ij s.	

midsomer charges.

spent in providing a horse for the Child	xviij d.
geuen to iij^e men to lead the Childes horse	ij s.
paid for prunes Comfettes apples & other thinges	xx d.
paid for bread and Cheese	vj s.
paid for half a barrell of the best beere	[viij s] vj s viij d 5
[half a barrel of smale beare	ij s vij d]
paid for wyne	ij s viij d
geuen to the musicioner	iij s [vj d]
geuen to the Cryer at the barres	iiij d
geuen to the Castell and to the northgate	xij d 10
paid for keping the banner	xij d.

...

f 59v

...   15

payd to the Stewardes of the drawers in dee for a Samon at
mydsomer watch for this Companie to theire banquett   vij s vj d.
...

Coopers' Records C: Company Book II   20
ff 25-5v *(13 January)*
...

Midsomer Charges 1622.

Inprimis payde to two picke men	xij d 25
more payde to foure men beinge musketers	ij s
more payde for powder and match	iiij s iiij d
more. payde for the loone of 2. payer of bandeleries of widdow	
locker	vj d
more payde for the lone of 2. pickes	iiij d 30
payde for drinke at the barrs vpon the Companye	xij d
more payde to the Cryer, Castell and northgate	xiiij d
more geven to apoore blynde boy	ij d |
payde for the boyes shooes	xx d
payde for his stockinges	ij s 35
payde for his gloves	xij d
payde for musicke	xviij d
payde for 2. payers gloves for the 2. men	ix d
payde for the loone of Ahatt for the boye	xij d
payde for apayer of gloves bestowed vpon willm pew Ioyner	xiiij d 40
payde for bere at our Alderman mr lynakers howse	vj d
payde for strong bere for our banquiett	iiij s

payde for bread	ij s
payde for Cheese	ij s vij d
payde for prvines suger synamond Corrant*es*	xiiij d
payde for Nuttes and aples	x d
payde for one pottell of wine	xvj d

...

A *Mayors List 5* BL: Harley 2125
f 54* *(Shrove Tuesday) Robert Whitehead*

...

on shroftusday diuers braue horses runing for the bell on Io
blanchard of chester bruer tould he would fach his mare out of
his trow & beat them all & laye wagers out w*hi*ch he p*er*formed
& won the bell & had his mare in such account as he had a great
price of her

...

Joiners, Carvers, and Turners' Records
CCA: Company Book G 14/1
f 105v *(25 March)*

...

Disbursments

...

Item spent in providinge a Child to Ride for the Companie on Midsomer Eve	iij d
Item paid for a paire of shooes for the Child	xiiij d
Item paid for stockings and garters	ij s ij d
Item paid for gloves	x d
Item paid for Musicke	ij s
Item paid to three men to Attend the boy	xij d
Item paid for dressinge the horse that the Child did ride vpon	iij d
Item paid for paintinge the staffe	xij d
Item spent at the borrowinge of a hatt	ij d
Item given to the Cryer at the Barrs, and to the prisoners at the Castle and Norgate	xij d
Item given vnto Sibdall a poore man	ij d
Item spent in wyne at the dressinge of the Child	viij d
Item spent in Beere vpon Midsomer Eve in severall places	vij d

...

Item spent vpon the Child after the watch and vpon those that did Attend him	xviij d

...

Mercers, Ironmongers, Grocers, and Apothecaries' Records
C: Company Book
pp 127-8 *(6 May)*

...

payde for 3. paiere of mens gloves . which did attend the Ladye
at the watch   ij s
paide the 3. men for theire paines   iij s
payde for one paier of Gloves for the girle   xvj d
payde for one paier of shoes and apaier of hoose for her   ij s x d
payde for Ribine for shoe tyes and for the horse head. 2 yardes   1?
                                                                   xij d
payde for silke Rybine. more for her dressinge   iiij d
payde vnto Sir Henrye Bumberies man for dressinge and Leadinge
the horse   ij s vj d
more spente in Raph willsons at the barres   ij s   1?
payde the Cryer at barres   xij d
Geven vnto the prisoners at Castell and at the Northgate   iiij s
Geven to apoore blynde boye that drumed   vj d
payde to the musitions   vj s viij d
payde for halfe abarill of beere to Iohn brookes for our banquit   2?
                                                                  viiij d
payde for wallnuttes orrenges and Lemons   xiiij d
payde for Cakes and wafers   iiij s
payde for 2 li. Comffittes   iij s iiij d
payde for .4 quarter 4t of Conceites   x d ob.   25?
payde for 12 li. prunes   iij s
payde for .j li. 6. ounces of marmelat at 20d per li.   ij s iij d ob.
payde for j li. Suger   xvj d
paide for .2. ounces of Sinamond at   viij d
payde for Comffettes. and Conceites more   xx d | 30?
payde for one pottell of seacke and one pottell of Clarett wine
                                                              iij s iiij d
payde for one paier of bootes for the boye   iiij s vj d
paide for 3. mens gloves and wages   v s
paide for Rybbine for the horse head & dressinge   xij d   35
payde for apayer of gloves for the boye   ij s
...

Joiners, Carvers, and Turners' Records CCA: Minute Book G14/2
p 49 *(21 May)*   40
...

It is agreed that the stewards shall provide a Child to Ride for

the Company on Midsomer Eve in such Manner as heretofore
[they] hath bene accustomed and that at the same tyme they
shall provide a Banquett for the Companie as formerlie hath
bene vsed

...   5

1622-3
Drawers of Dee's Records CCA: Company Book G10/1
p 51* *(30 June)*
                                                                         10
...

geuen to the bearebruers for a salmon & for dressinge the Child
                                                                  x s

...

p 52   15

...

geuen to the bearebruers   x s

...

Painters, Glaziers, Embroiderers, and Stationers' Records   20
C: Account Book II
p 5 *(18 October)*

...

payd vpon Midsomer eue for all thinges concerning the boy
horse and Musick   xj s iiij d   25
spent at dressing the Child   vj d
payd for gloues for the Aldermen and Stewards   iij s iiij d
payd to the barres Castell and Northgate   xij d
Spent at the Stuards after the wache on midsomer eve   ij s vj d
for 4 silken banners for the speares and gilding 6 phoenixes   ij s   30
for 4 new Scockets for the speares   xv d

...

payd for Cullering the pickes   x d
...
                                                                         35

Treasurers' Account Rolls CCA: TAR/3/42
mb 2 *(November)*

...

Item paid to mr Richard Bennett draper for ten yardes & ahalf
grove cullour brode cloth to make the waytemen gownes at   40
Seaven and eight pence the yarde   iiij li. vj d

...

Item paide to the Stewardes of the Sadlers towardes their Bell
at Shrovetyde   vj s. viij d

...

Item paide vnto Guest the drummer on Shrove tewsday   xij d.
Item paide vnto henry Barton a Carpenter for takeinge downe
the pales at Roodee on Shrovetewsday and for settinge of them
vp and Nailes   xij d

...

mb 3   1

...

Item paide to Nicholas halwoodde and Robert Thorneley for
payntinge and Trymeinge of the Giantes and beastes and the
other thinges against midsomer Eve   xliij s. iiij d.

...   1

Item paid to Thomas prickett for makeing the new antient for
the Cittie   viij s.
Item paide mr Christopher Blease for ix elnes of Taffeta
Sercenett at vij s iiij d the ell, one yarde and ahalf of Crymson
and white Taffeta, Two ounces of Silke one yard and ahalf of   2
None so prettir / to make a new Auntient   iiij li. x s xj d.
Item paide ^'mr' Randull holme for his payntinge guildinge and
tryminge the Auntient with gold & Coullors   xij s.

...

Item paid to Nicholas hallwood and Robert Thorneleye for   2
payntinge and settinge forth of the maiors mounte

                                                    xxvj s. viij d.

...

Item paid Thomas wealche Cooper for his paynes to beare the
Citties Auntient on midsomer Eve   ij s. vj d   3

...

Cordwainers and Shoemakers' Records
CCA: Account Book III G/8/4   3
f 54 *(11 November)*

...

more payde vnto Roberte kellye for musicke   ij s

...

21 / None *italicized in MS*

f 55

payde for our Sixe gleaves vj s. and for berrage xviij d some is

                                                                  vij s vj d

...

more spent. in speakinge for A dynner at mr. Inces for the

Companye one Thursday at shrovetyde   vj d

Spente at mr Throppes howse after the horse Race in bere   vj d

payde to the wayte men and to Roberte kellye for musicke. at

shrove tyde   iiij s vj d

payde at an over plushe at shrovetyde at our ffishe dynner   vj s

payde for one quarte of seacke after the drinkinge at Randall.

Inces   xij d

...

f 55v

midsom*er*
Charge   paid to mr hoolmes for keepinge our baner   xij d

...

f 56

paide for one yarde of sylke Ryben   vj d

payde. for beere *with*out the barres   iij s ij d

payde to the Cryer at barres   vj d

paide to the prisoners at Castell and northgate   vj s

payde for three quartes of seacke at our banquitt   iij s

paide for the lone of A sadell for our boye   v d

paide for the loone of Ahat and feather for the boye   vj d

payde for his gloves   x d

paide for his stockinges and poyntes   ij s vj d

payde at the dressinge of the boye   xij d

Spente at mr Inces one the even at the Call of the book   xviij d

paide for two yardes sylke Rebyn for the horse   xij d

paid for the boyes shooes   xvj d

paide for our musicke   iiij s

paid to the man that did leade the horse   xviij d

paid to hym that Caried the banner   vj d

paid to one. other man that helde the boye   vj d

more Spent *with* mr Ince. one the Companyes busynesse   vij d

more Spente at an overplushe after our banquitt one midsomer

even   xx s

...

Beerbrewers' Records CCA: Company Book G 3 /2
ff 67-7v *(23 November)*

Midsomer Charges

Geven vnto Thomas Gillam at the Request of Sir Thomas Smith
knight then mayor ˄ˎbut the companie not to be bound thereby
hereafterˎ   v s.
payde for a payer of stockinges, and a payer of Shooes for our
boye   iiij s |
payde for a payer of gloves. for hym   xx d   1
Spente at the dressinge of the boye   ij s
more spente in provydinge, and in goeinge, to gett a goulde
cheane and other thinges to furnish our boye   ij s
payde vnto them that did attende the horse   viij d
payde for prvines Comfeattes, apples Lemons oringes and other   1
® xx d.   banqueitinge stuffe   iiij s
payde for Cheese Cakes and breade   vj s
® 8s.   payde for halfe a barill of march beere   x s
payde for wine at our banquett   iiij s viij d
payde the musicioners for musicke   vj s   2
payde for Lambe in steade of A Salmon which we shoulde a
had at our banquett   iij s iiij d
Geven vnto the Cryer at the barres   iiij d
Geven at the Castell and northgate   xij d
paide vnto mr Hoolmes for keepinge our banner   xij d   2
payde for mendinge the Iron of our banner which was broken
                                                            iiij d
...

Dean and Chapter CC: Treasurers' Accounts IV   3
p 146 *(Christmas)*
...
Item to a Watchman at Chrestmas   ij s vj d
...
                                                                    35
Coopers' Records C: Company Book II
ff 29v-30 *(13 January)*
...
Mydsomer Charge
Inprimis paide for stronge beere   v s   4

16, 18 / *the scribe has underlined the original sum and placed a new one in the right-
hand margin*

payde for Cheese   ij s vj d
paide for apples   ix d
paide for prvines   ix d
payde for Synamon and suger   ix d
paide for the boyes hoose and shooes   iij s viij d   5
paide for his gloves   xij d
payde for two payer of gloves for the two men   viij d
payde. for iij li powder and match at 14d p*er* li. is   iij s x d
payde for breade   ij s
payde for one quarte seacke & j quarte Clarrett   xx d.   10
payde & spente at the barres   xviij d
more geven the Cryer at barres   iiij d
payde & geven to the prisoners at Castell and northgate   x d
more geven vnto Richarde Clerke   iiij d
more spente at the dressinge of the boye   iiij d   15
payd to the 4 shott men and. 2 pickemen   iij s
paide for our musicke   xviij d |
more payde for. 2 payer of gloves for willm pew and will*i*am
Catherall Ioyners   xij d
payde for the loone of a picke and gorgett   iij d   20
...

Joiners, Carvers, and Turners' Records
CCA: Company Book G 14/1
f 108 *(25 March)*   25
...
                              Disbursments
...
Item for a hatt for the Child that did Ride for the Companie on
Midsomer Eve   iiij s   30
Item for a paire of stockings and garters for the Child   xix d
Item for a paire of Shooes for the Child   xvj d
Item paid for Ribbon for the horse head and for shooe tyes   x d
Item for one dozen of silke poynts and one paire of gloues for
the Child   x d   35
Item given vnto three men to Attend the Child   xij d
Item paid for wyne at the dressinge of the Child   viij d
Item paid for wyne at the Banquett   xvj d
Item given to the Cryer at the Barrs   iiij d
Item given to the prisoners at the Castle and Northgate   viij d   40
Item given to the Musicke   xviij d
Item given vnto a blynd boy   ij d

Item spent at Alderman Salisburie on Midsomer Eve   xij d
...

Mercers, Ironmongers, Grocers, and Apothecaries' Records
C: Company Book
p 135 *(2 May)*

...

Item paid for apair of gloues for the boy   00-01-08
Item 3 pair of gloues for 3 men that did attend him   00-02-00
Item paid for apair shewes j pair garter and a pair stockings for   1
ye boy   00-05-00
Item paid for the lone of a hat for him   00-01-00
Item ij l. ½ of Comfittes at 18d per l.   00-03-09
Item in Conseates 14d ¼ li. with sucket and ¼ l. dry 20d all
          00-02-10   1
Item in orringes and lemonees 10d wafers & cakes 4s all 00-04-10
Item xij li. prues 3s li. ¾ of marmelat 18d per li. 21s 7d ½ als
          00-05-07½
Item shuger j li. ¼ 18d senanent 2 oz 8d all   00-02-02
Item paid Iohn Blanchard for halfe abarrel of Beare   00-10-00   2
Ribin for the horse hed and tayle and for the boyes shewes
          00-01-04
Item paid 3 men to attend the boy 3s and to a man for dressing
the horse 14d all   00-04-02
Item to the musicke   00-06-08   2
Item to the presoners at northgate & Castle iiij s to the Cryer 12d
          00-05-00
Item spent at Raph Wilsons   00-02-00
Item 2 yardes 2d Ribin to tye the Iewe⟨.⟩ 4d to apoor man 3d
          00-00-07   3
...

Item 3 quartes sack and j pottl Claret: to the bancket   00-04-04
Item for aples & strawberyes   00-00-08
...

          3

Joiners, Carvers, and Turners' Records CCA: Minute Book G 14/2
p 55 *(11 June)*

...

All the Companie now present have Agreed that the stewards
shall provide a Banquett for the Companie vpon Midsomer Eve,   4
and the Companie to Contribute therevnto accordinge to Ancient
Custome

A *Rogers' Breviary* BL: Harley 1948
f 18*

A Breuarye or some Collectiones of the most anchant & famous
Cittie of Chester, Collected by the Reuerend: mr Robert Rogers.   5
Batchlor in Diuinitye Archdeacon of Chester, and Prebunde in
the Cathedrall Church of Chester, ͦͺ˙& parson of Gawsworth˙͗ͦ
written by his sonne Dauid Rogers, and reduced into these
Chapters followeinge,
...   10

f 58
                Now of the lawdable exercises and playes
                of Chester, yerelye there vsed:
...   15

(After the account of the homage to the Drapers [collated with
CCA: unnumbered MS, see pp 234-8] and the proclamations for
the Shrovetide festivities [collated with CRO: DCC 19, see pp
320-2] Harley 1948 continues:)
                                                                     20

ff 60v-4v
...
This is performed yearely on shrouetuesday, And the drapers
haueinge the homages done to them, they haue also the forfectures
if any neclect the same, as many presidentes, and yerely recoueryes   25
of them that performe not this homage: yea ye drapers haue
very anchant recoueries againste diuers that stoode in lawe with
that worshipfull Company of drapers, which Custom cannot be
Infringed:
    The Custom of the said drapers anchantly was after the balls   30
offered by the shooemakers & sadlers, and ye footeball playe
ended, to meete togeather, and to make them drinke, all 3.
companies togeather in token of societie [to] ˄ˈatˈ the charges of
the drapers:
    But as the alteration is more comendable, so the Charges to   35
the drapers is now agreate deale more Chargeible, for now the
said worshipfull Companye | of drapers, doe on the same
Shrouetuesdaye (in stid of one drinkinge togeather) after the
games be ended, feaste the mayor and aldermen in the Comon
hall, with the said 2. Companies of Shooemakers and sadlers,   40

7 / ͦͺ˙& ... Gawsworth˙͗ *in RH II's hand*

with bread and beere, & soe likewise on wenseday & thurseday
followinge all which is 3 dayes, which is indeede to the greate
Charge of the said worshipfull Companye of draperrs:

The Sheriffes Breakfast
on monday in Ester weeke

Beinge a moste anchant Custome, there, on the said monday in
Ester weeke the 2. sherifes of ye Cittie to shoote for abreakefast
or dinner, of Calues heades & Bacon, the mayor Recorder &   1
Aldermen takeinge parte with on sheriffe or the other, and all
other gentlemen yeomen, or good fellowes, yat will there shoote
on either side beinge chosen, doe shote there 3 shootes, beinge
bettered still by the winers side which 3 shootes beinge so won,
they all take parte togeather of the same diner or breakefast, the   1
winners side payeinge, ij d apiece and the lossers side 4d apiece,
the origenall whereof, no mans memorie can remember, of which
anchant custome the time beinge very fittinge, the game beinge
moste lawfull, and the ende beinge the comforte societie and
recreation of the Cittizens it deserues not onlye great praise   2
and commendation but also perpetuall Continuance and
manteynance: |

The watches of the mayor &
Sheriffes at Christmas yerely vsed   2

Of which thoe mans memorie cannot remember the origenall, yet
the Collections of writers, doe shew the cause thereof: The time
of the begininge to be in the dayes of (William) the Conqueror,
who driueinge the ould Brittons or as is verylye ˏ'thoughte' the   3
walshe men who did here inhabitt, mixed with the ould saxons
seinge the Normans to haue gotten, the possession of this land
and had procured som rest & setled themselues in this Cittie
in peace, by force of conquest, at a season in the Cristmas when
all men giue themselues to securitie, The Walshmen neere   3
neighbors grudgeinge at theire securitie and possession, of theire
lande, (As late example we had of the Irishe, in london dery in
Ireland, and of later time about anno .1620. of the plantation
of the Englishe in Virginia) they walshe men came in the nighte
time and made a sudden Inuasion, and spoyled and burned som   4
parte of this Cittie, wherevpon the Conqueror gaue landes, with
the concente of Hugh Lupe his sisters son & Earle of Chester, to
diuers who should watche & warde and be readye to defende the

Cittie by any seruice, at all times, the which landes are come to
the possessions of diuers honorable, & worshipfull persons, &
others, which now is called the Gable rente at which time of
Cristmas allwayes after, they vsed to sett the said tennantes with
all theire forces | accordinglye to watch at that season, to   5
preuente ye like danger, of the walshmen, The which seruice is
required, and the houlders of those landes ˄ᶜand᾿ doe theire
homage before ye mayor & sheriffes at theire watchcourtes at
Christmas yearelye to this daye, with other seruices proper
to that tenure only when they are required or commanded,   10
This was the origenall the cause and the continuance of this
Custome:

The vse now:
of ye watches,

    The vse now yat is made thereof is, to preserue the seruice
of the anchant tenure, And to cause there apparance before
them, there to watch 3 nightes togeather, with [⟨.⟩] most stronge   15
& well appoynted armore, not fearinge ˄ᶜnot᾿ now the Inuasion
of forraigne or Ciuill enemye, by reason of the perfecte and longe
blessed peace we haue enioyed, from God and our gratious
Princes, and kinges precedent, But now We vse the same, as to
keape the Cittie from danger of fire, theues, dronknes and   20
vncueete mettinges, & drinkeinges in the nightes which mighte
be causes of perturbation of peace, and sin againste God, which
to these times and moste Incidente, this is the cause of the
Continuance thereof now: And after the Courte of theire
apparance of the tennantes aforesaid, and the watch there   25
ordered, and giuen, by the Mayor or sheriffes the 3. firste [⟨.⟩]
nightes in Christmas, The mayor Aldermen and shereffes, doe all
goe togeather to the howses of the mayor & sheriffes as theire
nighte | is in course, and doe there banquet togeather, in Ioy as
the time requires, not only for the birth of our blessed redemer,   30
but also for, rememborance of gods greate mercie, in gramtinge
vs peace, and plentie, but also, these gratious meanes to preserue
our peace and quiet, both of our soules, howses, goods and
persons, which is in my opinion a moste meete honeste and
comendable thinge: whereat if anye repine, because there may be   35
sin, I say he ˄ᶜor they᾿ muste goe vp to heauen for perfection,
for vpon this earth it is not to be founde:

         Of the showe at midsomer in Chester:
                                                                                   40

The begiinge thereof beinge. vncertayne, but it is more anchante

---

31 / gramtinge *for* grauntinge, *minim omitted MS*

then the Whitson playes, which weare played yerely there for
aboue 200 yeares togeather, this midsomer showe, had [in it]
diuers thinges in it which weare ofenciue in anchant times, (as
Christe in stringes) men in womens apparell, with Diuells
attendinge, them, called cuppes & cannes, with a diuell in his
shape ridinge there, which preachers of Gods worde, and worthye
diuines there spake against as vnlawfull and not meete, with
diuers other thinges which are now reformed but for the decensie
of it now vsed, It is thoughte by all both decente fitt and
profitable to the Cittie: | 10

St Georges Race on the
Roode Dee, of late begone

St Georges race
made by mr
Robert Ambrye,
Irnemonger,
somtimes sherife
of Chester it
began: 1609.

In Anno domini :1609: mr William Lester, mercer beinge mayor   15
of Chester, mr Robert Ambrye Irnemonger & somtimes Sheriffe
of this Cittie vpon his owne coste, did cause 3 siluer bells, to be
made of good value, which bells he appoynted to be runne for
with horses on St Georges day vpon the Roode Dee, from the
newtower to the netes, & there torninge to runne vp to the   20
watergate, that horse which came first there to haue the best
bell, & the second to haue the second bell, for that yere puttinge
in money [and] for to rune, & shuerties to deliuer in the bells
yat day twelue month, and the winers had the money put in by
those horses that runne, and the vse of the bells, The other bell 25
was appoynted to be rune for the same day at the ringe, vpon the
like conditions, This was the firste begininge of St Georges race,
to which charges, it is sayd mr Ambrye had som allowance from

St Georges race
altered 1623 by
mr Iohn Brereton
then mayor of
Chester:

the Cittie: This continued vntill the yere 1623: In which yeare
mr Iohn Brereton ⸰ ⸢a worthie famous Cittizen of Chester⸣⸰ then   30
mayor of Chester, altered the said race, to runne from ⸢behonde⸣
the Newtower, & so rownd about the Roode Dee, And the bell
to be agreater value and afree bell, to haue it freely foreuer that
shall winne the same, to which he gaue liberallye, & caused the
oulde bells with more money to be put |out in vse the which   35
vse shoulde make the free bell yerely foreuer, There to be runne
for on the said St Georges day foreuer, This I heare to be the new
alteration the which if by reporte I [cr] erre I craue pardon &
desire it maye be truly corected, |

30 / ⸰⸢a ... Chester⸣⸰ *in RH II's hand*

Now of the playes of Chester
Called the whitson playes:

The author of
them:

The matter of
them:

The first time
played:

The players &
charges thereof:

The manner of
them:

The places where
ye played them:

The maker and first Inuenter of them was one Rondoll a monke
in the Abbaye of Chester whoe did transelate the same, into   5
Englishe, & made them into partes and pagiantes, as they then
weare played: The matter of them was the historye of the bible,
mixed with some other matter: The time they weare firste sett
forthe, and played was in an*n*o :1339: S*i*r Iohn ˏ⸌Arnewaye⸍
beinge mayor of Chester: The actors and players, weare the   10
occupations & Companies of this Cittie, the Charges and costes
ˏ⸌thereof⸍ w*hi*ch weare greate, was theires also: The time of the
yeare they weare played was on monday, tuesday & wenseday in
whitson weeke: The maner of these playes weare, euery Company
had his pagiant or p*ar*te w*hi*ch pagiants, weare a high scafolde   15
with 2. rowmes ahiger & alower, vpon 4 wheeles In the lower
they apparelled them selues, And In the higher rowme they
played beinge all open on the tope that all behoulders mighte
heare & see them,: The places where the played them was in
euery streete, They begane first at the Abay gates, and when the   20
firste pagiante was played, it was wheeled to the | highe Crosse
before the mayor, and so to euery streete, and soe euery streete
had a pagiant playinge before them at one time tell ˏ⸌all⸍ the
pagiantes for the daye appoynted weare played, and when one
pagiant was neere ended worde was broughte from streete to   25
streete that soe the might ˏ⸌come⸍ in place thereof, excedinge
orderlye and all the streetes haue theire pagiantes afore them
all at one time playeinge togeather to se w*hi*ch playes was greate
resorte, and also scafoldes and stages made in the streetes ˏ⸌in⸍
those places where they determined to playe theire pagiantes: 30

(The list of companies and their parts follow.)
...

35

f 67

... the laste time these playes weare played in Chester was an*n*o
do*m*ini :1574: S*i*r Iohn Sauage beinge mayor of Chester Iohn
Allen & william Goodman sheriffes thus in breife of the playes   40
of Chester:

1623-4
Drawers of Dee's Records CCA: Company Book G10/1
p 52 *(30 June)*

...

geuen to the bearebruers   x s

...

Painters, Glaziers, Embroiderers, and Stationers' Records
C: Account Book II
p 7 *(18 October)*

...

Payd for apayre of stockings apayre of showes a payre of gloues
and Showtyes for the child at Midsomer   iiij s. iiij d.
Giuen for gloues for the Aldermen and Stuards   iij s. viij d.
Giuen Thomas williamson Ioyner for Cutting a litle Phœnix   ij s.
ffor a Ryband for the horse head   vj d.
Giuen to the Barrs. Castell. and Northgate   xiiij d.
Spent at dressinge the boy   vj d.
Spent after the wache on Midsomer euen at the Stuard Thomas
Waytes howse   ij s. vj d.
Payd to xij men that carried the pikes   vj s.
ffor leading the horse. carr͜ 'y'inge the banners and garland
                                                     ij s. viij d.
Giuen to the 3 Trompetors.   v s. vj d.
ffor guildinge the litle phœnix. for 3 new banners for the pikes,
and for 4 phœnixes for the mens heads   iij s.

...

Cordwainers and Shoemakers' Records
CCA: Account Book III G/8/4
f 60 *(11 November)*

...

Inprimis payde the xj[th] daye of November 1623 beinge St
martens daye. at an over plush after our dynner   xviij s

...

payde to Roberte kellye for musicke at the same dynner ij s vj d

...

more payde for musicke at Stewarde wrightes howse when the
Companye wente to drinke with hym   ij s vj d

...

f 60v

...

Shroftyde. /

payde. vnto Greiffyth for the sixe gleaves   vj s   5
paide to the berrage   xij d
more payde. after our drinkinge at an overplush the Companye
beinge present   xiij s
more payde the same tyme for one pottell of seacke   ij s
paide to the waytmen   ij s   10
paide to Roberte kellye   ij s vj d

...

                                                                    15

f 61

...

°Stockinges for the Boey   iij s x d
Showties for the Boey   jx d
Poynts for the Boey   ij s ij d° 20

...

f 61v   25
Spent in dressinge the Boey   xij d
Payd for Gloues for the Boey   xiiij d
Payd for Ribben for the Horse   xij d
Payd for the lone of a Hatt   viij d
Payde to Maister Holems for the Banner   xij d   30
Payde to the men that did leade the horse   iij s
Spent at the Barrs   ij s vj d
Giuen to the Crier at the Barrs   vj d
Payd for the lone of a Saddle   vj d
Spent in drinkinge out of our Beare   xvj d   35
Giuen at the Castle   xij d
Giuen at the Northgate   xij d
Spent ouerplus att our banquet on Midsomar Eue   viij d
ffor a Pottle of sacke   ij s
Payd to Robart Kelley   iiij s   40
[Payd for the boyes shoues   xx d]

...

Beerbrewers' Records CCA: Company Book G 3/2
ff 70v-1 *(November)*

...

Mydsom*er* accomptes and suite.

Inp*r*imis for bread and Cheese at the banquett   iij s viij d
more for prunes Confy*ttes* Synamon, sugar Orringes and apples
    ij s
® 5s   more for halfe a barrell of Stronge beere   viij s
more spent at the dressinge of the boy as form*er*lie hath beene
vsed   ij s.
more at the banquett three pottles of wyne   iij s
more for a pound of Powder at our banquett by the Companies
appoyntm*ent*   xvj d
more paid to the drawers of dee for a Samon   vij s
payd to mr Holmes for the keeping of the banner   xij d
payd for mendinge the banner   [vj d]
payd for a payre of stockinges for the boy   ij s
® 12d   payd for a payre of gloves for the boy   ij s
® 8d   paid for a man to Carrie the banner   xij d
® 5s   payd to the Musition*ers*   vj s |
more for borrowinge of two chaynes, and Ieuels and other
necessaries   ij s

...

more given to the Cryer at the barres   iiij d
given to the prison*ers* at the Castle   vj d
given to the prison*ers* at the Northgate   vj s

...

Coopers' Records C: Company Book II
f 34 *(13 January)*

...

13. Ia 1623   Inprimis payde. at o*ur* william ffishers sheriffe at his howse,
for our dynner after our meetinge vpon the xiij[th] daye of
Ianuarye Anno d*om*ini 1623. for the wholl Companye   xx s

...

payde to Thomas williams for musicke at our dynner   ij s x d
more geven vnto the sayde Thomas Williams for musicke at
margerye phillippes howse   ij s

...

9, 19-21 / *the scribe has underlined the original sum and placed a new one in the right-hand margin*

f 35

The iijth of May 1624

Payd for musicke at mr fisheres at Owen Morris dimer	ij s vj d
payd more for beare	ij s
payd more for wyne	v s vj d

Midsomer Charge

payd for powder and mach	iij s vj d
payd for pruines & other spic	xv d
payd for Chese	ij s ix d
payd for gloues	xv d
payd for stockins for the boye	ij s viij d
payd for appell*es*	viij d
payd for bred	ij s.
payd for beare	v s vj d
payd for ij picke men	viij d
payd for iiij shote	ij s.
payd for Musicke	iiij s
payd at the barres	vj d
payd at the Castell	iiij d
payd at the Northgate	vj d
payd for gloues for the men w*hi*ch did Lead the Child	xvj d
payd for ij C wallnutt*es*	viij d
payd for a pottell of Clarett wyne j quart secke	ij s
payd vnto the man w*hi*ch Lead the horse	xij d
given vnto william Ashton for Lone of the horse	iiij d
given more vnto wayett	j d
Spent at the borroweing of one picke	j d

...

(5 August, the king's holy day)
payd at hireing of the Musicke   iiij d

...

f 35v *(2 November, at a dinner)*

...

payd vnto the Musicke   iij s vj d

...

---

4 / dimer *for* dinner, *minim omitted MS*

(13 January 1625*)
payd for musicke   ij s vj d
...

Joiners, Carvers, and Turners' Records
CCA: Company Book G14/1
ff 110-10v *(25 March)*
...

Disbursements

...

Midsom*er* Eve   Item paid for a hatt for the boy that did Ride for the Companie
on Midsomer Eve   iij s
Item paid for a paire of stockings and garters for him   ij s vj d
Item paid for a paire of shooes   xvj d
Item for gloves and points   xiiij d
Item for shooe tyes and Ribbon for the horse head   viij d
Item spent at Widow Pues *with*out the Barrs by the Alderm*an*s
appointment   xvj d
Item given to the Cryer At the Barrs   iiij d
Item given to the Prisoners at the Castle and Northgate   viij d
Item given to Clarke the Cowp*er* a poore man   ij d
Item given More for Ribboninge for the horse   vj d
Item given to a man for trimminge the horse   vj d
Item spent more vpon the same man   ij d
Item paid for a quarte of wyne at the dressinge of the Child viij d
Item spent the same day vpon the Companie at Alderman
Salisburies house   xvj d
Item paid for one quarte of wyne for the Companie at their
Banquett the same day   viij d
Item given vnto three footmen that did attend the Child   xij d
Item paid for paintinge of the staffe   xij d
...

Item paid vnto the Musitioners that did Attend the Companie
on Midsom*er* Eve   ij s
...

A   *Mayors List 6* BL: Harley 2125
f 126* *(23 April) John Brereton*
...

this maior caused first st Geo Rase on Roodey the 23 Aprell
1624 to be begone at the poynt behind new Tower & to Run 5
tymes about the Roodey & he that wan the last Course or

Trayne to haue the bell of a good valew of 8 or 10 li. or therabout
to haue it for euer. which moneyes was collected of Cittisens to
a some for same purposse the 3 former li. bells of mr Amoryes
beinge sould & a 100 li. more gathared the vse therof to find a
Cupp he Caused the new tower Gate to be enlarged for the sayd   5
horsrace which before was but a small gate for the rome of 3
horses to run in brest & caused the gutters to be filled in the
Roodey with the muckhill called pudinghill at the gate.

...

10

Mercers, Ironmongers, Grocers, and Apothecaries' Records
C: Company Book
p 139 *(7 May)*   15

...

the 19th of Iune 1624 for oringes & lemons	00.01.06
for Waffornes & Cakes	00.04.00
Cumffet*es* 2 li. ¾	00.04.01
Marmelate j li. ¾	00.02.07
Suger j li. ¼	00.01.06
Suger plates ½ li.	00.01.04
Wet suckett ¼ li.	00.00.05
Dry suckett ¼ li.	00.01.03
pruines 8 li.	00.01.08
Synomond 2 q*uarte*r	00.00.08
hallfe barell stronge beare	00.08.00
j pottell sacke j potell claret	00.03.00
bouttes for the boye	00.05.00
a p*ar*r of shewes for the gerlle	00.02.00
a p*ar*r of hose for her	00.02.06
a p*ar*r of garttrs	00.02.00
riben for shewes & both horse hed*es*	00.01.06
2 p*ar*r gloues	00.07.04
6 p*ar*r mens gloues	00.05.06
j dosone riben poynt*es* & band tie riben	00.02.04
to seavene men that did attend the Childrn	.07.00
to the Mvseke	00.06.08
spent att Willsones	00.02.00
to the Crier	00.02.00
to the presonrs in Castell & northgate	00.04.00

...

Joiners, Carvers, and Turners' Records CCA: Minute Book G 14/2
p 67 *(8 June)*

...

c   It is agreed that A banquett shall be provided by the stewards for
the Company vpon midsomer Eve and everie brother to pay
theire accustomed duties and to attend them selues and theire
watchmen as formerlie they haue done.

...

1624-5   1

Painters, Glaziers, Emboiderers, and Stationers' Records
C: Account Book II
p 9 *(18 October)*

...

payd for Stockyns, Showes, gloues and Showtyes for the Child   1
at Midsomer.   iiij s iiij d
payd for gloues for the Aldermen and Stewards   iij s. iiij d.
for a Riband for the horse head.   vj d
Giuen at the Barrs. Castell & Northgate.   xiiij d
Spent at dressing the boy on midsomer Eue.   vj d   2
Spent after the wach at Steward Inces house   ij s vj d
payd for Carriing the pikes, leading the horse and for Carriing
the banners and Garland.   viij s
Giuen to the Trompeter and drommer   v s. vj d.
payd for Silueringe new the ^'one of ye' tow banners ᵒthe   2
Other Was giuen by ^'Ald: Holmes'ᵒ   xxvj s. viij d.

...

Cordwainers and Shoemakers' Records
CCA: Account Book III G/8/4   3
f 69 *(11 November)*

...

ffor an over plus the xj^th of November 1624 at mr Ince his
house   iiij s
Item geven to Robert Cally the same day for musicke   ij s vj d   3

...

Item for Musique the same day at Steward Cloughe his house   ij s

...

25-6 / ᵒthe ... Holmes]• *in RH II's hand*   37 / l *of* Cloughe *written over* h

ff 69v-70v

...

Imp*ri*mis 2º. decemb*er* payed for Musique at Steward Hiltons
house   ij s
...   5

Shrovetyde — 1625

Imp*ri*mis payed for our Gleaves   vj s.
Item spent in barrage thereof   vj d
Item payed for sacque at sheriffe Glegg*es* howse, w*hi*ch was   10
sent to m͡air͡ about the Complaint of the drap*ers* against
shoemakers & Sadlers   ij s. vj d.
Item payed for one pint of Wyne at W*illia*m Larking*es* about
Ioh*n* Alderseyes brather   iiij d. |
Item payed to the Waytemen   ij s   15
Item payed to Robert Callye   ij s
Item payed at an overplus then   xvj s.

...

Midsomer Ewe / 1625.

                                                                           20
Imp*ri*mis payed to Tho*mas* Crosse the Shopkeep*er* for
banquettinge stuffes   xviiij s
To the gouldsmith for mendinge Iewell*es*   xviij d.
Item payed for orrenges & leamons   xij d
Item payed more for Sugar   x d. 25
Item payed for gloves for the boy   xiiij d.
Item for stocking*es* for the Boy   xviij d.
Item for shoes   xviij d.
Item for the loane of a hatt   viij d
Item given to the Man w*hi*ch brought the horse   xij d   30
Item to the 2 leaders of the horse   xij d
Item given to the Cryar   vj d
Item given to the p*reso*ne*rs* in the Northgate and the Castell   ij s
Item 600. of wallnutt*es*   ij s |
Item spent in dressinge the Boy   vj d   35
Item for half a Barrell of Beere   vj d
Item for fyue Cakes   xij d
Item for other Cakes and bread   iiij s
Item for Cheeses   v s ij d
th Iuly   Item payd for the Banner   xij d   40
...

Item for Sacke on Midsomer Eve   iiij s

Item given the Musicke iiij s

...

Item spent when the drapers Called vs before mr. maior the last
Tyme xviij d

...

Item for Sackq att Randle Bennettes dynner ix s
Item for Musique ij s vj d
Item for stronge Aell the same day vij s

Beerbrewers' Records CCA: Company Book G3/2
f 76 *(23 November)*
...

Midsomer Inprimis paid for the Childes shooes xvj d
Charges Paid for his Stockinges xx d
Paid for a paire of gloves xvj d
Spent att dressinge the Child ij s
Spent in Providinge the horse xij d
Given to three men that ledd the Childes horse ij s
Paid for Prunes Comfittes Apples & other thinges xx d
Paid for bredd & Cheese. vj s.
Paid for halfe a barrell of Stronge beere v s
Paid for A Samon vij s vj d
Paid for wyne ij s viij d.
To the Musick v s.
Given to the Cryer at the Barres vj d
Given to the Castle & Northgate xij d
Paid for keepinge the Banner xij d

...

Painters, Glaziers, Embroiderers, and Stationers' Records
CCA: Minute Book CR 63/2/131
f 5v *(23 November)*
...

Whether the banners shall be new siluered ayaynst Midsomer
[to b] to be siluered *(13 votes)*
...

Coopers' Records C: Company Book II
ff 37-7v *(13 January)*
...

payd for mending the Baner xj d
...

Midsomer charge

Payed for beare	v s vj d
payd for Chese	iij s
payd for gloues	ij s iij d
payd for powder and match	iij s vj d
payd for pruines and other spices	xviij d
payd for stockines and shoes for the boye and Riben for hes shoes	iij s j d
payd for dresinge the flage stafe	ij s	
Spent at William Pues	iij d
payd for a payre of gloues for william Pue	xij d
payd more Musicke	ij s iiij d
payd for beare at the barres	ij s
payd the Crier at the barres	vj d
payd at the Castell	iiij d
payd at the Northgatt	vj d
given vnto william Pues man	iiij d
payd for iiij shott and ij picke men	ij s xj d
payd for bred	ij s
payd for j pottell Claret wyne j quart secke	ij s iiij d

...

payd more for appelles and nuttes	xviij d
payd for the Lone of ij pickes iiij payre of bandeleros and dresing j gorgett	xx d
given vnto the man which did Lead the horse	vj d
payd for Lone of the hatte and feather	xij d

...

Joiners, Carvers, and Turners' Records
CCA: Company Book G 14/1
f 112 *(25 March)*

...

Disbursements

Imprimis for a paire of shooes for the Child vpon Midsomer eve	xiiij d
Item for a paire of stockeinges for the Child	xvj d
Item for one dosen of points	iiij d
Item for a paire of garters	vj d
Item for Ribboninge for the Childes shooes and for the horse head	xij d

Item for a quarte of Wyne at the dressinge of the Childe   vj d
Item [for] to a man for dressinge the horse   vj d
Item paid for a hatt for the Child   iiij s
Item paid for a paire of gloves   viij d
Item paid for a skaine of silke   j d
Item given to the prisoners at the Castle and Northgate   viij d
Item given to the Cryer at the Barres   iiij d
Item paid for a quart of sacke at the Banquett   xij d
Item paid to three men to Attend the Child   xij d
Item paid vnto the Musicke   ij s
Item spent vpon Midsomer Eve at Widow Pues house   xij d
...

f 112v

...

Item spent at Alderman Pues at the dynner made there by Iohn
Robinson for the whole Company   x s
...

Item given to the Musicke at the same tyme   vj d
...

Mercers, Ironmongers, Grocers, and Apothecaries' Records
C: Company Book
pp 149-50 *(6 May)*

Kat Chetlwood

...   li. s d

Memorandum the 22th of Iune 1625 to mr Bleaye for a paier
of stockinge j paier of garteres & j yard ribine   00-04-08
Memorandum for a paier of shewes for the boye yat ride Lord
    00-02-00
Memorandum for Ribine to macke him poyntes & ye hores
hed   00-02-03
Memorandum for a paier of gloues for him   00-01-03
Memorandum giuen at the Castell and Northegate   00-04-00
Memorandum paide to three men that attended the booeaye
    00-02-00
Memorandum paid for 3 payere of gloues for them   00-02-00

Calluen Bryanne ...

Memorandum paid for a paier of gloues for the ladie   00-01-00
Memorandum paid mr Bleayes for a payer of garteres   00-01-06
Memorandum Ribine for shewe tyes   00-00-09
Memorandum paid for a paier of shewes   00-02-00
Memorandum paid for a paier of stockinges   00-03-00

Memorandum paid at willsones at the barres   00-02-00
Memorandum paid to the Crier at the barres   00-01-00
Memorandum paid to the Mewsicke y*at* went w*ith* the Compeny
                                             00-06-08
Memorandum paid 3 men y*at* attended ye ladie   00-02-00 | 5

                                            li.   s   d
Memorandum paid for 3 paier of gloues   00-01-10
Memorandum paid for ribine for the horse hed   00-00-06
Memorandum giuen the halkep*er* at ou*r* mettinge   00-01-00   10
Memorandum 8 li. prewnes   00-01-08
Memorandum j li. Comfet*es*   00-01-06
Memorandum 2 q*uarte*r shuger plate 2 oz of marchepane   00-00-08
Memorandum dj li. mor of Comfett*es*   00-00-09
Memorandum j li. hard shuger   00-01-06   15
Memorandum j li. 6 q*uarte*r of marmelate   00-02-01
Memorandum in waffernes and Cakes   00-04-00
Memorandum iij quart*es* of seke   00-03-00
Memorandum iiij q*uarte*r of wette suckett   00-00-05
Memorandum A firken of Beayer   00-02-06   20
Memorandum 2 q*uarte*r of synament   00-00-08
...

1625-6
Painters, Glaziers, Embroiderers, and Stationers' Records   25
C: Account Book II
p 11 *(18 October)*
...

for Gloues to the Alderman & Stuards on midsomer eue
                                          iij s. iiij d. 30
for Stokyns. Gloues. Showes. & Showtyes for the Childe y*at*
ride on midsomer eue   iiij s. iiij d.
Spent at dressing ye childe   vj d.
for riband for the Horse heade   vj d.
Giuen at Barrs Castell & northgate.   xiiij d. 35
Giuen for Ca⌃ʳringe the banners & Garland & leadinge the
Horse   xviij d
Giuen the ⌃'2' Trompetors & drom*m*er   v s. vj d.
Spent in wine at ye Stuards howse at the banckett after ye
wach   ij s. vj d. 40
Giuen to xij men for Carringe the pikes on midsomer eue   vj s.
...

Treasurers' Account Rolls CCA: TAR/3/43
mb 5 *(November)*

...

Item paid to Raphe Hilton drap*er* for the 4 waytemens gownes
against Christyde. 14 yard*es* of broade Cloth*e* at 7s 6d p*er*
yarde   v li. v s

...

Item paide to the Steward*es* of the Sadlers toward*es* the silver
bell againste Shrovetusdaye   vj s viij d

...   1●

Item paid to Roger Gueste for drum*m*inge the same daye   xij d

...

mb 8

...   1●

Item paid to the Paynters for repayreinge the Gyant*es* againste
Middsomer   xliij s iiij d

...

mb 9

...   2●

Item to Roger Gueste for drum*m*inge on Middsom*er* daye at the
showe   xij d
Item paid to the Paynters for dressinge the Maiors mounte on
Middsomer eve   xxvj s viij d

...   2●

Item to 2 men for keepinge the horsemen of the rood=eye on
St Georges daye   xij d
Item paid to Gueste for druminge before the Maior that daye xij d

...

Item paid for Bearinge the Auncyant on Middsomer Eve to   3●
Welche the Cowper   ij s vj d

...

Cordwainers and Shoemakers' Records
CCA: Account Book III G/8/4   35●
f 76 *(11 November)*

...

Imprimis geven to a poore widowe by Ald*erman* Ince his
Appointm*ent*   xij d
It*em* for musique that day & at nighte   iij s. iiij d   40
It*em* to Geo*rge* Hiltons boy then for singeinge   vj d
To the Musique at steward Allens house   ij s vj d

...

Item spent at mistris Inces at an over plus when william Gregorye
was Chosen Alderman   iij s

...

5

f 76v

Item payed for musique at our Alderman Gregories the same
Daye   ij s

...

Item spent in meetinge the sadlers 3 seuerall tymes about the   10
Drapers   vij d
Item spent when wee mett them in the Churchyard   xij d
Item spent in procuringe Evydence on our syde ⌃ᶜagainst the
Drapers⸍   xvij d
Item geven to the Baredge at makinge the gleaves   iij d   15

...

f 77

...

Item spent on the day and tyme of Assemblie with the Drapers   20
and sadlers in the Taverne   viij d
Item spent in the pentice at the same assemblie   ij s
Item spent with the Drapers after the assemblye at the blacke
hostes   xiij d
Item spent vpon Mr Henrye Annyon and given to him to resygne   25
his place to our companie   vj s v d
Item payed to the Clearke for Wrytinge our Request to the
Assemblie   vj d
Item payed for our gleaves   [vij s] vjj s
...   30
Item payed to the waytemen   ij s

...

Item payed to Robarte Callye   ij s vj d
Item spent in wyne   x s.
...   35

f 77v

...

Midsomer Charge ./

40

Layed out and allowed by our Companie   xxv s
  videlicet for Cheese   v s. viij d

ffor Beere	vij s. ij d	
ffor Bread	iiij s.	
ffor Banquetinge stuffe	ix s	
Item to 3 men to Attend the Boy	xviij d	
Item for his gloves	xiiij d	
Item for his point*es*	xvij d	
Item for Rybon for the horse heade	vj d	
Item for Musique	iiij s	
Item for stocking*es* ∧ ʿand shoesʾ	ij s vj d	
× [Item for his shoes	xij d]	1
Item for shoetyes	vj d	
× [Item for Rybon for his Baner	vj d]	
Item spent at dressinge the Boye	vj d	
Item to mr Holmes for keepinge the Banner	xij d	
Item to the Cryar	vj d	1
Item to the pr*iso*ne*rs* at the Northgate	xij d	
Item at the Castle	xij d	
Item for a pottle of sacque to our Banquett	ij s	
Item spent without the Barres the same Daye	iij s	
Item for bread when wee made an end of our Drincke	iiij d.	2

Beerbrewers' Records CCA: Company Book G3/2
f 79 *(23 November)*   2

...

Midsom*er* charges	Inpr*imis* payd for the Child*es* Shooes	xvj d	
	ffor his Stocking*es*	xx d.	
	ffor a paire of gloves	xvj d	
	Spent at dressinge the Child	ij s	30
	Spent in providinge the horse	xij d	
	Given to three men that led the child*es* horse	ij s	
	Paid for prunes Apples Comfytt*es* & other thing*es*	xx d.	
	Paid for bread & Cheese	vj s	
	Paid for half a barrell stronge beere	vij s	35
	Paid for a Samon	[vij s vj d] viij s	
	Paid for wyne	ij s viij d	
	To the musick	v s	
	Given to the Cryer att the barres	vj d	
	Given to the Castle & Northgate	xij d	40
	Payd for keepinge the banner	xij d	

...

Coopers' Records C: Company Book II
ff 40-40v *(13 January)*

...

Midsoumer Accountes

5

Item for Beare	v s vj d
Item for breed	ij s
Item for Chese	iij s
Item for Pruines with ther spices	xviij d
Item for appelles and nuttes	xviij d 10
Item for ij payre of gloues of them which Lead the. horse	xij d
Item for j payre gloues for william Pue and the Child	ij s
Item for iij li pouder and matches	iiij s ij d
Item for shoes and stockines for the boye and riben	iij s |
Item for Lone of the Childes hatt	xij d 15
Item for musicke	ij s iiij d
Item spent at the barres	iiij d
Item given vnto the Cryer	iiij d
Item at the Northgate	vj d
Item at the Castell	iiij d 20
Item for the Lone of one picke j gorgett	iiij d
Item for ij picke men iiij shote	iij s
Item spent vpon the agreement with Cartwright	v d
Item j pottell White wyne j quarte secke	ij s
Item spent at William Pues vpon the Companeyes busines	iiij d 25
Item spent at oure Aldermanes vpon midsomer hauen	iiij d

...

Assembly Books CCA: AB/2
ff 6v-7* *(17 February)*

30

•An order for the diffrences betwene the Company of Drapers showmakers sadlers att Shroftyde:•

Whereas some difference hath hertofore for many Yeares beene
betweene the Company of Drapers And the seuerall Societies
or Companyes of Shomakers and Sadlers within this Citty &
many litigious passages and discontented complaintes hapened 35
amongst the said Companyes concerninge the Yearly presentinge
of certaine gleaves Horse & bell vpon euery Shrovetuesday, Mr
Maior earnestly desireinge not onely to take away all present
discord & dissencion but also to prevent all future dangers suits
and inconveniences which might arise thereby, And to haue the 40
auncient and laudable customes of this Citty maynetained & to
settle a perfect peace and vnity for euer amongst the said

Companyes hath beene pleased to moue the said seuerall
Companies to referre themselues to the order of this howse

•Proclemation of
Homage of
Shoomakers &
sadlers to be
done at High
Crosse befor mr
maior goe to ye
Roodey •

wherevnto they willingly condiscended Now vpon readinge of
two orders thone made in the time of the Maioraltie of Mr Henry
Gee & thother in the Maioralty of Mr William Stiles Coueringe
the said differences and vpon veiuinge of some other Antiquityes
& full [ad] and deliberate hearinge of thereasons and allegacions
of the drapers Shomakers & Sadlers it is generally & with one
consent ordered Concluded & determined That the Proclamacion
or Call of the Shomakers and Sadlers vpon Shrovetuesday for
euer hereafter touchinge theire homage shall be made and read
at the high Crosse imediately before theire goeinge to the Roodee

the same for ye
sadlers

in these words followinge Videlicet The Aldermen and Stewardes
of the Society and Company of Cordwayners within the Citty
of Chester Come forth and doe your homage in giueinge your
Attendance vpon the Right Worshipfull the Maior of the Citty

the same for ye
sadlers

of Chester vpon payne of tenn pownds And that the proclamacion
or call concerninge theire presentmentes shalbe made and read
vpon the Roodee in theise words followinge Viz The Aldermen

•Proclemation of
ye gleaues to be
made on ye
Roodey to be
giuen to the
Drapers who
are imediatly to
giue them to
mr maior •

and Stewardes of the Societie or Company of Cordwayners
within the Citty of Chester Come forth giue and deliuer your
Gleaues to the Master and Wardens of the Company of Drapers
within the said Citty to bee by them immediatly presented to
the said Maior & afterwards disposed of at the discretion of the
said Maior and Drapers accordinge to auncient orders vpon payne
of tenn pownds And it is further ordered That the Aldermen and
Stewardes both of the company of Shomakers and Sadlers and
euery member of the said Companyes shall accordingely vpon

•showmakes &
sadlers in their
gownes to wayt
on mr maior to
& fro the Roodey
& to the Comon
hall, also the tow
days folowinge
from pentice to
Comon hall &
back vpon payn
of x s to be leuied
by distresse •

euery Shrovetuesday foreuer doe theire said homage vnto the
Maior for the time beinge in giueinge theire Attendance vpon
him orderly and decently in theire gownes from the Pentice to
the Roodee and thence back againe to the Common Hall And
likewise vpon the two dayes followinge shall giue theire Attendance
vpon Mr Maior for the time beinge decently in their gownes
from the Pentice to the Common Hall and thence back againe
to the said Pentice vpon payne of tenn shillinges to be payd [to
be paide] to the Treasureres for the vse of the Citty by euery
person absentinge himselfe except good cause bee shewed to Mr
Maior for his excuse And that if any person soe absentinge
himselfe shall refuse or delay the payment of the said forfeiture
then the same to bee levyed by distresse at the appoyntment of
Mr Maior for the time beinge And moreouer the said Aldermen

& Stewardes of the Company of Shomakers shall giue and
deliuer vp vnto the drapers in the presence of Mr Maior vpon
Shrovetuesday next & soe Yearely foreuer six siluer gleaves |
of the same fashion & more value then heretofore at any time
within the space of tenn Yeares now last past they haue   5
accustomed to bee by them ymediately presented vnto the Maior
& afterwards disposed of at the discretion of the said Maior and
Drapers as in and by the said proclamacion & auncient orders
made to that Purpose is expressed And likewise vpon
Shrovetuesday next and soe Yearely vpon the same day for euer   10
the Aldermen and Stewardes of the Company of Sadlers shall
show and present theire Horse in as Rich and Comely manner as
[⟨...⟩fully] ˏ'formerly' they have done And shall also giue [n] and
deliuer vp vnto the Master and Wardens of the Drapers one siluer
bell of the same value as at any time for the space of tenn Yeares   15
now last past they haue done vpon payne of tenn pownds
        And it is further ordered that the said Aldermen and Stewards
of the said Companyes of Shomakers and Sadlers shall vpon
Shrovetuesday morninge next and soe Yearely foreuer afterwardes
Deliuer vnto the Maior for the time beinge in writeinge the names   20
and Sarnames of euery particuler person free of theire said
Companyes vpon payne of forfeiture of the samme of tenn
Shillings to and for the vse of the said Citty & to bee levyed as
aforesaid.
        It is further ordered that the Master and wardens of the   25
Company of Drapers shall vpon Shrove [s]tuesday next & the
two dayes ˏ'next' followinge & soe Yearely for euer hereafter
maytaine and continue vpon them Costs and Charges of the said
Company of Drapers their potacion & drinkeinge and other
Customes in as large and ample manner & forme and at as great   30
Charge & expence in euery particuler as at any time within the
space of tenn Yeares they haue accustomed vpon payne of tenn
powndes And it is also ordered That the said seuerall orders
made in the seuerall maioraltyes of Mr Gee and Mr Stiles and
euery thinge therein contayned & not by this presente order   35
altered added or augmented are by this howse with one full
Consent allowed ˏ'ratified' and confirmed as well on the parts
and behalfes of the said Company of Drapers as also of the said
Companyes of Shomakers and Sadlers & of euery of them
And further it is ordered that the said Company of drapers and   40
euery of them shall vpon euery Shrovetuesday giue theire seuerall
Attendance vpon Mr Maior for the time beinge at the Roodee in

•showmakers to deliuer to the Drapers on ye Roodey 6 siluer gleaues & they mediatly to giue them Mr Maior to be disposed of with ye Drapers•

•sadlers show their horse to mr maior & deliuer their bell to ye Drapers &c.•

•showmakers & sadlers giue mr maior a note of the names of their companyes on payn of x s•

•Drapers to mantayne the potation or drinkinge to mr maior for ye 3 days as of ould on payne of x li.•

•Drapers to attend mr maior in yer gownes on Shroftusday & to receue the bell & gleaues to giue mr maior•

theire gownes there to receive the said gleaves & bell & to present
the same to the Maior as is before ordered & declared Lastly
it is ordered that if any person free of or admitted into any of
the said seuerall Companyes of Drapers Shomakers and Sadlers
shall at any tyme hereafter giue out publish or divulge any   5

•no companye
to wronge other
in words or
acctions vpon
paine of x li. •

outbraueing scandalous or disgracefull termes either against the
other two Companyes or either of them in generall or any
member of the same in particuler Concerninge theire professions
liberties and Customes And espetially towchinge the
presentmentes of gleaues and bell — which is by this howse   10
finally ended determined & ordered or to doe or offer any
violence which may any way occasion any tumult grudge or
dissencion amongst the said Companyes that then the partie
offendinge in this kind vpon proofe thereof made before Mr
Maior & some of his brethren by two or more sufficient witnesses   15
shall forfeit and pay vnto the Company wronged and offended
the summe of tenn powndes

...

Joiners, Carvers, and Turners' Records   20
CCA: Company Book G14/1
f 114 *(25 March)*
...
Disbursements
...   25
Item paid for a hatt for the Child that did Ryde for the
Companie on Midsomer Eve   iij s x d
Item paid for his stockeings, garters, points, shooetyes and Ribon
for the horse head   ij s x d
Item paid for a paire of shooes for the Child   xvj d   30
Item paid for a staffe that the Child did Carry in his hand   vj d
Item paid for a quarte of Wyne bestowed at the dressinge of the
Child   viij d
Item given to the Cryer at the Barrs, and to the prisoners at the
Castle and Northgate   xij d   35
Item spent at Alderman Salisburies vpon Midsomer Eve   xviij d
Item spent at steward Bollands the same day   iij d
Item paid for a quarte of Sacke and a quart of Clared wyne at
the Banquett on Midsomer eve   xx d
Item given to the Musitioners for theire attendance on Midsomer   40
Eve   ij s
Item paid for a paire of gloves   viij d

Item given vnto three men that did attend the horse and the
boy   xij d
Item paid for dressinge of the horse   ij d
...

Mercers, Ironmongers, Grocers, and Apothecaries' Records
C: Company Book
p 153 *(2 May)*
...

given 1 paire of gloaues for the Lady   iij s
given the C[a]ryer att Bars   xij d
paid for 1 payre of stockins   iij s
paid widow wilson att Bars   ij s
paid for Ribin for the horse head   vj d
paid mr Blease for garters and shooe tyes   ij s x d
paid for j payre of shooes   xx d
given att the Castell   ij s
paid for gloaues for men and their paynes   iiij s viij d
...

payd by the Appoyntment of our Aldermen for two wachmen
2 dayes and 1 night and a peece of a day   v s
...

p 154
...

By one Thomas Crosser	li. -s -d
Item j paire woosted hosser and j paire silk garters att	00-05-08
Item j paire shewes att	00-02-00
Item for Ribin for poyntes shewtyes and horse head	00-05-00
Item j paire gloues att	00-01-03
Item for 3 men to Tend the lord	00-02-00
Item for 3 paire of gloues for the men	00-02-00
Item 8 li. prunes att	00-01-04
Item j li. & halfe Comfittes att	00-02-03
Item In marchpanes and sugar plates	00-00-08
Item j li. hard sugar att	00-01-04
Item 14 quarter marmelett att	00-01-04
Item in wafars and Cakes	00-04-00
Item 2 quartes sack and 2 quartes Clarett att	00-03-00
Item j ferkin of Strong beere att	00-02-06
Item 4 quarter wett suckett and 2 quarter sinemond att	00-01-01
Item for painting the staffe	00-01-00

Item for Mussike   00-06-08

...

1626-7
Painters, Glaziers, Embroiderers, and Stationers' Records
C: Account Book II
p 13 *(18 October)*

...

for gloues to ye Aldermen & Stewards at midsomer.   iij s iiij d.
giuen to the Trompetor   iij s. iiij d.   10
to the tow Drommers   xx d.
Giuen to xii men for Carring the pikes   vj s
Giuen for leading ye Horse Carring the banners & Garland.   ij s
for a Ruben for the Horse Head   vj d.
Spent at dressing the child which ride for ye Company   vj d   15
for hose Showes gloues & Showtyes for ye Child   iiij s. iiij d
Spent at ye barres while we Stayed for mr maior   xij d
giuen at Barres Castell & northgate   xiiij d
Spent in wine at ye Stuards howse after ye wach   ij s vj d
...   20

payd to mr Robert Ince for Bayes to make xii Coates   xliij s
for 8 peces of Inkell to lace the Coates   v s ix d
for white & red threed   xv d
for making the Coates   vj s j d
to Rafe Dauis for Cutting all the Cottes   xvj d   25
for a yard of yelow buckrom ˄'to mak a bagge' to keep ye
Coates in   ix d
...

Dean and Chapter CC: Treasurers' Accounts IV   30
p 180 *(25 November)*

...

Item the waytes at the audit   ij s

...   35

Treasurers' Account Rolls CCA: TAR/3/44
mb 2 *(November)*

...

Item payd mr Bennett for 14 ydes of Cloth for 4 of the
weatemens gownes vij s vj d per yd v li. v s & in Money to   40
Clement Pemberton 26s 3d   vj li. xj s iij d

...

Item payd Richard Warmisham Sadler towards the bell vsually
rune for at Shroftyd   vj s viij d
Item payd Gest drumer   xij d
Item payd Richard Gregorye which he layd out for a locke 16d
and nayles for the payles j d & Rushes iiij d at Shroftyd   xxj d   5
...

mb 2d

...

Item payd Nicolas Hallwood & Robert Thorneley for midsomer   10
worke   xliij s iiij d

...

Item payd Nicolas Hallwood & Robert Thorneley for the Maiors
mounte   xxvj s viij d
Item payd Roger Geust the drumer   xij d   15

...

mb 3
Item payd Thomas Welch for Carryinge the Cytties Collers at
mydsomer   ij s vj d   20

...

Cordwainers and Shoemakers' Records
CCA: Account Book III G/8/4
f 87 *(11 November)*   25

...

Item for gleaves at shrovetyde, and the Beuerage   vj s vij d
Item to the waytes   ij s
Item to the Callyes   ij s
...   30
Midsomer Charge videlicet ./

Item for banquettinge stuffe   ix s
Item for gleaves   xiiij d
for stockinges and pointes   iij s iiij d   35
ffor shoes and shoetyes   xviij d
for Rybon for the horse head   vj d
for 2 Cheeses   vj s
for keepinge the Bannor   xij d
for Beere   vj s vj d   40
for bread   iiij s
for musique   iiij s

Item spent dressinge the Boy   vj d
Item given to him that brought the horse   xij d
Item to them that lead the horse   xij d
Item spent at Hugh Mowsons   xij d
Item spent at wydow Willsons   vj d
Item geven to the Cryar   vj d
Item to the prisoners in the Castle   xij d
Item to the prisoners in the Northgate   xij d
Item for the loane of a hatt for the boy   viij d
...

f 87v *(11 October)*
...

Item for musique the same Day   *(blank)*
...

Beerbrewers' Records CCA: Company Book G 3/2
f 84 *(23 November)*

Midsomer
charges.
Item for the Childs Shooes & Stockinges   iij s
Item for his gloves   xvj d.
Item spent at dressinge the Child   xvj d.
Item spent in providinge the horse   vj d
Item paid for prunes Aples Comfittes & other thinges   j s viij d
Item paid for bread & Cheese   v s.
Item paid for halfe barrell beere   vj s
Item paid for a Sammon   viij s.
Item paid for wyne   ij s viij d
Item paid the musicke   v s.
Item given to the Cryer, Castle & Northgate   xviij d.
Item to mr Holme for keepinge the banner   xij d
...

Coopers' Records C: Company Book II
f 44 *(13 January)*

Midsoumer Accoumptes

Item payd for shoes and stockines and riben for the Boye   iij s
Item for powder and Match   iiij s iij d
Item for Lone of iiij payre bandeleroes   vj d
Item for ij payre gloues for william Pue and the Child   ij s
Item for ij payre of gloues for them which did Lead the horse xij d

Item for Lone of A hatte	xij d
Item for iiij shote ij pickes	iij s
Item mendinge j pece	ij d
Item for beare	vj s
Item for breed	ij s
Item for Chese	iij s
Item for Appelles with other spices	iij s
Item payd at oure Aldermans vpon midsoumer haven	xx d
Item payd fir beare at the barres	xvj d
Item payd vnto the Cryer at the barres	iiij d
Item payd at the Castell	iiij d
Item payd. at the Northgate	iiij d
Item payd for ij pottelles Wyne	ij s viij d
Item payd for Musicke	ij s vj d
Item payd a piper	xij d.

...

(1 August)

Item payd to the Musicke	iij s iiij d

...

Joiners, Carvers, and Turners' Records
CCA: Company Book G14/1
ff 116-16v *(25 March)*

...

Disbursements

...

midsomer
Charge

Item payed for stockinges for the Boy	xviij d
Item for Shoes	xvj d
Item for garters, gloves, pointes and shoetyes	iij s.
Item for a quarte of Wyne att dressinge the Boye	vj d
Item for a Topp for the Banner	ij d
Item for Rybon for the horse head	vj d
Item to the Cryar and the presoners	xij d
Item spent at Alderman Salisburyes	xviij d
Item more at widowe Pues	ij s. vj d
Item to 4 men to Tend the Boy and horse	xvj d │
Item for a pynt of wyne in procuringe the Boy to Ryde	iiij d
Item for a quarte of Wyne at the Banquett	vj d
Item for dressinge the horse	iiij d
Item to our Musitioners	xx d.

...

Item payed for the wydowes & ye Clearkes dynner att william

Pues and for drincke   x s.

...

Item for musique   iiij d

Mercers, Ironmongers, Grocers, and Apothecaries' Records
C: Company Book
p 160 (12 May)

...

Item for paynting the staffe   0- 1-00

...   1

Item for the Lord j paire gloues   0- 1- 3
Item j paire of woosted hosse and j paire of silke garters 0- 5- 8
Item j paire shewes   0- 2- 0
Item 3 Men to tend the lord   0- 2- 0
Item 3 paire gloues for the men   0- 2- 0   1
Item for Ribin for poyntes for the [horshed] lord & Ribin for
the horse head   00- 4- 6
Item for Ribin for shewtys   00-00-0⟨.⟩

...

                                                                   2

p 161
R by Iohn Bennett the xxiiij^th of Iune 1627

Item payed for 3 parr of gloues at be   xviij d
Item payed for 1 parr silke garters   xviij d   2
Item in riben for shuties   ix d
Item payed for 1 parr shues for ladie   ij s
Item payed for 1 parr fine wosted hose for her   iij s
Item payed to the Musicke   vj s viij d
Item payed 3 men to Attend the ladie   ij s   3
Item payed for 3 parr gloues for them   ij s
Item payed for riben for the horse head   vj d
Item viij li. of prunes   xvj d
Item j li. of Cumfetts   ij s vj d
Item ij half of suger plates   [plates] iiij d   3
Item ij half March paynes   iiij d
Item j li. of suger at   xx d
Item in wafernes and Cakes   iiij s
Item iiij half of sucket   v d
Item ij half synomond   x d   4

22 / 1627 *underlined in MS*   34 / *first* t *of* Cumfetts *written over* e

Item for Aferken of stronge Beare	iij s
Item j pottell of sacke	ij s viij d
Item ij pottells of Clarret	ij s viij d
Item payed for payntinge stafe	xij d
...	5
Item giuen the Cryer att barres	xij d
Item giuen att the Castell	ij s
Item giuen att the northgate	ij s
...	
	10

AC **1627-8**
Midsummer Giants BL: Harley 2150
ff 209v-9* *(4 July)*

Memorandum vpon the iiijth Day of Iuly 1627 in the third yeere   15
of our soueraigne Lord Charles by the grace of god of greate
Brittaine ffrance and Ireland kinge &c. Randle Holme of the
Cittie of Chester Alderman of the Companie of painters Nickholas
Hallwod and Robert Thorneley of the said Cittie painters
wittnesseth that whereas the aforesaid Randle Holme the elder   20
Nickholas Hallowod [and] william Handco⟨...⟩ and Robert
Tharneley haue bin weare and are Lawfull possesse⟨...⟩ and
interressed as of theire owne proper goodes ever since the tyme
of the Mayraltie of the Right worshipfull mr Iohn Rattclife
Late of Chester Deceased in which yeere the parties abouesaid   25
did vppon theire owne proper costes make new the Giantes
beastes and Mayors Mounte with other theire apurtenances
belonging to the Midsomer watch to theire then great Charge
receiveinge from the Cittye but the ordinary and accust⟨.⟩med
fees for the same. It then was and now ys of meaneinge and   30
agreement that after the decease of any of theese parties the
whole and entire profittes and receites from the Mayor sheriffes
Treasuerers & Leevelokers to fall and properly belonge to the
surviuors, Now whereas william Handcock one of the aforesaid
parties is deceased and his afore mencioned fallen amonge the   35
said Randle Holme the elder Nicholas Hallwod and Robert
Thorneley yet notwithstandinge the the said parties do hereby
allow vnto Gwen Handcocke late wife to the said william
handcocke deceased vj s viij d out of the proffittes of the said
Gyant woorke every other yeere dureinge her widdowhoode.   40

37 / the the MS *dittography*

And likewise whereas Randle Holme the elder hath for some
valuable consideracion made sale of his quarter parte of the said
worke to the said Nicholas Hallwod for and dureinge the life of
the said Nicholas which parte after the Decease of the said
Nicholas by force of surviuorship retarnes to the said Randle   5
Holme the elder againe or to the surviuor of the said Randle
Holme and Robert Thorneley Now so it is that the said Nicholas
Hallwod beinge an aged old man and weake of boddie and not
able to performe the Moytie of the worke as formerly he hath
done doth with the conscent and assent of him the said Nicholas   10
Hallwod Randle Holme and Robert Thorneley for and in
consideracion of the sume of Twentie shillinges sell bargaine
asigne and sett over his one ⟨...⟩ parte of the said Giantes with the
apertinances | Dureinge the naturall life of him the said Nicholas
together with the other quarter parte formerly the parte of   15
the said Randle Holme the elder to Iohn wright of the said Cittie
of Chester painter to haue hold occupie and enioye as his owne
proper goodes and to worke and receive the profittes as he the
said Nicholas formerly hath don But and if it so happen that the
said Nicholas Hallw⟨...⟩ die then the whole to become due to the   20
said Randle Holme and Robert Thorneley and the surviuor of
the⟨.⟩ and if it shall so happen that the said Iohn wright die
before the said Nicholas the said Nicholas to reenter a partener
againe as before otherwise the said Iohn wright to enioye his
bargaine accordinge to the true intent of this agreement. In   25
wittnes whereof we haue herevnto putt our handes the day and
yeere abou⟨.⟩ written. /

       Randle Holme
       nicholis NH hallowood   30
       Robert Thornley

Whereas in ˄'the' writinge aboue specified Iohn wright was   35
interressed in the premisses by reson the said Nichola⟨.⟩ Hallowod
made a bargaine and sale vnto him of his parte now vppon the
day afforesaid for diuerse resons by the said Nicholas Hallowod
deliuered the said Ioh⟨.⟩ wrighe was content to relinquish the
said bargai⟨.⟩ provided alwayes that the said Nicholas shall not   40
sett on worke or sell his saide parte to any man whatsoever
without the assent and conscent of Ra⟨...⟩ Holme and Robert

Thorneley vnlesse it be vnto th⟨.⟩ said Iohn wright afforesaid
in wittnes whereof I putt to my hand.

Nicholas NH Hallowed

Painters, Glaziers, Embroiderers, and Stationers' Records
C: Account Book I
f 155v* *(18 October)*

...

for Inkele & making it	xij d	10
for gloues for the Aldermen & Stewards	iij s iiij d	
for hose shewes gloues and sutyes for the Child	iiij s iiij d	
spent at dressing the Child	viij d	
spent at the barrs tarring for mr maior	xiij d	
for Ribyn for the horse head	vj d	15
giuen at bares Castle & northgate	xiiij d	
for leading the horse caring the garland & baners	ij s vj d	
to the Trompeter	iij s iiij d	
to the Dromer	xij d	
giuen to xij mem for Cariing the pickes	vj s	20
spent in wine & bere at Steward Robinsons howse	ij s vj d	
for taffity Sarcenet & Ruben for ˏˈitˈ to make a trumpet baner		
	iiij s vj d	
for gilding the pheonix on it & for fring	*(blank)*	

(p marks appear in left margin beside "for Ribyn for the horse head" and "for taffity Sarcenet...")

...

Painters, Glaziers, Embroiderers, and Stationers' Records
C: Account Book II
p 15 *(18 October)*

...

payd to mr *willia*m Allen for red Bays to make the Dromer a cote	iij s. x d.	30
payd for white Inkell and making the Cote	xij d	
payd for gloues for ye Aldermen and Stewards	iij s. iiij d.	
payd for hose Showes Gloues and Shewtyes for the Child	iiij s iiij d	35
Spent at dressinge of the childe w*hi*ch ridd for the Company	viij d.	
Spent at the Barrs while we stayed for mr maior	xiij d	
payd for Riben for the horse head	vj d	40

20 / mem *for* men, *extra minim MS*

Giuen at the Barrs. Castle and northgate   xiiij d
Giuen for leading the horse, Carring the bannors and Garland
                                                            ij s vj d
Giuen to the Trompetor   iij s. iiij d.
Giuen to the dromer   xij d.
payd to xij men for Carringe of the pikes   vj s
Spent at Steward Robinsons on midsomer eue after the wach
                                                            ij s vj d
payd for ˄'greene' Taffaty Sarcenet to make a Trompet banner
and for Riben   iiij s. vj d.   1
payd for gilding the phœnix on it and for fringe ˄'the
workmanshipp bestowed by mr Holme & his sonne'˳   v s
...

Cordwainers and Shoemakers' Records   1
CCA: Account Book III G/8/4
f 92 *(11 November)*
...

Imprimis for musique at mistris Inces   ij s
...   2
Item for musique at Steward Woodcockes   ij s
...
Item for Musique at our steward Leys   ij s
...
Item for our gleaves, and the Berrage & spent in payinge for them   2
at mistris Inces   vij s. j d
...
Item to the waytes att Shrovetyde   ij s
...
                                                                    3

f 92v
...

                        Midsomer Charge /

Item for halfe abarrell of Beere   vj s. vj d   3
Item for Bread   xij d
Item for short Cakes   iiij s
Item for Cheese   iiij s x d.
Item for Apples   vj d

11-12 / *˙˄'the ... sonne'˙ in RH II's hand*

Item for banquettinge stuffes	vij s. iiij d
Item for Musique	iiij s.
Item for gloves for the boy	xvj d.
Item for Bootes and Spurrs	iiij s.
Item for Rybon	xij d
Item for keepinge the Bannor	xij d
Item to him which brought and did leade the horse	xij d
Item to 2 men to tend the Boy	xij d
Item spent at the Barrs	ix d.
Item to the Cryar	vj d
Item to the prisoners in the Castle	xij d
Item to them in the Northgate	xij d

...

Beerbrewers' Records CCA: Company Book G3/2
f 88 *(23 November)*

Midsomer charges /

ffor the Childes Stockines & Shooes	iiij s vj d.
Item for his gloves.	xvj d.
Item for a Samon.	vj s
Item for wyne	ij s viij d.
Item for bread & cheese	iiij s.
Item for beare	[iiij s] vj s
Item given to the Cryer, Castle and Northgate	xviij d
Item to the Musick	v s
Item to Mr Holme for keepinge the banner	xij d
Item spent at dressinge of the Child	xij d.

...

Dean and Chapter CC: Treasurers' Accounts IV
p 206 *(25 November)*

...

(Audit day)

Item waites and other musike	iiij s

...

p 228 *(Christmas)*

...

Item to Smalshew for the wach	ij s vj d

...

AC *Proclamation at the Christmas Watch* BL: Harley 2150
f 77

the proclamation at the Christmas watch.

oyes thrise

the right wor*shipfu*ll the maior of this Citty chargeth and
Comandeth all *p*ersons here asembled to keepe the peace and
be of quiet & Ciuill behauiour duringe the tyme of the wach   1
now in hand vpon payne of Imprisonment & a fine at his
worshipes pleasure

oyes thrise

all thos who [w*h*ich owe]´hould land by´sute seruice & homage   1
to this Court Come forth and make your apparance in answaringe
to your names vpon payne & perill that will fall theron

Coopers' Records C: Company Book II   2
f 47 *(13 January)*

...

Midsoumer Charge

It*em* payd for powder and Matche	iiij s iij d 2
It*em* payd for breed	ij s
It*em* payd for Chese	iij s
It*em* payd for Beare	vj s
It*em* payd for hose and shoes for the Boye and riben	iij s
It*em* payd for the Lone of ij payre bandeleroes	vj d 3
It*em* for Appel*les* with other spices	iij s
It*em* payd for Lone of hatte	xij d
It*em* payd for Mendinge iij peces	vj d
It*em* payd vj men	iij s
It*em* payd for iiij payre gloues	ij s vj d 3
It*em* payd at oure Aldermans	viij d
It*em* at the Barres	viij d
It*em* payd the Cryer	iiij d
It*em* payd at the Castell	iiij d
It*em* payd at the Northgatte	vj d 4
It*em* payd for a quarte of secke	xvj d
It*em* payd for Musicke	ij s iiij d

Item payd for a pottell of beare at the dressinge of the boye iiij d

Joiners, Carvers, and Turners' Records
CCA: Company Book G14/1
f 118v *(25 March)*

...

Item for a hatt hose poyntes Rybon & gloves for the Childe
vj s. iiij d
Item for a payer of shoes xiiij d.
Item for a quarte of wyne att dressinge the Childe viij d
Item spent att Alderman Salisburyes on Midsomer Eve ij s. iij d.
Item the same day att widowe pues ij s.
Item for Powder vj d
Item to the Musicke iij s.
Item at furnishinge the horse iiij d
Item for wine at the banquet xvj d
Item spent att Richard Bollandes, steward xviij d
Item given to 3 men to leade the horse xij d

...

more laid out on midsomer to the Cryar, the presoners in the
Castle, & northgate xij d

...

Mercers, Ironmongers, Grocers, and Apothecaries' Records
C: Company Book
p 166 *(12 May)*

...

more payed by mee at Midsomer 1628

Item j parr gloues for the ladie ij s vj d
Item j parr [silke garters] 'shewes' xviij d
Item in riben for shues. ix d
Item j parr fine hose 3s j parr silke garters 2s v s
Item giuen 3 men to Attend the ladie ij s
Item payd for 3 parr gloues for them ij s

...

p 168
Laid out by Thomas Drinkwater Iune 1628

videlicet.
paid for paintinge the staffe xij d

paid for a paire of gloues for the Lord   xvj d
paid for a paire of wosted stocknes and apaire of silke garters
                                                                               v s. viij d
      paid for apaire of shewes   ij s
      paid for 3 men to attende the Lord   ij s
      paid for 3 payre of gloues for them   ij s
      paid for poynts for the Lord & riben for the horse head   iiij s
      paid for a pare of roses for his shooes   xij d
      prunes 8 li.   ij s viij d
      Comfits j li. ½   iij s   ⬤
      in sugr plates & march paines   viij d
      in whitt suger   ij s
      in wafrons & cakes   iiij s vj d
      in sinoment & sucket   xviij d
      for a firken of stronge beare   iij s   ⬤
      sacke apotlle   ij s 8d
      clarit 2 potlles   ij s 8d
      paid without bares for the compay drinkinge   ij s vj d
      paid the Crier at the bares   xij d
      paid the prisoners at the castle   ij s   ⬤
      paid the prisoners at northgatte   ij s
      ...
      paid to the musicke   vj s. 8d
      ...

                                                                                        ⬤

AC   *Note on the Whitsun Plays* BL: Harley 2124
      flyleaf*

      The Whitsun playes first made by one Don Randle Heggenet o
      Monke of Chester Abbey who was thrise at Rome before he   ⬤
      could obtaine leaue of the Pope to haue them in the English
      tongue.

      The Whitsun playes were playd openly in pageants by the
      Cittizens of Chester in the Whitsun Weeke.   ⬤

      Nicholas the fift then was Pope in the year of our Lord 1447.

Anno 1628.   Sir Henry ffrancis sometyme a Monke of the Monestery of
      Chester, obtained of Pope Clemens a thousand daies of pardon,   ⬤
      and of the Bishop of Chester 40. dayes pardon, for euery person
      that resorted peaceably to see the same playes and that euery

person that disturbed the same to be accursed by the said Pope,
vntill such tyme as they should be absolued thereof.

1628-9
Painters, Glaziers, Embroiderers, and Stationers' Records
C: Account Book II
p 17 *(18 October)*

...

Payd Hose Gloues Showes & Sutyes for ye Child y*a*t Ridd

	iiij s. iiij d.
Spent at dressing of ye Child and berrage of his clothes	xiiij d.
Payd for a Ruben for ye horse head	vj d.
Spent at ye barrs while we stayd for mr Maior	xij d.
Giuen at ye barrs Castell & northgate	xiiij d.
Giuen to ye Trompeter	iij s. iiij d.
Giuen to ye Drum*m*er	xij d.
Giuen for Carriage of ye banners garland & leading ye horse	ij s.
Payd to ye xij pikemen.	vj s.
Spent at Stewards Bromefeild howse after ye wach	ij s. vj d.

...

Payd for Gloues for ye Aldermen & Stewards   iij s. iiij d.

...

Cordwainers and Shoemakers' Records
CCA: Account Book III G/8/4
f 97 *(11 November)*

...

(St Martin's Day)
Item for Musique   ij s

...

Item for our Gleaues and the Beuerage   vij s. iij d

...

ff 97v-8
Item to the waytes at Shrovetyde   ij s
Item to Robert Callye   ij s
Item for an overplus at our Ald*erman* Gregories at shrovetyde v. s

...

Midsom*er* Charge

Imprimis for halfe a barrell of beere   vij s
Item for bread and Cakes   iiij s viij d
Item for 8 li. of pruynes   ij s
Item for banquettinge Stuffe   v s

Item for one ould Cheese	iiij s iiij d
Item 2 new Cheeses	iiij s iiij d
Item for musique	iiij s
Item to the Cryar	vj d
Item spent at the barres	ij s v d
Item to the prisoners at the Castle	xij d
Item to the prisoners att the northgate	xij d
Item for a quarte of sacque at our banquett	xvj d
Item for stockinges for the boy	xvj d ⎯
Item for shoes for the boy	xij d
Item for keepinge the Banner	xij d
Item spent at dressinge the boy	vj d
Item geven to the man which brought and ledd the horse	xviij d
Item for Rybon for the horse head	vj d
Item geven to the [boy] men which attended the boy	xij d
Item for shoetyes for the boy	vj d

...

Beerbrewers' Records CCA: Company Book G 3 / 2
ff 99-9v *(23 November)*

...

Midsomer charges	Inprimis paid for the Childes shooes & Stockinges	iiij s vj d.
	Item for his gloves	xvj d
	Item for A Samon	x s.
	Item for wyne	ij s viij d
	Item for bread & cheese	iiij s. ⎯
	Item for Beere	vj s
	Item to the Cryer Castle and Northgate	xviij d
	Item to the Musick	v s.
	Item to Mr holme for keepinge the banner	xij d
	Item spent at the dressinge of the Child	xij d

...

Glovers' Records C: Company Book
p 30 *(January)*

...

Midsomer Charges	Inprimis payd for the boye his bootes	iij s x d
	Item for apaire of gloves for him	viij d
	Item payd for three paire for the men	xviij d
	Item paid for Rybbon for the horse	xij d
	Item paid to the Cryer Castle & Northgate	xviij d
	Item spent at mr ffletchers vpon some of the Company before	

our goeinge vp	xviij d
Item spent at the barres	vj s iiij d
Item to Mr Holme for the Bainer	xij d.
Item to the Musick	vj s.
...	5

Coopers' Records C: Company Book II
f 50v *(13 January)*

...

Inprimes	Payd at oure Aldermanes vpon the Election daye	xxiij s 10
	Payd the musicke	vj d

...

f 51

Midsomer Charge 15

Impr*imis* payd for powder and mache	iiij s iij d
Item more p*ay*d for a payre of stockins for the boye	xv d
Item more p*ay*d for a payre of shues for the boye	xviij d
Item more p*ay*d for apayre of gloues	xij d 20
Item more p*ay*d for the lone of a hatt	xij d
Item more p*ay*d for Ribban for shue tyes and for the horse hed	
	ix d
Item more p*ay*d for Aples prewnes and other spises	iij s
Item more payd for Cheesse	iij s 25
Item more payd for bredd	ij s
Item more p*ay*d for three payre of gloues for themen that led	
the horse and to Richard Boland	ij s
Item more p*ay*d for beere	vij s
Item more payd the pikemen and shott	iij s 30
Item more p*ay*d for the loane of 2 pikes and 2 bandelores	xij d
Item more p*ay*d for a pottell wyne and one quart of Sacke	
	ij s viij d
Item more p*ay*d for musicke	ij s vj d
Item more p*ay*d att our Aldermanes and the barres	xiiij d 35
Item more giuen the Cryer att the barres	iiij d
Item more giuen att the Castell	iiij d
Item more giuen att the northgate	vj d
Item more giuen to Robert nicholas for the loane of his peese	
and bandelerowes one quart of beere	ij d 40
Item more p*ay*d for mendinge of 2 peeses	vij d
Item more p*ay*d att the dressinge of boye	iiij d

Joiners, Carvers, and Turners' Records
CCA: Company Book G14/1
f 120v *(25 March)*

Disburcement*es.* 1628

...

Midsom*er*
Charge. /

Item paid for a hatt, stockinges, shoes, garters & Ryboninge for the boye   vij s +
Item for Musique   ij s vj d +
Item to them 3. that attended the boy on horsbacke   xij d
Item for Wyne at dressinge the boye   viij d   1
Item for a quarte of wyne att our banquett   viij d +
Item spent at widowe Pues   ij s.
Item to the prison*ers* in the Castle, the Northgate and to the Cryar   xij d
Item spent att our Ald*erman* Salisburies   xiiij d.   1
...

Mercers, Ironmongers, Grocers, and Apothecaries' Records
C: Company Book
p 169 *(8 May)*   2
...

Item paide for i p*air* wosted Stockinges for the Lord   00.0[.].06
Item paid for j p*air* silke garters   00.01.06
Item paid for j p*air* shooes   00.01.06
Item paid 3 men to attend the Lord   00.02.00   2
Item paid for 3 p*air* gloues for them.   00.02.00
Item paid for 〈.〉 Riben for the horse head   00.00.06
Item paid for Showetyes for the boye   00.00.10
Item paid without bares   00.02.06
Item paid the Cryer   00.01.00   3
Item paid prisoners at Castle & Northgate   00.04.00
...
Item paid for musick   00.06.08
...
Item paid for j p*air* gloue*es*. for the Lord   00.01.02   3
...

p 170
...

Imprymis 2 y*ardes* of 6d yellowe Ribben for the Lady   xij d   4
Item ½ yard 3d fferritt Riben. & j skeane silke & making Roses
                                                                                                          xix d

Item 2 yardes. of Carnation. Ribben 6d for garters   xij d
Item 2 yardes. of 6d Ribben for. horse. head.   xij d
Item j yard ¼ whitt 6d Ribenes   jx d
Item j pair of yellowe woosted hose.   iij s
Item 3 pair glouees.   ij s   5
Item j parr showees   ij s
Item 3 men to tend the Lady   ij s
Item j parr of gloues for. the Lady   iiij s
for the banquett   0.18.08
Item 8 li. prunees   ij s viij d   10
Item j li. ½ Comfites   ij s. vj d
Item 2 quarter suger platees   iiij d
Item j li. suger   xx d
Item in waffornees & Cakes   iiij s
Item 4 quarter Suckett   v d   15
Item 2 quarter Cynamon   x d
Item j pottle sack   ij s viij d
Item ij pottles Clarrett   ij s viij d
Item for beare   ij s vj d
Item. 2 quarter marchpanes   viij d   20

...

1629-30   25
Painters, Glaziers, Embroiderers, and Stationers' Records
C: Account Book II
p 19 *(18 October)*
...

Payd for gloues hosen Showes ˏ˒&˒ Showtyes for ye boy that   30
ridd   iiij s. iiij d.
Spent at dressing ye Child and berrage of his Clothes   x d
Spent at ye Barrs while we stayed for mr maior   xij d.
Giuen at ye Barrs Castell & northgate   xiiij d
Payd for a Ruben for ye horse head   vij d   35
Giuen to ye Trompetor   iij s. iiij d.
Giuen to ye Drummer   xij d.
Giuen for Carring the banners garland & leading ye horse   ij s.
Payd to ye xij pike men   vj s
Payd for Gloues for ye Aldermen & Stewards   iij s. iiij d.   40
Spent at Stewarde Prickets howse after ye wach   ij s. vj d.

...

Cordwainers and Shoemakers' Records
CCA: Account Book III G/8/4
f 102 *(11 November)*
...

Item for musique at dynner   ij s
...

Item for musique at Steward Wright*es*   ij s
Item for Musique at Steward Heathes   ij s
...

                                                                              1

f 102v
...

Shrovetyde   Item to the waytes   ij s
Item to the Callyes   ij s
Item at an overplus att our drinckinge vpon Thursday at our   1
Ald*erman* Gregories   x s
Item for a pint of sacque for m*istr*is Ince   viij d
Item for the 3. brethrens dynners w*hi*ch wayted at the Hall   xviij d
...

Item spent in provydinge a boy to ryde   vj d   2
...

f 103
Midsomer Charge 1630 /

                                                                              2

Inpr*i*mis for Beere   vij s. vj d
Item for bread   iiij s viij d
Item for pruynes   ij s
Item for banquettinge stuffes   v s.
Item for an ould Cheesse   iiij s. j d   3
Item for 2 new Cheeses   iiij s. vij d
Item to Robert Callye for musique   iiij s.
Item to the Cryar   vj d
Item spent att the barres   iij s.
Item to the pr*i*son*er*s in the Castle   xij d   3
Item to the pr*i*son*er*s in the Northgate   xij d
Item for stockinge for the boy   ij s. vj d
Item for shoes for the boye   xx d.
Item for keepinge the Banner   xij d
Item spent at dressinge the boye   xij d   4
Item payed to the man w*hi*ch brought and ledd the horse   ij s. vj d
Item for Rybon for the horshead   vj d

Item to them *which* tended the boy	xij d
Item for shoetyes	vj d
Item for gloves	xiiij d.
Item for poynt*es* for the boye	ij s
Item for apples at the banquett	xij d
Item for the loane of a hatt	viij d
Item for the loane of a Saddle	vj d

...

Beerbrewers' Records CCA: Company Book G 3/2
f 101v *(23 November)*

Inp*ri*mis paid for the Child*es* Shooes & Stockinges	4s 6d
Item for his gloves	xvj d.
Item for a Samon	x s
Item for wyne	ij s. viij d
Item for bread & Cheese	iiij s.
Item for Beere	vj s
Item to the Crier Castle & Northgate	xviij d
Item to the Musick	v s.
Item to Mr holme for keepinge the bann*er*	xij d
Item spent at dressinge of the Child	xij d /

Midsomer charges

...

Glovers' Records C; Company Book
pp 37-8 *(January)*

...

Item paid for hose and shooes for the boye	iij s vj d
Item paid for Ribbin for the horses head	xij d
Ite*m* p*ai*d for Glo*u*es for the boye	viij d
Ite*m* paid for Glo*u*es for the leaders of the horse	xviij d
Ite*m* spentt att the barrs	ix s vj d
Item spentt att George ffletchers by the Aldermens appointm*ent*	v s.
Item p*ai*d to the Musicke	v s.
Item Gi*u*en att the barr*es* Castle and Northgate	xviij d

Midsomer Charge

...

Coopers' Records C: Company Book II
ff 55-5v *(13 January)*

...

Ite*m* more p*ai*d the musicke the 3 daye of maye att Raph

Sharplesse his dinner   iij s iiij d

...

midsomer Charge

Item more spent att my Alderman Linackers on midsomer
eauen   ij s
Item more paid for apayre of shues for the boy   xviij d
Item more paid for apayre of stockins   xviij d
Item more paid for 2 yardes of Ribbin   x d
Item more paid for 3 payre of gloues   ij s j d
Item more paid for haulfe abarrell of beere   vij s vj d
Item more paid for Cakes   ij s |
Item more paid for prewnes and other spyces   ij s iij d
Item more in aples and walnuttes   xij d
Item more paid for powder and Mach   iiij s x d
Item more paid for beere att the barres   xij d |
Item paid the Cryar att the barres   iiij d |
Item paid att the Castell   iiij d
Item paid att the northgate   vj d
Item paid for a Cheese   iij s
Item more paid for 6 men to Carry armes   iij s
Item more paid for lone of bandeleryes and peecesses iiij d |
Item more paid for musicke   iij s
Item more paid for wyne   ij s x d

...

Item more paid for Lone of the boyes hatt   xij d.

...

Item more paid for wyne att william welshe his dinner the
second of August   vij s

...

Item more paid for musicke   iiij s iiij d

...

Item more payd at Ambrose Sharplesse dynner for wyne iiij s iiij d
Item more payd for musicke   ij s vj d

...

Item more payd for payntinge the staffe for the banner xvj d

...

Joiners, Carvers, and Turners' Records
CCA: Company Book G 14/1
f 123 *(25 March)*

Disburcementes ...

Midsomer Charge

...

Item given to Richard Bolland to provyde necessaries for his

sonne to Ryde for our Companie, by Consent   vij s
Item given to a man to dresse the horse   iiij d
Item for Rybon for the Horse head   vj d
Item for a quarte of wyne at dressinge the boye   viij d
Item spent at our Alderman Salisburyes   xx d   5
Item spent att at wydowe Pues   ij s
Item to the Cryar, and the presoners in the Castle and the
Northgate   xij d
Item spent att William Williams   xiiij d
Item for a quarte of wyne att our banquett   viij d   10
Item for three men to Attend the boy   xij d
Item for our musique   ij s iiij d

...

Mercers, Ironmongers, Grocers, and Apothecaries' Records   15
C: Company Book
pp 183-4 *(7 May)*

...

Item for apaire hose ^'2s 10d' garteres ^'2s 2d' shootyes for the
boye & 'shooes'   vj viij d   20
Item for a parr of hose, '2s 8d' gartees, '18d' & rosses ^'12d'
for the gerle   v s ij d
Item a parr shooes for the gerle   xx d
Item ribbine for dressing her head & 'silke'   xij d
2 parr of gloues for them both   iiij s   25
Item ribbine for the both horseheads   xij d
Item 3 men to attend vpon the boye & gloues 'for them'
         iiij s vj d
Item 3 men to attend the gerle & 3 parr gloues   iiij s vj d
Item gaue to Sir Henry Bunburyes horskeeper for bringing &   30
dressing the horse   ij s
Item gaue a boye yat brought the other horse   vj d

...

paid at Widow wilsons for beare   ij s vj d
paid the Cryare at bares   xij d   35
paid the Castle & northgatt prisoners   iiij s
spent while we rested the Childrn at glouerstone   iiij d
Item paid for musicke   vj s viij d
Item gaue [xij d] for wyne to bestowe on them yat dressed
the gerle   xij d | 40

6 / att at *MS dittography*   30 / gaue *written over* paid

It*em* 8 li. of prunes 2d li	xx d
It*em* j li. ½ of comfit*es*	ij s vj d
j li. suger	xx d
2 q*uarter*s sinnamon	[x] viij d
marchpane stuffe & conceiptes	xvj d
j pottle of sacke	ij s
j gallone of clarret	ij s

...

1630-1

A   *Mayors List 5* BL: Harley 2125
f 60 *(18 September) Christopher Blease*

...

vpon the xviij^th day of septenber 1630 Came to chester being
saterday the duches of Tremoyle of france and motherinlaw to
the lord Strange and many other great estates and all the gentry
of Cheshier flintshier & denbighshier went to meete her at hoole
heath with the Earle of Darby being at least 600 horse also the
gentle men of the Artilery yard latly erected in chester mett her
in Cowlane in very statly manner all with great white & blew
fithers & went before her Chariot in a march to the bushops
pallas & making a gan let her through the midest & then gaue
her 3 voleys of shot & so returned to their yard also the maior
Aldermen in their best gownes & Aparrell weare on a stage in the
Estgat Street to entertayn her & the next day. she Came to the
pentise after the sermon in the after noone to a banquet being
invited p*er* the maior & the next day went to whichurch but it
was reported that so many knights Esquiers & gentlemen neuer
were in chester to gether no not to meet king Iames when he
Came to chester

...

Painters, Glaziers, Embroiderers, and Stationers' Records
C: Account Book II
p 21 *(18 October)*

...

Payd for a payre of Bootes for the boy that did ride ⌐yat was mr⌐ Harper sonne⌐	iiij s.
Payd for a payre of Gloues for the [child] boy y*a*t ridd	xij d.
Spent at ye Barrs while we Stayd for mr Maior	xij d.
Giuen at the Barrs Castell & northgate	xiiij d.
payd for a Rubyn for ye horse head	vj d.

payd for Gloues for ye Aldermen & Stewards   iij s. iiij d.
Giuen to the Trompetor   iij s. iiij d.
Giuen to the Drummer   xij d.
Giuen to the xij Pike men   vj d.
Giuen for Carring the banners. Garland. & leading the horse   ij s.   5
Spent at Steward Bromfeilds howse after ye wach   ij s. vj d.

...

Cordwainers and Shoemakers' Records

CCA: Account Book III G/8/4   10
f 107 *(11 November)*

...

Item to Robert Callye for musique at Martinmas at our Alderman
and 2 stewardes   vj s.

...   15

Item for the Gleaves and Beuerage at shrovetyde   vij s. vj d
Item for musique to the waytes and Callyes   iiij s

...

f 107v   20

...

Imprimis for Beere	viij s
Item for Cheese newe & ould	vij s.
Item for banquetinge Stuffe	vij s. xj d
ffor bread and Cakes	iiij s
Geven to Mistres Shingleton to buie Stockinges gloves & pointes	
	iij s
Item for shoes	xx d.
Item spent att the dressinge the boy	xij d.
Item for Ribon for the horse head	vj d.
Item for Mr Shingletons menn for tendinge the boy	ij s
To Mr Glaseours mann which brought and ledd the horse	xviij d
ffor shoeinge the horse	[xvj d]
To mr Holmes for keepinge the bannor	xij d.
To the Cryar	vj d.
To the Castle and Northgate	ij s.
Item Spent att the barrs	ij s vj d.
Item to Robert Cally for musique	iiij s

Midsomer
Charge

f 108   40

...

Item for musique when Edward Eaton came into our Companie

to bee a *Maister*   ij s.

...

Beerbrewers' Records CCA: Company Book G 3/2
f 102v* *(23 November)*

Midsamer
Chardges 1631 /

Inprimis payd for the Child Boote*es* and spure*es*   vj s
Item for his glowes   xvj d
Item for Samond   vj s viij d
Item for wine   ij s viij d   1
Item for Bread and Cheese   iiij s.
Item for Beere   vij s
Item too the Crier at Castle and Northgate   xviij d.
Item too the musick   v s
Item too Mr Holme for keepinge the banner   xij d   1
Item spent at the dressinge of the Child   xij d

...

Dean and Chapter CC: Treasurers' Accounts IV
p 249 *(Christmas)*   2

...

It*em* to Smalshoe for ye watch   ij s vj d

...

Glovers' Records C: Company Book
p 43 *(January)*   2

...

Midsommer
charges

p*ai*d for Gloues bootes and spurrs for the boye   v s
p*ai*d for the banner   xij d
p*ai*d for lone for a hatt for the boy   vj d   3
p*ai*d for Ribben   xij d
p*ai*d for Gloues for the men   xviij d
Giuen to the Cryer, castle, & Northgate   xviij d
Spentt att the barrs   ix s vj d

...   3

Coopers' Records C: Company Book II
ff 59v-60 *(13 January)*

...

midsomer

It*em* payd for apayre of shues for the boye   xij d   4
It*em* more payd for apayre of stockins   xviij d
It*em* more payd for apayre of gloues   xij d
It*em* more payd for ribbeninge for the Childe*es* shues and for the

horse hed	viij d
Item more payd for the lone of ahatt	xij d
Item more payd for 3 payre of gloues for the foote men	xviij d
Item payd for a Cheese	iij s
Item payd for bred	ij s vj d 5
Item more payd for haulfe ⟨.⟩ barrell of stronge beere	vij s vj d	
Item more payd for the Loane of 2 muskettes and 3 pikes	x d
Item more payd for Aples and other spicese	iij s v d
Item more payd [⟨.⟩] for Carringe of 3 pikes & 3 peeceses	iij s
Item more payd for mache and powder	xxiij d 10
Item more payd for wyne	ij s ix d
Item more payd for musicke	ij s
Item more payd att our Alderman Linakers on midsumer eue	xij d
Item more payd the Cryer	iiij d
Item more payd att the Castell	iiij d 15
Item more payd att the Northgate	vj d
Item more payd for beere att the barres	iiij d
Item more payd for dressinge of 2 peecesses	iiij d

...

20

Joiners, Carvers, and Turners' Records
CCA: Company Book G 14/1
f 125 *(25 March)*

...

Disburcmentes
1630 ...

Item to Richard Bolland to furnish his boy for to ryde on	25
Midsomer eve	viij s
Item to the Cryar, the presoners in ye Castle & northgate	xij d
Item at our Alderman Pues on Midsomer Eve	ij s ij d
Item att widowe Pues then	iij s
Item att Iohn whitbies	ij d 30
Item to the ^ '3' men which ledd the horse	xij d
Item for wyne	xij d
Item for Musique	iij s

...

Item for musique at william Catteralles dynner	xij d 35

...

Mercers, Ironmongers, Grocers, and Apothecaries' Records
C: Company Book
pp 189-90 *(6 May)*

40

...

Item layd out at midsomer following for the banquet	
8 li. pruines	00-02-00

Item more j li. of w*hit*t sugar   [00] -01-08
Item 2 oz. of synim*en*t   00-00-09
Item j li. ½ of Comfyt*es* 20s   00-02-06
Item march pane stufe & concept*es*   00-01-04
Item payd ffor waffers and Cakes   00-04-06
Item payd for appells   00-00-06
Item layd out for the boye and gerell for 2 payer of garters
                                                                       00-03-04
Item 2 yardes of ryben for the horsses head*es*   00-01-00
Item 2 payer of hose for the boye and the gerell   00-05-04   1
Item 2 yardes of ryben for the gerells head and 2 yardes rybyn
for there sue tyes   00-02-00
Item for making the ryben in to rosses   00-00-04
Item 2 payer of Childrens shues   00-02-08
Item 2 paier of Childrens gloues   00-04-00   1
Item 5 payer of mens gloues   00-03-04
Item payd 5 men for attending the Children   00-05-00
Item payd the man that brought the horse for the boye 00-02-00
Item payd the Mussissioners   00-06-08
Item payd the prissoners at Castell and at the northgate 00-04-00   2
Item payd the Cryer   00-01-00
Item layd out at wilsons *with*out bares   00-02-06
Item at mr Tayllors layd out   00-00-06 |
Item payd for j ferkyn of beyre   00-03-0⟨.⟩
Item payd for 6 quartes of Claret wyne vnto the banquet   2
                                                                       00-03-00
Item more j quarte wyne at the dressing of the Children 00-00-06
Item j potele and j pynt of sacke   00-0[⟨.⟩]'2'-11
...
                                                                         3

1631-2
Painters, Glaziers, Embroiderers, and Stationers' Records
C: Account Book II
p 23 *(18 October)*
...   3

Payd for Gloues for ye Aldermen & Stewards at Midsomer
                                                       iij s. iiij d.
Payd for a payre of Bootes for the boy that did Ride   iiij s.
payd for a payre of Gloues for him   xij d
Spent at dressinge of him   x d   4
payd for a Ruben for ye horse head   vj d
Spent at Barrs while wee stayd for mr Maior   xiiij d.
Giuen at ye Barrs Castell & northgate.   xiiij d.

Giuen to ye Trompetor   iij s iiij d
Giuen to ye Drommer   xviij d.
Giuen for Carriage of ye banners. Garland & leading ye horse   ij s.
Giuen to the xii pikemen   vj s.
Spent at Iohn Taylers howse after ye wach on midsomer eue   5
     ij s. vj d.

...

Cordwainers and Shoemakers' Records
CCA: Account Book III G/8/4   10
f 114 *(11 November)*

...

Inprimis To Roberte Callye at our Alderman Gregories vpon the
Eleccion daye   ij s.
...   15
Item payed for our Gleaves, and Beuerage   vij s. iiij d
Item to the Waytes at Shrovetyde   ij s.
Item to the Callyes   ij s.

...

     20
f 114v

...

Midsomer Charge	Item for Beere	vj s. vj d
	Item for Ryban for the horsehead & shoeties	x d.
	Item for Banquettinge Stuffe	vij s. vj d 25
	Item more for Apples & Nuttes	ij s
	Item for Stockinges shoes & gloves	iij s iiij d
	Item for 2 Cheeses	vj s. vj d
	Item for bread	v s.
	Item for 2 quartes of Sacque	ij s. 30
	Item for Musique	iiij s
	Item to them which attended the boy	ij s
	Item spent at dressinge the boye	vj d
	Item spent at Barrs	ij s
	Item to the Cryar	vj d 35
	Item to the prisoners in the Castle & northgate	ij s.
	Item to mr Holmes for keepinge our banner	xij d

Beerbrewers' Records CCA: Company Book G 3/2
ff 109-9v* *(23 November)*   40

Midsommer
Chardges

Imprimis paijd for ten poundes of prunes and one pound of
succar   iij s iiij d

Item paijd for hoose showes & garters for the Child	vj s x d
Item paijd for ʽoneʼ oold Cheese apples & ʽwalʼnuttes	v s
Item paijd for a paijre of glowes for the Child	x d
more for one greene Cheese	ij s vj d
more for Comeffeates and sinamond	iij s iiij d
more at dressinge the Child	xij d
[more for pepper and viniger	j s iiij d]
more vnto Mr Holmees for keeppinge the banner	xij d
more for stronge beere	vij s
more for Riband for the horse	vj d
more at Barres for beere for oure men	xij d
more to the Crier at Castle & Northgate	xviij d
more in wine and sack at Banquet	xviij d
more for 2 sammondes	viij s
More given vnto oure Musick	v s
More given vnto too footmen & one that Carried the Banner	ij s
More for white bread & Cakes	ij s vj d
More for a Riband for the Child	iij d
[More Bestowed one our Musick at parting	iiij d]
More bestowed vpon Mr Birkenhead his man for bringinge the horse	vj d
[More for too samondes	viij s]

...

Glovers' Records C: Company Book
pp 46-7 *(January)*

...

midsomer charges

Item paid for bootes spurres and gloues for the boye	v s ij d
Item paid for the Loane of a hatt	vj d
Item paid for Ribben for the horse	xij d
Item paid for 3 paire of gloues for the men	xviij d
Item Spentt att the Barres	x s vj d
Item Giuen to the Cryer, Castle, and Northgate	xviij d
Item paid to mr Holmes for the Banner	xij d
Item paid to the Musicke	vj s viij d

...

Coopers' Records C: Company Book II
f 63 *(13 January)*

...

Item more payd for beere at Richard Smithes dynner	viij s
Item payd the musicke	iiij s

...

Item more payd for the flagstaufe   xvj d

...

Item more payd for anew Banner to mr Holmes	iij li. xj s	
Item more payd the Cryer att the barres	vj d	5
Item payd att the Castell	vj d	
Item payd for mach	ij d	
Item payd for beere	vj s vj d	
Item payd for prewnes	viij d	
Item payd for 3 pound of powder	iij s iij d	10
Item payd for 4 mens wagges	ij s	
Item payd for Cakes	ij s vj d	
Item payd for the boyes bootes	iiij s	
Item payd for Lone of the hatt	xij d	
Item payd for the boyes gloues	x d	15
Item payd for 2 payre of gloues for the 2 men	xiiij d	
Item more payd for 2 men	xij d	
Item more payd for Cheese	ij s viij d	
Item more payd for aples	vj d	
Item more payd att our Alderman Linackers on midsumer eue		20
	xxij d	
Item more payd for musicke	iij s	
Item more payd for other spyces	xv d	

midsomer Charge (margin, left of "Item payd att the Castell" area)

Joiners, Carvers, and Turners' Records   25
CCA: Company Book G14/1
f 127v *(25 March)*

Disburcem*en*tes ...

Item at mr. Parkers	iij s. iiij d	30
Item for a head for the Banner and paintinge the staffe	v s. viij d	
Item for ffurnishinge the Childe at Midsomer	viij s.	
Item for Rybon for the horsehead	vj d	
Item for dressinge the Childe a pint of sacque	vij d	
Item to the Cryar and prisoners at Midsomer	xij d	35
Item spent then at Ald*erman* Pues	iij s	
Item at Widowe Pues belowe the barres	iij s. vj d	
Item at Steward Bolland*es*	iij s	
Item at Steward Williams	ij s	
Item to the men w*hi*ch ledd the Horse	xvj d	40
Item for Musique	ij s. vj d	

*midsom*er (margin, left of "Item at mr. Parkers")

...

Mercers, Ironmongers, Grocers, and Apothecaries' Records
C: Company Book
p 201 *(4 May)*

...

Item layed out for the boye j payer of wosted stockinges	00-03-00	5
Item for j payer of silke garters	00-02-00	
Item for j payer of sues	00-01-06	
Item j payer of knottes for the sues	00-00-08	
Item j payer of gloues for the boye	00-01-06	
Item for ryben for the horse and man	00-01-00	10
Item payd for dressing and leading the horse	00-03-00	
Item payd 2 men for atending the lord	00-02-00	
Item payd for 3 payer of gloues for 3 men	00-02-00	
Item Layde out for the lady at midsomer j payer of stockinges		
	00-02-04	15
Item j payer of garters	00-01-06	
Item j payer of gloues	00-03-09	
Item [f] payd for j payer of sues	00-01-06	
Item j payer of Rosses	00-01-00	
Item rybens for the ladyes horse	00-01-06	20
Item payd for 6 [me] payer of mens gloues	00-06-00	
Item payd the musissioners for goinge before the Company at midsomer	00-06-08	
Item payd the Cryer for Calling the Company at the bares		
	00-01-00	25
Item more at midsomer payd for a ferkin of stronge beire	00-03-00	
Item layed out for wyne the same tyme	00-0[0]'7'-00	
Item payd for Cakes from the ladye	00-01-00	
Item for waffers prunes fruite sugar syniment and other banquetting stufe	00-14-11	30
Item layd out at wilsons without the bares	00-02-06	
Item given the prissoners at the northgate and at the Castell		
	00-04-00	
Item [spe] layed out vpon the Company in the northgate street vpon the eyven, the daie being very rayenny and foule	00-01-00	35

...

1632-3
Painters, Glaziers, Embroiderers, and Stationers' Records
CCA: Minute Book CR 63/2/131   40
f 20v *(29 June)*

a meeting houlden the 29 June 1632

...

Absent on midsomer eue

Mr humphreys
[William bromfield for Absent & tar 2 meetinges *(1 vote)*   vj d]   5
Io Souch
Tho berchley
Tho pricket sen
Tho pricket & William bromfield for not Coming in their gownes
[deferd to next meeting]   10

...

f 21
Iohn Souch for being absent on midsomer Eue [diuers tymes] &
absent from diuers meetings *(12 votes)*   v s   15
vj s viij d *(1 vote)*
0 *(1 vote)*
ij s vj d *(2 votes)*
...
      20

Painters, Glaziers, Embroiderers, and Stationers' Records
C: Account Book II
p 25 *(18 October)*
...   25
Payd for Gloues for Aldermen & Stewards   iij s iiij d
Payd for Gloues hosen Showes Ruben for ye horse &c: to the
pike men Drumer Trompeter & other matters on midsomer
eue   xxv s vj d
Payd for new Silk for the Trompet banner   v s   30

...

Payd for 2 new Banners on Taffaty Sarsnett fringed for Silke
for the pickes, new pheonixs & Guilding for mens heads: 4
litle Banners of Silke 4 vpon paper 4 Escutions for Garland
      v li. x s   35

...

Payd for Red & Greene Taffaty for ye Typpetts for Silke and
making °for ye tow Stewards°   xx s

...

38 / °for ... Stewards° *added by RH II*

AC *City Treasurers' Accounts* BL: Harley 2158
f 72v *(November)*

...

payd to Roger Geste for beating the drume vpon Shrove*wsdaye*
                                                    xij d

...

payd to the Stuards of the Sadlers towards the bell for
Shrovetewesdaye   vj s viij d

...

f 73

...

payd to Roger Gest for beating the drum the same daye   xij d

...

ff 74v-5*

...

payd to 4 men with halbards by mr maiors apoyntment to keepe
the Compen*n*ys in order vpon mydsomer Eve   iiij s
payd to Edward parry and to his mate for leading and keeping
in order the armed men and shott   ij s iiij d
payd to Thomas Walshe for Carying the Citties Cullers at the
watch °on midsomer Eue°   ij s vj d

...

payd to Roger Gest for beateinge the Drum at the watch   xij d
payd to Robert Thornley and Iohn Wright for their worke
for the watch °for payntinge Giants°   xliij s iiij d
payd more to them for the maiors mount   xxvj s viij d

...

payd to 3 wiflers to keepe Compeny out before the Compenes
at the Comeing in of the lorde deputye   xviij d
payd for a potle of whitewyne with suger a pynte of Sacke and
Cheres by mr maiors appoyntment to bestoe vpon the lady
St Iohn the lady manwaring lady Brerton with others in the
pentiz to staye the lorde deputes Comeing   iij s j d
payd to 2 porters for Carying awaye of dirt from about the
kings boord °in watirgate Street°° and other places by mr
m*ai*ors apoyntm*ent*   vj d
payde for 6 borne of Rushes to stroe in the street where mr
maior aldermen sheriffs sheriff peers and fortye stoode at the

Comeinge of the lorde deputye ˌlord strafford˳   xviij d |
payd for a bankett the *(blank)* of Iuly for the lorde Deputey
the lorde of Castle-haven the lorde bushopp of Chester dyvers
knights and a great number of worthy gentlemen and for wyne
to the said bankett as by a noate of the perticulers it maye   5
appeare   vij li. xij. s j d
payd to the wayetmen by mr maiors appoyntment for playeing
when the lord deputy Came in and the daye after at the bankett
            ij s vj d
payd to mr Gwyne for Rushes and flowers for the pentiz when   10
the lorde deputye Came to the bankett   xviij d
payd to Iames Raffeenscroft for 2 great Venas glasses on of them
a Co*uer* ont it borrowed of him at the banket for the lord deputy
then booth broke   iiij s
...   15

f 75v

...

payd ˄ ʹfor a banket and wyneʼ vpon the xvj th daye of Septemb*er*
by mr maior and aldermans appoyntm*ent*, for the lorde strange   20
and his ladye all their followers *with* many other lades and great
parsonages, as by the perticulers maye appear   vj li. iij s ix d
...

Cordwainers and Shoemakers' Records   25
CCA: Account Book III G/8/4
f 120 *(11 November)*

...

Impr*i*mis for Musique at our Alderman Gregories on St martins
daye   ij s   30

...

It*e*m for musique at Steward Bennett*es*   ij s.

...

Item for Musique at Steward ffletchers   ij s

...   35

f 120v *(7 February)*

...

Item payed for our Gleaves at shrovetyde   vij s
Item to the Waytes at Shrovetyde   ij s. 40
Item the same tyme to Rolent Callie   ij s

...

f 122

Midsomer Charge /

Imprimis. for halfe a barrell of Beere	vij s.
Item for shoeties for the boy and Rybon for ye horsehead	x d
Item for Banquettinge stuffes	vij s. vj d
Item for Aples and Nuttes	ij s
Item for stockinges shoes and gloves	iij s vij d
Item for 2 Cheeses	vj s. j d
Item for Breade ˄ ˈand Cakesˈ	v s. 1
Item for 2 quartes of Sacque	ij s
Item for Musique	iiij s
Item to them which attended the boy and led the horse	ij s
Item spent att dressinge the boy	vj d
Item spent att the barrs	ij s ij d 1
Item to the Cryar	vj d
Item to the Prisoners in the Northgate & Castle	ij s
Item at Alderman Hiltons on Midsomer Eve	xxij d
Item for keepinge the Banner	xij d
...	20

Beerbrewers' Records CCA: Company Book G 3/2
f 112v *(23 November)*

Midsommer
Accomptes

Imprimis payd for hoase showes and garteres and gloves for the Child	25 vj s x d
Item payd for one ould Cheese	iiij s ij d
Item payd for a greene Cheese	ij s iij d
Item payd for one pound of sugar	j s viij d
Item for one pound of Coumfeites	j s viij d 30
Item for prunees	j s x d
Item for sinamant	oo - x d
Item for vinigar	j s
Item for walnuttes	ix d
Item for Lemondes and orengees	x d 35
Item for white bread and Cakees	ij s x d
Item for wine and sack	iij s
Item given vnto our Musick	v s
Item given for triming of the horse and for a Riband for the horse	j s 40
Item given three men to Carry the Banner and to atend the Child	xviij d

Item given to the Crier and at Castle and Northgate   xviij d
Item given vnto Mr Holme*es* for keeping the Banner   xij d
Item for beere att the Barr*es* for our men   xij d
Item for strong beere at Banquet   vij s
Item payd vnto the drawer*es* in dee for 2 saman*es*   x s   5

...

Glovers' Records C: Company Book
p 53 *(January)*   10

Midsom*er*
Charges. /

p*ai*d for powder and match   xiij s vj d
p*ai*d for hose, shooes, gloues, and for lone of a hatt for the boye
    vj s viij d
p*ai*d for Riben for the horse   xij d   15
p*ai*d for 3 paire of gloues for the men   xviij d
p*ai*d and Spentt att the Barrs   vij s
p*ai*d and giuen to the Cryer castle & Northgate   xviij d
p*ai*d to m*aster* Holmes for the Banner   xij d
p*ai*d and Giuen to the Musicke   vj s viij d   20

...

Joiners, Carvers, and Turners' Records
CCA: Company Book G 14/1   25
f 129v *(25 March)*

Disburcem*en*tes ...

Midsom*er*
Charge

It*em* for a pynte of Wyne at dressinge the Childe   vj d   30
It*em* for furnishinge the Childe   vij s. vj d
It*em* for musique   ij s. viij d
It*em* to the Cryar and the prison*ers*   xij d
It*em* to them w*hich* attended the boy and ledd the horse   ij s.
It*em* for Rybon for the horse head   vj d   35
It*em* for wyne att our Banquett   xvj d

...

3º december

It*em* at Ald*erman* Salisburies for stronge drincke at our dynner
and supp*er*   xvj d
...   40
It*em* for Musique   ij s

...

Mercers, Ironmongers, Grocers, and Apothecaries' Records
C: Company Book
p 212 *(9 May)*

...

Item for a paier of hose for the lord	00-03-00.
Item for j payer of sues for the lord	00-01-08
Item for Ryband to make knottes for his sues	00-01-00.
Item for ryband to make tyes for his [sue] knottes	00-00-02
Item for ryband for his bande	00-00-03.
Item for j payer of silke garters	00-02-00.

Item Sir henry Bunberres man for bringeing and dressing the
horse for the lord 00-02-00.
Item paid to 3 men to lead the hors & tend the lord 00-03-00.

Item for 3 paier of gloues for 3 men	00-02-00.
Item for j paier of gloues for the lord	00-02-00
Item for the lady j payer of hose	00-02-08.
Item j payer of gloues for her	00-03-00.
Item j payer of knottes and j payer of sues	00-02-06
Item rybandes for her horse	00-02-00.
Item 4 payer of gloues	00-04-00.
Item payd a fellowe that Caried the banner	00-01-00.
Item for bringeing the horse	00-01-00

...

Item to the prissoners of the Castell and north gate 00-04-00
Item payd the Cryer at the barrs 00-01-00
Item to the wydowe wilson at the barres and that was spent on
the Company there 00-02-06.
Item for ryband for the horse head and tayell 00-01-00
Item to Thomas williams man for the loan of brydell and sadell
00-01-06

Item for 8 li. of prunes	00-01-04
Item j li. of sugar	00-01-08
Item 2 oz. syniment	00-00-11
Item j boxe of marmylet	00-02-00
Item in Comfettes and other bankqueting stufe	00-05-00
Item payd for Cakes and waferns	00-04-00
Item for j ferkin of stronge beer	00-03-00
Item for j pottell of sacke	00-02-00.
Item for j gallon of Claret and white wyne	00-02-00.

p 213

...

Item payd to the mussitions for goinge be for the Companey

at Midsomer   00-06-08

...

1633-4

A   *Mayors List 5* BL: Harley 2125   5
   f 61* *(15 July) William Spark*

...

15 Iuly 1633 Vescont wentworth lord deputy of Irland Came to
chester to goe for Irland the maior & Aldermen stoode in the
Estgate street in Scarlett to receue him the stood from   10
milkestoopes arowe downe street also the Companyes with their
baners stood on eich side street to the Estgate: he lay at the
bushops pallas & was next day banqueted at pendice & so
departed to Irland

...   15

Painters, Glaziers, Embroiderers, and Stationers' Records
C: Account Book II
p 27 *(18 October)*   20

...

for gloues for ye Aldermen & Stewards   iij s. iiij d.
for gloues hosen showes for mr Sheriffs sonne that rid at
midsomer & for Ruben for ye horse   v s
to the pike men & halbert man   vj s. vj d. 25
for Carringe the banners & garland & leading the horse iij s. vj d.
to the dromer & Trompetor   v s. iiij d.
Giuen at barrs Castell & norgate   xx d.
Spent at barrs while we Stayed there   xxij d.

...   30

Cordwainers and Shoemakers' Records
CCA: Account Book III G/8/4
f 132 *(11 November)*   35

...

Item given to the Musique at our Alderman Pembertons howse
                                                       0-2-0.
Item given at our Alderman Ioynsons for the like   0-2-0.

...   40

Item paide for Musique at our Steward Cases howse   0-2-0
Item paid at our Steward Martins for the like   0-2-0

...

f 132v

...

Item paid for the Gleaves at Shrovetyde	00-06-00
Item given to the Barrage	00-01-04
Item given to the weates the same tyme	00-02-00
Item given to other Musique	00-02-00
Item paid for beere	00-00-02

...

ff 133-3v

...

Midsomer Charge.

Middsomer
Charge.

Imprimis for halfe a barrell of beere	00-07-00
Item for Ribon for the horse and shoe tyes	00-01-00
Item for j. payre of Stockinges for the boye	00-02-06
Item for a payre of gloves	00-01-00
Item to the men for leadinge the horse	00-01-00.
Item given to the prisoners of the Castle & Northgate	00-02-00
Item more to the Cryer	00-00-06
Item spent at the barrs	00-03-00
Item paid for 5. pyntes of secke	00-02-06.
Item for Nuttes & apples	00-02-00
Item for secke at dressinge the boye	00-00-06
Item for banquetinge stuffe	00-07-00	
Item for 2. Cheeses	00-07-09
Item for bread & Cakes	00-06-00
Item for the boyes shooes	00-01-04
Item for Musique	00-04-00
Item for keepinge the banner	00-01-00

...

f 134

(St Martin's Day)

...

Item for Musique	iiij d

...

Beerbrewers' Records CCA: Company Book G3/2
ff 118v-19 *(23 November)*

...

Midsomer
Chardgees

Imprinis for hose showees and garters ´glouees` for the Child

vj s 10d

Item payd for one ould Cheese	[v] iiij s xj d
Item payd for one greene Cheese	ij s vj d
Item payd for two samond*es*	x s │
Item for sugar	xxiij d
Item for Comfeat*es*	xx d
Item for sinamont	xij d
Item for twelve pound*es* of prune*es*	xxij d
Item for five quart*es* of vinigar	xx d
Item in Lemond*es* and orange*es*	viij d
Item for apple*es*	viij d.
Item for walnutt*es*	x d
Item for bread & Cake*es*	v s
Item for strong beere att Banquet	vij s
Item payd for keeping the Banner	xij d
Item given vnto the Crier att Barrs Castle and Northgate	xviij d
Spent att vallantine ffletcher vpon our men	ij s
It*em* given for a Riband for the horse	viij d
Item given to the Musicke	vj s
Item given vnto Robert denson to buie him ij love*es* for tending the Child	viij d
Item given vnto the man that brought the salmond*es*	vj d

...

City Waits BL: Lansdowne 213
ff 326-6v*

...

The next Morning we were early vp, being rous'd from *our* sweet │
sleep by the Citty Wayts, whose absence we had rather desir'd,
nott for the Charge, but for *our* Rest, yet thereby were we the
earlier, and readier to performe *our* mornings Deuotions at their
Cathedrall, and to heare a graue Prebend preach in his Surplice. ...

f 327

...

The Citizens retaine an old Order, & Custome, w*hi*ch is this,
allwayes on Christmas euen the Watch begin, & the Mayor,
Sheriffs, Aldermen, & fortie of the Com*m*on Counsell, goe about
the Cittie, in triumph, w*i*th Torches, & ffire-workes. The Recorder
making a Speech of the Antiquity of her, founded by Gyants: On
Midsummer euen, the Giants, & some wild Beasts (that are
constantlie kept for that purpose) are carry'd about the Towne. ...

Glovers' Records C: Company Book
p 61 *(January)*

<table>
<tr><td>Midsomer
charges</td><td>paid for powder and Match</td><td>xx s vj d</td><td></td></tr>
<tr><td></td><td colspan="2">paid for hose shooes gloues and the loane of a hatt for the boye</td><td></td></tr>
<tr><td></td><td></td><td>vj s viij d</td><td></td></tr>
<tr><td></td><td>paid for Ryben for the horse</td><td>xviij d</td><td></td></tr>
<tr><td></td><td>paid for 3 paire of gloues for the men</td><td>xxij d</td><td></td></tr>
<tr><td></td><td>paid for [⟨..⟩y] Gloues for Aldermen and Stewards</td><td>vj s viij d</td><td></td></tr>
<tr><td></td><td>paid att the Barrs Castle and Northgate</td><td>xviij d</td><td>1</td></tr>
<tr><td></td><td>paid to the Musicke</td><td>vj s viij d</td><td></td></tr>
<tr><td></td><td>paid to Carry their lowd Instrum*en*ts</td><td>vj d</td><td></td></tr>
<tr><td></td><td>paid for the Banner</td><td>xij d</td><td></td></tr>
<tr><td></td><td>Spentt att the Barrs</td><td>iij s</td><td></td></tr>
<tr><td></td><td>...</td><td></td><td>1</td></tr>
</table>

Joiners, Carvers, and Turners' Records
CCA: Company Book G14/1
f 131v *(25 March)*   2

Disburcem*en*tes ...

<table>
<tr><td>Midsom*er*
charge</td><td>Item for a newe Banner</td><td>iij li.</td><td></td></tr>
<tr><td></td><td>Item for the banner staffe</td><td>xvj d</td><td>2</td></tr>
<tr><td></td><td>Item for peecinge the Rodd for the Banner</td><td>iij d</td><td></td></tr>
<tr><td></td><td>Item gevinge to the Beu*er*age at makinge the Banner</td><td>vj d</td><td></td></tr>
<tr><td></td><td>Item for Charg*es* fornishinge the Boy</td><td>viij s</td><td></td></tr>
<tr><td></td><td>Item for a quarte of wyne ^ ꞌ& sugerꞋ dressing the boy</td><td>viij d.</td><td></td></tr>
<tr><td></td><td>Item for Rybon for the horsehead</td><td>vj d</td><td>3</td></tr>
<tr><td></td><td>Item for powder for Tho*mas* Willi*a*mson</td><td>vj d</td><td></td></tr>
<tr><td></td><td>Item for dressinge the Horse</td><td>vj d</td><td></td></tr>
<tr><td></td><td>Item to the Cryar att the Barres, & the p*re*son*er*s in the Castle
and the Northgate</td><td>xij d</td><td></td></tr>
<tr><td></td><td>Item for Wyne att our Banquett</td><td>vj d</td><td>3</td></tr>
<tr><td></td><td>Item for stronge beere att our banquett</td><td>xij d</td><td></td></tr>
<tr><td></td><td>Item to 4 men attendinge the boy & the Horse at the shewe</td><td>ij s</td><td></td></tr>
<tr><td></td><td>Item for hurte w*hic*h the Horse did at Chattertons, breakinge
his Mugge, and his Wall</td><td>vj d</td><td></td></tr>
<tr><td></td><td>Item for Musique</td><td>ij s. viij d</td><td>4</td></tr>
<tr><td></td><td>Item spent at our Ald*erman* Davies</td><td>ij s vij d</td><td></td></tr>
<tr><td></td><td>Item at Widowe Pues at the barres</td><td>ij s</td><td></td></tr>
<tr><td></td><td>...</td><td></td><td></td></tr>
</table>

Mercers, Ironmongers, Grocers, and Apothecaries' Records
C: Company Book
p 220 *(2 May)*

...

Item paid at midsomer for the lady. for j paier of gloues and j   5
paier of sues 3s. & 18d   00-04-06
Item j paier of hoes & j paier of knottes   00-03-04
Item ryband for the horse   00-02-00
Item for fore men 4 paier of gloues   00-04-00
Item for caringe the banner   00-01-00   10
Item paid the man that brought the horse   00-01-00
Item paid to the prissonrs at the northe gate and Castell 00-04-00
Item paid the Crier   00-01-00
Item paid at widowe wilsons for the Roome and for the
Company   00-05-00   15
Item the lord j paier of gloues   00-02-06
Item for sues stockinges & rosses   00-05-00
Item 5 yardes ryband 20d: 3 paier mens gloues 2s: in all 00-03-08
Item 3 men to atend the [ladye] ˊBoyeˋ   00-03-00
Item paid the man that brought the horse and for driuinge him   20
                                                        00-02-00
Item for 8 li. prunes 16d: j li. suger 20d   00-03-00
Item for siniment j box of marmylett for comfetes and other
banquetinge stufe   00-07-11
Item for Cakes and Wafers   00-04-00   25
Item paid for j ferkin stronge beer   00-03-00
Item paid for j potell sacke j gallowen of whitt and Clarett
wyne   00-04-08
...
                                                                  30

p 221

...

Item paid mr Alderman holmes for payntinge and gildinge
the banners Anewe   04-00-00
...   35
for musicke att Midsomer   00-06-08

...

Painters, Glaziers, Embroiderers, and Stationers' Records
CCA: Minute Book CR 63/2/131   40
f 25 *(11 June)*

it is ordred that the 2 banners shall be made new agaynst midsomer

also it is ordred that the drinking on midsomer Eue shall be
abolished & no drinking at all but dressing of the child according
to the ould custome

no drngkdig after after wach 'at all all' *(19 votes)*

[wheras hertofore there hath byn a bancquet or Colation made by
the Stewards vpon midsomer eue after the show for the bretheren
of the Company according as the tymes then were; and benge
made of the Stewards owne charges the Company only payng   1
ij s vj d for beeare but at last the sayd Colation was turned to
a banquet or feast to the great charg of the stewards & also
Caused the Company to exceed in expeces of wyne & beare
aboue the Auntiente alowaice: as may be seene by seuerall
acconts hertofore: for auoydinge of the sayd excesse thein both   1
of the [stewards] Company & stewards & because midsomer eue
is a bussy tyme for all our brethern eich desiring to follow his
bussnesse: few ʌ 'of them' comig to the sayd banquet aforsayd it
is therfore ordred by a generall Consent the xi Iune 1633 that
euery brother after the wach is ended may be at his owne liberty   2
to goe home if he please & [that the steward shall make noe
drinkinge]'banquet' on midsomer eue at all nor haue no allowance
if he make any banquet or Colation but only the ij s vj d auntienty
vsed to make the bretheren drink who accompany the boy that
ridd to the Stewards howse]   2

1634-5

A   *Mayors List 5* BL: Harley 2125
    f 61v* *(24 July)* *Randle Holmes*

      ...   3

24 Iuly Came to chester the ʌ 'lady Anne' Countice of Ancoram
da*ughter* to the E*arl* of Darby & the 25 Iuly had a banquet in
the pentice of chester of w*hi*ch was the E*arl* of Darby & diuers
great ladyes w*hi*ch tooke the same very thankfully the same
month Came to chester the E*arl* of bridgwater lo*rd* president   3.
of the marches & his wife & dyned at mr Recorders howse
where was exeding great entertaynment after the had a banquet

---

5 / drngkdig *for* dringkdig, *minim omitted MS*
5 / after after *MS dittography*   5 / all all *MS dittography*
14 / alowaice *for* allowance, *minim omitted MS*
15 / thein *for* therin
18 / comig *for* coming, *2 minims omitted MS*

in the pendice w*hic*h the tooke very thankfully as also for his
entertaynment at his Coming in the Companyes standing on
eich side bridgstreet from the Recordes dore where the maior
etc: stood the Companys downward toward bridg

...   5

Painters, Glaziers, Embroiderers, and Stationers' Records
C: Account Book II
p 29 *(18 October)*

...   10

Item payd for clensing the meetinghouse of ye ould rushes &
mendinge of ye Phenixes and ´for new Rushes our part`   ix d

...

Item for gloues hosen Showes for the boy that ridd at midsomer
& for Ruben for ye horse   v s   15
Item to ye horse leader & garland bearer   xij d
Item to ye tow banner bearers & 2 men that held ye child   ij s
Item spent at barrs while we stayd for mr Maior   xij d

...

Item for gloues for ye Aldermen & Stewards   iij s iiij d   20
Item giuen at Barrs Castell & northgate   xx d
Item giuen to the Trompitor   iij s iiij d
Item giuen to ye Drummer   xviij d
Item spent at ye Stewards howse afte ye wach on midsomer
Eue   ij s vj d   25

...

Cordwainers and Shoemakers' Records
CCA: Account Book III G/8/4
f 140 *(11 November)*   30

...

Impr*i*mis paide to the Musique on Saint Martins att our Alderman
Pemb*er*tones howse   00-02-00
Item paide att Iohn Ioynsons howse for musique   00-02-00
Item paid att George Hiltons howse for musique   00-02-00   35

...

f 140v

...

Item given to the Berridge at Makinge the gleaves   00-0[1]-00   40

...

Item paid vnto Mr Edward*es* for the gleaves   00-06-00

...

f 141

Item paide to the Waytes & Calleys att Shrovetide	00-04-0

...

f 141v

Middsomer Charge.

Imprimis for halfe a barrell of beere	0-7-6	
Item for Rybon & shooe tyes for the boye & the horse	0-1-0	
Item for stockinges for the boye	0-2-6	↑
Item for a payre shoes	0-1-4	
Item for a payre of gloves	0-1-0	
Item for the man that brought the horse	0-0-6	
Item for leadinge the horse to 2. men	0-1-0	
Item given to the prisoners	0-2-0	1
Item given to the Cryer	0-0-6	
Item spent at the barrs	0-3-0	
Item spent in wyne at dressinge the boye	0-0-6	
Item paid for banquetinge stuffe	0-9-4	
Item paide for Cheese	0-6-8.	2
Item paide for bread & Cakes	0-6-0	
Item paid for a pottle of secke at the banckett	0-2-0	
Item paide for Musique	0-4-0	
Item for keeinge the banner	0-1-0	
Item spent in beere	0-0-2	2

...

f 142

...

Item paid att mr Alderman Gregories the same daye	0-3-8	3
Item paid to the Musique	00-02-00	

...

Beerbrewers' Records CCA: Company Book G 3/2
f 123v *(23 November)*

3

...

<table>
<tr><td rowspan="7">Midsomer
Chardges</td><td>Item payd for hose Showees and garteres for the Child</td><td>00-06-10</td><td></td></tr>
<tr><td>Item for one ould Cheese</td><td>0-05-00</td><td></td></tr>
<tr><td>Item one greene Cheese</td><td>0-02-4</td><td></td></tr>
<tr><td>Item 2 salmondes</td><td>0-10-0</td><td>4</td></tr>
<tr><td>Item one poundes of sugar</td><td>0-01-8</td><td></td></tr>
<tr><td>Item one pound of Coumfeytes</td><td>0-01-7</td><td></td></tr>
</table>

Item 12 poundes of prunees	0-01-8
Item for sinnamot	0-01-0
Item for vinigar	0-01-9
Item for Lemondes and orayngees	0-00-6
Item for walnuttes	0-01-00
Item for whyte bread and Cakees	00-02-8
Item for stroung beere att Banquet	0-07-6
Item for keeping the Banner	0-01-00
Item for a Ryband for the horse head	0-00-6
Item unto the Crijar att the barres Castle & Northgate	0-01-6
Item spent att vallantine ffletcher on our men	0-02-0
Item given to the Musick	0-06-0
Item given vnto the too men for tending the Child	01-4
Item given the men that brought the salmondes	0-00-6
Item given for wyne and sack	0-04-0

Glovers' Records C: Company Book
p 68 *(January)*

...

Midsomer
Charges.

Paid for Match and Powder	xx s
paid for gloues for Aldermen and Stewards	vj s viij d
paid for bootes Spurrs and gloues for the boye and for loane of a hatt	v s. iiij d
paid for gloues for the men	xxij d
paid for Ribben for the horse	xviij d
paid to the Musicke	vj s viij d
paid for the Banner	xij d
Giuen att barres Castle and Northgate	xviij d
Spentt at the Barres	iij s vj d

...

Coopers' Records C: Company Book II
f 68 *(13 January)*

...

more paide at the dinner of George watt for beere and musick	jx s iiij d

...

f 68v

...

midsomer
charge

paide vnto m Hollmes ffor the banner	xij d

...

more paid to Thomas Malbone the smith for a hoope for the
staffe   xij d
more paide for halfe a barell of beere   viij s
more paide for the boyes bootes   iiij s
more paid for the boyes gloues and ij paire for the ij men   ij s
more paide for powder and match   iiij s
more the dressing of ij musketts and for the lone of ij bandilleros
    xij d

more for cakes   ij s vj d
more nutts pruines [pr] and apples and other spise   ij s vj d
more paid ffor wine   iij s vj d.
more paid for cheese   iij s iiij d
more paide for musicke   iij s iiij d
more spent at the barres   ij s
more giuen to the crier at the barres   iiij d
more giuen at the castle and northgate   xij d
more paide five men for there wages   ij s vj d
more for a bridle and ribbeninge for the horse   xxij d
more giuen Thomas Bauche a ˄ˈpaire ofˈ gloues and money   xij d
more paid for the lone of a hatt   xij d
...

Joiners, Carvers, and Turners' Records
CCA: Company Book G14/1
f 133v *(25 March)*
    Disburcement*es* ...

Midsom*er*
Charge

Item spent att hyringe our Musique for Midsom*er*   ij d
Item to the Cryar, the p*re*sone*rs* in ye Castle & Northgate   xij d
Item att our Ald*erman* Davies   iij s. iiij d
Item for Musique   ij s viij d
Item for keepinge our Banner   xij d
Item spent att Widowe Pues   iij s.
Item for Wyne att dressinge the boye   viij d
Item for Rybon for the horsehead   vj d
Item to them W*hi*ch ledd the horse & attended the boye   xviij s
Item for furnishinge the Boye   viij s
Item for dressinge the Horse   iiij d
...

f 134
...

not allowed

+ It*em* payed for furniture w*hi*ch our Steward William Williams had provyded for a boy to ryde at Mydsomer   viij s +

...

Mercers, Ironmongers, Grocers, and Apothecaries' Records
C: Company Book   5
p 228 *(8 May)*

...

Item paid at midsomer for stockings for the boy	00-02-08.
Item paid for ribon &: for roses for his shooes	00-01-02
Item paid for j paire gloves & j pair siclk garters	00-04-04
Item paid for his shooes	00-01-08
Item paid for 8 l. proynes with j l. Lose suger	00-03-00
Item paid for Cinomon & marmalate	00-03-00
Item paid for banquettinge stuffe and waforns	00-09-00
Item paid for Ribon for the horse	00-01-00.
Item paid widow willson at midsomer for ye Compan	00-05-00.
Item paid the prisoners at the Northgate & Castill	00-04-00.

...

Item paid the Crier	00-01-00
Item paid twoo men for bringing the horse & leading him bee	
very vnrulie	00-03-00.
Item paid for 3 paire of gloues for 3 men	00-02-00
Item paid 3 men for tending the boy	00-03-00.
Item paid for musicke	00-06-08.
Item paid for stronge beare	00-03-06
Item paid for wyne	00-04-08.

...

Item Laid out for the geirle; for. shooes stockings roses & gloues	
⌜& Ribon ye horse⌝	00-11-02
Item paid for attending the ladie	00- 2-06
Item paid for gloues fore 4 men	00- 3-00

...

1635-6
Painters, Glaziers, Embroiderers, and Stationers' Records
C: Account Book II   35
p 31 *(18 October)*

...

Item for Gloues Bootes & Ribband for ye ⟨...⟩ Child yat Ridd	
& for furniture for ye horse at Midsomer	vj ʃ
Item spent at dressinge of ye Childe	xij d
Item to ye horse leader & Garland bearer	xij d
Item to ye 2 banners bearers & ye 2 men yat heald ye Childe	ij s

Item spent at ye Barrs Staying for mr Maior   xij d
Item giuen at ye Barrs Castell & northgate   xx d
Item giuen to ye 12 Pikemen & Halbert man   vj s vj d
Item giuen for gloues to ye Aldermen & Stewards   iij s iiij d
Item giuen to the Trompitor   iij s iiij d
Item giuen to Preston ye Trompitor by ye Aldermens
appoyntment.   xij d
Item giuen to Tho Ashton the Drummer   xviij d
...
Item Spent at Stewards howse after midsomer Eue   ij s vj d
...

Cordwainers and Shoemakers' Records

CCA: Account Book III G/8/4
f 147 *(11 November)*
...

(Election Day)
Item for Musique att our Alderman Gregories   ij s
...
Item for musique at steward Totties   ij s
Item for musique at steward Tyrers   ij s
...
Item spent vpon the gouldsmith when wee spake for the gleaves
                                                                                       ij d
...

f 147v
...

30. ffebruarij	Item to mr Edwardes the gouldsmith for our gleaues and to the Beuerage	vij s.
3. Martij	Item to the Waytes at shroovetyde	ij s
3. Martij	Item to the Callies	ij s
	...	
31. Martij	Item spent on our Clarke in settinge downe our shroovetyde Accomptes and other reaconinges	iiij d
20 Iunij	Item spent on our Clarke takinge a note of Midsomer charges and other thinges	ij d
	Item spent in gatheringe the money for powder on Midsomer Eue	ij d
midsomer Charge 1636.	Item for halfe a barrell of Beere	vij s. vj d
	Item for Rybon for the horsees shoeties for the boye	xij d
	Item for stockinges for the boye	ij s. vj d

Item for shoes for the boye	xvj d.
Item for gloves	xij d
Item to him Which brought the horse	vj d
Item to 3 men which ledd the horse and attended the boye	xviij d
Item to the Cryar	vj d
Item spent att the barres	iij s. viij d
Item to the prisoners in ye Castle & northgate	ij s.
Item in Wyne att dressinge the boye	vj d
Item for banquettinge stuffes	ix s. vj d
Item for Cheeses	vj s. viij d
Item for bread & Cakes	vj s. vj d
Item for a quarte of sacque at our banquett	xij d
Item for Musique	iiij s
Item for keepinge the Banner	xij d

f 148 *(August)*

...

Item to mistris Gregorie at an overplus at Arthur Willsons Admittance	ix s. vj d

...

Item for Musique then	ij s

...

Item more for beere bestowed on the Musique	vj d

...

Beerbrewers' Records CCA: Company Book G 3/2
ff 128-8v *(23 November)*

...

Item payd by mee Iohn lloyd out of the quarterayge moneij vnto Mr Holme for keepinge the Banner	xij d	
payd the same tyme of the same money for mendinge the Banner bij mee Iohn lloyd	xij d	
Item for one ould Cheese	iij s vj d	
Item for one pound & halfe of sugar	ij s jx d	
Item for 10 poundes of prunees	j s viij d	
Item for Lemoundes	jx d	
Item for applees	xij d	
Item for Cakees	xij d	
Item Bakeres Cakees	ij s	
Item for white Bread	ij s	
Item for Cheriees	vj d	
Item for Comfeitees	iij s iiij d	

Midsomer
accomptes /

Item for sinamond   vj d
Item for vinagar   ij s
Item [for] to the man that brought the samant   vj d
Item for stroung beere   vjj s vj d |
Item for Rybond for the horse mane   j s 9d
Item payd for a Ryband for the horse   vj d
Item for a quart of sack & ij pottlees of wine[es]   iij s
Item for walnuttes   xiiij d
Item for them that led the horse   ij s
Item to the Cryer   xij d
Item att Castle and Northgate   xij d
Item given to the [muske] Musick   vij s
Item for the Childes hose and shewees   vj s 10d
Item for two samandes   10s
...

Glovers' Records C: Company Book
p 72 *(January)*

Midsomer
Charges

Paid for Match and powder   xviij s
paid for Gloues for Aldermen & Stewards   viij s
paid for hose shooes and gloues for the boye   v s iiij d
paid for Gloues for the men   xxij d
paid for Riben for the horse   xviij d
paid for the Banner   xij d
paid & Giuen to the Musicke   vj s viij d
Giue att Barrs Castle and North gate   xviij d
Spentt att the Barrs   iiij s
...

Coopers' Records C: Company Book II
f 72 *(13 January)*
...

midsom
Charg

more paide for halfe a barell of beere   vij s vj d
more paide for a paire of stockings for the boy   ij s iiij d
more paide for a paire of gloues for the boye   xiiij d
more for powder and mach   iij s
more for a paire of shooes for the boye   xvj d
more for Cakes   iij s ij d
more apples nutts pruines and other spice   iij s ij d
...

more paide for the lone of 2 peecses and 2 bandelers   vj d

more paide for the dressing of 3 peeses	viij d
more for ribben for the horse hed	vj d
more paide for a bridle for the horse	xiiij d
more paide mr Holmes for keeping the banner	xij d
more paide for Cheese	iij s	5
more paide at the barrs for beere	ij s ij d
more paid at at the barrs Castel and northgate	xij d.
more paide for musike	ij s vj d
more paide for 3 paire of gloves for 3 footemen	xx d
more paide for five mens wages	ij s vj d	10

...

f 72v

...

more paide to the musick at the dinner of George Richardson   15

iij s

...

Joiners, Carvers, and Turners' Records   20
CCA: Company Book G14/1
ff 136-6v *(25 March)*

...

Disbursementes ...

     25

Midsomer
Charges

Item for furnisheinge the boy	viij s.
Item for a quarte of Wyne	vj d.
Item for a Ribben for the horse	vj d.
Item to the Cryar & the prisoners	xij d
Item spent att our Alderman Pewes	iiij s	30
Item spent att Widdow Pewes att the Barrs	iij s viij d
Item att our Steward Baguleys att our banquett in stead of Wyne	ij s. vj d.
Item for 3 men attendinge the Child	xij d.	
Item spent att the hyringe of the Musique	ij d	35
Item paid to the Musique	ij s viij d
Item for keepinge the Banner	xij d.

...

7 / at at *MS dittography*

Mercers, Ironmongers, Grocers, and Apothecaries' Records
C: Company Book
p 234 *(6 May)*

...

It*em* p*ai*d for shooes stockings Roses gloues and [Ribbon]	
ʹgirdlesʹ for the geirle	00-09-0[4 4]
It*em* for Ribband for the horsse	00-02-00
p*ai*d for Ribband for knotts for ther lady	01-06
It*em* p*ai*d for j. pottle of wtt wine	
It*em* j. pottle of clarett. j. pottle	00-05-00
It*em* of ye best sack	
It*em* p*ai*d for banquettinge stuffe	00-05-00
It*em* for Cakes & Wafers	00-04-00
It*em* for Cynamond & marmilott	00-03-00
It*em* for prunes & sugar	00-03-00
It*em* for stronge beere	00-03-06
It*em* to the prisoners att the [barrs]	00-04-00
It*em* Castle & northgate	
It*em* [pd] giuen the Cryer att the Barres	01-00
It*em* giuen to Widdow Wilson for	00-05-00
It*em* the Roome. & beere	
It*em* p*ai*d for 4 paire of gloues and	00-06-00
It*em* for triminge the horsse	
It*em* p*ai*d for Cariinge the banner	00-01-00
It*em* p*ai*d for Musick	00-06-08

...

p 235

...

It*em* Iune ye 21th layd out for ye boy j paire of hose	02-08
It*em* j. paire of Garters	02-00
It*em* for Riband & Roses	01-02
It*em* for A paire of gloues	02-00
It*em* for a paire of spanish leather shoo*es*	01-08
It*em* for ij yards of Ribband	01-00
It*em* for iij paire of gloues for .3. men	03-00
It*em* for atendinge ye boy to .3. men	03-00
It*em* giuen mr. Harpurrs man for	02-00
It*em* triminge & leadinge ye horsses	

17 / to *written over* for   17 / att *written over* aft

1636-7
Smiths, Cutlers, and Plumbers' Records C: Account Book II
pp 16-17 *(July)*

...

Midsomer
Charge

Item for Powder and Match	ix s	5
Item for a quart of Wyne att dressinge the Childe	vj d ‖	
Item for keepinge the Banner	xij d.	
Item to the Cryar att the barres & the prisoners in the Castle and Northgate	xviij d.	
Item for Rybon, for the horse & Scutchion	xvij d	10
Item for 3 men which ledd the horse and attended the Boy	iij s. vj d.	
Item for our Musique	vj s. viij d	
Item spent att Robert Iohnsons at the Barres	ij s. viij d.	
Item att our steward Ryders fetchinge the Boy and horse	xviij d	15
Item for our banquett on Midsomer Eve	xxj s.	

...

Painters, Glaziers, Embroiderers, and Stationers' Records
C: Account Book II   20
p 33 *(18 October)*

...

Item for hose Showes and gloues for ye Child yat Ridd at midsomer	v s	
Item giuen to ye 12 pikemen & ye halbert man	vj s vj d	25
Item giuent to ye drummer	xviij d	
Item giuen to the Trompeter	iij s iiij d	
Item spent at ye barrs Stayinge for mr Maior	xij d	
Item giuen at ye barrs Castell & Northgate	xx d	
Item giuen for gloues for ye Aldermen & Stewards	iij s iiij d	30
Item Spent at dressinge the child yat Ridd according to Custom	xij d	
Item giuen ye horsleader garland & baners bearers & 2 that heald the child	iij s	
Spent at ye Stewards howse after ye wach on midsomer Eue	ij s vj d	35

...

Cordwainers and Shoemakers' Records
CCA: Account Book III G/8/4   40
f 153 *(11 November)*

...

Imprimis to the Musitioners at our Aldermans	ij s

...

| Ianuarij 1636. | Item payed for musique When Iohn yonge, Richard ffletcher & Robert ffletcher weare admitted | ij. s |

...

Item payed for the Gleaves ⌃'& for the Beuerage˺   vij s vj d

...

ff 153v-4

Shrovetyde	Item geven to the Waytes	ij s
	Item spent on them in drincke	ij d
	Item to the Callyes	ij s
	Item spent on them	ij d

...

Midsomer charges	Item for halfe a barrell of Beere	viij s.
	Item for the horse & shoeties for the boy	xij d
	Item for stockinges	ij s. vj d
	Item for shoes	xx d
	Item for gloves	xij d
	Item to him Which brought the horse	vj d
	Item to 3 men Which ledd the horse & attended ye boy	xviij ⟨.⟩
	Item spent att the barres	iij s. viij d
	Item to the Cryar	vj d.
	Item to the prisoners in the Castle & northgate	ij s.
	Item for Wyne dressinge the boy	vj d
	Item for banquettinge stuffs	ix s. vj d
	Item for Cheese	vj s. viij d	
	Item for bread & Cakes	vj s. vj d
	Item for a quart of sacque att our banquett	xiiij d
	Item for Musique	iiij s
	Item for keepinge the Banner	xij d
	Item payed for Match & powder	xvij s. iiij d
j Iulij	Item spent on our Clarke settinge the midsomer charges downe, and castinge vp our Accomptes vntill this day	iiij d

...

Beerbrewers' Records CCA: Company Book G 3/2
f 130v *(23 November)*

Midsomer Accounts   L.   s   d

Imprimis for keepinge & mendinge the Banner by dickason
00-01-06

Item for an ould Cheese   00-03-06
Item for sugar   00-02-09
Item for prunes   00-01-08
Item for Alemonds   00-00-09
Item for apples   00-01-00   5
Item for Cakes   00-01-00
Item for Bakers Cakes and white bread   00-04-00
Item for Cherries.   00-00-06
Item for Comfeittees   00-03-04
Item for sinnamond   00-00-06   10
Item for vinigar   00-02-00
Item to the man that brought the samanes   00-00-06
Item for strounge beere   00-07-06
Item for Ryband for the horse maine   00-01-09
Item another Riband for the horse   00-00-06   15
Item for wine and sack   00-03-00
Item for walnuttees   00-01-02
Item to them that tended the horse   00-02-00
Item to the Cryer   00-01-00
Item att Castle and Northgate   00-01-00   20
Item to the Musick   00-07-00
Item the Childs hose and showes   00-06-10
Item allowed for samonds   00-10-00
...

                                                                                          25

Glovers' Records C: Company Book
p 74 *(January)*   30
...

Item paid for powder and Match   xviij s viij d
Item paid for bootes & spurrs for the boy & Ribben for the
horse   v s.
Item paid for Gloues, for Aldermen & stewards   viij s   35
Item paid for Gloues for the boy, & the three men thatt guided
the horse   iij s ij d
Item paid for the banner   xij d
Item Spentt att the barres   iiij s
Item Giuen att barrs Castle & Northgate   xviij d   40
Item paid to the Musicke   vj s viij d
...

Coopers' Records C: Company Book II
f 75v *(13 January)*

Midsomer Charge

Paide for the boyes. stockings	ij s iiij d
more paide for the boyes gloues	xxj d
more paide for a paire of shooes for the boye	xx d
more for powder and match	iij s ij d
more paide for Cheese	iij s iiij d
more paide for the mending of 3 kaleevers	vj d
more pade for the footemens gloues	xviij d
more paide to mr Houlmes for keeping the banner	xij d
more paide for ribbeninge for the horse hed	vj d
more paide for beere at the barrs	xxij d
more giuen at the bars Castell and northgate	xviij d.
more paide for Cakes	iij s
more for v mens wages paide	ij s vj d.
more paide for musick	ij s vj d
more paide for a potle of Clarett a potle of white and a quart of sack	iij s
more paide for halfe a barell of strong beere	viij s
more for nutts pruines apples and othe spice	iij s vj d
more spent at my Alderman Tottyes	vj d

...

Joiners, Carvers, and Turners' Records
CCA: Company Book G14/1
f 139 *(25 March)*

Disburcem*entes* ...

Midsom*er* Charg*es*

Item for a quarte of wyne att dressinge the boy	viij d
Item for furnishinge the boye att Midsom*er*	viij s
Item for Rybon for the horse	xij d
Item for 2 quart*es* of Wyne	xvj d
Item spent att Ald*erman* Catteral*les*	v s. iiij d
Item att the Barres to the Cryar	iiij d
Item to the pr*esoners* in the Castle & Northgate	viij d
Item to him W*hich* ledd the horse	vj d
Item to 2 men attendinge the boy	viij d
Item for beere att on overplus att. steward Callcotes	ij s
Item for Musique	ij s. viij d
Item to mr Holmes for keepinge & mendinge the Banner	ij s

...

Mercers, Ironmongers, Grocers, and Apothecaries' Records
C: Company Book
p 240 *(5 May)*

...

Item the 19th Iune for Cloath taffety & silk for the lyverys	00-15-09
Item paid for makinge of them	00-04-00.

...

Item the 23th Iune paid the Cryer	00-01-00.
Item paid at widowe wilsons	00-05-00.
Item paid to the prissoners at Castell and the northgate	00-04-00
Item paid 6 men to attend vppon the lorde and lady	00-06-00
Item paid for 6 paier of gloues	00-06-00
Item paid the mussioners	00-06-08
Item paid for Ryband for the 2 horsses	00-03-00.
Item paid for the lordes hose garters shues [and] rosses and gloues	00-10-00.
Item paid for the ladyes furniture hose shues gloues and rosses with her shue tyes	00-09-10
Item paid for j ferkin stronge beere	00-04-00.
Item paid for Cakes and waffers	00-03-00
Item paid 8 l. prunes	00-01-04
Item j l. ¼ whitt sugar & j oz. syniment	00-02-06
Item j l. ¼ marmylett	00-02-00.
Item for sweet meates	00-05-011
Item for 3 pottells wyne & j pottell sacke	00-04-04

...

A *Rogers' Breviary* Liverpool: Liverpool University MS 23.5
f 1

Certayne Collections, of anchante, times conceringe the Anchant
and ffamous Cittie of Chester, collected by That Reuerend man
of god mr Robert Rogers. Bathlor of deuinitie, Archedeacon of
Chester. parsone of Gooseworth and Prebunde in the Cathedrall
of Chester, beinge but in scatered notes. and by his sonne Reduced
in to these Chapters followinge. viz.

...

34 / T *of* That *written over* mr

ff 25-7v*

...

Of the Sheriffes breakefaste.

There is, an anchant, Custome, in this Cittie of Chester the memory of man, now liueinge, not knowinge the originall, that vpon monday in ester weeke yearelye: comonly called blake mondaye: the twoe sheriffes of the Cittie, doe shoote for abreakefaste of Calueheades and bacon, comonly called ye Sherifes breakfaste the maner beinge thus. The daye before the drume sowndeth throughe the Cittie, with proclamation. for all gentellmen, yeomen and good fellowes, that will come, with theire, bowes, and arowes, to take parte with one sherife or ye other, and vpon monday moringe on the Rode dee, the Mayor sherefes Alldermen, and any other gentlemen that wlbe there, the one sherefe chosinge, one, and the other sherife chosinge an other. and soe of the Archers, then. one sherife. shoteth. and the other sheriffe he shotethe to shode him, beinge at length. some twelue score: soe all the archers, on one side. to shote till. it be shode and soe till. three shutes be wonne, And then all the winers side goe vp. together firste with arowes. in theire handes, And all the loosers. with. bowes in theire handes, together, to the Comon hall of the Cittie, where the Mayor Alldermen and gentlemen and the reste. take parte togeather of the saide brekfaste, in loueinge manner, this is yearelye done, it beinge a conendable exercise, agood recreation and loueinge assemblye: |

Of St Georges Race. of late time
Inuented. & when altered

In Anno domini .1609: mr William Lester, mercer beinge mayor of Chester, one mr Robert Amerye Ironmonger, somtime sherife of Chester in Anno. domini. 1608: he withe the assente of the Mayor, and Cittie, at his owne coste cheifelye, as. I conceaue, caused .3. siluer cupps of good vallue, to be made, the which saide siluer cuppes, weare vpon St Georges daye. foreuer, to be this disposed, all gentlemen that woulde bringe theire horses to the Roode Dee, that daye and there Ronne, that horse which with speede did ouerrune the Reste shoulde haue the beste cuppe there presently deliuered, and that horse which came seconde. nexte to the firste before the reste. had the seconde cuppe there also. deliuered.

And for the. third Cuppe. it was. to be runne for at the Ringe.
by any gentlemen that woulde rune for the same, vpon the saide
Roode Dee, and vpon St Georges. daye. beinge thus. decreed
that euery horse put in soe much money. as made the value of
the Cupps or bells, and had the money, which horses did wine   5
the same, and the vse of the cupps till that day tweluemonth.
beinge in bonde to deliuer in the said cupps. that day: so also.
for the Cuppe for the Ringe. which was yearely continued
acordingly vntill. the yeare. of our. lord. 1623. Iohn Brereton
Inholder beinge mayor of Chester. he altered the same, after this   10
manner and caused the three cupps to be soulde, and caused,
more money to be gathered and added, so yat the Intreste
thereof. woolde make one faire siluer cuppe of the value .8s. as
I suppose, it maye be more worthe, and the race to be altered.
viz. from beyonde the New tower, a great distrance, and soe to   15
rune fiue times, from that place rownde aboute the Roode dee,
and he that ouer ranne all the reste, the. laste. Cowrse, to haue
the Cuppe, freelye, foreuer, then and there deliuered which is
continued to this daye.

But heare I muste not omitt, the charge and the solemnitie   20
made the firste St Gerges daye, he had apoett one. mr dauies,
whoe made speches and poeticall verses. which weare deliuered
at the highe crosse before the mayor and aldermen, with shewes |
of his Inuention, which. booke was Imprinted and ˄ʽpresented·
[deliuered] to that ffamos prince Henry, eldest sonne to. the   25
blessed King Iames of famous memorie, Also he caused a man to
goe vpon the spire of St Peters steeple in Chester and by the fane,
at the same time, he sownded a drume and displayed a banner,
vpon the tope of the same spire, And this was the origenall of
St Georges. with the change. thereof. as it is now vsed.   30

Also. the said ˄ʽmr· Robert Amerye, caused the Iacks or boyes
which strike quarterlye at St Peters. at highe crosse to be made
and erected, in. Anno domini .16(blank)

Now of the playes of Chester,   35
called the whitson playes

These playes weare the worke of one Rondoll. higden a monke in
Chester Abaye, whoe, in a good deuotion transelated the bible,
in to seuerall partes, and playes soe as the Comon. people mighte,   40

32 / second r of quarterlye written over l

heare the same, by theire playinge, and alsoe by action, in theire
sighte, And the firste time, they weare acted or played was. in
the time of Sir Iohn Arnewaye ˄ 'about' the firste yeare of his
Maroltie: aboute anno. domini. 1328. we muste Iudge this
monke, had noe euill Intension, but secrett deuotion there in.
soe also the Cittizens that did acte and practize the same. to.
their gret. coste.

Here I muste showe the manner of the performinge of these
anchante. playes. (Which was) all those Companyes and
occupationes which weare Ioyned togeather, to acte or performe
theire seuerall partes, had, pagents. which was. a buildinge of a
greate heighte, with a lower and higher rowme, beinge all open,
And sett vpon fower wheeles, and drawne from place to place,
where they played. The. firste place where they begane, was.
at the Abaye gates, where the monks and Churche mighte haue
the firste sight: And then it was drawne. to the highe Crosse
before the mayor and Aldermen. and soe from streete to streete.
And when one pageant was endend an other came. in the place
thereof till. all that weare appoynted for that daye was ended,
thus of the maner of the playes. all beinge at the Cittizens
charge, yet profitable for them, for [both] all bothe farr and
neere came to see them. |

> Now follow, what occupationes, bringe forth at
> theire charges. the playes of Chester, and on what
> dayes, theye are played. yearely. these playes or
> dard sett forthe. when the are played, Vpon, monday.
> tuesdaye and, wensedaye in the whitson weke.

...

*(The list of companies and their parts follows, ff 26v-7v; see
collation, pp 248-52)*

f 27v

...

These. 7. pagientes. aboue written. weare played vpon the 3d.
day beinge wensedaye in whitson weeke: these whitson playes
weare played. in anno domini. 1574: Sir Iohn Sauage, knighte,
beinge mayor of Chester, which was the laste time they weare
played, and we may praise god, and praye yat we see not the
like profanation of holy scripture, but .o. the mercie of god. for
the time of our Ignoraunce god he regardes it not, as well in
eueri mans. particuler, as alsoe in generall causes.

1637-8
Smiths, Cutlers, and Plumbers' Records C: Account Book II
p 19 *(July)*
...

Item for Match and Powder	viij s.	5
Item for furniture for the Boy	v s.	
Item for Rybon for the horse & men	xv d.	
Item for a quarte of Wyne dressinge the boy	vij d.	
Item spent at our Stewardes	vj d.	
Item for keepinge our Banner	xij d	10
Item to 3. men which ^'attended' the boy & horse	ij s vj d	
Item spent at Robert Iohnsons	ij s. viij d	
Item to the Cryar, the prisoners in Castle and Northgate	xviij d	
Item for our Musique	v s.	
Item for our banquett on Midsomer Eve	xx s. iiij d.	15

...

Painters, Glaziers, Embroiderers, and Stationers' Records
C: Account Book II
p 35 *(18 October)*   20
...

Item payd for Gloues for ye Aldermen & Stewards for Midsomer eue.	iij s. iiij d.	
Item payd for hosen Showes Gloues for ye Child that Ridd and for a Rubyn for ye horse head	vj s	25
Spent at dressinge of ye Child that ridd according to Custome	xij d	
Item Spent at ye Barrs Stayinge for mr Maior	ij s	
Item giuen to ye Citty Crior '12d' at ye Barrs: & to ye Prisoners '4d' of the Castell and northgate '4d'	xx d	30
Item Spent at Steward Taylers howse on midsomer Eue	ij s vj d	
Item Spent more in wyne the Same tyme by the Alderman Inces & the bretherens Consent then present; & to be allowed off	ij s. iiij d	
Item payd to ye xij Picke men & halbert man at Midsomer	vj s vj d	35
Item Giuen to ye Drummer for drumminge on midsomer Eue	xviij d.	
Item Giuen to ye Trompiter for Soundinge same day at showe tyme.	iij s iiij d	
Item Giuen vj d apeece to ye horsleader Garland bearer ye 2 banner Carriors: & 2 which heald ye Child on horsback	iij s.	40

...

Cordwainers and Shoemakers' Records
CCA: Account Book III G/8/4
f 158 *(11 November)*

...

11 November	Imprimis for Musique att our Alderman Gregories	xij d
	...	
	Item for Musique at our Alderman Gregories	ij s
	...	
January	Item payed ffor our Gleaves & the Beuerage	vij s. vj d
	...	
	Item to the Waytemen att Shrovetyde	ij s
	Item to the Callies the same tyme	ij s
	...	

f 158v

...

Midsomer Charges	Item for halfe a barrell of Beere	viij s
	Item for Rybon for the horse & shoeties for the Boy	xij d
	Item for stockinges for the boy	ij s vj d.
	Item for Shoes	xviij d
	Item for gloves	xij d
	Item to him Which brought the horse	vj d
	Item to 3 men Which ledd the horse & attended the boy	xviij d
	Item spent att the barres	iij s.
	Item to the Cryar	vj d
	Item to the prisoners in the Castle & Northgate	ij s.
	Item for Wyne at dressinge the boy	vj. d
	Item for banquettinge Stuffes	ix s
	Item for 2 Cheeses	vj s viij d
	Item for bread and Cakes	vij s
	Item for Musique	iiij s
	Item for keepinge our Banner	xij d.
	Item for Matche and Powder	xxj s.
	...	

f 159

Item spent when wee agreed to have our banquett on Midsomer
Eve at Mr Gregories   viij d

...

Beerbrewers' Records CCA: Company Book G 3/2
f 135v *(23 November)*

...

Rc H: pad by him for makeinge the tippett*es*   00-02-00

...   5

R H: given to the prissoner*es* the same tyme   00-00-06

...

R H: payd the musick   00-00-[06]

...

Middsomer accompt*es* in toto   03-00-00   10

...

Dean and Chapter CC: Treasurers' Accounts IV
p 269 *(Christmas)*

...   15

It*em* to Smallshoe for 3 night*es* watching   ij s vj d

...

Glovers' Records C: Company Book
p 79 *(January)*   20

...

Midsomer Charges

paid for Mattch and Powder   xij s
paid for bootes and spurs for the boy and Ribben for the horse v s   25
paid for Gloues for the boy   xiiij d
paid for Gloues for Aldermen & Stewards   viij s
paid for gloues for the three Men, thatt attended the horse xxij d
paid to the Musicke   v s. vj d
paid att barrs Castle and Northgate   xviij d   30
Spentt att the Barrs   iiij s

...

Coopers' Records C: Company Book II
f 79 *(13 January)*   35

...

midsomar   for the lone of a goone & bandeleros   ij s
               for the lone of too pyks & dresing 3 goons   j s
               for furnetur for the boye   v s

4, 6, 8 / *initials are for Richard Harison, one of the stewards for the year*

for Cakes	iij s
for wallnuts & other spyses	iij s iij d
spent at our allderman Totys howse	iiij d
for pouder & mach	iiij s ij d
for Ribin for the horse hed	viij d 5

f 80

paid for a brydel f of the horse	j s ij d
paid for the foot mens gloues	j s
paid for 5 mens wages	ij s vj d 10
paid for meusick	ij s vj d
paid for drinke at the bars	j s x d
giuen at the bars Castel & norgat	j s
paid for half a barell of beare	viij s vj d
paid for wyne & sacke	iij s vj d 15
paid for keeping the bannar	j s

...

(at a dinner)

paid for meusick	ij s

...   20

Painters, Glaziers, Embroiderers, and Stationers' Records
CCA: Minute Book CR 63/2/131
f 40v *(31 January)*

25

Cominge without gounes f

    Ed bellen Steward   William Tayler
    Tho Robinson
    Io Tayler   30
    Ios prickett
    Rog banester   all Iorymen
    Moy dalby
    Tho Edmuds
    Io Sidall   35

[the tow Stewards iiij d a peece
all the rest ij d apeece
⟨..⟩ a generall consent of the rest

8 / f *not cancelled*   37 / t *of* tow *converted from* E
37 / d *written over* s *in* iiij d

notise was giuen accordingly by Midsomer the yonger bretheren
to provide gownes accou'

Iohn Souch & William Walker for not Coming on midsomer Eue
& refuse Cominge to meeting & Kinges holy day iij s iiij d a   5
peece by a generall Consent]

Joiners, Carvers, and Turners' Records
CCA: Company Book G14/1
f 142 *(25 March)*   10
...

Disburcementes ...

Item for furnishinge the boy	viij s
Item for keepinge the Banner	xij d
Item for Wine dressinge the Boy	vj d
Item for Wine att our banquett	xij d
Item for Rybon	viij d
Item dressinge the Horse	vj d
Item for 3 men attendinge the boy & the horse	xij d
Item to the Cryar att the Barres	iiij d
Item to the Prisoners in the Castle & Northgate	viij d
Item att our Alderman Bollandes	iij s iiij d
Item att widowe Pues	iiij s iiij d
Item for Musique	iij s
Item for beere att steward Bennettes	v. s

Midsomer
Charges

...

Mercers, Ironmongers, Grocers, and Apothecaries' Records
C: Company Book   30
p 248 *(4 May)*
...

Item the 23th Iune 1638 paid for the lordes gloues and [the
ladyes] gloues for they men that attended him   00-06-00.
Item more paid the men that attended him   00-03-00   35
Item paid for j paier stockings   00-03-00
Item paid for garters and Rosses for him   00-03-10.
Item paid for j paier of sues for the lord   00-02-00.
Item more 3 yardes ryband that was tyed about the horse
                                                     00-01-06   40

Item gloues for the Ladye hose sues furniture rybande rosses
& other nessesaires   00-01-00

Item gloues for the men that waieted vppon the ladye   00-03-00.
Item more paid the men that attended vppon her   00-03-00.
Item for sweet meats and banketinge stufe of all sort*es* as hath byn vssuall   00-19-01
Item for beer and wyne at the bankequet   00-08-04
Item paid the prisson*ers* at the Castell & northgate with the Cryer   00-05-00
...

Item to the mussicke paid   00-06-08
Item paid for ryband for the ladyes horse   00-02-08   1
...

1638-9
Smiths, Cutlers, and Plumbers' Records   C: Account Book II
p 23 *(July)*   1
...

Midsomer
Charg*es*

Item for stocking*es* shoes & gloues for the Boy and Rybon for the horse   viij s. vj d.
Item att dressinge the Boy   vij d
Item to the 3 hansemen   ij s   20
Item to the Musique   ij s. vj d.
Item for Match and powder   iiij s. x d.
Item spent att the Barres   iij s. iiij d.
Item to the Cryar & att the Castle & Northgate   xviij d.
...   25

Item for our banquett on Midsomer Eve   xx s. ij d.
...

Painters, Glaziers, Embroiderers, and Stationers' Records
C: Account Book II   30
p 37 *(18 October)*
...

Item for Gloues for the Aldermen & Stewards on midsomer Eue.   iij s iiij d
Item payd for the childes Gloues hosen Showes & Ruben for the horse head   vj s   35
Spent at dressinge of the child that ridd   xij d
Spent at the Barrs   xij d
Giuen to ye Crior at the barrs xij d, to the Prisoners at ye Castell iiij d and to ye Prisoners of ye Northgate iiij d in all   xx d   40
Spent at Steward Bellens howse after ye wach   ij s vj d
Item payd to the xij pikemen & halbart man   vj s vj d

Item Payd to the Drummer   xviij d
Item Payd to the Trompiter   iij s iiij d
Item giuen vj d a peece to the. Horsleader, Garland bearer, the
2 Banner Carriors & 2 which held the child   iij s
...   5

Treasurers' Account Rolls CCA: TAR/3/47
f 3v *(November)*

Item Paid to Robertt Thorneley & Iohn wright for the Giantts,   10
Mount, beasts and other workes for Midsomer Eve   04 00 00

...

Item Paid to Henry Ioanes for mendinge the two drumms &
Anchient staffe, with sockett, Pike & silke tassells   01 02 00
...   15

Item Paid to the Prissoners   00-02-00
Item Paid to the waytmen playinge vpon Sct Georges day 00-01-00
Item Paid to the drummer vp Sct Georges day   00-01-00
...
                                                                        20

f 4
...
Item to 2 Pypers on Midsomer Eve before the Gyants   00-02-00
Item to Guest the drummer the same tyme   00-01-00
Item to Perrye & others, Appointed by Mr Mayor to kepe the   25
Armedmen on Midsomer Eve in order   00-05-06
...

f 4v
Item Given to the Earle of Northumberlandes Trumpiter   30
                                                         00-02-00

...

Cordwainers and Shoemakers' Records
CCA: Account Book III G/8/4   35
f 165 *(11 November)*
...
Imprimis given to the Musicke at our Aldermans on our Eleccion
day   ij s
...   40
19 November: Item the same day for Musique at our Steward Bennettes   ij s
...

ff 165v-6

...

21th ffebruary / Item payed for our Gleaves and the Beuerage att Shrovetyde

vij s. vj d

Item to the Waytemen   ij s.

Item to our Musique the Callies   ij s

Item spent then on them   iiij d

Item spent on our Clark Wrytinge all our names fayer ohes to

be Deliuered vpp at Shrovetyde   ij d

Item more spent Wrytinge downe our Shrovetyde Accomptes ij d   1

...

Midsomer   Item for halfe abarrell of Beere   vij s
Charges /   Item to him which brought the horse and dressed him   xij d

Item to mr Holmes for keepinge the banner   xij d

Item for shoes for the boy   xx d   1

Item for gloves   xviij d

Item for stockinges & shoeties   ij s x d

Item for Rybon for the horse   xiiij d.

Item to 3 men Which attended the boye and the horse   xviij d

Item for bread & Cakes   vij s   2

Item for 2 Cheeses   vj s. viij d

Item for banquettinge Stuffes   ix s.

Item spent att the barres   iij s iiij d

Item to the cryar   xij d |

Item to the Prisoners in the Castle & northgate   ij s.   2

Item spent att dressinge the boye   vj d.

Item for Wyne att our banquett   xiiij d

Item for [Wyne] Musique   iiij s.

Item for Matche & powder   xvj s. j d.

...   3

Dean and Chapter CC: Treasurers' Accounts IV
p 287 *(Christmas)*

...

Item for a watchman at Christmas   ij s vj d   3

...

Item to Thomas Malbon for a dragoon, flask headpeice & buckle
to ye dragoone   xxxviij s

8-9 / ohes is uncertain and the word rendered Deliuered seems to be De with a tittle.
The phrase may refer to the beginning of the Shrovetide Proclamation o yes and the
call to deliver up the gleaves.

Item to Thomas Malbon for a sword, cap, belt, dragoone girdle
& a Knapsacke   xv s. x d

...

Glovers' Records C: Company Book   5
pp 82-3 *(January)*

...

Midsomer Charges

paid & disbursed for Match & powder more then wee Receaued   10
from the Company the some of   iiij s viij d
paid for bootes and Spurrs for the boy   v s.
paid for [for] Gloues for Aldermen, Stewardes, Child, and other
the Attendants   xxj s ij d
Item paid for the banner   ij s   15
Item paid for Ribben for the horse   xij d
Item Giuen to the Castle, Norgate & att the barrs   ij s |
Sentt on the Company att the Barrs   ix s ij d
paid to the Musicke   vj s viij d

...   20

Coopers' Records C: Company Book II
f 84 *(13 January)*
                    midsomer charge

                                                                     25

Paide for halfe a barell of Stronge beere   vij s vj d
paid for powder and mach   iiij s
paid for ffurnishing of the boye   iiij s viij d
paide to the musick   ij s vj d
paide for cheese   iij s   30
paide for bred   iij s
paide for nutts apples and plumes and other spice   iij s vj d
paid for ribeninge for the horse   xij d
paide for the ffootmens gloves   xviij d
paide for 6 mens wages   iij s   35
paide for beere at the barrs   ij s
paide for lone of pikes and gorgets and ffore dressing the peeces
                                                              viij d
paid to the cryer castell and northgate   xviij d
paide for wyne at oure banquett   ij s xj d   40
paide mr Hollmes for keeping oure banner   xij d
paide at oure alderman Tottyes   vj d

...

f 84v

...

It*em* more paid for stronge beere at the diner of Thomas Linaker
the 4th of November   viij s
It*em* more paide for musick the same daie   ij s vj d

...

(Nicholas Welsh's dinner)
It*em* more paid the same daie in margerie Pphilips for wyne   jx s.
It*em* more paid for musick   iij s

...   1

Joiners, Carvers, and Turners' Records
CCA: Company Book G14/1
f 145 *(25 March)*

...   1

Disburcem*entes* ...

Midsom*er*   Item for furniture for the boy   viij s
Charg*es*   Item for keepinge the fflagge   xij d
                 Item for a quart of Wyne att dressinge the Boy   vij d   2(
                 Item for Rybon for the horse   xij d
                 Item for dressinge the horse   vj d
                 Item to three men to attend the Boy & leade the Horse   xviij d
                 Item spent widowe Pues   v. s
                 Item to the Cryar and the Prisoners in the Castle & Northgate   2(
                                                                           xij d
                 Item for Wyne att our banquett   xiiij d
                 Item for Musique   iij s. iiij d
                 Item for Beere att an overplus att our Steward*es* amongst the
                 Companie   iiij s.   3(
                 ...
At our dynner / Item to the Musique   iij s. iiij d

Mercers, Ironmongers, Grocers, and Apothecaries' Records   3!
C: Company Book
p 256 *(8 May)*

...

paid for Colleringe of the stafe for the flage 14th Iune 1639
                                                                       00-00-10   4(
paid for the Lords Gloues and gloues for the men that Atend
him   00-07-00

paid the men that Atended him	00-03-00	
paid for a peare of hose for him	00-03-00	
paid for gartters and Roses for him	-00-03-00	
paid for a peare of shewes for him	-00-02-00	
paid for ribon that was for the horse	00-01- 6	5

paid for the Ladij hose shewes furniture Ribon rosses and other
Nessesaryes	00-10-00	

paid for the [⟨.⟩s] mens Gloues that wayted one the Ladij
	00-03-00	
paid the men that Atended her	00-03-00	10
paid for Ribon for the Ladij horse	00-01- 6	

paid for sweete meates and Banketinge stufes of all sorts *which*
hath ben vsiall	00-19- 1	
paid for beare and wynne at Banquit	00-08- 8	
paid the prisinors at Castell & norgat	00-04-00	15
paid the Crier	00-01-00	
paid widow wilson at the bares	00-05-00	
paid the man that Carride the Banor & gl⟨...⟩s	00-01- 8	
paid vnto the Mussicke	00-06- 8	
...		20

1639-40

Smiths, Cutlers, and Plumbers' Records   C: Account Book II   25
p 26 *(July)*

...

midsomer Eve Charge 1640

for match and powder	0-7-4	30
for bootes spurs & gloues for the boy that Rode	0-7-4	
for Rybbon	0-0-6	
given at the barrs the northgate & the Castle	0-1-6	
for musicke	0-4-0	
given to the honncemen	0-3-0	35
for keepinge of the banner	0-1-0	
for a q*ua*rt of sacke dressinge the boy	0-1-2	
spent at Robert Ionesons	0-5-4	
ffor our bankquett on midsomer Euen	0-11-2	
...		40
It*em* p*ai*d for a new Banner	3-06-08	

...

Painters, Glaziers, Embroiderers, and Stationers' Records
C: Account Book II
p 39 *(18 October)*

...

payd for tynn for the garland for Inkell for the picke banners
& phœnixs for the mens heads and pastbord for som new
phœnexes   xij d.
Spent in berrage to the banners   vj d
giuen to the pickmen °& halbertere°   vij s vj d
to the drummer xviij d to the Trumpiter iij s iiij d   iiij s x d
Spent at the barrs xiiij d to the Crior xij d to the Castell &
norgate viij d   ij s x d
for gloues for Aldermen & stewards   iij s 4d
for bootes '&' gloues for the boy that Rid for rubyn for the
horse head   vj s.
to the men that led the horse & Carried the banners   iij s
Spent att dressinge of the boy   xij d
Spent at Stewards howse ij s vj d & a q*uart* of Sack °by ˄ 'Alder*man*
Inces word'°   iij s

...

payd for new guildinge & Silueringe of the Tow banners & new
workinge the Trompett baner for blew & yelow Silke for banners
for the pikes for new gildinge all the phenexes for the mens heads
for new workinge the Escutions for the boys pheonex: & the
garland: new cullringe the Staues °˄'workmanship giuen by Ald
Holme & his sonne'° etc   3li. 13s. 4d

...

Cordwainers and Shoemakers' Records
CCA: Account Book III G/8/4
f 170 *(11 November)*

...

Imp*ri*mis spent att our Alder*man* Inces vpon the Eleccion day att
night 'for musike'   ij s

...

It*em* paid for o*ur* Gleaues att Shroutyde   vij s

...

It*em* giuen to the weates att Shrouetyde   ij s
It*em* giuen to Robe*rt* Kelley   ij s

...

8 / b *of* banners *written over* p

ff 170v-1

Midsomer
Accomptes

...

Item for halfe a barrell of Beere	vj s
Item to him that brought the horse and dressed him	xij d
Item to Mr Holmes for keepinge our banner and paintinge	5
our staffe	xvj d
Item for shoes for ye boy	xx d
Item for Gloves	xviij d
Item for stockings & Roses	ij s x d.
Item for Ribbin for ye horse	xiiij d 10
Item for 3 men for tendinge boy & horse	xviij d
Item for bread & Cakes	vij s
Item for 2 Cheeses	vj s viij d
Item for banquettinge stuffe	ix s.
Item spent att the barres	iij s iiij d 15
Item giuen to the Cryer	xij d
Item giuen to ye prisoners Castle and Northgate	ij s.
Item spent att dressinge ye boy	vj d
Item paid for a pottle beere att Aldermans house	iij d |
Item for a quart of sacke att banquett	xvj d 20
Item for musicke	iiij s
Item for matche & powder	xxiij s

...

25

Glovers' Records C: Company Book
p 86 *(January)*

Midsomer Charges   30

Paid for Match and Powder	viij s x d
Paid for Bootes & spurs for the boye	v s.
Paid for Gloues for the Aldermen, Stewardes & Child and for	
the men	xij s vj d 35
Paid for the Banner	xij d
Paid for Ribben for the horse	ix d
Paid for loane for a hatt for the boye	xij d
Spentt on the Company att the barrs	iiij s iiij d
Giuen att Barrs, Castle, & Northgate	xviij d 40
Paid to the Musicke	vj s viij d

...

Coopers' Records C: Company Book II
f 87v *(13 January)*

midso*m*mer charge

It*em* paid for 2 li of gunpowder	iij s viij d
paide for mach	ij d
paide for 1 pounde and halfe of curance	jx d
paid for 4 pounde of pruines	viij d
paid for halfe a pounde of sugar	viij d
paid for synamon pouder	iiij d
paid for stockings for the boye	ij s iiij d
paide for ribeninge	xvj d
paide for a paire of garteres for the boye	iij s viij d
paide for a paire of roses for the boye	vj d
paid for a paire of shooes for the boye	xviij d
paid for nuts and apples	x d.
It*em* more spent at the barrs	xij d
It*em* more giuen at bars castle and northgate	xviij d
It*em* more paide for a paire of gloves for the boye	xij d
It*em* more paid for 3 paire of gloves for the men	ij s
It*em* more paide for 6 mens wages	iij s
It*em* more paid for a bridel for the horse	xvj d
paid for beere	vj s
paid for cheese and bred	vij s
paide for mr Hulmes for the fflag	ij s
paid for borowing and dressinge of gunnes	ij s
paid for wyne at oure banquet	iiij s
paid to the musik	iiij s vj d
paid at oure aldermans vpon midsomer eve	xxij d
...	

Joiners, Carvers, and Turners' Records
CCA: Company Book G 14/1
f 148 *(25 March)*

Disburcem*entes* ...

...

midsom*er*
charge

It*em* for ffurniture for the Boy	vj s.
It*em* for keepinge the banner	xij d
It*em* spent at our Ald*erman* Davies	iij s. vj d
It*em* att widowe Pues	v s. vj d
It*em* to the Cryar & the pr*eso*ne*rs* in the Castle & Northgate	xij d
It*em* for Rybon for the horse	xij d

Item for a quart of wyne dressinge the boy   vij d
Item to 3 men w*hich* ledd the horse & attended the boy   xviij d
Item for dressinge the horse   vj d
Item to the Drummer   ij s
Item for Musique   iij s iiij d   5
Item for a pottle of Wyne att our banquett   xiiij d.
Item for beere att an overplus att our steward*es*   iij s.

A   *Mayors List 5* BL: Harley 2125   10
     f 64v *(5 April) Robert Harvey*

     ...

     the sheriffs caused a peece of plate of 13 li. 6s 8d to be run on
     Tewsday in Ester weeke the reason was to haue had no Calues
     head feast w*hich* they had on black minday also but no longe   15
     tables out in Comon hall but only in bar for Maior Ald*ermen*
     sh*eriffs* gent*lemen* & the Archers

     ...

A   *Mayors List 6* BL: Harley 2125   20
     f 133* *Robert Harvey*

     ...

     the maior Caused the sheriffs breckfast vsed on monday in Easter
     weeke to be made into a more p*ar*ticular pr*i*uat dyner for the
     Ald*ermen* gent*lemen* & archers only and no other loose people   25
     to troble the hall and ordred the ouerpluss of that charge was
     Conuerted to tow flagans of siluer worth 8 li. & he that gott
     most after 3 Courses to wyn the same w*hich* mr spurstow of
     Spurstow horse did wyne

     ...   30

A   *Mayors List 11* BL: Add. 29779
     f 49v *Robert Harvey*

     ...

     This yeare the sheriffs of this Cittie caused a peese of platte to   35
     be made to the vallwe of xiij li. vj s viij d and ʌ⸢to beʼ run for in
     twesdaye in Easter weeke. and mayde the break fast on mondaye
     notwithstanding for the maire & his breethr*en* the sheriffes
     peeres & all that was leaue lookers, & gentlemen & archers as
     afore tyme / saveinge the tooke awaye the too long tables w*ith*out   40
     the bar that straggling people came to

     ...

Mercers, Ironmongers, Grocers, and Apothecaries' Records
C: Company Book
p 262 *(8 May)*
...

p*ai*d for the lord*es* and for the men*es* gloues that tended him	00.07.00
p*ai*d 3 men to tend him	00.03.00
p*ai*d for p*ai*r hose	00:03:00
p*ai*d for garter*es* and Roses	00:03:00
p*ai*d for a p*ai*r of shues	00.02.00
p*ai*d for Riband for the house	00.01.06
p*ai*d for the ladies hoase shues & furneture	00.10.00
p*ai*d the men that tended her and for 3 p*ai*r gloues	00.06.00
p*ai*d for Riband for the Ladyes horse	00.01.06
p*ai*d for sort*es* of sweett meat*es* which haue beene vsuall	00.19.01
p*ai*d for beare and wine	00:08:08
p*ai*d the prisneres at Norgate & Castle	00.04.00
p*ai*d the Cryer	00.01.00
p*ai*d widow willson at bars	00.05.00
p*ai*d the man that Carrijed the banner	00.01.08
p*ai*d to the Musisuenes	00.06.08

...

p*ai*d mr Hoolmes the 2 of Iulij 1640 for macking new banners — according to the Aldr*eme*n*es* direction	06.06.08

...

Painters, Glaziers, Embroiderers, and Stationers' Records
CCA: Minute Book CR 63/2/131
f 43 *(15 June)*

at a meetinge houlden at Goulden Pheonix the 15 day of June 1640
...
It was agreed ˄'by a generall Consent' that the Company banners being spoyled last midsomer Eue by Rayne should be vewed and beinge vewed [at this]'by the' Company at this meetinge, it is ordred vpon the sight of them that they should be new Siluered and other there needfull done and for the payment for doinge of them is referred to the Aldermen & Stewards.

1640-1
Smiths, Cutlers, and Plumbers' Records C: Account Book II
p 29 *(July)*
...

Midsom*er*
Charges

Paid for bootes, & gloues & Ribben, for the boy & horse	xj s	5
Spentt att dressinge the Child	xij d	
Paid mr holmes for the Banner	xij d	
Paid for a trunchion & painteinge itt	xij d	
Paid to the Musick	v s. vj d	
Giuen att Barrs, Castle, & Northgate	xviij d	10
Giuen mr Leicesters man of Tabley in gratuity for bringinge obtayneinge & leadinge the horse	v s.	
Giuen to the two Hance men, thatt Carried the banner & leaded, the boye	ij s	
Spentt att ouer Steward Morris his new house behinde the barrs	v s.	15
Spentt more att Iohn Morris house behinde the barrs	ij s vj d	
Spentt att ouer banquett att Alderman Holmes. his house on midsomer Eve	xv s. iiij d	
...		20
Paid for Gunpowder	viij s.	
Paid for Match	vj d	

...

Painters, Glaziers, Embroiderers, and Stationers' Records
C: Account Book II
p 41 *(18 October)*
...

payd for Gloues Stokens showes for the boy that Ridd & Rubyn for the horse head	vj s	30
Spent at the barrs while we stayd for mr Maior	xij d	
giuen to the Crior and at the Castell and norgate	xx d	
Spent at dresinge the boy that ridd °for the Company°	xij d	
payd for gloues for the Aldermen and Stewards	iij s iiij d	
Spent at the Stewards howse after the wach	ij s vj d	35
giuen to the Trompiter	iij s iiij d	
giuen to the drommer.	xviij d	
giuen to them that Carried the banners & led the horse	iij s	
payd for a quart of Sack at the Stewards howse	xvj d	
giuen to the pikemen & halbertman	vij s vj d	40

...

Treasurers' Account Rolls CCA: TAR/3/48
mb 1d *(November)*

...

p*ai*d for xiiij yardes of Cloth to make the fower waytemen
gownes at vij s vj d the yard Amo*unts* to   v li. v s.

...

Cordwainers and Shoemakers' Records
CCA: Account Book III G/8/4
f 175 *(11 November)*

	s	d
November 11 1640 Impr*i*mis for Musicke att Ald*erman* Gregories	2	0

	s	d
Impr*i*mis for musicke att Ald*erman* Thropps	2	6
It*em* Steward Bennett for ye like	2	0
It*em* Steward Payne for ye like	2	0

...

It*em* for bearage for ye gleaues   0 - 3

...

It*em* for Gleaues att Shrouetyde   6 - 6
It*em* giuen to the weats   2 - 0
It*em* giuen to Robe*r*t Kelley   2 - 0

...

f 175v

...

Midsom*er*   Impr*i*mis for beere   vj s vj d
Accompt*es* It*em* for bread   vij s
It*em* for Cheese   vj s viij d
It*em* for banquetting stuffe   ix s
It*em* att dressing of the boy ‸ ⌐spent⌐ in a pynte of wyne   vj d
It*em* for shoes for the boy   xx d
It*em* for Gloues for the boy   j s vj d
It*em* for stockinges & Roses   ij s x d
It*em* disburst for Powder ‸ ⌐and match⌐   xvj s - ij d
It*em* to giuen to him that brought the horse   xij d
It*em* for Ribbins for the horse ⌐and dressinge⌐   j s vj d
It*em* spent att the barres   ij s vj d
It*em* giuen to the Cryer   xij d
It*em* spent att mr Gregories house when we brought the ‸ ⌐boye⌐
downe before th shight or watch   viij d

Item for the Carrying the Coulers   vj d
Item for 3 men tendinge the boy & leading the horse   xviij d
Item paid to mr Holmes for keeping the banner & paynting the
staffe   xvj d
Item giuen to the Prisoners in Northgate & Castle   ij s   5
Item to George Kelley giuen   iiij s
Item spent att mr Gregories house when we wayghed the powder
& diuided the match   iiij d
Item for a quarte of sacke att the banquett   xij d
...   10
Item spent att makeing vp our Midsomer Accomptes   vj d
...

Painters, Glaziers, Embroiderers, and Stationers' Records
CCA: Minute Book CR 63/2/131   15
f 46v *(26 November)*

Iohn Souch for not Cominge to the Company this iij yeares and
also for not Coming on midsomer Eue nor Kinges holyday
hauinge byn fined before in iij s iiij d it is now ordred he shall   20
pay for all neglects
...
it is ordred that no prentices of any brother of the Company
shall acte any part in playes vnder payne of a fine as the Company
think fitt ˏ ⸢there in is⸣ to be fined   25

Glovers' Records C: Company Book
pp 88-9 *(January)*
...
Midsomer Charges   30

Paid for Gunpowder and Match   xiij vj d
Paid for Ribben for the horse   xij d
Paid for bootes & spurs for the boy   vj s
Paid for loane of a hatt   xij d   35
Paid for Gloues for the Aldermen, Stewardes, boye, and three
men   xij s vj d
Paid and spentt att the Barrs   vj s vj d |
Giuen att the Bars, Castle and Northgate   xviij d
Paid to the Musicke   vj s viij d   40
Paid for keepeinge and mendinge the banner   ij s
...

Coopers' Records C: Company Book II
ff 92-2v *(13 January)*
...

midsomer charge

It*em* paid for 2 li. of gunpowder and 3 yardes of mach	iij s
It*em* more for suger and currance	xvj d
paid for riboning for the horse	xiiij d
paid for the boyes gloves	x d
paid for cheese and bred	vij s
paid for nutts and apples	xij d
paid for pruines and si*n*namon powder	xiij d
paid for shooes and rosses	ij s
paid for a hatt for the boye	ij s
paid for stockings	ij s
paid for the lone of 4 peeces and bandeleros and for dressing the peeces	ij s
paid for 3 paire of gloves for the men	ij s
paid for a bridel for the horse	xiiij d
paid for beere at oure aldermans	xij d
paid for beere at the bars	ij s 4d
paid at Castel barrs and northgate	xviij d
paid mr Hulmes for keeping the ba*n*ner	xij d
paid to the musick	iiij s
ffo*r* 6 mens wages	iij s	
It*em* more paid for wyne and sack at oure banquett	iij s x d
paid for halfe a barell of strong beere	vj s

...

Joiners, Carvers, and Turners' Records
CCA: Company Book G14/1
f 151 *(25 March)*

The Disbursments ...

Midsomer Chardge	It*em* spent and p*ai*d for ffurniture for the Boy	00-08-00
	It*em* for keepinge and mendinge the Banner	00-01-06
	It*em* for Musick	00-05-00
	It*em* for Riband for the horse	00-01-00
	It*em* for Dressinge the horse	00-00-06
	It*em* for 3: men to attend the boy	00-01-06
	It*em* for one quart of wine att Dressinge the Boy	00-00-08

Item spent att Alderman Davies	00-02-08
Item spent att widdow Pues the same Day	00-04-00
Item given vnto the prissoners att Castle and Northgate	00-01-00
Item for stronge beere att Bankett by our selves	00-03-00
Item for apottle of wine att the Banckett	00-01-04

...

Mercers, Ironmongers, Grocers, and Apothecaries' Records

C: Company Book

p 268 (7 May)

...

paid for the Lordes glovees and the menes gloves that tended him	0-7-06
paid the men to tende him	0-4-00
paid for hoose for him	0-3-00
paid for garteres & Rosees	0-3-00
paid for shues for him	0-2-00
paid for Ribbin for hose	0-2-00
paid for the Ladyees hose shues & furniture	0-10-00
paid the men that tended her and for .3. paire gloves	0-7-00
paid for Ribbin for the Ladyes horse	0-2-00
paid for sweett meates att midsomer which have bine Usuall	0-19-06
paid for beere & wine	0-6-00
paid widdow willson att barres	0-5-00
paid the Crier	0-1-00
paid to the keeperes of northgate & Castle	0-4-00
paid the men that caryed the banneres	0-2-00
paid the musissioneres	0-6-8

...

1641-2

Drawers of Dee's Records CCA: Company Book G10/1

p 56 (30 June)

...

payd the Stuards of the brewars tourds the bannar	00-13-4
payd for tow salmans for the brewars	00-5-0

...

payd for two ffishis fore the Brewars	00-1-00

...

Smiths, Cutlers, and Plumbers' Records C: Account Book II
p 31 *(July)*

...

<table>
<tr><td rowspan="14">Midsom*er* Charges</td><td>P*ai*d for powder and Match</td><td>v s viij d</td></tr>
<tr><td>P*ai*d for mendinge the Banner & keepeinge itt</td><td>vij s viij d</td></tr>
<tr><td>P*ai*d for Ribbon for horse & men and to hange the badge & pistoll in</td><td>iiij s [⟨...⟩] d</td></tr>
<tr><td>P*ai*d for a bridle for the horse</td><td>xviij d</td></tr>
<tr><td>p*ai*d to the three haunsmen</td><td>iij s</td></tr>
<tr><td>Spentt att Alderman Meacock*es* on Midsom*er* Eve after the watch</td><td>xix s. ij d</td></tr>
<tr><td>p*ai*d for Musick</td><td>v s.</td></tr>
<tr><td>Giuen to the Cryer, Castle & Northgate</td><td>xviij d</td></tr>
<tr><td>Spentt att bringeinge the Child home and att the dresseinge of him</td><td>iij s iiij d</td></tr>
<tr><td>Spentt, the same day att Steward Evan*es*</td><td>iij s</td></tr>
<tr><td>P*ai*d for Gloues, Stockings, & shoo*es* for the boye</td><td>vj s</td></tr>
</table>

...

Painters, Glaziers, Embroiderers, and Stationers' Records
C: Account Book II
p 43 *(18 October)*

...

Payd for Gloues for ye Aldermen & stewards	iij s iiij d
Payd for hosen showes Gloues for ye Child that ridd and for Rubyn for ye Horse head	vj s
Spent at dressinge the child	vj d
Spent stayinge at Barrs	xx d
Giuen to the Cryor	xij d
to the Prisoners at ye Castell	iiij d
to ye Prisonors of ye northgate	iiij d
Spent at the Stewards Howse after ye wach	ij s vj d
more at same tyme for sack & white wyne	xviij d
Giuen to the 14 pike men & Halbart man	vij s vj d
Giuen to ye Drommer	xviij d
Giuen to ye Trompiter	iij s iiij d
to the Horse leader Garland bearer the 2 banner bearers & one to hould ye Child that ridd	iij s

...

Treasurers' Account Rolls CCA: TAR/3/49
mb 3 *(November)*

p*ai*d to the Steward*es* of the Sadlors toward*es* the Shrouetyde
Bell   vj s vij d   5

...

p*ai*d to Gwest the Drumer for his paynes on Shrouetewsday   xij d

...

p*ai*d to Robart Thorneley, and Iohn Wright Painters for there
Annuall ffee for makinge of the Giant*es*   iiij li.   10

...

p*ai*d to Edward Parry, and other Conduct*ou*rs of the Companies
at Midsomer   v s vj d
p*ai*d to Gwest the Citties Dru*m*mer for his paines at Midsomer
          xij d   15

...

Cordwainers and Shoemakers' Records
CCA: Account Book III G/8/4
f 179 *(11 November)*   20

Imp*ri*mis for Musicke att Ald*erman* Inces   ij s
It*em* for Musicke att Steward Iohn Whittles   ij s

...

It*em* spent on Gerard Iohnes for the berrage of the Gleaues   vj d   25

...

It*em* paid vnto Gerard Iohnes for Gleaues   vj s vj d
It*em* paid to the Wayts   ij s
It*em* paid to Rob*ert* Kelley ye same day   ij s

...   30

f 181

...

It*em* for beere   vij s vj d
It*em* for bread & Cakes   vij s viij d   35
It*em* for Cheese   vij s x d
It*em* for banquetting stuffe   x s
It*em* spent att Dressing of the boy in a quarte of wine   vj d
It*em* for shoes for the boy   xx d
It*em* for Gloues for the boy   ij s   40
It*em* for stockings and Roses for the boy   iiij s

Margin notes:

ffeb. 4

ffeb 18
ffeb. 25

Midsom*er*
Chardg*es*

Item for Powder & Match   xiiij s
Item for him that brought & dressed the horse   xij d
Item for Ribbins for the horse   xv d
Item for 3 men for Leading the horse & houlding the boy   j s vj d
Item spent att the barres   iij s iiij d
Item spent att mr Gregories when the boy was brought downe
before the watch   xij d
Item giuen to the Cryer   xij d
Item for Carying the Coulers   vj d
Item giuen to Mr Holmes for keeping the banner & a new sockett
for the banner   ij s viij d
Item giuen to the Prisoners att Castle and Northgate   ij s
Item giuen to Robert Kelley   iiij s
Item spent att buying the powder & Match   iiij d
Item a quarte of sacke att our banquett   xij d
Item a quarte of sacke for the wiues   xij d
...

Dean and Chapter CC: Treasurers' Accounts IV
p 303 *(Christmas)*
...
Item for a watchman at christmas. 1641   ij s vj d
...

Coopers' Records C: Company Book II
ff 95-5v *(13 January)*
...

midsomer Charge

paide for Cheese   iiij s j d
paide for halfe a barell of strong beere   vij s vj d
paide for shooes for the boye   xviij d
paid for a hatt for the boye   ij s
paid for 2 pounde of gunpowder and 3 yardes mach   iij s
paid for suger and Currante   xvj d
paid for 4 pounde of pruines   viij d
paide for stockings for the boye   ij s ij d
paide for garters for the boye   iij s vj d
paide for rosses for the boye   vj d
paide for the boyes gloues   xij d
paide for synament powder   v d
paide for ribeninge for the horse   xij d

paide for 3 paire of gloues for the men	ij s
paide for nuts and appels	xij d
paide for beere at oure aldermans vpon mydsomer even	viij d
paide for beere at the barrs	xvj d
paide for a bridle for the horse	xv d
paide at the barrs Castel and norgate	xviij d
paide for 6 mens wages	iij s
paide for musicke	iiij s
paide mr Hulmes for the fflagg	xij d
paide for Cakes	iij s 4d
paide for dressing 2 peeces	vj d
paide for wyne	iiij s

...

Joiners, Carvers, and Turners' Records
CCA: Company Book G14/1
f 154 *(25 March)*
...

The Disbursments ...

Midsomer Chard	Item for ffurishinge the Boy	00-08-00
	Item spent att dressinge the Boy	00-00-08+
	Item paid vnto Mr Holme for keepinge the Banner	00-01-00
	Item for Riband for the horse	00-00-06.
	Item for Dressinge the horse	00-00-06.
	Item for 3. men attendinge the horse and boy	00-01-00
	Item at Barrs Castle and Northgate to the prisners	00-01-02
	Item paid the Musick	00-02-08.
	Item Spent att Alderman Pues the same Day	00-02-00
	Item spent att widdow Pues the same Day	00-03-00
	Item for one quart of wine att Bankett	00-00-08+
	Item spent in stroinge beere att Bankett att steward Cattralls	00-03-04.

...

A *Minstrels Court* CRO: DLT/B3
ff 143-4v* *(24 June)*

Concerninge the auntient Custome of the ridinge before all the
minstrells in Cheshire on the ffeast of St Iohn Baptist at Chester
&c. Belonginge to the heires of Dutton de Dutton in the same
County.

As touchinge the originall Institution of the power & authorite
ouer ye whole minstrellrie in Chesshire, I finde that when Randle
surnamed Blundevill Earle of Chester was beseiged by the
welshmen at Rut῾h᾽lent Castle, about the ῾begining of King
Iohn's᾽[end of the] Raigne [of K Henry the Second], The said
Earle sent vnto his Constable of Chesshire (who was ye Baron of
Halton) that hee should come & bringe what ayde hee could
immediately to succour him in this his distresse: The Constable
vpon this Message (for it was then the faire=tyme at Chester)
gathered forthwith all the merry persons hee could meete with in
the Citty of Chester, As Coblers, ffidlers, merry Companions,
Whores, & such routish Company, & marched speedily with that
his promiscuous Army consistinge both of men & weomen
towards the said Castle where the Earle was beseiged: The Welsh
seeinge A great multitude comming, left the seige & fledd: The
Earle thus deliuered cometh backe with his Constable to Chester,
& for his service graunteth him power ouer all kind of such Loose
persons residinge within the County of Chesshire: The said
Constable passed it ouer vnto Hugh de Dutton, whose heires
enioye it at this day

Circa Annum
domini 1186.
for Iohn
Constable of
Chesshire dyed
in the holy land
13ᵗ: Ric: the .l.
Hoveden:: pag:
685. / Leccator
signifies A
ryoutous
debauched
person, Aroaringe
boy, A Taverne
Hunter ·A letcher,
vnde nomen
Leccator·

The originall Deed of ye Constable of Chesshire
vnto Dutton remayninge in ye hands of ye heire
of Dutton de Dutton.

Sciant presentes et futuri quod ego Iohannes Constabularius
Cestriae dedi et concessi et hac praesenti charta mea confirmavi
Hugoni de Dutton et heredibus suis magistratum omnium
Leccatorum et meretricum totius Cester-shiriae, sicut liberius
illum magistratum teneo de Comite: Salvo Iure meo mihi et
haeredibus meis. His Testibus Hugone de Boydele, Alano fratre
eius, Petro de Gonenet, Liulfo de Twamlowe Ada de Dutton
Gilberto de Astun, Randulfo de Kingestey Hamone de Bordington,
Alano de Waleie, Willelmo filio Richardi Martino Angevin,
Willelmo [de ⟨...⟩] ₍῾Carill᾽₎, Galfrido et Rob[erto]῾in᾽ filijs
meis, Bletheris, Herbard de Waleton, Alano Mulinton, Galfrido
de Dutton.

David Powell in his History ₍῾pa: 296῀ is vtterly mistaken:
whome Cambden in his Brittannia Tit: Chesshire seemeth to
followe: for both these make Raph de Dutton to bee the only
man in deliueringe the Earle of Chester & that the Earle gaue
this power immediately vnto him: as for ye name of Raph de

Dutton; There was neuer any such man in ye right line of Dutton
de Dutton; nor I beleiue in all the oblique line w*h*ich liued about
that tyme: [Excepte Radulpho Dispensatore: which Ralph
although hee was originally descended from Hadard, yet hee was
called Dispensator from his office w*h*ich hee had vnder ye Earle   5
of Chester & not by the name of Dutton: whose posteritie wholly
retayned the name of Spenser by Contraction from the Latine
word Dispensator, which as I said before was A name of office;
And from him is lineally descended, the Lord Spencers a family
flourishinge at this day.] | 10

2ly (a) But
Dutton was
Steward of
Halton vnder
the Baron

Secondly as for the i*m*mediate graunt of ye Earle to Dutton
you see the originall deed aboue named doth evidently prove
the contrary: Howbeit I deny not but that Hugh de Dutton (who
hath his privilidge giuen him from the Constable) might p*er*happs
haue accompanied the aforenamed Iohn Constable of Chesshire   15
in that service for the Earle, & for his reward had this graunt
from the Constable, salvo Iure suo &c: as it is in the Deed: (a)
[There is one other mistaken concerninge the Custome w*h*ich
I haue mett withall, & that is an auntient Parchment Rowle
remayninge in ye hands of Thomas Starkey of Stretton in the   20
County of Chester Esq*uire* wherein is contayned the descents
of the Barons of Halton, & is A monument very truly & accurately
drawne in euery point, saveinge the mistake of the man touchinge
the originall of this Custome, wherein Roger Constable of
Chesshire is there named to haue rescued the Earle in stead of   25
Iohn his ʽsonneʼ[father]] And thus much of the originall
Institution: Now followeth ye manner of the solemnite of it as
it is vsed at this day: v*idelice*t 1642. Iune the: 24th

ffirst the lord of Dutton, or his Deputy, rideth vpp w*i*th many
Gentlmen of his frends & acquaintance (haueinge A Banner   30
displayed before him[,], & A Drumm & trumpett) vntill they
come a litle aboue the Eastgate in the citty of Chester, where
there is Proclamac*i*on made in the streete before the said heire,
or his deputy, sittinge on horsbacke, as followeth:

                                                                   35

The forme of the proclamac*i*on.

Vnder the Royall grace of the Kings most excellent ma*ie*stie &
his most Ho*nora*ble Counsell, The right Ho*nora*ble Robert
Viscount Killmurrey, Lord, Leader, conducter, & (vnder his   40
highnes) Protecter of all & euery music*i*ons and Minstrells
whosoeuer, either resident or resortinge w*i*thin or to ye County

Pallatine of Chester, And within or to the County of ye Citty of
Chester, By vertue & authoritie of the auntiente vse, custom,
preheminence, and speciall royalltie of the Predecessors of the
Mannor of Dutton, straightly chargeth & commaundeth all &
euery the said Musicions & Minstrells & others whosoever,
acknowledginge, vseinge, & professinge the noble art, worthy
science, & high misterie of musique and minstrellzie within the
said Countyes, or either of them, To approach this presente
place & attend this presente Proclamacion, And presentely
heere to drawe forthe their sundry Instruments of Musique &
Minstrellzie, And to play heere before ye said Robert Viscount
Kilmurrey or his Deputy, heere presente vnto the accustomed
place in dutifull manner & order customablie vsed by his
Predecessors before tyme, soe longe that the memory of man can
not Witnes to the contrary, which royalltie hath beene allwayes
annexed & resigned to the said auntient Predecessors of the
mannor of Dutton, & now come vnto the said Robert Viscount
Killmurrey in the right of Dame Elinour now wife of the said
Robert Viscount Killmurrey, & sole daughter & heire of Thomas
Dutton, late of Dutton aforesaid, Esquire deceased, & her heires,
as parcell & Porcion of her inheritance, And in like good dutifull
order to retorne from the said place, playinge vpon their said
severall Instruments vnto the Courthouse, And there to make
their severall apparances: Alsoe to doe all other such Hommages,
duties, & services, as by vertue thereof belongeth to the aforesaid
Court of ye said Robert | Viscount Killmurrey: and from thence
in like good order, playinge vpon their said sundry Instruments,
to his Lodginge, & not to departe without License, This omitt
you nott, as you will at your perills avoyde the displeasure of
the aforenamed Robert Viscount Killmurrey, the rebuke of the
Court, forfeiture of your Instruments, & imprisonments of your
Bodyes. God save the Kings maiesty, his most Honorable Counscll,
And the lord of Dutton, And send vs peace. Amen.

    The Proclamacion beinge ended, the said heire of Dutton or
his Deputy rideth down in like solemne manner vnto St Iohn's
Church in Chester, all the Minstrells attendinge & playinge on
their severall Instruments before him. As soone as they come
vnto the said Church of St Iohns, the saide heire or his Deputie
allighteth from his Horse, & goeth into the said Church, & all
the Gentlemen likewise, which in good will accompany him,
seating themselves in the Chauncell thereof; In which place A
sett of the Lowd Musique vpon their Knees playeth A solemne

Lesson or Two; which ended they arise vpp with this congratulation, God blesse the Kinge, And the heire of Dutton. And soe ye deputy returneth in like manner as hee came, vnto the place where the Court is kept. Assoone as hee is come hee sitts awhile to heare the Court called, which in the Court Rolles is stiled, Curia Minstralciæ, &c. And then the Steward of the Court calleth the suitors one by one, and after the apparance made impannelleth A Iurie, & soe proceedeth to his charge, which consisteth of Three heads, ffirst, that if they knowe of any Treason against the Kinge or Prince, in that Court they ought to present it. Secondly, if any hath exercised his Minstrellzie without the License of the lord of this Court, or by any other License than from the Lord of this Court, it is heere presentable; And whether any ˏ'of them' have prophaned ye Sabboth by playinge vpon that day, vnlesse they have had speciall License for it from the Lord of this Court or his Steward. and whether any ˏ'of them' hath beene drunke, or the like. Thirdly, whether they haue heard any scandalous words tending to the prejudice of the heire of Dutton, & by whome, The Iury is heere to present it; As also to present the default of all such Suitors as ought to haue appeared that day &c.

The Charge beinge given, the Deputie goeth out of the Court to dinner, which is provided for him & what Gentlemen hee shall please to invite, At the close of all; after dinner (when the Court is ended) One of the order deliuereth vp on his knee the Pole or launce whereon the Banner was carryed vnto the Deputy, which is his due, soe that euery yeare there is A new Launce, But the Banner is preserued. Note also that euery one exerciseinge the Art of Musique in this County, doth or ought yearely to renew his License, for which he payeth vnto the Steward 02s. 02d. And that those who are vpon the Iury the yeare before doe the next yeare after weare Long Linen Towells over their Shoulders in manner of A scarfe, to signifie they were elected on the Iury — Et sic de cæteris. / |

This is the manner as it is solempnized at this day, yet perhapps in part altered from the ffirst Institution in point of ceremony; for I believe auntiently only A court was kept for the preservinge of the Authoritie, and noe more adoe

In the Clayme of Dutton de Dutton: 14: Hen: 7 I finde it thus Recorded, vpon A quo warranto brought against him.

So it was 1642, but now 1666 the Steward takes 2s. 6d. for each Licence

5

10

15

20

25

30

35

40

Laurentius Do*mi*nus de Dutton clamat quod omnes Minstrelli infra Civitatem Cestriæ, et infra Cestriam manentes, vel officia ibidem exercentes, debent convenire coram ipso vel Seneschallo suo apud Cestriam, ad ffestum Nativitatis *San*cti Ioh*annis* Baptistæ annuatim et dabunt sibi ad dictum ffestum Quatuor Lagenas vini, et vnam Lanceam: et insuper quil[l]ibet eorum dabit sibi Quatuor Denarios. et vnum obolum ad dictum ffestum, et habere de qualibet Meritrice infra Comitatum Cestriæ, et infra Cestriam manente et officium suum exercente, Quatuor Denarios p*er* Annum ad ffestum praedictum &c. Et etiam quo warranto clamat habere pro se et haeredibus suis, Liberam Warrenam in Villis suis de Dutton, Weston, Preston, Leigh, et Berterton in Comitatu praedicto &c.

owre bottles of wine /

another quo warranto ag*ainst* Laurence Dutton and (.)ten his brother 27 Ed: 3

Copia Concordat*a* cum originali in Scaccario Cestriæ de Recordo remanente

Lastly Notandum est, That whereas ffidlers are by Acte of Parliament construed to bee in the Condic*io*n of Roagues and Vagabonds: 39: Eliz: Cap: 4. Yet there is A speciall Proviso in that Acte, whereby those authorized by Iohn Dutton of Dutton Esq*uire* are exempted, as belonginge to his auntient Custome and privilidge

ffinis.

1642
Dean and Chapter CC: Treasurers' Accounts IV
p 306 *(26 September)*

...

It*em* to his mayestyes footmen their fees for ye canopie & carpet. Sept*em*ber 26 1642 iij l.

It*em* to ye ringers at his maiestys being here sept*em*ber 27 v s.

A *Mayors List 5* BL: Harley 2125
f 65v* *(23 September)* *Thomas Cooper*

...

on friday 23 Sept 1642 *King* Ch*arles* ʌ᾿(who by the Parliaments barringe to Him perceyid there was no Safety but in Armes)᾿ came to chester w*ith* the exch*equer* & lodged at the bushopp pallas & stayid all twesday after & went to wrixham the maior & Cittizens entertayned him w*ith* all Companyes & their banners in order on both sides street the maior Ald*ermen* Sh*eriffs* on a

scaffolde in Estgate street where the Recorder on his knees made
a speech & the maior did deluer the sword to him who gaue it
him agayne & then gott on horsback & Carried it before the
King & the Earl of darby the Castell ^ᐟor Excheqier˙ Sword to
the Abby the Citty gaue him in a purse 200 li. & to the prince   5
100 li. in gould which was taken very thankfully etc.

    at his goinge out of towne to wrexham the maior Aldermen
sheriff peares & Counsell in their best habetts on horsback in their
order the yongest forty first & so by degrees ridd 2 & 2 before
him the maior Carring the City Sword before the King to the end   10
of hand bridge in bromfeld lane where the King because of his
Iurney would not lett them go farther then they alighted & all
did kisse his hand & so he departed & the back

A   *Mayors List 9* BL: Add. 11335   15
f 24v* *(23 September) Thomas Cooper*

...

The 23 of september 1642 Thomas Cowper Ironmonger being
major, being fryday of Kings Majesty that now is being King
Charles the first, who had leyne long at shrewberry he came to   20
Chester with prince Charles his eldest sonne with him, he lay in
the Bishops palace, the King and prince were at sermon on
sunday following in the Quoire. and on tuesday his Majesty with
the prince went to Wrexham to one mr Richard Loyd house
whom he knighted, the Cittie gave his Majesty 200 li. in gould   25
and to the prince £100, the Major and Aldermen in Scarlett on
horse back with sherriffes peers attended the King and prince the
Major bearing the citty sword afore the King through the Cittie
to handbridge where his majesty tooke leave of the Major and
citizens   30

...

1 Undated Entries

Treasurers' Account Rolls CCA: TAR/1/6
mb 1d*

...

De Meronar*ijs* p*ro* Carigij sui auisamento   vj d
De pannar*ijs* p*ro* consil*io*   viij d   5

...

Barber Surgeons' Records C: Company Book
p 21*

...   10

        An order for the stewardes for the settinge
        out of our shew [of] vppon mydsomer even

21 Item yt is further. ordered. and agreed vpon, by the saide
company That upon everye Mydsomer even. at the watch. at   15
the companyes charge the stewards for the tyme beinge is to
p*ro*vyde against that tyme & tymes one to Ride abraham and a
younge stripleinge or boy to Ride Isaacke and they to be sett
fourth accordinge to Auncient custome. as hath bene before
tymes vsed in the saide companye / and the saide stewardes for   20
the tyme beinge, to doe theire best in the settinge fourth of
the saide showe, for the better creditt of the saide societie and
company °in payne of vj s°

22 Item more it is further agreed vpon that everie brother of the   25
sayd company shall vpon everye mydsomer even against the
watch. attende vpon the aldermen and stewardes for the tyme
beinge and everie one of the saide company to ˌ ˋhaueˋ his man
eyther in armour or otherwise accordinge to auncient custome.

4 / auisamento *for* aysamento

as other companyes vse & soe to repayer with theire show to
the barres. where it is to be sett out in paine to everye one that
doth not performe this order to paye vnto the sayde company
in the name of afyne / ij s

Butchers' Records C: Company Book
f 247v

(16)
Allowance of
the boy that
rides at
Midsomer /

...

It is Ordered That fifteene Shillings is to bee allowed by The
said Company and noe more for and towards the setting forth of
such boy as shall bee Appointed by the Aldermen and Stewards
to ride att Midsomer Shue succesiuely /

...

Cappers, Pinners, Wiredrawers, and Linendrapers' Records
C: Order Book
f 4

7 An order, what is allowed vnto the stewardes. to spend vpon
midsomer even with other orders to be obserued at that tyme

® 6s 8d

Seauenthlie it is agreed vpon with the Consent of all the said
Companie That the said Companie [doe] ₍shall₎ allowe vnto the
stewardes of the same Companie vpon euery midsomer even, yf
the Watch be sett out at A drinckinge after the watch the some
of six shillinges eight pence

prouided yf the stewardes. for the tyme beinge doe exceede
aboue the said some of vj s viij d at the said watch, the said
stewardes. to pay the ouerplus them selves

® 10s

More it is agreed vpon that the stewardes for the tyme being
shall against euery midsomer even against the watch prouide
some comlye boy to Ride vpon balams Asse before the Companie
And also to see that the said boye & Asse be trymmed & sett
furth accordinge to Auncient Custome for the credit of the same
Companie on paine of forfeyting for anie such default in monie

® iij s iiij d

More ouer it is agreed vpon that euery brother of the same
Companie shall vpon euery Midsomer even at the Watch attend
vpon the Aldermen of the same Companie with ech brother an
Armed man as it is vsed in other Companies to attende vpon the

aldermen vnto such place as the said watch is sett out at in paine
for eu*er*y default to pay

Mercers, Ironmongers, Grocers, and Apothecaries' Records
C: Company Book   5
p 14*

An order as Conc*er*inge the settinge out
the shooe vpon mydsomer even.

10

8 / Item more yt is further ordered concluded and agreed vppon by
the same companye. That vpon midsomer even at the watche.
shalbe set forth at the charges of the wholl companye of mercers
and Iremongers. for the saide show. and the stewards for the
tyme beinge, to pr*o*vyde against that tyme, some comely striplinge   15
or boye. to Ride before the same companye, and also to get some
other childe, to Ride as agentelwoman or ladye, in respecte that
the said companyes of m*er*cers and Iremongers are vnited and
made one companye and fellowshipp, whereas before they were
two companyes, and the saide boye and ladye to Ride vpon two   20
seu*er*all horses by them selves, and the saide Stewardes for the
tyme beinge, to bye for eyther of said children, at the companyes
charge. eyther of them a suit of app*ar*ill fyttinge for the said
shew. not exceedinge aboue the some of five poundes of Currant
money, and soe the same sutes of apparill, to contynue to the   25
companyes vse, from tyme ∧˹to tyme˺ at theire pleasures. /

An order that everye brother Attend vpon the
Aldermen at the watch vpon midsomer even

30

9 / Item more it is further ordered and agreed vppon by the same
companye of m*er*cers and Iremongers. that all the said brethren
shalby lawfull warninge giuen them by the steward*es* Attende
at aplace appoynted, attende vpon the Aldermen and everie
brother to haue attendinge one them eich one his armed man or   35
watchman. either in armore. or w*i*th Iacke, head peece, and
blacke. bill, and soe eich man in his place indecente order to
accompany theire saide aldermen w*i*th theire boye and ladye to
the barres. where the watch is to be sett out, excepte the haue
leave giuen them by the Aldermen to the contrarie, In paine of   40
forfeature everye tyme soe offendinge. to the stewardes, for the
vse of the same Companye in name of a fyne in Currant Englishe
money to be duely levied vpon everye such offender   v s

Goldsmiths' Records CCA: Minute Book G12/1
p 12*

...

Item it agreyed by the Consent of the Alderman and Steward of
the gouldsmyths that whoe soe ever shall make the bell that   5
shalbe made a gainst Shrouftide ffor the Sadlers shall haue ffor
his paines iiij s iiij d and yf any of the Compeney shall offend in
the premisses shall pay vnto the Alderman and Steward and the
Reste of the Compeney being   iij s 4d

                                                                     10
And if all the oulde bells shalbe broke and not any of the
Compeney to by any to be newe burnished or sould to the
peneltie a ffore said

...
                                                                     15

Dean and Chapter CC: Treasurers' Accounts I
p 155

In primis to William Calw for wachyng   xij d
...   20

A C *Treasurers' Accounts, St Werburgh's* BL: Harley 1994
f 32*

...

                        Dona et Regarda.   25
                                                    li.- s-d
Et solutum diuersis Nuncijs et histrionibus tam domini
Regis quam aliorum magnatum per diuersas vices eidem
Abbatti accidentibus   13-6-8
...   30

A C *Smiths, Cutlers, and Plumbers' Records*
BL: Account Book I Harley 2054
f 14v*

...   35
payd in mr dauid midleton Tauarne   ij d
in mr daueson Tauern   vj s
at william locker dimner   viij d
payd at Simon Mounfort at the Cominge in of Io doe the
weeteman   vj d   40

---

38 / dimner *for* dinner, *4 minims in MS with a tittle above*

...
wach at midsomer eue at night   vj d
Spent on St Clemants day in St Iohns   viij d
...

5

A C   *Smiths, Cutlers, and Plumbers' Records*
      B L : Account Book I Harley 2054
      f 25*

& that ⌈diuers⌉[the Companys] that haue relation to oure &   10
others Artes haue Ioyned themselues in on society or Company
may appeare from the tyme of *Sir* Io Arnway K*nigh*t Maior of
this Citty in tyme of K H 3 [ab] about 410 yeares since when the
Auntient playes vsed in this Citty comonly called whitson plays
wherin they Ioyned for their pagients showes & when the vse   15
therof was layd downe and the wach or showe on midsomer eue
began in tyme of Rich dutton maior 1498 the sayd Artes misterys
societyes Craftes occupations or by what other stille they were
called by, did also Ioyne to gether in the sayd show as on Company

20

a booke I haue   And that the Company of Smythes furbers or Cutlers & pewterers
and founders the rest of their associates were acompany then by
the sayd ould bookes of the whitson playes appereth & what
p*ar*t the acted in the sayd playe tyme out of mynd.
...

25

f 26

witson plays made & first began by Ran Higden a moonk temp
Io Arnway maior about 50 H 3 ⌈1266⌉ yeares since then the   30
⌈Company of⌉ Smyth ffurbors & pewterers Ioyned in the play
called the purification of our lady on Twesday in witson weeke
after w*hi*ch tyme others tooke p*ar*t w*ith* them as mettall men
vilzt

35

A C   *Poem of Children's Games*   B L : Harley 2057
      f 14v*

...

Auntient Customes in games vsed by boys & girles merily sett

---

13 / 410 *written over another date, possibly* 1266, *of which only* 66 *is certain*
29 / m *in* made *written over* b

out in verse

> any they dare chalenge for to throw the slen͜d'ge ͵
> to Iumpe or leape ouer dich or hedge
> to wrastle, play at Stooleball, or to Runne;
> to pich the barre, or to shoote off a gunne
> to play at Loggets, nine holes; or Ten pinnes
> to trye it out at footeball; by the shinnes
> at Tick tacke, Irish, noddy, Maw, & Ruffe
> at hott cockles, leape frogge, or blindman buffe
> to drinke the halph potts or deale at the whole Can:
> to play at chesse or pen and Inkehorne Iohn
> to daunce the morris play at barly breake
> at all exployts a man can thinke or speake
> a shoue groate venterpoynte or Crosse & pile
> at beshrow him thats last at any Style
> at leapinge ore a Christmase eue bonefier
> or at the drawinge dunne out of the myer
> at shoote Cocke: gregory. Stoole ball & what not
> picke poynt topp & scourge to make him hott

AC   *Midsummer Proclamation* BL: Harley 2150
f 161v*

> °The proclamacion at the setting out of
> the watch on midsomer eve.°

The Aldermen and stewards of everie societie and Companie draw yourselues to your said severall Companies accordinge to Ancient Custome, and soe to appeare with your said severall Companies everie man as you are Called vpon paine that shall fall theron.

°If any Iustice of peace be of the company of any society then called the worshipfull•

1 The Aldermen and stewards of the worshipfull Companie of Tanners Come forth with your shewes according to Ancient Custome

2 The Masters and wardens of the societie and Companie of the worshipfull drapers

3 The Masters Aldermen and stewards of the worshipfull Companie of Beerebruers waterleaders and drawers in dee.

4 The Aldermen and stewards of the Barber surgions and Tallow Chandlers

5 The Aldermen and stewards of Cappers, Pinners, Wyredrawers Bricklayers and linnen drapers

6 The Aldermen and stewards of the wrights and sclaters.

7 The Aldermen and stewards of the Ioyners Carvers and Turners

8 The Aldermen and stewards of the worshipfull Companie of Painters Glasiors embroderers and stationers

9 The Aldermen and stewards of the Companie of gouldsmiths and Masons

10 The Aldermen and stewards of Smyths Cutlers pewterers Cardmakers and Plummers °spurriors & girdlers hedmakers°

11 The Aldermen and stewards of the societie and Companie of Butchers.

12 The Aldermen and stewards of the worshipfull Companie of glovers.

13 The Aldermen and stewards of the Companie of Cordwainers

14 The Aldermen and stewards of the Companie of Bakers

15 The Aldermen and stewards of the Companie of ffletchers Bowyers Cowpers and stringers.

16 The Aldermen and stewards of the worshipfull Companie of Mercers °& appothecaries°

17 The Aldermen and stewards of [Cookes and worshipfull Inhoulders and victulers.]'the Companie of worshipfull Ironmongers.' °‚& grocers‚°

18 The Aldermen and stewards of Cookes and worshipfull Inhoulders and victulers.

5

10

15

20

25

30

35

40

19 The Aldermen and stewards of the Societie and worshipfull Companie of Skinners and feltmakers.

20 The Aldermen and stewards of the Companie of Sadlers.

21 The Aldermen and stewards of the Companie of Taylors.

22 The Aldermen and stewards of the Companie of fishmongers.

23 The Aldermen and stewards of the Companie of Clothworkers and walkers.

24 The Aldermen and stewards of the Companie of dyers and Hewsters.

25 The Aldermen and stewards of the Companie of Weavers.

26 The Masters and wardens of the worshipfull Companie of Marchants and Mariners

AC   *Shrovetide Proclamation* BL: Harley 2150
f 162

out of mr
knights bookes

the proclemations on the Roodey vpon
S[⟨.⟩]phTusday oes. oes. oes.

The Right worshipfull the maior of this Citty of Chester willeth & requireth and in the queenes maiestyes name stretly chargeth & Comandeth all & euery person & persons of what degree & Callng soeuer he or they be now Asembled together or shall Asemble to gether to see the Auntient games heretofore Acustomed to be played on this day to the coumfort of the maiesties subiects then present that they & euery of them doe obserue & keepe her maiestyes peace & good behauiour durng the tyme of the sayd games vpon payne that shall fall theron

The Aldermen & stuards of the sosiety & company of Sadlers within the Citty of chester com forth and doe your homage with your horse & bell vpon payne of x li.

The Aldermen & stuards of the Society & company of Cordwyners within the same Citty come forth & doe your

homage with your gleaues and presentments vpon payne of
x li.

All maner of person[s] or persons that haue byn mairied
within the Citty of Chester or els where & dwell within the   5
same during this last yeare now ended Come forth and doe
your seuerall homages with your gleaues & presentments
euery man vpon payne of x li.

...
                                                                      10

AC   *Midsummer Show* BL: Harley 2150
     f 201*

              The Auntient forme & payments
                of midsomer wach or show,   15

The materialls of the Giants the beastes etc. were the proper
goods of the paynters ˻& by them mayd in tyme of Io Ratlife
maior 1601˼ and the Citty maior sheriffs and leauelokers payd
yearly for the repayre videlicet   20

out of the Threasury of the Citty auntiently for aboue this 80
yeares for the payntinge of the Giants and the other beastes
                                                    xliij s iiij d
                                                                      25

more payd by the Treasurers which was auntienly payd by
mr Maiore himselph for the Citty or Maiors Mount till mr
Edwards tyme   xxvj s viij d

              So the citty payd in all, iij li. x s.   30

Mr Maior payd yearly for his 6 mens garlaits and balls for his
burches to the paynters   x s
beside [Carriage] payinge aman to Carry the Maiors mount ij s vj d
& the men new gloues & their wages & for the burches   (blank)   35
mr Maior made Companys drink as the passed by beare & the
Councell & Aldermens wine & a banquet at alightinge or wyne
& cakes

The Sheriffs   40
payd yearly for the payntinge of the Elophant v s a peece to the
paynters   x s

and payd the corriors and cupitt   *(blank)*
payd for their ˄'8' garlands betwene them   xij s
for their balls to ther burches betwene them   ij s
for their 2 haunce staues xx d apeece   iij s iiij d
for their burches, gloues, and wages to the halbeters   *(blank)*   5

for the dragon at paynters charge only   charge
for the Carriage & payinge 6 naked boys at the sheriffs &
leaulookers   *(blank)*
                                                                              10
the Leauelokers payd yearly for payntinge the 4 beastes & 4
hobby horses equialy betwixt them   xliij s 4d
the payd the Carrors & dancers beside
for the morris dancers ˄'had x s from citt but now' haue no fee
but the Curtesye after the show at eich house what the please   15

the mayor payeth yearly to the paynters   xij s vj d
the Threasurers for the Citty   iij li. x s
the sheriffs   xxvij s 4d
the leauelookers   xliij s iiij d   20

AC   *Midsummer Show* BL: Harley 2150
     f 201v*

Wheras there hath byn an auntient and laudable Custome in this   25
Citty Comonly called midsomer show or wach ˄'caused to besett
forth &'approued of by our ˄'Ancestors the'Maiestrates
[thetofore] for the great [vtility of that citty by] drawing in of
Strangers by ther great Comerse and trafick for the benifite of
the sayd citty & Cittizens w*h*ich by late obstructiue tymes hath   30
byn much hindred it is thought meet ˄'at the last generall
assembly'[for the tranquility therof] and taken into Consideration
the sayd show may be agayne reuiued for the publick benifite
of this City and for the [your] good approbation and furtherance
therin in respect diuers thinges of Consernment ˄'therin' are   35
wantinge, to know [what] what willingly your Company is
pleased to contribute to ward the sayd charge that it may not be
retarded and to be subscribed here vnder the hands of your
Alder*men* or [&] Stewards to se whether the some ˄'in generall
gathared' will equilize the Charge of expences, it beinge a   40
*p*articular *pro*fite to eich one & honor to the Citty to *pr*eserue
theis auntient Customs

AC *Midsummer Show* BL: Harley 2150
ff 202-2v*

in Mr Holmes accounts 1632

4 men with halberts to keepe the Companys in order at the
show   iiij s
to sargant parry & his mate for leadinge & keepinge in order the
Armed men at wach   ij s vj d
To Tho welch Citty Ensigne for carring citty cullers at wach
                                                                            ij s vj d
to Gest citty drummer for beatinge drome at wach   xij d
to Robert Thornley & Io wright for their worke about the
Giants & other payntinge at midsomer show   xliij s iiij d
payd for fittinge of the Maiors mount   xxvj s viij d

leauelookers   for paynting of the beastes & hoby horses at midsomer 'both
1610   leauelokers parts'   xliij s iiij d

sheriff 1615   to Iasper gillam for 4 garlands for harness men   4s
               to the 4 men that carried the Armor   4s
               gloues for harness men   xvj d

⟨...⟩t Iunior   to 4 men that carried the 2 beastes   4s. vj d.
leaueoker 1628 to the 5 men that held the boys that ridd   ij s vj d
                to the 2 boys that danced the hobby horses   *(blank)*
                to chatterton the piper my part   xij d
                for payntinge the beasts at midsomer my part   xxj s 8d

for mr maior   for 16 burches & carriage   ix s vj d
1633   the burches are sett vp by harnesse men   *(blank)*

                to the 6 harnisse men that carried halberts 3s for 6 payre of
                gloues ij s ij d
                to welch ned for Carriage of maiors mount   ij s vj d
                to Robert Thornley for 6 garlands for harnisse men heads   ix s

mr Sheriff   for 12 byrches & Carrage   ix s vj d
                for balls for the trees   xij d
                to the 4 men that Carried Armor v s [⟨...⟩] for gloues xviij d
                for hier of Armor   iij s vj d
                citty wayts   xij d

payd 2 porters to Carry Elofant my part mr byrd pad as much

xij d

to the boy that ridd on it my part   vj d

payd R Thornley for my part payntig the Elophant v s mr byrd

payd as much   5

payd him for making 4 garlands for harnis men vj s, mr byrd
as much for his |

vpon Conference with Io wright about makinge the 4 Giants etc.
⌐& other thinges for midsomer⌐ by the aminge ‸⌐only⌐ at the   10
charges of the particulars as neere as Could be the workm⟨..⟩
excepted to be payd for
we compute great hoopes dale bords Couper worke nayles
size cloth ‸⌐bastbord paper⌐ for bodyes sleue ⌐&⌐ skirts to be
Cullered Tinsilld Arsedine Cullers & ⌐cariage of them⌐ the thinges   15

⟨.⟩ x li.   for one Giant with an other to be with workmanshipp the least
to be v li. a pee⟨..⟩ all beinge new to be made & the stronger &
firmer will be better for the future to saue the Citty charge /
for the Elophant with the Castell for hoopes cloth Cullers
⌐Tinsile for Castell⌐ & makinge   20

⟨..⟩ li. 10s   for Airows & skyns for the naked boy & workmanshipp all
new wrought
the leaste with workmanship will be l s

v li.   the 4 beastes for the leauelokers the Antilope flowerdeluce
l. s d   vnicorne & Camell all matterialls this yeare to be new, will   25
[⟨...⟩]   be about [30s]⌐36s⌐⌐[vj]⌐ apeece

li. s   the maiors mount new made this yeare with all matterialls
⟨..⟩ 10   will be at least l s beside bays to be hired & a man to Carry it

50s   for the Marchant mount all to be new made with maiormen
etc & the shipp 50s beside cloth to be hired & men to Carry it   30

2 li.   for the 4 hobby horses for the leauelokers [xiij s 4d] peece

4s   for 2 hance bills for the sheriffs boys   iiij s
for garlands for mr maior ‸⌐6⌐ harnesse men as vsuall ⌐&

1 li. 1s.   sheriffs 4 apeece⌐ hath byn xviij d apeece

                                                                        35

the maior sheriffs Threasurers & leauelokes pay yearly among
them 7. 10 8d to the paynters the rest on the paynters charges

this to be this yeare to goe on the generall charge because of new
makinge & an order for future the thinges made to be payd   40
accordinge to ould Custome
or if this be Contynued by them as Auntiently then the same

is to be deducted out of the generall charge of agreement

payd yearly to the paynters for new triminge of the marchants
mount by the Company of marchants   xxxiij s 4d

                                                       5

AC *Midsummer Show* BL: Harley 2150
ff 203-3v*

a Compute of the charges about midsomer show all thinges to
be made new by reason the ould modells were all broken w*hi*ch   10
was m*r* holmes & Io wrights goods & yearly repayred ˌ'hertofore'
by the Citty Threasury [and theirby] one p*art*, and the maior
sheriffs & leauelokers the rest

Impr*imis* for ˌ'finding of' all the materialls w*i*th the workmanshipp   15
of the 4 great Giants all to be made new as neere as may be like
as the were before at v li. a Giant the least that can be in all 20 li.
for 4 men to Carry them   x s
for the new makinge the Citty mount Called the maiors mount
as auntiently it was and for hyringe of bayes for the same & a   20
man to Carry it   iij li. vj s 8d
for makinge anew the marchant mount as auntiently it was w*i*th
a shipp to turne hyringe of boys & 5 to Carry it   iiij li.
for makinge a new the Elaphant & Castell & Cupitt to sute out
of it & 2 men to Carry it   lvj s viij d 25
for makinge new the 4 beastes for the leauelookers Called the
Vnicorne the Antilop the fflowerdeluce & Camell at 33s 4d a
peece   vj li. xiij s 4d
for 8 men to Carry them   xvj s
for 4 hobby horses at vj s viij d apeece   xxvj s 8d 30
for 4 boys to Carry them   [⟨..⟩] ij s
for the 2 hancestaues for the boys that Ride for the sheriffs
                                                          vj s viij d
for 6 garlands for m*r* maiors halberts & 4 a peece for m*r* sheriffs
at xx d a peece   [xix s 8d] xxiij s 8d 35
for balls for the maior & sheriffs burches   x s
for the makinge new the dragon   v s
& for 6 naked boyes to beat at it   vj s
the ˌ'6' morris dancers & Tabrett & pipe   xx s

                                                       40

the whole some the paynters findinge all this yeare as abouesayd
is and Carrors   [xlij li. ⟨...⟩s 8d]

[44 li. ⟨...⟩s 8d]
[45 xj s 8d]
45 9 8d

to borrow the hall as before for them
mrs maiores berrage
the tyme will be halph a yeare dowing ⎸   5

If so much moneys of the Companys as to pay 45 li. 9s 8d then
the ∧ʿCittyʾ maior sheriffs leauelookers & Company of marchants
pay nothing this yeare because as is made new it is very probable
some Companys will giue much more then orther because the   10
benyfite more and with the generall Collection by the ⟨..⟩nstables
of others beside the remaynder to be put into the Citty stocke
toward their charges herafter

If the Companeys gratuitys fall short, the Citty maior sheriffs   15
leauelookers & marchants to pay as auntiently and to be added
to what is gathared

if the moneys gathared be satisfactory ∧ʿfor the payntersʾ that
an order of Agreement be sett downe by assembly or otherways   20
that after this yeare the Citty maior sheriffs leauelookes &
marchants may pay yearly as auntiently the ould fees before
mentioned for keepinge the giants & the rest in repayre as
formerly was vsed

                                                                               25

AC *City Treasurers' Accounts* BL: Harley 2158
f 36v*

Watergatestrete   30

...
mercatoribus Ciuitatis Cestrie pro vna vacua placea ibidem   vj d
...

f 37*   35

...
panniparijs Ciuitatis Cestrie pro quodam aysiamento   viij d
...

Watergate Street

...   40
all rest as in 9 Roll

f 40*

...

Estgatestrete

...

senescall*is* Tellairij C*iuita*tis Cestr*ie* *pro* gardin iuxta truants   5
hole   4d

f 41

...

Watergate streete   10

...

marchants   meraner*ijs* *pro* Carriagiy ib*ide*m Aysiamento   vj d
panneri*orijs* *pro* Consil*io*   vj d

...

                                            15

f 43v*

...

Watergate stret

...

mercatoribus C*iuita*tis Cestr*ie* *pro* vna vacua placea ib*ide*m   vij d 20

...

drapers de Cite Cestr*ie* *pro* aysamento   ij d

5 / Tellairij *for* Sellarij   5 / gardin *for* gardino

2 Printed Documents

1531
Alleged letter to an unknown nobleman from the Mayor and Corporation of Chester John Payne Collier, *The History of English Dramatic Poetry to the time of Shakespeare: and Annals of the Stage to the Restoration,* I (London, 1831)   5
pp 114-16*

'Our moste humble duetye to your right honorable Lordshypp premysed, we holde it convenyent and proppre to infourme your good Lordshyppe of a play, which som of the companyes   10
of this Cittye of Chester, at theyr costes and charges, are makynge redy, for that your good Lordshyppe maye see wether the same be in any wyse unfyttynge for them, as honest menne and duetyfull subjectes of his Majestye. The sayde playe is not newe at thys tyme, but hath bin bifore shewen, evyn as longe   15
agoe as the reygne of his highnes most gratious father of blyssyd memorye, and yt was penned by a godly clerke, merely for delectacion, and the teachynge of the people to love & feare God and his Majestye, and all those that bee in auctoryte. It is callyd Kynge Robart of Cicylye, the whiche was warned by an Aungell   20
whiche went to Rome, and shewyd Kyng Robart all the powre of God, and what thynge yt was to be a pore man; and thanne, after sondrye wanderynges, ledde hym backe agayne to his kingdome of Cicylye, where he lyved and raygned many yeres.

   Thys muche we thought it mete to shewe to your right   25
honorable Lordshyppe, for that your good Lordshppe myght knowe the holle of theyr entent that goe aboute to playe this playe on Saynt Peter's day nexte ensewing; and yf your good Lordshyppe shold holde the same unfytte or unwyse at thys tyme, thanne theis pore artifycers will of our knowlege staye   30
the same and'

1620
Cappers, Pinners, Wiredrawers, and Linendrapers' Company
Order Book: T. Hughes, 'Midsummer Show'
p 244

5

Whereas the Companye of Bricklayers within this citty are to
be at charges in settinge forth of the SHOWE or WATCH at
MYDSOMER of Balaam and Balaam's asse, whereunto as well
the freemen of the Lynnen drapers, brickemakers, and bricklaiers
of this Cittye, as also the forreners inhabitinge w'thin this cittye, 10
and usinge the trades aforesaide, have bene acoustomed to bee
contributarye. These are theirfore to authorise Roberte Ridley
and George Antrobus, Aldermen of the companye of Bricklayers,
and Roberte Goodaker and Thomas Markes, stewards of the same
companye, to collecte of everye of the said p'sons aforesaide all 15
such somes of money as they haue bene heretofore accustomed
to paye, and as hath bene accustomed to bee collected towardes
the Charge aforesaide. Dated the xxjth of Maie, 1602.

JOHN RATCLIFFE, Maior. 20

...

That thereafter the said company doth alow vpon Mydsomer
even after the WATCH for theire drinkeinge vnto the stowards of
the sayd company the some of vjs. viijd.; and yf the said stewards
for the tyme doe make any more charge, or exceed above the 25
said some of vjs. viijd., the said stewardes to pay the overplushe
themselves.

1603
Cappers, Pinners, Wiredrawers, and Linendrapers' Company 30
Minute Book: T. Hughes, 'The Whitsun Plays'
p 231

June 1. fforasmuch as it appeareth that of aunciente tyme the
Companye of Capp'rs, pynners, and wyardrawers within this 35
cittie haue yearelye ioyned to geather in settinge foorth their
pagines both at plaies at Whitsontyde and at the Watch on
Mydsomer, And that afterwards, upon decaie of the pynners
and Wyardrawers, the Companye of Lynnen Drapers within
the said Cittye have ioyned in all Contribution' with the saide 40
Cappers; w'ch companye of Capp'rs beinge lykewise decayed,
the companye of bricklayers have borne the charge with the saide

lynnen drapers yearely in settinge forth the Shew or Mydsomer Watch, Accordinge to auncient Costome; which saide lynnen Drapers doe nowe refuse to ioyne or Contribute in the same, It is therefore ordered that the saide Lynnen Drapers and bricklayers shall contynue the settinge foorth of the said showe vpon Midsomer Eve, and be Contributors one w'th the other for the doeinge theireof, as they have bene accustomed for the space of manye yeares.

	HUGH GLASEOURE, MAIOR.	1
WILL'M ALDERSAYE	EDMUND GAMUELL	
JOHN RADCLYFF	THOMAS LYNEALL	
EDWARD DUTTON	JOHN FYTTON	
THOMAS GAMUELL	FFOULKE ALDERSAY	
RICHARD BAVAND		1

More, it is fully agreed vpon that the Stewardes for the tyme beinge shall, against everye Midsomer even against the Watch, provyde some comely boye to Ryde upon Balahams Asse before the companye, and also to see that the said boye and Asse be trymed and sett fourth accordinge to Auncient Custome for the Creditt of the same companye, in paine of forfeaytinge for any such defaulte in money . . . . 10s.

1606-8
Cappers, Pinners, Wiredrawers, and Linendrapers' Company
Order Book: T. Hughes, 'Midsummer Show'
p 244

...

payd for Caringe of Balams Ase		vijd.
payd to the minstrylles		viijd.
for stokengs, showes, and glovs for the boye	iijs.	viijd.
for dressing of the beast	iijs.	iiijd.
It. for the bankett	iijs.	iiij d.
It. in drenk before the Wache		vjd.

...

1673
Minstrels' Court   Sir Peter Leycester, *Historical Antiquities*
pp 141-2 *(Randle Blundevill, earl of Chester, 1181-1232)*

...

This *Randle* among the many Conflicts he had with the

Welsh, as I find in an ancient *Parchment* Roll, written above two
hundred Years ago, wherein the Barons of *Halton* with their
Issue were carefully collected, was distressed by the *Welsh,* and
forced to retreat to the Castle of *Rothelent* in *Flintshire,* about
the Reign of King *John,* where they Besieged him: He presently   5
sent to his Constable of *Cheshire, Roger Lacy,* sirnamed *Hell,* for
his fierce Spirit, that he would come with all speed, and bring
what Forces he could towards his Relief. *Roger* having gathered
a tumultuous Rout of Fidlers, Players, Coblers, debauched
persons, both Men and Women, out of the City of *Chester* (for   10
'twas then the Fair-time in that City,) marcheth immediately
towards the Earl. The *Welsh* perceiving a great multitude coming,
raised their Siege and fled. The Earl coming back with his
Constable to *Chester,* gave him Power over all the Fidlers and
Shoemakers in *Chester,* in reward and memory of this Service.   15
The Constable retained to himself and his Heirs, the Authority
and Donation of the Shoemakers, but conferred the Authority
of the Fidlers and Players on his Steward, which then was *Dutton*
of *Dutton;* whose Heirs enjoy the same Power and Authority
over the Minstralcy of *Cheshire* even to this day; who in memory   20
hereof keep a yearly Court upon the Feast of *St. John Baptist* at
Chester, where all the Minstrels of the County and City are to
attend and Play before the Lord of *Dutton:* And none ought to
use their Minstralcy but by Order and Licence of that Court,
under the Hand and Seal of the Lord *Dutton* or his Steward,   25
either within *Cheshire* or the City of *Chester.* And to this day
the Heirs of *Dutton,* or their Deputies, do in a solemn manner
yearly upon *Midsummer-day,* being *Chester* Fair, Ride attended
through the City of *Chester,* with all the Minstralcy of *Cheshire*
playing before them on their several Instruments, to the Church   30
of *St. Johns,* and at the Court renew their Licences yearly.

I cannot here pass by the gross mistake of *Powel* on the
Welsh History, *pag.* 296. whom *Cambden* in his *Britania* seems
to follow; where *Raufe de Dutton* is said to have gathered this
Army, and to have rescued the Earl: whereupon he had the   35
Power over the Minstralcy granted immediately from the Earl. |

For first, there was never any such an Heir of *Dutton* of
Dutton, that was called *Rafe de Dutton.* But I shall, for more
satisfaction, transcribe the Original Deed made to *Dutton,*
remaining among the Evidences of that Family, which now by a   40
Daughter and Heir is devolved to the Lord *Gerard* of *Gerards*
Bromley in *Staffordshire.*

Lib. C. fol. 139.

Sciant præsentes & futuri, quod ego Johannes *Constabularius* Cestriæ, *dedi & concessi & hac præsenti Charta mea confirmavi,* Hugoni de Dutton, *& Hæredibus suis, Magistratum omnium Leccatorum & Meretricum totius* Cestershiræ, *sicut liberius illum Magistratum teneo de Comite; Salvo jure meo mihi & Heredibus meis. Hiis Testibus,* Hugone de Boidele, Alano *Fratre ejus,* Petro de Goenet Liulfo de Twamlow, Ada de Dutton, Gilberto de Aston, Radulfo de Kingsley, Hamone de Bordington, Alano de Waleie, Alano de Mulinton, Willielmo *Filio* Ricardi, Martino Angevin, Willielmo de Savill, Galfrido & Roberto *Filliis meis* Bletheris,* Herdberd de Waleton, Galfrido de Dutton.

*It is either thus, as I have put it; or, *Galfrido & Roberto Filiis meis, Blethero Herberd de Waleton, &c.* I leave it to the Reader to judge.

In which Deed it is, *John Constable of Cheshire* (not the Earl of *Chester) grants to* Hugh de Dutton (not to *Raufe de Dutton) the Authority over all the Letchers and Whores of all Cheshire; Salvo jure meo.* So as the Right was the Constables, which he held of the Earl; but now transfers it over to *Hugh Dutton,* about the end of King *John's* Reign. By the ancient Roll it should seem *Roger Lacy* rescued the Earl, and now *John* his Son transferrs this Power to *Dutton:* Which Original Grant mentioneth nothing of the Rule of Fidlers or Minstrels; but ancient Custom hath now brought it onely to the Minstrelsie: For anciently I suppose the Rout which the Constable brought to the Rescuing of the Earl, were debauched Persons drinking with their Sweet-hearts in the Fair, Fidlers, and such loose kind of Persons as he could get; which tract of time hath reduced onely to the minstrels.

I find in the Records at *Chester, inter placita* 14 *Hen.* 7. a *Quo Warranto* brought against *Laurence Dutton* of *Dutton,* Esq; why he claimed all the Minstrels of *Cheshire,* and in the City of *Chester,* to meet before him at *Chester* yearly, at the Feast of Saint *John Baptist,* and to give unto him at the said Feast *quatuor Lagenas Vini, & unam Lanceam;* that is, four Bottles of Wine, and a Lance: and also every Minstrel to pay unto him at the said Feast four Pence half-penny: And why he claimed from every Whore in *Cheshire,* and in the City of *Chester, Officium suum exercente,* four Pence to be paid yearly at the Feast aforesaid, &c. Whereunto he pleaded Prescription.

And whereas by the Statute of 39 *Eliz. cap.* 4. Fidlers are declared to be Rogues; yet there is an especial *Proviso* in the Statute, for the exempting of those in *Cheshire,* Licensed by *Dutton* of *Dutton,* as belonging to his ancient Custom and Privilege: So that the Fidlers of *Cheshire,* Licensed by the Heirs of *Dutton* of *Dutton,* are no Rogues. But enough of this.

...

p 251 *(Hugh Dutton of Dutton)*

...

® See the Deed at large *supra pag* 142. made about the end of King *Johns* Reign, or the beginning of *Henry* the Third.

He had also the Magistracy, or Rule and Authority, over all the Letchers and Whores of all *Cheshire,* granted unto him and his Heirs, by *John* Constable of *Cheshire,* and Baron of *Halton,* as freely as the said *John* held the same of the Earl of *Chester;* saving the Right of the said *John* to him and His Heirs: Which are the very words of the Deed, onely rendred by me in *English: Lib. C. fol.* 154. *h.* So that he holds it, as it were, under the Baron of *Halton,* who reserves his own Right by a special Reservation.

This Privilege over such loose Persons was granted first unto *Roger Lacy* Constable of *Cheshire,* under *Richard* the First, by *Randle,* sir-named *Blundevill,* Earl of *Chester,* in memory of his good Service done to the Earl in raising the Siege of the *Welsh-men,* who had beset the Earl in his Castle of *Rothelent* in *Flintshire:* For the Constable having got a promiscuous Rabble of such like Persons together, and Marching towards the said Castle, the *Welsh* (supposing a great Army to be coming) raised their Siege, and fled: So saith the ancient Roll of the Barons of *Halton: Lib. C. fol.* 85. *b. Monasticon Anglicanum,* 2 *Pars, pag.* 187. This Roll saith, the Rabble consisted of Players, Fidlers, and Shoe-makers. The Deed here toucheth Letchers and Whores. The Privilege and Custom used at this day by the Heirs of *Dutton,* is over the Minstrelsie and Common Fidlers; none being suffered to Play in this County, without the Licence of the Lord of *Dutton,* who keeps a Court at *Chester* yearly, on *Midsomer-day,* for the same, where all the Licenced Minstrels of *Cheshire* do appear, and renew their Licences: So that the Custom seems to have been altered to the Fidlers, as necessary Attendants on Revellers in Bawdy-houses and Taverns.

And it is to be observed, That those Minstrels which are Licensed by the Heirs of *Dutton* of *Dutton,* within the County Palatine of *Chester,* or the County of the City of *Chester,* according to their ancient Custom, are exempted out of the Statute of Rogues, 39 *Eliz. cap.* 4.

...

Translations: The Records

The Latin and Anglo-Norman documents have been translated as literally as possible in order to aid the reader in understanding what the documents say. The arrangement of the translations parallels that of the text. No indication is given of words or passages in English surrounding those in Latin. Place names and Christian names have been normalized but not surnames. Capitalization and punctuation are in accordance with modern practice. As in the text, diamond brackets indicate obliterations and square brackets cancellations. No indication is given of interlineations in the text. Round brackets enclose words not in the original language but needed for grammatical sense in English.

1398-9
Mayors' Books CCA: M/B/1
ff 55v-6* *(30 May)*

Inquest taken at Chester before the sheriffs of Chester on Friday, the day after Corpus Christi in the twenty-second year of the reign of King Richard the second, on the oath of Richard de Draycote; John the glover; Henry the corviser; William Mody; John Russell, porter; William de Hulfeld, cooper; John Chirche, corviser; Richard Short, shipman; Andrew the freeman; Robert de Thenwall, skinner; William the tailor; and Richard del Halgh. The jurors say on their oath that William de Wybunbure, senior; Henry de Felday, weaver; Thomas Bragot, weaver; William de Stretton, walker; Thomas the chaloner of Eastgate Street; Thomas de Brymstath, dyer; Richard de Werburton, weaver; William Cay, chaloner; Roger the chaloner of Foregate Street; Hugh de Thurstanton, weaver, Richard del Hope, weaver; Henry Huntebach; William Shagh, weaver; Richard Whyt, fuller; William

Butt, dyer; Richard Byrne, weaver; John le Erle, chaloner; Richard Gardeyn, fuller; William Bryn, fuller; William Porter, fuller; Richard de Hale; William Thomassone, dyer; John Howell, weaver; Hugh Bargeyn; Hugh de Legh; John de Ince, senior; David Broun, weaver; John Mair, weaver; [John de Berkeswell, senior]; William the shearman; Nicholas the shearman; John the shearman; Thomas Jakes, shearman; John de Shottum, shearman; [Hugh de Aston, chaloner]; John the chaloner of Saint John's Lane; William the chaloner; [cr⟨...⟩rins the chaloner; John le Smyth, weaver]; Richard Getegode, weaver; William Haslore, weaver; Thomas le Spencer, weaver; Henry Denys, weaver; John the weaver of Castle Lane; Simon the weaver of Hawardyn; John [de Bromley] de Frodesham; William Capemaker; and many other master weavers came with force and arms, with pole-axes, (?) staves, daggers, and other diverse armaments, by a premeditated plan on Thursday, the feast of Corpus Christi, in the twenty-second year of the reign of King Richard the second, opposite the church of Blessed Peter of Chester. Also, those gathered together insulted William de Wybunbure, junior, Thomas del Dame, and very many others, their servants, called journeymen, in a great affray of the whole population of the city, against the peace of the lord king. They say they are not guilty. And on the next Thursday following after the feast of the apostles Peter and Paul, it was learned by the inquest taken that Thomas Bragot, Richard Whyte, Richard de Werberton, ⟨Wi⟩lliam the chaloner, John the chaloner, John Howell, William de Stretton, Hugh Bargayne, ⟨Jo⟩hn le Smyth, weaver, and William Cadewalleshened are not guilty of the aforesaid insult, but they ⟨say⟩ that they are guilty in the aforesaid fray. Therefore it was concluded, etc. |

Item they say that William de Wybunbure, junior; Henry Penkyth, fuller; John de Merton; John de Hull, weaver; Richard le Spencer, weaver; John Thomasson, weaver; Robert de Derbyshyre, fuller; Thomas del Dame, weaver; Richard Stubbok, chaloner; John Chestre, junior; Henry Bragot; John de Sucton, weaver; William le Smyth, weaver; John de Acton, weaver; Reginald de Merford; Roger Pyme; John de Holand; William Wodewarde, servant of Richard de Hale; Thomas Werforde; John Dernak, weaver; Thomas del Mosse; Roger, servant of Richard de Hale; Robert, servant of William Porter; Edward Brounsworde; Bellyn, servant of William Shawe; Henry Bragot; Hugh Bragot; [William] Nicholas,

Richard, and David, servants of Richard Whyt; [John de Londes-
dale]; Thomas de Byrchomley; John de Hale, junior; David
de Moldesdale; [Thomas le Sheuacre, chaloner]; John de Chestre,
senior; William and Robert, servants, the servants of Thomas de
Brymstath; John Gredyn; David, servant of Henry Penkyth;
William Kydde, servant of William Porter, weaver; William le
Wodewarde, servant of Richard de Hale; John Skelo, servant of
David Broun.

1421-2
Coopers' Records C: Loose Papers*
(20 April)

Memorandum that discord and action at law have arisen between
the Ironmongers of the city of Chester on the one side, and the
Carpenters of the same city on the other side, whether one side
or the other should have all the Fletchers, Bowers, Stringers,
Coopers, and Turners of the same city to help them in the
Corpus Christi Play of the same city. Finally, with the assent
of each side, an inquest was taken in the full portmote held at
Chester on the next Monday after the close of Easter, in the
tenth year of the reign of King Henry the fifth after the conquest, before John Hope, mayor of the aforesaid city, to find
out the truth of the aforesaid issues, whether they ought ⟨to be
attached⟩ to one side or the other, or not, viz, on the oath of
John de Hatton, senior, William Hope, Richard Weston,
Alexander Hennebury, Adam de Wotton, John de Hatton,
junior, Robert Wolley, Richard Lynakre, William de Pykton,
Thomas de Hellesby, John William, and Richard Thomworth,
jurors. They say on their oath that the aforesaid ⟨Fletchers⟩,
Bowers, Stringers, Coopers, and Turners ought not to play nor
are they held to play nor to be participants with one side or
the other, with the aforesaid Ironmongers or with the aforesaid Carpenters, in their pageants of the aforesaid Corpus Christi
Play, but they say that they are held to support by themselves
their own pageant for the same play, viz, from the flagellation
of the body of Christ, with those things belonging to it, according to the original made of it (ie, the play), as far as the crucifixion of the same Jesus Christ as far as is contained in the said
original, and that the aforesaid Ironmongers ought to support
the play of the Crucifixion as the aforesaid ⟨...⟩ and the aforesaid
Carpenters ought to support their pageant according to the

aforesaid original. In testimony of which thing the aforesaid mayor caused the seal of his office of the mayoralty to be affixed to this present inquiry. Given on the day and year aforesaid.

1429-30
Portmote Court Rolls CCA: M/R/4/85
mb 1* *(19 May)*
...

Pleas of the portmote of the city of Chester held at Chester before John Walssh, mayor of the said city, on the Monday next after the feast of St Dunstan in the ⟨eighth⟩ year of the reign of King Henry the sixth after the conquest.

Let it be remembered that on the Monday next after the feast of St Dunstan in the seventh year of the reign of our most sovereign lord, King Henry the sixth after the conquest, before John le Walssh, mayor of the city of Chester, the sheriffs, and the twenty-four aldermen of the said city: by the consent, agreement, and good will of Richard de Hawardyn and Richard de Brogheford, stewards of the crafts of the Weavers, Walkers, Chaloners, and Shearmen of the said city upon a petition made in full portmote by the said mayor, sheriffs, ⟨.⟩ twenty-four aldermen ⟨...⟩, it was ordained, established, and agreed that it shall be in perpetuity, that each person of whatever estate or condition who practises or sets up in any of the said crafts within the said city be contributory ⟨...⟩ or cause to be paid all ⟨...⟩ of which he is or will be assessed to pay by the stewards of the said crafts for the time being towards the costs and expenses ⟨...⟩ the light of Our Lady St Mary and of Corpus Christi and for the play of Corpus Christi, both for the one and the other and for each and every time ⟨...⟩, that it shall happen that the said light is carried or the said play is performed and that each one who does not send the sum which he is assessed by the said stewards shall pay within the month ⟨in which⟩ the said assessment, (or) it shall be that he shall incur the for⟨feit ...⟩ pain of 13s 4d, that is to say, 6s 8d to the sheriffs of the said city for the time being and 6s 8d to the ⟨stewards⟩ of the same crafts who will be for the time being, and the said sum to be levied as a distraint.

And that it is allowed as well to the said sheriffs for the 6s 8d which is allotted to them, ⟨so also the⟩ said stewards for the 6s 8d which is allotted to them, and ⟨...⟩ for the said sums thus assessed to distrain any person on whom the said sum has thus been assessed ⟨..⟩ (who) refuses to send or pay the said

distraint to anyone unless the said case of non-payment be agreed
to be given and held unfulfillable ⟨...⟩ always. In testimony of
which declared (?) ⟨...⟩ ordinance, decision, and agreement
indented and enrolled as well the said mayor for himself, the said
sheriffs, and twenty-four aldermen (has set) the seal of office of
the mayoralty ⟨and also⟩ the said ⟨...⟩ stewards for themselves
and all the craftsmen of the crafts mentioned aforesaid have set
their seals. Given at Chester on the day and year mentioned
above.

...

1437-8

AC *City Treasurers' Accounts* BL: Harley 2158
f 33v *(November)*

...

The steward of the Mercers for the rent of Shipgate   8d

...

1438-9

AC *City Treasurers' Accounts* BL: Harley 2158
f 33v* *(November)*

...

From the stewards of the Fishers of Chester for a certain piece
of land   6d

...

1439-40

AC *City Treasurers' Accounts* BL: Harley 2158
f 33v *(November)*

...

From the stewards of the Tailors of Chester for a certain piece
of land   6d
From the stewards of the Fishers for a certain piece of land   6d

...

1440-1

AC *City Treasurers' Accounts* BL: Harley 2158
f 34 *(November)*

...

From the stewards of the Tailors of Chester for a certain piece
of land   6d

...

f 35v *(Arrearages)*

...

From the Fishers of Chester for a certain piece of land   *(blank)*

...

1441-2

AC   *City Treasurers' Accounts* BL: Harley 2158
f 34v* *(November)*

...

From the Tailors of Chester for a piece of land   6d

...

From the Fishers of Chester for a piece of land   6d
From the stewards of the Mercers for a piece of land in Shipgate   8d

...

f 35
... the Mercers' steward 8d

...

1442-3

AC   *City Treasurers' Accounts* BL: Harley 2158
f 35v *(November)*

...

From the Mercers' stewards for their rent   8d

...

1465-6

AC   *City Treasurers' Accounts* BL: Harley 2158
f 51* *(November)* *(Arrearages)*

...

The Mercers of the city of Chester   *(blank)*
The Drapers of the city of Chester for *(blank)*   *(blank)*

...

1466-7

AC   *City Treasurers' Accounts* BL: Harley 2158
f 51* *(November)* *(Arrearages)*

...

The Mercers of the city for the house for their carriage   *(blank)*

...

1467-8

AC *City Treasurers' Accounts* BL: Harley 2158
f 39* *(November)*

...

From the stewards of the saddlercraft of the city of Chester
for a garden next to Truantshole   4d

...

f 39v

...

From the stewards of the Shearmen for accommodation for
their carriage   4d

...

f 40

...

® before (the entry) from the Merchants

From the (?) Mariners for accommodation for their carriage
there   6d
From the Drapers for the council   8d

...

f 52

...

From the Mercers of the city for one empty plot (of land)
there   8d

...

f 52v

...

The Drapers of the city of Chester for a certain accommodation
                                                                     8d
From the Mercers of the city for a certain accommodation for
the carriage   8d

...

1469-70

AC *City Treasurers' Accounts* BL: Harley 2158
f 56 *(November) (Arrearages)*

... from the Drapers of Chester 4d ...

1470-1

AC   *City Treasurers' Accounts* BL: Harley 2158
f 54v* *(November) (Arrearages)*

...

From the Drapers of the city of Chester   *(blank)*

...

1471-2

Treasurers' Account Rolls CCA: TAR/1/4
mb 1d* *(November)*

...

From the Mercers of the city of Chester for one empty plot
(of land) there   6d

...

Saddlers' Charter PRO: CHES 2/144
mb 7 *(8 March)*

Letters patent
of the Saddlers
of the city of
Chester

Edward, by the grace of God king of England and France and
lord of Ireland, to all to whom the present letters may have
come, greetings. Know that since it has been made known to us
by our beloved subjects, Richard Sadiller and Henry Ellome,
stewards, Richard Ellome, John Yong, Richard Yong, and Henry
Yong, aldermen, and the resident masters and occupiers of the
art and trade of the Saddlers within our city of Chester, how,
because of unauthorised trespasses, settings up, and occupations
of the same art within our aforesaid city by foreign persons, and
out of the unruliness of people of obstinate disposition in not
helping them to support the burdens and costs of the play and
pageant assigned to occupiers of the same art and city, (which)
portions of the play and light of Corpus Christi (are) to be
supported and watched over annually for the honour of the same
by the occupiers of the same art and trade in the aforesaid city,
and (in not helping them to support) other manifold burdens
ordered annually for the honour of God and of our aforesaid city
and supported by the same craftsmen within our aforesaid city,
thus our aforesaid subjects have been gravely impoverished, and
thus, impoverished of their goods, that they are not able to
continue the same burdens or to sustain them in future without
our favour and remedy on that account. We therefore, having
intimate consideration of the aforesaid, by our special grace have

conceded to our aforesaid subjects, stewards, aldermen, and
resident masters, and to the occupiers of the same art and trade
of Saddlers and to their successors being stewards, aldermen, and
resident masters and occupiers of the same art and trade of
Saddlers within our city of Chester in future, that no person or
persons, for the remainder of the term of the next forty years,
shall enter or set up or occupy the aforesaid art and trade of the
Saddlers within our said city or in any place of its liberty without
the will, assent, licence, and agreement of our aforesaid subjects
and of their successors as stewards, aldermen, masters, and
occupiers of the same art of Saddlers, or of the greater part of
them living within our aforesaid city, under pain of forfeiture
of a hundred shillings by any person doing thus, as often as he,
without such licence, shall enter, set up, or occupy the aforesaid
art or trade without the will, assent, licence, and agreement of
the aforesaid, with half of the abovesaid same hundred shillings
to be forfeited to us, to our heirs and to our successors, the other
half of the same hundred shillings to be forfeited to the aforesaid
stewards, aldermen, masters, and occupiers of the same art and
trade of Saddlers being within our city for the time being, for
the support of the pageant, light, and play mentioned above,
and it is to be levied by those who are our sheriffs of our aforesaid city for the time being. And in addition, by our greater
grace, we have conceded to the aforesaid subjects and to their
successors as stewards, aldermen, masters, and occupiers of the
said art of Saddlers living in the aforesaid city and its liberty
afterward, that it shall be permitted to them in future, as often
as shall be proper for them through necessity, to ordain, make,
and compose among themselves such ordinances and constitutions
to be kept within and among the stewards, aldermen, masters,
and occupiers of the same art within the said city as might be
able to provide more beneficially for the convenience of the
ordained support of the pageant of the play of the art and
trade of the aforesaid Saddlers within the aforesaid city and its
liberty. In testimony of which thing, we have caused these
letters patent to be made. Witnessed by me, myself, at Chester,
on the eighth day of March in the twelfth year of our reign.

By a writ of the privy seal and
of the authority of parliament granted.

1472-3

AC *City Treasurers' Accounts* BL: Harley 2158
f 55v *(November)*

...

From the Mercers of the city of Chester for one empty plot
(of land) there   6d

...

From the Drapers of the city of Chester for accommodation   8d

...

f 56v *(Arrearages)*
... from the Mercers of the city for an empty plot (of land), 6d ...
from the Drapers of the city for accommodation, 8d ...

1473-4

AC *City Treasurers' Accounts* BL: Harley 2158
f 56v *(November) (Arrearages)*

...

The Mercers of Chester   6d

...

From the Drapers of Chester   8d

...

1476-7

AC *City Treasurers' Accounts* BL: Harley 2158
f 58 *(November)*

...

From the Mercers of the city of Chester for an empty plot of
land, etc   6d

...

From the Drapers of the city by a wall for accommodation   8d

...

Minstrels' Court PRO: CHES 2/149
mb 11 *(23 June)*

Commission of
the abbot of
Chester and
others for
holding a court
of the minstrels
of Chester

Edward etc, to all to whom the present letters may have come,
greetings. Know that we, fully confident of the fidelity, circumspection, and industry of our beloved and faithful Richard,
abbot of the monastery of Saint Werburgh of Chester, Hugh
Mascy, mayor of our city of Chester, and Master William Thomas,
have constituted and ordained them, the abbot, mayor, and

William, as our seneschals, jointly and individually, for the purpose of holding a court of the minstrels of Chester in the aforesaid city for this time only, (which court) is now in our hands because of the minority of Laurence, son and heir of Roger de Dutton, recently lord of Dutton, now deceased. And for the purpose of performing and carrying out all things which pertain to performing the duty of the aforesaid office of seneschal for this time. And therefore we order you to be attentive to the same abbot, mayor, and William in all things which pertain to the aforesaid duty for this time, aiding, strengthening, and answering (them) in every respect. In (testimony of) which thing, etc. Witnessed by me, myself, at Chester, the twenty-fourth day of June in the seventeenth year of the reign of our said prince.

1477-8

AC *City Treasurers' Accounts* BL: Harley 2158
f 61 (*November*)

...

From the Mercers of the city of Chester
From the Drapers of the same city

...

1478-9

Minstrels' Court PRO: CHES 2/151
mb 5d* (*23 June*)

...

Edward, first born of Edward the fourth, king of England and France and lord of Ireland, prince of Wales, duke of Cornwall, and earl of Chester, to all to whom the present letters may have come, greetings. Know that we, fully confident of the fidelity, circumspection, and industry of our beloved and faithful Richard Soderen, bishop, abbot of the monastery of Saint Werburgh of Chester, Robert Natervile, mayor of our city of Chester, and Peter Dutton the elder, have constituted and ordained them, the bishop, mayor, and Peter, as our seneschals, jointly and individually, for the purpose of holding a court of the minstrels of Chester in the aforesaid city for this time only, (which court) is now in our hands, by reason of the minority of Laurence, son and heir of Roger de Dutton, recently lord of Dutton, now deceased. And for the purpose of performing and exercising all things which pertain to performing the duty of the aforesaid office of seneschal for this time. And thus we order you to be attentive to the same bishop, mayor, and Peter, in all things which pertain to performing the aforesaid duty for this time, aiding, strengthening, and answering (them) in every respect. In testimony of which thing we have caused these letters patent to be made. Witnessed by me, myself, at Chester, the twenty-third day of July in the nineteenth year of our said prince.

1479-81

AC   *City Treasurers' Accounts* BL: Harley 2158
f 64v *(November)* *(Arrearages)*

...

The Mercers of the city (for) two years 19 20 Edward 4   12d
From the Drapers of the city (for) two years   16d

...

1480-3

AC   *City Treasurers' Accounts* BL: Harley 2158
f 63v *(November)*

...

From Thomas Rokley and John Smyth, stewards of the saddler-craft within the city of Chester for a certain accommodation of their pageant   4d

...

f 64

...

The Mercers of the city of Chester for a plot of land for the accommodation of their carriage (for) three years   18d
The Drapers of the city for the rent of another plot (of land) for their carriage (for) three years   2s

...

1483-4

Mayors' Books CCA: M/B/6
f 72* *(November)*

...

Memorandum of Richard Benet, minstrel, to keep the peace with Richard Dalby and Henry Dalby until the next portmote of the city of Chester to be held at Chester and then etc, viz Thomas Dedwode, John Rithebon, Edward Dolby. Under penalty of   £40

...

Memorandum of Richard Dalby to keep the peace with Richard Benet and Elisabeth his servant until the next portmote, etc, viz Ralph Hunt Thomas Truer, and Thomas. Penalty   £40

1495-6
Minstrels' Court PRO: CHES 2/166
mb 3 *(24 June)*

...

Commission of the mayor of Chester [and others] for holding a court of the minstrels of Chester

Arthur, etc, to all to whom the present letters may have come, greetings. Know that we, fully confident of the fidelity, circumspection, and industry of our beloved and faithful Richard Werehall, mayor of the city of Chester, William Tatton, and Hamon Hassall, have constituted and ordained them, the mayor, William, and Hamon, as our seneschals, jointly and individually, for the purpose of holding a court of the minstrels of Chester in the aforesaid city for this time only, (which court) being in our hands from the time of the death of Roger Dutton, esquire, now deceased, and being held of us by military service; and for the purpose of performing and exercising all things which pertain to the duty of the aforesaid office of seneschal for this time. And thus we order you to be attentive to the same mayor, William, and Hamon, in all things which pertain to performing the aforesaid duty for this time, aiding, strengthening, and answering (them) in every respect. In (testimony of) which thing, etc. Witnessed by me, myself, at Chester, on the twenty-fourth day of June in the eleventh year of the reign of our said prince.

...

1538-9
Carriage House, Property of the Carmelite Friars
PRO: S.C.6 / Henry VIII / 7384
mb 82*

...

The rent of the house of the Carpenter(s) in the same place for putting their pageants in *(blank)* ...

1574-5
Treasurers' Account Rolls CCA: TAR/1/15
mb 6 *(November)* *(Watergate Street)*

...

Nicholas White for the next house adjacent to a house called

the Drapers' carriage house   3s 4d
...

From the stewards of the Mercers for their carriage house   6d
...

mb 7
To one John Allen outside the district, to pay for the tunic of
Thomas Bennet, paver, and for the waits' gowns   £7 10s 7d
To the stewards of the Saddlers for their fee   6s 8d
...

Assembly Books CCA: AB/1
f 159v* *(30 May)*
...

At the assembly held in [the interior of the Pentice] the Common
Hall of Pleas of the city of Chester [held there], on the thirtieth
day of May in the seventeenth year of the reign of Queen
Elizabeth, etc.
...

1575-6
Assembly Books CCA: AB/1
ff 162v-3* *(21 November)*

In the time of the aforesaid Henry Hardware, mayor of the aforesaid city, at a meeting held there in the interior of the Pentice
of the same city on Monday, viz, the twenty-first day of November in the eighteenth year of the reign of Queen Elizabeth, etc.
...

1576-7
Treasurers' Account Rolls CCA: TAR/1/16
mb 4 *(November)*
...

Nicholas White for the next house adjacent to a house called
the Drapers' carriage house   3s 4d
...

From the stewards of the Mercers for their carriage house   6d

... And paid to John Hankie, alderman, for the gown of Richard
Veale, officer of the aforesaid city, by the order of the aforesaid
mayor, 24s 4d. And paid to the steward of the Saddlers for their

little bell, by order of the mayor, 6s 8d ...

And paid to Thomas Gillam for his leaping, called dancing, in the play called 'morris dance', on the vigil of St John the Baptist last past, 6s 8d ...

1589-90
Treasurers' Account Rolls CCA: TAR/1/19
mb 2 *(November)*

... And paid for nineteen and a quarter yards of linen cloth for the employees of the said city called the 'waitmen' and Jasper Gillam and Crowfot, £7. ... And paid to Richard Bromley and Laurence Warmincham, stewards of the craft of Saddlers, (which craft was) assigned by the city to the job of making the horsebell, 6s 8d. And paid to Raymond Stockton for the gunpowder, £40. And paid for cartage thence, 2s ...

1641-2
A   *Minstrels' Court* CRO: DLT/B3
f 143* *(24 June)*

...

Let those present and future know that I, John, constable of Chester, gave, granted, and by this my present charter confirmed to Hugh de Dutton and his heirs the magistracy of all lechers and whores in all Cheshire, just as I freely hold that magistracy from the earl, saving my right for myself and my heirs. These witnesses: Hugh de Boydele; Alan, his brother; Peter de Gonenet; Liulf de Twamlowe; Adam de Dutton; Gilbert de Astun; Ralph de Kingestey; Hamon de Bordington; Alan de Waleie, William, son of Richard; Martin Angevin; William [de ⟨...⟩] Carill; Geoffrey and Rob[ert]in, my sons, the babblers; Herbert (?) de Waleton; Alan Mulinton; Geoffrey de Dutton.

...

f 144v

...

Laurence, lord of Dutton, claims that all minstrels within the city of Chester, and staying within Chester or carrying out their jobs there, ought to meet before him or his seneschal at Chester on the feast of the nativity of St John the Baptist every year, and shall give to him on the said feast four gallons of wine and one lance; and moreover, each of them shall give him 4½d on the said feast;

and [he claims] to have from each whore within the county of Chester, both remaining within Chester and carrying on her job, 4d per year on the aforesaid feast, etc. And also, in *quo warranto* proceedings he claims to have for himself and his heirs free warren in his towns of Dutton, Weston, Preston, Leigh, and Berterton in the aforesaid county, etc.

> With a copy agreeing with the original remaining of record in the exchequer of Chester.

...

Translations: Appendix 1

Treasurers' Account Rolls CCA: TAR/1/6
mb 1d*

...

From the Mariners (Mercers) for accommodation of their
carriage   6d
From the Drapers for advice   8d

...

Treasurers' Accounts, St Werburgh's BL: Harley 1994
f 32*

...

                        Gifts and gratuities

And paid to divers messengers and actors (or minstrels?) both of
the lord king and of other magnates upon divers occasions for
extraordinary services to the same abbot   £13 6s 8d

...

AC   *City Treasurers' Accounts* BL: Harley 2158
     f 36v*

     ...

     From the Mercers of the city of Chester for one empty plot (of
     land) there   6d

     ...

     f 37*

     ...

     From the Drapers of the city of Chester for a certain accommo-
     dation   8d

     ...

f 40*

...

From the stewards of the saddlercraft of the city of Chester for
a garden next to Truantshole   4d

f 41

...

From the Mariners (Mercers) for accommodation for a carriage
there   6d
From the Drapers for advice   6d

...

f 43*

...

From the Mercers of the city of Chester for one empty plot
(of land) there   7d

...

The Drapers of (the) city of Chester for accommodation   2d

Translations: Appendix 2

1673

Minstrels' Court   Sir Peter Leycester, *Historical Antiquities*
pp 141-2 *(Randle Blundeville, Earl of Chester, 1181-1232)*

(as Minstrels' Court document above 1641-2, pp 505-6)

End-notes

3 Add. 11335 f 22v
The entry also appears in Stowe 811, ff 19v-20, DLT/B37, f 36, and Add. 29780, f 61. Arnewaye was mayor in 1268-78; see Add. Charters 50004-6 and Salter, *MDC,* p 116, notes 7 and 10. Salter, *MDC,* p 37, published the Stowe version. The reference to Randall Higden places the composition of the entry after that of the Late Banns (c 1561), the first document to attribute authorship to the monk. The assertion that the last performance occurred during Hankey's term, 1571-2, is erroneous and suggests that the list of events was compiled before 1575, the date of the last performance. The plays were not performed at Whitsun until the sixteenth century.

3 Harley 2125 f 91v
See the note on the preceding entry. The language of the entry recalls that in the Late Banns. The entry is duplicated in DLT/B37, f 36. Randle Holme's marginal note indicates that he was aware of the inaccuracy of the traditional claims of authorship.

4 Harley 2125 f 23v
The probable source for the entry is the Late Banns, which only give the first name of the monk Randall. The surname 'heggenett' was probably derived from the flyleaf of the play manuscript, Harley 2124, which was in the Holme collection. The flyleaf entry is dated 1628 and could have been made by Randle Holme II's father. Holme apparently corrected Add. 29779 (see next entry) to 'higgden' because he found it in other Mayors Lists or thought that the 'heggenett' was an error for the famous Higden; however, he disputes this attribution in his note to the Harley 2125 entry above. David Rogers attributes authorship of the plays to the monk Randall in the first four copies of the 'Breviary' and adds the surname only in the last, dated c 1637; however, his copy of the Mayors List in Harley 1944 (c 1619) attributes the plays to Higden. It seems likely that the Late Banns intended to attribute authorship to Randall Higden, but did not use the surname; that there was a tradition that this surname was 'heggenett', and this accounts for its appearance in the flyleaf note (1628) which was available to Holme and was the probable source for his correction of Harley 2125, f 23v; that he became aware of the Higden tradition from another source, possibly the Harley 1944 'Breviary', which was available to him, and that he later concluded that the attribution was erroneous when he found a List which placed the invention of the plays in the late thirteenth century.

4 Add. 29779 f 11v
See the note on the preceding entry.

4 Harley 2125 f 100

The note is made by a late seventeenth-century scribe, possibly Randle Holme II. The numbers are probably indexing references.

5 M/B/1 ff 55v-6

The document has been published by Morris, pp 405-8. The document may seem to end abruptl however, it does not fill the entire second folio and therefore must be complete. Morris also pub lished a list of the fines, most of which were for three shillings and four pence, but the list is not reproduced here because it simply repeats the names.

6 Loose papers

The document is faded and there are holes in the places denoted by diamond brackets. The text was published by Salter, *Trial*, pp 7-8. Professor Robert Lewis checked my original transcription and offered a few clarifications.

7 M/R/4/85 mb 1

Several persons have worked on this transcription. Dr Cameron Louis read the original under ultra-violet light after I had and was able to add a large portion to my original transcription. Professor Alfred David and Dr Bella Schauman worked with a poor xerox copy between my reading of the original and that of Dr Louis; they made some suggestions about readings. This final reconstruction was worked on by Lynette Muir and Peter Meredith at the University of Leeds, and Brian Merrilees at the University of Toronto.

8 Harley 2125 f 27v

The entry is dated 1429 for 1429-30, but Hope was not mayor until 1430-1. The entry was added by Randle Holme.

8 Harley 2158 f 33v

The word 'senescall*is*' has been consistently expanded with the ablative case ending here and else-where in the Harley 2158 extracts. The expansion is based on surrounding entries in the same accounts where the ablative is regularly used.

A number of Latin words with corrected expansions appear as footnotes to the Harley 2158 extracts in this volume. Words like 'parcell' (p 9, l 1) have no brevigraphs in the Harley MS, but do require case endings in context. 'parcell', for example, would need the ablative -a expansion after '*pro* quad*am*'. The lack of brevigraph can probably be attributed to the antiquarian omittin marks which may have been in the original MS.

9 Harley 2158 f 34v

The last entry is on a different roll, but both rolls are dated 20 Henry VI. It is possible that the rolls are for two different years or that the Mercers rented two different pieces of property. See The Documents, pp xlviii.

10 Harley 2125 f 29

The entry is listed under Nicholas Daniel here and in Add. 29777, item 127, but in the latter, the year is given as 1452-3. Harley 2125, f 107v, dates the event to John Cottingham's term in 1455-6

10 Harley 2054 f 36v
The charter is dated 2 Edward IV, ie, 4 March 1462 - 3 March 1463. The excerpt has been published by Salter, *MDC*, p 47, and Morris, p 316. Randle Holme notes on f 38v that the charter was
later amended: 'vide post 60 a grant from the Citty in tyme of *willia*m glasior maior 6 E 6 wherin
the words about whitson pleas are put out'. Glaseor was mayor in 1551-2; the second Bakers'
charter, ff 39-40, contains no reference to the plays.

11 Harley 2158 f 51
At the end of each entry is a series of dashes to indicate the roll was fragmentary.

11 Harley 2158 f 51
There are three dashes at the end of the entry to indicate that the roll was fragmentary.

11 Harley 2158 ff 39-40, 52-2v
The last three entries are from roll 24 which is dated to the same year as roll 13 from which
the first four entries come. Holme notes, ff 52v and 53, that the accounts for 1468-9 and 1469-
70, respectively, are the same as those in roll 24.

13 Harley 2158 f 54v
Roll 29, f 56, contains the following arrearages from the period 9 to 14 Edward IV: '...
mercator*ibus* Ci*uita*tis vj d. pannarijs Ci*uita*tis viij d ...'

13 TAR/1/4 mb 1d
It is not clear whether the account is for 1471-2 or 1472-3.

15 M/B/5 f 216
There are holes in the places denoted by diamond brackets; however, Morris, p 572, apparently
could read more of the entry.

16 Harley 2125 f 30
The entry is dated 1474 for 1474-5. All Mayors Lists associate the visit with Mayor Southworth
except for Add. 29777, item 150, which places the entry under Hugh Massey; however, all Lists
except the one transcribed date the visit to Southworth's second term in 1475-6. The Mayors'
Book for 1476, M/B/6b, f 33, lists the committee assigned the task of preparing the visit. A
similar entry appears in Massey College MS, f 15.

17 CHES 2/151 mb 5d
Ricardi Soderen (p 18, l 4): Dugdale lists Richard Oldham as bishop of Chester and abbot of
St Werburgh in 1479 (Wm. Dugdale, *Monasticon Anglicanum,* John Caley *et al* (eds), II (London,
1846), 375). Richard was made abbot in 1453 and about twenty years later was promoted to the
see of the Isle of Man, usually called Sodor and Man. Richard's surname, therefore, is derived
from the second office. Dr Cameron Louis resolved the problem. Randle Holme gives a précis
of the commission in his notes on the records in the Exchequer of Chester. Harley 2009, ff 37v-
8, and lists the custom of the Dutton heir in inquisitions dated 23 Edward I and 1 Edward III
in Harley 2065, ff 42 and 56 respectively.

19 Harley 2158 f 62v

The first two entries are from roll 34, the second two from roll 35; both rolls are dated 21 Edward IV.

20 M/B/6 f 72

These are sample entries of the form used to bind persons over to the portmote court. There are additional entries concerning minstrels in M/B/6c, f 44; M/B/7d, f 142v; M/B/7e, f 164; M/B/8c, f 75; M/B/24, f 29v; M/B/27, f 41, *et passim;* however, since the crime is never stated, similar entries have not been transcribed for this volume.

20 Harley 1046 f 161v

The entry is dated 1488 for 1488-9. The entry also appears in Harley 1944, f 76v, where it is listed for the year 1490-1. The early part of Harley 1046 seems to be off by a year, so the Harley 1944 date may be more accurate. Salter, MDC, p 50, accepts the earlier date.

20 Harley 2125 f 31

The entry is dated 1488 for 1488-9.

20 Add. 29777 item 163

The entry is dated 1488 for 1488-9. The following words are rubricated: 'In', 'Assumption of our Ladye', 'Bridgestrete of Chester', 'Lorde Strange'.

21 Harley 2057 f 26v

The entry erroneously attributes the Watch to 1498 because it dates mayoral terms according to the majority of the mayor's term; however, Goodman seems to have been mayor in 1498-9, and if the Show began in his term, it must have occurred in 1499. Add. 11335, f 23; Add. 29779, f 19; Add. 39925, f 18; and Massey College MS, f 16v all date Goodman's term by the year of accession, 1498, but say that the Show began that year. Add. 29780, f 124, and Stowe 811, f 48, date the beginning of the Midsummer Watch to 1495, but on ff 62 and 20 respectively, date it to 1498. These latter two entries are from a list of events common to some of the 'Antiquities' compilations; the first two entries are from Aldersey's List of Mayors which, in its earliest state, seems to be off by two or three years, particularly in the entries before the early sixteenth century. Harley 2125, f 32, misdates Goodman's term to 1497-8. If the visit occurred in Goodman's term, then it took place in 1499; however, the event may have taken place in 1498 and drifted into an association with Goodman because of the practice in some Lists of dating his term to the year of accession. See the note on the entry which follows.

Shorter notices of Arthur's visit also appear in Harley 2133, f 36; Add. 29780, ff 62-3 and 124 (under the entry for 1496; this is the List that is off a few years); Add. 29777, item 173 (under the entry for John Clyffe, 1498-9, who was mayor in 1499-1500); Add. 39925, f 18; Stowe 811, ff 20 and 48; Harley 1944, f 77v; Harley 2105, f 93; and DLT/B37, f 52v.

21 Harley 2125 f 32

The MS dates the entry 1497 for 1497-8. Holme, who made the additions in this entry, may be responsible for the assertion that the play was performed in two places. In his notes on the Smiths' Company, Harley 2054, f 25, he makes the following comment and attributes it to the 'maiors booke':

likewise it appereth by diuers manuscripts that ˏ´only´ the sayd occupations of smythes etc. Ioyned all in one Company: played about 4 Aug 1498 their play called the purification of our Lady before prince Arthur at Abby gate & high Crosse

The reference to 'diuers manuscripts' unfortunately suggests that Holme's source of information was not the 'maiors booke' but the Lists of Mayors.

22 Account Book II f 1v
Holme probably derived the date 14 Henry VII, which would be 1498, from one of the Mayors Lists which misdate Goodman's term of office to 1497-8.

22 Harley 2104 f 4
The list has been published by Greg, *Trial*, pp 170-1. Greg dated the list to 1500 on the basis of the handwriting but we can only be certain that it comes from the period 1474-1521. See Clopper 'The History and Development of the Chester Cycle'.

23 Add 11335 f 23
See the similar entry in Add. 29780, f 63, and Stowe 811, f 20v. Harley 2125, f 33; Add. 29780, f 126; Stowe 811, f 49; Add. 39925, f 18v; DLT/B37, f 53v; and Massey College MS, f 17v, also note the beginning of the Breakfast Shoot.

23 A/F/1 f 5
The MS is partially torn on the right side. Rathbone was mayor from November 1514 to November 1515 and Henry's seventh year began 22 April 1515; therefore, the ordinance was passed in 1515 between 22 April and the end of Rathbone's term. The order was reconfirmed 13 December 1566 (A/F/2, f 10).

23 Harley 2125 f 33v
The entry was added by Randle Holme.

24 M/B/12 f 24v
The document has been published by Morris, pp 349-50, note 1.

25 Harley 1996 f 120
The petition is an original document preserved in an antiquarian collection. It is undated. David Middleton was mayor in 1523-4 and 1538-9; however, the earlier date is probably the correct one since Henry Gee, mayor in 1533-4, reissued verbatim (in A/F/1, f 19) Middleton's response to the Cappers' complaint that others were interfering in their trade. There are two Thomas Smiths in this period: the senior Smith served in 1504-5, 1511-12, 1515-16, 1520-1, and 1521-2, and his son in 1530-1 and 1535-6. The document was published by Morris, pp 316-17, note 4, and dated 1523.

26 Harley 2133 f 39
Holme added this entry to Harley 2125, f 34v.

26 Add. 29777 item 204

The words 'In', 'kinge Roberte of Scissill', and 'highe Crosse in Chester' are rubricated. Chamber *The Mediaeval Stage,* II, 356, said he found a reference to this play in the State Papers, but Salter *MDC,* p 114, note 27, was unable to locate it. See Appendix 2, p 484.

26 A/F/1 f 11

The right side of the page is torn and it is impossible to determine if the first line read 'xxiii' (ie, 1531) or 'xxiiii' (ie, 1532). Except for those in the first word, the diamond brackets indicate the torn edge of the page. The document was published by Morris, p 317, note 1.

27 A/F/1 f 12

The right side of the page has been torn off, but a seventeenth-century copy (Harley 2013, f 1*) made by Randle Holme before the damage occurred, was pasted into the front of one of the play texts. In post-Reformation times, a scribe went through the archives MS correcting and deleting material in order to make the proclamation conform to Protestant sensibilities. The proclamation has been printed in T. Hughes, 'The Whitsun Plays,' *The Cheshire Sheaf,* 1st series, 1 (1879), 30; Morris, pp 317-18, note 2; Salter, *MDC,* pp 33-4; and Wickham, I, 340-5.

It is obvious that all of the statements about the plays' history cannot be true. Arnewaye was not the first mayor (see The Documents, pp xxxvi-xliii). The association of the invention of the plays with the establishment of the office of mayor, furthermore, is suspiciously coincidental; clearly, the link was forged to grant authenticity and authority to the plays. The plays were, the proclamation implies, as old as the freedoms of the city and, therefore, equally sacred.

The reference to Pope Clement is not helpful in determining the origin of the plays because none of the popes so named can be attached to any documented event in the cycle's history. Clement IV (1265-8) overlaps Arnewaye's term of office and it might be argued that the bull was 'fabricated' to lend additional support to the Arnewaye claim; however, there is no evidence that the Chester antiquarians dated Arnewaye's term to the thirteenth century before the Aldersey List of 1594. Clement V (1304-14) and Clement VI (1342-56) held office long before there is any documentary support for the plays, and while Clement VI's reign overlaps Randall Higden's mature life, there is no extant claim for Higden's authorship before the writing of the Late Banns (c 1561). Clement VII (1523-34) is an unlikely candidate because he overlaps the life of Newhall and could not conceivably be associated with Arnewaye even by the most uncritical antiquarian. The remaining possibility is that the tradition of Pope Clement's bull derives from the days of the Corpus Christi procession when such pardons were granted. If this is the case, the bull should probably be dated to Clement V's papacy during which the feast was established throughout Europe (1311).

The only part of the history which may have some authenticity, therefore, is the claim that Henry Francis wrote the plays; unfortunately, the assertion does not prove particularly enlightening because we know little more than his name. A Henry Francis appears in three lists of monks dated 1377, 1379, and 1382 (Burne, *Monks of Chester,* p 99). Since the earliest extant record of the guild play is the Coopers' and Ironmongers' dispute of 1422, it is conceivable that the play originated during Francis' lifetime.

29 Harley 2177 f 19v

The entry is dated 1532.

29 Harley 2054 f 87v
The charter is dated, f 87, 'Hen 8; MCCCCCXXXIIIJ.' An eighteenth-century copy follows on
88; a second copy is enrolled in CHES 2/323, 13-14 Charles 2, mb 4. In his notes on the Painters'
Guild, f 85v, Holme says that 'before H7 tyme the were a society of paynters & barbors'.

30 P/20/13/1 f 5
The last entry probably refers to a picture or a statue.

31 S.C.6 / Henry VIII / 7384 mb 82
The entry was published by J.H.E. Bennett in 'The White Friars of Chester,' p 28.

31 Harley 2150 ff 85v-8v
The text has been printed by Greg, *Trial,* pp 130-9, and by Salter, 'The Banns of the Chester
Plays,' pp 137-41.
  The Early Banns are included in a transcription of the 'white booke of the pentice' which
begins on f 49 of Harley 2150, but which itself is part of a Holme manuscript collection entitled
Deedes & customes with other notes conserning the Citty of Chester'. Many, but not all, of the
entries in this section of the manuscript are identical with those preserved in the Chester Assembly
Book (A/B/1) and generally appear in the same order; consequently, Harley 2150 and the Assembly
Book, each leaving parts uncopied, must have been compiled from a common prototype, or Harley
2150 is a copy of a city record kept at the Pentice, and the extant Assembly Book is a separate,
nearly-duplicate record kept at another location. Two hands are evident in the transcription: the
primary one is a legal hand of the last half of the sixteenth century, the second is the loose secretary
hand of Randle Holme. Most of the Banns entry is in the legal hand, except for lines 136-210 and
the marginalia, which are in Holme's hand. Greg distinguished a third hand in some of the marginalia, but I think that this is a printed hand occasionally used by Holme and I have not distinguished it in the text. If the reader wishes to see where the hands supposedly differ, he may check
them in Greg. Lastly, Holme drew lines around some of the text and indicated in the margin that
these sections had been erased from his exemplar.
  There are three items in the entry: a List of Companies and the parts they had in the plays, a
revised Newhall Proclamation, and the Early Banns themselves. The proclamation is a Protestant
version of the Newhall Proclamation of 1531-2 from which have been deleted all references to
Henry Francis, a monk and supposed author of the plays, Pope Clement's bull, and the granting
of pardons. The revised proclamation puts the extant version of the Banns in post-Reformation
times, and the inclusion of the entire entry amidst items from Henry Gee's mayoralty in 1539-40
establishes the *terminus ad quem* for the document as a whole.
  The List of Companies differs from the Early Banns in omitting the Wives' Assumption and in
assigning the Mercers the Magi play rather than the Presentation; it is probable, therefore, that the
List postdates the Early Banns and was added by the scribe who copied the remainder of the
entry. In any event, the List corresponds to one in existence in the late sixteenth century and
reflects the contents of the extant play texts which also postdate the Early Banns.
  In summary, the Early Banns were copied by a late sixteenth-century scribe who may have
inserted the List of Companies before the Banns entry and who left uncopied the descriptions of
fifteen pageants; in the seventeenth century, Randle Holme collated Harley 2150 with the White
Book of the Pentice, copied the omitted lines, and marked the passages which had been erased

subsequent to 1539-40. For further discussion of the document, see Lumiansky and Mills, vol I and Clopper, 'The History and Development of the Chester Cycle.'

39 AB/1 ff 64-5
The entry was published by Morris, pp 342-4. A hand has been drawn in the MS in the followin[g] places: after 'Laues' (p 40, l 19), 'Chester' (p 40, l 27), 'Inconuenynce' (p 41, l 1), 'Accordingly' (p 41, l 15).

42 Harley 2125 f 35
A condensed version of this notice appears in the same List under the years 1533-4, Gee's first term of office (f 34v), and in DLT/B37, f 56, under 1539.

43 P/Cowper [1956] I.188
The entry has been added by the original scribe around the entry for Gee's term.

46 Harley 2177 f 21v
The entry may be for 1545-6. At the head of the entry, in the left margin, is the note '1545 & 1546'; however, in the heading itself, the churchwardens are said to have been chosen on 12 Ap[r] 1546. Since the dates are contradictory, I elected to follow the one in the heading.

46 Harley 2054 f 15
Many of the earlier Smiths' accounts are undated, but from 1558 onward the sequence is compl[ete] enough that accounts can be dated according to their position in the sequence. The early accou[nts] are obviously disarranged and there must remain the possibility that Holme may have misdated some when he copied the records. Dates have been assigned on the basis of internal evidence an[d] patterns in the sequence; though the evidence is fragmentary, it is possible to see short sequence[s] which may indicate that Holme was working with a manuscript whose initial leaves were loose a[nd] easily reversed. Stewards were elected on St Loy's Day in July.

I Undated, f 14v (see p 472). 'Io harrison & simon founder', stewards. No ascertainable date.

II Undated, f 14v. 'Rich Scryui‸'n`er & Gilbert Knoys', stewards. A later account, X (see p 54, 1554-5), names the same stewards and is dated 1554; it is the account for 1554-5. This may be a part of the same account.

III 1554, ff 14v-15 (see p 53, 1553-4). 'Robert handcock & william locker', stewards. The entry includes expenditure for the Whitsun plays. The Smiths apparently kept the play accounts separate from their regular accounts; see the lists of assessments for 1561, 156[5] 1568, and the play accounts for those years.

IV Undated, f 15 (see p 46, 1545-6). 'Io a leygh & Rog ledshom', stewards. 'Io a leygh' do[es] not appear in the 1561 assessment and therefore must have been steward before then. [He] was steward in 1547-8, but the account cannot come from the period 1548-53 because [it] contains an expenditure for Corpus Christi Day, and the feast had been banned in 1548. Further, the account cannot be for the period 1553-61 because there are extant accoun[ts] for all those years. It is possible the entry begins the sequence completed by the two following accounts, those for 1546-7 and 1547-8.

V 1547, f 15 (see p 46, 1546-7). The account specifies an expenditure for Corpus Christi,

1547. No stewards are listed; nonetheless, the account must be separate from the preceding account and the following one, which is also dated 1547, because each of the three contains a Corpus Christi reference.

VI   1547, f 15 (see p 47, 1547-8). 'Io alee & simon founder', stewards.

VII   Undated, f 15v (see p 55, 1555-6). 'Ric skremner & Io parssevay', stewards. The account includes a payment to Sir John Smith for the 'Reggenall'. Smith finished Hugh Aldersey's term in 1546-7 and was himself mayor in 1555-6. Since there is an account for the earlier term, this account should be dated to 1555-6.

VIII   Undated, f 15v (see p 60, 1557-8). 'Rich barker & hugh stocken', stewards. The account includes a payment to the baron of Kinderton's minstrels, a group hired by the Shoemakers in 1556-7. The Shoemakers' and Smiths' accounting years overlap from July 1557 to November 1557. Since there is a clearly dated Smiths' account for 1556-7 (IX), this account should be dated 1557-8.

IX   1556, f 15v (see p 58, 1556-7). 'Io harryson & Iohn ball were made stewards ... 4 Iuly 1556'. Holme added immediately afterwards, 'I Conseaue 1556', perhaps to indicate his uncertainty about his exemplar; nevertheless, the date appears to be correct.

X   1554, f 15v (see p 54, 1554-5). 'Rich Strymner & gil*bert* Knowys', stewards.

XI   1558, f 16 (p 61, 1558-9). 'hough stoken & Io doe', stewards.

47 Harley 2177 f 22

The entry may be for 1546-7, but see the preceding entry on p 46 and the end-note. In the heading is the statement that the payments and the account were made on 17 April 1547, which would suggest that the accounting year ended that day; however, since this would conflict with the information in the heading of the preceding entry, I assume that the churchwardens backdated the account.

48 G/8/2 f 10

The account is dated '3 Edw 6' at the beginning; this must refer to the time the account was copied because there is an undated account which follows, but which itself precedes the account for 1550-1. In addition, the account includes expenditure for Corpus Christi Day, which means it had to have been made up before the feast was banned in 1548.

49 G/8/2 ff 16-16v

The account is undated but comes at the end of those for 3 Edward 6 (1549-50) and before those begun in the term of Edmund Gee, mayor, 1550-1. The account is probably for a performance in 1550.

53 Harley 2054 ff 14v-15

The account has been published by Salter, *MDC*, pp 76-7. For the date, see the note to the Smiths' accounts for 1546.

54 Add. 29777 item 228

The entry appears under that noting Mary's accession, 6 July 1553. The words 'Also' and 'Playes' are rubricated.

54 Harley 2054 ff 15v-16
For the date, see the notes to the account for 1546-7, pp 518-19.

55 Harley 2054 f 15v
For the date, see the notes to the 1546-7 account, pp 518-19. Sir John Smith was the mayor in 1555-6.

56 AB/1 f 85
See the copies in Harley 2015, f 64, and Harley 2150, f 128v. The latter erroneously dates the ordinance to John Webster's term, 1556-7.

58 Harley 2054 f 15v
The account is undated; see the notes to the 1546-7 entry, pp 518-19.

60 Harley 2054 f 15v
The account is undated; see the notes to the 1546-7 entry, pp 518-19.

65 Harley 2054 ff 16v-17
The play accounts were kept separate from the regular accounts in this year.

67 Add. 29780 f 130
The entry also appears in Harley 2057, f 28v; Harley 2125, f 192; Add. 29777, item 235; Add. 29779, f 24v; Add. 39925, f 20; DLT/B37, f 58v; and Massey College MS, f 20v.

71 Harley 2150 f 208
The agreement is an original document bound in an antiquarian collection. A copy of the agreement has been entered in Harley 1968, f 38.

72 Harley 2125 f 39
The entry was added by Randle Holme. Mr Mann was headmaster of the Grammar School founded by Henry VIII, 1563-7. See M.G. and C.D.R., 'Schoolmasters in Elizabethan Cheshire,' *The Cheshire Sheaf,* 4th series, 4 (1969), 3.

73 Add. 29777 item 238
The following words are rubricated: 'In', 'Tryvmpth', 'Aeneas', 'Dido of Carthage', 'Trivmpthe', 'Roode Eye', 'Two ffort*es*', 'Shippe'. The entry was published by Salter, MDC, p 24.

74 TAR/1/12 mb 2
Bamvell was mayor in 1562-3.

75 Add 29780 f 130
The date 1566 is probably an error. Add. 29780 contains Aldersey's List in its earliest state; the entry was dropped in such later editions as Harley 2057 and 2133, Add. 39925, and the Liverpool copy of the 'Breviary'. The entry should be for 1566-7.

76 A/F/2 f 10
The right side of the MS is faded and the upper right corner torn off.

77 Harley 2054 ff 18-18v
The play accounts were kept separate from the regular accounts in 1566-7. The regular accounts, p 75, are dated 1566 in the margin; the play account is dated 1567. It might seem that the two are not part of the same accounting year because William Locker is listed as one of the stewards in the regular account but not in the play entry; however, since Locker is also missing from those who were assessed for the play, it is possible that he died and was replaced by another steward. In any event, the two accounts fit into the sequence of accounts for the year 1566-7.

78 Add. 29779 f 25
See also Add. 29777, item 241; Harley 2057, f 29; Harley 2125, f 39; Add. 39925, f 20v; DLT/ B37, f 58v; and Massey College MS, f 21.

78 Account Book I f 38
The early accounts transcribed from the Painters, Glaziers, Embroiderers, and Stationers' Records (1567-87) are cancelled in the MS, but it is unclear whether the cancellations were made by a contemporary or later hand.

80 Harley 2125 f 39
The entry also appears in Add. 29779, f 25.

80 M/B/19 f 45v
The entry was published by Morris, p 315, note 2. Salter, *MDC*, pp 50-1, discusses the document, but also see Clopper, 'The History and Development of the Chester Cycle'.

80 M/B/19 ff 52-2v
The entry was published by Morris, p 304, note 2, and Nelson, *The Medieval English Stage*, pp 159-60. Nelson's discussion, pp 160-1, distorts the sense of the document; see Clopper, 'The History and Development of the Chester Cycle'.

81 Account Book I ff 35-7v
The play accounts were kept separate from the regular accounts this year. The account has been published by Bridge, 'Items of Expenditure,' pp 157-63, but the transcriptions are untrustworthy.
   In the space to the right of three items on f 36 (p 82, ll 37-9) 'Tomas Pentney' practised writing his name and also wrote 'Item layd'.

84 Treasurers' Accounts II p 52
The entry was published by Bridge 'The Chester Miracle Plays,' p 97, and Burne, 'Chester Cathedral in the Reigns of Mary and Elizabeth,' p 61.

84 Harley 2054 ff 18v-19
The play accounts were kept separate from the regular accounts this year.

86   Harley 2133 f 42v
The entry also appears in Add. 39925, f 20v.

86   Add. 29777 item 242
'In' and 'Playes' are rubricated.

87   Account Book I f 1
The entry was published by Salter, *Trial,* p 14.

89   Account Book I f 1v
The entry was published by Salter, *Trial,* pp 14-15.

89   Harley 2177 f 28v
The entry was published by Salter, *MDC,* p 21.

90   Account Book I f 2v
The entry was published by Salter, *Trial,* p 15.

91, 93   Account Book I ff 47-8, 48v
The account has been published by Bridge, 'Items of Expenditure', pp 166-70, but the transcriptions are not trustworthy.

95   Account Book I ff 3-3v
The account has been published by Salter, *MDC,* pp 72-3.

97   Harley 2133 f 43
See also Add. 29780, f 131; Add. 39925, f 20v; Harley 2057, f 29; and Massey College MS, f 21v all of which reproduce the above; DLT/B37, f 59v, which gives a slight variant; and Harley 1944, f 86, and Add. 29779, f 25v, both of which merely note the performance.

97   Add. 29777 item 246
'In' and 'Playes' are rubricated.

99   Account Book I f 4v
Part of this entry has been published by Salter, *Trial,* p 17.

100   Account Book I ff 55, 56
These two entries follow the accounts for 1573-4, but since there is no evidence for a performance of the play after 1572 and before 1575, I think that it must be business left over from the 1572 performance. It is also possible that the entries do not belong with this account at all; between some of the regular accounts in the early part of this book, there are additional notes and entries and these may be strays from the regular accounting sequence.

101   Harley 2172 p 17
Salter, *MDC,* p 125, note 11, prints the Latin text and cites his source as Harley 2009, f 41v; however, he obtained his text from Harley 2020, f 41v. The Latin text records the measurements

in 'virgatas regias'. The deed, of which this is the abstract, is recorded in the Corporation Lease Book (CHB/3, f 8v) and in Harley 1996, f 263. Upon his decease, Hill's fee farm was returned to the Tailors and they, on 1 February 1630, petitioned the city to allow them to rebuild on their property, the old carriage house having been torn down when Newgate was built. A copy of their petition is entered in Harley 2104, f 192.

102 Harley 2172 p 17
The lease, of which this is an abstract, can be found in the Corporation Lease Book (CHB/3, ff 24v-25). In Harley 2172, f 15 (CHB/3, f 17) is another lease which grants a fee farm to Nicholas White in Greyfriars Lane 'by a certayne stone wall called grayfreere wall on the south & betweene the Queenes high way Called grayfrere lane on the Est side, & a certayn buildinge Called the drapers Carriage howse on the south ...'

103 A/F/3 f 25
The oughts are a record of the votes cast. Note that the tally on the left is inaccurate.

104 AB/1 f 159v
The order has been published by Morris, p 319.

105 Harley 1989 f 26
The entry is said to be 'out of the black booke'.

106 Account Book I ff 59-60
The play accounts were kept separate from the regular accounts in this year. The account has been published by Bridge, pp 171-2, but the transcriptions are untrustworthy.

108 Account Book I ff 7-8
The account has been published by Salter, MDC, pp 74-6, but he misdated it to 1574.

109 Harley 1046 f 164v
The entry is not dated in the MS. It has been published by Salter, MDC, pp 51-2.

110 Harley 2133 f 43v
See also Add. 29780, f 131; Add. 39925, f 20v; Harley 2057, f 29; and Massey College MS, f 21v, which reproduce the above; DLT/B37, f 60, which gives a slight variant; and Harley 1944, f 86v, and Add. 29779, f 26, which merely note the performance.

110 Add. 29777 item 249
'The' is rubricated.

110 Account Book I Harley 2054 f 21
The accounts are not dated, but Holme noted that they 'should be 1575 & part 1576'.

111 M/B/21 f 187v
The entry has been published by Morris, pp 304-5.

112   CHB/3 f 28
The letter has been published by Morris, p 319. A seventeenth-century copy is preserved in Harle
2173, f 107v.

113   AB/1 ff 162v-3
The certificate has been published by Morris, pp 319-20.

114   CHB/3 f 28v
The right side of the page has been damaged; the readings at the bottom of the page have been
made from the sometimes free seventeenth-century copy preserved in Harley 2173, ff 107v-8. Th
certificate has been published by Morris, pp 321-2.

122   Account Book I f 67v
The MS is blotted at the two places indicated by square brackets.

124   Harley 2133 f 44
See also Harley 1944, f 87, and DLT/B37, f 60.

135   Treasurers' Accounts II p 304
The entry has been published by Burne, *Monks of Chester,* p 61.

135   Account Book f 6
The item on f 6 is not part of an entire account but a note. The account is on ff 9-9v.

136   Harley 2173 f 90
The items from f 90 are part of an audit made in 1585 according to the heading of this entry.

139   Harley 2125 f 42
The entry also appears in Add. 29779, f 27v.

139   Add. 11335 f 23
The entry also appears in Stowe 811, ff 20v, 54; Add. 29780, ff 63, 133; Add. 39925, f 21v; and
Harley 2133, f 44v.

142   Harley 2150 f 5v
The entry was published by Morris, pp 235-6.

152   Account Book I ff 23-3v
At some point between 1583 and 1590, the Coopers shifted their accounting year from November
to January, which must have resulted in one accounting year being fourteen months long. The las
entry to be dated 20 November is for the accounting year 1582-3; the earliest entry to be dated
13 January is for the year 1590-1. The date of the other accounts in the period 1583-90 can
sometimes be determined if there is a reference to the mayor or other matters. There are occasional expenditures of money on St Edmund's Day, the election day, up to 20 November 1587;
consequently, the shift from November to January may not have occurred before January 1588.

There are two accounts which mention Robert Brerewood as mayor (ff 21-1v and 23-3v), but it is only possible for him to be cited in both accounts if the stewards of the first cited the mayor in office at the time that they made up their accounts at the end of the year, and if the next set of stewards cited the name of the mayor in office at the time they started their accounts. The first of these accounts contains money spent for drink on St. Edmund's Day at the end of the year; therefore, the first account must have run from 20 November 1586 to 19 November 1587. The second account must have begun on 20 November 1587 and may have run until either 19 November 1588 or 13 January 1589. The account which follows on f 24 is dated 1588 at the top when Robert Brock was mayor (1588-9), and could have started at either November 1588 or January 1589. Subsequent accounts begin in January and can be accounted for throughout the rest of the sequence.

156   Harley 2125 f 43
The entry was added by Randle Holme.

156   Account Book I f 24
For the date, see the note (pp 524-5) to the preceding Coopers' account.

159   Treasurers' Accounts III p 45
The entry has been published by Burne, *Monks of Chester,* p 61.

162   Treasurers' Accounts III p 80
The entry has been published by Burne, *Monks of Chester,* p 61.

166   Treasurers' Accounts III p 109
The entry has been published by Burne, *Monks of Chester,* p 68.

169   Account Book II f 2v
The last numeral in the date has been cut away; however, a similar order copied by Holme can be dated 1592.

183   Account Book I f 13v
The order was subsequently copied in Account Book II, f A1.

184   AB/1 f 243v
The entry has been published by Morris, pp 333-4.

193   AB/1 f 253
The entry has been published by Morris, p 476.

194   Add. 29780 ff 63-4
See also Stowe 811, f 20v and Add. 29780, f 141.

194   P/65/8/1 f 139
The 'frame' may not be the sepulchre reported in earlier inventories.

198   Harley 2125 f 45v

The entry may combine actions from two or three of Hardware's terms (1559-60, 1575-6, and
1599-1600). There are two different suppressions which can be traced in the records: 1) the gian
in the Midsummer Show; and 2) the devil in his feathers. The most useful records would be the
City Treasurers' accounts, were they not so fragmentary. There are only twelve extant from the
period 1559-1600 and none of these belong to Hardware's term of office. Nevertheless, the city
accounts provide some evidence: in 1554-5 (TAR/1/8), the city paid 38s 6d for the Midsummer
Watch to the Painters; Hardware's term intervened in 1559-60; in 1564-5, the city retroactively
paid the Painters for the show set out in Mayor Bamvill's term, 1562-3; in 1564, the city agreed
to pay 40s annually for the giants and other pageants in the Show; and Mayor Dutton was commended in 1567-8 for, among other things, setting out the Show. If Hardware suppressed the
Show in 1560, it seems to have been revived almost immediately; however, even though there is
the 1564 agreement for an annual production, there is no expenditure for the giants until 1590-1
(TAR/1/20). We can be reasonably sure that Hardware suppressed the Show in his second term,
1575-6, because Mayors List 3 tells us that Thomas Bellin revived it in 1578. There is payment
for the giants in 1590-1, 1591-2, and 1592-3 (TAR/1/20-22), and several guilds issued orders in
1592 for the Midsummer Watch. It is possible that the Show was suppressed by Hardware, revivec
by Bellin, but then suppressed again until the 1590s. It is probable that the Show was suppressed
again in 1600, but there is no evidence for this other than the Mayors Lists and the Drapers' order
for the Show in 1602.

   The Butchers' accounts do not survive from this period; however, most of the characters from
the plays had disappeared from the Watch by 1572, and the woman and the devils, or 'cuppes
and canes', appears only sporadically in the Innkeepers' accounts in the late sixteenth century,
but had ceased to appear by 1597-8, three years before Hardware supposedly suppressed the
Butchers' devil. It seems likely, therefore, that Hardware suppressed the remnants of the Whitsun
plays in 1575, and that these were sporadically revived but had totally disappeared before his last
term in 1600. According to the Massey College List of Mayors, the Butchers' devils, as well as
others, were revived in Edward Button's term in 1616; since the List was copied in 1618, we can
assume that its facts are accurate.

   The final piece of evidence that a suppression occurred earlier than 1600 is Archdeacon Rogers
commendation of Hardware. The statement in the 'Breviary' is written in the first person and one
might assume that it was made by David; however, if he were not resident in Chester, as seems to
be the case, it is odd that he would take such a vehement stance against the customs, especially
so long after the fact. I think that the attack on the Show, like those on the Whitsun Plays, was
written by Archdeacon Rogers before his death in 1595, and that Hardware suppressed some of
these customs in 1576 and possibly as early as 1560. The antiquarian compilers of the Mayors
Lists may, therefore, be responsible for attaching the entry to Hardware's term in 1600 alone.

   Add. 29779, f 31v, contains the complete passage as in Harley 2125, ff 44-5v; Harley 2125,
f 123, contains the same information but in a different order.

206   Morris, *Chester in the Plantagenet and Tudor Reigns* pp 324-5

The Drapers' Company Book was not available; consequently, I have published Morris' transcription

206   Harley 2125 f 46

There is external evidence for Holme's claim that Radcliffe revived the Show in the Linendrapers'
order for the Midsummer Show dated 21 May 1602. The entry was added by Randle Holme.

211   Harley 2125 f 47
The entry was added by Randle Holme.

214   Company Book p 19
The entry has been published by Salter, *Trial,* pp 21-4.

216   Company Book G10/1 pp 19-20
The bottom of page 19 has been damaged and poorly repaired.

217   Harley 2150 f 162v
A notice of this entry appears in Add. 16179, f 60.

218   Add. 29779 f 34
There are similar entries in Harley 2133, f 46v, and Harley 2125, f 48. Harley 2133 says they 'did
dance and vault'.

226   A/F/8 f 18
The petition is undated, but included among the files for 1608-10.

232, 234   unnumbered MS unnumbered folio, ff 1, 17-23
The Harley 1944 description of the Whitsun Plays has been cited many times, but see Greg, *Trial,*
pp 146-7, or Salter, *MDC,* pp 55-6, for a standard text. The Chester Archives copy was published
in Clopper, 'The Rogers' Description of the Chester Plays,' pp 84-5.
      Greg published a text of the Late Banns from Harley 1944 in *Trial,* pp 146-63, and discussed
the three copies known to him on pp 140-5. Salter published Bellin's copy from the 1600 text
of the plays (Harley 2013) and added the continuations from Bodley and Harley 1944 ('Banns',
pp 142-8). Neither seems to have been aware of the Chester Archives copy which antedates
Harley 1944. For the date of the Late Banns, see Salter's article, 'The Banns of the Chester Plays,'
Lumiansky and Mills, vol II, and Clopper, 'The History and Development of the Chester Plays.'
      The sections of the 'Breviary' which are nearly duplicates of the first edition are collated here
and not repeated in their separate entries under the years 1619 and 1623. The texts of the later
editions which are printed in this volume (pp 320-6, 351-5) pick up at the point where considerable
revision or rewriting makes a collation impossible.

258   Harley 2150 f 185
Other entries about expenditures for the St George's Day Race have not been included in the
volume.

258   Harley 2150 ff 186-6v
The early edition, *Chesters trivmph in honor of her Prince. As it was performed vpon S. Georges
Day 1610. in the for said Citie.* (London, 1610), has been edited by Thomas Corser for the Chet-
ham Society, 1st series, III (Manchester 1844).

261   A/F/8 f 38
The petition is undated; however, since it must have been made not long after the event, I have
dated it to 23 April 1610.

262   Add. 29779 f 35
Briefer, less detailed notices appear in Harley 2125, f 49; Harley 2133, f 47; and Harley 1944, f 92v.

268   Add. 29780 f 156
The entry also appears in Stowe 811, f 62, and Add. 39925, f 26v; a variant is included in Harley 2125, ff 49-9v.

272   Minute Book G12/1 p 13
The entry has been published by Morris, p 345.

279   Company Book G10/1 p 45
It is not clear why there is a double entry, but both are dated to the same year.

285   M/B/30 f 22
The regnal term is inaccurate; it should be 12 and 47 James. On 4 June 1614, Robert Calley, musician, and Thomas Fisher, musician, were placed under bond to appear at the next portmote court on unspecified charges (f 22).

286   Harley 2177 f 84
The entry has been published in L.M. Farrall (ed), *Parish Register of the Holy & Undivided Trinity,* p 81.

289   A/F/10 f 53
The document is waterstained and partially faded. There are holes in line 5 (p 290) and line 35; the last line is entirely faded. The sentence in lines 22-3 , 'and the ... dinogte' is interlined and very faint.

292   AB/1 f 331v
The entry has been published by Morris, pp 353-4.

297   STAC 8 156/22
The excerpt comes from a complaint made to the king by Richard Grosvenor and William Barlowe concerning an attack made on Barlowe.

301   Company Book II ff 4-4v
The entry has been published by Salter, *Trial,* pp 20-1, but he misdates it to 1616-17.

304   AB/1 f 336
Further action was necessary in order to collect the assessment: the 'sessors' for the entertainment were appointed, f 340, an order issued on 20 October 1618 to arrest non-payers, f 346v, and a renewal of the order on 20 October 1619, f 352v.

305   Harley 2133 f 47v
Add. 29780, ff 161-2; Stowe 811, f 63v; Add. 39925, f 27v; Harley 2125, f 51v; and Add. 29779, f 37v, contain brief notices of the visit.

306   Add. 11335 ff 23v-4
The entry also appears in Stowe 811, f 21; Add. 29780, f 64; and Harley 2125, f 125. There is
a briefer version in Harley 1944, f 93v.

306   Add. 29780 ff 161-2
The entry also appears in Stowe 811, f 63v, and Add. 39925, f 27v.

320   DCC 19 unnumbered folio
For the date, see the MS description (p xxviii). The play description has been published in Clopper,
'The Rogers' Description of the Chester Plays,' pp 86-7.

326   DCC 19 ff 112v-13
In the paragraphs immediately prior to this passage, David says that there are Lists of Mayors
which show Sir Walter Lynnett to have been mayor in the time of Henry III, and that these lists
are to be believed before the more numerous ones which begin with Sir John Arnewaye in 1329.
He attributes the error to the fact that the succession of mayors did not begin to be recorded until
the reign of Edward III (ff 110v-11v).

331   Harley 2125 ff 52v-3
See Add. 29779, f 39 for a briefer account. Though Add. 29779 lists the incident under Williamson's term in 1619-20, the entry states the event occurred on 2 October 1621. The entry also
states that the mayor was in the 'vtter pentise' for the baiting.

336   Harley 2125 f 53v
A similar entry appears in Add. 29779, f 39v. Holme corrected the passage to indicate that
Francis Gamull, Randle Holme (his father), and others in Bridge Street were responsible for the
show at Whitsun.

338   Harley 2057 f 36
The entry is divided into two columns. The second column begins with '5 Touching' (p 339, l 19).

343   Harley 2125 f 54
A briefer note appears in Add. 29779, f 40v. The entry was added by Randle Holme.

345   Company Book G10/1 p 51
It is not clear why there is a double entry, but both are dated to the same year.

351   Harley 1948 f 18
For the date, see the MS description (p xxviii). The play descriptions have been published in Greg,
Trial, pp 165-9, and Clopper, 'The Rogers' Description of the Chester Plays,' pp 87-8.

360   Company Book II f 35v
This entry is included among a list of expenses dated 13 January 1624 (1625, new style), which
occurs at the end of the 1624-5 accounts. Apparently the guild spent an amount of money for a
party on the last day of the budget year to use up the funds remaining. These expenses were thus
charged to the 1624-5 year, although technically they could be charged to the 1625-6 year instead.

The yearly headings in the Coopers' Records say that the accounting year runs from 13 January t
13 January (not to 12 January) of the next year. The company could therefore legitimately
charge any expenses dated 13 January to either the preceding or the following year.

360   Harley 2125 f 126
A brief note appears in Add. 29780, f 163.

371   AB/2 ff 6v-7
Fair minutes of the dispute are to be found in A/F/12, ff 10-12, but these sheets are torn off at
the bottom and mended at the upper right and there are holes through the middle.

381   Harley 2150 ff 209v-9
The sheet has been reversed; it starts on f 209v and continues on 209. The document is an origina
which has been bound in an antiquarian collection. On f 210, a similar document, dated 30 April
1632, transfers part of the giant works to John Wright, and on ff 211-12v, in a document dated
1668, Wright acknowledges that the costs, charges, and profits of the giants, etc, belong to Randle
Holme and that Wright has a part in them in consequence of a payment of thirty shillings.

383   Account Book I f 155v
The entry is in Randle Holme's hand. At the lower left of the page is the date '1628'. It may be
a rough copy for the account which follows from Account Book II.

388   Harley 2124 flyleaf
Harley 2124 is one of the play texts. The entry has been published by Salter, MDC, pp 38-9. The
hand could be Randle Holme I; however, it might be an italic-like hand that Randle Holme II
seems to use occasionally for marginalia.

400   Company Book G3/2 f 102v
The entry is duplicated on f 105v.

403   Company Book G3/2 ff 109-9v
The entry is duplicated on ff 110-10v.

408   Harley 2158 ff 74v-5
The item 'payd to Iames Raffeenscroft ... iiij s' (p 409, ll 12-14) is interlined and partially indis-
tinct. The MS reading of 'Co*uer* ont it' is uncertain. The 'Co' is followed by a flourish, a space
and 'ont', a space and 'it'. It is possible that this is one word describing a kind of Venice glass.

413   Harley 2125 f 61
A briefer notice appears above this one and in Add. 29779, f 45. See also Add. 11335, f 24;
Add. 29780, f 65; and Stowe 811, f 21.

415   Lansdowne 213 ff 326-6v
The entry has been published in L.G. Wickham Legg (ed), *A Relation of A Short Survey of 26
Counties ...*, pp 49-52.

418   Harley 2125 f 61v
The mayor is Randle Holme II's father.

434   Liverpool University MS 23.5 ff 25-7v
For the date, see the MS description (p xxix). The play description has been published in the
Rev. Daniel and Samuel Lyson's *Magna Britannia,* II, ii, 584, note u, and pp 590-1, and in Clopper,
'The Rogers' Description of the Chester Plays,' pp 88-9 (from their MS notes in Add. 9442, f 295).

451   Harley 2125 f 133
See also DLT/B37, f 81v.

461   DLT/B3 ff 143-4v
The section on the history of the minstrels' court was published in Sir Peter Leycester's *Historical
Antiquities,* II, 141-2 (reproduced in Appendix 2, pp 486-9 of this volume); the section on the
1642 ceremony was published in George Ormerod's *History of the County Palatine and City of
Chester,* I, 484, note r.

466   Harley 2125 f 65v
A briefer notice appears in Add. 29779, f 51.

467   Add. 11335 f 24v
The entry also appears in Stowe 811, f 21v, and Add. 29780, f 67.

End-notes Appendix 1

469   TAR/1/6 mb 1d
The roll is endorsed on the outside to Henry VII's reign, but I do not think the note is contemporary
with the document.

469   Company Book p 21
The entry has been published by Morris, p 324. The marginal numbers are the numbers of the
orders.

471   Company Book p 14
Order 8 has been printed by Salter, *Trial,* pp 10-11. He dates it to 1606.

472   Minute Book G12/1 p 12
Morris dated the order to 8 March 1603 and printed it on p 344.

472   Harley 1994 f 32
Salter, *MDC,* p 27, says the entry is 'apparently for 1525'; however, I see no date. Holme says
this roll was among some ancient parchment rolls in his custody 'dec 2 1667' and that this is a
copy of one of those rolls. He adds that he put two other parchment rolls (dated 29 Henry VI and
24 Henry VII - 1 Henry VIII) into this book and retained two others.

472   Harley 2054 f 14v
The entry is undated and no date can be established for it. See the notes to the 1546-7 entry (pp 518-19).

473   Account Book I Harley 2054 f 25
The manuscript is defective at this point. Holme had numbered the folio as 30 originally but the preceding one is numbered 21; consequently, the entry appears either to begin in the middle of a document, a charter, perhaps, or it is simply a note. In any event, the book that he says he was copying from had the date 1499 on its first leaf.

473   Harley 2057 f 14v
For a similar version of this poem, see the fourth satire of Samuel Rowlands, 'The Letting of Hvmovrs Blood in the Head-Vaine,' *The Complete Works of Samuel Rowlands 1598-1628*, I (Glasgow, 1880), 64-5.

474   Harley 2150 f 161v
Randle Holme added the title, the marginalia, and the items noted in the text. Harley 2150, f 204, contains an abstract of the list in Holme's hand. At the top is noted the 'whole charge' to the Painters of '45 li 9s 8d', and at the end are appended the following:

'Ale wiues of notrade
bonelace weauers
other gent*lemen*

the Constables to goe in euery ward for their free beneuolence & giue it & the note
to mr maior'.

477   Harley 2150 f 201
A similar list of fees is entered on f 205; on f 206v is another computation, the latter half of which is similar to the latter half of the above. It was published by Morris, pp 326-7, note 1. Morris also lists the materials used in rebuilding the giants, etc, on pp 327-8.

478   Harley 2150 f 201v
The entry is in Holme's hand.

479   Harley 2150 ff 202-2v
Morris prints part of this entry, pp 328-9.

481   Harley 2150 ff 203-3v
A similar list of charges is entered on f 206 where there is also this note on the amount to be paid from the city treasury:

...

Of this antiently paid out of the Tresurie of the Cittie by the tresurers for the yearely
painting of the gian*tes*   xliij s iiij d
More paid now by the Cittie tresurers w*hi*ch was before Antiently was p*ar*ticulerly

paid by the Maior for the Mayors Mount or Cittie Mount till master Edwards his time

xxvj s viij d

Some from the tresurie now
is iij li. x s

...

482   Harley 2158 ff 36v-7
The entries are from roll 9; see the description of the MS (p xlviii). The only entries in roll 9 for Watergate Street are for the Mercers and the Bakers.

483   Harley 2158 ff 40, 1
Holme says the roll is from Henry VII's reign; see the MS description (p xlviii).

483   Harley 2158 f 43v
Holme says the roll is from the latter end of Henry VI's reign and the beginning of Edward IV's (see p xlviii).

End-notes Appendix 2

484   John Payne Collier, *The History of English Dramatic Poety to the time of Shakespeare: and Annals of the Stage to the Restoration,* I pp 114-16
Attempts to trace the letter from which Collier quotes have been unsuccessful. Collier (p 114) prefaces the citation as follows:

... among the unarranged papers of Cromwell in the Chapter-house, Westminster, I found a valuable letter, (not indeed addressed to Cromwell, because he was not even knighted until 1531,) from the Mayor and Corporation of Chester, stating the nature and object of the play ['Robert of Sicily'], and asking permission to have it represented. This document has in part been destroyed by damp, so that it has no name nor date, but nearly all the rest has been preserved, and there cannot be the slightest doubt that it refers to this very transaction. The back of the letter having been torn off, it cannot be ascertained to what nobleman in the Court of Henry VIII. it was addressed.

Glossaries: Abbreviations

abl	ablative	part	participle
adj	adjective	perf	perfect
adv	adverb	phr	phrase
CL	classical Latin	pl	plural
conj	conjunction	poss	possessive
EG	English Glossary	pp	past participle
f	feminine	pr	present
fut	future	prep	preposition
impers	impersonal	pron	pronoun
indecl	indeclinable	prp	present participle
inf	infinitive	sg	single
m	masculine	subj	subjunctive
ML	medieval Latin	tr	transitive
n	noun	v	verb
nt	neuter	vb	verbal

Glossaries: Introduction

The glossaries are intended to make the documents as accessible as possible to the reader. English words which occur in Latin passages are found in the English glossary, although words not easily recognized as English have been listed alphabetically in the Latin glossary with a cross reference to the English (EG).

Words are included in the Latin glossary if they are not to be found in Lewis and Short, *A Latin Dictionary*, the standard reference work for classical Latin. Words listed in Lewis and Short which have had a change or restriction of meaning in medieval Latin are also cited. Many words in these documents are common classical Latin words using medieval spellings. Such variations have not been considered significant, ie, as producing new words. They are:

> ML *c* for CL *t* before *i*
> ML *cc* for CL *ct* before *i*
> ML *d* for CL *t* in a final position
> ML *e* for CL *ae* or *oe*
> ML *ff* for CL *f,* especially in an initial position
> ML addition of *h*
> ML omission of CL *h*
> ML *n* for CL *m* before *m* or *n*
> intrusion of ML *p* in the CL consonant cluster *mn* or *ms*
> ML doubling of CL single consonants and singling of CL double consonants

In addition, medieval Latin words can vary in spelling by alternation between *i* and *e* before another vowel. Scribal practice has been followed in such cases, as well as with *i/j* and *u/v* variants. Headwords are given in the standard form: ie, nouns are listed by nominative, genitive, and gender; adjectives by the terminations in the nominative singular; verbs by their principal parts. Where the same word occurs in spellings which differ according to the list above, the most common spelling is designated as standard and used for the headword. Anomalous inflectional forms are dealt with in one of two ways: they are listed separately and cross referenced to the main entry or, if they follow the headword alphabetically, they are listed under that headword and set apart by bold-face type.

Words or phrases which may be unfamiliar to a reader of modern French are included in the Anglo-Norman glossary. Some Anglo-Norman words beginning with *d'* or *l'* in the text do so as a result of elision of a preceding *de* or *le, la* with the initial vowel. Such words are glossed under their initial vowel. Headwords have been chosen according to frequency of usage. All variant spellings are listed.

Forms of English words interesting from a purely phonological or morphological point of view have generally not been included in the English glossary. It is assumed that the reader is familiar with common spelling alternations (eg, medial and final *d/th,* initial *en/in*) in otherwise easily understood words. Where variant spellings of the same form occur, the first spelling in alphabetical order has normally been chosen as headword. However, where this would result in an odd or rare spelling becoming a headword, a more common spelling has been given precedence. Spellings separated from their main entries by more than two intervening ones have been cross referenced.

Manuscript capitalization has been ignored. Only the first three occurrences of each word are given with page and line number separated by an oblique stroke. If the word occurs in marginalia, this is indicated by a lower-case *m* following the page and line reference.

Works consulted:

Du Cange, Charles du Fresne. *Glossarium mediae et infimae latinitatis.* 6 vols (Paris, 1733).

Godefroy, Frédéric. *Dictionnaire de l'ancienne langue française et de tous ses dialectes du ixe au xve siècle.* 10 vols (Paris, 1880-1902).

Greimas, A.J. *Dictionnaire de l'ancien français jusqu'au milieu du xive siècle.* 2nd ed (Paris, 1968).

Holland, Robert. *A Glossary of Words used in the County of Chester.* English Dialect Society XVI (London, 1886).

Kelham, Robert. *A Dictionary of the Norman or Old French Language* (London, 1779).

Kurath, Hans and Sherman M. Kuhn. *Middle English Dictionary.* Fascicules A.1-N.2 (Ann Arbor, 1952-79).

Latham, R.E. *Dictionary of Medieval Latin from British Sources.* Fascicule 1, A-B (London, 1975).

— *Revised Medieval Latin Word-list from British and Irish Sources* (London, 1965).

Leigh, Egerton. *A Glossary of Words used in the Dialect of Cheshire* (1877; rpt East Ardsley, Yorkshire, 1973).

Lewis, Charlton T. and Charles Short. *A Latin Dictionary* (Oxford, 1879).

The Compact Edition of the Oxford English Dictionary. 2 vols (New York, 1971).

Latin Glossary

abbas, -atis *n m* abbot of a monastery 17/7m, 17/9, 17/12

affraia, -e *n f* fray, brawl 5/39, 6/7

agrementum, -i *n nt* agreement, assent 14/26; agreamentum, -i 14/19

aldermannus, -i *n m* alderman 13/31, 14/9, 14/11, etc

alternus, -a, -um *adj* other, another 18/28

annuatim *adv* each year, yearly 13/39, 14/1, 466/5

appono, -ere, apposui, appositum *v tr* affix (a seal) 7/20

apronarius, -i *n m (?) synonymous with* meronarius 11/36

armiger, armigeri *n m* esquire (title) 21/8

armitura, -e *n f* armament, arms 5/34

ars, artis *n f* craft, art, craft guild 13/31, 13/37, 13/39, etc

artifex, -icis *n m* craftsman 14/3

asyamenta, -e *n f* easement, accommodation 12/10

aysiamentum, -i *n nt* easement, accommodation 11/29, 11/36, 12/11, etc; aysamentum, -i 15/20, 483/22

baslardus, -i *n m* dagger 5/34

beatus, -a, -um *adj* blessed; (as a title) Saint 5/36

beneficialius *comparative adv* more beneficially 15/5

bletherus, -i *n m* babbler, young child (?) 462/36, 488/11

campanilla, -e *n f* (small) bell 120/16

capio, -ere, cepi, captum *v tr* hold (a legislative or judicial proceeding) 5/5, 6/2, 6/42, etc

cariagium, -i *n nt* carriage, cart 19/6, 19/11, 19/13, etc; caragium, -i 11/36, 12/11; carigium, -i 469/4; carragium, -i 11/29, 18/29; carriagium, -i 11/14, 18/27, 483/12

carpentarius, -i *n m* carpenter 6/35, 7/10, 7/17, etc

Cestershira, -e *n f* Cheshire 462/29, 488/4

Cestria, -e *n f* Chester 5/5, 6/35, 17/22, etc; Cestra, -e 15/6

charta, -e *n f* charter 462/27, 488/2

clamo, -are, -avi, -atum *v tr* claim 466/1, 466/10

clausum pasche *n phr* first Sunday after Easter 6/40

comes, -itis *n m* earl 18/1, 462/30, 488/5

comissio, -ionis *n f* commission (of a person to an office or task) 17/7m, 21/1m

comitatus, -us *n m* county, region of the authority of an earl 466/8, 466/12

conquestus, -us *n m* conquest 6/41

constabularius, -i *n m* constable 462/26, 488/1

constitucio, -ionis *n f* decree or constitution of any body or magistrate 14/40

continuo, -are, -avi, -atum *v tr* continue, continue with 14/5

copia, -e *n f* copy 466/15

Cornubia, -e *n f* Cornwall 18/1

crucifixio, -onis *n f* crucifixion 7/14, 7/16

curia, -e *n f* court 17/9m, 17/13, 18/9, etc

custus, -us *n m* cost 13/36

de necessario *adv phr* necessarily 14/38-9

depauperatus, -a, -um *adj* impoverished 14/4

dies, diei *n m* day; — iouis *n phr* Thursday 5/35, 5/40; — lune Monday 6/40, 7/27, 113/6; — veneris Friday 5/5-6

dominus, -i *n m* lord (ie, hereditary title) 5/39, 17/16, 18/1, etc

dux, ducis *n m* duke 18/1

ereccio, -onis *n f* setting up (of a shop or workshop by a master of a craft) 13/33

erigo, -ere, erexi, erectum *v tr* set up (a shop or workshop) 14/16(2), 14/25

etas, etatis *n f* age; *only in idiom* minor etas minority 17/15, 18/11

existens, -entis *prp* being; *especially in idiom* pro tempore existens for the time being 14/14, 14/32, 14/34

exopposito *prep* opposite, across from 5/36

feodum, -i *n nt* fee, fief 102/38

festum, -i *n nt* feast-day 466/5, 466/7, 466/10; — corporis christi *n phr* Corpus Christi (Thursday after Trinity Sunday) 5/35; — apostolorum Petri & Pauli (29 June) 6/1; — nativitatis sancti Iohannis Baptistae (24 June) 466/4

forincecus, -a, -um *adj* foreign, strange 13/34

forisfacio, -ere, -feci, -factum *v tr* forfeit 14/28, 14/29

forisfactura, -e *n f* forfeiture 14/23

franchesia, -e *n f* franchise (of a town), privileged area within which the liberties or freedoms apply 14/37, 15/4

Francia, -e *n f* France 13/26, 17/40

gardinum, -i *n nt* garden 11/21

gero, -ere, gessi, gestum *v tr only in idiom* pacem gerere keep the peace 20/5, 20/11

heuster *E G*

Hibernia, -e *n f* Ireland 13/26, 18/1

histrio, -onis *n m* minstrel 17/10m, 17/14, 18/9, etc

infuturo *adv* in future 14/38

inordinatus, -a, -um *adj* unauthorized 13/33

inquisicio, -onis *n f* inquest 5/5, 6/2, 6/42, etc

intrusio, -onis *n f* trespass 13/33

irrigimen, -minis *n nt* indiscipline, unruliness 13/35

iurator, -oris *n m* juror 5/11, 7/6

ius, iuris *n nt* right, privilege 462/30, 488/5

lagena, -e *n f* gallon 466/5

leccator, -oris *n m* lecher; man who frequents prostitutes 462/29, 488/4

littere, -arum *n f pl* letters 15/6, 17/7, 18/17; littere patentes *n phr* letters patent 13/26m, 15/6, 18/17-18

ludus, -i *n m* play; *apparently synonymous with* pagina *in some documents* 13/36, 13/37, 14/33, etc

lumen, -inis *n nt* light; *specifically* the lights carried in the Corpus Christi procession 13/38, 14/32

lusus, -i *n m* play; *apparently synonymous with* pagina *in some documents* 6/38, 7/10, 7/12, etc

magister, -tri *n m* master (of a craft) 5/33, 13/31, 14/10, etc

magnas, -atis *n m* magnate 472/28

maior, -oris *n m* mayor 6/42, 7/19, 14/22, etc

maioratus, -us *n m* mayoralty 7/19

meranerius, -i *n m* 483/12 *see* meronarius

mercator, -oris *n m* merchant, mercer 11/5, 11/37m, 12/5

mercerus, -i *n m* mercer 19/11

meronarius, -i *n m* mariners 11/36, 469/4

militaris, -e *adj* military, pertaining to a knight; *here only in legal idiom* **servicium militare** *n phr* knight service, a form of feudal tenure of land or office in return for military service or an equivalent fee 21/9

minor, minus *adj* 17/15, 18/11 *see* **etas**

minstrellus, -i *n m* minstrel 466/1; **mynstrellus, -i** 20/5

nuncius, -i *n m* messenger, herald (?) 472/27

obolus, -i *n m* half-penny 466/7

occupatio, -ionis *n f* trade, business 13/32, 13/39, 14/10, etc; act of occupying a shop as its principal craftsman and proprietor 13/33

occupator, -oris *n m* occupier; practitioner of a craft with a shop of which he is the principal craftsman and proprietor 13/31, 13/37, 13/38, etc

occupo, -are, -avi, -atum *v tr* occupy, a shop as its proprietor and chief craftsman 14/16, 14/17, 14/25

officiaris, -is *n m* official, officer 120/15

ordinatio, -ionis *n f* ordinance, decree (of any body) 14/40

ordino, -are, -avi, -atum *v tr* order, decree 14/2, 14/39, 15/2, etc

originale, -is *n nt* original (copy or version) 7/14, 7/15, 7/18, etc

pagens, -entis *n nt* pageant-cart 31/11

pagina, -e *n f* pageant, one of the component parts of the Corpus Christi Play 7/10, 7/12, 7/17, etc

pannarius, -i *n m* draper 11/37, 13/5, 13/11, etc

pannerioriis *n m abl pl for* **pannariis** 483/13 *see* **pannarius**

panniparius, -i *n m* draper 15/20, 16/31, 482/37

parcella, -e *n f* portion, small part or piece (of land) 9/1, 9/8, 9/9, etc

patens, -tis *adj see* **littere**

pertinentium, -i *n nt* appurtenance 7/13

placea, -e *n f* plot, piece (of land) 12/5, 13/20, 15/24, etc; **placa, -e** 15/18, 18/26, 18/28; **placia, -e** 19/13

placitum, -i *n nt* plea 104/25

portmotum, -i *n nt* portmote 6/39, 20/6, 20/12

posterim *adv* afterwards 14/37

premitto, -ere, -isi, -issum *v tr* send before; *hence* say or mention before 14/8

premitum, -i *n nt* (?) 5/34

princeps, -ipis *n m* prince 17/23, 18/1, 18/19, etc

quarter *n indecl* one quarter (¼) 159/36

quo warranto *n phr* name of a legal writ whereby one was cited to produce the warrant by which one exercised a right or franchise 466/10

recordum, -i *n nt* record; *in idiom* **de recordo** of record 466/16

redditus, -us *n m* rent 8/35, 10/5, 18/28, etc

regardum, -i *n nt* wages, gratuity 472/25

salvus, -a, -um *adj only in idiom* **salvo iure meo** reserving my right 462/30, 488/5

scaccarium, -i *n nt* exchequer 466/15

sellaria, -e *n f* saddlercraft 11/21

sellarium, -i *n nt* saddlercraft 483/5

sellarius, -a, -um *adj* pertaining to the Saddlers 19/5

sellator, -oris *n m* saddler 13/27m, 13/32, 14/11, etc

senescalcia, -e *n f* office of seneschal 17/18, 21/10

senescallus, -i *n m* seneschal; steward of a guild

8/35, 8/42, 9/8, etc

senoscalcie *n f* 18/13 *see* **senescalcia**

serviens, -ntis *n m* servant 5/38, 6/19, 6/20, etc

shopa, -e *n f* shop 18/28

sissor, -oris *n m* tailor 9/8, 9/16, 9/28

supporto, -are, -avi, -atum *v tr* support, sustain 13/36

sustentacio, -ionis *n f* upkeep 14/32, 15/3

toga, -e *n f* robe, gown 120/14

tribuenus, -i *n m* employee 159/37

vicecomes, -itis *n m* sheriff 5/5, 14/33

vicinetum, -i *n nt* district, neighbouring area 102/36

vigilitas, -tatis *n f* eve 120/19

villa, -e *n f* town 466/11

virgata, -e *n f* yard 159/36

Wallia, -e *n f* Wales 18/1

warrantum, -i *n nt* 466/9m, 466/10 *see* quo warranto

warrena, -e *n f* warren; *in legal idiom* **libera warrena** free warren, the right to keep or to hunt certain kinds of game and game birds 466/11

Anglo-Norman Glossary

achescun *adj* 8/5 *see* **chescun**

apprendra *v fut 3 sg* be allotted (?) 8/12, 8/13

artes *n m pl* crafts, craft guilds 7/35, 7/39, 8/2, etc

ascun *pron* each one, any one 7/39

assent *n m sg* consent 7/34

assesse *pp* assessed 8/1, 8/7, 8/14, etc

astate *n f sg form of* **estate** state, condition 7/39

auiendra *v fut 3 sg* will be agreed (?) 8/16

bene lite *v impers* (?) *for* **bene licet** (CL) it is allowed 8/11

cestassauoir *for* c'est à sauoir that is to say 8/9

chescun *adj* each 7/38, 8/5, 8/14, etc

costages *n pl* costs, expenses 8/2

danere *v inf form of* **donner** to give 8/17

deinz *prep* within 8/7; **denz** 7/40

demesne *adj* own; same (?) 8/10

destre *v inf see* **estre**

distrendre *v inf* to constrain, compel, distrain 8/14

distresse *n f sg* distraint, seizure 8/11, 8/16

encourge *v subj 3 sg* incur 8/8

endente *pp* indented 8/18

estable *pp* established 7/38

esteauntz *pr part adj in phr* le temps esteauntz the time being, present 8/2, 8/10-11

estre *v inf* to be 8/5, 8/6, 8/11; **fust** *perf 3 sg* 7/38

face *v pr subj 3 sg of* **faire** make, do 7/40

fortz qe *conj* unless 8/16

fust *see* **estre**

ioures *n pl in phr* toutz ioures always 8/17

irreplenisable *adj* unable to be fulfilled, completed 8/17

issint *adv* thus 8/14; **issait** 8/15

iwe *n sg* play 8/4

lan *n sg for* l'an year 7/31, 8/22

lassent *n m sg* 7/34 *see* **assent**

lumeir *n m sg* light; *here* one of the torches, called 'lights' of Corpus Christi procession 8/3; **lumier** 8/5

mose *pp* declared (?) 8/18

moyse *n sg* month 8/7

ordeigne *pp* ordained 7/38
ordenance *n f sg* ordinance 8/18

payne *n m sg* pain, penalty 8/8
perpetaute *n sg* perpetuity 7/38
portemote *n sg* portmote, borough court 7/37

seal *n sg* seal 8/20; seales *pl* 8/21
seneschalles *n m pl* stewards, officers of a craft
   7/35, 8/1, 8/7, etc

septyme *adj* seventh 7/32
si bene *adv phr for* si bien as well 8/11-12
sieur *n m sg* lord, possessor of a fief 7/31

temoignage *n sg* witness, evidence, testimony
   8/17
tressouerein *adj* most sovereign 7/31

viscountz *n m pl* sheriffs 7/33, 7/37, 8/9, etc
voier *v inf* to send 8/15; voiet *subj 3 sg* 8/6

English Glossary

abeareach *see* baredge

abode *n* temporary staying 219/32

aferken *see* ferkin

affrey *n* sudden disturbance, attack 28/20; afrey 33/29

all exployts *n phr pl* game of some kind 474/14

amesomar *adv* at midsummer 79/5

aminge *vb n* guessing, estimating 480/10

anchient *see* antient

angells *n pl* angel nobles, gold coins having the archangel Michael as a device, worth a varying amount 139/15, 157/37, 193/26, etc; angelles 158/4; angels 157/34m

anoverplushe *see* over plushe

antient *n* ensign, banner 174/4, 222/23, 346/16; anchient 443/14; aunciante 151/25; auncyant 368/30; auntient 174/3, 346/21, 346/23, etc

apotle, apotlle, apottell, apottle *see* potell

apt *adj* suited, qualified 165/11

arfflaye *n* orphrey, gold embroidering 117/22

arisedene *see* arsedine

arowe *adv* in a row, line 413/11

arsedine *n* gold-coloured alloy of zinc and copper, rolled into a thin leaf 152/7, 155/34, 170/13, etc; arisedene 139/37; arsedon 99/15; arsedyne 100/9, 269/29; arsideine 186/31; arsladyne 145/31

aunciante, auncyant, auntient *see* antient

awarrante *v pr 3 pl* guarantee as true 242/11

backsides *n pl* back premises, back yards, out-buildings 143/10

bandeleros *n pl* broad belts worn across the breast, used for hanging a wallet or charges for a musket 365/24, 439/37, 456/16; bandeleries 342/28; bandeleroes 378/40, 386/30; bandelerowes 391/40; bandelers 426/42; bandeleryes 396/20; bandelores 391/31; bandilleros 422/7

banes *n pl* proclamation of a play 49/32, 53/14, 66/13, etc; banees 81/35

barage *n* carriage, transport 162/39, 181/12, 189/27, etc; bariage 117/16; barige 186/20; barrage 160/9, 207/42, 213/14, etc; barrich 200/36; barrych 210/5; baryage 92/7; bearage 454/19; beirage 282/24; berag 299/33; berage 228/32, 270/24; bereage 123/14; berecche 145/27; bereche 134/6; beredge 183/26; berege 148/23, 152/1; bereghe 95/30; beriage 125/27, 132/9, 217/14, etc; bericche 141/11; berige 174/19; berradge 340/14, 340/24; berrag 66/22, 295/18; berrage 66/17, 120/33, 127/18, etc; berrecche 127/24; berreiche 103/10; berricche 128/5; berridge 155/24, 419/40; berrige 167/13; berygh 95/29; byryche 147/31

bardes *n pl* protective coverings for horses 106/32

baredge *n* drink-money 369/15; abereach 148/10; berage 326/30; bereache 148/8; bereghe 99/15; berrage 58/14, 332/30, 448/8, etc; beryg 82/14; beyrech 49/38

bargaine *v pr 3 pl* agree to sell 382/12

bariage, barige *see* barage

barkers *n pl* tanners of hides 22/37, 31/32, 50/19, etc

barly breake *n phr* country game, in which one couple is required to catch one of two other couples, who are allowed to 'break' or change partners 474/13

barr *n* barrel 220/15, 224/41

barrage, barrich, barrych *see* **barage**

barre *n* pole used for throwing in contests 474/6

baryage *see* **barage**

bastbord *n* pasteboard, board substitute made by pasting sheets of paper together 480/14

bated *pp* lessened, decreased 84/9

baxters *n pl* bakers 22/38

bays *n pl* baize, coarse woollen stuff 383/31, 480/28

be dene *adv phr* together 36/39

beadman *n* one who prays for the souls of others 184/36

bearage, beirage *see* **barage**

beiskie bread *see* **biskett breade**

belfounders *n pl* casters or makers of bells 33/1; **bellfownders** 251/26

bentes *n pl* ornamental straps 215/37

berag, berage, bereage, berecche, bereche, beredge, berege, bereghe, beriage, bericche, berige, berradge, berrag, berrage, berrecche, berreiche, berricche, berridge, berrige, berygh *see* **barage**

berage, bereache, bereghe, berrage, beryg *see* **baredge**

besene *adj* arrayed 37/1

beshrow him thats last at any style *n phr* game of some kind 474/16

beyrech *see* **baredge**

biskett breade *n phr* ie, biscuits 274/28, 285/19; **beiskie bread** 279/22

black minday *n phr* Easter Monday 451/15; **black munday** 23/14; **blake monday** 323/1; **blake mondaye** 253/25-6, 434/7-8; **blake munday** 299/3-4

blacke bill *n phr* type of halberd 471/37

bobbyde *v perf 3 pl* buffeted 37/6

bogyttes *n pl* leather bags or bottles 92/22

bone *v inf* prepare, make ready; dress 92/40;

bowne 151/1; **boning** *vb n* 154/15; **bouning** 201/1; **bounninge** 190/16; **bounying** 157/2; **bowinge** 108/42; **bowning** 181/19; **bowning** 109/6, 109/26, 151/3, etc; **bownnynge** 137/43, 146/13; **bownyng** 134/25; **bownynge** 141/34, 197/23; **boynynge** 149/27

borne *n* load 408/39

bouninge, bounninge, bounying *see* **bone**

bourne *n* water from a well 85/39

bouttes *n pl* boots 361/29

bowier *n* maker of bows 169/27, 169/29, 170/1; **bowers** *pl* 6/37, 7/8, 12/19, etc; **bowyers** 37/4m, 37/4, 475/32; **boyeres** 245/10; **boyers** 245/12m, 250/23

bowinge, bowne, bowning, bowninge, bownnynge, bownyng, bownynge, boynynge *see* **bone**

braceng *vb n* tightening up 281/24

breauary *n* summary, short account 320/20; **breauarye** 248/4; **breuary** 232/10, 232/24; **breuarye** 351/4

brebynge *vb n* breaking (?) 106/40

brode clothe *n phr* fine, plain-wove, dressed, double width, black cloth, for men's garments 84/26, 314/18, 314/21, etc; **broadcloth** 327/18; **broade cloth** 154/38; **broade clothe** 368/5; **broadecloth** 308/11; **brode cloth** 314/22-3

broderers, brotheres *see* **embroderers**

brute *n* rumour 292/33

brvyles *n pl* broils, disturbances 324/2

buckle *n* buckler, small round shield 260/4, 444/37; **buckler** 259/6

buckrom *n* fine linen or cotton fabric; or coarse linen cloth stiffened with paste 274/6, 309/17, 376/26; **buceram** 215/8; **buckeram** 122/30, 152/35; **buckram** 187/31, 218/33

bull ringe *n phr* place where bulls were baited 197/38, 198/19, 332/13; **bullringe** 199/1; **bulringe** 270/4

bumbast *n* cotton-wool 191/14, 215/20; **bumboist** 163/5

buskens *n pl* foot-coverings stretching to the calf or knee 134/27, 137/20, 141/17, etc; **buskines** 152/9, 200/1; **buskins** 148/28, 150/42, 154/13, etc; **buskkyns** 140/32;

buskyns 140/29, 145/8, 202/37, etc;
busquins 182/28; busquyns 178/40
butchafte *n* arrow 238/8
byryche *see* barage

calico *n* cotton cloth, imported from the East
30/16, 144/16
cape papper *n phr* a kind of wrapping paper
147/5
cardmakers *n pl* makers of cards for combing
wool 32/30, 37/19m, 475/19; cardemakers
251/10
cattes *n pl* cat-stick, used in children's games
92/28
challoner *n* maker of blankets or coverlets
5/14, 5/16, 5/20, etc; chaloner 6/3, 6/4
chandlers *n pl* makers or sellers of candles 31/
35, 35/5m, 242/28, etc; chaundlers 35/4
chauernes *n pl* wigs; or, frontlet for the ass (?)
50/10
chelder *n pl* children 50/31; childers *poss*
302/31, 302/32
cheue *v inf* succeed 35/2
chonchyse *n pl* conch-shells (?); shallow vessels
(?) 50/23
choryed *n* cord 149/12
ciertall *see* curtall
clapes *n pl* clasps 109/4
clar *n* claret 119/11
cleaves *see* gleaue
clid *n form of* child 298/22
cloues *n pl* gloves (?) 187/19
clouts *n pl* flat-headed nails used to fasten the
'wain-clouts' or coverings of the axle-trees
of a wagon 91/7
cobler *n* shoe repairer 300/1, 313/5, 318/33,
etc; coblers *pl* 462/11, 487/9
cobweb lawne *n phr* fine, transparent linen
262/23
codlinges *n pl* type of apple 267/29, 273/40
coierse *n poss form of* conerse (?) (ale) conner's,
ale tester's 165/27
colation *n* small meal 418/11, 418/23
color *n* semblance 293/6

comfettes *n pl* sweetmeats made of fruits,
roots, etc preserved with sugar 221/17, 226/
14, 231/38, etc; comeffeates 404/5;
comfeates 415/5; comfeattes 348/15;
comfeitees 425/42; comfeittees 431/9;
comfetes 310/15, 367/12, 417/23;
comffettes 319/6, 337/29, 344/30;
comffittes 344/24; comffyttes 274/26;
comfites 393/11, 398/2; comfits 388/10;
comfittes 350/13, 364/19, 375/34, etc;
comfytes 402/3; comfyttes 370/33;
comphettes 312/23; confyttes 358/7;
coumfeites 410/30; coumfeytes 420/42;
cumfettes 302/38; cumfetts 380/34;
cumffetes 361/19
cominaltie *n* community 34/15; cominal(..)
commons 28/13; comynaltie 33/21
comoditie *n* advantage 115/14
comphettes *see* comfettes
compute *n* reckoning 481/9
compute *v pr 1 pl* count 480/13
comynaltie *see* cominaltie
conceates, conceiptes, conceites, conceptes
see conseates
condecendet *pp* agreed 24/19, 24/39;
condecendent 24/33; condescended 26/37;
condiscended *v perf 3 pl* 372/3
confyttes *see* comfettes
conseates *n pl* fancy trifles for the table, kick-
shaws 285/20, 296/37, 319/8, etc; conceates
274/27, 279/25; conceiptes 398/5; conceites
344/25, 344/30; conceptes 402/4; conseites
312/29
consorte *n* company of musicians 195/6
conveighinge out *vb n phr* stealing 143/10
cordwainers *n pl* shoemakers 475/27;
cordwayners 372/14, 372/20; cordwyners
476/42
cornett *n* horn or instrument like a horn 281/
18, 281/21, 285/41; cornetes *pl* 164/41
corriors *n pl* carriers, porters 478/1
coruesters *n pl* shoemakers 250/17
coruyser *n* shoemaker 5/8; coruesers *pl* 36/34;
coruisers 22/37, 36/34m; coruysers 244/
22m, 244/22; corvesers 32/17
costage *n* expense 38/15

coumfeites, coumfeytes *see* comfettes

cowerds *n pl* cords 67/2

cowper *n* maker and repairer of casks, tubs, etc
170/10, 360/21, 368/31, etc; couper 5/9,
480/13; coupers *pl* 6/37, 7/8, 37/4m, etc;
cowpers 16/3, 16/14, 16/20, etc

crabefysshes *n pl* crabs 82/31

cressets *n pl* iron vessels for carrying fires
59/28

crocke *n* earthen pot 66/32; crokes *pl* 66/32

crosseweeke *n* Holy Week 64/19; crosse weeke
47/16, 59/24, 63/1

cumfettes, cumfetts, cumffetes *see* comfettes

curier *n* colourer and dresser of tanned leather
192/17, 192/18, 192/19, etc

curtall *n* kind of bassoon 170/30; ciertall 165/
29; curtayle 285/40

cussocke *n* long gown 136/1

cuttler *n* repairer of knives 336/1; cutlers *pl*
32/12, 475/18

dale bords *n phr pl* boards of fir or pine,
probably ones less than seven inches wide
and three inches thick 480/13

damaske *n* rich silk fabric, usually woven with
designs 36/7

dary *adv form of* daily 40/23

daubers *n pl* renovators of old clothes or
clothing 249/21; dowbers 31/39

deuise *n* dramatic representation 240/9;
devyses *pl* 261/23

diadem *n* crown 78/16, 91/17

dinogte *n* dignity (?) 290/23

dispensator *n* steward of the goods of another
463/5, 463/8

doble beere *n phr* strong beer, stout 226/20,
293/40; dubble beare 212/12, 224/41

doblet *n* close-fitting body garment worn by
men 279/10; dublet 163/5; dublett 212/43,
303/16; dvblete 164/22; dvblitte 164/26

dome *n* judgement 16/6

dowbers *see* daubers

drawers in dee *n phr* carriers of water from the
river Dee 230/4, 242/24m, 249/8, etc;

drahers of dee 22/27; draweres in dee 411/
5; drawers of dee 31/34, 34/39m, 34/39, e

dring *n* drink 105/38

drombandarye *n* kind of camel, with one hum
and especially light and fleet 72/9

dubble beare *see* doble beere

dublet, dublett, dvblete, dvblitte *see* doblet

dur *n* measure of length probably equal to thr
inches 215/11, 215/16; small amount
215/12

dye manes *n poss* demon's 140/4, 176/2, 179
27; dye men *pl* 173/8; dye mene 183/36,
184/2; dyemen 176/16; dye menes *poss*
183/23, 184/1; dyemenes 176/10

dyght *v inf* adorn, decorate 36/20

dysaneates *n pl* designs, emblems (?) 135/29

embroderers *n pl* those who ornament with
needlework 475/13; broderers 35/23;
brotheres 32/1; imbrauderers 29/41;
imbrauderreres 30/8; imbrautherers 35/24m
imbrotherers 249/25; ymbroderers 281/11

enui *n* 'annoy', disturbance, trouble, vexation
40/24

eschochions, escutions *see* scotchen

evies *n pl* ivy leaves 258/42

ex wensdaye *n phr* Ash Wednesday 64/35;
ex wensdey 52/13, 52/18; ex wenssdaye
68/22; ex wyenesdey 49/9; exwendey
60/27; exwenesdaye 71/5

exbursmentes *n pl* disbursements 44/14

excheqier *n* officer charged with custody of
money collected by the departments of
revenue 467/4; exchequer 466/39

exwendey, exwenesdaye *see* ex wensdaye

fane *n* temple (or banner ?) 91/17; weather-
cock 435/27

faunounce *n pl* embroidered bands, attached to
the left wrist of the officiating priest and of
the deacon and subdeacon at mass 59/30

faxe *n* wig (or beard ?) 66/43; ffaxe 105/40;

faxes *pl* 78/17

fee farme *n phr* kind of tenure whereby land is held in fee-simple subject to a perpetual fixed rent 102/1m, 102/14, 102/16m, etc

feltmakers *n pl* makers of hats 258/23, 476/2

ferkin *n* small cask, about a quarter of a barrel 375/40, 406/26, 412/37, etc; aferken 381/1; ferkyn 402/24; firken 293/40, 367/20, 388/15

ferrett *n* stout tape made of cotton or silk 338/14; fferritt 392/41

ffaxe *see* faxe

fflecchers *n pl* makers of arrows 6/37, 12/19, 32/21; fflecherus 22/39; ffletchares 245/10, 250/24; ffletchars 245/11m; ffletchers 16/2, 16/19, 475/31; flechers 37/4, 37/5m

fflight *n* light arrow for long-distance shooting 129/12; flighte 238/8

fflowerdeluce *n apparently a misunderstanding of* 'luce', lynx 480/24, 481/27 *see* luce

ffounders *see* founderer

ffreytyng *vb n* furnishing (or decorating ?) 49/37

ffrysers *n pl* those who make frieze-cloth or put nap on cloth (*error for* 'fustors' ?) 246/1, 246/3m

ffurbors *n pl* those who polish or burnish weapons, armour, etc 473/31; ffurbours 32/11; forbers 250/8; furbers 473/21; furbors 36/19m

ffurishinge, ffurnished, ffurnishing, ffurnishinge *see* furnish

ffurniture *see* furniture

ffusters *n pl* saddle-tree makers 32/32; foysters 37/23, 37/24m; fusters 251/16

ffynd *see* fynd

firken *see* ferkin

flagans *n pl* metal bottles 451/27

flaxson *adj* flaxen, made of flax 49/40

flechers *see* fflecchers

flighte *see* fflight

flues *n pl* pieces of down or fluff 145/10, 154/15; flewes 145/33

foote cloth *n phr* large, richly ornamented cloth laid over the back of a horse and hanging down to the ground 305/30; foote clothe

155/35; foote clothes *pl* 320/11m; fotclothes 320/12

forbers *see* ffurbors

forme *n* framework; bench 78/6

fornishinge *see* furnish

forreners *n pl* those not of the guild, non-freemen 206/9

fotclothes *see* foote cloth

founderer *n* caster of metal or maker of articles from cast metal 53/28; ffounders *pl* 24/12, 24/21, 24/23, etc; founders 473/22

foysters *see* ffusters

frest *adj* first 106/8

frettes *n pl* ornaments 95/37

frettinge *vb n* decorating 66/27

furbers, furbors *see* ffurbors

furbisher *n* one who burnishes and polishes armour, weapons, etc 32/11

furnish *v inf* prepare, equip 284/10, 348/13, 401/25; ffurishinge *vb n* 461/21; ffurnishing 445/28; ffurnishinge 405/32; fornishinge 416/28; furnisheinge 427/26; furnishinge 387/15, 411/31, 422/37, etc; ffurnished *pp* 183/8

furniture *n* accessories 151/25; clothing apparel 331/13, 422/43, 423/40, etc; ffurniture 450/37, 456/36; furnetur 439/39; furneture 452/12; furnytures *pl* 72/8

fusters *see* ffusters

fustian *n* coarse cloth made of cotton and flax 215/7, 215/38, 262/34, etc

fydder *n* feather 155/36

fynd *v inf* support, maintain, furnish 27/19, 38/6; fynde 168/42; ffynd *pr 3 pl* 37/39; fynde 36/35; fynding *vb n* 35/18; fyndyng 24/34

gambone *n* gammon, ham 92/20

gan *n* passage 398/22

gannokes *n pl* oatmeal cakes (or gannets ?) 92/21 *see* ianokes

garbyche *n* entrails used for food 107/6; garbyge 83/21

garne *v inf* prepare, decorate 95/30

garnyshe *n* adornment, ornament 83/25

girdlers *n pl* makers of belts 37/20m, 475/19; gyrdlers 32/31, 251/13

girke *n* jerkin, close-fitting jacket 145/36

glaseers *n pl* makers of glass 243/16m, 243/16; glasiars 35/23; glasiers 35/24m; glasiores 249/26; glasiors 475/13; glasiours 32/1; glassiers 29/41, 30/8; grasiors 281/11

gleaue *n* arrow or small spear 237/4m, 237/16m; cleaves *pl* 315/22; geyffes 46/36; glaues 50/3; glaves 162/38, 162/39, 167/12, etc; glayfes 68/19; gleaues 41/4, 235/13(2), etc; gleaufees 57/14; gleaves 42/35, 51/35, 151/40, etc; gleeves 42/32m, 42/32, 71/1, etc; glefes 63/40; gleives 74/20; gleues 200/35, 272/24; gleuys 62/8; gleves 75/37, 79/20, 87/12, etc; glevys 69/10; gleyffes 54/5; gleyues 52/8, 60/23; gleyves 47/41, 49/7; gleyvese 51/12

goddartes *n pl* drinking-cups, goblets 179/15; goddertes 158/33, 158/38

goodtides *n* Shrovetide 155/6; goottedes 71/2; goted 52/9; gotedes 46/37, 47/42, 48/27; gotetees 57/14; gotted 54/7, 54/8, 54/9, etc; gottedes 52/10, 52/19; gottes 68/20; gottets 64/33; gottyes 63/34; goutted 51/13, 51/14; gouttedes 60/23; govtted 54/6; gowtyt 62/9; gutted 69/11, 69/13, 74/20, etc; guttedes 69/6, 74/22, 79/21, etc; gutteds 308/38; guttes 128/6; guttides 51/34; guttydes 51/36

gorgett *n* piece of armour for front of the throat 349/20, 365/25, 371/21; gorgets *pl* 445/37

gorse *n* furze 78/10

goted, gotedes, gotetees, gotted, gottedes, gottes, gottets, gottyes, goutted, gouttedes, govtted, gowtyt *see* goodtides

goteddesdaye *n* Shrove Tuesday 234/10; gottedesday 40/38; guttedday 132/11

grasiors *see* glaseers

grayth *n in phr* in grayth in proper order 37/35

greiffes *n pl* wrongs, injuries 280/33

grone *n* nose of a pig or boar 83/7

grove *n* 'grave', dull, sombre 345/40

gutted, guttedes, gutteds, guttes, guttides,

guttydes *see* goodtides

guttedday *see* goteddesdaye

gyrdlers *see* girdlers

gyse *n pl* guide ropes 49/35

hagays *n* haggis, minced entrails boiled in a sheep's stomach 83/16; haggassys *pl* 83/2 hagocyes 93/6; hagoosscys 92/9; hagosses 107/7

halbert *n* weapon having sharp-edged blade ending in a point and a spear-head 413/25 424/3, 429/25, etc; halbart 442/42, 458/3 halbards *pl* 408/18; halberts 479/6, 479/3 481/34

halbertere *n* bearer of a halberd (*see* halbert) 448/9; halbeters *pl* 478/5

halbertman *n* bearer of a halberd (*see* halbert 453/40

hance bills *n phr pl* hand bills, small halberds 480/32

hance men *n phr pl* bearers of hances (small halberds) 453/13; hansemen 442/20; haunsmen 458/9; honncemen 447/35

hancestaues *n pl* hand-staffs, small poles 481 32; haunce staues 478/4

hard shuger *n phr* candy of some kind 367/1 hard sugar 375/36

harnes *n* defensive or body armour 59/5, 160 41, 168/1, etc; harness 479/20, 479/22; harnesse 138/41, 163/27, 168/42, etc; harneys 89/40; harnis 480/6; harnise 53/1 harnisse 479/33

harnest *pp* dressed in harness armour 179/24 179/30, 182/2

hasthel *n* hostel or storage place 46/27

haunce staues *see* hancestaues

haunsmen *see* hance men

hedmakers *n pl* hatmakers 475/19

heuster *n* dyer 5/15, 5/19, 5/22; heusters *pl* 23/7; hewsters 33/1, 38/13m, 38/13, etc

hight *v pr 3 sg* is called 37/36, 38/16; hyght 36/21, 36/36

hogshed *n* large cask for liquids 136/31

holland cloathe *n phr* linen fabric from Holla*n*

province 147/41

hollyn *n* holly 59/26, 59/29; **hollyns** *pl* 59/26

honncemen *see* **hance men**

hoope *n* dry measure for grain 91/11; **hoppe** 66/34, 66/37; **hoopes** *pl* 78/10

horsbread *n* bread for horses 73/33, 160/21, 167/29, etc; **hores brid** 138/6; **horsbreade** 163/10; **horsbred** 55/1, 85/27, 90/40, etc; **horsbredd** 205/8; **horsbrede** 147/9; **horse bread** 122/39, 153/36, 159/26, etc; **horse breade** 155/33, 173/20, 175/31, etc; **horse bred** 136/17, 152/10, 154/17, etc; **horse bredd** 161/38; **horse brede** 151/8, 183/38, 201/14; **horse breid** 135/4; **horsebread** 171/41, 266/26, 277/40; **horsebred** 99/18, 100/6, 119/14, etc; **horss bread** 172/9; **horssbred** 168/11; **horsse breade** 208/29; **horsse bred** 134/22; **horsse bredd** 101/16, 123/13, 125/37, etc; **horsse brede** 83/1, 128/30, 146/19; **horsse bridd** 175/12; **horssebread** 98/13; **horssebrede** 141/39; **horstebred** 131/3

hortyng *vb n* hoarding 93/4

hosiers *n pl* makers of hose and underclothing 31/33, 34/35m, 249/5

hostelers *n pl* innkeepers 32/24, 37/15; **hostlers** 22/42, 251/3

hott cockles *n pl* game in which a player conceals his eyes and tries to guess which other player has struck him 474/10

houke *n* (shepherd's) hook 92/32

houlle *n* owl (?) 92/25

hyght *see* **hight**

hyrms *n* winter 339/31

iacke *n* stuffed or quilted tunic, used for defence 471/36

iacks *n pl* figures of men which strike the bell on the outside of a clock 435/31

iacobins *n pl* Jacobuses (name of English gold coins) 305/40

ianokes *n* oatmeal cake 107/18 *see* **gannokes**

ieane *n* twilled cotton cloth 338/3; **iene** 215/6; **ienes** *pl* 215/40

ieans *n pl* giants 72/8

ieren *n* iron (?) 95/32; **ierne** 93/8

ierken *n* garment for the upper body 279/10; **ierkine** 166/2, 192/14; **ierkinge** 192/13; **ierkyne** 166/3, 171/2

imbrauderers, imbrauderreres, imbrautherers, imbrotherers *see* **embroderers**

in brest *adv phr* abreast 361/7

in fere *adv phr* together 35/23, 37/11

inckle *n* a kind of linen tape 262/22, 269/15; **inkele** 383/10; **inkell** 376/22, 383/33, 448/5; **inkle** 121/17, 123/36; **ynckill** 91/18

intromedill *v inf* interfere 24/25; **intromedelyng** *vb n* 24/30

ipocrise *n* cordial drink made of wine flavoured with spices 136/34

irish *n* game resembling backgammon 474/9

kaleevers *n pl* kind of musket 432/10

knottes *n pl* bows 406/8, 412/7, 412/8, etc; **knotts** 428/8

la wire *n phr* lace wire 262/34

lape *v inf* wrap 147/5, 199/19

lasses *n pl* laths 49/34

lawne *n* clothing made from a kind of fine linen 92/34

leauelooker *n* municipal officer with certain inspection duties 327/17; **leaueoker** 479/25m; **leaue lookers** *pl* 451/39; **leauelokers** 477/19, 478/11, 479/18, etc; **leauelokes** 480/36; **leauelookers** 197/41, 199/4, 478/20, etc; **leauelookes** 482/21; **leaulookers** 478/9; **leave lookers** 198/19-20; **levelokers** 62/1

lethes *n pl* lungs ('lights') 92/26

lett *n* hindrance 27/11, 42/14, 178/14; **let** 42/20

lett *v subj 2 pl* hinder 35/1

leuarse *n pl* livers 92/26

list *v pr 3 pl* desire 43/12m; **lust** *subj 2 sg* 38/29

loggets *n pl* game in which the participants

throw missiles at a stake in the ground 474/7

luce *n* lynx 72/9 *see* **fflowerdeluce**

lust *see* **list**

malvesey *n* malmsey, a strong sweet wine 58/3

mandelion *n* loose coat or cassock 134/25

mane *n* money 53/29, 53/37

marcers, marsers *see* **mercer**

march beere *n phr* strong beer brewed in March 348/18

march pane *n phr* confectionery composed of a paste of pounded almonds, sugar, etc 402/4; **marchepane** 367/13; **marchpane** 398/5; **march paines** *pl* cakes made of this composition 388/11; **march paynes** 380/36; **marchpanes** 375/35, 393/20

markes *n pl* units of money worth 13s 4d 304/35; **marks** 193/25

maunday *n* Last Supper 36/40; **maundy** 250/20

maw *n* card game using a piquet pack 474/9

meathe *n* mead, liquor made from honey 98/26

medsore *n contraction of* midsummer 199/18 *see* **amesomar, mesomer**

menyssheth *v pr 3 sg* diminishes 40/13

mercer *n* dealer in small wares 215/24, 323/14, 354/15, etc; **marcers** *pl* 22/31, 35/37m, 61/32; **marsers** 55/12, 56/41; **mercers** 9/31, 9/35, 10/35, etc

mesomer *n contraction of* midsummer 91/39m; **messemar** 182/12, 182/16; **messemare** 177/22, 182/13, 182/20; **messemer** 175/6, 175/11; **messomar** 19/4; **mycommer** 65/3 *see* **amesomar, medsore**

milners *see* **myllner**

misterys *n pl* craft guilds 473/17

mockadone *n* mockado, a kind of cloth 144/18

modells *n pl* representations 481/10

moytie *n* half 382/9

murrey *n* cloth of a blood-red or purple-red colour 218/2

mycommer *see* **mesomer**

myllner *n* miller 179/19, 183/38; **milners** *pl* 36/40m; **mylners** 32/19, 250/21

nayle *n* unit of cloth length, equal to two and a quarter inches 337/39; **neale** 231/29; **nayles** *pl* 480/13; **neyles** 338/4

nerve *n* narrow bands 154/38

nheghet *n* night 68/35; **nheghte** 68/37

noddy *n* game resembling cribbage 474/9

none so prettir *n phr* some kind of cloth 346/21

occutione *n* occasion 219/33

oestas *n* summer 339/25

onerated *pp* burdened 25/28

oryell *n* oil (?) 183/27

outbraueing *v prp* defying 374/6

over plushe *n phr* extra amount over specified sum 288/33, 300/25, 309/2, etc; **anoverplushe** 309/39, 316/7; **ouer plous** 127/2; **ouerplus** 119/25, 357/38, 470/31; **ouerpluss** 451/26; **over plus** 362/33, 369/2; **over plush** 356/36; **overplus** 363/17, 389/37, 394/15, etc; **overplush** 341/9, 357/7; **overplushe** 228/42, 256/7, 265/11, etc

packe threed *n phr* stout thread used for sewing or binding 84/29; **pake thryd** 50/23; **pakethryde** 106/41; **paketryde** 92/30

pagent *n* one of the plays in the Mystery Cycle or, one of the carriages or wagons on which the plays were performed 33/10, 35/30, 38/6, etc; **pagan** 105/29; **pageant** 325/14, 436/18; **pageante** 242/29, 246/13; **pagen** 106/2; **pagend** 36/24, 36/32, 37/26; **pageon** 244/18; **pagiant** 238/27, 325/15, 325/25, etc; **pagiante** 239/5, 242/5, 243/18, etc; **pagient** 339/9; **pageanntes** *pl* 247/21; **pageantes** 4/29, 110/8, 241/6, etc; **pageants** 317/28, 388/34; **pageanttes** 240/13; **pagens** 34/16; **pagents** 32/6, 32/27, 436/11;

pageons 113/12; **pagianntes** 242/7; **pagiantes** 238/16, 238/25, 239/10, etc; **pagiants** 355/15; **pagientes** 436/35; **pagients** 473/15; **pagions** 55/20, 115/7, 115/18, etc; **pagyns** 31/26

pales *n pl* stakes used to form a fence 275/33, 275/36, 281/34, etc; **payles** 377/5

parbolyng *vb n* thorough boiling 83/21

parcell *n* portion, part 464/21; **parceles** *pl* parts of a text 108/21; **parcells** 66/16, 66/19, 78/17

pascall *n* great Easter candle 30/24

passynares *n pl* singers of the Passion on Palm Sunday 45/5; **passyners** 45/30

paste balye *n phr* ball made of paste (?) 108/1

paulle *n* rich robe 35/34

paxe *n* Paschal candle-stick 31/3

payles *see* pales

penon *n* long triangular flag or streamer 338/41

phenix *n* emblem in shape of a phoenix 298/30, 314/10, 314/11, etc; **pheonex** 448/24; **pheonix** 383/24; **phœnix** 356/16, 356/26, 384/11; **phenexes** *pl* 448/23; **phenixes** 419/12; **pheonixs** 407/33; **phoenexes** 448/7; **phoenixes** 345/30; **phoenixs** 448/6; **phœnixes** 356/27

picke *n* weapon consisting of a long wooden shaft and an iron pointed head (or, a man so armed) 349/20, 359/30, 371/21, etc; **pike** 443/14; **pyke** 269/31, 336/25; **pickes** *pl* 342/30, 345/33, 365/24, etc; **pikes** 340/27, 340/28, 356/22, etc; **pyks** 439/38

picke poynt *n phr* children's game of some kind 474/20

pike men *n phr pl* men armed with pikes 393/39, 399/4, 407/28, etc; **picke men** 342/25, 359/18, 365/19; **pickemen** 349/16; **pickmen** 448/9; **pikemen** 389/18, 391/30, 403/4, etc

pillers *n pl* posts, supports 66/19; **pillers** *poss pl* 66/43

pinners *n pl* makers of pins and other small wire objects 475/4; **pynners** 31/37, 35/9, 249/16

plummers *n pl* workers in lead 475/19

pointes *n pl* tagged laces or cords usually used for attaching hose to doublets 220/37, 223/12, 271/35, etc; **points** 360/15, 365/39,

374/28; **poyntes** 82/26, 214/41, 217/28, etc; **poynts** 349/34, 357/20, 388/7; **pynttes** 92/30

polaxes *n pl* battle axes or halberds 5/33

pompes *n pl* kind of slipper 99/1, 132/25; **pumpes** 83/15

poppyngee *n* parrot 36/8

postie *n* authority, power 241/27

potell *n* liquid measure equal to half a gallon 111/18, 131/23, 160/29, etc; **apotle** 185/29; **apotlle** 388/16; **apottell** 145/1; **apottle** 145/18, 145/19, 457/5; **potele** 402/28; **potle** 155/41, 156/1, 269/42, etc; **pottel** 48/40; **pottell** 58/3, 74/24, 74/27, etc; **potter** 226/17, 331/10; **pottl** 350/32; **pottle** 133/4, 204/17, 204/18, etc; **potelles** *pl* 131/27; **potells** 71/4; **potlles** 388/17; **potteles** 65/4; **pottelles** 379/13; **pottells** 212/12, 221/26, 381/3, etc; **pottlees** 426/7; **pottles** 307/19, 314/4, 314/7, etc; **pottls** 292/15

pottares *n pl* pushers (of a carriage) 93/1; **pottarres** 92/36; **potters** 50/20, 50/21; **pouters** 107/29; **poutters** 107/10; **puteres** 83/19; **putters** 82/38, 96/3, 109/14

powldauie *n* coarse canvas or sacking 338/4

poynters *n pl* makers of points (*see* **pointes**) 32/31, 37/19m, 251/12

poyntes, poynts *see* pointes

prebunde *n* holder of a prebend (canon's stipend) 351/6, 433/36; **prebundes** *pl* 320/23

presentmentes *n pl* things presented 322/14, 372/18, 374/10; **presentments** 477/1

princebiskie *n* type of biscuit 267/31

pumpes *see* pompes

purseuant *n* warrant officer 109/37, 110/1; **pursevant** junior heraldic officer 44/1

puteres, putters *see* pottares

pye *n* magpie 135/38

pyks *see* picke

pynners *see* pinners

pynttes *see* pointes

queare *n* choir 226/4; **queer** 306/8; **queere**

306/7; quoire 306/28, 467/23

regalls *n pl* small organ 78/15

regenall *n* original copy 53/39, 107/37; reggenall 55/40; regynale 108/34; regynall 109/24; ryegenalle 96/8

renish wyne *n phr* Rhine wine 258/2

reparile *n* dress, apparel 147/28

repine *v subj 3 sg* complain 353/35

rombe *in n phr* in the rombe of instead of 42/33

ropers *n pl* makers of ropes 32/23, 37/5m, 250/30

rout *n* crowd 487/9, 488/22; route 242/2; rowte 36/4

routish *adj* disorderly 462/12

ruffe *n* card game 474/9

ryegenalle *see* regenall

saccloth *n* coarse textile fabric 215/31; sackcloth 274/7

sack *n* Spanish white wine 119/5, 119/11, 179/1, etc; sacke 69/9, 69/14, 121/24, etc; sackq 364/6; sacque 363/10, 370/18, 390/8, etc; sake 65/4, 99/22, 133/4, etc; seacke 223/25, 229/13, 256/1, etc; seake 226/17; seck 159/13, 225/11; secke 71/4, 74/24, 74/27, etc; seke 99/30, 110/35, 280/23, etc

sadd *adj* dark 154/38

safforn *n* orange-red spice used for colouring and flavouring 78/11

salueringe *vb n* silvering 207/18

sarcenet *n* fine, soft silk material 383/22, 384/9; sarsnett 407/32; sassenet 151/24; sercenett 346/19; sersnett 36/8

scheremen *see* sharemon

sclaters *see* slaters

scotchen *n* shield on which a coat of arms is depicted 91/19; scutchion 429/10; eschochions *pl* 340/17; escutions 407/34, 448/24

scouring *vb n* rubbing to clean and polish 61/4;

skowryng 45/10; skowrynge 45/35

seacke, seake *see* sack

seawater *n* a shade of green 215/36

seck, secke, seke *see* sack

selles *n pl* sills 95/25

semet *n* vest or undershirt 132/42

sences *n pl* censers (?) 59/26, 59/28; senses 52/38, 63/2

sercenett, sersnett *see* sarcenet

serge *n* woollen fabric 215/16, 274/10

sharemon *n* shearer of woollen cloth 81/31; shermon 5/25(2), 5/26, etc; scheremen *pl* 23/6; shermem 29/15; shermen 11/29, 29/13, 32/37, etc; shermens *poss* 246/17m

sheriffes peere *n phr* former sheriff 304/35; sheriffpeere 138/35; sheriff peers *pl* 408/40; sheriffes peeres 114/4-5, 114/13, 451/38-9; sheriffs peeres 218/3; sheriffspeeres 289/39; sherifs peeres 305/29; sherriffes peers 139/26, 467/27

shoote cocke *n phr* game using bird as an archery target 474/19

shootes *n pl* archery contests 352/13, 352/14

shot *n* collection for drink money 63/34, 68/22, 68/23, etc; shoost 150/23; shote 57/18, 62/20, 63/36, etc; shott 63/11, 63/15, 84/19, etc; shotte 46/37, 47/42, 49/10, etc; shoute 48/27, 50/2, 52/14, etc; shoutte 54/7, 60/25; shovtte 52/31, 57/33; showte 62/9, 71/20; shutte 60/24, 60/36, 60/40; shotes *pl* 68/21, 68/22; shovtes 52/11

shott *n* bowman 349/16, 365/19, 391/30, etc; shote 371/22, 379/2

shoue groate *n phr* shuffle-board 474/15

shuger plate *n phr* dainty sweet in the form of of flat cake 367/13; sugar plates *pl* 375/35; suger platees 393/12; suger plates 337/29, 361/22, 380/35; sugr plates 388/11

shute *n* suit 214/42; shvtte 175/6

shutte *see* shot

shype hoke *n phr* shepherd's crook (?); or, ox (?) 93/22

sil *n abbreviated form of* silk (?) 331/20

skaine *n* quanitity of thread or yarn wound around a reel 366/5; skayne 215/32; skeane 392/41; skine 273/39; skaines *pl* 215/36;

skaynes 215/19, 302/33; skeanes 231/29; skines 274/11; skynes 215/10, 221/15, 278/36

skluesynge dayes *n phr pl* term for Shrovetide 57/17

skowryng, skowrynge *see* scouring

slaters *n pl* those who lay slates on roofs 31/39, 35/14, 35/15m, etc; sclaters 243/8m, 249/19, 475/7

slayth *n* skill 37/34

slendge *n* sling 474/3

smiters *n pl* devices for ringing the bells of a clock 262/8

snyges *n pl* small eels 106/39

solens *n pl* stakes (?); balls (?) 52/38

sossed *pp* assessed 111/37

soure *n* sir 106/19; sovre 106/28

spens *n* expense 326/40

spicers *n pl* dealers in spices or apothecaries 249/32; spycers 32/4

spungyes *n pl* spangles (?) 147/3

spurriors *n pl* spur-makers 475/19

stables *n pl* staples 230/14; stabylles 92/16

stacioners *n pl* booksellers 281/11; stationeres 29/41; stationers 30/8, 475/13

stocke *n* fund set aside for certain expenses 482/12

stoole ball *n phr* country game resembling cricket 474/19; stooleball 474/5

stringers *n pl* makers of strings for bows 6/37, 7/8, 37/4m, etc; stryngers 32/21

stryke *n* dry measure, probably equal to a bushel 49/39

stryngers *see* stringers

suckett *n* fruit preserved in sugar 267/31, 279/23, 312/28, etc; sucket 350/14, 380/39, 388/14; suckettes *pl* 274/29

sugar plates, suger platees, suger plates, sugr plates *see* shuger plate

svttinge *vb n* shooting 129/32; svttinges *pl* 147/7

sweet meates *n pl* sweet food, such as cakes, pastries, confectionery, etc 433/25; sweet meats 442/3; sweete meates 447/12; sweett meates 452/15, 457/23

tabrett *n* small tabor or drum 244/9, 481/39

taffyta *n* plain-wove glossy silk 36/8, 188/26, 212/43, etc; taffata 145/34; taffaty 384/9, 407/32, 407/37, etc; taffeta 218/27, 346/18, 346/20; taffety 433/5; taffita 214/29, 231/26, 337/39; taffity 383/22

tallowchandler *n* maker of candles from hard animal fat 284/10; tallow chandlers *pl* 35/5-6m, 475/1-2; tallowchaundlers 280/34, 280/37, 281/7

tanners *n pl* those who tan hides for leather 31/32, 34/25, 34/32, etc

tapsters *n pl* those who draw beer or ale in a tavern 22/42, 32/24, 251/2

tawny *adj* of a brownish-yellow colour 339/28

tenekell *n* vestment worn over the alb by subdeacons 96/1; tunecle 91/29

tenor *n* wording 115/34

thacchors *n pl* roofers 31/40; thatchares 249/22

tinker *n* mender of metal household utensils 230/12

tippettes *n pl* parts of garments hanging from hoods or sleeves or loose 231/28, 331/18, 439/4; tippites 205/21, 205/23; tippittes 231/27; typpetes 190/37; typpetts 407/37

topas *n poss sg* of a ram 107/4; tuppes 83/10

torteaux *n* tortoise 339/19

trayne *n* retinue 139/25; audience 241/20; riding course 361/1

tressell *n* bench or trestle support 105/34; trestle 78/6

tret *adj* third 106/8

triumph *n* show or spectacle, play 72/31; trivmpthe 73/13; trivmthe 70/29, 70/32; tryumph 73/2; tryvmpth 73/11; trivmphes *pl* 124/35; tryumphs 125/3

trunche *n* staff, truncheon 291/32

trunchion *n* staff 453/8; trunchon 236/4

trunke sleeves *n phr pl* full, puffed sleeves 215/38

tryne *adj* wooden 92/35

tryumph, tryumphs, tryvmpth *see* triumph

tunecle *see* tenekell

tuppes *see* topas

turners *n pl* those who turn objects on a lathe 32/22, 37/5m, 250/27; turnours 6/37, 7/8
typpetes, typpetts *see* tippettes

vayle *n* piece of silk used to cover a crucifix, chalice or image 30/41, 31/18, 45/22, etc; vale 44/26, 44/33; veyle 45/42
venas glasses *n phr pl* drinking vessels made near Venice, of a fine, delicate glass 409/12
venterpoynte *n* game of some kind 474/15
ver *n* spring 339/22
veyle *see* vayle
victulers *n pl* suppliers of food and provisions 475/38, 475/42
vinteners *n pl* sellers of wine 35/29m, 243/22, 243/25m, etc; vynteners 26/39, 27/8, 27/12, etc; wynteners 22/30 *see* vynters
vnbowninge *prp* undressing 67/10; *vb n* 109/8
vncueete *adj* uncouth 353/21
voyd *adj* empty, unoccupied 287/32
vynters *n pl* sellers of wine 32/2 *see* vinteners
vysar *n* mask 109/5

wach *n* vigil 30/4
wach *n* revel on midsummer eve 21/22m, 21/35, 75/11, etc; wacche 79/34, 101/9; wache 55/20, 71/40, 72/7, etc; watch 21/22, 22/4, 168/18, etc; wattche 144/31
waches *see* watch
waite *n* musician 290/7; waites *pl* 43/18, 180/15, 184/37, etc; wayetes 150/37; wayets 228/7; waytes 43/9, 43/10m, 91/16, etc; wayts 459/28, 479/42; weates 414/5, 448/38; weats 454/22; weytes 119/11; wyettes 49/1, 49/17, 49/19, etc *see* waite man
waite man *n phr* musician 181/1; waiteman 222/41; weeteman 472/40; waitemen *pl* 163/19, 167/14, 180/1, etc; waitesmen 164/39, 165/4; waitmen 160/6, 160/10, 160/32, etc; watemen 174/20; watmen 162/40; wayetmen 409/7; wayte men 119/3, 125/25, 136/42, etc; waytemen 93/39,

97/31, 120/27, etc; waytmen 60/9, 185/2, 185/16, etc; waytsmen 164/37; waytte men 154/39; wayttmen 155/1; weatemenne 13(
37; weatement 166/36; weatmen 148/24, 148/41, 152/2, etc; weattemen 94/35; weete men 98/28; weetmen 211/20; wetemen 151/18, 200/30; wetmen 94/16, 210/7, 210/16, etc; wettmen 57/16, 57/26, 99/31, etc; wheate men 132/5, 132/10, 13: 32, etc; wheatemen 128/6, 134/31, 137/14 etc; wheete men 117/19, 125/29; wheeteme 117/17, 125/42; whetemen 117/10; wyete men 52/6; wyettemen 52/20; waytemens *poss* 314/19, 368/4; waytmens 327/18; wayttmens 57/3; weatemens 376/40; wetemens 191/29; wettemens 55/27; wheat mens 174/7 *see* waite
walker *n* fuller of cloth 5/14, 5/19, 5/20, etc; walkers *pl* 23/8, 33/2, 38/19m, etc
watch *n* patrol of streets to maintain order 4/37; waches *pl* 211/37
watch courte *n phr* court in which certain tenants had to produce watchmen to be charged by the mayor 324/15; watchcourt 324/21; watchcourtes *pl* 353/8
watemen, watmen *see* waite men
waterleaders *n pl* those who cart water for sale 34/39m, 242/22, 242/24m, etc; water leder 34/39; waterleders 31/34
wax chandlers *n phr pl* makers of wax candles 31/35; wax chaundlers 35/4; waxe chandler 242/28, 242/30m; waxechandlers 249/9
wayetmen, wayte men, waytemen, waytemens, waytmen, waytmens, waytsmen, waytte men wayttmen, wayttmens *see* waite man
wayetes, wayets, waytes, wayts *see* waite
waytship *n* office of wait (*see* waite) 280/6m
weatemenne, weatemens, weatement, weatmen weattemen, weete men, weeteman, weetmen wetemen, wetemens, wetmen, wettemens, wettmen *see* waite man
weates, weats, weyttes *see* waite
webster *n* weaver 5/13, 5/16, 5/18, etc
wheate men, wheatemen, wheete men, wheetemen, whetemen *see* waite man
whysteles *n pl* shrill pipes 82/24; wyestlles

92/17; **wystelles** 106/33; **wystyles** 92/42

wiflers *n pl* persons used to hold back crowds 408/30

woodmen *n pl* huntsmen; or wild men 338/35

wort *n* pottage; or pig's snout 166/16

wyer candles *n pl* candles strengthened with wire 61/4; **wyred candles** 59/29

wyerdrawers *n pl* those who draw metal into wire 31/37, 249/15; **wyredrawers** 475/4

wyestlles *see* **whysteles**

wyete men, wyettemen *see* **waite man**

wyettes *see* **waite**

wynteners *see* **vinteners**

wypcord *n* thin, tough kind of hempen cord, which is used to make whip-lashes 50/23

wyred candles *see* **wyer candles**

wyredrawers *see* **wyerdrawers**

wystelles, wystyles *see* **whysteles**

yarne *n* iron 92/16

yede *n* head 92/29

ylott holes *n phr pl* holes in cloth for the passage of string or lace (eyelet-holes) 147/42

ymbroderers *see* **embroderers**

ynckill *see* **inckle**

Index

The Index combines subject headings with places and names for ease of reference. Where the same word occurs in two or more categories, the order of headings is people, places, subjects, and book or play titles (eg, Dutton, Edward precedes Dutton, manor of).

Place names and titles appear in their modern form where this is ascertainable; surnames are cited in the most common or simplest form used in the text and are capitalized (ff is, therefore, rendered F in the headword). Both places and surnames are followed by a list of their variant spellings. Trade and place names appearing as surnames are so treated. Names of saints are indexed under 'St'. *The Handbook of British Chronology* (F. Maurice Powicke and E.B. Fryde [eds], 2nd ed [London, 1961]) and *The Compact Edition of the Dictionary of National Biography* (2 vols [London, 1975]) have been consulted for identification of peers and ecclesiastical officials. Where the family name is known for these dignitaries, it has been chosen as the main headword, with a cross reference from the official's title (eg, Essex, earl of *see* Devereux). The pattern for ordering page references is as follows: name with no modifier, royalty, peerage in descending order, ecclesiastical authorities, civic officials, personal designation of status (eg, widow or mister), modernized Christian names in alphabetical order.

Modern subject headings are provided with some complex groupings such as Whitsun Plays to aid research. Thus, individual pageants in the Chester cycle are listed under Whitsun Plays; their titles accord with the Lumiansky and Mills edition of *The Chester Mystery Cycle*. When a subject occurs regularly in a set of documents, a general reference is given rather than many page numbers. These references are usually to annual guild accounts; where a combined guild is involved, its name is simplified in the citation to the first element (eg, *see accounts of Smiths*, not *see accounts of Smiths, Cutlers, and Plumbers*).

The number of occurrences of a place or name on a page in the text is given in round brackets after the page number (eg, Crocket, Robert 84(2)). A similar number is provided for subject entries to indicate when the subject appears in two or more documents on the same page.

Antrobus (Anterbous), George 206, 485; John 208
apes
in 1621 Show 339
apostles
in Christ on the Road to Emmaus 32, 251
in Last Supper 32
See also **disciples**
Apothecaries *see under* **guilds**
apprentices xxi, lix, 12, 86, 165, 293
archers 39, 323, 434, 451(3)
archery li-lii, 39, 237-8, 323, 434
revival of 40-2
See also **Breakfasts**, of sheriffs; **homages**
arms and armour
for Christmas Watch li, 204, 212, 257, 271, 289, 310, 353, 444
for Midsummer 168-9, 179, 182, 198(2), 408, 443, 470-1, 478-80
for 1610 Show 259-60
for 1621 Show 338
See also Coopers' and Painters' accounts 1621-42, and **lances**
Arnewaye (Aneway, Arneway, Arnway), Sir John, mayor xii, xxv-xxix, xxxi, xxxvi-

carriages *see* **pageant carts**
carriage houses *see under* **guilds; pageant carts**
Carter, Jacob 328, 333
Carthage 72-3
Carvers 475
Cary, Lord, deputy of Ireland xxxi
Cases, Steward 413; Mr 221
Casker, John 93
cassocks
    for Midsummer lady 136
Castellane *see* **Castle Lane**
Castle, of Chester lv, lviii, 32; *see also* guild
    Midsummer accounts
Castlehaven *see* **Tuchet**
Castle Lane (Castellane) 5
Catterall (Catherall, Catteralles, Cattralls),
    Alderman 432; Steward 461; William 225,
    349, 401
Cay, William 5
chains *see under* **costumes**
Chalewoddes *see* **Hallwood**
Challoner (Chalners, Chaloner), John le 5-6;
    Roger le 5; Thomas le 5; Thomas 136, 159;
    William 5-6
Chaloners 7
Chanter (Chaunter), Mr 77-8
Chantres (chantrelles), Roger 127(2)
Charles I xxxviii, 466-7
Charles II 467
charters xlvii
    Bakers' 10
    Fletchers and Bowers' 12
    Painters, Glaziers, Embroiderers, and Sta-
      tioners' xxv, 29-30
    Saddlers' 13-15
Chatterton 416, 479
chess 474
Chester, city of
    allegorical, in 1610 Show 259
    attacks on li
    mayors of, terms of xlii-xliv; *see also*
      Mayor's Mount; antiquarian compilations,
      Lists of Mayors and Sheriffs; **Christmas,**
      watch for
    rentals of xii, xv-xvii, xlvii-xlix
    streets and wards of xii, xxxii, xlvii

See also **bars; liberties**
Chester, county palatine of
    chamberlains of 139, 145, 306
    constables of li; *see also* **Lacy**
    earls of xvii, xxx; *see also* **Blundevill,**
      Randle; Lupus, Hugh
Chester, diocese of
    archdeacons of 320, 351, 433
    bishops of *see* **Bishop's Palace; Bridgeman,**
      John; Chester Cathedral; Coventry and
      Lichfield; Downham, William
Chester Cathedral
    clerks of 78
    dean and chapter of liv, lviii-lix, 84, 96,
      135, 159
    See also **St Werburgh's Abbey** *and under*
      ecclesiastical records
Chestre, John de, senior 6; John, junior 6
Chetlwood, Katherine 366
children
    for Midsummer Show liii, lx; *see also*
      accounts of Beerbrewers, Coopers, Cord-
      wainers, Drawers of Dee, Innkeepers,
      Mercers, Painters, and Smiths 1571-1642;
      and under **costumes**
    naked 82
    of Israel 32, 36, 50
    of Noah 242
    to dance hobby horse 69
    See also **boys; girls; innocents; ladies**
Chirche, John 5
Cholmondeley, Charles xxviii
Christ
    in Annunciation and the Nativity 31, 243,
      249
    in Antichrist 246
    in Ascension 32, 251
    in Christ at the House of Simon the Leper
      32, 250
    in Christ and the Doctors 53, 67, 70, 73, 75,
      78, 86, 88, 91, 105
    in Christ on the Road to Emmaus 37, 246
    in Harrowing of Hell 37, 244
    in Last Judgement 246
    in Last Supper 32, 245, 250
    in Passion 32, 37, 245, 250